Civil Society and Political Change in Asia

Civil Society and Political Change in Asia

Expanding and Contracting Democratic Space

Edited by

Muthiah Alagappa

Stanford University Press, Stanford, California, 2004

Stanford University Press
Stanford, California
©2004 by the Board of Trustees of the
Leland Stanford Junior University
Printed in the United States of America

Library of Congress Cataloging-in-Publication Data

Civil society and political change in Asia : expanding and contracting democratic space / edited by Muthiah Alagappa.

p. cm.

Includes bibliographical references and index.

ISBN 0-8047-5061-0 (cloth : acid-free paper) —

ISBN 0-8047-5097-1 (paper : acid-free paper)

1. Civil society—Asia. 2. Democratization—Asia.
3. Non-governmental organizations—Asia. 4. Social movements—Asia.
I. Alagappa, Muthiah.

JQ36.C58 2004
300'.95—DC22 2004013177

This book is printed on acid-free, archival-quality paper.

Original printing 2004

Last figure below indicates year of this printing:
13 12 11 10 09 08 07 06 05 04

Typeset at Stanford University Press in 10/13 Minion

Contents

Tables and Figures

Tables

Figures

Preface

Beginning in the 1980s, civil society gained worldwide prominence as a political force in the context of fundamental global geopolitical and economic changes, and in the wake of numerous transitions to democracy all over the world. Political leaders and scholars, especially in the West, credit civil society with having played a crucial role in the collapse of communism and authoritarianism and in the accompanying democratic transitions. Perceived as a normative ideal, civil society is deemed as having the potential to liberate citizens from the oppressive state and to confer full economic and political freedom on them. Some present civil society as a program and an alternative to the domineering state. Viewing it as a positive force for the development of democracy, Western international aid agencies and foundations, along with advocates of democracy in the academic community, target the development of robust civil societies in new democracies and seek to sow the subversive seed of civil society in nondemocratic states. Along with the rule of law, enhancement of legislative capacity, growth of political parties, and development of the capitalist economy, promotion of civil society in developing countries has become a key goal of Western governments and, to a lesser degree, of the Japanese government.

The growing political prominence of civil society stimulated a great deal of thought about the concept in the scholarly community as well. Civil society has been used as a lens to understand politics and deployed as a key variable to explain democratic political change, especially in developing countries. Democratic change in South Korea, Taiwan, Chile, Poland, Czechoslovakia, South Africa, Nigeria, and Benin, among other countries, it is argued, cannot be comprehended without reference to civil society. Others have asserted that studying civil society provides a clearer understanding of the interface between society and government, and that it holds the key to the political legitimation of governments. Furthermore, it is posited that the absence of a vigorous civil society hinders sustained political reform, improved governance, and viable state-society-economy relations in developing countries. In his 1998 book *Civil Society: Old Images, New Visions*, John Keane goes so far as to claim that its emergence is a sign of "the end of a long century of political thinking dominated by statist ideology" and the move of civil society, reborn on grand scale, to "occupy the center-ground of contemporary political thought." Some scholars contend that civil society is relevant to understanding political development not only in developing countries but also in the postindustrialized countries in which the concept originated. A reconceived theory of civil society, it is argued, can make important contributions to ongoing debates in the developed states on elite versus participatory democracy, rights-oriented liberalism versus communitarianism, and the free market versus the welfare state. Others connect the erosion of social capital and decline of civil society to disarray and disaffection with democracy in advanced industrialized countries.

Many of the best works on civil society are grounded in the experience of the southern, central, and eastern European countries. Experience in Latin American countries also informs some of the major works on democratic transitions and consolidation and, indirectly, civil society. Asia has been much less central in this literature. In part this neglect is due to the persistence of communist and other authoritarian regimes in the region and the belief in several quarters that Asian values are distinct, and that their nondemocratic features are immune to the general worldwide trend. A substantial segment of the Asian political and scholarly community argued in the 1980s and early 1990s that liberal democracy is not suited for Asia, and that the Western concept of civil society is alien and inapplicable to Asian situations. The "Asian values" argument and the presence of multiple political systems have not prevented scholarly work on civil society. Such works, however, have been limited in number, mostly empirical, and country-specific. There are very few Asia-wide studies, and almost none of them are conceptual in orientation or comparative in nature.

This book seeks to contribute to filling the gap in the literature. It is a comparative inquiry into the nature of civil society and the role of organizations in this realm in advancing (or retarding) change in twelve Asian countries in the direction of open, participatory, and accountable politics. It advances four sets of findings: on the nature and development of Asian civil societies; the connection between civil society and democracy; the implications of the rise of civil society for the state and for state-civil society relations; and the relationship between civil and political societies. On the nature and development of civil societies in Asia, the study presents six propositions. First, contrary to the claim that the idea of civil society is alien, civil society organizations not only exist in Asia but have experienced dramatic growth since the mid-1980s; in some cases civil societies have relatively long histories. Second, development of civil society is social-reality specific; multiple factors have fueled the development of civil societies in Asia. Anticolonial mobilization, weaknesses of states, resistance to repressive rule, government sponsorship of organizations, increase in democratic space, economic growth, the information and communications revolutions, change in the international normative structure, and growing international support have all stimulated the development of civil societies. Their salience has varied with circumstance and over time. Third, civil societies in Asian countries are highly diverse in composition, resource endowment, and goals; they are arenas of power, struggle, and cooperation. Fourth, the composition and dynamics of civil societies have altered dramatically over time in several countries, and more change is in prospect. The spread of open political systems, market economies, and globalization is likely to fuel further change in Asian civil societies, including their transnational and global dimensions. Fifth, contemporary Asian civil societies display features of both the neo-Tocquevillean and neo-Gramscian frameworks. As the state and its political institutions become more legitimate, the neo-Tocquevillean framework tends to dominate. Sixth, the dramatic growth in the number of civil society organizations has not, however, been accompanied by institutionalization of the nonstate public sphere. The full measure of rights and rules necessary to construct and protect the autonomy of this realm is still not in place in several countries, including democratic ones. Civil society in Asia is viewed largely in instrumental terms to bring about or prevent political change in the state and its institutions; it is less commonly viewed as an autonomous arena for self-governance.

On the connection between civil society and democracy, the study advances four propositions. First, there is no necessary connection between civil society and democratic change. Civil society organizations have both expanded and contracted democratic space. Some groups have been in the forefront in preparing the ground for and even taking the lead in advocating political liberalization, political reform, and democratic transition; others, especially those with totalizing missions and that employ violence to achieve political ends segment society and undermine democracy. Second, civil society supports democracy when its dominant discourse is rooted in democratic ideals and prodemocratic organizations acquire critical mass. Third, the specific democratic role of civil society is contingent upon a number of factors: the political opportunity and constraints, stage of political development, and the strength, orientation, and role of the state and political society in a country. Fourth, civil society is a necessary but not sufficient condition for democratic development. On its own, civil society has a limited effect; in fact, it faces an uphill battle in promoting and consolidating democratic change.

The next set of findings relates to the implications of the rise of civil society for the state and for state-civil society relations. Here we advance four propositions. First, the rise of civil society has limited the power and reach of the state, although the latter continues to be the most powerful institution in Asia. Second, the state has had a strong impact on the nature and development of civil society. Third, state-civil society interaction in Asia is not necessarily confrontational. The relationship varies widely across countries and has undergone transformation in several of them. Fourth, present civil society-state relations in Asia span a broad spectrum. A wide range of organizations covering a broad range of issues now populate the realm of civil society; their interaction with the state ranges from co-optation through mutual respect and interaction on the basis of accepted norms to outright confrontation. The final set of findings centers on the relationship between civil and political societies. Here we advance two propositions. First, there is much overlap between civil and political societies; the boundary separating them is porous. Second, the development of civil society is not necessarily detrimental to the development of political society. There is much synergy between them. In establishing the above propositions, this study as a whole draws on, refines, and in certain cases refutes the arguments advanced in the literature on civil society and political change, demonstrating the contribution that can be made by studies of Asian civil societies.

In line with my goal over the past decade to promote a new generation of scholars on Asia, I invited mostly younger scholars to contribute chapters, while inviting senior scholars and nonregional specialists to discuss and review these contributions. In addition to concentrating some of the best minds on the project, this approach has helped create new networks. The authors and senior scholars met in two stimulating and productive workshops, in Honolulu (March 16–19, 2002) and Phnom Penh, Cambodia (October 24–28, 2002). Covering twelve countries (fourteen were originally included, but for various reasons, Thailand and Bangladesh had to be omitted), involving fourteen contributors, twenty-eight senior scholars, and twenty-three readers, and spanning three years, the study has been a major undertaking. Many people have helped in bringing it to a successful conclusion.

I would like to thank the contributors to the book. Their knowledge—not only of the country of their specialization but also of other countries in the region—is remarkable, and their willingness to ground their inquiry in a common definition of civil society and conceptual framework and to rework their contributions several times is admirable. Our readings of one another's chapters at various stages and regular interaction during and after the two workshops have contributed to the book's coherence. I greatly value the opportunity I have had to work with them. The senior scholars gave generously of their time and expertise. Participating in both workshops, Michael Foley, Niraja Gopal Jayal, Susan Pharr, and Geoffrey Robinson read and reread several chapters; some of them commented on the penultimate drafts. Charles Armstrong, Richard Baker, Vannath Cheah, Chua Beng Huat, Harold Crouch, Larry Diamond, Gerard Finin, Steven Fish, Shiaw-Chian Fong, Peter Hershock, Ben Kerkvliet, Choong Nam Kim, Sankaran Krishna, Christopher McNally, Charles Morrison, Norani Othman, Minxin Pei, Sheila Smith, Ok Serei Sopheak, Arun Swamy, Yutaka Tsujinaka, Guobin Yang, and Xue-Liang Ding participated in one of the two workshops and commented on one or more chapters.

Patricio N. Abinales, Terrell Carver, Neera Chandhoke, Tun-Jen Cheng, Bruce Dickson, William W. Grimes, Ayesha Jalal, James Jesudason, Ku-Hyun Jung, Sudipta Kaviraj, Hagen Koo, William Liddle, Patricia Martinez, Katherine H. Moon, Andrew Nathan, Mochtar Pabotinggi, Morton B. Pederson, Kevin Quigley, Garry Rodan, Frank Schwartz, David I. Steinberg, Nira Wickramasinghe, and Thongchai Winachakul read one or more of the penultimate drafts. Byron Bocar, Saturnino Borras Jr., Steven Drakeley, Greg Fealy, Anton Lucas, Angus McIntyre, Michelle Miller, Manuel Quiambo, Ben Read, and Olle Tornquist commented on individual chapters. Ben Kerkvliet read the entire manuscript. To all these scholars I would like to express my deep appreciation and thanks. They made an enormous contribution to the project; it has been my privilege—professionally and on a personal basis—to interact with them. Although not a direct participant in the project, Carolyn Fleisher provided strong support for it.

Thanks are also due to the Japan Foundation Center for Global Partnership for providing funding support, the Asia Foundation, Cambodia, for co-hosting the second workshop in Phnom Penh; Charles Morrison and Ralph Carvalho of the East-West Center for their support; Don Yoder for his copyediting; Kevin Downey and Tomoko Okano, who served as my research assistants for the project; Jane Smith-Martin for so ably organizing the two workshops; Nancy Hopkins for her assistance in organizing the second workshop; and Ann Takayesu for so efficiently word processing the entire manuscript, as well as compiling it for submission to Stanford University Press; Deborah Forbis, Jeremy Sutherland, Luke Johnson, and Tae-Eun Song for proofreading; and Muriel Bell, Carmen Borbon-Wu, and John Feneron for shepherding the manuscript through the review and production processes.

Finally, I would like to express my deepest appreciation to my wife Kalyani. Her understanding and unstinting love and support has made this and the other books in the past decade possible. My daughters Radha, Shanthi, and Padmaja, and especially Vikram and Arjun continue to remind me that life is much more than just work. Being close to them has been a source of strength, joy, and pride.

Muthiah Alagappa

Selected Acronyms and Abbreviations

AARP	American Association of Retired Persons
ABIM	Angkatan Belia Islam Malaysia (Malaysian Islamic Youth Movement)
ABSDF	All-Burma Students' Democratic Front
ACFTU	All-China Federation of Trade Unions
AMP	Association of Malay Muslim Professionals (Singapore)
APLA	All Peasant Leader Assembly (Philippines)
APWA	All-Pakistan Women's Association
AWARE	Association of Women for Action and Research (Singapore)
BAYAN	Bagong Alyansang Makabayan (New Patriotic Alliance) (Philippines)
BCP	Burma Communist Party
BD	Bajrang Dal (India)
BEPRPA	Blue East Port River Protection Association (Taiwan)
BJP	Bharitya Janata Party (India)
BSPP	Burma Socialist Program Party
BTI	Barisan Tani Indonesia (Indonesian Peasants' Front)
CARP	Comprehensive Agrarian Reform Program (Philippines)
CCEJ	Citizens' Coalition for Economic Justice (South Korea)
CCP	Chinese Communist Party
CPAR	Congress for a People's Agrarian Reform (Philippines)
CPP	Communist Party of the Philippines
CSE	Center for Science and Environment (India)
CSGE	Citizens' Solidarity for General Elections (South Korea)

CSMNAIGO	Citizens' Solidarity for Monitoring the National Assembly Inspection of Government Offices (South Korea)
CYDF	Chinese Youth Development Foundation
CYL	Communist Youth League (China)
DAR	Department of Agrarian Reform (Philippines)
DFID	Department for International Development (UK)
DPP	Democratic Progressive Party (Taiwan)
DVA	Domestic Violence Act (Malaysia)
FBC	Free Burma Coalition
FCRA	Foreign Contribution Regulation Act (India)
FFF	Formosans for a Free Formosa (Taiwan)
FOSSO	Field Operations and Support Services Office (Philippines)
FP	Federal Party (Sri Lanka)
GHF	Garden of Hope Foundation (Taiwan)
GNP	Grand National Party (South Korea)
GONGO	government-organized NGO
HKTI	Himpunan Kerukunan Tani Indonesia (Indonesian Peasant's Harmony Association)
HRCP	Human Rights Commission of Pakistan
INGI	International NGO Forum on Indonesia
INPACT	Initiative for Political and Conflict Transformation (Sri Lanka)
ISA	Internal Security Act (Malaysia, Singapore)
ISI	Interservices Intelligence (Pakistan)
JAG	Joint Action Group Against Violence Against Women (Malaysia)
JSS	Jathika Sevaka Sangamaya (National Worker's Union) (Sri Lanka)
JVP	Janatha Vimukthi Peramuna (People's Liberation Front) (Sri Lanka)
JYC	Jaffna Youth Congress (Sri Lanka)
KFEM	Korean Federation of Environmental Movements
KMT	Kuomintang (Taiwan)
KMP	Kilusang Magbubukid ng Pilipinas (Peasant Movement of the Philippines)
KOMPIL	Kongreso ng Mamamayang Pilipino (Congress of Filipino Citizens)
KPA	Konsorsium Pembaruan Agraria (Consortium for Agrarian Reform) (Indonesia)
LBH	Lembaga Bantuan Hukum (Legal Aid Institute) (Indonesia)

LTTE	Liberation Tigers of Tamil Eelam (Sri Lanka)
MKSS	Majdoor Kisan Shakti Sangathan (Organization for the Empowerment of Workers and Peasants) (India)
MMA	Muttahida Majlis Amal (United Action Forum) (Pakistan)
MRD	Movement for Restoration of Democracy (Pakistan)
MTBIA	Mandalay Traders, Brokers, and Industrialists Association (Burma)
MWF	Modern Women's Foundation (Taiwan)
NAPCU	National Association for the Promotion of Community University
NCWO	National Council of Women's Organizations (Malaysia)
NDF	National Democratic Front (Philippines)
NFTSR	National Front for Tribal Self-Rule (India)
NGO	nongovernmental organization
NGORC	NGO Resource Center (Pakistan)
NHA	neighborhood association (Japan)
NKDP	New Korea Democratic Party
NPA	New People's Army (Philippines)
NPC	National Peace Council (Sri Lanka)
NPO	nonprofit organization
NRSP	National Rural Support Program (Pakistan)
NSS	Nature Society Singapore
NSS	National Sample Survey (India)
NU	Nahdlatul Ulama (Awakening of the Islamic Scholars) (Indonesia)
OPP	Orangi Pilot Project (Pakistan)
PA	People's Alliance (Sri Lanka)
PAN	Partai Amanat Nasional (National Mandate Party) (Indonesia)
PAP	People's Action Party (Singapore)
PARRDS	Partnership for Agrarian Reform and Rural Development Services (Philippines)
PAS	Parti Islam seMalaysia (Pan-Malaysian Islamic Party)
PBU	professional business unit (China)
PDF	Pattan Development Foundation (Pakistan)
PEACE	Philippine Ecumenical Action for Community Empowerment Foundation
PECCO	Philippine Ecumenical Council for Community Organizing
PERGAS	Persatuan Guru-Guru Agama Islam Singapura (Singapore Islamic Scholars and Religious Teachers Association)

PILER	Pakistan Institute for Labor Education and Research
PIP	public-interest legal person (Japan)
PKB	Partai Kebangkitan Bangsa (National Awakening Party) (Indonesia)
PKI	Partai Komunis Indonesia (Indonesian Communist Party) (Indonesia)
PML-N	Pakistan Muslim League Nawaz
PML-Q	Pakistan Muslim League Quaid-e-Azam
PNA	Pakistan National Alliance
PNF	Pakistan NGO Forum
PNI	Partai Nasional Indonesia (Indonesian National Party)
PPP	Pakistan People's Party
PPP	Partai Persatuan Pembangunan (United Development Party) (Indonesia)
PRC	People's Republic of China
PRD	Partai Rakyat Demokratik (People's Democratic Party) (Indonesia)
PRIA	Society for Participatory Research in Asia (India)
PRRM	Philippine Rural Reconstruction Movement
PSPD	People's Solidarity for Participatory Democracy (South Korea)
PUCL	People's Union for Civil Liberties (India)
PUDR	People's Union for Democratic Rights (India)
RIT	Rangoon Institute of Technology (Burma)
RSC	Remaking Singapore Committee
RSS	Rashtriya Swamsewak Sangh (National Volunteer Corps) (India)
SCAP	Supreme Commander Allied Powers (Japan)
SDF	SUNGI Development Foundation (Pakistan)
SDPI	Sustainable Development Policy Institute (Pakistan)
SEWA	Self-Employed Women's Association (India)
SLFP	Sri Lanka Freedom Party
SLORC	State Law and Order Restoration Council (Burma)
SMO	social movement organization
SPDC	State Peace and Development Council (Burma)
SPDC	Social Policy Development Center (Pakistan)
SSP	Sipah Sahaba Pakistan (Army of the Prophet's Companions)
SWRC	Social Work and Research Center (India)

TWC	The Working Committee Network (Singapore)
TWRF	Taipei Women's Rescue Foundation (Taiwan)
UBCCI	Union of Burma Chamber of Commerce and Industry
UCCM	United Coordinating Council of Muslims (Sri Lanka)
ULD	United Liberal Democrats (South Korea)
UMCCI	Union of Myanmar Chamber of Commerce and Industry
UMNO	United Malays National Organization
UNF	United National Front (Sri Lanka)
UNORKA	Pambansang Ugnayan ng Nagsasariling mga Lokal na Samahang Mamamayan sa Kanayunan (National Coordination of Autonomous Local Rural People's Organizations (Philippines)
UNP	United National Party (Sri Lanka)
UPFA	United People's Freedom Alliance (Sri Lanka)
USDA	Union Solidarity and Development Association (Burma)
VHP	Vishwa Hindu Parishad (World Hindu Council) (India)
VWO	voluntary welfare organization (Singapore)
WADECOR	Worldwide Agricultural Development Corporation
WLAW	Warm Life Association for Women (Taiwan)
WUFI	World United Formosans for Independence (Taiwan)
YMHA	Young Men's Hindu Association (Sri Lanka)

Contributors

MUTHIAH ALAGAPPA is director of the East-West Center Washington. He received a Ph.D. in international affairs from the Fletcher School of Law and Diplomacy at Tufts University. His research interests include international relations theory, international politics in the Asia Pacific region, and comparative politics in Asia.

EDWARD ASPINALL is lecturer in the Department of Chinese and Southeast Asian Studies and Department of History, University of Sydney. He received a Ph.D. in political science from the Australian National University. His research interests include Indonesian politics, especially democratization, civil society, and social movements, as well as Indonesian nationalism and the secessionist movement in Aceh.

AMITABH BEHAR is program officer of the Swiss Agency for Development and Cooperation, New Delhi. He received an M.Phil. in political science from the Centre for Political Studies, Jawaharlal Nehru University, New Delhi. His research interests are governance and civil society, especially decentralized rural self-governance and social movements in central India.

NEIL DEVOTTA is assistant professor of political science at Hartwick College. He received a Ph.D. in political science from the University of Texas at Austin. His research interests include civil society and democracy, ethnicity and nationalism, ethnic conflict resolution, globalization and Third World development, and South Asian politics and security.

YUN FAN is assistant fellow at the Institute of Sociology, Academia Sinica. She received a Ph.D. in sociology from Yale University. Her research interests include social movements, civil society, and collective action.

JENNIFER C. FRANCO is an independent researcher in the Philippines and in the Netherlands. She received a Ph.D. in politics from Brandeis University. Her main research interests are peasant movements, land reform, and rural democratization.

MARY E. GALLAGHER is assistant professor of political science at the University of Michigan, Ann Arbor. She received a Ph.D. in politics from Princeton University. Her research interests include legal mobilization, state-society relations, and the politics of economic reform in developing and transitional states.

SUZAINA KADIR is assistant professor in the Department of Political Science, National University of Singapore. She received her Ph.D. in political science from the University of Wisconsin–Madison. Her research interests include religion and politics, state-society relations, as well as political change and development in Southeast Asia.

SUNHYUK KIM is associate professor in the Department of Public Administration at Korea University. He received a Ph.D. in political science from Stanford University. His research interests include comparative democratization, comparative policy analysis, international institutions, and regional integration.

KYAW YIN HLAING is assistant professor in the Department of Political Science at the National University of Singapore. He received a Ph.D. in government from Cornell University. His research interests include state-society relations, social movements, political culture, democratization, and conflict resolution.

ROBERT PEKKANEN is Luce Junior Fellow in Asian Studies and assistant professor of political science at Middlebury College. He received his Ph.D. in political science from Harvard University. His research interests include Japanese civil society, the transformation of indigenous conglomerates in Southeast Asia after the financial crisis of 1997–98, and the effects of electoral system change on political parties and legislative institutions.

ASEEM PRAKASH is a fellow at the Institute for Human Development, New Delhi. He received an M.Phil. in political science from Jawaharlal Nehru University, New Delhi. His research interests include the political economy of development, caste and communal politics, governance and decentralization, and environmental politics.

AQIL SHAH is a visiting scholar at the International Forum for Democratic Studies in Washington, D.C. Beginning fall 2004, he will be a doctoral candidate in political science at Columbia University.

MEREDITH L. WEISS is assistant professor of international studies at DePaul University. She received her Ph.D. in political science from Yale University. Her research interests include social movements and protest in Malaysia and Singapore, Malaysian electoral politics, and the changing nature of ethnicity and communalism in Malaysia.

Civil Society and Political Change in Asia

Introduction

MUTHIAH ALAGAPPA

> Civil society and its movement are the central forces leading our society.
>
> —Roh Moo-hyun, president of the Republic of Korea, 2003

> In Korea, where political parties, the media, and the judiciary still remain weak and underinstitutionalized, civil society organizations, which have persistently pursued public good, are the only social force[s] that give us hope.
>
> —Park Won-soon, secretary-general, People's Solidarity for Participatory Democracy, Republic of Korea, 2002

> To solidify our democracy, we will reinforce the teaching of democratic ideals and establish a civil society built upon a foundation of liberty and self-discipline broadening the concept of human rights and advocating respect for diversity.
>
> —Chen Shui-bian, president, Republic of China (Taiwan), 2002

> From now on we require a new arrangement, one in which citizens, local governments, business, and the national bureaucracy face each other as equals around the table of "public affairs" . . . so as to create a locus of public interest values. This is an important part of what we mean by shifting from a state-centered society to citizen-centered society.
>
> —Yukio Hatoyama, co-equal chairman of the Democratic Party of Japan, 2002

> The power of our civil society has come from [the] popular conviction that democratic governments must be founded by the people and for the people. . . . People power was responsible for the demise of two dictators. [People power] movements emerge when governments fail to give real democracy to the people.
>
> —Corazon Cojuango Aquino, first post-Marcos president, Republic of the Philippines, 2001

> We have to clarify that civil society is not monolithic. . . . Sometimes we will disagree on our attitude toward the government. This is not the time to abandon the government. This is the time to link arms and to work at pursuing the political, social reforms that are still badly needed by our society.
>
> —Jose Luis Martin "Chito" C. Gascon, member of the national council of the Congress of the Filipino Masses, 2002.

> The relationship between the Thai state and civil society is not always an easy one. The government often sees the NGOs as ill-informed adversaries [who constitute] an obstacle to state plans. For their part, civil society groups need to learn how to use the right to assemble and articulate their demands through the free press before resorting to acts of civil disobedience. . . . Without willingness to compromise in reasonable ways, conflict is inevitable.
>
> —Boontun Dockthaisong, second vice president of the senate, Thailand, 2000

> In today's era of reformation, we are all resolved to forge a new spirit and vitality in national life for the attainment of a democratic civil society.
>
> —B. J. Habibie, president, Republic of Indonesia, 1998

> In the civil society that we envisage, it is incumbent upon the elected leadership to inculcate certain fundamental principles and put them into practice. Chief among these would be the rule of law, the clear separation of powers among the various branches of government, freedom of belief, freedom of speech, and freedom of assembly. Citizens must not only be accorded these liberties; they must be made aware of them.
>
> —Anwar Ibrahim, deputy prime minister of Malaysia, 1998

> Civil society is almost always portrayed as an unmitigated good. . . . The truth, however, is that like government and the private sector, there is good as well as bad civil society. . . . The countries of Southeast Asia must seek to foster a vibrant civil society that works with the government and the private sector for the common good. The onus does not rest with civil society alone.
>
> —Abdullah Badawi, deputy prime minister of Malaysia, 2001

> A battlefield is not necessarily a place where people are shooting at each other. In civil society where basic human rights are ignored, where the rights of people are violated every day, it is like a battlefield where lives are lost and people are crippled.
>
> —Aung San Suu Kyi, leader, National League for Democracy, Burma, and Nobel laureate, 1999

Despite its Western pedigree, the term *civil society* has entered Asian political discourse and analysis in a substantive manner. As the preceding epigraphs illustrate, leaders in government and political society through much of Asia acknowledge the existence, power, and role of civil society groups and organizations in the politics of their respective countries and in the region at large. Certainly, there are wide variations in the conception of civil society and in the attitude of governments and political leaders to civil society organizations. Viewing such organizations as a positive force in the advancement of democracy, some governments have instituted rules and rights to facilitate the development of a sphere of organization and governance that is independent of the state. Civil society organizations in these countries have been actively involved in drafting and ratifying new constitutions, monitoring elections, maintaining oversight of the state, and policymaking. Other governments have adopted a more negative attitude. Viewing nonstate organizations as a cause of instability and an obstacle to their visions and policies, these governments seek to suppress if not eliminate the space and role of such organizations. Still other governments seek to limit, penetrate, co-opt, control, and manipulate civil society organizations for their own benefit. Notwithstanding the differences in orientation, considerations relating to civil society have become a significant factor in the calculations of the Asian political elite. Except in a case like North Korea, political leaders can no longer hold on to state power or govern on the assumptions that society does not matter or that they know best what is good for society. For their part, leaders and members of nonstate organizations and participants in mass movements regard themselves and their organizations or movements as belonging to civil society. They seek to create public spaces and organizations free of state control, articulate the interests of their respective constituencies, be a voice for minorities, the marginalized, and the poor, and bring about (or prevent) change in the nature of the state and its agencies, in the political system or incumbent government, and in government polices. In the process, civil society organizations contribute to a restructuring of the state and political societal relations among state, society, and the economy.

The importance of civil society as a political force gained worldwide prominence beginning in the 1980s in the context of fundamental global geopolitical and economic changes and in the wake of numerous transitions all over the world from authoritarian and communist regimes to democracy—what Samuel Huntington (1991) has called the Third Wave of democracy. By the mid-1990s, liberal political leaders, scholars, and activists were celebrating the triumph of democracy, free-market capitalism, and human rights throughout the world. The Soviet Union and indeed the whole European communist world had collapsed, and the command economy model was bankrupt. More than sixty countries had adopted some form of democratic government between 1974 and the mid-1990s. Victory on the ideological and geopolitical battlefields had so discredited communist and authoritarian systems that one observer was led in a widely criticized article to proclaim the end of history (Fukuyama 1989). Others claimed that historians would look back on the last quarter of the twentieth century "as the greatest period of democratic ferment in the history of modern civilization" (Diamond and Plattner 1996: ix).

Western political leaders—along with participants in the dramas that unfolded in various regions of the world and liberal scholars—credit civil society with having played a crucial role in the collapse of communism and authoritarianism and in the accompanying transitions to democracy. Civil society has become a normative ideal. It is perceived as having the potential to liberate citizens from the oppressive state and to confer full economic and political freedom on them. Some present civil society as a program and an alternative to the domineering state. Viewing civil society as a virtue and a positive force for the development and consolidation of democracy, as well as a site for subverting the remaining communist and authoritarian states, Western international aid agencies and foundations, along with advocates of democracy in the academic community, target the development of vigorous civil societies in the new democracies and seek to sow the subversive seed of civil society in undemocratic states. Along with rule of law, enhancement of legislative capacity, growth of political parties, and development of capitalist economy, promotion of civil society in developing countries has become a key goal of governments in the West and, to a lesser degree, of the Japanese government (Carothers and Ottaway 2000). A substantial portion of international aid money has been earmarked for programs to aid the development of civil society.

Although the democratic transitions in eastern Europe in the wake of the Soviet collapse were the most celebrated, Asia too had its share of dramatic moments. The prominence of civil society in Asia is due in substantial part to the mass rallies and protests by citizens' organizations and movements that played a central role in the delegitimation and ouster of a number of authoritarian governments in the past two decades and to the challenge they continue to pose for the remaining communist and authoritarian states. The 1986 mass protest by some one to two million Filipinos played a key role in the ouster of President Marcos and his authoritarian government. And mass protest has continued to be an important feature in the politics of that country. In 1997, on the twenty-fifth anniversary of Marcos's declaration of martial law, some 600,000 citizens protested the anticipated lifting of the one-term limit on the office of the president and forced Fidel Ramos's supporters to abandon their campaign. In 2001, in the context of an impeachment stalemate in the Philippine senate, a massive public protest called People Power II resulted in the arrest of the legitimately elected but massively corrupt Joseph Estrada and installation of Gloria Macapagal-Arroyo as president.

Mass rallies and protests have also figured prominently at critical junctures in South Korea, Thailand, Bangladesh, Indonesia, Burma, and the PRC. In 1987, a highly mobilized civil society in South Korea compelled President Chun Doo Hwan to accept the demands of the opposition (including a speedy constitutional reform) and to hold elections under a new constitution. Mass action by civil society organizations played a central role in the major turning points in post–World War II Thai politics, including the ouster of the military government in 1973 and prevention of a return to military-dominated rule in 1992. A mass protest organized by the two leading political parties and the All-Party Student Union in 1990 led to the resignation and subsequent arrest of General Hosain Muhammad Ershad, Bangladesh's president since 1982, and the holding of free elections in 1991 under a caretaker government headed by the chief justice. Mass protest also figured prominently in the events leading to the dramatic resignation of President Suharto in 1998, paving the way for a new, and in many ways uncertain, democratic era in Indonesia. Mass student-led demonstrations in Burma in 1988 jolted the military that had ruled the country since 1962, compelling the leadership to organize multiparty elections. A massive democracy demonstration in Beijing in 1989 severely challenged the legitimacy of the Chinese Communist Party.

Although they are dramatic and capture the popular imagination, mass movements, rallies, and protests are only one manifestation of civil society and its activities. Indeed, mass movements and rallies are not the everyday expression of civil society. They erupt at moments of crisis and opportunity when a number of organizations (students, teachers, journalists, workers, farmers, merchants, professionals, religious orders) combine efforts to mobilize public opinion with the purpose of expressing support or disapproval of an incumbent government and to demand or prevent change in the political system, the incumbent ruler, or a specific policy. Frequently, such mass protests fuse elements of political and civil societies and, because they are based on a minimal set of demands in times of acute crisis, lack the capacity for permanent organization and representation. Consequently, they disband soon after their immediate purpose is realized, or they simply run out of steam. Civil society in Asian countries, as elsewhere, is an arena of power, inequality, struggle, and cooperation that is populated by a wide array of voluntary and nonvoluntary groups whose political orientations, interests, resources, capacities, and methods span a wide spectrum. These nonstate groups, operating in urban and rural areas and at times in foreign countries, function independently or in small networks to advance specific causes and interests that may diverge and conflict with one another.

An undue focus on mass rallies and protests may overstate the strength and consequence of civil society—obscuring the relevance of other domestic and international actors, as well as fissures in the government and the military that may provide an opening for the "resurrection of civil society." A selective emphasis on mass protests may also obscure the more mundane and less visible functions of civil society in normal times, functions that may be just as crucial as its actions in moments of crisis. Civil society organizations may be consequential in all stages of politics at the national, regional, and local levels. In a country undergoing democratic change, for example, prodemocracy organizations, subject to their critical mass and inclinations, may play key roles in the liberalization, transition, and consolidation phases. In the *liberalization* phase, their focus may include the construction of individual rights and a public space free of state control. In the *transition* phase, their focus may include delegitimating and ousting the incumbent system of government or ruler, drafting and ratifying a new constitution, fleshing out and institutionalizing a system of individual and group rights, constructing the framework for a legitimate public sphere, supporting the development of political parties, drafting and overseeing the implementation of an electoral system and legitimating its outcome, maintaining oversight of the state, and preventing a rollback of democracy by ensuring a balance of power in favor of democratic forces. In the *consolidation* phase, their focus may widen to include the substantive dimensions of democracy: improving socioeconomic equity, making the system more inclusive, increasing the transparency and accountability of government, demanding change in specific policies, and assisting in the delivery of services. This catalog of roles points out the relevance of civil society organizations in all phases of democratic development, not just in the ousting of an undemocratic regime. Civil society organizations can also play important roles in policy advocacy and in constraining state power in nontransitional states and countries where full democratization is unlikely. It is pertinent to observe here, however, that antidemocratic forces in civil society may be working simultaneously to limit and even reverse certain democratic developments.

There is a tendency in Asia, as elsewhere, to bracket civil society, idealize it as the moral conscience of society, and project its development as critical for democratic transition and consolidation. Although its role as a moral force is important, only occasionally and for brief moments does civil society assume the image of a moral force in the eyes of the public. Even at points of maximum mobilization, when its components endeavor to portray themselves as united, civil society is often divided, with struggle and competition among groups simply held in abeyance. As noted earlier, civil society is an arena of power and struggle among competing interests. In the Philippines, for example, EDSA 1 clearly deprived Marcos of moral authority, but the People Power movement, which comprised disparate groups, soon fragmented. A constant struggle has ensued in that country over a range of issues between civil society organizations rooted in middle-class values and those of the Left. Similarly, civil society in South Korea comprises both so-called moderate and radical elements, with substantial differences in their visions of democracy (Kim 1997): the moderate groups emphasize the minimum procedural elements of democracy; the radical groups' vision stresses socioeconomic equality, labor rights, and other features of substantive democracy. Liberal and conservative elements in civil society also compete to influence the political direction of Thailand. Although most evident during the 1973–76 period, such competition—especially between urban and rural organizations, whose political orientations and interests vary substantially—continues to be a key driving force in Thai politics. Not all civil society organizations support democracy. Civil society groups in Asia, as elsewhere, have also supported authoritarian governments: significant elements supported Marcos in the early years of his dictatorship; urban groups did not oppose, and indeed welcomed, the military's seizure of power in Thailand in 1991; and a substantial segment of the Indonesian middle class supported the authoritarian government of Suharto well into the 1990s. And even among groups supporting democracy, visions of democracy may vary significantly. Depending on the structure and composition of civil society, the autonomy and inclination of nonstate organizations, and the prevailing political and economic circumstances, civil society organizations have displayed both democratic and antidemocratic tendencies.

With civil society organizations becoming more numerous and consequential, it is crucial to understand the nature of the nonstate public sphere in Asian countries, the strength and orientation of the organizations that populate this realm, their relationship to the state, society, and the economy, and their political import. This is especially important in Asia, which is still home to multiple political systems and confronts several fundamental challenges of political change arising from nation building and the development of legitimate and durable political systems. North Korea is a totalitarian state; the PRC, Vietnam, and Laos still have communist political systems; Pakistan and Burma have military governments; Brunei is a monarchy; Malaysia and Singapore are quasi-democracies; Sri Lanka is an illiberal democracy; Thailand, the Philippines, Mongolia, Bangladesh, Indonesia, and Cambodia are in various stages of transition to democracy; South Korea and Taiwan are becoming consolidated democracies; India and Japan are democracies of relatively long standing.

The ideological basis of the governing political systems in Vietnam, the PRC, Pakistan, and Burma has eroded considerably or is bankrupt. Governments in these countries seek to enhance their legitimacy by stressing economic performance, nationalism, and security and tinkering with aspects of the existing system. But good economic performance, even if sustained, cannot provide durable legitimacy (Alagappa 1995). In fact, it creates forces and conditions that challenge the monopolization of political power by a single party or dictatorial rule. Nationalism and security do not translate into durable political institutions. And tinkering with the details cannot satisfy the forces of change. The democratic systems in several countries—especially in Indonesia, Bangladesh, and Cambodia—are still fragile and subject to many challenges, or even reversal. And the deepening of democracy in Thailand and the Philippines confronts serious problems. Even the long-standing democracies face fundamental political challenges, including political immobilism in Japan and a crisis of governance and erosion of secularism in India. The rise of religious fundamentalism is of grave political concern in several Asian countries, especially those with a Muslim majority. The challenge of political change is made more complex in Asia by the distributional consequences arising from the embrace of capitalism and economic reform, along with the integration of national economies into the global capitalist economy. Although tension is particularly acute in countries with closed political systems and relatively open economies, it is by no means limited to them. Both capitalist and democratic development, still in an early phase in Asia, create new groups that alter the distribution of power, making for conflicting interests and tension between the forces of change and the status quo.

Purpose, Definitions, and Propositions

The role of civil society organizations in the challenge of political change confronting many Asian countries is the subject of this study. Our purpose is not simply to argue that civil society exists or that it matters, but to go beyond such assertions to investigate the state of the nonstate public sphere in Asia and the importance of civil society organizations relative to other domestic and international actors, and the specific functions and consequences of civil society organizations in promoting or preventing political change in the direction of open, participatory, and accountable political systems. Specifically, the study investigates:

— The nature of Asian civil societies and the progress made in constituting a legitimate public sphere that is free of state control. Here the concern is with:

The nature and development of civil society organizations. Investigation of this dimension focuses on the structure, composition, and dynamics of organizations that populate the realm of civil society, with particular attention to their political inclinations, and the fissures, struggles, and cooperation that characterize their interaction, as well as the strategic relations and interaction of civil society organizations with other domestic and international actors. The study also considers the general trend in the development of Asian civil societies and the factors underlying it.

The development of a nonstate public sphere. Here investigation focuses on the institution of a set of rules and rights to facilitate the development of autonomous nonstate organizations that can affect state power, engage in self-governance, and make demands on the state in pursuit of public interests.

— The role of civil society organizations in fostering or inhibiting political change in the direction of open, participatory, and accountable political systems and institutions. Here the concern is with:

System transformation and within-system change, including policy change. This includes changes in regime, government, and government policy, as well as in the realization of key systemic features, such as participation, transparency, and accountability.

Restructuring the state and its agencies. Closely related to system change, the focus in this dimension is on the role of civil society organizations in fostering (or preventing) change in state structure and monitoring developments in the relevant state agencies (for example the bureaucracy, military, and the judiciary) in line with the tenets of an open political system.

Relationship to the state and political society. The implications of the growing political significance of civil society organizations for the development of the state and political society, and the changing relationship among actors in all three domains, are the issues investigated in relation to this dimension.

Civil society is the independent variable in this study, and political change is the dependent variable. But political change can occur in many arenas, including the realm of civil society. When civil society itself is the object of change, it becomes part of the dependent variable. These variables are elaborated in Chapter 1. Drawing on that discussion, civil society in this study is defined as a distinct public sphere of organization, communication and reflective discourse, and governance among individuals and groups that take collective action deploying civil means to influence the state and its policies but not capture state power, and whose activities are not motivated by profit. The four aspects of this definition are: a distinct space for organization by nonstate, nonmarket groups; a site for communication and discourse; a site of governance; and a means to influence the structure and rules of the political game. In the first aspect, civil society consists of the voluntary and nonvoluntary organizations that populate the realm located in the interstices among the state, political society, the market, and the society at large and take collective action in the pursuit of public interests. In the second perspective, civil society is a distinct sphere of rights, political discourse, critical reflection, and construction of normative ideals through interaction on the basis of ideas and arguments. The third aspect identifies civil society as an important site of self-governance that is independent of the state. The final feature draws attention to the collective action role of civil society organizations in constructing, protecting, and expanding the public sphere, limiting state power, making demands on the state, affecting the political system, and restructuring the relations among actors in the different realms. It is crucial to note here that civil society is not a monolithic force but a diverse group of actors, whose interests may span a wide spectrum. Although they may be distinguished for analytical purposes, the four aspects are interrelated. And, moreover, the definition advanced here is necessarily a broad one, meant to capture the multiple meanings and features of civil society.

Political change can take many directions. Our concern in this study is with change in the direction of open, participatory, and accountable politics. Although Asia is still home to a variety of political systems, we believe that popular sovereignty and participatory politics are in the ascendance and that the fundamental political challenges confronting most Asian countries arise from the clash between efforts to advance and consolidate change in this direction and those that seek to forestall such changes. Since 1980, Asia has witnessed democratic transitions in the Philippines, Taiwan, South Korea, Thailand, Bangladesh, Mongolia, Cambodia, and Indonesia. Even in a country like the PRC, which cracked down on the 1989 democracy movement, a measure of liberalization (especially at the individual and professional group levels) has occurred, and the economy is becoming substantially free of state control. Although some of the democratic transitions and liberalization are fragile and could suffer setbacks, it appears unlikely that the trend can be reversed without intense opposition, conflict, and suffering. A more likely option for incumbent rulers is to explore ways to accommodate new groups and pressures for change by modifying prevailing systems while holding on to state power.

To capture this complex trend, political change in this study is defined to include all change in the direction of open, participatory, and accountable politics. Democratic change is a key concern of our study, but not its exclusive focus. Furthermore, our concern is not only system change but within-system change. And such change is not limited to the level of the state, as is common in the democratic transition and consolidation literature. In this study, political change is expanded to include change in the realm of civil and political societies and in the structure of relations among civil society, political society, and the state.

The study advances four sets of findings. On the nature and development of Asian civil societies, it presents six propositions. First, contrary to the claim that the idea of civil society is alien, civil society organizations not only exist in Asia but have experienced dramatic growth since the mid-1980s; in some cases, civil societies have relatively long histories. Second, development of civil society is social-reality-specific; multiple factors have fueled the development of civil societies in Asia. Third, civil societies in Asian countries are highly diverse in composition, resource endowment, and goals; they are arenas of power, struggle, and cooperation. Fourth, the composition and dynamics of civil societies have altered dramatically over time in several countries, and more change is in prospect. Fifth, contemporary Asian civil societies display features of both the neo-Tocquevillean and neo-Gramscian frameworks. As the state and its political institutions become more legitimate, the neo-Tocquevillean framework tends to dominate. Sixth, the dramatic growth in the number of civil society organizations has not, however, been accompanied by institutionalization of the nonstate public sphere. The rights and rules necessary to construct and protect the autonomy of this realm are still not all in place in several countries, including democratic ones. Civil society in Asia is viewed largely in instrumental terms, as bringing about or preventing political change in the state and its institutions; it is less commonly seen as an autonomous arena of self-governance.

On the connection between civil society and democracy, the study advances four propositions. First, there is no necessary connection between civil society and democratic change. Civil society organizations have both expanded and contracted democratic space. Second, civil society supports democracy when its dominant discourse is rooted in democratic ideals and organizations advocating democracy acquire critical mass. Third, the specific democratic role of civil society is contingent upon a number of factors: the political opportunity and constraints, the stage of political development, and the strength, orientation, and role of the state and political society in a country. Fourth, civil society is a necessary but not sufficient condition for democratic development. On its own, civil society has a limited effect; in fact, it faces an uphill battle in promoting and consolidating democratic change.

The next set of findings relates to the implications of the rise of civil society for the state and for state-civil society relations. Here we advance four propositions. First, the rise of civil society has limited the power and reach of the state, although the latter continues to be the most powerful institution in Asia. Second, the state has had a strong impact on the nature and development of civil society. Third, state–civil society interaction in Asia is not necessarily confrontational. The relationship varies widely across countries and has undergone transformation in several of them. Fourth, present civil society–state relations in Asia span a broad spectrum. The final set of findings centers on the relationship between civil and political societies. Here we advance two propositions. First, there is much overlap between civil and political societies; the boundary separating them is porous. Second, the development of civil society is not necessarily detrimental to the development of political society. There is much synergy between them. These propositions and the future prospects, including challenges confronting the institutionalization and development of civil society, are elaborated in the final two chapters of the book.

Civil Society's Relevance in Asia

Although it has gained prominence since the 1980s, the concept of civil society has a longer history in Asia than is commonly acknowledged. In Japan, for example, the 1920s and early 1930s witnessed the emergence of new sociopolitical forces, such as trade unions and "new religions," that were not under state domination, and interest groups mushroomed in the first two postwar decades (Sheldon Garon cited in Schwartz 2003). *Civil society* was a widely used term in the post–World War II period (Carver et al. 2000). Deploying an idealized notion of civil society in Britain and France, Japanese historians and social scientists characterized Japanese society as immature and lacking the ethos of civil society. The failure to cultivate the ethos of modern society, including the distinction between public and private spheres, was advanced as a fundamental reason for the militarism and ultranationalism that characterized prewar Japan. Thus prescriptions for postwar Japan ranged from the democratization of family life to the encouragement of free enterprise in the commercial sector through the adoption of modified Western political and social arrangements. Political activists in this period exploited the idea of civil society, especially in the 1960s, in their opposition to government policies—for example, the revision of the U.S.–Japan security treaty. With the wide sweep of the state, especially the all-pervasive influence of the bureaucracy, and an expanding market, combined with Japan's rapid economic development and the wide distribution of its benefits, the idea of civil society, especially the Marxist interpretation that dominated Japanese academic circles in the immediate postwar period, waned in political influence. Beginning in the early 1990s, however, growing distrust of politicians and the bureaucrats and the inability of the state and the private sector to respond to social needs contributed to disaffection with government (Pharr 2000) and a reinvigoration of the nonprofit, or "third," sector. The dramatic shortcomings of the state in responding to the great Hanshin-Awaji earthquake and the outpouring of voluntary effort boosted the image and role of civil society organizations in Japan (Schwartz 2003; Takao 2001).

Although the term *civil society* itself was not used, self-governing nonstate associations that sought to influence state politics and policies were a feature of several Asian countries both during the precolonial and colonial eras and in the postindependence period. In India, for example, the origins of civil society may be traced to the emergence of a number of social reform movements in the mid-nineteenth century that questioned the caste system and position of women in the Hindu tradition (Jayal 2001). In British India, peasants established resistance groups, collected funds for litigation, and sent petitions to the British government of India (Pandey 1988). Peasant groups, traditional caste and religious groups, and elements of the exploited classes often organized and mobilized themselves independently—posing a dilemma for the educated bourgeois leadership of the Indian nationalist movement in the early twentieth century and sparking a controversy in the Indian National Congress (Low 1988). Some observers consider the Indian National Congress itself to have been a vast network of organizations constituting civil society in British India (Jayal 2001). Civil society in pre-independence India is credited with having provided the cultural basis for the development of democratization in that country. The social transformation goal articulated by Mahatma Gandhi stimulated the formation of several movements and organizations (advocating Hindu-Muslim unity, the abolition of untouchability, raising the status of women and tribal people, labor welfare, the prohibition of alcohol, and so on) that in many ways were the precursors of the contemporary voluntary sector in India (Varshney 2001). In postindependence India, with important segments of civil society moving to occupy positions in the state and in political society, civil society receded into the background. The state, which enjoyed a high degree of legitimacy, became the focal point of authority and governance. However, the growing crisis of governance arising from a lack of state capacity and repressive rule during the 1975–77 emergency substantially reinvigorated civil society, especially in the development sector and in the area of civil liberties. Today, completing the unfinished project of substantive democratization is the main rationale and purpose of civil society organizations in India (Jayal 2001). Civil society in India and in many Asian countries is thus not a novel feature, although its manifestations and aims may have altered over time and differ from place to place.

Nevertheless, scholars do not always agree on the relevance and utility of the concept for Asian societies. One group of scholars argues that civil society is a Western concept that is not applicable to Confucian societies, contending that the search for it in such societies is tenuous. Citing tradition—conformity and orthodoxy, benevolent rule by a dominating state, and the penetration of society by the state—these scholars often advance a cultural distinctiveness argument that in many ways mirrors the Asian values debate of the 1980s and early 1990s (Steinberg 1997). Adrian Chan (1997), for example, labels the contemporary search for civil society in China as a Holy Grail that, like the search in the 1950s for "sprouts of capitalism," rests on a "mistaken theoretical premise." Chan contends that there is no room for a Habermasian public sphere in a Confucian state: "If China is to become Confucianist, then she cannot be expected to sprout civil society." Scholars of this persuasion see little analytical value in the concept. In fact, they argue, analysis based on this concept is misleading (Ding 1994). Because civil society in Confucian states like China and South Korea is manipulated by the state and conservative forces to control democratic movements, some say the term should be dropped. William Callahan (1998) says that the concept of "new social movements" is more helpful than the notion of civil society in understanding popular politics in China and South Korea. Others advance concepts such as "plural institutionalism," the "third realm," and "amphibious institutions" as alternatives to the state/society binary dichotomy (Gu Xin 1998; Huang 1993).

At the same time, a number of scholars have begun to deploy the concept of civil society to explain political developments, not only in contemporary China, but also in late imperial China and the republican era. These scholars trace the origins of civil society in China to the reform effort since 1978 and the sustained growth of the Chinese economy, which is perceived to have substantially increased personal freedoms and the autonomy of society (Saich 1994; Strand 1990; Gold 1996). The rise and failure of the 1989 Tiananmen democracy movement (or incident, or tragedy, depending on one's perspective) is attributed by these scholars to the weakness of the incipient civil society. To break away from autocratic rule, they argue, a reconfiguration of state-society relations must occur in China—a process that would feature the development of a strong civil society.

Viewing the economic reform that began in 1978 as a resumption of the unfinished modernization of the republican era, several Western historians of China deploy the civil society concept to understand "the growth and transformation of Chinese cities, as they accelerated during the Republican era, and for asserting the relevance of such historical developments to the present-day situation" (Bergere 1997: 310). David Strand argues that by the end of the 1920s, "a major proportion of city people in China had reached a level of political consciousness commensurate with their formal status as citizens of a Republic" (cited in Bergere 1997: 324). Others, such as Frederic Wakeman (1993), claim that urban residents remained transients from other provinces, that increased fragmentation of urban society contributed more to the development of corporatism than to public spirit, and that there was a growth in autocratic power. Arguing that state power was not reinforced in the early republican era, but nearly disappeared when the warlords took over, Marie-Claire Bergere attributes the successes of the Shanghai bourgeois to the decline of central power, which favored the partial lifting of bureaucratic constraints and the rise of autonomous social forces. The debate among China scholars about the relevance of the concept of civil society has also stimulated research on the development of a civil society with Chinese characteristics that is much more complex than that posited by the state/society dichotomy.

Like most debates in the social sciences, the controversy over the existence of civil society in China and its role in political change is unlikely to be resolved in a definitive manner through abstract discussion. As observed earlier, however, the concept has entered political discourse in many Asian countries—including Confucian states like South Korea and Taiwan—with consequences for the interaction of state and society and for political change. A similar controversy surrounds the relevance of the civil society concept to Islamic societies (Kazemi 2002). Some Western scholars, such as Ernest Gellner, assert that the idea of civil society is antithetical to Islam, because the latter is a social order that "seems to lack much capacity to provide countervailing institutions or associations" and "operates without intellectual pluralism" (Gellner 1994: 29). Conservative and fundamentalist Muslims also reject the concept, because it is perceived as alien, antireligious, and designed to pollute and undermine Muslim societies. Other Muslims argue that it is a universal concept that is applicable to all societies, including Islamic ones. In this view, classical Islam is archaic and irrelevant. Yet a third (reformist/modernist) perspective argues that classical Islam has elements that can be developed through creative reinterpretation to reflect modern social needs. All three perspectives are reflected in the spectrum of Muslim political societies; there is, in fact, no one uniform type of civil society in the Muslim world (Hanafi 2002). Advocating the modernist view, Hasan Hanafi argues that diffusion of power to limit the power of political authorities is not alien to Islam. Although the rights and obligations of Muslims as members of the same religious community command the highest priority, Hanafi contends, Islam does not prohibit nonreligious identities and affiliations. "Islamic theory and practice sustain a number of legitimate human groupings between the state and the individual," and Islamic theory "provides a number of institutions to operationalize the concept of civil society." However, the concept of civil society in Muslim societies, Hanafi argues, must find its roots in the ingredients of Islam and not simply replicate civil society in the West.

Shades of the radical and modernist views are represented in countries with Muslim majorities and minorities in Asia. In Indonesia, for example, there are groups that advocate an Islamic state, but these are in the minority. Robert Hefner (2000) argues that the great majority of Indonesian political groupings advocate a pluralist, democratic nation-state. He posits that "civil pluralist Islam" in Indonesia affirms "democracy, voluntarism, and a balance of countervailing powers in a state and society." However, Hefner asserts that Indonesian democrats are less liberal in spirit than their counterparts in the Atlantic world. Society for them is much more than autonomous individuals, and democracy is more than the market and the state. Contrary to the assertion that civil society is incompatible with Islam, Muslim voluntary associations in Indonesia were in the forefront of nonstate public life during the colonial and postindependence periods, as well as in advocating democracy during the Suharto era. Muslims in Indonesia, Malaysia, Pakistan, and Bangladesh (all Muslim-majority countries) have non-Islamic identities as well and belong to nonreligious organizations, although religious identity overrides all others in a country like Malaysia. Islam in Asia is also not monolithic; there are variations across countries and competing interpretations in nearly every Asian country. As the studies in this volume and others (e.g., Mitsuo, Siddique, and Bajunid 2001) illustrate, the concept and language of civil society have been widely embraced by Muslim groups both in Asian countries where Islam is the majority religion and in countries like the Philippines and Thailand, where Muslims are a minority community.

Throughout much of Asia, organizations and individuals, self-consciously identifying themselves as belonging to civil society, seek to affect the identity and structure of their respective states, as well as government policy on such matters as political and civil rights, minority and women's rights, the environment, and socioeconomic conditions. Moreover, considerations relating to civil society figure in the calculations of the political elite. This study proceeds on the assumption that civil society, however weak and penetrated, does exist and does affect political development in Asian countries. At the same time, it acknowledges that civil society's meaning, nature, and composition will vary with circumstances, not only across countries, but also over time in a country. This assumption is not peculiar to Asia. Even in western Europe, where the concept originated, the meaning of civil society has varied across countries and philosophical traditions and shifted over the course of time. Just as in Asian languages, when translated from English into other European languages, such as German, the term does not convey the same meaning. As amplified in Chapter 1, the meaning and definition of *civil society* are historically contingent, but this does not imply static cultural relativism and incomparability. Culture in our view is not static and can support more than one way of political life. And the impact of culture is best taken into account by connecting it to actors (liberals, conservatives, traditionalists, religious movements) and their organizations, power, interests, and influence in society. Thus culture in our framework is not accorded a fixed and privileged status, but informs, is informed by, and competes with other forces, such as capitalist development and ideational change, in explaining the emergence, development, and role of civil society.

The Significance of the Study

The growing prominence of civil society in democratic transitions throughout the world, including Asia, has stimulated a great deal of thinking about the concept. Civil society has been used as a lens to understand politics and deployed as a key variable to explain democratic political change, especially in developing countries. Many analysts view civil society organizations such as Charter 77 in Czechoslovakia and Solidarity in Poland as crucial elements in the collapse of communism. Certainly, those who took part in the dramas that unfolded in eastern Europe have emphasized the importance of civil society. Václav Havel, for example, has argued that civil society is the key to the survival or defeat of totalitarian political regimes. Writing on the earlier democratic transition in Spain, Victor M. Perez-Diaz (1993: 3) credits civil society: "The gradual emergence of liberal democratic traditions of institutions and values in civil society preceded and prepared the way for the political transition of the 1970s, and . . . those societal traditions enhanced the chances for the consolidation (and institutionalization) of the new regime."

Larry Diamond (1996) writes that democratic change in South Korea, Taiwan, Chile, Poland, Czechoslovakia, South Africa, Nigeria, and Benin, among other countries, cannot be comprehended without reference to civil society. Jean Cohen and Andrew Arato (1992: 2) insist that the concept of civil society is indispensable to understanding the dramatic changes that occurred in Latin America and eastern Europe—especially "to understanding the stakes of these transitions to democracy as well as the self-understanding of the relevant actors." In seeking to explain the democratic political transitions in Africa in the early to mid-1990s, as well as post-transition politics on that continent, John Harbeson (1994: 1–2) advances the proposition that the idea of civil society enables a clearer understanding of the interface between society and government. Civil society, he says, was the "missing key to sustained political reform, legitimate states and governments, improved governance, viable state-society and state-economy relationships, and prevention of the kind of political decay that undermined the new African governments a generation ago." Michael Bratton (1994: 59) asserts that "civil society is sovereign," because the right of an elite to exercise state power is ultimately dependent on popular acceptance, a key resource that is "manufactured by the institutions of civil society." In other words, civil society holds the key to political legitimation of governments.

Some scholars contend that civil society is relevant to understanding political developments not only in the developing world but also in the postindustrialized countries in which the concept originated. Cohen and Arato (1992: 17–18), for example, argue that a "new theory of civil society"—reconceived around the notion of "self-limiting democratizing movements seeking to expand and protect spaces for negative liberty and positive freedom and to recreate egalitarian forms of solidarity without impairing economic self-regulation"—can make important contributions to three ongoing debates in settled democracies: elite versus participatory democracy; rights-oriented liberalism versus communitarianism; and the free market versus the welfare state. Based on the idea that "social connections and civic engagement pervasively influence our public life, as well as our private prospects," Robert Putnam attributes the "disarray" in American democracy to the substantial erosion of social capital (features of social organizations such as networks, norms, and social trust) and a notable decline in civil society (1996: 290–306).

Many of the best works on civil society are grounded in the experience of the southern, central, and eastern European countries. Experiences in Latin America inform some of the major works on democratic transitions and consolidation and, indirectly, civil society. Asia has been much less central in this literature. In part, this neglect is due to the persistence of communist and authoritarian regimes in the region and the belief in several quarters that Asian values are distinct, and that their nondemocratic features are thus immune to the general worldwide trend. A substantial segment of the Asian political elite and scholarly community argued in the 1980s and early 1990s that liberal democracy was not suited to an Asia with its own distinctive value system, which, they claimed, supports a strong state, one-party-dominant political arrangements, and the developmental-state economic model. The outstanding performance of the East and Southeast Asian economies, labeled "miracle economies" by the World Bank, lent weight to this claim. But the 1997 financial crisis, the ensuing recognition of the weaknesses of the developmental-state economic model, and need for political reform, highlighted by the traumatic transition to democracy in Indonesia, badly dented claims for a distinctive Asian value system and suggested that Asia may not be immune to the broad trend in the rest of the world after all. Nevertheless, as observed earlier, Asia still has four of the five remaining communist governments in the world, the military still dominates politics in Burma and Pakistan, and authoritarian legacies still linger in several countries.

The "Asian values" argument and the persistence of multiple political systems have not prevented scholarly work on civil society. Such works, however, have been limited in number, mostly empirical, and country-specific. There are very few Asia-wide studies, and almost none of them are conceptual in orientation or comparative in nature. This book seeks to make a modest contribution in filling the gap in the literature. Although it has an Asian focus, the study is of broader relevance. Because Asia is still home to multiple political systems, several of which suffer legitimacy problems or are in the early stages of change, a comparative study such as this can highlight the complex and changing role of civil society across political systems and across the different stages of democratic development. By drawing attention to the struggles in civil society, and to its democratic as well as its antidemocratic potential, the study can lead to a deeper understanding of the contingent connection between civil society and democracy. Moreover, Asia is a good laboratory for testing and refining propositions on civil society and democracy based on experiences in other regions.

About the Book

This study is a comparative inquiry into the nature of civil society and the role of organizations in this realm in advancing (or retarding) change in twelve Asian countries in the direction of open, participatory, and accountable politics. Political change can be investigated at many levels. This study focuses on the level of the political system: both system change and within-system change. Our concern is not limited to change in the system of government (democracy, communist, authoritarian, monarchy) at the level of the state, however, but includes related changes in political society, in the nonstate public sphere, and in the interaction of actors in all these spheres.

The book has five parts. Part I provides the conceptual perspective for the study. Chapter 1 traces the history of the concept, outlines the contemporary frames of civil society, defines civil society and political change for the project, explores the connection between civil society and democracy, and suggests possible roles for civil society in fostering change in the direction of open, participatory, and accountable politics. The twelve country studies in Parts II to IV investigate the nature of civil society and the role of nonstate organizations in advancing or hindering open politics in the context of the circumstances prevailing in each country. The twelve countries are grouped into three categories. Indonesia, the Philippines, South Korea, Taiwan, India, and Japan constitute the first category (Part II). Although the nature and space for civil society varies widely, there is growing acknowledgement in these countries of the legitimacy of the nonstate public realm. Negotiations over delimitation, purpose, and roles of civil society are a key feature of their politics. Grouping these countries together also enables investigation of the role of civil society in different stages of democratic development. Malaysia, Sri Lanka, and Singapore constitute the second group (Part III). Malaysia and Singapore in this group are quasi-democracies with relatively stable political systems that display strong authoritarian features. Sri Lanka is an illiberal democracy that has denied equal citizenship rights to its Tamil minority, the militant elements of which have been engaged in an armed struggle for an independent homeland for the past nineteen years. The space for civil society in Singapore is severely restricted, while nonstate organizations in Malaysia and Sri Lanka are heavily communalized. Pakistan, Burma, and China constitute the final group (Part IV). The first two countries have military regimes. In Pakistan, a military dictator seeks to legitimate himself through certain pseudodemocratic measures and with American support in the context of the war against terrorism. Refusing to transfer power to the National League for Democracy, which won an overwhelming victory in the 1990 elections, the military in Burma continues to dominate the state and politics there. China, although still formally a communist state, has substantially freed its economy and has also engaged in limited political liberalization. The repressed and truncated civil society in Pakistan is co-opted and coerced by the military state, while the military state in Burma severely suppresses civil society organizations, forcing their members to flee underground and into exile. Although it allows greater personal and professional freedom, the Chinese communist party-state is deeply suspicious of and forbids independent nonstate organizations. In all three countries, the present political systems are not viable in the long run, and they will have to be substantially modified or replaced. Indeed, a fundamental challenge for many Asian countries is the construction of legitimate and durable political systems (Alagappa 1995). Despite the severe restrictions, however, civil society is not absent in these countries. Grouping them together facilitates comparative investigation of the state of civil society in such countries, how they function, and their role in fostering political change in closed and repressed societies.

Drawing on the definitions and analytical framework of Chapter 1, each country study addresses a common set of questions posed in this introduction. Contributors have been allowed wide latitude in expanding and enriching the core framework in a manner they consider appropriate to their country of study. The two chapters in Part V take a regional perspective. Based on the twelve case studies and other published material, Chapter 14 compares the conception, nature, and development of the nonstate public sphere, and the composition, orientation, and dynamics of the organizations that populate this realm in the countries investigated in the study. Chapter 15 summarizes and compares the role of civil society organizations in fostering or hindering change in the direction of open politics. In the process, it seeks to advance several propositions on the role of civil society in political change in Asia and also refines propositions derived from experience in other regions.

Works Cited

Alagappa, Muthiah. 1995. "Seeking a More Durable Basis of Authority." In Muthiah Alagappa, ed., *Political Legitimacy in Southeast Asia: The Quest for Moral Authority*. Stanford: Stanford University Press.

———. 2001. "Asian Civil-Military Relations: Key Developments, Explanations, and Trajectories." In Muthiah Alagappa, ed., *Coercion and Governance: The Declining Political Role of the Military in Asia*. Stanford: Stanford University Press.

Bergere, Marie-Claire. 1997. "Civil Society and Urban Change in Republican China." *China Quarterly* 150: 309–28.

Bratton, Michael. 1994. "Civil Society and Political Transition in Africa." In John W. Harbeson, Donald Rothchild, and Naomi Chazan, eds., *Civil Society and the State in Africa*. Boulder: Lynne Rienner.

Callahan, William. 1998. "Comparing the Discourse of Popular Politics in Korea and China: From Civil Society to Social Movements." *Korea Journal* 38(1): 277–322.

Carothers, Thomas, and Marina Ottaway. 2000. "The Burgeoning World of Civil Society Aid." In Thomas Carothers and Marina Ottaway, eds., *Funding Virtue: Civil Society Aid and Democracy Promotion*. Washington, D.C.: Carnegie Endowment for International Peace.

Carver, Terrell, Shin Chiba, Reiji Matsumoto, James Martin, Bob Jessop, Fumio Iida, and Atsushi Sugita. 2000. "Civil Society in Japanese Politics: Implications for Contemporary Research." *European Journal of Political Research* 37: 541–55.

Chan, Adrian. 1997. "In Search of Civil Society in China." *Journal of Contemporary Asia* 27(2): 242–51.

Cohen, Jean L., and Andrew Arato. 1992. *Civil Society and Political Theory*. Cambridge, Mass.: MIT Press.

Diamond, Larry. 1996. "Toward Democratic Consolidation." In Larry Diamond and Marc F. Plattner, eds., *The Global Resurgence of Democracy*. Baltimore: Johns Hopkins University Press.

———. 1999. *Developing Democracy: Toward Consolidation*. Baltimore: Johns Hopkins University Press.

Diamond, Larry, and Marc F. Plattner. 1996. "Introduction." In Larry Diamond and Marc F. Plattner, eds., *The Global Resurgence of Democracy*. Baltimore: Johns Hopkins University Press.

Ding, X. L. 1994. "Institutional Amphibiousness and the Transition from Communism: The Case of China." *British Journal of Political Science* 24(3): 293–318.

Fukuyama, Francis. 1989. "The End of History." *National Interest*, Summer: 3–18.

Gellner, Ernest. 1994. *Conditions of Liberty: Civil Society and Its Rivals*. New York: Allen Lane, Penguin Press.

Gold, Thomas B. 1995. "Democratic Scorecard." *Free China Review* 45(11): 47–49.

———. 1996. "Taiwan Society at the Fin de Siècle." *China Quarterly* 148: 1091–1114.

Gu Xin. 1998. "Plural Institutionalism and the Emergence of Intellectual Public Space in Contemporary China: Four Relational Patterns and Organization Forms." *Journal of Contemporary China* 7(18): 271–301.

Hanafi, Hasan. 2002. "Alternative Conceptions of Civil Society: A Reflective Islamic Approach." In Simone Chambers and Will Kymlicka, eds., *Alternative Conceptions of Civil Society*. Princeton: Princeton University Press.

Harbeson, John W. 1994. "Civil Society and Political Renaissance in Africa." In John W. Harbeson, Donald Rothchild, and Naomi Chazan, eds., *Civil Society and the State in Africa*. Boulder: Lynne Rienner.

Hefner, Robert W. 2000. *Civil Islam: Muslims and Democratization in Indonesia*. Princeton: Princeton University Press.

Huang, Philip C. 1993. "Public Sphere / Civil Society in China? The Third Realm Between State and Society." *Modern China* 19(2): 216–40.

Huntington, Samuel P. 1991. *The Third Wave: Democratization in the Late Twentieth Century.* Norman: University of Oklahoma Press.

Jayal, Niraja Gopal. 2001. "India." In Tadashi Yamamoto, ed., *Governance and Civil Society.* Tokyo: JCIE.

Kazemi, Farshad. 2002. "Perspectives on Islam and Civil Society." In Sohail H. Hashim, ed., *Islamatic Political Ethics.* Princeton: Princeton University Press.

Kim, Sunhyuk. 1997. "Civil Society and Democratization in South Korea." *Korea Journal* 38(2): 214–36.

Low, D. A. 1988. "Congress and Mass Contacts 1936–1937: Ideology, Interests, and Conflict over the Basis of Party Representation." In Richard Sisson and Stanley Wolpert, eds., *Congress and Indian Nationalism: The Pre-Independence Phase.* Berkeley: University of California Press.

Ma, Shu-yun. 1994. "The Chinese Discourse on Civil Society." *China Quarterly* 137 (Mar.): 180–93.

Nakamura, Mitsuo, Sharon Siddique, and Omar Farouk Bajunid. 2001. *Islam and Civil Society in Southeast Asia.* Singapore: ISEAS.

Pandey, Gyanendra. 1988. "Congress and the Nation, 1917–1947." In Richard Sisson and Stanley Wolpert, eds., *Congress and Indian Nationalism: The Pre-Independence Phase.* Berkeley: University of California Press.

Perez-Diaz, Victor M. 1993. *The Return of Civil Society.* Cambridge, Mass.: Harvard University Press.

Pharr, Susan J. 2000. "Officials Misconduct and Public Distrust: Japan and the Trilateral Democracies." In Susan J. Pharr and Robert D. Putnam, eds., *Disaffected Democracies: What's Troubling the Trilateral Countries?* Princeton: Princeton University Press.

Putnam, Robert D. 1996. "Bowling Alone: America's Declining Social Capital." In Larry Diamond and Marc F. Plattner, eds., *The Global Resurgence of Democracy.* Baltimore: Johns Hopkins University Press.

Saich, Tony. 1994. "The Search for Civil Society and Democracy in China." *Current History* 93 (584): 260–64.

Schwartz, Frank. 2003. "Civil Society in Japan Reconsidered." *Japanese Journal of Political Science* 3(2): 195–215.

Steinberg, David I. 1997. "Civil Society and Human Rights in Korea: On Contemporary and Classical Orthodoxy and Ideology." *Korea Journal* 37(3): 145–65.

Strand, David. 1990. "Protest in Beijing: Civil Society and the Public Sphere in China." *Problems of Communism* 39(3): 1–19.

Takao, Yasuo. 2001. "The Rise of the Third Sector in Japan." *Asian Survey* 41(2): 290–309.

Varshney, Ashutosh. 1997. "Postmodernism, Civic Engagement, and Ethnic Conflicts." *Comparative Politics* 30(1): 1–20.

———. 2001. "Ethnic Conflict and Civil Society: India and Beyond." *World Politics* 53: 362–98.

Wakeman, Frederic. 1993. "The Civil Society and Public Sphere Debate: Western Reflections on Chinese Political Culture." *Modern China* 19(2): 108–38.

PART I

Conceptual Perspective

CHAPTER ONE

Civil Society and Political Change

An Analytical Framework

MUTHIAH ALAGAPPA

The principal objections to democratical or popular government are taken from the inequalities which arise among men in the result of commercial arts. . . . How can he who has confined his views to his own subsistence be intrusted with the conduct of nations?

—Adam Ferguson, *An Essay on the History of Civil Society*

The differing interests of producers and consumers may come into collision with each other, and even if, *on the whole*, their correct relationship re-establishes itself automatically, its adjustment also needs to be consciously regulated by an agency [the state] which stands above both sides.

—G. W. F. Hegel, *Elements of the Philosophy of Right*

What we can do . . . is to fix two major superstructural levels: one [is] "civil society," that is the ensemble of organisms commonly called "private," and [the other is] that of "political society" or the "state." These two levels correspond on the one hand to the function of "hegemony" which the dominant group exercises throughout society and on the other hand to that of the "direct domination" or command exercised through the state and "juridical" government. . . . The superstructures of civil society are like the trench systems of modern warfare. . . . The question [is] whether civil society resists before or after the effort to seize power.

—Antonio Gramsci, *Prison Notebooks*

The most democratic country on the face of the earth is that in which men have . . . carried to the highest perfection the art of pursuing in common the object of their common desires and have applied this new science to the greatest number of purposes. Is this the result of accident, or is there in reality any necessary connection between the principle of association and that of equality?

—Alexis de Tocqueville, *Democracy in America*

Civil society is a popular, normatively charged concept that does not have a single meaning. As illustrated by the epigraphs to this chapter, the concept of civil society and its perception as a problem or solution to the ills of society and state have varied with intellectual tradition and the prevailing sociopolitical and economic conditions. Concepts of civil society in eighteenth- and nineteenth-century Europe emerged in the context of the development of the commercial sphere and the modern state. Conceived essentially, but not exclusively, as a sphere of market relations, civil society was viewed by Scottish Enlightenment thinkers and Hegel as a positive development, which nevertheless posed a problem for social order that had to be overcome by appealing to the moral sentiments of society or state guidance and arbitration. Later, Marx viewed civil society as an arena of alienation and exploitation that had to be overcome through revolution. Tocqueville, in contrast, viewed civil society as a positive force in sustaining democracy in a condition of social equality and a weak central government.

The idea of civil society has traveled far from its origins in Western philosophy, to the United States, Latin America, southern, central, and eastern Europe, Africa, and Asia. Until the early 1980s, debates on civil society were largely confined to the history of ideas in Western political philosophy. With the third wave of democratization, however, especially the dissolution of the USSR and the emergence of the public sphere as legitimate in the post-Soviet central and eastern European states (Poland, Czechoslovakia, Hungary), discussion of the proper relationship between the individual, society, state, and market came to the fore, sparking widespread debate over the meaning of civil society and its place in politics. Civil society has entered the discourse of policymakers, scholars, journalists, NGOs, and laypersons in much of the world. Along with this global spread of civil society, certain scholars envisage the emergence of an international civil society (Keck and Sikkink 1998; Smith, Chatfield, and Pagnucco 1997). They say that the global spread of civil society is not just talk. According to John Keane (1998: 33), it is a sign of "the end of a long century of political thinking dominated by statist ideologies" and the move of civil society, reborn on a grand scale, "to occupy the center-ground of contemporary political thought" (65).

Yet controversy surrounds the meaning of civil society and the universality of the concept. The argument against universality is rooted in the Western origin of the idea and its perceived incompatibility with different traditions or substantially different circumstances in other parts of the world. The cultural relativist argument, which has been quite pronounced in Asia, assumes a single Western conception, which has remained unchanged. But, as we shall see, the meaning of the term has varied over time and the framing of civil society has depended on intellectual tradition and social reality. At present, there are several understandings of civil society. And the place of civil society in the structure of domination and its role in politics, including political change, are not settled issues. In the 1980s, for example, the "antipolitics" notion governed the visions of civil society leaders in central and eastern Europe and Latin America (Arato 2000; Baker 2002). Emphasizing society itself as the arena of politics and change, the antipolitics conception did not envisage directly affecting the state, its politics, and policies. The primary purpose of the "society-first" conception was to liberate society from the totalitarian "lie" of the state and to promote "self-management" in a situation of truth. By the 1990s, however, this conception had given way to an instrumental notion in which the focus of civil societies in central and eastern Europe shifted to their power to limit and influence their respective states, politics, and policies, or to capture state power.

This chapter explicates two contemporary formulations of civil society and develops a framework in which to investigate the relationship between civil society and political change—especially in the direction of open, accountable, and participatory politics. Specifically, I want to address four questions: What is civil society? How is it defined for this study? Is there a causal connection between civil society and democracy? And what is the role of civil society in promoting political change in a democratic direction?

Civil Society: Contemporary Frames

The history of the idea of civil society and its formulation in the different streams of Western political thought over the past two millennia—classical liberalism, liberal-egalitarianism, critical theory, pluralism, Marxism, and democracy, for example—and in the religious traditions of the West and East, including Christianity, Islam, Buddhism, and Confucianism, have been the subject of a number of books (see, e.g., Cohen and Arato 1992; Seligman 1982; Gellner 1994; Keane 1998; Ehrenberg 1999; Kaviraj and Khilnani 2001; Post and Rosenblum 2002; and Chambers and Kymlica 2002). A detailed historical account of the concept's evolution is beyond the scope of this chapter. Here I simply want to develop in broad terms an understanding of how the concept has evolved and to outline the key features of the two predominant contemporary frameworks of civil society.

Early European articulations contrasted civil (or good) society with society in a state of nature or with despotic government. There was no attempt to distinguish civil society from the community and political society at large. With the development of the commercial state in eighteenth-century Europe, civil society, conceived essentially as a market-organized sphere of production and competition, came to be viewed as a distinct, legally protected public realm, separate from family and state. Modern accounts of civil society usually trace the term to Adam Ferguson, a leading thinker of the Scottish Enlightenment. Ferguson viewed commerce and trade and more generally the development of the "commercial state" as ending the corrupt feudal system and reinforcing liberty and personal security (Varty 1997). But he was also concerned about the divisive and disintegrative effects of a market-constituted civil society for social order. The specialization and division of labor, the consequent separation of the commercial from the political arts, and the "avarice and vanity" of the commercial elite were perceived by him as undermining the communal bonds and public virtues (magnanimity, courage, love of mankind) on which democratic government rested (Ferguson [1767] 1995). The market had to be reined in, but not by the state. Asserting that political control would do more harm than good, Ferguson made the case for a self-regulating market that is free of state interference. His solution to the negative consequences of the "separation of the arts and professions" appealed to the moral sentiments of society.

Despite his articulation of the idea of civil society, Ferguson did not distinguish between civil society and the polity. He believed that "society cannot be detached from its form of government, nor can economic man be torn, in practice or abstraction, from the political man" (Oz-Salzberger 1995: xix). The German conception of civil society, which drew its inspiration from Ferguson and Adam Smith did, however, make a firm distinction between the civil society, the family, and the state. Asserting that civil society is a product of the modern state and that its development presupposes a state, Hegel conceptualized civil society as a sphere of market relations, regulated by civil law, intervening between the family and the state (Hegel [1821] 1991: 220; Ehrenberg 1999: 121–32; Ioannidou 1997: 49–62). The acquisitive urge of the burgher class and the ensuing competitive interplay of private interests that breeds poverty and inequality led Hegel to view civil society as prone to periodic instability and conflict, despite its tendency toward a natural equilibrium. To ensure "civility" and stability, he concluded, the state—which in his view was the only entity capable of representing the unity of society and furthering the freedom of citizens—had to order civil society. Hence state intervention to guide and govern civil society was legitimate. Since the time of Ferguson and Hegel, formulations of civil society, irrespective of their political philosophy, have shared a common root. They arose in the context of changing theories of power, legitimacy, and sovereignty, stimulated by the ascendance of centralizing monarchies, their succession by nation-states, the development of self-regulating markets as a separate realm, and the emergence of movements for political freedom. "No longer understood as part of a universal commonwealth," civil society came to mean "private property, individual interests, political democracy, the rule of law, and an economic order devoted to prosperity" (Ehrenberg 1999: xii).

Two contemporary formulations of civil society—that of the New Left and that of the neo-Tocquevillean, or liberal-democracy, model—are relevant to this study. Although they differ in diagnosis, purpose, and strategy, both the New Left and the liberal-democracy school share a positive take on civil society. The New Left conception is rooted in the Gramscian formulation of civil society, which departs significantly from that of Marx. Orthodox Marxists view civil society, constituted by production, class, and their attendant social and political relations, as a structural problem to be overcome through revolution. Marx, in contrast to Hegel, viewed the state as a superficial structure in the service of the dominant capitalist class and depicted civil society as coterminous with the socioeconomic base of the state (Bratton 1994: 54–55). For Marx, therefore, civil society was a problem that had to be overcome, not by the state, which was its captive, but through a revolution that would put the proletariat in the driver's seat. With the workers' party in power, civil society would dissolve into the state, which would represent the true public good. Marx's depiction of civil society as an arena of alienation and exploitation that had to be abolished deprived it of analytic value in orthodox Marxism (Baker 2002: 5).

Committed to the same goal, and using Marxist categories, Antonio Gramsci arrived at a conception of civil society that differed significantly from that of Marx. Viewing civil society as not coterminous with the socioeconomic base of the state, he located it in the political superstructure. Differentiating state and civil society, Gramsci stressed the crucial role of the cultural and ideological support provided by civil society for the survival of European capitalism (Ehrenberg 1999: 208–11). The hegemony of capitalism, according to Gramsci, rested not only on material and coercive foundations but also on a measure of "consent, cooperation, and collaboration" that issued from cultural and ideological support. He therefore urged Western Marxists to pay serious attention to the cultural and ideological institutions that supported capitalism. Advocating a protracted war of position, rather than a simple revolution, as in peasant Russia, he depicted civil society as providing many sites to undermine existing values and inculcate new ones in the counter-hegemonic struggle against capitalism. Gramsci's conception of civil society includes all social institutions that are non-production-related, nongovernmental, and nonfamilial, ranging from recreational groups to trade unions, churches, and political parties.

The voluntarism and political agency accorded to civil society in Gramsci's account inform much contemporary thinking of the New Left on civil society (Baker 2002: 7). Robert Cox (1999), for example, posits civil society as a surrogate for revolution—a key terrain of strategic action to construct "an alternate social and world order." Depicting globalization of production and neoliberal economic orthodoxy as benefiting the integrated class and encouraging "exclusionary and covert politics," he views civil society as the "crucial battleground" for citizens to regain control of public life and as a potential agent for transformation of the state. Others, like Jürgen Habermas (1984; 1996), with due recognition of the pluralism that pervades modern society, view civil society as necessary to defend democracy against the threat posed by modern state bureaucracy, which seeks to encompass more and more of social life. Rather than posing a problem, as in earlier Marxist accounts, civil society is now viewed as providing a solution. The self-reflexivity of society and the institutions of civil society are seen as vital to protect autonomous public opinion and the integrity of the public sphere, two pillars of democracy.

Making a clear distinction among civil society, the state, and the economy, the New Left sees civil society as an important site for counterhegemonic struggle and assigns it a key role in defending society against the state and market and in formulating democratic will to influence the state.

Gramscian analysis and strategy have also been appropriated by advocates of the neo-Tocquevillean conception of civil society, the origins of which can be traced to the response to centralizing monarchs and a powerful state in early-eighteenth-century France. Civil society as conceived in that context emphasized intermediate organizations and notions of community. Seeking to protect the privileged position of the French aristocratic class from royal absolutism, and admiring the balanced constitutional structure of Britain that preserved the interests of the commons, the lords, and the king, Montesquieu advanced an elitist notion of civil society (Ehrenberg 1999: 144–49). Inasmuch as the power and property of the aristocratic class was independent of "the will of the king and the passion of the crowd," he argued, it was "the only estate that could mediate between them" (145). The mediating role of such intermediary organizations, however, rested on certain norms and the existence of laws that would guarantee the integrity of civil society. Montesquieu located "intermediate bodies in the heart of republican theories of civil society." His contribution, together with the notion of community advanced by Rousseau and the defense of custom, tradition, and local power by Burke culminated in Tocqueville's emphasis on political and civil associations as key pillars of democracy in the United States.

Based on his observations of French history and American democracy—and contrasting the centralized French state with decentralized administration in the United States and the "vibrant culture of local activity" in New England—Tocqueville (bk. 1, chap. 12; bk. 2, chaps. 5–7), who does not use the term *civil society*, crafted his conception of associations as performing several key functions: meeting unmet social needs in the context of a weak central government; intermediating between personal or local interest and the national common good; preventing the tyranny of the majority (a major concern of Tocqueville's in light of despotic excesses in France); limiting state power; and preventing abuse by the state. His "civil society," operating in conditions of socioeconomic equality and political freedom, is composed of voluntary associations that cooperate for collective purposes. The interplay of the interests of these associations would guard against domination by a single interest and check the tyranny of the majority and other excesses of democracy. Tocqueville's conception of civil society is based on a limited state that would confine itself to the political sphere and guarantee the legal framework and other conditions (such as socioeconomic equality) necessary for the effective functioning of civil society. It was less state-centered and less certain of the relationship between the state and civil society (Whittington 2001: 22–23). In fact, he viewed the associations in New England as compensating for the deficiencies of a weak central government. Several observers have noted that Tocqueville's assumption about American equality did not take account of the substantial economic and racial inequalities in American society. Thus he was effectively blinded to the negative effects on civil society of the inequalities that pervade capitalist societies (Foley and Edwards 1997).

The intermediation and limitation of state power functions that Tocqueville assigned to associations also inform the neo-Tocquevillean formulation of civil society. But whereas Tocqueville was equivocal about a generalized connection between associations and democracy, contemporary scholars posit a logical link between civil society and democracy. One important stream holds that participation in associations produces social capital that is vital to healthy democracy (Putnam 1993; 1996). In this view, a strong civil society is a prerequisite for effective democracy. The democratic-transition literature assigns civil society an important role in the prelude to the transition, although not in the transition itself (Arato 2000). And the democracy-consolidation literature posits the institutionalization of civil society as a key condition for the consolidation of democracy, making it the only game in town. Democracy advocates also view civil society, in a Gramscian fashion, as a site for the development of democratic culture, with the goal of democratizing the remaining authoritarian regimes.

The liberal-democratic school and, to a lesser degree, the New Left conceive of civil society and its institutions in instrumental terms vis-à-vis the state (protecting the public sphere from the intrusive state, influencing state policy, or altering the regime type) and not as a distinct site for governance and reform that is independent of the state. Consequently, they do not capture the "society-first" formulation that dominated the thinking of Polish and Czech civil society leaders in the 1970s, which emphasized "self-organization," "self-management," and "self-limitation." That conception envisaged a hybrid political system that would limit but not overthrow party-state control (Arato 2000; Baker 2002). The idea was to liberate society from the all-pervasive totalitarian ideology of the party-state, recover social autonomy, expand civil liberties and human rights, and create democratic space (in education, culture, media, and the like) outside the party-state. Although these actions would indirectly challenge the legitimacy of the party and the state, the primary purpose was not to change the party-state or to capture state power. The locus of action was society itself. This notion of civil society as a democratic end in itself was eclipsed in the early 1980s by a more instrumental view that merged with the neo-Tocquevillean notion of civil society. The "ethical society" notion that informed the central and eastern European formulation and the two predominant frameworks discussed here have all been stimulated by a system of needs and outcomes of a process of historical transformation. The ideas were developed and deployed in the context of specific social realities to produce, justify, legitimize, or resist a certain distribution of power, to appropriate certain privileges and roles, or as a strategy for action. This is not to argue for cultural relativism, or to deny the possibility of comparative study, but to point out that the framing of civil society must relate to concrete realities.

Defining Civil Society for the Study

In light of its multiple meanings, and mindful of the need to problematize civil society and its connection to democracy, this study adopts a definition that posits civil society as, first, a realm in the interstices of the state, political society, the market, and the society at large for organization by nonstate, nonmarket groups that take collective action in the pursuit of the public good; second, a distinct sphere for discourse and construction of normative ideals through interaction among nonstate groups on the basis of ideas and arguments; third, an autonomous arena of self-governance by nonstate actors in certain issue areas; and, fourth, an instrument for collective action to protect the autonomy of the nonstate public realm, affect regime type, and influence the politics and policies of the state, political society, and the market. Although distinct, the four aspects are interrelated and affect one another. The political discourses among the self-organized, self-governing, nonstate, nonprofit, nonprivate organizations and the collective actions they take deploying civil means, for example, affect the autonomy of civil society and the prospects for governance that is independent of the state. They also influence society's relations with the state, political society, and the market, and the rules of the games in these arenas. The study does not view civil society intrinsically as a virtue, solution, or problem, but focuses on the discourses, values, and interactions of civil society organizations that are oriented directly or indirectly toward influencing the distinctiveness of the realm of civil society itself, as well as the rules of the political game, in the direction of open, participatory, accountable politics. Several features of the definition—recognition of civil society as a distinct sphere; the depiction of civil society as a space and a site of action; conferment of agency; membership and means of civil society; and the relationship of civil society to the state, political society, and the market—require elaboration.

Civil Society as a Distinct Sphere

It is crucial to view civil society as an arena of governance in its own right, not just an adjunct or means to influence the state, political society, or the market. The notion of civil society as an end in itself is relevant not only to totalitarian and authoritarian states but also to liberal-democratic states. In totalitarian and authoritarian states, this formulation captures the effort of nonstate groups to carve out areas of governance outside the control of the all-embracing party-state without seeking to alter the regime type. As a strategy, the self-organization and self-limiting approach may be less threatening and thus have a better chance of success. Contraction or expansion of the realm of civil society as an arena of self-governance is indicative of the depth and scope of political liberalization in authoritarian states. In liberal-democratic states, the state, in theory, is limited to providing order and security, establishing a system of rights, and enacting broad constitutive and regulatory rules within which nonstate institutions and the market organize much of the social and economic interaction of society. Civil society institutions are the normal means for sustaining governance over a wide range of issues. Viewed in these terms, the scope and vitality of governance in civil society are useful indicators of the emancipation of society from state domination, decentralization, and democratization of governance. They can also be a useful measure of democratization and the consolidation of democracy in societies undergoing political transition.

Civil Society: Space, Site, and Agency

Thus far, I have referred to civil society at various points as a space, a site, and an actor. It is all three. Conception as *space* indicates the location of civil society in relation to other spheres and preserves the integrity of the public realm by not tying it to specific actors who may move in and out of this space, which may contract or expand in terms of sectors, issues, actors, and roles. The space conception also permits the construction of civil society as a *site* for governance and strategic action. It is useful here to recall Gramsci's notion that civil society, as the cultural and ideological repository of hegemony, can be the battlefield in a war of position against capitalism. Civil society in his conception becomes the site for the construction of a counterhegemonic narrative. Neoliberals have also appropriated the notion of civil society as a site for struggle in their endeavor to subvert and eventually replace the remaining communist and authoritarian regimes. Civil society has been used, as well, to denote *agency*, although it should not be treated as a single collective actor. Like the society at large, civil society is a realm of power, inequality, struggle, and conflict among competing interests. It is populated by diverse formal and informal groups and organizations, and although these may choose to cooperate on certain issues or reach accommodation of their conflicting interests, there is no necessary consensus among them. Civil society is invariably competitive and heterogeneous. Agency applies to organizations that populate the civil society space, not to civil society as a single entity. The tendency to use civil society in a shorthand fashion may mask the diversity, inequality, and struggle within the realm. Analytically, it is more useful to speak in terms of specific actors or groups of actors in civil society. This raises the question of membership in civil society: Which organizations qualify and on what basis?

Membership and Means

The preceding elaboration cited certain characteristics of units that populate the realm of civil society: self-organized, self-governing, nonstate, nonprofit, nonprivate institutions that employ nonviolent means to achieve a public interest or good through collective action. With the exception of nonviolent means, these features are not controversial, although in certain cases, it may be difficult to determine whether an organization is indeed self-organized, self-governing, and pursuing a public good, and whether it is penetrated and exploited by the state, political society, or the market. It should be noted that the pubic good in the definition refers to the nonprofit and nonprivate interest of particular groups, not that of the entire community.

Two controversies—one omitted from the definition (voluntary associations with nonexclusionary membership) and the other spelled out in the definition (civil means)—attend the membership question. First: Should membership in civil society be restricted to voluntary associations of individuals? Or should it include ascriptive and other groups that limit membership on the basis of ethnicity, religion, or class? The neo-Tocquevillean conception identifies civil society with voluntary associations, in which membership is by consent and open to entry and exit by all qualified citizens without loss of status or benefits. Individuals can move freely among groups, shift involvement in them, and join more than one association. The emphasis is on the individual's autonomy to choose. Associations in this conception (organized around professional and other interests, social causes, or the pursuit of status and power) represent limited and specific purpose or interest; they do not pursue totalizing goals, which, if realized, would deprive other groups of public rights and benefits. A plural and fluid civil society that permits shifting and crosscutting identities (making possible escape from hereditary and ascriptive attachments) and operates within an agreed political and legal framework is frequently associated with the functions of intermediation and limitation of state power.

Limitation of civil society to voluntary associations, however, excludes other groups (based on religion, heredity, ethnicity, class, and other such features) that are not open to all citizens—groups in which membership is by assent, rather than consent, and exit is not a real option. Because such groups do exist in the public realm, their exclusion by definitional fiat would truncate our understanding of the composition and dynamics of civil society. Inclusion of such groups highlights the complex nature of civil society and the struggles and tensions that pervade it, reminding the observer that civil society comprises heterogeneous groups with diverse and competing goals. Civil society groups are not always supportive of democracy, as is sometimes assumed by proponents of democracy. Limiting civil society to prodemocracy voluntary associations also creates a circularity problem in exploring the connection between civil society and democracy. Furthermore, recognition of the potential for struggle in civil society accommodates the New Left conception of civil society as an arena for the construction of a counterhegemonic narrative. It also provides insights into the perception and reaction of governments, especially authoritarian ones, to demands from civil society groups. As observed by Robert Post and Nancy Rosenblum (2002: 4–8), civil society is, in fact, a continuum of fluid and segmented organizations. But they assert that "segmentation within civil society must have limits" and add that the "freedom that produces pluralist associations should be prized and enforced." The society must afford autonomy to individuals and groups, but the balance should favor the individual's freedom to associate. When this right is curtailed, civil society fragments into rigid groups. In their view, the persistence of civil society "depends upon a complex equilibrium among diverse groups and associations."

We come now to the second controversial issue: What makes civil society civil? Many analysts advance two criteria: the absence of violence and the absence of the will to dominate the entire public realm. In the abstract, civil society is a public realm guaranteed by civil laws of the state, which has a monopoly on the legitimate use of violence. In this context, society is pacified, and violence is excluded as a legitimate means for the pursuit of particularistic interests by organizations functioning in a state-protected realm. In practice, however, many states are not internally pacified. A weak state may not be able to guarantee law, order, and security to all its citizens. Both strong and weak states may unleash state violence against certain segments of the population. In such situations, groups, especially certain ascriptive ones, may have to resort to their own private agencies to ensure the security of members. Such use of violence may be legitimate if deployed for purposes of protection. Intimidation and terrorization of other groups cannot, however, be legitimate tactics to advance a public interest. Groups that avowedly resort to violence to achieve political goals, like the various liberation movements, cannot be part of civil society. This does not imply that their goals and methods are necessarily illegitimate. But such organizations operate more in the realm of political society. There will certainly be gray areas. The military wing of an organization may rely on violence, for example, while the social wing operates in civil society deploying nonviolent means. This issue illustrates the difficulty of applying the civil society concept to weak and contested states—supporting the claim that civil society (as a legally protected realm) is difficult to conceive of without a sufficiently strong state structure. This problem was not absent in strong states like Nazi Germany and Fascist Italy, however, where state violence against a certain segment of society was deemed legitimate by key segments of civil society. Violence is antithetical to civil society, but civil society is also the container of such violence. The control of violence is a major problem for civil society and the state.

Similarly, the will to dominate is not a clear-cut issue. In principle, a will to dominate that denies other citizens their public status and rights, especially the right to associate, is incompatible with civil society. As observed earlier, however, the exclusion of such organizations distorts analysis by obscuring important dynamics of civil society. Groups espousing totalizing missions may not pose a problem if they have little hope of realizing their objectives and the balance clearly favors groups pursuing limited objectives. But this may not always be the case. Overall, the analytical benefits of inclusion would appear to outweigh the benefits of exclusion. In this study, civil society comprises formal and informal voluntary and ascriptive organizations including churches, labor unions, farmers' organizations, academic and student groups, debating societies and reading groups, nonstate media, NGOs, occupational associations, business federations, and sports and leisure groups. Social movements "based on underlying social networks and resonant collective action frames," and that engage in contentious politics when the "political opportunity structure" opens up, are also part of civil society.[1] New social movements that seek radical policy reform in specified areas are part of civil society as well. Transnational and global organizations and movements, as well as diaspora and exiled communities, that significantly influence the composition and dynamics of civil society in a country should also be taken into account.[2] Although the composition of civil society is necessarily broad, it can be narrowed to focus on the key groups and actors that are relevant to the purpose at hand.

Relationship to Other Spheres

Although conceptually distinct, civil society in practice is not fully independent of the other spheres. There is considerable overlap among them, with numerous avenues for interpenetration and mutual influence. Just as civil society organizations may influence the distribution of power, norms, and policies of institutions in the other realms, the structure of civil society and the purposes and interaction of its constituent units are shaped by many elements: the normative and material structures of the society at large; the divisions, inequality, and struggles that characterize society (although civil society need not mirror society at large); the structure, vitality, and policies of state institutions; the vibrancy of political society; and the distribution of intellectual and material resources, which in good part relate to the structure and function of the economy. The scope, representativeness, and effectiveness of institutions in these spheres determine the potential for expansion or contraction of the realm of civil society, its population density, the formal or informal nature of its organizations, whether they seek to engage, constrain, alter, overthrow, or retreat from the state and the market, the resources available to such organizations, and their methods of operation.

Especially critical is the relationship to the state. Civil society cannot exist in a condition of total anarchy—that is, where government is unable to maintain civil order, define personal and group rights, and enforce them (Post and Rosenblum

2002: 7). With political authority, a monopoly on legitimate violence, a stable legal framework, and representing the common good, the ideal Weberian state provides internal law and order, ensures external security, and establishes the rights and entitlements of individuals and groups. It creates the political, legal, bureaucratic, and tax framework within which civil society organizations can pursue their particularistic interests in a civil or nonviolent manner. The scope, purposes, and roles of civil society organizations are all closely connected to the type of regime. The space for civil society is greatest in a liberal-democratic system and least in totalitarian, authoritarian, and paternalistic regimes. In theory, such regimes severely restrict or even eliminate the space for civil society. They also seek to control, manipulate, and deploy civil society organizations to serve the interests of those in power. In practice, totalitarian and authoritarian governments have not always been successful in controlling and manipulating civil society organizations and have proved even less successful in eliminating them. But in contrast to democratic states, where civil society is a legally protected realm, in totalitarian and authoritarian states certain (non-state-sponsored) civil society organizations exist in fear of the state and often go underground. Control and manipulation are not absent in democratic states, however, and the space for civil society and the functions of civil society organizations may vary from one democratic state to the next.

The relationship of civil society to the state is often depicted as confrontational and zero-sum. This may be the case in certain situations. But in most cases the state and civil society are mutually dependent for survival. As noted earlier, civil society requires governance to survive and governments, at least democratic ones, draw their strength from civil society (Post and Rosenblum 2002). The relationship of civil society to the state can take many forms: co-optation and manipulation of civil society by the state, deep penetration and influence over the state by certain civil society actors, productive tension between the two in a context of overall agreement on the political and economic framework, contestation over certain fundamental issues, alienation and isolation of civil society organizations from the state, or outright rejection of the state by key segments of civil society. Although interconnected, civil society groups must be distinct from the state if they are to influence governance, and the state must have autonomy to protect the rights of all its citizens. This arrangement has been referred to as the principle of double autonomy.

Another important sphere in the continuum between private life and the state is political society. Popularized by Alfred Stepan (1988: 3–4), the concept of political society denotes, at least in democratic states, the realm of formal competition for the acquisition and exercise of state power. Political parties, the primary actors in this realm, seek to mobilize public support and to constitute winning coalitions in the formal competition and management of state power through elections and the constitution of legislatures. Civil society is distinct from political society. While they seek to influence the rules of the game and affect policies, civil society organizations do not organize themselves on a partisan basis to aggregate interests and formally compete for state office. In practice, however, the relationship between civil and political society is often blurred. Many civil society organizations—trade unions, churches, the media, and certain interest groups—affiliate with certain political parties on ideological or ascriptive grounds. They may also wield state power through the political party in office. In the process, they become partners in governance, compromising the distinctiveness and autonomous quality of civil society. Blurring also occurs when the actors and activities of political society are banned or co-opted in totalitarian and authoritarian regimes—dissidents may take refuge in civil society to survive, to construct counternarratives, and to develop networks that can be deployed when the "political opportunity structure" opens up. The distinction between civil society and political society and their merging in practice are useful indicators of the existence of civil society even in the most authoritarian and totalitarian states in a defensive or underground form (Bratton 1994). Such differentiation is also useful during moments of political transition when proto-party elites exit civil society to form political parties and compete for state office. Civil society then reverts to its conventional state.

To conceptualize civil society without reference to economic society—especially the market—is to miss crucial insights into civil society and its operation. As observed in the previous section, eighteenth-century conceptions of civil society in Europe were rooted in the recognition of the market as a distinct public realm and the competition arising from growing specialization and division of labor as a problem for social order. Subsequently, Marx linked civil society to a particular stage in the development of capitalism. Today, some New Left intellectuals posit civil society as a defense against the encroachment of the state and the market and the threat of global capitalism. By assuming socioeconomic equality or defining civil society as a nonprofit sector, the Tocquevillean and neoliberal formulations decouple civil society from the economic sphere such that the "material bases of civil society and the negative effects of the market on civil society are erased from view" (Howell and Pearce 2001: 76). The structural inequality of markets has consequences for political and civil societies. It makes it difficult to rid the public sphere of relations of power and inequality. Functioning in a nonstate, nonprofit sphere, civil society organizations, to protect their autonomy, should in theory have independent sources of revenue. But unlike the state, which relies on tax revenues, and the market, which accumulates wealth through capital accumulation, civil society can meet only a portion of its financial requirements from service fees, subscriptions, and donations. A substantial part comes from state contributions, private giving, and international aid (Salamon and Anheir quoted in Howell and Pearce 2001: 79–80). These contributions empower certain groups more than others, shape their agendas, affect the structural and discourse dynamics of civil society, and influence the demands placed on the state. Furthermore, the growing dominance of the mass media—newspapers, journals, and especially radio and TV stations, often owned privately or by the state—subverts the public communication that is central to the formation of democratic will. Without an independent financial base and access to media, the autonomy of civil society is undermined. The key point is this: Although civil society is conceptually distinct, in practice it is not completely autonomous. Its structure and function are heavily influenced by its material base and its relations with the state and market. Civil society's boundary, especially in relation to the state and political society, is porous, at times highly contested, and subject to redefinition through struggle. Actors may inhabit more than one space, act simultaneously in multiple arenas, or move in and out of arenas.

Civil Society in New Democracies

All civil societies are not equal. Some are more developed than others. Before discussing its role in governance and political change, we need to have a good understanding of how civil society operates in a particular country. This section sketches in broad terms the likely contours of civil society in a new democracy. Although civil society organizations may be in the forefront in ousting authoritarian or communist regimes, they are likely to be weak in the postouster phase (Whitehead 1997: 109–10). Usually, civil society organizations are dominated by a small elite, many of whom had privileged standing in the previous regime. They are likely to be few in number and not well organized. The norms associated with civil society—autonomy, deliberation, collective action, civility—will be underdeveloped. Moreover, the new government, often cobbled together from diverse groups, confronts many challenges, including drafting a new constitution and legal system. It may not be able to protect the rights of individuals and groups and establish laws to secure and regulate the public realm. Political and economic equality and rule of law, key conditions for a civil society, may exist only in aspiration. And civil society may be unevenly developed across the geographic and social terrains. Thus, while collective action by a coalition of diverse forces may bring about the ouster of an authoritarian or communist government, civil society often fragments in the aftermath of the political revolution. Some personalities and organizations move on to occupy the vacant state and political society; others simply lose their rationale and disappear from the scene. But in their place, new organizations may mushroom, mostly in the urban areas.

Thus, with few exceptions, civil society is unlikely to be well developed and institutionalized in new democracies. The weakness of civil society may be exacerbated if the incumbent political system or government lacks legitimacy, the nation-state as constructed is contested, and the government is unable to maintain law and order and lacks the capacity to address socioeconomic problems. An overbearing state and the market may also limit the space for civil society and distort its organization and agenda. The legacy of the authoritarian regime, especially its old actors in new garb, as well as criminal organizations, liberation movements, and the like, may also compete with civil society organizations for the public realm. The democracy-promoting effect of civil society organizations may be limited; some may be antidemocratic. Although this sketch may appear pessimistic, it is essential to recognize such possibilities. Civil society must be defined and analyzed in the context of a country's prevailing circumstances.

Two sets of issues are important in understanding how civil society operates in a country. First is the size and quality of the realm of civil society. Can citizens associate freely? Can such associations function in all issue areas? Or do certain restrictions apply? With what consequences? Is a system of rights, fundamental to the functioning of civil society, institutionalized? Investigation of these questions should yield a good measure of the size, quality, and institutionalization of civil society in a particular country. Second: Is civil society plural and fluid with opportunities for multiple identities? Or is it segmented and polarized? Or do features of both coexist? Do civil society's actors partake in a system that is widely acknowledged as legitimate? Or is the system contested in a fundamental manner by certain groups? Do groups employ violence in the pursuit of their interests? In sum, then, it is crucial to gauge the mix of organizations that constitute civil society, as well as their structural locations, purposes, and methods, if we are to understand their democratic (or antidemocratic) potential and their role in political change.

Civil Society and Democracy

For different reasons, both neo-Tocquevillean and the New Left associate civil society with democracy. Civil society has also not only been deployed in the democratization literature to explain political liberalization and democratic transition but has been advanced as a precondition for democratic consolidation. Reviewing these linkages, this section makes the following claims: There is no necessary connection between civil society and democracy; civil society can have both democratic and antidemocratic effects; and the actual effect in practice hinges on the ideas, purpose, and the distribution of power among the organizations that make up civil society, the strategic connections between organizations and leaders in civil society with their counterparts in political society and the state, and the international context.

The Neo-Tocquevillean Connection

Among the early theorists of civil society, Tocqueville made an explicit connection between civil society and democracy. Convinced that the profusion of voluntary public associations underpinned America's robust democracy (by protecting individual liberty, preventing tyranny of the majority, decentralizing power and authority, and fostering active engagement of citizens in politics and governance), he posited civil society as an indispensable component of a stable democracy (Whitehead 1997: 98–99). Today, a remarkable consensus has emerged among democratic theorists around Tocqueville's proposition that "the virtues and viability of a democracy depend on the robustness of its associational life" (Warren 2001: 3).

There is, however, an important difference between the connection made by Tocqueville and that of the neo-Tocquevilleans. Tocqueville himself regarded civil society as a key site for governance and decentralization of democratic governance. For neo-Tocquevilleans, the locus of activity is not society but the state. Their primary concerns relate to the core democratic institutions and processes at the state level. Civil society is viewed as a supporting structure to democratize the state. Associational life is thought to provide the social infrastructure for liberal democracy, supply the means to limit, resist, and curb the excesses of the state and market, present alternatives when they fail, facilitate service delivery at the local level, assist in conflict management, deepen democracy (by cultivating civic virtues, establishing democratic norms, and spreading democracy to more domains of life), offer a voice to disadvantaged groups, and promote economic development. Armed with such beliefs, scholars have tried to explain the degree of robustness of democracies in Western industrialized states, connect civil society to democratic change in the developing world, and prescribe policy for national governments, international donors, and multilateral lending agencies.

An important stream of contemporary thought has focused on the critical role of small face-to-face voluntary associations in promoting civic engagement, and the role of such engagement in producing social capital. Robert Putnam (1996) argues that the norms and networks of civic engagement have a powerful influence on the quality of public life, including the performance of representative government. Such networks foster the development of "generalized reciprocity and encourage the emergence of social trust," which in turn facilitate "coordination and communication, amplify reputations, and thus allow dilemmas of collective action to be resolved" (292). Dense civil networks broaden participants' self-conception, helping to transform the "I" into "we." These are crucial resources for collective action in the pursuit of the common good. The structural resources, habits, and attitudes inculcated through participation in voluntary associations promote healthy democracies. To explain this phenomenon, Putnam relies on the concept of social capital, which he defines as "features of social organizations such as networks, norms and social trust that facilitate coordination and cooperation for mutual benefit" (292). Voluntary associations produce social capital; quality of life and representative government are better in a community with a high stock of social capital; a decline in voluntary associations leads to a reduction in social capital that erodes the vitality of democracy. Although it is based on the study of Italy and the United States, Putnam claims that his conclusion that civil society is the "key to making democracy work" is relevant to the new democracies as well. His impact on policymakers has been substantial (Howell and Pearce 2001: 47).

The concept of social capital and its connection to democracy as articulated by Putnam has generated much debate within the intellectual community, producing critiques from several perspectives (see, e.g., Edwards, Foley, and Diani 2001; Bermeo 2000; Nord 2000; Howell and Pearce 2001). Several criticisms are relevant here. First is the issue of definition. Trust is both a precondition and an output of social networks (Newton 2001). The inclusion of functions and products as part of the definition of social capital creates a circularity problem and muddies empirical investigation. Second, social capital produced by small face-to-face organizations may be important for primary democracy (direct citizen participation) but not for democratic governance in a large, complex modern society. Institutions such as the media and education may be more important in creating the abstract trust that is necessary for the functioning of complex large-scale societies (Newton 2001). Third, Putnam takes a narrow view of democracy that focuses on performance, rather than on deepening and extending the democratic process (Howell and Pearce 2001: 48). Fourth, the benefits of civil society for democracy are uncertain. As Philip Nord (2000: xv) has observed: "Burgeoning civil society translate[s] into a democratization of public life in certain instances but by no means always." Putnam does not consider the antidemocratic norms, values, and practices that inform civil society. If these are taken into account, civil society organizations may be a threat to democratic institutions (Whittington 2001). Voluntary associations may deepen conflict in society, create excessive demands on the government, and hasten the disintegration of democratic regimes (Berman 2001). Thus, while social capital is an important tool for achieving a social goal, the consequence for democracy depends on the political ends for which social capital is used. Finally, to ascertain whether a robust civil society will produce beneficent or harmful consequences for democracy, it must be examined in the proper political and constitutional context and be related to the capacity of political institutions. A healthy democracy depends not only on a vigorous civil society but also on effective political institutions—a point made by Samuel Huntington decades ago (Berman 2001).

Thus the claim that associational life builds civic virtues (reciprocity, trust, recognition), which in turn underwrite democracy, should be qualified in two respects. First, democracy may build on civic virtues, but such virtues are not uniquely democratic. They may underwrite other forms of government (Nazism in Germany, Fascism in Italy, apartheid in South Africa) as well. Much depends on the political and constitutional context and the political ends for which the social capital is deployed. Second, the democratic process may itself erode the civic virtues that are supposed to underwrite democracy, which "is a way of dealing with conflict in the face of pressures for collective action" (Warren 2001: 150). Reciprocity and trust may be fractured by strategic political maneuverings, while democratic politics may sharpen differences of identity. Nevertheless, a background of cooperation may very well lead to empathetic connections that make deliberation more likely, bargaining and compromise less threatening, and democracy easier. But democratic potential depends on associational types, their purposes, and political circumstances, issues that we shall take up later. Next, we explore the second take on the connection between civil society and democracy.

The New Left and Society-First Perspective

The New Left shares certain aspects of the neo-Tocquevillean perspective: for example, it emphasizes the recovery of civil society in order to defend society against the intrusive state and the threat from the capitalist market. Moreover, civil society is assigned a key role in democratizing the state and influencing its politics and policies. Yet there are major differences. Political participation and communicative action, not the production of social capital and its connection to democracy, are the key themes of certain New Left scholars, such as Jürgen Habermas (1984), and Jean Cohen and Andrew Arato (1992). Acknowledging the pluralism in modern society, these scholars focus on the formulation of public will to influence the politics and policies of the liberal-democratic state. Other scholars, such as Robert Cox (1999), view civil society as a site for struggle and construction of a counternarrative for an alternative version of democracy that will cater to the needs of the excluded classes. It is unclear what this form might be. Neither of these perspectives, however, conceives of civil society as a democratic end itself. The society-first approach, in contrast, projects a vision of democracy with multiple sites, of which civil society is an important arena of governance. This notion suggests a more complex connection between civil society and democracy. In addition to the function of civil society in affecting democratic institutions and governance at the level of the state, it draws attention to democratic governance in other sites and the decentralization of power, resources, and authority to local and nonstate institutions in order to promote self-governance and liberate society from domination by the political center (Howell and Pearce 2001: 54–55). Although it developed in the context of communist regimes in central and eastern Europe and has since lost some of its early luster, the society-first perspective alerts us to a much neglected aspect of the link between civil society and democracy.

The Democratization Literature

Although observers and participants celebrate the role of civil society in the political changes that swept central and eastern Europe and Asia, this is less the case in the democratization literature, which focuses heavily on Latin America and elites. Little attention is paid to civil society's origins, its composition, or its democracy-producing effects. Viewed as a given, civil society is conceived of primarily in instrumental terms for bringing about change in the state, not as a distinct area of democratic governance. In fact, such an idea is considered dangerous for democratic politics, because it creates a "parallel to state power" (Stepan 1997). The basic premise of the democratization theorists is that the locus of governance is the state, not society. In this context, civil society is viewed in one of three ways: as a positive but subordinate factor in explaining political liberalization and democratic transition; as a negative force obstructing the development of political society and the democratic state in the postouster phase; and as a precondition for the consolidation of democracy.

"Elite dispositions, calculations, and pacts," write Guillermo O'Donnell and Philippe Schmitter (1986: 48), determine in large measure whether there is an opening and set "important parameters on the extent of possible liberalization and democratization." Once soft-liners prevail, they argue, opportunity opens up for general mobilization, which they call the "resurrection of civil society." This hypothesis is rooted in the belief that authoritarian and totalitarian states eliminate independent civil society organizations, that the public arena is dominated by state-controlled organizations, and that discussion in this arena conforms to codes and rules established by the state. Aside from a few highly motivated individuals, the majority of citizens, it is presumed, confine themselves to private pursuits. Once the government lowers the barriers, however, collective action mushrooms into an "explosion of civil society." The rapid changes undermine the legitimacy of the soft-liners who seek to perpetuate themselves in government and increase the cost of a coup by the hard-liners (53). The diverse layers of civil society come together in a "popular upsurge" that pushes transition even further (56). O'Donnell and Schmitter argue that the popular upsurge is "always ephemeral," however, leaving behind "a persistent problem for consolidation of political democracy that can only be 'tamed' by the holding of elections." This leads to the demobilization thesis: once the authoritarian government has been ousted, civil society loses its relevance and should make way for political society to take the lead in negotiating pacts and constituting the democratic state; civil society, which invariably fragments in the aftermath of a political revolution, must be reconstituted in the context of a new framework put in place by political society and the new democratic state (Arato 2000: 29–30, 63).

The popular top-down thesis is open to challenge for at least two reasons. First, authoritarian and totalitarian states have not been able to emasculate civil society except in a formal sense. Civil society in these regimes may operate informally under different guises or go underground. In the absence of such associations, it is difficult to account for the explosion of civil society. Indeed, the account offered by O'Donnell and Schmitter on the resurrection of civil society relies heavily on the activities and effects of such organizations. Moreover, pressure from below is necessary—as in Thailand, South Korea, and the Philippines—to create and augment differentiation among the elite and extract concessions from the government.

Rather than being an all-elite affair (agency), openings for liberalization and democratization hinge on political and economic inequality and dissatisfaction in society at large, on the international context (structure), and on the actions of individuals and groups in dissident political society and civil society (agency). While structure cannot cause a specific occurrence, agency alone cannot succeed in the absence of propitious conditions. To be successful, moreover, synergy is required between soft-liners in government and leaders in dissident political society and civil society. This synergy often is found in the interaction of bottom-up and top-down pressures for liberalization and democratization. The salience of civil society for political liberalization and democratization increases sharply when viewed as an arena of democratic governance in its own right. Although important, concessions relating to individual civil rights do not free citizens from control and regulation by the party-state. The locus of authority and activity is still the state. Self-governance, by contrast, results in the creation of space outside the control of the party-state, shifts the locus of activity at least partially, and constitutes an acknowledgment by the party-state that citizens can govern themselves and issues can be regulated without its involvement. Development of civil society as an independent realm of governance is a critical feature of political liberalization.

Second, a sharp dichotomy in the relevance of political society and civil society is not warranted. Juan Linz and Alfred Stepan (1996) disagree with the demobilization thesis, arguing that it is "not only bad democratic theory but also bad democratic politics." In their view a robust civil society, capable of generating political alternatives and monitoring government, can "help start transitions, help resist reversals, help push transitions to their completion, and help consolidate and deepen democracy" (299). In a similar vein, Arato (2000) argues that negotiated transitions to democracy have the best prospects for consolidation—and civil society, he says, is a crucial prerequisite for successful transition. The power and legitimacy provided by civil society shore up the bargaining position of political leaders in negotiating and implementing pacts and drafting new constitutional and electoral frameworks.

A full democratic transition, Stepan asserts, must involve both political society and civil society. To be representative, political society has to be subject to the pressures in civil society and be periodically renewed by it. For its part, civil society cannot go it alone. "At best, [it] can destroy a non-democratic regime" (Stepan 2001: 8). Civil society needs a strong political society to carry the transition through to completion. Stepan's primary point is that while a robust civil society is indispensable, it should not be unduly privileged, and care should be exercised to avoid making false contradictions between civil society and political society and the state. Larry Diamond (1999) agrees that democratic change cannot be understood without reference to civil society but warns against a "one-dimensional and dangerously misleading" conceptualization in understanding democratization. Linz and Stepan draw attention to the danger that civil society may pose for the development of political society by the idealization of certain norms and practices that may be appropriate to civil society but not to political society.

There is general agreement among analysts on the need for a strong civil society in the consolidation of democracy. A "free and lively civil society" is the first of five necessary conditions cited by Linz and Stepan (1996) for a democracy to be consolidated. Schmitter (1997) lists several ways in which civil society can contribute to democratic consolidation: aggregating and stabilizing expectations, inculcating civic conceptions of interests and norms of behavior, supporting inclusive political processes, reducing the burdens of governance, and checking the abuse of power. Equally important, civil society may inculcate in the society at large the cultural and normative foundations of democracy. Arato (2000: 67–70), for his part, views the crucial role of civil society—in self-limitation, adherence to rule of law, providing sociological legitimacy, and limiting popular demand—as vital to the consolidation of a negotiated transition to democracy.

Nevertheless, civil society is not an unmitigated blessing for democracy (Schmitter 1997). Certain types of civil society may make the formation of majorities more difficult, build biases into the policymaking process, lead to pork-barrel politics, and segment the political community to the point of stimulating secession. Thus civil societies may produce a mixture of positive and negative consequences for democracy—and there is no guarantee that the positive effects will always outweigh the negative ones.

Democratic Effects of Civil Society

Civil society, like other realms, is an arena of power, inequality, struggle, conflict, and cooperation among competing identities and interests. It is populated by diverse formal and informal organizations with widely varying structures, resources, purposes, and methods. Not all civil society organizations have the purpose, potential, or consequence of advancing democracy. Some are decidedly antidemocratic or have such an effect (Whittington 2001; Warren 2001: 10–12). Business organizations, for example, can use their greater access to financial resources to undermine deliberative power and voting—two key means of democratic influence. Hate groups undermine democracy through their racism, secrecy, and frequent resort to violence. Fundamentalist religious organizations and groups advocating racial superiority can transform pluralism into parochialism, breeding intolerance in political life. Thus to ascertain the democratic potential and role of civil society, it is crucial to gauge the mix of organizations in civil society and identify those that can directly or indirectly advance or hinder democratic development. To highlight those that promote democracy while neglecting those that retard democratic development is to present a misleading picture.

Furthermore, the democratic potential of associations varies by type (voluntary versus nonvoluntary), structural location (pro- or anti-status quo), and purpose (individual or exclusive social good versus inclusive public good), with certain associations having a greater potential than others to generate certain democratic effects. The most useful work here is that of Mark Warren (2001). Unlike those who exclude nonvoluntary organizations from civil society by definitional fiat, Warren says that both voluntary and nonvoluntary associations may have democracy-producing effects. Voluntary associations, because they are self-selecting and externalize political conflict, achieve a higher degree of solidarity, develop a distinctive voice in the public sphere, and have more capacity for subsidiarity, resistance, and representation. They may also be better at cultivating the civic virtues of trust, reciprocity, and recognition. But they are likely to be impoverished in giving voice to dissent and resolving conflict. Nonvoluntary associations, by contrast, because of the high cost of exit, are compelled to provide a voice for dissenting groups and internalize and manage conflicts over purpose and methods, and they thus have greater capacity for deliberative and political skills.

Associations rooted in social relations are likely to have democratic effects akin to those of voluntary associations. From the perspective of political change, associations embedded in the political-legal sphere, and to a lesser degree the market medium, are likely to have greater democratic effects. Adversarial expectations make debate and conflict—and the development of political skills to manage them—the norm in these organizations. Both status quo organizations and those that seek change have democratic potential so long as they work in a context in which issues are forced onto the democratic terrain. They are bad for democracy if their power positions allow them to escape institutional bargaining and public accountability. Status quo associations have a greater capacity for subsidiarity, coordination, and representation, but limited capacity for resistance and transformation of the system. Non-status quo institutions (unions, feminist movements, consumer groups, new social movements) supply the issues of representation and resistance and have greater potential for change and transformation.

The democratic potential of associations is affected by their purposes as well. Some may aim to contribute directly to a certain aspect of democratic governance: extending citizenship rights and political participation to excluded groups (women, minorities, lower castes, social outcasts), broadening and democratizing public policymaking, increasing government accountability in specific domains, promoting the rule of law, advocating distributional justice, and so forth. Although the primary purpose of most organizations may not be to promote democracy, they may nevertheless have democratic consequences that are more significant than those whose primary purpose is to advance democracy. Associations pursuing public material goods through collective action, for example, are likely to have a broad range of democratic effects. Associations pursuing status goods are less likely to contribute to democratic processes and may in fact nurture uncivil attitudes. Those pursuing exclusive identity goods, by enhancing solidarity and efficacy, enable agency—especially for disadvantaged groups—and contribute to diversity and pluralism in the public realm. They may also, however, make the development of shared identity, the discovery of commonality, and cooperation more difficult. If exclusive identity representation develops in response to oppression and suppression, they may "serve as the conscience of a democracy, challenging public judgment, and stretching the boundaries of public agendas" (Warren 2001: 131). Associations devoted to social goods such as political reform and securing civil liberties play an important role in "underwriting public sphere and political processes." Because of the wide variation in the democratic effect of organizations and the presence of antidemocratic forces in civil society, it is important to gauge the mix and ascertain the balance of power among them.

Even when important groups in civil society support democracy, their effects are likely to be conditioned by the response of the state, by the connection among civil society, political society, and legislatures, and by the international context. In responding to formal and informal associations and their activities, a state may legally sanction, suppress, or merely tolerate them (Bermeo 2000). Legal sanctions might be advantageous up to a point, but they could also lead to co-optation and control, limiting the democratic potential of associations and in the long run undermining their credibility. Suppression might be stultifying, but it could also create martyrs and provoke uprisings that undermine the legitimacy of the incumbent government and enhance the image and power of dissident groups. De facto toleration of the activities of civil society groups, according to Nancy Bermeo (2000: 249), had the greatest democratic consequences in nineteenth-century Europe. Tolerance in the legal, semilegal, or extralegal realm allowed civil society groups to survive, to grow, and to expand democratic space.

The impact of groups advocating democracy can be substantial if they connect with political society and the legislature. An alliance between such civil society groups and political society can pose a credible challenge to authoritarian governments. An alliance with the reformist elements in a communist state can open up political space. It may also lead to suppression of certain civil society groups and the elimination of reformist elements within the government. Such suppression is not, however, without cost. In a new democracy, alliances with political society and the legislature can enhance the influence of civil society groups in policymaking. Strategic connections in general have the power to enhance the effect of prodemocracy groups in civil society. For such alliances to occur, political society must be sufficiently differentiated; reformist elements should be present in communist states; the social structure should be open; national, local, urban, and rural areas should be linked; and legislatures should be effective. An independent and accessible media committed to promoting democracy can significantly enhance the influence of civil society as well.

The democratic effect of civil society organizations can be amplified or hindered by the international environment. The contemporary context is certainly favorable for democratic development. Democracy has no alternatives. Ideologies like Nazism, Fascism, and Marxism-Leninism are not viable; possible alternatives such as techno-bureaucratic-authoritarianism, one-party-dominant political systems, and the developmental state economic model have been discredited. Although there are several holdouts, especially in Asia, formal commitment to democracy is widespread in the international system. Leading states are more supportive of democracy today than they were during the Cold War. (Consider the Clinton administration's democracy enlargement policy, for example.) The alliances forged by the United States with military and autocratic governments in the wake of September 11, 2001, suggest, however, that in certain cases strategic considerations still outweigh the goals of promoting democracy and protecting human rights. Nevertheless, good governance and the development of civil society continue to feature in the programs of international lending agencies. Associations in developed countries and transnational movements devoted to human rights and the environment have significantly enhanced the political resources available to domestic actors in developing countries (Keck and Sikkink 1998). The global media and technological revolutions (radio, TV, fax, the Internet) have minimized the negative consequences flowing from the control of media by the state or antidemocratic groups. And the dissemination of information with greater ease and the ensuing demonstration effect have become much more consequential.

Although the international structure and the disposition of key actors and agencies are conducive to democratic development, there are constraints as well. In the wake of September 11, promoting democracy has been subordinated to fighting terrorism. And in countries like Burma, the Western states have limited influence. The involvement of external forces, especially foreign funding, tarnishes the credibility of indigenous associations and provides opponents with a nationalist card. Dependence on international support affects the agenda of associations and prevents them from developing indigenous roots and networks (Hudock 1999). The dominant role of international lending agencies in policymaking reduces the responsiveness of the executive to the electorate and undercuts popular trust in legislatures. Thus both opportunities and constraints characterize national and international conditions.

Civil Society's Role in Political Change

Thus far, discussion has highlighted several points: Civil society is a space, an arena of governance, and organizations populating this space can be a force for affecting institutions and governance in political society, the state, and the market; civil society is not monolithic; there is no necessary connection between civil society and democracy; certain civil society organizations have greater democratic effect than others, while some may have an antidemocratic effect; the democratic effect and role of a country's civil society organizations depend on its specific domestic and international circumstances; successful democratic transition and consolidation require civil and political societies to have strong democratic forces; these forces are more consequential when they complement one another and act in mutually supporting ways; and the role and influence of civil society actors must be examined in conjunction with other actors in both the domestic (political society, the market, the state) and the international arenas.

System Legitimacy and Change

Moreover, the specific functions and roles of civil society organizations will vary with the legitimacy of the nation-state and political system, the type of political system, and the stage of political development. If the nation-state and political system are widely acknowledged as legitimate, most civil society organizations are likely to emphasize reform, accountability, representation, and subsidiarity. In a nation-state that is contested or where a political system lacks legitimacy, it is highly probable that disengagement, resistance, construction of counternarratives, formation of clandestine organizations, and mobilization of domestic and international support will feature prominently. In a system in the midst of transition, the role of civil society can be expected to change as well. In an entrenched communist or authoritarian system, civil society groups may seek to carve out public space in certain domains. In the prelude to the ouster of such governments, civil society groups in combination with segments of political society may play the vanguard role. In the subsequent transition phase, civil society groups may become involved in drafting a new constitution, in strengthening and monitoring political society and the state, in institutionalizing civil society, and in fostering public participation in politics and policymaking. In the consolidation phase, civil society groups may seek to expand the space for civil society and correct the deficiencies of the new democracy (including greater transparency and accountability)—all with the goal of making democracy the only game in town. The effectiveness of these civil society roles hinges on prodemocracy groups acquiring and retaining a favorable balance of power in the different phases. This may at times be difficult to accomplish. Many analysts have drawn attention to the fragmentation of civil society in the aftermath of the velvet revolutions in central and eastern Europe. The point is simply this: the process of political change often is not linear, and the composition and role of civil society groups in this process are bound to alter as circumstances change.

Autonomy and Institutionalization of the Public Sphere

The role of civil society in political change must also be examined in terms of the arenas of political discourse and governance, which includes civil society itself, political society, and the state. Civil society is a distinct and crucial sphere of democratic governance. Here the concern is with decentralization of power, authority, and resources to local levels and nonstate institutions such that social, cultural, and some political interaction are regulated by associations free of state intervention. Citizens acquire the right to self-determination and governance in matters of immediate relevance. Civil society also provides the space and means for articulating and aggregating public interests, forming public opinion, developing agendas outside the state and the market, and creating the means to influence them. Unlike the state and market—whose primary organization and transaction mediums are power and money respectively—freedom of association and unfettered public discourse that enable representation (of differences and commonalities), influence, and communicative power are the central pillars of the nonstate public sphere. The public sphere cultivates and shelters the political autonomy that in turn facilitates collective judgment and decision making to support self-governance by citizens and influence political society, the state, and the market (Warren 2001). Roles that expand (or contract) the space of the public realm in terms of the domain for societal self-governance—as well as in terms of institutions, actors, and agendas that enable collective action to influence political society and the state—constitute political change in the realm of civil society.

The second change involves the transformation of civil society from a group of social movements to a set of institutions (Arato 2000: 71–74). Institutionalization of civil society involves a guarantee of fundamental rights that presupposes a constitution, separation of powers, and an independent judiciary; a politically accessible media that is independent of state and market; decentralization of power, authority, and resources to local governments and nonstate institutions; acceptance of domestic and international NGOs as legitimate actors; and financially secure associations. In other words, civil society becomes a legally protected realm distinct from the state and political society. The third change relates to the development of the communicative mode of rational action. In this mode, agreements are arrived at through rational discourse and interpersonal interaction, not through power, money, or violence. Actors with divergent interests coordinate their interaction by negotiating definitions of the situation and remedies through discourse and reinterpretation of norms (Cohen and Arato 1992: 435).

Central to these three changes is the establishment of a system of individual and group rights—a fundamental feature of civil society. Cohen and Arato (1992: 441–42) cite three key sets of rights: freedom of thought, speech, and communication, which pertain to cultural production; freedom of association and assembly, which pertain to social integration; and the rights of privacy, intimacy, and inviolability of the person that secure socialization. They also cite rights that mediate between civil society and the market (rights of property, contract, and labor) and between civil society and the state (political and welfare rights of citizens). The establishment of rights is a good measure of the progress made in the institutionalization of civil society (from social movements to a settled civil society) and its constitution as a legally protected realm. In such a realm, communicative action becomes the norm. Although power and money are not absent, transactions in an institutionalized civil society hinge substantially on the force of ideas and arguments in defining a situation and remedies.

Change in Political Society and the State

At the level of political society, the concern is with structures and rules for interest aggregation and representation, competition for state power, and the power and responsiveness of legislatures to demands from civil and political society. Civil society can assist (or hinder) the development of political parties and a party system, the institution of an electoral system, public participation in elections, monitoring of elections and legitimating outcomes, and the constitution and functioning of the legislature. In addition to developing political society and monitoring its activities, civil society organizations may build links to political parties and legislators in order to channel and realize the interests of their specific groups and bolster democratic elements in civil society.

Turning to the state, the concern is with change (reform or transformation) in the basis of political community, type of political system, and specific policies of domination and governance. Such changes may be discerned in a number of sites, including the ideational foundation of the nation-state, the structure of the state (unitary or federal state; creation of autonomous regions; presidential, semipresidential, or parliamentary systems), change within a political system (political liberalization in an authoritarian system, for example, or change in the base of the vanguard party in a communist state), change in the political system itself (from authoritarianism or a communist party system to democracy, or vice versa), change in incumbent government, redefinition of the state's relationship with economic society, political society, and civil society, and change in state institutions and policies in specific areas of governance. In a system that is recognized as legitimate, civil society groups may play a variety of roles in shaping the course of such changes: setting norms, representing interests, promoting transparency and democratic accountability, and contributing to policymaking. In a system that is contested and widely regarded as illegitimate, in contrast, resistance, change, and transformation may inform the role of prodemocracy groups.

Socialization Function

Apart from these roles in relation to the three arenas (civil society, political society, and the state), civil society organizations perform a socialization function that applies across the board. This function encompasses roles that relate to citizens'

TABLE 1.1
Functions and Roles of Civil Society

Level/arena and function	Examples of specific roles
Individual/group	
Socialization (applies across arenas and different stages of political development)	Develop political skills Promote political participation Educate for democracy or other political systems Develop identities Disseminate information Develop trust, reciprocity, civic virtues
Civil society	
Construct and strengthen autonomy of nonstate public sphere	Institutionalize system of individual and group rights and rights to mediate between civil society–state and civil society–market
Develop and regulate self-governance in civil society	Develop nonstate institutions, agendas, resources Find and solve problems in society at large; generally expand domain of nonstate governance at local and national levels Prevent abuse of state power and limit state intrusion in private, social, and economic lives of citizens
Develop communicative mode of rational action	Develop structures for articulation, aggregation, representation of public interests Inculcate normative foundations for communicative action
Political society	
Facilitate and monitor development of political society	Input into structure and rules of party and electoral systems Assist and monitor conduct of elections and legitimate outcomes
Build connections to political society and legislatures	Assist development of party leadership, cadres, and platforms and generally help develop strong parties with clear policy alternatives Develop channels to communicate group interests to political parties and legislatures and means to ensure their responsiveness
Augment power of democratic parties	Build democratic coalitions; resist antidemocratic forces and practices
State	
Intermediation	Affect function and policy of state through: —Aggregating and representing interests —Forming public opinions —Advocating policy change
Accountability	Watchdog role to ensure transparency, accountability, effective functioning of state agencies
Service delivery	Supplement state in economic development and service delivery, especially in rural areas
Political system	
System maintenance and reform	System reform and maintenance roles may include: —Legitimating system by naturalizing norms associated with it and maintaining favorable balance of power —Strengthening participation in and support base for system

TABLE 1.1—*cont.*

Level/arena and function	Examples of specific roles
[System maintenance and reform]	—Overseeing and encouraging conformity with rules of the game —Promoting effective functioning of system —Furthering reform and development of system including correction of perceived defects
System change	Promote system change through: —Resisting and denying domestic and international legitimacy for incumbent government and political system —Constructing alternative visions, norms, institutions —Providing refuge and support for political counterelite —Mobilizing domestic and international support for alternative elite and system Form social movements and mobilize public at crucial moments to oust incumbent government

skills and communication of information—critical elements in the development of an individual's capacity for autonomous judgment and participation in the democratic process—as well as those that relate to the virtues of trust, reciprocity, and recognition, which can serve as a foundation for the robustness of the public sphere and democratic institutions of a community. Roles that belong to the socialization function include those identified by Larry Diamond (1999), such as stimulating political skills and participation, education for democracy, development of cross-cutting identities, and dissemination of information to empower citizens, as well as others that relate to the creation of civic virtues.

The role of civil society in political change may be investigated in several ways. Taking into account the purpose of this study—to investigate political change in the direction of open, accountable, and participatory politics—and the importance of conceptualizing civil society both as an arena of governance and as a force for bringing about change in political society and the state, Table 1.1 sets out the roles of civil society in the abstract by arena, functions, and examples. These functions and roles are illustrative, however, not exhaustive. They will vary with the type and legitimacy of political system and stage of system change. In the democratization literature, for example, discussions of the role of civil society indicate how and why the role may alter in different stages of the process. In the following chapters, as we shall see, the contributors modify the functions and roles of civil society to make them relevant for investigation of political change in their respective countries.

Notes

1. On social movements, see Tarrow 1998 and Cohen and Arato 1992.
2. On transnational social movements, see Smith, Chatfield, and Pagnucco 1997.

Works Cited

Arato, Andrew. 2000. *Civil Society, Constitution, and Legitimacy*. Lanham, Md.: Rowman & Littlefield.

Baker, Gideon. 2002. *Civil Society and Democratic Theory: Alternative Voices*. London: Routledge.

Benjamin, Barber R. 1999. "Clansmen, Consumers, and Citizens: Three Takes on Civil Society." In Robert K. Fullinwider, ed., *Civil Society, Democracy, and Civic Renewal*. Lanham, Md.: Rowman & Littlefield.

Berman, Sheri. 2001. "Civil Society and Political Institutionalization." In Bob Edwards, Michael W. Foley, and Mario Diani, eds., *Beyond Tocqueville: Civil Society and the Social Capital Debate in Comparative Perspective*. Hanover, N.H.: University Press of New England.

Bermeo, Nancy. 2000. "Civil Society after Democracy: Some Conclusions." In Nancy Bermeo and Philip Nord, eds., *Civil Society Before Democracy: Lessons from Nineteenth Century Europe*. Lanham, Md.: Rowman & Littlefield.

Bratton, Michael. 1994. "Civil Society and Political Transitions in Africa." In John W. Harbeson, Donald Rothchild, and Naomi Chazan, eds., *Civil Society and the State in Africa*. Boulder: Lynne Rienner.

Chambers, Simone, and Will Kymlicka, eds. 2002. *Alternative Conceptions of Civil Society*. Princeton: Princeton University Press.

Cohen, Jean L., and Andrew Arato. 1992. *Civil Society and Political Theory*. Cambridge, Mass.: MIT Press.

Cox, Robert W. 1999. "Civil Society at the Turn of the Millennium: Prospects for an Alternate World Order." *Review of International Studies* 25(1): 3–29.

Diamond, Larry. 1999. *Developing Democracy: Toward Consolidation*. Baltimore: Johns Hopkins University Press.

Edwards, Bob, and Michael W. Foley. 2001. "Civil Society and Social Capital: A Primer." In Bob Edwards, Michael W. Foley, and Mario Diani, eds., *Beyond Tocqueville: Civil Society and the Social Capital Debate in Comparative Perspective*. Hanover, N.H.: University Press of New England.

Edwards, Bob, Michael W. Foley, and Mario Diani, eds. 2001. *Beyond Tocqueville: Civil Society and the Social Capital Debate in Comparative Perspective*. Hanover, N.H.: University Press of New England.

Ehrenberg, John. 1999. *Civil Society: The Critical History of an Idea*. New York: New York University Press.

Ferguson, Adam. [1767] 1995. *An Essay on the History of Civil Society*. Edited by Fania Oz-Salzberger. Cambridge: Cambridge University Press.

Fine, Robert. 1997. "Civil Society: Theory, Enlightenment, and Critique." In Robert Fine and Shirin Rai, eds., *Civil Society: Democratic Perspectives*. London: Frank Cass.

Foley, Michael W., and Bob Edwards. 1997. "Escape from Politics? Social Theory and Social Capital Discourse." *American Behavioral Scientist* 40(5): 550–61.

Gellner, Ernest. 1994. *Conditions of Liberty: Civil Society and Its Rivals*. New York: Penguin Books.

Gramsci, Antonio. 1971. *Selections from the Prison Notebooks of Antonio Gramsci*, ed. and trans. Quintin Hoare and Geoffrey Nowell Smith. New York: International Publishers.

Habermas, Jürgen. 1984. *The Theory of Communicative Action*, vol. 1. Boston: Beacon Press.

———. 1996. "Further Reflections on the Public Sphere." In Craig Calhoun, ed., *Habermas and the Public Sphere*. Cambridge, Mass.: MIT Press.

Hegel, G. W. F. [1821] 1991. *Elements of the Philosophy of Right*. Edited by Allen W. Wood. Cambridge: Cambridge University Press.

Howell, Jude, and Jenny Pearce. 2001. *Civil Society and Development: A Critical Exploration*. Boulder: Lynne Rienner.

Hudock, Ann C. 1999. *NGOs and Civil Society: Democracy by Proxy*. Cambridge: Polity Press.

Ioannidou, Anastasia. 1997. "The Politics of the Division of Labour: Smith and Hegel on Civil Society." In Robert Fine and Shirin Rai, eds., *Civil Society: Democratic Perspectives*. London: Frank Cass.

Kaviraj, Sudipta, and Sunil Khilnani, eds. 2001. *Civil Society: History and Possibilities*. Cambridge: Cambridge University Press.

Keane, John. 1998. *Civil Society: Old Images, New Visions*. Stanford: Stanford University Press.

Keck, Margaret E., and Kathryn Sikkink, eds. 1998. *Activists Beyond Borders: Advocacy Networks in International Politics*. Ithaca, N.Y.: Cornell University Press.

Linz, Juan J., and Alfred Stepan. 1996. "Toward Consolidated Democracies." *Journal of Democracy* 72 (Apr.): 14–33.

Newton, Kenneth. 2001. "Social Capital and Democracy." In Bob Edwards, Michael W. Foley, and Mario Diani, eds., *Beyond Tocqueville: Civil Society and the Social Capital Debate in Comparative Perspective*. Hanover, N.H.: University Press of New England.

Nord, Philip. 2000. "Introduction." In Nancy Bermeo and Philip Nord, eds., *Civil Society Before Democracy: Lessons from Nineteenth Century Europe*. Lanham, Md.: Rowman & Littlefield.

O'Donnell, Guillermo, and Philippe C. Schmitter. 1986. *Transitions from Authoritarian Rule: Tentative Conclusions about Uncertain Democracies*. Baltimore: Johns Hopkins University Press.

Oz-Salzberger, Fania. 1995. "Introduction." In Adam Ferguson, *An Essay on the History of Civil Society*. Cambridge: Cambridge University Press.

Post, Robert C., and Nancy L. Rosenblum. 2002. "Introduction." In Robert C. Post and Nancy L. Rosenblum, eds., *Civil Society and Government*. Princeton: Princeton University Press.

Putnam, Robert. 1993. "The Prosperous Community: Social Capital and Public Life." *American Prospect* 13: 35–42.

———. 1996. "Bowling Alone: America's Declining Social Capital." In Larry Diamond and Marc F. Plattner, eds., *The Global Resurgence of Democracy*. Baltimore: Johns Hopkins University Press.

Schmitter, Philippe C. 1997. "Civil Society: East and West." In Larry Diamond et al., eds., *Consolidating the Third Wave Democracies: Themes and Perspectives*. Baltimore: Johns Hopkins University Press.

Seligman, Adam. 1992. *The Idea of Civil Society*. New York: Free Press.

Smith, Adam. [1759] 2000. *The Theory of Moral Sentiments*. Amherst, N.Y.: Prometheus Books.

Smith, Jackie, Charles Chatfield, and Ron Pagnucco, eds. 1997. *Transnational Social Move-*

ments and Global Politics: Solidarity Beyond the State. Syracuse, N.Y.: Syracuse University Press.

Stepan, Alfred. 1988. *Rethinking Military Politics: Brazil and the Southern Cone*. Princeton: Princeton University Press.

———. 1997. "Democratic Opposition and Democratization Theory." *Government and Opposition* 32(4) (Autumn): 657–73.

———. 2001. "Reflections on Problem Selection in Comparative Politics." In Alfred Stepan, *Arguing Comparative Politics*. Oxford: Oxford University Press.

Tarrow, Sidney. 1998. *Power in Movement: Social Movements and Contentious Politics*. New York: Cambridge University Press.

Tocqueville, Alexis de. [1835–39] 1994. *Democracy in America*. With an introduction by Alan Ryan. New York: Knopf.

Varty, John. 1997. "Civic or Commercial? Adam Ferguson's Concept of Civil Society." In Robert Fine and Shirin Rai, eds., *Civil Society: Democratic Perspectives*. London: Frank Cass.

Warren, Mark E. 2001. *Democracy and Association*. Princeton: Princeton University Press.

Whitehead, Laurence. 1997. "Bowling in the Bronx: The Uncivil Interstices Between Civil and Political Society." In Robert Fine and Shirin Rai, eds., *Civil Society: Democratic Perspectives*. London: Frank Cass.

Whittington, Keith. 2001. "Revisiting Tocqueville's America: Society, Politics, and Association in the Nineteenth Century." In Bob Edwards, Michael W. Foley, and Mario Diani, eds., *Beyond Tocqueville: Civil Society and the Social Capital Debate in Comparative Perspective*. Hanover, N.H.: University Press of New England.

PART II

Legitimate Civil Society

Negotiating Democratic Space

CHAPTER TWO

Indonesia

Transformation of Civil Society and Democratic Breakthrough

EDWARD ASPINALL

Few countries provide clearer evidence than Indonesia that there is no simple correlation between a dense civil society and democracy. In the 1950s and 1960s, despite high levels of poverty and illiteracy, Indonesia's citizens were deeply engaged in associational activity. Labor unions, women's organizations, and peasant associations, as well as similar bodies for artists, students, and other groups, flourished. By the mid-1960s, a large majority of the adult population were either members of, or closely identified with, political or social associations.

This flurry of organizational activity did not produce a benign outcome in terms of democratic political change. Instead, there was escalating and increasingly violent conflict between contending sociopolitical currents and a drift toward more authoritarian rule. This trend culminated in 1965 with one of the late twentieth century's bloodiest massacres and the inauguration of one of its most durable authoritarian regimes, the "New Order" of President Suharto (1966–98).

By the 1990s, after three decades during which the military-led state had prevented, impeded, and controlled potential challenges from civil society, a revival of independent associational life was visible. Previously docile corporatist organizations became more assertive; a variegated and energetic nongovernmental organization (NGO) sector emerged; there were even attempts to organize previously repressed groups like industrial workers and peasants. Yet the extent of popular participation in this new civil society was limited compared to the 1960s. This far weaker civil society in the 1990s, however, contributed to the overthrow of the Suharto regime and a transition toward a more democratic form of rule. Suharto's immediate successors, Presidents Habibie (1998–99) and Abdurrahman Wahid (1999–2001), proclaimed that they intended to construct a new democratic order in which *masyarakat madani* (civil society) occupied pride of place.

One explanation for the different outcomes lies in the very different nature of associational life in the two periods. In the 1950s and 1960s, civil society was deeply polarized, as was political life more generally. Most large civil society organizations were affiliated to political parties that aimed to hold or seize political power, and that had conflicting ideological visions for Indonesian society. Associational life thus inflamed cleavages in society—both along class lines and between socioreligious groups. Civil society became a mechanism, not for generating civility and "social capital," but rather for magnifying sociopolitical conflict and transmitting it to the very bases of society. Subsequent decades of authoritarian rule not only greatly weakened and fragmented civil society; they also meant that the state became the central problematic of political life for the emergent civil society. Groups in civil society no longer viewed their civilian foes as their primary adversaries, nor were most of them extensions of political parties that aimed to attain state power. A new political discourse emerged that emphasized the creation of a "system of rights" (Blaney and Pasha 1993) and constraint of the state.

Put most simply, the Indonesian experience supports the proposition advanced in Chapters 1 and 15 that only a civil society that is truly *civil* supports democracy. Where the primary modes of action in civil society are violent or confrontational, maximalist, and given to polarization, democratic rule is unlikely to survive. This is especially the case where associational life reinforces and exacerbates societal and political cleavages. In a civil society where actors moderate their most ambitious goals for remaking state and society and no longer view each other as their primary adversaries, by contrast, the political environment is likely to be more conducive to democracy. Key conditions for such an outcome include minimal societal consensus about the desired nature of the social and political order and at least some civil society organizations that cut across, rather than reinforce, cleavages in society.

It is important to stress, before moving on, that I do not contend that a relationship of simple causality connects civil society and political change. It was not only the conflictual nature of Indonesian civil society that contributed to the decline of democracy in the 1950s and 1960s. Conflict in civil society itself reflected broader political, class, and cultural conflict. Moreover, many other factors played a crucial role—above all the fateful decisions and interventions by central political actors (especially President Sukarno and the army leadership) at key junctures. The same can be said about the downfall of Suharto in 1998. The changed nature of civil society was not the only, or even necessarily the predominant, element contributing to this political transition. Civil society was important in many ways, however, not least in setting the limits of possible political change: enabling actors to make certain political choices while disabling other choices or making them more costly.

Civil society, I argue, performs this function especially by contributing to an underlying ideological climate in society. It played an especially significant role in the end of the Suharto regime by undermining the ideological foundations of authoritarian rule. In the 1950s and 1960s, by contrast, it amplified the ideological conflicts within society.

With this caveat in mind, a key question arises: how is a conflictual civil society, which may be destructive to democracy, replaced by a peaceable civil society that allows it? The following pages suggest that in seeking to answer this question, there is little alternative to detailed historical analysis. By examining the evolution of civil society primarily through the prism of associational activity concerning land and rural issues, I demonstrate that three factors were especially important in the Indonesian case (although the list is by no means exhaustive). The first factor was the changing international context, especially the impact of international linkages on domestic civil society. The second was the impact of capitalist development on civil society, its changing class structure, and the extent to which different social classes were able to assert dominance within it. The third factor was the changing relationship between the state and civil society—especially the state's structuring of civil society—as well as how groups in civil society came to view the state.

The Antecedents of Civil Society

Civil society does not always support democracy. Sheri Berman (1997: 402), for example, has suggested that "a robust civil society actually helped scuttle the twentieth century's most critical democratic experiment, Weimar Germany." She argues that this was primarily because associational life exacerbated social cleavages: "Germany was cleaved increasingly into distinct subcultures or communities, each of which had its own, separate associational life" (425). This deeply fractured civil society undermined the legitimacy of national political institutions and provided a pool of cadres who supported the Nazis' destruction of the parliamentary regime.

The Indonesian experience during the first two decades of independence (1945–65) shared certain parallels with Weimar Germany. During this period, Indonesia had a dense associational life. Society at all levels was highly mobilized and politicized. This dense associational life did not produce positive outcomes in terms of ameliorating conflict, encouraging civility within society, or democratizing the state. On the contrary, during the 1950s and 1960s, conflict between rival sociopolitical groups became more violent and unconstrained, accompanied by increasing political authoritarianism, including a growing role for the military. These trends culminated in the establishment of Suharto's military-based New Order regime in 1966.

In Germany, Sherman argues, civil society undermined the party system; in Indonesia, however, civil society was closely linked to the political parties, especially the major communist, Islamic, and nationalist parties. The deep politicization and organization of Indonesian society in the 1950s and 1960s took the form of "*aliran* politics," a term that was first introduced by Clifford Geertz and subsequently became highly influential in studies of Indonesian politics. In an article titled "The Javanese Village," Geertz (1959: 37) defines an *aliran* in the following way:

> An aliran consists of a political party surrounded by a set of voluntary social organizations formally or informally linked to it. In Java there are only four such alirans of importance: the PNI or Nationalists; the PKI or Communists; the Masjumi, or Modernist Moslem; and the NU, or Orthodox Moslem. With one or another of these parties as the nucleus, an aliran is a cluster of nationally based organizations—women's clubs, youth groups, religious societies, and so on—sharing a similar ideological direction or standpoint. . . . An aliran is more than a mere political party, certainly more than a mere ideology; it is a comprehensive pattern of social integration.

The *aliran* pattern of social organization had its immediate roots in the deep politicization of Indonesian society during the revolutionary period and, later, in the logic of national political competition. In 1945–49, parties, mass associations, and militias proliferated. Although their overriding aim was to rid Indonesia of the Dutch colonialists, there was considerable conflict between groups with different visions of how an independent Indonesia should be constituted—leading to social revolutions in some areas, violent conflict between communists and Muslims, and the proclamation of an Islamic revolt. After the Dutch relinquished sovereignty, the infant republic had to construct a workable political order. Many of its impoverished and war-ravaged citizens had high expectations that *merdeka* (freedom) would satisfy their widely varied material and other needs. Under parliamentary democracy in the 1950s, especially in the three years preceding the 1955 election (the period during which Geertz conducted his fieldwork in Java), electoral competition impelled the parties into a fierce competition to expand their mass organizations. Later in the decade, amid widespread political and social conflict, as well as considerable public disillusionment with the political parties, President Sukarno, with army support, abolished parliamentary rule. During "Guided Democracy" (1959–65), he presided over an unstable balance between the contending mass-based sociopolitical forces—playing rival groups off against one another and considerably exacerbating political tensions. Mass mobilization and organization became means for the parties to demonstrate loyalty to Sukarno's anti-imperialist order and secure a place in national government.

The flourishing of *aliran* politics partly stemmed from a failure of the state. Geertz argued that the colonial and postcolonial state had failed to penetrate village society effectively, at least insofar as integrative and reconstructive functions were concerned. As a result, the *aliran* became the basic skeleton of social organization by performing numerous religious, educational, economic, and other integrative functions and organizing the "reconstruction of vigorous village life" (Geertz 1959:

37). These networks of mass organizations, each centered on a political party, substituted for effective state institutions. Through the *aliran*-linked organizations, villagers could arrange loans, secure assistance to harvest their crops or repair their houses, learn about national and international affairs, participate in or watch cultural performances, and engage in many other useful activities. (It should be admitted, though, that groups linked to the Indonesian Communist Party, the PKI, were by far the most effective in performing such functions, and that grassroots associational activity by the other *alirans* may have declined markedly after the 1955 elections.)[1]

If we use a minimalist definition similar to that advanced in Chapter 1—viewing civil society as merely that zone of organizational life, located between private or family life and the state, where citizens form associations and pursue joint interests—then it seems reasonable to describe associational life before the New Order as a kind of civil society. The picture becomes less clear, however, if we add a criterion of civil society frequently insisted upon by liberal-pluralist writers: component groups of civil society do not aim to attain state power for themselves but, rather, wish to influence the state. According to Larry Diamond (1994: 6): "Civil society *relates to the state* in some way but does not aim to win formal power or office in the state. Rather, civil society organizations seek from the state concessions, benefits, policy changes, relief, redress or accountability. . . . [But they do not have] a desire to capture state power for the group per se." The picture that Diamond presents is one in which the denizens of civil society view the political and social order as fundamentally legitimate. They may seek to benefit from the state, even to mold it to their advantage, but they do not attempt to capture, overthrow, or fundamentally reconstruct it.

In Indonesia during the 1950s and 1960s, there was little underlying consensus on fundamental questions about the social and political order. The *alirans* not only sharpened social cleavages but came to constitute them, as each *aliran* increasingly resembled a self-contained social universe. The two major Islamic *alirans*, those formed around Masjumi and Nahdlatul Ulama (NU), wanted to establish, if not a theocratic Islamic state, at least one in which sharia'ah would be binding on all Muslims. Essentially, they aimed to impose their interpretation of religious doctrine on other Muslims. We must be careful, however, not to overstate the totalizing aims of the major Islamic *alirans*. Both Masjumi and NU cooperated with noncommunist nationalists and Christians in national government; NU was especially amenable to cooperation so long as the interests of the NU community were safeguarded. Nevertheless, the nationalist and communist *alirans* derived part of their cohesion in reaction to Islamic claims and identity and drew their adherents mostly from nominal Muslims and religious minorities.

It was the rapidly expanding communist *aliran* that most seriously threatened the political and social order. Its aims were ultimately revolutionary, and it sought explicitly to appeal to the lower classes. Moreover, its growth came in the wake of major communist victories in China and North Vietnam, at a time when, as Benedict Anderson (1994) has argued, Indonesian communists believed they were part of a worldwide historical wave that would eventually sweep them to victory. To be sure, the party had learned from previous defeats. For much of the 1950s and early 1960s, it downplayed class struggle and even recruited locally influential headmen and other patrons to assist its expansion in village society. But the PKI was essentially engaged in a classical Gramscian "war of position" within the terrain of civil society (although its leaders did not use these terms). By organizing and mobilizing a massive base among subordinate classes, the party effectively sought to establish a counterhegemonic movement that would "undermine the foundations of state and class rule" (Keane 1998: 15; Alagappa, Chapter 1). The short-term aim, during Guided Democracy at least, was to force the PKI's enemies to allow it to participate in national government. But this "national-democratic" phase was preparatory to a second "socialist stage" of the revolution during which, the experience of other countries suggested, the PKI would assert dominance.

The state was not clearly delineated from the *aliran* system. At the local level, state officials were frequently party bosses; at the national level, various ministries became fiefdoms for the different political parties. The communists were the only *aliran* that did not have a significant foothold in the state apparatus, and the party's gradualist strategy was largely aimed at securing such a position. The army was virtually the only state institution that became increasingly coherent and whose leaders developed a distinct corporate identity during the 1950s and early 1960s. But the army, too, was deeply involved in inter-*aliran* conflict by virtue of the implacable hostility of most of the officer corps toward the PKI. In such circumstances, there was little possibility that the state could effectively mediate between competing sociopolitical groups or create the institutional and legal framework within which a nonpartisan civil society could grow. Instead, state functionaries were themselves involved in the mounting conflict between different *aliran*s with incompatible, maximalist political goals.

Case Study: Land Conflicts in Rural Java During Guided Democracy

Inter-*aliran* conflict became particularly acute in rural areas. In the 1960s, Indonesia remained an overwhelmingly agrarian society and the PKI's rapid growth was largely a rural phenomenon. Borrowing from the strategy of the Chinese communists, the PKI emphasized recruitment among small and landless peasants and explicitly aimed at the eventual abolition of landlordism.

The PKI's main front organization in rural areas was the Barisan Tani Indonesia (BTI; Indonesian Peasants' Front). Established in November 1945, the BTI had initially been relatively independent of the party, and it retained many independent-minded members right to the end. Nevertheless, the BTI became, in the words of one contemporary observer, "next to the party . . . the principal agency concerned with the implementation of Communist policy objectives" (Van der Kroef 1965: 197). It was also huge: although such claims are impossible to verify, by 1962, it claimed five and a half million members, equivalent to 25 percent of the adult peasant population (Hindley 1966: 169). It grew by performing many basic integrative functions in village society—offering its members literacy training, teaching them new agricultural techniques, and running campaigns to raise productivity and destroy rats (with the nationwide death toll of rodents published in the organization's bimonthly journal, *Suara Tani*).

In late 1963, however, marking a departure from the "national united front" approach, the party and BTI initiated a vigorous campaign of unilateral actions (*aksi sepihak*) in the countryside in which poor peasants seized land owned by landlords. In the short term, this campaign was designed, as Rex Mortimer (1974: 277) argues, to be "an additional lever" to force the party's opponents to give it a share of power in national government. In the longer term, "in the event of untoward developments at the political center, the party would by its radicalization of the villages provide itself with a firm base for continuing the struggle outside the bounds of the system" (277–78). In launching *aksi sepihak*, the PKI and the BTI stressed their legality. They intended, they said, the proper implementation of the 1960 Basic Agrarian Law, a piece of legislation that embodied much of the egalitarian spirit of the independence struggle. One of the law's basic provisions set an upper limit on land (five hectares in densely populated wet-rice areas) that could be owned by a single family; land in excess of this limit was to be redistributed to landless peasants. By mid-1963, however, the law had met considerable resistance from landlords, local government officials, and leaders of the noncommunist parties—three categories that overlapped greatly—and its implementation was stalled in many regions.

Even so, as Olle Törnquist (1984: 195–96) notes, PKI and BTI slogans such as attacks on the "seven village devils" went far beyond the provisions of the Basic Agrarian Law.[2] Land-hungry peasants seized property held by landlords who controlled less than the 5-hectare limit, sometimes surprising party and BTI leaders by their vehemence. But the essential aim of the campaign was to secure the communist movement a base in the countryside by increasing class polarization. As the BTI vice-chair, Dahliar (1964: 5), put it at a conference of peasant women:

> The *aksi sepihak* have provided a revolutionary education to the peasants, women and men. They have educated the peasantry to trust in their own strength, to trust the organization, and to trust the leaders. The peasants increasingly understand who sides with them and leads them in winning their just demands, who is indifferent toward the peasants and derides them, and who confronts the peasants with unsheathed bayonet.

The campaign attracted much support from poor peasants: by late 1964, the BTI claimed 8.5 million members (*Suara Tani* 15, nos. 9–10 [1964]: 4). But it also met with violent resistance. The police and military frequently backed landlords, who were themselves often leaders of noncommunist political parties who could mobilize their own clients and party supporters in opposition to land claims. As a result, in many places the conflict, at root about class and control of the means of production, frequently took on the character of a horizontal clash between the peasant followers of different *alirans*.

The conflict became most severe in areas of rural Central and East Java where the Nahdlatul Ulama was strong. Many of the more prosperous peasants and landlords were *santri*, or orthodox Muslims, affiliated to NU. Moreover, NU was founded on the institution of the rural *pesantren*, or Islamic boarding school. The *kyai*, or religious scholars, who ran these boarding schools were venerated by their followers as the bearers of sacred Islamic knowledge and scholarly tradition. They were also frequently large landowners in their own right, as well as managers of land donated to their *pesantren* by wealthy members of the community. Students at *pesantren* frequently worked on both types of land as payment for their education.

In their land reform campaign, the communists frequently targeted land owned by *kyai* and other NU leaders, who in turn described the campaign as an attack by atheists on religion and urged their followers to resist in the language of jihad. The result, especially in East Java, was extreme violence:

> The clashes were marked from the outset by acts of violence such as stabbing and kidnapping, and before long large scale confrontations between opposed forces armed with *kris* and other weapons were taking place. Factions took to burning down the houses of hostile elements and destroying their crops in the fields. In a number of places, police intervention led to serious loss of life and injury. (Mortimer 1974: 317)

In most cases, the communists got the worst of it. NU groups tended to be more disciplined and tenacious, and in some places they were backed by local military and police units. Resistance became so tough that in the final months of 1964, PKI leaders admitted defeat and attempted to terminate the unilateral actions.

These conflicts over land in 1963–65 set the scene for far greater mass violence in 1965–66. In October 1965, following the kidnapping of six senior army officers in a left-wing coup attempt ("the September 30 movement"), the army leadership and its civilian allies launched a campaign to wipe out the communist *aliran* once and for all. In the ensuing massacres, between 500,000 and one million people, mostly members and sympathizers of the PKI and its affiliated organizations, including the BTI, were killed.

The 1965–66 bloodshed was partly a conflict between state and society. It certainly involved a high degree of central army direction and planning, and soldiers did their share of the killing. But to borrow a phrase from another recent work on twentieth-century Germany, there were also many civilian "willing executioners" (Goldhagen 1996). The killings tended to be most severe in areas where the land reform campaign had been strongest; in some places, there was barely a break between the two rounds of violence. In East Java, for example, there was serious violence on a weekly basis through August and September 1965, prior to the "coup attempt," and in early October, some NU supporters began to kill communists even before they were instructed to do so by the military (Sulistyo 2000: 155, 162–63). The large-scale killings by NU members, which began later in the month, involved close coordination with the military, although many NU *kyai* urged their followers forward by issuing "*fatwa* declaring that the PKI were *kafir harbi* (unbelievers who are belligerent toward Islam) and *bughat* (rebels against the legitimate government) against whom it was obligatory for Muslims to wage war" (Fealy 1998: 255). In Bali, although the army "orchestrated and incited the violence" (Robinson 1995: 295), many of those who conducted the killings were supporters of the nationalist PNI who had only months earlier fought against their communist victims during the land reform campaign. On the other hand, leaders of the *aliran* hostile to the PKI were themselves frequently embedded in, or attached to, the state. For instance, PNI leaders and landlords were frequently state officials; indeed, the PNI and the state bureaucracy were virtually identical at the local level throughout much of Bali, Java, and elsewhere. Even NU controlled the Department of Religion.[3]

In sum, the conflicts that led to the great violence of 1965–66 and subsequent establishment of Suharto's authoritarian regime were not simple clashes between state and civil society. There was certainly a state-society dimension to the violence, but the *aliran* system fundamentally blurred the boundaries between state, parties, and civil society. Enemies of the Left could draw upon the state apparatus to mobilize violence, but they also used their networks of societal organizations for the same purpose. The PKI primarily relied upon its mass organizations and mobilization, and its progress in expanding its mass base was the main trigger for the violent backlash. The party was also, however, making modest inroads into parts of the state bureaucracy and even the armed forces. The main lines of conflict thus split society itself (and, to a lesser extent, the state apparatus), along class lines and between *alirans*, reflecting the absence of minimal societal consensus about the desired shape of the political and social order. Conflict *within* civil society, in other words, was a crucial part of the wider class and sociocultural polarization, and it contributed to the breakdown of civility and democratic rule.

But we must be careful to avoid an impression of inevitability here. I do not mean to suggest that "too much" social participation and radicalism gave rise to authoritarianism. Nor is it my intention to blame the communists for their own murder. Maximalist, even revolutionary, aims do not in themselves doom civil society and democracy, nor does affiliation to political parties mean that associations should not be considered part of civil society. As Michael Foley and Bob Edwards (1996: 42) point out, the Italian region of Emilia-Romagna, which Robert Putnam (1993) famously holds up as exemplar of his thesis that a dense civil society may generate the "social capital" that enables democracy to flourish, was an area where the Italian Communist Party (along with the Christian Democrats) dominated associational life. In retrospect, the very scale and horror of Indonesia's 1965–66 bloodletting make it hard for us to imagine alternative outcomes. But we must not forget that Indonesia might have taken a different path. The Indonesian communists (like their Italian counterparts) might eventually have been peacefully accommodated within the political system had their enemies been willing to provide them the democratic space and role in government they sought. Indeed, it is worth recalling that at least one contemporary observer of the PKI (Hindley 1962) believed that Sukarno's attempts to constrain the party during Guided Democracy were already leading to its "domestication."

At this point, I must emphasize, like Neil DeVotta in his contribution on Sri Lanka (Chapter 9 in this volume), the importance of interventions by political actors at crucial junctures. The key in the Indonesian case was not so much the mere existence of divisions, as the fact that the anticommunist groups (in both state and society) were not prepared to countenance civil society's expansion to incorporate the demands of their adversaries, particularly radical calls for redistribution. It was this logic that pushed the military state to the fore. From at least the early 1960s, fearing an eventual confrontation, the major anticommunist *aliran* all cultivated support within the military (for NU efforts in this regard, see Fealy 1998: 236–37) and threw their lot in with the army when the time came. The elimination of the PKI was the primary goal of the civilian anticommunists. Many of them (including NU leaders) also hoped that removing the PKI would facilitate greater representation of their own interests in government. They became bitterly disillusioned when this did not eventuate. The more farsighted elements—the many urban liberal students and intellectuals, for example, who supported the army through the anticommunist and anti-Sukarno "Action Fronts"—knew that a period of military dominance was unavoidable. Some Christian and secular urban intellectuals, believing that political Islam would otherwise assert dominance, actively favored military control (Ward 1974: 35–36). By the terms of this Faustian bargain, the anticommunist political groups ceded a large measure of political control to the army in exchange for the elimination of their main foe, the reestablishment of social order, and a commitment to economic growth.

Civil Society in the New Order

The establishment of President Suharto's New Order was in one sense the bloody culmination of the *aliran* politics of the 1960s. The military-led government, however, also set about cutting through the conflictual nature of *aliran* politics and establishing social and political consensus by force. In the 1965–66 massacres, it had eliminated one wing of Indonesian organizational life (the communist party and its affiliates) that aimed to capture and reconfigure state power. Later it put severe constraints on the other wing (political Islam), whose goals were almost as ambitious. Moreover, the military leadership had what Richard Tanter (1990) has described as "totalitarian ambitions," in that it attempted to extend state control to the furthest reaches of associational life. State violence and the constant threat of it, reinforced by memories of the bloodletting of 1965–66, allowed the army to begin to achieve these ambitions. Organizations of the lower classes were either eliminated or corralled into state-controlled "sole organizations." (Attempts to do the same with middle-class groups like lawyers and students were somewhat less successful.) The army forced the surviving political parties to fuse into unstable agglomerations, which were then subject to constant state supervision and intervention. Although it was more difficult to dominate the major religious, especially Islamic, organizations, they too were effectively controlled by a mixture of patronage rewards for leaders prepared to cooperate with the state and judiciously applied repression of those who challenged it. Overall, civil society became a denuded and barren landscape compared to the richness of the parliamentary and Guided Democracy periods.

Civil society consisted of three main categories of organizations for much of the New Order period. First were the exclusionary corporatist *sole organizations*, the products of enforced fusion of the surviving, noncommunist organizations representing subordinate classes. In 1973, for example, surviving peasant organizations were shepherded into a new body called Himpunan Kerukunan Tani Indonesia (HKTI; Indonesian Peasant's Harmony Association). HKTI, like equivalent bodies for labor and other groups, was dependent on the state for direction. It was affiliated to the state party (Golkar). Its leaders were often military officers or other state functionaries (frequently from the Department of Agriculture). It did not attempt to build an active mass membership base. And although its leaders occasionally offered carefully worded criticisms of government policies, they never tried to mobilize against them. The most striking feature of New Order civil society when compared to that which preceded it was thus the changed class basis produced by the systematic eradication of independent organizations representing the lower classes and their replacement by corporatist bodies, like HKTI, that were effectively instruments of state power.

The corporatist organizations did not represent the sum total of associational life, however. Numerous other organizations were allowed to survive, provided that they respected certain limits: they had to profess loyalty to the state ideology of Pancasila; they could not make any direct claim on political power; and they could not attempt to mobilize lower-class groups. This second category comprised a spectrum of *semicorporatist organizations* that, while independent in their origins and aspirations, compromised with the state in order to survive or prosper, participated in regime structures such as parties and parliaments, supported at least some official policies, and experienced some degree of state interference in their internal workings. Among the most important of these groups were the large Islamic mass organizations, Nahdlatul Ulama and Muhammadiyah. These groups were allowed to survive essentially intact, as was the network of institutions on which they were based (*pesantren* in the case of NU; modern schools, universities, and healthcare institutions for Muhammadiyah). At times, the army leadership used open force and intimidation against these organizations. NU followers were victims of considerable state violence during the 1971 election campaign, for example, a time when the organization's leaders were already embittered by the political marginalization they had experienced after the destruction of their communist foes. But the state also remained a critical source of patronage resources for them. When relations were good, government funds became available for *pesantren* development programs, mosque construction in local communities, and the like—to say nothing of the business opportunities and more straightforward bribes available to the most cooperative leaders. Although many NU leaders still criticized the government when they believed the core interests of the Islamic community were threatened, most were ultimately anxious to cooperate with it.

After the New Order's first decade, a third category, which might be called *proto-oppositional civil society organizations*, began to emerge. These organizations strove to maintain greater autonomy from state intervention and sometimes adopted a critical stance toward state policies and actions. They mostly avoided repression by emphasizing particularistic goals rather than pushing for systemic change. The largest group in this category were the nongovernmental organizations active in fields like legal reform, environmental protection, and alternative community development. Early on in the New Order, many NGOs, research institutes, and similar bodies were led by middle-class intellectuals who had allied with the army in its conflict with the Left. Thus they shared a degree of ideological affinity with state officials. Early NGOs such as the Lembaga Bantuan Hukum (LBH; Legal Aid Institute) frequently described themselves as part of the New Order. Their leaders also maintained many political and financial links; for example, LBH and several other NGOs that eventually numbered among the New Order's staunchest critics were initially sponsored and funded by prominent New Order ministers and generals. By the 1990s, however, the NGO sector had become a prominent player on the Indonesian political scene. In 1996, the Coordinating Minister for Politics and Security, Soesilo Soedarman, estimated there were some eight thousand NGOs in the country (*Republika*, November 4, 1996). While most of these engaged in development-oriented activities compatible with the government's own aims, some became key sources of political criticism.

Associational life during the New Order was marked by two significant features. In the first place, there was again a blurring of the boundary between state and civil society, although this took a very different form from that which occurred in the pre-New Order *aliran* system. The blurring now was predominantly a product of the central role the state played in restructuring civic life and the ubiquity of state supervision and intervention in legal organizations, especially those with mass membership. As a result, challenges to the New Order were frequently characterized by what X. L. Ding (with reference to Dengist rule in China) describes as "institutional amphibiousness," in which official or semiofficial institutions were utilized for purposes that ran counter to their official aims. This blurring remained characteristic of Indonesian political life until the end of the New Order. A famous example, in the early 1990s, was the attempt by a section of the modernist Islamic community to colonize the state from within via the Ikatan Cendekiawan Muslim se-Indonesia (ICMI; Indonesian Muslim Intellectuals' Association). Although this organization was established with considerable popular support, it acquired the sponsorship of Suharto's favored technology minister, B. J. Habibie, and, through him, of Suharto himself.

A second characteristic of New Order civil society was its frequently defensive character. From the beginning, many political actors retreated from the explicitly political sphere (especially parties), where they were likely to attract the hostile attention of the state, into officially "apolitical" activities such as community development, cultural expression, and religious life. Activists from political parties and student groups, for example, established NGOs as a means to maintain their own networks and reach out to broader social constituencies: a group of young intellectuals formerly associated with various Muslim, socialist, and Christian student groups established the prominent research institute LP3ES; several prominent members of the nationalist *aliran* established the Consumers' Foundation. This defensive shift was also evident in the later behavior of Nahdlatul Ulama. During the 1970s, NU relations with the government hit a low point, with many of the organization's leaders harshly criticizing what they saw as the government's hostility to the interests of the Islamic community and its legitimation of secular norms. In 1984, the organization officially severed its relations with formal politics by withdrawing from the Islamic-based Partai Persatuan Pembangunan (PPP; United Development Party). It also accepted the state philosophy of Pancasila as its "ideological foundation." These moves strengthened NU's relations with the government and led to the release of greatly increased development funds to NU *pesantren*. But it was also noteworthy that the NU leader Abdurrahman Wahid justified this move as a way to preserve the organization's integrity, its links with its membership base, and its relative freedom of movement (Ramage 1995: 56). It was no coincidence that the NU chair had been both active in the Jakarta NGO world and a leading advocate of the cultural and economic modernization of the traditionalist Islamic community. He also encouraged the development of a network of NU-linked NGOs and, in the government's final decade, became one of the country's better-known exponents of the idea of civil society (although he never advocated confrontation with the government).

As disillusionment deepened among the New Order's most liberal former allies in the early 1970s, there were those in the emergent civil society who argued (while not opposing the New Order state in toto) that citizens—and by extension a civic space—should be protected by subjecting the state to an impartial rule of law. As Daniel Lev (1978; 1987; 1990) has argued, private lawyers were particularly prominent in promoting this argument, giving rise to institutions like LBH. Such groups were a kind of minority vanguard of civil society. Most organizations avoided overt confrontation with the state and sought to carve out niches that were congruent with state policies or that at least would not provoke confrontation and repression. The dramatic growth of community-development NGOs in the 1970s was one product of this tendency. But even this kind of activity generated an incremental ideological shift. In the world of community-development NGOs, a perspective evolved seamlessly from an emphasis on "basic needs" in the late 1970s through "people's participation in development," and "popular empowerment" in the 1980s, to the development of "civil society" by the mid-1990s (although, to be sure, many of the major developmentalist NGOs still avoided such critical language).

Through a myriad of similar processes, by the late Suharto years, the idea of civil society as a guaranteed realm of freedom from state interference—in short, as an *aim* of organizational life as much as a sphere in which citizens organized—became increasingly influential in public political discourse. (For a parallel development in Poland in the late 1970s and 1980s, see Arato 1981: 23.) The idea of civil society (*masyarakat sipil* or *masyarakat madani*) was achieving something like hegemonic dominance among NGO activists, critical intellectuals, and students.

The "Civilizing" of Civil Society

By the mid-1990s, although the old corporatist structures and institutional amphibiousness remained ubiquitous, there was also an increasingly vigorous civic life independent of the state. The NGO sector continued to grow; there was a new and resilient student activism; early efforts to organize lower-class groups were visible. Some organizations adopted a more confrontational stance toward the state. Many NGOs began to promote democratization openly. New student groups even declared that they wanted to overthrow the New Order. There were also attempts to assert the independence of semicorporatist and corporatist organizations—giving rise to major internal battles for control, such as one inside Nahdlatul Ulama in 1994 when Abdurrahman Wahid and his supporters successfully resisted a government-engineered attempt to oust him (Fealy 1996).

The new associational life was very different from that which prevailed before the New Order. In the 1960s, civil society was not only highly organized but was also a terrain for bitter contestation between groups with very different political visions. By the late 1990s, civil society had become far weaker institutionally. It was also the site of much less intense ideological contention. Different groups still had different visions of the ideal society, but there was an emerging political consensus that the state and social order were not fundamentally illegitimate (although many groups viewed the New Order government and regime in this way). Instead, the primary aims of politics were conceived as pressuring, lobbying, or otherwise influencing the state to achieve desirable policy outcomes; constraining state intervention in (and carving out a domain for) autonomous civil initiatives; and subjecting the state and its officers to an impartial rule of law. Different groups varied in the extent to which they were prepared to articulate these goals openly, of course, and many had entirely different views on their strategic implications. (Some groups believed that it was ultimately necessary to overthrow the New Order government to achieve these goals; others believed in incremental reform; most still refrained from political action.) In one way or another, however, this set of ideas became central to the emergent civil society. Some NGO activists and intellectuals explicitly argued, in neo-Gramscian terms, that they were engaged in a kind of long-term, incremental "war of position" or "counterhegemonic struggle." Unlike in the early 1960s, however, this was not a war of position between subordinate and dominant classes. Instead, it was conceived as a contest between certain groups in civil society and the state (see, e.g., Billah 1994).

Several factors underpinned the slow and painful growth of civil society, as well as the new mood of restraint associated with it. The first, ironically, was the consolidation and dominance of the state itself. For much of the New Order period, the state was unquestionably dominant. It moved resolutely against all forms of illegal opposition, and its overthrow appeared impossible. This dominance made the state the central problematic of political life for those who wanted reform. At the same time, the state was not indiscriminately repressive. As we have seen, it allowed many organizations to survive so long as they respected certain limits. The combination of repression and toleration imposed high costs on the promotion of alternative totalistic ideas and allowed a shift in the conceptual frame toward incremental reform and containment of the state. During the New Order period, for instance, many Islamic activists abandoned the long-cherished goal of an Islamic state and embraced the secular compromise embodied in the state philosophy of Pancasila, saying that rather than an Islamic state, they now sought to achieve an "Islamic society." There was also a more subterranean diffusion of ideas traditionally associated with the Indonesian Left. Even when new radical left-wing groups emerged among student activists in the 1990s—groups such as the Partai Rakyat Demokratik (PRD; People's Democratic Party)—they combined traditional leftist ideas (such as class analysis and hostility to capitalism) with suspicion of the state and commitment to political pluralism. Meanwhile, the consolidation of an increasingly institutionalized, ambitious, and effective state from the late 1960s on created many new interfaces for state-society interaction of the sort typical of the liberal-pluralist vision of civil society (as in the design and execution of economic development policy, for instance: a policy area that attracted considerable lobbying and similar efforts by NGOs). The increased dominance and consolidation of the state made possible the conceptualization of a state-society delineation in a way that was impossible during Guided Democracy because of the interpenetration of state, parties, and associational life.

Changes in the economy and class structure constituted a second important influence on civil society. Under the New Order's "repressive-developmentalist" rule (Feith 1980), the Indonesian economy expanded dramatically. Growth produced considerable social disruption among the poor, eventually triggering new forms of civil society activity by lower-class groups. One of the chief beneficiaries of growth, however, was the urban middle class. In 1965–66, the threat of a violent overturning of the social order drove much of this group into the arms of the military. As time passed, the middle class became larger and more robust. Although most continued to value social and political order, their fears of a revolutionary threat from below gradually receded, adding to their political confidence. This process should not be exaggerated: many scholars have stressed that much of the middle class remained tied economically to the state and were either politically ambivalent about authoritarianism or supported it. Most of the middle-class civil society organizations likewise maintained an ambivalent posture—often seeking an increasingly autonomous sphere for their own action but retaining multiple financial, political, and other links with state institutions and sponsors. But as the middle sectors became increasingly vigorous, at least a vocal minority increasingly sought to constrain state interference in their affairs. This shift, combined with restrictions on lower-class political activity, meant that civil society became increasingly a vehicle, not only for the articulation of a middle-class worldview, but even for the inculcation of middle-class values among subordinate classes.[4]

A third factor was the shifting international environment. In the 1960s, the Cold War encouraged polarization in Indonesian society. The communist *aliran* viewed itself as part of, not merely an international movement, but an epochal wave in world history. Its foes, especially in the army, derived much support from the United States and the other capitalist powers. Shifts in global politics, especially the end of the Cold War, created an environment much less prone to polarization. Indeed, the United States sometimes criticized the New Order for violations of human rights. Moreover, civil society derived such sustenance from international links that from the mid-1970s on, it becomes increasingly difficult to speak of Indonesian civil society as a discrete national entity. A large majority of NGOs, especially the outspoken critics of the government, became dependent on foreign funding for their survival. Indonesian NGOs also readily adopted and disseminated major trends in international civil society discourse (not least the promotion of "civil society empowerment" in the 1990s)—a phenomenon encouraged by the need to comply with project criteria set by foreign donor organizations. Foreign funding also meant that many NGOs became more professional, with financial plans, budgetary guidelines, project objectives, offices to rent or purchase, and salaried staff with middle-class lifestyles and career ambitions. Such institutional ballast meant that most NGOs were reluctant to risk provoking the state by straying too far toward radicalism.

Case Study: Land Conflicts in the 1980s and 1990s

The New Order regime took extraordinary measures to repress, control, and proscribe independent organization and mobilization among subordinate classes. One aim of these policies was to facilitate capitalist development, upon which the regime relied in large part for its legitimacy. In the late 1980s and early 1990s, however, lower-class protest began to have a significant impact on national politics. This protest was to a large extent fostered by the very pattern of capitalist development promoted by the state. One sign was an unprecedented wave of strikes from 1990 on by workers in the new industrial estates that had sprung up around the big cities following a government shift toward export-oriented industrialization policies in the 1980s (Hadiz 1997). Prior to this, protests by farmers and other members of rural communities had attained considerable coverage in the national press. The most celebrated of these cases occurred in Kedung Ombo, Central Java, when the government attempted to relocate approximately thirty thousand people to make way for a massive reservoir being built with funds from the World Bank and other sources. Residents complained they were being offered inadequate compensation and claimed that the military was using violence, intimidation, and deception to force them to leave (Stanley 1994). Many of them refused to comply. Local NGOs and student activists became involved. The International NGO Forum on Indonesia (INGI), the major umbrella group for Indonesian NGOs and their foreign counterparts, also campaigned internationally on the issue, provoking President Suharto's ire. Students accompanied residents to the national capital, Jakarta, where they held rowdy demonstrations. Although the dam was filled with water in early 1989, many residents still refused to accept the government's miserly offers of compensation or relocation. The case dragged on for years. There were court challenges, frequent articles in the national press, even plays. The Kedung Ombo case became a cause célèbre of the late New Order.

Apart from its public prominence, Kedung Ombo was in many ways typical of the land dispute cases of the 1980s and 1990s. Unlike the land conflicts of the 1960s, most such disputes concerned *penggusuran* (expropriation) when local residents were forced off their land to make way for private and public development projects such as golf courses, hotel complexes, plantations, agro-industry projects, factories, refineries, residential housing, and the like. In most cases, developers offered little or no compensation. (In the Cimacan case in West Java, farmers complained they were offered the equivalent of the price of an egg for every square meter of their fertile land.) Security forces frequently used intimidation to force peasants to leave, sometimes accusing resisters of harboring PKI or BTI sympathies, a terrifying label that justified all manner of abuse. When resistance persisted, security forces often arrested, beat, or tortured ringleaders. In many cases, their houses or crops were burned down or wrecked, often in the dead of night. There were many hundreds of such cases: between July 1994 and September 1996, the National Human Rights Commission recorded 891 instances of human rights abuses in land cases (Lucas and Warren 2000: 223).

Landholders employed diverse forms of resistance. Typically, these began with a few of the bravest residents making individual representations to local officials. The next step was often involvement by outside groups, either NGOs or student activists. Eventually, court challenges might result—as well as direct action such as coordinated refusal to sign acquisition papers, occupation and symbolic planting of dispossessed land, protests in district and provincial capitals, press campaigns, and the like. Such campaigns frequently resulted in physical confrontation on the land itself, as in Jatiwangi in West Java, where land belonging to eight villages had been claimed by the air force since the 1950s. In 1988, residents collectively refused to pay land rents, while some of the old women in the community stripped naked in the fields to dramatize their impoverishment. The following year, two thousand farmers attempted to work their fields, resulting in violent confrontation with military forces, detainment, and torture.[5]

Campaigning over land disputes involved broad networks of civil society. From the mid-to-late-1980s, it drew on an array of middle-class activists, who brought with them the political ideas that had been gestating in urban civil society groups—especially interest in the rule of law, human rights, and democratization. Often, the first outside groups to become involved in land disputes were NGOs. LBH, the private institution best known for defending the legal rights of the disenfranchised, was often the first resort for landholders. It began dealing with land acquisition cases in the early 1970s, when the Jakarta city administration (then under the control of the organization's sponsor, Governor Ali Sadikin) displaced the residents of slum areas for urban redevelopment projects. Early on, the organization's leaders viewed land disputes as primarily legal matters to be fought in the courts. By the late 1980s, LBH had developed a concept of "structural legal aid" in which legal conflicts were no longer viewed as merely matters to be litigated but were now seen as foundations for broad social movements focusing on the legal empowerment of those involved. Along with labor, environmental, and political cases, the organization viewed land disputes as a high-priority issue where campaigning could most enhance collective rights against state interference (Aspinall 2000: 134). Although LBH lawyers still took cases to court, they also worked with other NGOs (by the mid-1990s, there were several dozen that focused on land issues) and student groups. The aims were to publicize and condemn land expropriation and to encourage victims to organize to defend their rights.

In the late 1980s, student activists too became involved in land disputes. Many of these students had been radicalized by the government's suppression of campus political activity since the 1970s and had concluded that it was necessary to mobilize popular sectors if they wanted to democratize the regime (Aspinall 1993). In some cases, student activists first encountered rural communities as voluntary researchers for NGOs like LBH. Elsewhere, student activists independently visited villages where land disputes were occurring, collected information, and then organized seminars or protests on campus. Some formed ad hoc campaign committees and stayed in affected villages for months at a time. Generally, the aim was to give farmers a basic political education and practical skills for organizing resistance campaigns (*pemberdayaan*, or empowerment, as a catchphrase of the early 1990s put it).[6]

A subterranean form of organizing also developed in the affected communities. Frequently assisted by students and NGOs, but sometimes independently, landholders threatened by or experiencing displacement organized themselves. Often the pattern of organization was based on a highly participatory, consensus model, assisted by the cohesion of small rural communities, in which issues were discussed and decided upon by all those affected. But these groups often manifested a considerable degree of organizational sophistication involving democratic selection of their leaders, role specialization, and acute consciousness of the need for secrecy.[7]

Such efforts culminated in attempts to organize peasant resistance on a permanent basis. The radical student-based PRD, for example, established the Serikat Tani Nasional (STN; National Peasants' Union), and a group of student and NGO activists around the Bandung-based Lembaga Pendidikan dan Pengembangan Pedesaan (LPPP; Rural Education and Development Institute) assisted the formation of several *ikatan petani* (peasants' associations) in West Java in the early 1990s. These organizations, centered on the most motivated peasant-activists at land dispute sites, remained rudimentary and mostly underground affairs. Primarily, they aimed to assist networking between farmers affected by similar cases of land expropriation. In 1994, the Konsorsium Pembaruan Agraria (KPA; Consortium for Agrarian Reform) was formed; within a year, it involved more than sixty-five NGOs and six peasant associations. It campaigned for "people-oriented land reform" and the "defense of victims of land disputes" (KPA 1995).

There were similarities between the land dispute campaigns of the late New Order and those of the 1960s. The student and NGO activist practice of living in rural communities, for example, resembled the old PKI "going down" (*turun ke bawah*) campaigns when the party sent its urban cadres to experience the realities of rural life. More radical student activists were motivated by Marxist class analysis. By the mid-1990s, the KPA and allied groups began to formulate demands for thorough agrarian reform (*pembaruan agraria*)—the centerpiece of which was a call for the reinvigoration of the old 1960 Basic Agrarian Law, which they called a "masterpiece" of the Sukarno era (see, e.g., Fauzi 2001). Such steps required great courage given the stigma attached to land reform due to its prior association with the PKI and BTI. Senior government officials accused groups like the KPA of harboring communist tendencies.

But the differences between the land disputes of the 1980s and 1990s and the *aksi sepihak* of the 1960s were obvious, too, and revealed much about changes in Indonesia's civil society in the intervening decades. In the land reform campaign of 1963–64, a primary schism was within village society itself—whether along class lines (poor and landless peasants versus the "seven village devils") or those of *alirans* (PKI versus NU, nominal versus traditionalist Muslims, and so forth). The land conflicts of the 1980s, in contrast, generally pitted entire rural communities against *external* forces—either the state, private developers, or, most commonly, an alliance between the two. This shift happened despite a continued "objective basis" for conflict within rural society, with landlessness and land concentration apparently more pronounced since the 1960s (Pincus 1996; Fauzi 1997: 165). Even so, the shift also flowed from the pattern of capitalist development encouraged by the regime. Indonesia was becoming an increasingly industrialized society, and land acquisition typically resulted from intrusions by urban-based, capital-intensive development into rural areas (Setiawan 1997: 205).[8] Such development, moreover, involved a close alliance between state officials and the nascent capitalist class. Indeed the latter group was largely emerging out of the bosom of the former in the shape of various types of crony capitalism (Robison 1986). It was precisely this alliance that confronted peasants in land disputes: urban-based private and public investors working hand in glove with local officials and the military to secure cheap access to land.[9] This does not mean there was no division within rural society. On the contrary, developers and officials frequently attempted to divide rural communities—for example, by bribing village heads to falsify land documents. Village heads, big landowners, and other village notables had profited considerably from New Order policies of increasing agricultural production. Even so, in *penggusuran* cases, they too often lost land to developers. Indeed, they often stood to lose the most. As a result, such individuals were frequently at the forefront of resistance.[10]

Moreover, conflicts over land did not give rise to horizontal *aliran* conflict in the 1980s and 1990s. Unlike in 1963–64, when NU was violently hostile to PKI land reform campaigns, from the 1980s on, traditionalist NU communities were often victims of expropriation and local *kyai* sometimes defended them against pressures to vacate their land. (One notorious case occurred in 1994 in Nipah, on the island of Madura, when a large crowd of peasants resisting the construction of a dam were fired on by security forces, killing four of them.)[11] In some places, such as Jenggawah in East Java, traditionalist communities consulted *kyai* to attain Koranic justification for their resistance (Hafid 2001: 151). Some students from NU families studied leftist literature, formed action committees (*komite aksi*), and became involved in anti-*penggusuran* campaigns. In some places, there was confrontation, even violence, between these activists and NU groups (especially from the youth organization Ansor) close to local officials, who accused the activists of communist sympathies.[12]

A second difference from the 1960s was that there were now far greater obstacles to organization. In the 1960s, organizational life had permeated the very fabric of rural society. *Aliran*-linked peasant associations had millions of members. The PKI and BTI had been able to take *offensive* action to redistribute land to poor and landless peasants. The campaigns of the 1980s and 1990s, by contrast, were primarily *defensive*; they usually aimed at regaining or defending villagers' land from the clutches of developers or, when this proved impossible, obtaining adequate compensation. Moreover, it was now extremely difficult to build lasting and effective organizations among peasants, let alone ones that aimed at land redistribution and class-based mobilization. This was largely a product of repression. From the start, the New Order regime had applied depoliticization policies especially rigorously in the countryside. (See Fauzi 1997: 123–24 for a summary of the state's control apparatus in rural society.) Student activists reported that it was very difficult to conduct organizing work in village communities given the high level of surveillance and intimidation they experienced. Military personnel sometimes tortured student activists involved in land dispute campaigns (a relatively rare event for those who confined their antigovernment activities to campus). Farmers who protested were routinely subjected to even greater violence.

Difficulties in organizing were also caused by the structural nature of the disputes. In the 1960s, the PKI had organized its campaign for land reform on the basis of structural inequalities in landownership and control that it identified throughout rural society. Now, although there were thousands of land disputes across the country, each was essentially a specific, hence isolated, "case." Student and NGO activists who dreamed of fostering class consciousness among the peasants, and mobilizing them against the regime, frequently complained that these campaigns tended to peak around the time of land expropriation itself. If the developers offered sufficient compensation to satisfy a sizable proportion of the residents—or if a majority of them simply became exhausted and moved away in search of employment—the campaigns fostered by activists tended to fade away.[13]

As a result of these obstacles, organizing over land disputes took the form of a proliferation of small groups, whether NGOs, student groups, or groups of farmers and landholders. Although there was a great deal of effective networking, the overall pattern was characterized by ad hoc, underground, and semiunderground methods. Unlike in the 1960s, when associational life in rural society consisted of large, cohesive blocs, the associational efforts of the 1980s and 1990s are better imagined as forming a kind of spiderweb: faint to the eye but nevertheless remarkably resilient. And the fact that the state was so central to these conflicts—either as the direct agent of disenfranchisement or the main obstacle to organization—meant that land disputes were more readily perceived by those who participated in them in "state versus society" terms, whereas in the 1960s, rural society itself was divided into warring camps.[14]

Finally, we must consider the impact of the international context on the new pattern of civil society activity. In the 1960s, those advocating redistribution of land had readily linked their struggle to a world-historical wave promising the coming of a classless social order. By the late 1980s, even though some middle-class land activists again viewed agrarian conflict through a Marxist lens, the international communist movement was in decline, along with attempts to establish egalitarian rural regimes and collective agriculture in other parts of the developing world (Low 1996). Now groups involved in land disputes were often linked to NGOs that in turn, as noted earlier, were part of an emerging global civil society movement. As a result, the new campaigning on land issues was embedded in a new global discourse in which the basic references were no longer the international class struggle but the evolving architecture of universal human rights. As one activist involved in rural NGOs put it (after the fall of Suharto): "Agrarian problems are problems of basic human rights. And in the struggle to fulfil and protect human rights, including the basic rights of peasants, the basis is international law, namely, the Universal Declaration of Human Rights of 1948" (Damanik 2002: 34.)

Civil Society and the Democratic Breakthrough

Civil society campaigning, like that around land disputes, did not mount an immediate threat to the New Order state. But it did have a significant political impact. The unjust terms of land acquisition, as well as the brutal techniques used by the military to suppress those who resisted, generated much discussion in the media, academia, and other public forums. Campaigning thus added to the mounting burden faced by the regime of maintaining its aura of legitimacy. The cumulative effect of such activity, from the early 1990s onward, shifted the ground of public discourse under the feet of the regime and greatly undermined its legitimacy. It was here that civil society made its central contribution to the transition to democratic government: it eroded the ideological foundations of authoritarian rule.

In the end, however, the collapse of the Suharto regime was dictated not so much by processes within civil society as by processes internal to the state—combined with a massive external shock. As I have argued elsewhere (Aspinall 1998, 2005), the growing "sultanization" of government ruled out the possibility of a negotiated transition. Suharto's predominance in the political structure—and the identification of his and his family's interests with those of the New Order—helped to clarify what had previously been a blurred line between state and society and imparted to the transition the character of a society-initiated *ruptura*. Indeed, after the devastating impact of the 1997 Asian financial crisis, the sudden collapse of the Suharto regime caught many in civil society organizations unprepared. It did not fit their schema of a long-term, incremental "war of position."

Even so, the fall of the Suharto government was reminiscent of the 1989 "victories of civil society" in eastern and central Europe. The mass democratic movement of February–May 1998 drew extensively on the language and ideas of various efforts over previous decades to carve out a civic space. This was most apparent in the demands of the student protesters, whose political program was essentially a culmination of all such efforts and drew extensively on the discourse of NGOs and radical social movements. One of the popular slogans of student groups in Java, for example, *menolak tunduk, tuntut tanggungjawab* ("refuse to submit, demand accountability"), had according to one account initially been coined in 1996 by peasants involved in the Wedoro Anom land dispute with the military in East Java (Firmansyah et al. 1999: 95). Some groups even chose names reflecting the hegemony of the civil society idea. (Hence when the former Suharto minister Emil Salim mounted a challenge to the candidacy of B. J. Habibie as vice president, he called his support group the Gema Masyarakat Madani, or "Echo of Civil Society.") Some civil society organizations played important roles in increasing pressure on the regime during the crisis. (For example, the Legal Aid Institute launched a highly effective public campaign against a series of military abductions of political activists.)

But we must not overstate the role played by organized civil society in the fall of Suharto—especially the degree to which it led or managed the mobilizations that drove the political transition. The established organizations that made up civil society were mostly too weak to organize antiregime mobilizations or were ill suited to playing this role. Organizations of subordinate social groups like workers and farmers remained fragmented and were reeling from the impact of the economic crisis. They played little part in the key mobilizations. NGOs were mostly professional, middle-class bodies without solid links to a mass base. Corporatist or semicorporatist bodies were reluctant to risk their institutional and financial resources by challenging the state. In the case of Nahdlatul Ulama, for instance, although many of the organization's students and younger members participated in the anti-Suharto protests, its leader, Abdurrahman Wahid, had in 1997 effected a dramatic and expedient reconciliation with Suharto and his regime. As a result, the NU leadership vacillated for most of the crucial final months (Mietzner 1999).

The social groups whose protests drove the transition—students and the urban poor—were precisely those most suited (albeit for different reasons) to relatively spontaneous and unstructured political action. In the case of the students, a huge number of organizations were involved in the protests leading to Suharto's downfall. Although these groups drew on the legacy of previous decades of student political activity, many of them were ad hoc and temporary, even anarchic, in their organizational style. In the case of the urban poor, whose rioting played a key role in impelling sections of the political elite to finally break with Suharto, their action—violent rioting in the streets—was the very antithesis of an organized and moderate civil society. The violence of the transition, especially the rioting of the urban poor, was itself largely a product of the New Order's previous restrictions on organizing among subordinate classes. Lacking avenues for peaceful expression, the political frustrations and interests of lower-class groups remained unmediated. The unintended result of the regime's policy was, therefore, an absence of organizational means for instilling civility in much of the population. Combined with the many lessons in violence that the New Order itself had given society down the years, this absence added considerably to the potential for explosive unrest in Indonesian political life after the democratic transition.

In short, we must be cautious in conceptualizing the relationship between the organizational infrastructure of *civil society* (NGOs, student organizations, religious bodies, and the like) and the more amorphous *society* in democratization—especially in conditions of popular upsurge such as those that accompanied the fall of Suharto. In the literature on democratic transitions, the popular upsurge is frequently described as a "victory of civil society." The Indonesian transition, however, was marked by a degree of fluidity, spontaneous expression, and violence that bore little relationship to the models of political change nurtured in much of organized civil society.

After the Breakthrough

The downfall of the Suharto regime was followed by a series of political reforms that went a long way toward establishing a more secure legal framework for civil society. From virtually the moment that B. J. Habibie was sworn in as president, the ideas about political and social order generated in the vanguard elements of civil society (such as human rights NGOs) over the previous decade were accepted as an ideological foundation for the new political order. In the face of a highly mobilized society, there was now little open resistance expressed from within the state to notions of democracy, accountability, supremacy of law, even civil society itself.

But even as civil society provided the ideological foundation for democratization, certain inherited characteristics of civil society undermined the momentum of reform. Militant prodemocracy groups in civil society were weak, marginalized, and disunited as a result of decades of repression. The semicorporatist organizations often had better-organized mass followings, but their leaders (Abdurrahman Wahid, head of the 40-million-strong Nahdlatul Ulama was an obvious example) had been deeply affected by the politics of compromise and deal making under the New Order. The disunited, dispersed organizational character of civil society and its political moderation—two elements that had helped it survive under the New Order—now meant that democratic forces lacked the political cohesion, institutional resources, and clarity and unity of purpose to seize control of the reform process and stamp their authority on it. As a result, the state elite survived the downfall of Suharto largely intact, and many of the patrimonial, rent-seeking, and repressive practices of the Suharto years carried over into the post-breakthrough phase.

Even so, in the new Reformasi era, there were significant changes in civil society and its interaction with the state. The most obvious was a dramatic expansion of civil society. In a pattern typical of *ruptura* democratizations, the resignation of President Suharto was the signal for great social energization and popular mobilization. Keeping the focus on rural and land issues, the first sign was a wave of land occupations. All across the archipelago, in places where land had been expropriated during the New Order years (and in some cases long before), peasants occupied land, dug up golfing greens, chopped down coffee trees, and planted their own crops (Lucas and Warren 2000: 227–31). One of the most symbolic examples was in Tapos, West Java, where, within a few hours of Suharto's resignation on May 21, five farmers began to dig plots on land that had been taken from them some twenty-five years earlier to make way for a cattle ranch owned by President Suharto himself (Bachriadi and Lucas 2001: 62–63)—and many more joined them over the following days. Eventually, according to one activist from the rural-oriented NGO Bina Desa, "hundreds of thousands" of hectares of land were seized by farmers across the archipelago in the years following Suharto's resignation. The total far exceeded that occupied during the unilateral actions of 1963–64.[15]

There was also a rapid expansion of associational activity. In the rural sector, new NGOs formed, and there was a rash of seminars and conferences to discuss issues of agrarian reform (Lucas and Warren 2000: 227). The most striking development, however, was the rapid expansion and formation of peasants' unions (*serikat petani*). Usually formed on the basis of the subterranean networks established during the preceding fifteen years, several dozen such organizations were formed or declared themselves openly for the first time. In some cases, they were soon able to mobilize large numbers. A Lampung Peasants' Association was launched at a mass meeting of 12,000 farmers in March 2001 (*Kompas*, August 20, 2001). By mid-2002, the Serikat Petani Pasundan in West Java claimed some 200,000 members. These new unions were integrally concerned with land occupations, but they also began to mobilize in favor of more general policy demands. In September

2001, for example, approximately 10,000 farmers organized by the Aliansi Petani Indonesia (Indonesian Peasants' Alliance) were blocked by security forces from entering the West Javanese capital of Bandung, where they had intended to lobby members of the People's Consultative Assembly who were discussing a draft decree on agrarian reform (*Kompas*, September 15, 2002).

In superficial terms, it seemed that rural politics was reverting to the pattern of the 1960s, with mass-membership peasant organizations (although still only a fraction of the size of the old BTI) and national campaigns for agrarian reform and absolute equality in the countryside. In the words of a "Declaration of the Rights of Indonesian Peasants" produced by a conference of peasant organizations and NGOs in April 2001 (Damanik 2002: 63): "Improvement in the fate of the peasants can only be brought about by total agrarian reform, beginning with equal distribution of control over and use of the land, water, and natural wealth." The new campaigning differed from the land reform offensive of the 1960s, however, insofar as the primary focus was now the *restitution* of land that had been unfairly expropriated during preceding decades. Thus Pri Suhardi, coordinator of the Ikatan Petani Lampung, stressed that although most of the organization's members were landless, "we only struggle for land that we used to own but that is now controlled by others; it must be returned" (*Kompas*, August 20, 2001). In fact, many of the occupations involved previously landless peasants taking over plantation lands that had been state-owned since colonial times. But even here it is significant that the new agenda for agrarian reform stressed the redistribution of *state-owned* plantation land in which usage rights were granted to state enterprises and private investors (and that amounted, by some estimates, to 60 percent of productive land), rather than land in the hands of small-scale landlords, as in the 1960s.[16]

In short, the post-Suharto burst of associational activity substantially continued the trend set during the late New Order whereby civil society was primarily a domain of organizations that eschewed the ambitious, maximalist aims of the 1960s.[17] Indeed, most civil society organizations had a rather limited conceptualization of their own goals. They did not seek to utterly transform the state or social order but focused instead on restraining, seeking redress from, or gaining other desirable policy outcomes from the state. In the words of a rural activist: "The obligations of the state are the central point, namely, the obligations to protect, fulfill, and advance the rights of the peasants" (Damanik 2002: 51).[18]

A second significant change in civil society after the fall of Suharto concerned its relations with political society. The New Order had attempted to sever the links between civil society and political parties. In the post-breakthrough climate, there was a partial renewal of the bonds between civil and political society that was in some ways reminiscent of pre–New Order conditions. Some organizations representing core sociopolitical traditions (*alirans*) created or resurrected political parties. Abdurrahman Wahid and other leaders of Nahdlatul Ulama, for example, created the Partai Kebangkitan Bangsa (PKB; National Awakening Party), while some leaders of Muhammadiyah, the chief modernist Islamic organization, sponsored the Partai Amanat Nasional (PAN; National Mandate Party). In this sense, post-breakthrough politics resembled a reawakening of the old *aliran* pattern in which each major sociocultural grouping had its own political party.

The boundaries between the different sociocultural streams are far less clear, however, than in the 1950s and 1960s. PAN and PKB, for example, consciously strove to reach out (albeit with minimal success) beyond their core modernist and traditionalist Islamic constituencies and even attempted to recruit non-Muslims. More important, there is less conflict between the revivified *alirans* than in the 1960s. Although there has been considerable violence (see below), there is little of the sense of looming social conflagration that dominated Indonesian political life in the 1960s. To some extent, this reflects the emergence of a much larger buffer zone of organizations that lack *aliran* affiliation. Thus, in dramatic contrast to the 1960s, none of the larger new farmers' unions are linked to political parties. Instead, when they seek certain legislative outcomes (such as a 2001 People's Consultative Assembly decree on agrarian reform), these organizations and allied NGOs lobby all the major parties—speaking in terms of "bargaining power" rather than class struggle and viewing themselves as "pressure groups" or "lobby groups" (Damanik 2002: 40 and 45).

Equally important, the sociocultural element of *aliran* identity (the division between major religious groupings) is no longer reinforced and exacerbated by class conflict. The only party that pursues a rigorous class line is the PRD, a product of the student radicalization of the 1980s and 1990s, but this party attained less than 0.1 percent of the vote in the 1999 election. Some of the larger political parties campaigned on *penggusuran* issues and tried to portray themselves as advocates of farmers' interests, but mostly in a fitful and casual manner. When it comes to determining policy on land, they have been influenced more by international financial agencies promoting a brand of agrarian reform that aims to create a more efficient and better-regulated market in private land (Bey 2002). Overall, ideological conflict between the *alirans* is far less intense today than in the 1950s and 1960s.

A third feature of post-breakthrough civil society, however, has been its inability to prevent serious violence and social breakdown in many parts of the country. The Indonesian transition has been marked by outbursts of violence occasioned by the suppression of secessionist movements in East Timor, Papua, and Aceh, severe ethnic and religious conflict in some regions, and a widespread breakdown of law and order. A detailed examination of the sources of this violence is beyond the scope of this chapter. One important factor contributing to these phenomena, however, is the legacy of state suppression of civil society during the long Suharto period. The state's restriction of organization meant that many members of society had few avenues for venting their grievances peacefully and little experience of associational activity to impart the habits of tolerance, mutual respect, and trust sometimes ascribed to civil society interaction. Once political controls were lifted, a pattern of patron-client pyramids extending from the state apparatus down to social groups (including criminal gangs) combined with competition for scarce resources to produce severe communal conflict in some areas (Van Klinken 2001a, 2001b; Bertrand 2002).

Moreover, after the fall of Suharto, it became apparent that the appearance of a strong state in Indonesia had been deceptive. The "strong state" was in fact primarily dependent on military repression in dealing with challenges from society and dependent on patrimonialism for maintaining internal cohesion (Crouch 1998). After the democratic breakthrough, therefore, the state was increasingly prey to predatory attack as numerous political and business forces sought to gain access to its resources for their own rent-seeking purposes, frequently impeding the functioning of its machinery in the process. This phenomenon has been especially pronounced at the local level, where old alliances between business and state elites have been rapidly reconstituted in many areas through the institutions of the new democratic order, such as parties and parliaments (Hadiz 2003; Robison 2002). In many regions, this process has seen the establishment of what Jennifer Franco in Chapter 3 refers to as local "authoritarian enclaves"—in which conflict between business and the state, on the one hand, and civil society groups representing subordinate groups, on the other, largely follows the pattern established under the prior authoritarian regime.

This continuity of violence is apparent in the new rural campaigning. The land occupations and farmer activism that followed 1998 still faced powerful and violent adversaries. The partial political retreat of the armed forces has meant that developers make increased use of private hoodlums (*preman*) when attempting to force farmers off disputed land. When this first line of privatized violence fails, however, police and military forces have frequently intervened on behalf of developers. (See Collins 2001 for case studies of conflict in South Sumatra.) In many cases, security forces have arrested farmers occupying land or used violence to oust them; several have been shot dead.[19] In regions where land disputes have been particularly severe, as in the plantation zone of North Sumatra, local conditions have come to resemble civil war—with private "ninjas" and estate employees (sometimes guarded by police mobile brigade troops) regularly attacking villages, burning down homes, schools, and houses of worship, destroying property, beating whomever they find, and sometimes killing them. In response, farmers have formed their own militia-like groups and proclaimed themselves ready to "fight to the death."[20]

As severe as it became in some parts of the country, this kind of conflict does not presage a headlong descent into societywide massacres like those of 1965–66. There is nothing resembling the deep ideological conflict within civil society of the sort that predated the New Order. Nor does the new pattern of violence pose an immediate threat to the liberal-democratic shell that has largely replaced the authoritarian political structures of the New Order. Rather, such violence says much about the *kind* of democracy being constructed in Indonesia (Robison 2002). It suggests that although civil society faces severe challenges, its continued expansion will be necessary to extend the benefits of democratization to subordinate groups.

Building a *Civil* Society

Civil society in Indonesia has contributed differently to political change in different periods. In the 1960s, civil society was an important arena of the intense political conflict that preceded a tremendous massacre and a long period of authoritarian rule. In the 1990s, civil society became an arena where many groups attempted to expand space for political participation, constrain the state, and promote democratization. Civil society contributed to the transition to formal democracy, especially by undermining the ideological foundations of the authoritarian political order.

In general terms, civil society was much tamer in the 1980s and 1990s than it was in the early 1960s. As we have seen, however, it would be wrong to say that civil society was no longer violent or conflictual. Instead, the nature of the conflict had substantially changed. The violence was mostly no longer *within* civil society as it had been during the 1960s when the party-linked mass associations faced each other across a deep ideological gulf and viewed one another as mortal enemies. Land disputes in the 1980s and 1990s demonstrated not only that civil society remained a site of considerable violent conflict but also that this conflict was more readily perceived by participants in "state versus society" terms. Of course, conflictual relations were not the only, or even dominant, mode of civil society interaction with the state. Especially in corporatist and semicorporatist organizations, as well as middle-class associational life, there was considerable overlap and accommodation with the state. But the fact that civil society grew under the New Order as a defensive attempt to carve out a sphere for independent action meant that it generated a political dynamic and discourse that cumulatively did much to undermine the legitimacy of authoritarian rule (especially in combination with the process of atrophy visible in state institutions). This erosion of the ideological foundation of authoritarianism was civil society's primary contribution to Indonesia's democratic breakthrough in 1998.

One reason that a democratic system was able to emerge and survive after 1998 (even if the quality of that democratic system is, to say the least, uneven) was that civil society was no longer a terrain for such bitter contestation as in the 1960s. It was no longer divided into vertically aligned blocs, each linked to a political party, each representing distinct socioreligious and socioeconomic constituencies, with incompatible goals for reconstructing Indonesian state and society. Instead, much of civil society now imagines itself to be inherently limited, in the sense of forgoing aims of overthrowing or fundamentally reordering the state and social order and instead seeking from the state Diamond's "concessions, benefits, policy changes, relief, redress or accountability"—as well, we might add, as political space guaranteed against state interference and violence. Features of the neo-Tocquevillean framework outlined in Chapter 1 are becoming dominant.

In explaining the emergence of such a civil society in Indonesia, this chapter has emphasized three factors. The first, which explains a great deal, is the changing international setting. The end of the Cold War meant that the broad international context did not exacerbate polarization in Indonesian society as it had in the 1960s. By the time of Suharto's fall, there was even a large international "democracy aid" industry ready to disburse funds to encourage precisely the kind of groups that accord with Diamond's vision of a limited civil society.

Second, we have seen that changes in economic structures and the dynamics of class conflict had a large impact on the evolution of civil society and hence political change. Class conflict in the countryside made a crucial contribution to the violent collapse of Indonesia's political system in 1965–66. Under the New Order, despite an all-pervasive security apparatus that aimed to suppress mobilization by subordinate classes, class conflict did not pass from the picture. On the contrary, our survey of agrarian politics suggests that class conflict remained severe. But the particular type of capitalist development that flourished under the New Order meant that the *form* of class conflict, and its impact on civil society, changed. Because the main engine of economic growth—and hence the main cause of social dislocation—was an alliance between the developmentalist state and an emergent urban-based capitalist class, the main fissure of conflict no longer divided small rural communities against themselves. Instead, class conflict set entire rural communities against powerful forces far removed from them in the social hierarchy. The enmeshment of the new capitalist class with state officialdom—and the role played by the security apparatus as main protector and enforcer for capitalist development—also meant that class conflict was now more readily conceived in "state versus society" terms. In the countryside, the agents of land alienation came dressed in the uniforms of the civil service corps and the military. If disenfranchised landholders were to defend themselves, they needed to fight state officials to establish even minimal civic space. As a result, the dynamic of class conflict reinforced other trends promoting an orientation toward civil society constraint and control of the state.

The third factor was the evolution of the state, its structuring of civil society, and the way it was consequently viewed by groups in civil society. We have seen how the state became supremely dominant during the New Order. This dominance—especially as exercised by the repressive apparatus—meant that the state itself became the primary problematic, and the primary focus, of civic life. Almost every group that sought to organize itself, to further its members' interests, or to achieve other social and political aims had to confront this behemoth in one way or another. Many groups attempted to cooperate with it; others resisted; most used some combination of cooperation and resistance. But the very fact that all civil society groups, including those descended from different *alirans*, shared a common condition of subordination to the state meant that the focus of political life (including political conflict) to a large extent shifted away from the hostile axes of competition between different societal groups and toward their individual relations with the state.

During the long New Order years, Indonesian civil society thus gave rise to a discourse that viewed the state as the primary problem of political life and its constraint as a foremost political goal. This antiauthoritarian, antistatist impulse represented an ideational foundation of the social convulsion that removed Suharto from power. It meant that Suharto's fall was immediately followed by unequivocal movement in the direction of greater political democracy. After this breakthrough, civil society expanded rapidly—although it also faced severe challenges and revealed many weaknesses that had been created by decades of military rule (in a way reminiscent of Aqil Shah's account of Pakistan in Chapter 11). In this sense, the survey of Indonesian civil society presented in this chapter supports Robert Hefner's (2000) formulation (based on an analysis of Indonesian Islamic politics) that a "civil society requires a *civil state*."

But the Indonesian case illustrates a more fundamental proposition: if civil society is to emerge, it also requires a *state*, in the sense of a distinct set of state institutions and political interactions that have separated themselves from the world of political party and associational life. Indonesia's New Order was in few senses civil. It was authoritarian, violent, and manipulative. Yet it was precisely in counterpoint to this state that an Indonesian civil society began to emerge.

Notes

1. This point is suggested, for instance, by R. William Liddle's (1970) study of political party and associated activity in Simalungun regency in North Sumatra. (I am thankful to one of the anonymous reviewers for Stanford University Press for this observation.) J. Eliseo Rocamora (1973: 144), by contrast, suggests that the political organization of the PKI, PNI, and NU *alirans* actually improved under Guided Democracy.

2. The seven village devils were "wicked landlords and wicked boat-owners (in fishing areas), usurers, crop speculators, wicked brokers, bureaucratic capitalists, wicked officials, and village bandits" (*Suara Tani*, nos. 5–6 [1964]: 1).

3. I am indebted to one of the anonymous reviewers for pointing out this complication.

4. For example, although NGOs were middle-class organizations, generally their raison d'être was to organize lower-class groups, if only for credit, income generation, or alternative technology schemes. Eventually, many middle-class NGO and student activists sought to promote more political forms of organization in lower-class groups, even to radicalize them. Often, however, they did this by seeking to channel and "civilize" lower-class political activities and recast them in a middle-class mold. NGO activists engaged in early labor organizing efforts, for example, generally emphasized teaching workers their legal rights and encouraged them to seek legal redress for their complaints rather than engage in disorderly or violent protest.

5. See "Sejarah tanah pertanian Jatiwangi yang dirampas AURI," *Suara Petani*, Mar. 10, 1990.

6. Numerous manuals circulated among student and NGO activists explaining how to conduct such empowerment activities. Often these were translations of books produced by similar movements in the Philippines, South Korea, and elsewhere. These efforts also produced a rich underground literature. Bulletins, magazines, and journals with titles like *Suara Petani* (Voice of the Peasants) and *Suara Rakyat* (Voice of the People) proliferated, praising the virtues and dignity of the farmers' life, detailing disputes, outlining landholders' legal rights, and incorporating antigovernment material.

7. For case studies of several such organizing attempts all across the archipelago, see Firmansyah et al. 1999. During a visit to the site of the Jatiwangi dispute between farmers and the air force in October 1993, I was impressed by the great sophistication of local networks. Not only could large meetings of the local community be assembled to meet me on very short notice, but local people were able to keep a close watch on the movements of local military personnel, shepherding me from village to village to avoid contact with them.

8. As a result, many of the new generation of rural activists argued that it was now "pointless" to explain agrarian conflict by reference to division between feudal landlords and peasants (Setiawan 1997: 203).

9. It is worth noting that some of the bitterest conflicts, in which the greatest violence was used against local communities, involved the military as developer—as in the village of Wedoro Anom in East Java, where the Brawijaya military command initially claimed it was acquiring land for a military base, although it was later revealed that real estate speculation was the motive (Firmansyah et al. 1999: 88).

10. Thus, in the Jatiwangi case, student activists suggested that the chief leaders of resistance were several wealthy farmers, retired civil servants and soldiers, and even certain local officials of the New Order's corporatist peasant association (HKTI).

11. See, e.g., the interview with the famous *kyai*, K. H. Alaway Muhammad, in *Forum Keadilan*, Dec. 9, 1993, 19.

12. After NU university students in Jombang demonstrated against military repression of a strike in a factory, local authorities and Ansor leaders organized intimidatory counter-demonstrations, accusing the students of being communists. See "Tandingi aksi buruh, Kades turun ke jalan," *Surya*, Oct. 24, 1995.

13. It should be noted, however, that even when landholders were forced off their land and overt resistance declined, in most cases they still rejected the legitimacy of the acquisition and remained ready to take over their land when conditions allowed (as indeed occurred in 1998–99). Some groups even chose names that underlined their patient refusal to surrender their claims; one in North Sumatra that had been involved in a decades-long dispute

called itself the Badan Perjuangan Rakyat Penunggu Indonesia (Struggle Organ of the Waiting People of Indonesia).

14. It is significant, for example, that the new generation of land campaigners complained that the old Basic Agrarian Law of 1960 gave unfettered rights to the *state* to control land (KPA 1995, 3–4).

15. Interview with Syaiful Bahari, May 26, 2002.

16. Ibid.

17. There were, however, obvious exceptions, such as some Islamist groups and ethnic associations that were involved in violent activity.

18. Outside the rural sector, this trend was especially apparent in the rapid growth of watchdog NGOs—not only human rights organizations of the traditional kind but also an array of corruption-watch, judiciary-watch, parliament-watch, and election-watch groups. These groups were overwhelmingly middle-class, and their growth was made possible by a huge inflow of "democracy aid" from foreign governments and private foundations after the fall of Suharto. (During the elections alone, for example, USAID gave financial support to some two hundred Indonesian NGOs; see Clear 2002.)

19. See, e.g., "Bentrok antara Massa dan Aparat Kepolisian: Satu Orang Tewas Diterjang Peluru," *Media Indonesia*, Nov. 30, 2001.

20. See, e.g., "Penggarap Ancam Sabung Nyawa Dan Kibarkan Bendera SM Raja XII," *Waspada*, Dec. 10, 1999.

Works Cited

Anderson, Benedict. 1994. "Rewinding 'Back to the Future': The Left and Constitutional Democracy." In David Bourchier and John Legge, eds., *Democracy in Indonesia: 1950s and 1990s*. Monash Papers on Southeast Asia, 31. Clayton, Victoria, Australia: Monash University.

Arato, Andrew. 1981. "Civil Society Against the State: Poland, 1980–1981." *Telos* 47: 23–47.

Aspinall, Edward. 1993. *Student Dissent in Indonesia in the 1980s*. Centre of Southeast Asian Studies Working Paper 79. Clayton, Victoria, Australia: Monash University.

———. 1998. "Opposition and Elite Conflict in the Fall of Soeharto." In Geoff Forrester and R. J. May, eds., *The Fall of Soeharto*. Bathurst, N.S.W.: Crawford House and Australian National University.

———. 2000. "Political Opposition and the Transition from Authoritarian Rule: The Case of Indonesia." Ph.D. diss., Australian National University.

———. 2005. *Opposing Suharto: Compromise, Resistance and Regime Change in Indonesia*. Stanford: Stanford University Press.

Bachriadi, Dianto, and Anton Lucas. 2001. *Merampas Tanah Rakyat: Kasus Tapos dan Cimacan*. Jakarta: Kepustakaan Populer Gramedia.

Berman, Sheri. 1997. "Civil Society and the Collapse of the Weimar Republic." *World Politics* 49(3): 401–29.

Bertrand, Jacques. 2002. "Legacies of the Authoritarian Past: Religious Violence in Indonesia's Moluccan Islands." *Pacific Affairs* 75(1): 57–85.

Bey, Idham Samudra. 2002. "Lonceng Kematian UUPA 1960 Berdentang Kembali: Menyoal Tap MPR Nomor IX/MPR/2001." *Kompas*, Jan. 10.

Billah, M. M., ed. 1994. *Gerakan Transformasi Sosial untuk Menegakkan Kedaulatan Rakyat di dalam Masyarakat sipil yang kokoh: Fajar baru bagi ornop. Laporan Workshop Perencanaan*

CPSM Tanggal 20–22 Januari 1994 Cimanggis-Bogor. Jakarta: Circle for Participatory Social Management.

Blaney, David L., and Mustapha Kamal Pasha. 1993. "Civil Society and Democracy in the Third World: Ambiguities and Historical Possibilities." *Studies in Comparative International Development* 28(1) (Spring): 3–24.

Clear, Annette. 2002. "International Donors and Indonesian Democracy." *Brown Journal of World Affairs* 9(1) (Spring): 141–55.

Collins, Elizabeth Fuller. 2001. "Multinational Capital, New Order 'Development,' and Democratization in South Sumatra." *Indonesia* 71: 111–33.

Crouch, Harold. 1998. "Indonesia's 'Strong' State." In Peter Dauvergne, ed., *Weak and Strong States in Asia-Pacific Societies*. Canberra: Allen & Unwin.

Dahliar. 1964. "Perkuat Front Persatuan Tani Lawan 7 Setan Desa: Laksanakan Dwikora Untuk Menghantjurkan 'Malaysia' dan Mengatasi Kesulitan Pangan." *Suara Tani* 5–6: 2–6.

Damanik, Jayadi. 2002. *Pembaruan Agraria dan Hak Asasi Petani*. Yogyakarta: Lapera Pustaka Utama.

Diamond, Larry. 1994. "Rethinking Civil Society: Toward Democratic Consolidation." *Journal of Democracy* 5(3) (July): 4–17.

Ding, X. L. 1994. *The Decline of Communism in China: Legitimacy Crisis, 1977–1989*. Cambridge: Cambridge University Press.

Fauzi, Noer. 1997. "Anatomi Politik Agraria Orde Baru." In Noer Fauzi, ed., *Tanah dan Pembangunan*. Jakarta: Pustaka Sinar Harapan.

———. 2001. "Revisi UUPA Perlu Dipikirkan." *Kompas*, Sept. 27.

Fealy, Greg. 1996. "The 1994 NU Congress and Aftermath: Abdurrahman Wahid, Suksesi, and the Battle for Control of NU." In Greg Barton and Greg Fealy, eds., *Nahdlatul Ulama: Traditional Islam and Modernity in Indonesia*. Monash Papers on Southeast Asia, 39. Clayton, Victoria, Australia: Monash Asia Institute.

———. 1998. "Ulama and Politics in Indonesia: A History of Nahdlatul Ulama, 1952–1967." Ph.D. diss., Monash University.

Feith, H. 1980. "Repressive-Developmentalist Regimes in Asia: Old Strengths, New Vulnerabilities." *Prisma* 19: 39–55.

Firmansyah, Esrom Aritonang, Hegel Terome, Nanang Hari S., and Syaiful Bahari. 1999. *Gerakan dan Pertumbuhan Organisasi Petani di Indonesia: Studi Kasus Gerakan Petani Era 1980-an*. Jakarta: Yappika and Sekretariat Bina Desa.

Foley, Michael W., and Bob Edwards. 1996. "The Paradox of Civil Society." *Journal of Democracy* 7(3): 38–52.

Geertz, Clifford. 1959. "The Javanese Village." In G. William Skinner, ed., *Local, Ethnic and National Loyalties in Village Indonesia*. New Haven: Yale University Cultural Report Series.

Goldhagen, Daniel J. 1996. *Hitler's Willing Executioners: Ordinary Germans and the Holocaust*. New York: Knopf.

Hadiz, Vedi R. 1997. *Workers and the State in New Order Indonesia*. London: Routledge.

———. 2003. "Power and Politics in North Sumatra: The Uncompleted *Reformasi*." In Edward Aspinall and Greg Fealy, eds., *Local Power and Politics in Indonesia: Democratisation and Decentralisation*. Singapore: Institute of Southeast Asian Studies.

Hafid, J. 2001. *Perlawanan Petani: Kasus Tanah Jenggawah*. Bogor: Latin.

Hefner, Robert. 2000. *Civil Islam: Muslims and Democratization in Indonesia*. Princeton: Princeton University Press.

Hindley, Donald. 1962. "President Sukarno and the Communists: The Politics of Domestication." *American Political Science Review* 56(4): 915–26.

———. 1966. *The Communist Party of Indonesia, 1951–1963*. Berkeley: University of California Press.

Keane, John. 1998. *Civil Society: Old Images, New Visions*. Stanford: Stanford University Press.

Konsorsium Pembaruan Agraria (KPA). 1995. *Konsorsium Pembaruan Agraria: Profil Organisasi*. Bandung: KPA.

Lev, Daniel. 1978. "Judicial Authority and the Struggle for an Indonesian Rechtsstaat." *Law and Society Review* 13(1): 37–71.

———. 1987. *Legal Aid in Indonesia*. Centre of Southeast Asian Studies Working Paper 44. Clayton, Victoria, Australia: Monash University.

———. 1990. "Notes on the Middle Class and Change in Indonesia." In Richard Tanter and Kenneth Young, eds., *The Politics of Middle Class Indonesia*. Monash Papers on Southeast Asia, 19. Clayton, Victoria, Australia: Monash University.

Liddle, R. William. 1970. *Ethnicity, Party and National Integration: An Indonesian Case Study*. New Haven: Yale University Press.

Linz, Juan J. 1970. "An Authoritarian Regime: Spain." In Erik Allardt and Stein Rokkan, eds., *Mass Politics*. New York: Free Press.

———. 1973. "Opposition in and under an Authoritarian Regime: The Case of Spain." In Robert A. Dahl, ed., *Regimes and Oppositions*. New Haven: Yale University Press.

Low, D. A. 1996. *The Egalitarian Moment: Asia and Africa 1950–1980*. Cambridge: Cambridge University Press.

Lucas, Anton. 1992. "Land Disputes in Indonesia: Some Current Perspectives." *Indonesia* 53: 79–92.

Lucas, Anton, and Carol Warren. 2000. "Agrarian Reform in the Era of Reformasi." In Chris Manning and Peter van Diermen, eds., *Indonesia in Transition: Social Aspects of Reformasi and Crisis*. Singapore: Institute of Southeast Asian Studies.

Mietzner, Marcus. 1999. "From Soeharto to Habibie: The Indonesian Armed Forces and Political Islam During the Transition." In Geoff Forrester, ed., *Post-Soeharto Indonesia: Renewal or Chaos?* Bathurst, N.S.W.: Crawford House. New York: St. Martin's Press.

Mortimer, Rex. 1974. *Indonesian Communism under Sukarno: Ideology and Politics, 1959–1965*. Ithaca, N.Y.: Cornell University Press.

Pincus, Jonathan. 1996. *Class Power and Agrarian Change: Land and Labour in Rural West Java*. Houndmills, Basingstoke, Hants.: Macmillan. New York: St. Martin's Press.

Putnam, Robert. 1993. *Making Democracy Work: Civic Traditions in Modern Italy*. Princeton: Princeton University Press.

Ramage, Douglas. 1995. *Politics in Indonesia: Democracy, Islam, and the Ideology of Tolerance*. London: Routledge.

Robinson, Geoffrey. 1995. *The Dark Side of Paradise: Political Violence in Bali*. Ithaca, N.Y.: Cornell University Press.

Robison, Richard. 1986. *Indonesia: The Rise of Capital*. Sydney: Allen & Unwin.

———. 2002. "What Sort of Democracy? Predatory and Neo-liberal Agendas in Indonesia." In Catarina Kinnvall and Kristina Jönsson, eds., *Globalization and Democratization in Asia: The Construction of Identity*. London: Routledge.

Rocamora, J. Eliseo. 1973. "Political Participation and the Party System: The PNI Example." In R. William Liddle, ed., *Political Participation in Modern Indonesia*. New Haven: Yale University Southeast Asia Studies Monograph Series.

Setiawan, Bonnie. 1997. "Perubahan Strategi Agraria: Kapitalisme, Agraria dan Pembaruan Agraria di Indonesia." In Noer Fauzi, ed., *Tanah dan Pembangunan*. Jakarta: Pustaka Sinar Harapan.

Stanley. 1994. *Seputar Kedung Ombo*. Jakarta: Elsham.

Sulistyo, Hermawan. 2000. *Palu Arit Di Ladang Tebu: Sejarah Pembantaian Massal yang Terlupakan (Jombang-Kediri 1965–1966)*. Jakarta: Kepustakaan Populer Gramedia.

Tanter, Richard. 1990. "The Totalitarian Ambition: Intelligence and Security Agencies in Indonesia." In Arief Budiman, ed., *State and Civil Society in Indonesia*. Monash Papers on Southeast Asia, 22. Clayton, Victoria, Australia: Monash University.

Törnquist, Olle. 1984. *Dilemmas of Third World Communism: The Destruction of the PKI in Indonesia*. London: Zed Books.

Van der Kroef, Justus M. 1965. *The Communist Party of Indonesia: Its History, Program, and Tactics*. Vancouver: University of British Columbia Press.

Van Klinken, Gerry. 2001a. "Indonesia's New Ethnic Elites." Paper presented to the Indonesia in Transition Workshop held in Yogyakarta, Aug. 22.

———. 2001b. "The Maluku Wars: Bringing Society Back In." *Indonesia* 7: 1–26.

Ward, K. E. 1974. *The 1971 Election in Indonesia: An East Java Case Study*. Monash Papers on Southeast Asia, 2. Clayton, Victoria, Australia: Monash University.

CHAPTER THREE

The Philippines

Fractious Civil Society and Competing Visions of Democracy

JENNIFER C. FRANCO

Contemporary post-Marcos Philippine civil society is a large and complex sphere of public action filled with a variety of associations and movements, some more enduring and autonomous than others. Its population, spread unevenly across the archipelago, uses local and national spaces in varied ways to pursue different ends. Its contours broadly reflect the contours of the post-Marcos Philippine state, where the rule of law is unevenly institutionalized below and beyond the national capital. Over the past thirty years, dynamics within this sphere have evolved in close tandem with national political turning points, including two national regime changes (1972 and 1986), and two series of within-regime political-electoral cycles (first 1978–86, then 1987–present). In contrast to the broad-based political unity that was gradually forged against the Marcos dictatorship in the 1980s, the post-Marcos era has seen the cyclical ebb and flow of intra–civil society political conflict and fragmentation, suggesting high porosity vis-à-vis an elite-dominated political society. Underpinning this fractious civil society, which seems to be exchanging political inhibition for political ambition at an ever faster rate, are competing visions of democracy (inchoate though they may be). This was certainly evident when one section of civil society mobilized to remove a popularly elected president only halfway through his term in January 2001, followed by a dramatic but unsuccessful countermobilization to restore him just three months later.

Before dawn on May 1, 2001, tens of thousands of mainly urban poor protesters left the symbolic EDSA Shrine after days of rallying and headed to Malacañang, official residence of the president.[1] The move had been expected, as politicians close to ousted president Joseph Estrada had been agitating the crowd for days. When they arrived at the palace, they were met by a phalanx of government troops. A fierce battle ensued as the protesters, armed with sticks and stones, tried to breach the palace gates. Meanwhile, EDSA 2 supporters who had been monitoring the situation, believing the newly installed government of Gloria Macapagal-Arroyo to be in danger, urged fellow citizens out into the streets to "defend Malacañang" and the "gains of EDSA 2." It might be recalled that EDSA 2 was the multiclass "uprising of civil society" (as one supporter described it) that had led to the ouster of President Joseph Estrada three months earlier.[2] After weeks of tension, a violent confrontation now loomed between supporters of EDSA 2—sparked when Estrada's impeachment was derailed by allies in the senate—and those of EDSA 3, sparked by his arrest on April 25.

To be sure, for many participants EDSA 3 was as much an outcry against the trashing of the deposed president's dignity—a degrading mug shot had appeared in all the newspapers—as it was a rejection of the corruption charges laid against him.[3] But it was also an indictment of EDSA 2 politicians perceived as elitist and corrupt; many ordinary Filipinos supported the mobilization, saying that the anti-Estrada politicians were even more corrupt, only more adept at hiding their misdeeds. Either way, the meaning of the mobilization became something else by the time the protesters decided to march. By then, they had endured a torrent of humiliating jokes and insults circulated by EDSA 2 loyalists via the media and text messaging that must have thrown salt on an already painful wound.[4] This rare appearance of the "silenced majority" had been dismissed from the start by many self-conscious civil society activists as mere manipulation by the pro-Estrada elite, although some may have quietly begun to wonder if perhaps something was off in the wholesale rejection of a mobilization attended by so many poor people.[5] For many, however, it was simply unimaginable that the protesters' "Poor Is Power" slogan might contain a "hidden transcript" (hidden in the open, as it were) based on real class antagonisms.

By late morning, palace troops had repelled the crowd past the security perimeter. Tired protesters shifted to classic urban poor warfare, including feigned loitering followed by quick incursions before melting back into the urban jungle. Meanwhile, there was looting and selective property destruction; protesters conspicuously went after vehicles of ABS-CBN Channel 2, a TV network closely associated with EDSA 2. But, by noon, the need for food, water, rest, and shade took over, making the assault unsustainable, and by afternoon, the uprising of Manila's "dirty and ignorant" underclass was more or less over. In the end, hundreds of protesters had been injured and four reportedly died. The president belatedly, but forcefully, declared a dubious "state of rebellion" and ordered zoning operations in urban poor neighborhoods, leading to hundreds of warrantless arrests, a draconian response praised by many EDSA 2 activists.

People Power Parallax

Following so closely on the heels of EDSA 2, the incident laid bare a series of fault lines beneath the crust of Philippine civil society. To its supporters, EDSA 2 had been an uprising of civil society that promoted democratization, even though, admittedly, it may have been "accomplished at some cost to constitutional democracy" (Tiglao 2001). As far as they were concerned, the campaign to oust Estrada had involved the rise of a broad-based nonviolent opposition that succeeded in replacing a corrupt, incompetent leader. From this angle, EDSA 3 was nothing less than an assault on democracy by elite-manipulated masses, although it was not made clear why the unconstitutional ousting of a president was more democratic than his election by a majority. In contrast, its critics contend that EDSA 2 was an essentially elitist uprising—one that undermined the democratic process by overturning the 1998 election results (which Estrada won by 39 percent of the vote) and preempting impeachment procedures.[6] In this view, the "civil society" campaign to oust Estrada had engendered a "maximalist" political culture, calling into question the purported link between civil society and democratic values and attitudes. Its singular focus on Estrada made it vulnerable to another kind of elite manipulation. Thus it ended up being unable to prevent, and perhaps even facilitated, a return of the traditional political elite, who, once back in power, backed away from promised reforms, reinforcing an inequitable status quo. From this angle, EDSA 2's civil society was simply a thin veil for intolerance and traditional elite democracy—a veil that EDSA 3 briefly tore away.

Such inflamed sociopolitical conflict might seem out of place in contemporary Philippine political history. After all, seventeen years ago, in 1986, a strong and broadly united civil society, aided by a military rebellion, was instrumental in bringing down a dictatorship at the first EDSA uprising, providing an example of civil society–driven regime change that activists elsewhere, such as in South Korea (see Sunhyuk Kim, Chapter 4, this volume), sought to emulate. It was then called on to help in consolidating democracy by deepening it beyond traditional elite political circles. Part of the motivating force behind this subsequent project was a widespread belief that persistent poverty in the Philippines, and the extreme social inequity that underlies it, would ultimately set limits on how far consolidation could go.[7] But any initial unity of purpose among civil society groups soon waned, along with the high hopes of a truly open and participatory democracy after Marcos that many Filipinos had harbored, based perhaps on romanticized images of civil society. Indeed, recent events have revealed the existence of what might be called a "people power parallax" with regard to this project. The term *parallax* refers to an apparent difference in the position or direction of an object when it is viewed from two different points. The underlying analytic issue is whether civil society always promotes democratization, taken here as a long process involving the struggle to extend basic democratic rights and freedoms to all citizens systemwide, or whether it can undermine this process as well. The Philippines offers a chance to explore this question in less than democratic settings before and after a national regime transition away from authoritarian rule.

Recent experience supports the proposition advanced in Chapter 1 that the relationship between civil society and democracy is indeterminate. Civil society in the Philippines has been both boon and bane for the postauthoritarian democratization project. At times, civil society interactions have helped to extend basic democratic rights and freedoms to previously excluded groups and to increase political competition. Yet past cycles of civil society organization and mobilization have not always fostered change in the direction of more open, participatory, and accountable politics. Instead, civil society's impact on democracy has varied from time to time and from one place to another. Even when groups espouse a democracy mission (and not all do), the variable impact of civil society on democracy is attributable in part to the contested meaning of democracy and the mechanics of democratization within contemporary Philippine civil society itself. In this sense, today's civil society is, among other things, a political battlefield marked by fault lines along which groups struggle for position and where values are either undermined or reinforced in the process.

One fault line is between those who subscribe to the dominant elite view of the meaning and purpose of democracy and those who hold a more popular view, the latter being akin to what Muthiah Alagappa calls "non–status quo institutions" (Chapter 1, this volume). In the Philippines' elite democracy, which traces back to political exclusion institutionalized under colonial rule, national political parties do not attempt to represent the poorest members of society, especially the rural poor, leaving them captives instead of local political monopolies, where access to the political process is restricted by regional elites through "guns, goons, and gold." Although most analysts tend to emphasize this dimension, elite democracy versus popular democracy has been an important theme in Philippine politics. Popular democracy refers broadly to a still unrealized institutional setting where effective access to democratic governance is available to the entire citizenry. A small but significant section of civil society has always worked around such a framework historically. Among those subscribing to a popular view in more recent decades, however, disagreement over how to get there, influenced in part by the difficult institutional obstacles associated with elite democracy, has created two broadly distinct currents concerned with system transformation, suggesting that even among non–status quo associations, "the place of civil society in the structure of domination and its role in politics . . . are not settled issues" (Alagappa, Chapter 1, this volume). One current flows along a political-electoral reform path—seeking to promote system change by seizing power from a corrupt traditional political elite through political-electoral means. The other flows along a social reform path—

aiming to promote change by exercising citizenship power in state policymaking and implementation. Historically, the two streams have complemented each other at key junctures, undermining authoritarianism and promoting open, participatory politics. But in recent years, as elite democracy has careened ever more wildly along, the relationship between these two currents has turned more competitive. The pull of elite-dominated political-electoral cycles—a prominent feature of the political system—has grown, exerting pressures that periodically redistribute power among civil society organizations, pulling some groups into the center while sending others out toward the periphery. In the process, the two currents have become disconnected and at odds, as seen especially in dynamics around agrarian reform, a long-standing social justice issue.

The Philippines has long had one of the most skewed distributions of landownership in the region—a legacy of colonial rule and the cumulative failure of past governments to democratically respond to organized demands for land and tenancy reform. Periodic outbreaks of social unrest in the countryside, combined with civil society advocacy, made agrarian reform an important political issue throughout much of the past century, leading to the passage of numerous agrarian reform laws by landlord-dominated legislatures that were, unsurprisingly, largely ineffective in actually curbing the power of the ruling class. Perhaps the American political scientist Samuel Huntington was right when he observed that a "basic incompatibility exists between parliaments and land reform" (1968: 388). But the Marcos dictatorship's dismal performance in carrying out its own land reform program, known as Presidential Decree (PD) 27, showed that the centralization of political power was no guarantee for achieving redistributive justice either. By the time of the first EDSA uprising and regime change away from centralized authoritarian rule in 1986, the country's agrarian problem was still unresolved, if not significantly worse. With a Gini coefficient in land redistribution of 0.647 as recently as 1988 (Putzel 1992: 30), with the rural poor comprising almost three-fourths of the country's poor (World Bank 2000), and with wealth in land still a key source of political power, inequality in landownership and control remains a major problem today, despite the passage of a new agrarian reform law in 1988.[8]

Notably, concerted civil society mobilization and advocacy played a key role in the passage of the 1988 law known as the Comprehensive Agrarian Reform Law (CARL), which then shifted the nature of the problem from national lawmaking to nationwide program implementation. Yet the civil society response to this shift has been mixed. Whereas the two popular democratic streams worked well together in putting agrarian reform onto the national agenda and pushing the first post-Marcos government to enact a law with real redistributive potential, this has not been the case since the law was enacted. Although gains in land redistribution have been made via the 1988 law, a relative political weakening of social reform pressures in favor of land reform, partly as a result of the strategic disconnect in civil society, has been discernible in recent years. Today, agrarian reform is no longer widely seen as a key national issue, despite the still pressing need for it, a fact that does not bode well for democratization. Precisely because in the country's exclusionary electoral democracy "[u]pper-class control is facilitated by the manipulation of rural voting blocs by large landowners" (Reidinger 1999: 184), weakening of social reform pressures has dimmed prospects for further democratic deepening and extension of democratic rights and governance systemwide. Indeed, the main premise of this chapter is that if the democratization process is to move beyond its still extremely narrow and shallow limits, civil society groups as well as reformists inside and outside the state will have to take seriously the concerns of the majority and give priority to unmet demands for radical rural reform, particularly redistributive agrarian reform. In taking up the case of agrarian reform, this chapter hopes to shed light on some of the difficulties rural civil society actors face in relation to a postauthoritarian popular democratization project.

Mapping Civil Society

I follow Alagappa (Chapter 1) in defining civil society as a public space between the state, political society, economic society, and private life where individuals attempt to build autonomous collective citizen engagement on different levels around issues that matter for public policy. Autonomous engagement refers to an ideal type of action involving an assertion of basic political rights and civil liberties, including freedom of association and expression. Not all attempts to build this type of engagement with the political environment succeed. There are obstacles related to collective action, or internal to civil society, or found in between civil society and the state.[9] The integrity of this public space is neither fixed nor uniform across issue areas or geographic place. Its boundaries are continuously shaped by the ongoing interplay of those in society and in the state who may try to expand or constrict them.[10]

In the Philippines, this definition resonates with Gramscian inspired popular-democracy discourse, which sees civil society as a localized "laboratory" and generalized "terrain of struggle" (Francisco 1994). Although it resists the tendency among Filipino activists, academics, and the media to equate civil society with NGOs and POs, this approach does share the literature's emphasis on the role of civil society groups in "open[ing] up the decision-making process to more than an elite few" (Silliman and Noble 1998: 10). But while including the "masses of citizens engaged in public protest, social movements, and NGOs acting in the public sphere," I refrain from a priori exclusion of political parties and "groups striving to gain control of the state through armed rebellion." Clear lines in theory may be blurred in reality—especially in flawed democracies where neither the state's nor society's respect for democratic rights and liberties is guaranteed in practice. The gray area

Alagappa talks about certainly obtains in the Philippines, where an armed Left, led by the Maoist CPP (Communist Party of the Philippines), its military wing, the NPA (New People's Army), and the NDF (National Democratic Front) "united front," has played a key role in constituting and reconstituting rural civil society over time. Under repressive centralized authoritarian rule, the rise of nonviolent antidictatorship opposition outside the cities in the 1980s would not have happened had it not been for CPP-NPA-NDF organizers. Yet in today's more open polity, this trio and their allies use civil society space to campaign against agrarian reform, while making "unholy alliances" with landed elites resisting redistribution and harassing local peasant associations pushing for it (in exchange for money, arms, and protection from the state). Such a presence, however slippery, cannot be ignored.

Meanwhile, the analysis also draws on Miriam Coronel Ferrer's view of Philippine civil society as a venue where the larger institutional context creates power differentials between groups that have a bearing on the democratization process. The role of state, societal, and economic institutions in determining resource distributions within civil society has been noted by Alagappa, and it may be obvious, as Ferrer (1997a: 13) suggests, that the overall context contributes to an uneven distribution of access to resources (money, technical knowledge, timely information, status) that matter for organizing public citizen engagement. This context is not static, however, but may shift because of extraordinary regime change or in relation to the ordinary rhythms of politics. In the Philippines, not only regime changes, but also political-electoral cycles periodically redistribute political access in civil society, empowering some groups and disempowering others, forcing them to alter their political strategies. Although power differentials within civil society are important, they may change, if only temporarily, presenting civil society groups with new sets of opportunities and constraints that matter for democratization.[11] Against this backdrop, at least some of what can be taken as civil society activity has involved ordinary Filipinos, including if not especially the rural poor, whose citizenship was not officially recognized or was compromised by authoritarian elites in state and society. The urban middle class–led political-electoral movements have often overlooked or underestimated this fact and its deeper political implications. Although not representative of all civil society activity, in the Philippines today, as in the past, popular mobilization on socioeconomic issues such as land reform remains a deeply political struggle by the traditionally excluded to obtain what Neil Harvey (1998) calls "the right to have rights."

Understood this way, Philippine civil society can be traced at least as far back as the late nineteenth century, when the archipelago was still subject to harsh Spanish colonial rule and calls for change were on the rise. According to Mary Racelis (2000), civil society in the Philippines originated in "nineteenth-century Spanish colonial welfare and Roman Catholic parish organizations" that, like their contemporary counterparts, ostensibly sought to "empower the marginalized." What "empower the marginalized" might mean in the context of the nineteenth century is perhaps hard to say, but it is important to note that these organizations existed alongside organized groups of natives and mestizos resisting colonialism. One of the issues that most fueled native unrest from the start of Spanish rule via the sword and the cross was the extremely oppressive nature of the latter. "The insolently fatuous attitude of the friars and their administrators in the various estates they held and unbearable exactions in taxes, tribute, and forced labor, led the peasants to commit atrocities that ordinarily would have been shocking, yet were natural and justified when no means were left to air their grievances and to get justice," Teodoro Agoncillo (2002: 3) explains. Peasant revolts against landgrabbing, onerous taxation, and forced labor emphasized egalitarianism and "division of land among the righteous" (Putzel 1992: 50).[12] Meanwhile, Filipinos living in Spain demanded civil and political rights through the Propaganda movement led by José Rizal, who was executed at the start of a major insurrection in the 1890s (Constantino 1975: 152–58).[13]

The insurrection was led by the Kataastaasan Kagalanggalangan Katipunan ng mga Anak ng Ating Bayan (Katipunan; Highest, Most Respected Society of the Children of Our Nation), a movement of resistance and transformation that began as a secret society among the working poor. A Manila laborer, Andres Bonifacio, described by Agoncillo as "the first truly Filipino democrat," founded the Katipunan after a split in Rizal's mutual aid association, Liga Filipina, between the more middle-class heirs of the Propaganda movement and the league's working-class rank and file (Constantino 1975: 152–90). The insurrection that began in 1896 was a complex affair that ultimately ended in defeat at the hands, not of the fading Spanish, but of the expanding American empire. The story has been told elsewhere and need not be repeated here, except to stress a point made by Reynaldo Clemeña Ileto: that is, the struggle for independence had plural meanings in a socially differentiated society. Whereas the original Katipuneros sought to create "a condition of brotherhood, equality, contentment and material abundance," their successors, who founded the first republic at Malolos in 1898, were concerned with "freedom from foreign domination" (Ileto 1979: 117). As "the leadership of the revolution came to rest increasingly in ilustrado [mestizo nouveau riche] hands, resulting in neglect of local problems" (ibid.: 120), those whose egalitarian aspirations were not satisfied by the mere establishment of a Filipino republic became restive. Renewed suppression of local Katipunero groups, especially in the countryside, followed, this time carried out by a rising Filipino elite ahead of advancing U.S. imperialism. When the elite capitulated to the Americans in 1901, armed resistance continued by those who "felt that something was terribly wrong with the way the revolution had been conducted in the recent past" (ibid.: 176).

U.S. colonial rule followed a brutal war by the Americans to quell widespread resistance, which decimated the native population, especially in the countryside (Zinn 1995: 305–9). Under American tutelage, new civil society organizations were formed to act as the carrot to the stick of military efforts to bring the new colony under control. This period saw the birth of "local versions of American or international associations, like the Philippine National Red Cross and . . . women's suffrage groups," "private nonprofit organizations in the form of religious and academic institutions," and "government-supported rural credit cooperatives" (Racelis 2000). But U.S. land and agricultural policies and the political entrenchment of the landed elite led to deepening discontent. A new cycle of resistance in the 1930s brought peasants briefly into a three-way conflict with landlords and the state over the direction of public policy and access to basic democratic rights.[14] Conflict between a restrictive elite version of democracy, favored by landowner-politicians (and reinforced by the Americans), and a popular democratic vision, championed by organized peasants and their allies in Manila's middle and working classes, had begun to play out, both electorally and nonelectorally, when interrupted by World War II.

Japanese occupation during the war reorganized rural society when landlords fled to the cities. A peasant-based anti-Japanese guerrilla movement took control of parts of the countryside, establishing local popular governments that resisted Japanese rule and redistributed hacienda land in their areas. But as in Korea, returning U.S. military leaders, fearing the spread of communism and, in the Philippines at least, allied with the landed elite, moved to dislodge these groups and nullify their gains on account of their leftist political leanings. This meant returning the landed elite to power at all levels by any means, and in some cases despite the stain of collaboration. A successful electoral campaign by organized peasants allied with a fledgling left-wing political movement in 1946 landed them in the national legislature. But the peasant-backed legislators were unjustly kept from taking their seats, leading to the Huk rebellion (Kerkvliet 1977: 136–37).

The arrival of the U.S. counterinsurgency operative Edward Lansdale in 1950 marked a revival of civil society aimed at complementing the military drive against the Huks. Lansdale's strategy included mobilizing nominally independent anticommunist groups such as the National Movement for Free Elections (NAMFREL) and Federation of Free Farmers (FFF) (Hedman 1997: 217). Similarly, this period also spawned "the community development approach to rural poverty," heavily funded by the United States and modeled after the Philippine Rural Reconstruction Movement (PRRM) founded in 1952 (Racelis 2000). But despite its origins, the controlled effort to build civil society as an impediment to communism unintentionally led to a revival of militant mass mobilization when it began to challenge the status quo. In the context of a repressive political environment and government failure to enact reforms that would redistribute power, non–status quo groups almost inevitably grew out of status quo intentions. Thus the FFF took on a life of its own after sections of it encountered anti-reform elites on the ground and imbibed

Vatican II's liberation theology and Mao's underground revolutionary ideology (Franco 2001a: 82–85).[15] In 1971, the FFF adopted a grassroots electoral strategy to further its evolving land reform agenda but ran up against local bosses using "guns, goons, and gold" to control the elections. Ironically, like the movement that it had once sought to displace, the FFF (or much of it) would eventually turn to armed struggle after finding all channels for real political participation blocked. Civil society became contested space where alternative visions of democracy competed for popular support, but under highly restrictive larger political conditions that, marked by intolerance of relatively autonomous participation of urban and rural working-class groups, favored maintenance of the inequitable and undemocratic status quo.

By 1970, popular discontent was focused on elite democracy. With the rise of a student movement alongside deepening urban and rural poor movements—as well as a new generation of church social action workers and a reinvigorated, if fractious, Left—civil society took a radical turn.[16] This turn was due in part to the founding of the Communist Party of the Philippines (CPP) in 1968 by a group of young, mainly middle-class, university-based intellectuals, who envisioned dismantling "the three evils of Philippine society"—namely "imperialism, bureaucrat[ic] capitalism, and feudalism"—via a two-stage revolution (national-democratic, then socialist) based on the Chinese model. Guided largely by this new ideological pole, issue-based mobilizations put socioeconomic and political reform back on the national agenda. But united against elite politics, activists also became increasingly divided between those who believed change could come through the ballot and those who insisted that bullets were needed.[17] An escalation came early in President Ferdinand Marcos's unprecedented second term in 1970, when students launched the "First Quarter Storm" (FQS).[18] The FQS created an "empowering consciousness" and spawned "democratic spaces" that people would later defend under the dictatorship (Reyes 2001: 12). Popular protest peaked at the 1971 constitutional convention. At stake was the form of government, since Marcos sought a shift to parliamentarism to extend his stay in power—a plan that rattled the political elite, who correctly perceived it as a threat to politics as usual.[19] Thus finding himself unable to overturn existing constitutional term limits via the established political process, Marcos declared a "democratic revolution from the center" and imposed martial law in September 1972.

The Road to EDSA 1

Thousands of student and church activists and labor and peasant leaders and organizers throughout the country were detained and tortured, killed, or disappeared, while prominent elite oppositionists were arrested or put under surveillance. Civil society changed dramatically overnight, virtually collapsing at first, as those who survived the initial crackdown went into hiding or adopted a low profile, as activists did in Burma in the mid-1960s (see Kyaw Yin Hlaing, Chapter 12, this volume). A relatively open space once teeming with dissidence was refracted into "aboveground" and "underground" segments, on the vertical dimension, and "urban centers" and "white areas" (rural plains in between the cities) and guerrilla-controlled mountainous "red areas," on the horizontal dimension, to borrow the language of the armed Left. The now much reduced aboveground space initially consisted mainly of a protected state-sponsored sector that, as in Burma, extended to nonpolitical social and religious groups. As will be seen, this curtailed area later included a furtive but tenacious "illegalized" opposition sector that insisted on trying to stretch the limits despite the risks. In the beginning, Marcos used repression selectively to eliminate opposition and recreate a circle of groups beholden to him, often splitting apart preexisting organizations and driving one portion underground, as with the FFF. But the deterioration of political conditions in urban centers and white areas alike increased the flow of people into armed struggle and diversified this option ideologically as groups other than the outlawed CPP now also embraced the use of force to dislodge the regime. Hidden links connected these various levels and spaces, enabling underground activists to try to shape developments aboveground.[20] In this way, throughout the 1970s and 1980s, dissident groups in urban centers and white areas, mostly tied to the outlawed CPP, increasingly engaged the dictator in what Anne Mackenzie (1987) has called "political jiu jitsu" that would eventually lead to his downfall.

At first, however, society's response to martial law was mixed. Manila's heavily Catholic middle class, whose disproportionate fear of communism—the Philippines was a far cry from Indonesia's *aliran* politics of the 1950s and 1960s (see Edward Aspinall, Chapter 2, this volume)—had been carefully stoked, gave the dictator tacit support (Tiglao 1988). Media controls prevented news of militarization in distant regions from reaching Manila, hindered news of suppression of basic rights from reaching foreign audiences, and shielded many from the brutal costs and dubious benefits of martial law. But while some Filipinos embraced martial law, and others saw little hope of resisting, still others detected weak spots in the authoritarian wall and turned to cracking them open through what might be called "rightful resistance."[21] The first breakthroughs came in urban poor communities in Manila that had been organized in the late 1960s by the Philippine Ecumenical Council for Community Organizing (PECCO), a community organizing agency (Constantino-David 1995). PECCO gathered church leaders, academics, and students and immersed them in poor neighborhoods, including those threatened with demolition to make way for a World Bank–funded "urban renewal" project. Pushed by a deteriorating economy and disregarding the risks after 1972, maverick PECCO organizers launched protest masses and prayer rallies, marches and street demonstrations, and dialogues with government officials (Franco 2001b). Mobilizations around immediate socioeconomic problems soon turned into open confrontation with the regime, which tended to respond harshly, favoring repression over concessions, causing a backlash among some of the more conservative PECCO leaders. The group broke into two ideologically determined factions—the anticommunist social democrats and the CPP-led national democrats, obscuring the underlying political issue of what the role of civil society could and should be in a dictatorship. The breakup of PECCO in 1977 unleashed these two contending organizing streams, the national democratic one far larger and more daring than its rival, propelling each to expand beyond the national capital, preparing the way for an extensive and largely national democratically oriented antidictatorship network.

Rising protest and exposure of human rights violations prompted Marcos to hold authoritarian elections in 1978.[22] In holding elections while withholding basic rights, he hoped to satisfy calls for "normalization" while undercutting democratic opposition. Manipulation enabled Marcos to win the election but cost him the battle by prompting defections from the ruling party, widening the rift with the elite opposition and fueling mass protest. There was a flowering of "cause-oriented groups" in urban centers and white areas (Ferrer 1997a: 8).[23] In the lingo of national democratic activism then dominant, most worked to "expose and oppose" the regime. Meanwhile, anticommunist oppositionists, convinced of the need to use force to dislodge Marcos, launched the "bourgeois bomber" urban insurrection campaigns of 1979–80, which failed to spark an uprising but did convince foreign audiences that a serious crisis was brewing (Thompson 1995: 82–95). To defuse the situation, Marcos again turned to an authoritarian electoral strategy that required restricting competition. For presidential elections in 1981, the national democrats initiated a boycott campaign that succeeded in denying Marcos a real opponent, forcing him to manufacture one (Rocamora 1994: 26). The election also spawned new protest streams, however thin organizationally, that helped heighten the profile of the antidictatorship movement. Then in August 1983, former senator Benigno Aquino was murdered, finally shaking the urban middle class out of quiescence and into the streets with the huge alliance called Justice for Aquino, Justice for All (JAJA).

Meanwhile, a social reform agenda began taking shape. This process was led by COMPACT, a new alliance between national democrats—the strongest voice for workers, peasants, women, students, and teachers at the time—and a group of independent elite politicians whose prominence lent political weight to pressing social issues (Lane 1990: 10). Meanwhile, part of Manila's business elite launched the Kongreso ng Mamamayang Pilipino (KOMPIL; Congress of Filipino Citizens) to unite the opposition behind an alternative to Marcos (Diokno 1988: 150–51). The 1984 national assembly elections led to more ruling party defections and strengthened the opposition. But the latter split into two competing forces: the "protest vote," led by the political-change-oriented KOMPIL, and the "boycott vote" led by the social-change-oriented COMPACT (Franco 2001a: 168–73).

Marcos's electoral strategy in 1984 sped up the regime's erosion—pushing him to call a snap presidential election in early 1986. U.S.-backed, elite-led opposition coalition building eventually crystallized around Corazon Cojuangco Aquino as the most viable candidate to run against Marcos (Cameron 1992: 240). Opposition consensus rested in part on a "declaration of unity" that, in a nod to groups on the left, endorsed major socioeconomic and political reform (Diokno 1988: 155). Thus promises of reform were made, raising hopes and encouraging ordinary Filipinos to join the campaign. To consolidate the reform pole, a new center-left coalition called Bagong Alyansang Makabayan (BAYAN; New Patriotic Alliance) was conceived. But the initiative fell apart amid fears that the majority national democrats would call for a boycott. And in spite of Aquino's popularity, the CPP leadership did just that. In the end, only the CPP-led national democrats remained in BAYAN, which parted ways with the rest of the antidictatorship movement at a most critical moment (Rocamora 1994: 33–37). Marcos's attempt to declare himself winner of the fraud-marred election sparked a nationwide civil disobedience campaign that ultimately led to the collapse of the regime.

In the end, Marcos's use of controlled elections and repression to maintain his grip on power had only strengthened opposition to the regime. That it did so was not automatic. As Benedict Kerkvliet (2001: xxvi) observes: it took "Filipinos who rolled up their sleeves and became involved, frequently at considerable risk to themselves and their families." Opposition in civil society was the key to breaking down the wall of silence, transforming authoritarian elections into real political battles, and pushing the system in a more democratic direction by helping to dislodge the dictator.

The Road to EDSA 2

After Marcos's departure, and even as many segments of urban and rural society became caught up in a brutal "low intensity" conflict between the military and the NPA that paralyzed portions of the country during the 1987–92 period, civil society underwent a remarkable revival that resulted in part from a steady fragmentation of the Left, including its heftier national democratic wing. The number of registered nonstock, nonprofit organizations alone grew from 27,100 in 1986 to between 60,000 and 95,000 by the year 2000—with 5,000 to 7,000 of these said to be "grassroots organizations whose organizers focus on empowering poor and excluded people" (Racelis 2000).[24] The range of issues expanded as well to include many "heretofore . . . not viewed as amenable to political action," such as domestic violence and the national debt (Silliman and Noble 1998: 19). Meanwhile, single-issue engagements slowly deepened beyond an orthodox "expose and oppose" framework, which typically focused only on state human rights violations, or HRVs, to include addressing HRVs by nonstate actors—such as multinational companies, despotic landlords, and more recently, even the NPA—and pressuring the state to do so as well. To be sure, continued militarization in suspected CPP-NPA influenced areas and in the southern Philippines, where Islamic separatist movements continued to challenge the state, meant that exposing and opposing state abuses remained a relevant mobilizing framework in civil society. Yet many groups also began trying to shape public policy, even reforming state programs by maximizing reformist provisions and opposing antireformist ones in existing laws, such as in agrarian reform (Borras 1999). Civil society also thickened as scaling up, coalition building, and networking built (and rebuilt) internal linkages that had been rent by splits or weakened by militarization.[25]

Still, in spite of the fragmentation of the old and explosion of the new in civil society, which to some extent marked a break with the past, much of the credit for a strong civil society vis-à-vis the state after 1986 certainly must go "to the political and social movements that have been built and nurtured by the politicized sectors of society throughout the decades" (Ferrer 1997b: 1). It is for this reason that many groups quickly "manifested a capacity to maintain autonomy from the state," on the one hand, and "demonstrated their potential as independent power sources and agents of change," on the other (Ferrer 1997b: 1). Yet the boundaries between civil society and other spheres remained highly porous. Karina Constantino-David's (1997: 23–26) typology is instructive. In addition to influential "nongovernmental individuals" and "ideological forces," there are various "membership organizations" and other institutions. The former include professional, academic, and civic organizations (PACOs) and grassroots people's organizations (POs), which are now subdivided into government run/initiated people's organizations (GRIPOs) and genuine, autonomous people's organizations (GUAPOs). Civic institutions now include development, justice, and advocacy NGOs (DJANGOs), traditional charitable, welfare, and relief NGOs (TANGOs), funding agency NGOs (FUNDANGOs), and mutant NGOs (MUNGOs). "The growing recognition of the role of NGOs, the avalanche of funds from foreign donors . . . and the government decision to engage NGO services in the implementation of programs resulted in the proliferation of organizations whose essence was really a mutation of the original spirit of NGOs," Constantino-David observes. The mutant NGOs include government run/initiated NGOs (GRINGOs), business-organized NGOs (BONGOs), and fly-by-night organizations set up by NGO entrepreneurs (COME N'GOs)—in other words, entities that represent attempts to circumvent boundaries between civil society and other realms and appropriate the language of civil society in order to cash in on the resurgence of a compelling idea.

Finally, after Marcos, civil society became more differentiated in terms of agenda. Within the broad Left, at least, most activists soon saw that "the task awaiting [them] during the post-EDSA years was not simply the restoration of democracy, but more importantly, its 'deepening.' . . . The task of looking into issues of social justice and equity was left largely in the hands of the Left" (Abao 1997: 274). Note, however, that this was perhaps an especially fractious section of civil society, with an ambivalent relationship with traditional political society and less-than-democratic electoral politics historically. Many groups have certainly tried to combine "directly political" agendas with socioeconomic change (Silliman and Noble 1998: 18). Yet two broadly distinct currents have become increasingly apparent in recent years—political-electoral reform versus social reform—reflecting contending views of the difficult challenge of democratization in a formal democracy dominated by entrenched regional authoritarian elites.

The political-electoral reform stream posits civil society as a democratizing national political actor whose main objective is to seize state power by wresting it away from notoriously selfish and corrupt "traditional politicians," mainly through political-electoral means. Unlike the Nakch'on/Nakson civil society campaign in South Korea's 2000 elections described by Sunhyuk Kim (Chapter 4, this volume), which concentrated on exposing and opposing corrupt politicians and endorsing "clean" ones, civil society–driven political-electoral reform in the Philippine case has stressed running for public office. Here, civil society itself has been posited as the source of the most promising democratic political alternative to the traditional guardians of the undemocratic status quo entrenched in national political office. The social reform stream, in contrast, posits civil society as the seedbed of empowered locally rooted social actors whose main objective is to exercise citizenship power in order to win redistributive gains mainly by engaging the state bureaucracy and making it accountable to traditionally excluded social groups. Here, civil society is the origin of potent democratizing social pressures from below on the state to reform and work with civil society in mobilizing against the inequitable and undemocratic status quo. In a setting such as the Philippines, where authoritarian elite political practices persist in large and small patches throughout the country, making the state accountable has involved, among other things, pressuring specific state actors to take concrete steps to actively guarantee poorer citizens' constitutionally defined social, economic, and political rights and civil liberties in particular, defend them against violations, and effectively punish violators, whether they be other state actors, such as the military or police, or nonstate actors, such as despotic landlords evading land reform. Although both streams are concerned with empowerment, as will be seen, their preferred means have led to a potential for conflict.

Lawmaking from Below

The first post-Marcos government coalition, forged under the special circumstances of a national regime change, had many "birth defects" (as Terry Karl has termed them in the context of Latin America), including the appointment of antireformists to key positions in the new cabinet. Yet reform advocates had several factors going for them, most important, a hugely popular president who had campaigned on a reform platform and had been given full lawmaking powers until a new national legislature could be convened. Moreover, many regional land-based elites who were expected to oppose reform had been weakened politically by years of centralized authoritarian rule, while the key role of social and political reform advocates in the antidictatorship movement offered an unprecedented opportunity to exploit the opening from both inside and outside the new government. This was a unique chance to reform the system, and one of the most prominent items on the civil society agenda at this time was land reform, which many considered a prerequisite to real political democracy and to addressing the root causes of communist insurgency.

The national democratic Kilusang Magbubukid ng Pilipinas (KMP; Peasant Movement of the Philippines) and various social democratic NGOs and POs began lobbying for reform in hopes of pressuring President Aquino to use her special powers to enact a land reform law right away. But when the president, who came from one of the largest landowning families in the country, failed to act, comparatively less effort was then put into trying to pack the legislature with reformists via an electoral strategy, in large part because of strong resistance from within the underground armed Left, which continued to assign only a marginal "tactical" role to electoral struggle in its overall strategy of "protracted people's war." As expected, and partly because of half-hearted efforts, the first post-Marcos congressional elections in May 1987 saw a massive return of the oligarchs to national power, with 167 out of 198 of those elected linked to the same large landowning families that had previously constituted the national elite, including many who had served in the Marcos legislature (IPD 1987). Reform advocates were thus left with the seemingly impossible task of trying to induce a landlord-dominated legislature to produce a truly redistributive agrarian reform law; maximum public pressure would clearly have to be applied if they were to have any chance of success.

Believing that their impact would be increased through unity, several peasant organizations, backed by allied political movements, rural development NGOs, academics, and church activists, formed a national coalition called the Congress for a People's Agrarian Reform (CPAR) on May 31, 1987 (Villanueva 1997: 82–84). Although CPAR came into being too late to influence the elections and faced a decidedly uphill battle in the legislature, its birth was nonetheless important. The coalition articulated the principles of what members believed was genuine land reform, embodied in its founding document, "The People's Declaration of Agrarian Reform" (Villanueva 1997: 84). Later, when the legislature convened, CPAR mobilized both inside and outside of it to influence the lawmaking process—not an easy undertaking, to be sure. Although relatively experienced in street activism, the

CPAR activists had to learn legislative lobbying and the finer points of lawmaking from below—a situation similar perhaps to that faced by Taiwanese women's groups in the early 1980s, as described by Yun Fan (Chapter 5, this volume). In the end, the landlords proved stronger. When a loophole-ridden land reform law was enacted in June 1988, CPAR responded by rejecting the Comprehensive Agrarian Reform Law (CARL) and publicizing its own more radical version, called the People's Agrarian Reform Code (PARCode).[26] It then launched an innovative but ill-fated campaign to recall the new law via an untested constitutional provision allowing voters to petition for legislative action (Putzel 1998: 95–96).[27]

The legislative struggle had exacerbated political divisions within the coalition, and the petition drive received only halfhearted support from members. On the one hand, with the passage of CARL, the social democratic NGO known as the Philippine Partnership for Development of Human Resources in Rural Areas (PHILDHRRA) began testing the law through a program called the Tripartite Partnership for Agrarian Reform and Rural Development (TriPARRD). Rather than reject CARL, the idea was to "explore areas of collaboration or coordination among NGOs, POs, donor agencies, and the government" for its implementation ("Workshop Report" 1988: foreword). Pilot testing began in 1989 in places "where there are voluntary offers to sell and in occupied lands" (ibid.: 13).[28] On the other hand, in the highly charged atmosphere of the government's "total war" counterinsurgency effort in the countryside, the national democratic bloc viewed CARL as evidence of the "antipeasant, prolandlord" character of the new government, clearing the way for a return to the expose and oppose mode in aid of an eventual armed seizure of state power. Forgoing the petition campaign, they embarked on a massive land occupation—a militant form of action the rest of CPAR was not prepared to take. The KMP's unverified claim is that it successfully occupied between 75,000 and 100,000 hectares between 1986 and 1990, although most if not all of this was later rolled back as a result of all-around unpreparedness in the face of heavy militarization and violent state retribution. In the end, the PARCode signature campaign gained little ground—partly because of halfhearted support from national democrats and social democrats alike, and partly because of a "misinterpretation of the law on CPAR's part" (Putzel 1998: 96).

Lack of consensus as to how to proceed was paralleled by member organizations continuing to "do their own thing" on the ground—leading them in opposite directions, while the anti-CARL/pro-PARCode petition drive fell into limbo somewhere in between. The strain led to a full-blown split during the May 1992 presidential elections. Despite prior agreement to back a progressive candidate (who was sure to lose), most non-national-democratic members of the coalition ended up endorsing Fidel Ramos (an army general and former defense minister who had led the Aquino administration's devastating total war counterinsurgency campaign and who supported raising the retention limit for landowners under CARL to 50 hectares). Ramos won the election with 24 percent of the vote. By then, however, the coalition was beyond repair, and it folded in 1993. In reality, it had ceased functioning much earlier.[29]

Redistributive Reform Innovations

The collapse of CPAR created a vacuum in the agrarian reform front in terms of both national agrarian reform advocacy and civil society linking mechanisms. Despite its problems, the coalition had nonetheless served a useful dual function—as a voice on the national stage for local grassroots organizations engaged in trying to redistribute land under the government law and as a place where agrarian activists from varied traditions could interact. Many activists soon saw a need for a different kind of coalition to fill the gap. This new coalition would have to steer a difficult course—between what had come to be seen by many activists as the social democratic movement's uncritical collaboration with the Ramos government and what remained the official national democratic movement's outright rejection of it—in order to effect "full and meaningful" land redistribution (Franco 1998).

A split in the CPP-NPA and national democratic movement in 1992–93 suddenly freed those who had previously questioned party leaders' rejection of the government program but been unable to redirect party policy. Until then, they had been prevented from fully pursuing an alternative approach being developed somewhat surreptitiously by the Philippine Ecumenical Action for Community Empowerment (PEACE) Foundation, a community-organizing NGO that was the national democratic offspring of PECCO. Although steeped in party ideology and practiced in organizing rural communities for guerrilla-zone preparation, PEACE veterans had also been schooled in CO methods, which enabled them to see the importance of immediate concrete gains for impoverished rural communities and pushed them to try to link struggling for concrete gains to the larger struggle to alter underlying power relations in the countryside. Later known as the *bibingka* strategy, the new approach, initially tolerated but eventually dismissed and later attacked by the CPP as "reformism" and "collaboration," involved combining militant reformist pressures from below (social movements) with reformist initiatives from above (state actors) (Borras 1999). The basic idea was that the Comprehensive Agrarian Reform Program (CARP) contained provisions that could be maximized for landless peasants and, moreover, that such state-society interaction could also be used to plug the prolandlord loopholes in the program. Ultimately, of course, this meant a radical and challenging shift in emphasis for PEACE from a framework of militarily seizing state power in the distant future to exercising militant citizen power now in order to exact power-altering concessions from the state in the form of real land redistribution.

The split permitted this group to continue in this vein unfettered by party orthodoxy. It also opened up space for other groups interested in pursuing a more sophisticated approach to CARP than the two main political movements could offer. Apart from the former national democrats now undertaking a *bibingka* strategy in agrarian reform, as well as those who were part of the so-called Movement for Popular Democracy stream, there were also activists associated with the independent socialist political group called Bukluran Para sa Ikauunlad ng Sosyalistang Isip at Gawa (BISIG; Unity for the Advance of Socialism in Theory and Practice). The birth of the Partnership for Agrarian Reform and Rural Development Services (PARRDS) in March 1994 formally brought these three fledgling "critical collaboration" streams together, helping to reinvigorate a largely defunct CARP implementation process and specifically to activate its redistributive mode via expropriation.

Political-Electoral Innovations

Innovations were also arising in political-electoral reform. Two changes that promoted new civil society mobilization around political-electoral reform were the Local Government Code and the party-list law. Each originated in provisions of the 1987 constitution. The 1991 Local Government Code (LGC) operationalized the provision for strengthening "local autonomy" through decentralization. Notwithstanding its potential for also strengthening unreformed local authoritarian enclaves (and not necessarily local democracy) in the process, as far as many activists were concerned, it offered a welcome corrective to the twin problems of an overcentralized state and weak local participation, which had been inherited from the colonial period (Gonzales 2000). The code devolved "power and resources to local government units at the provincial, city, municipal and barangay levels" and allowed for "people's participation in local government and development" (Gonzales 2000). Notably, and quite auspiciously given the persistence of antireform landed elites in local governments across the archipelago, it did not extend to the Department of Agrarian Reform (DAR), the agency charged with implementing CARP.[30] The LGC opened up a new mobilization frontier that drew many civil society groups who, in spite of the persistence of "guns, goons, and gold" in local politics, saw it as a real opportunity to influence the local political process if not reform the system at the local level.[31]

The party-list law, too, originated in the 1987 constitution. Here, the basic idea was to open up the national legislature to unrepresented sectors of society. Many activists embraced it as "the best hope for the transformation of the trapo (traditional political) system into one with more programmatic parties, more responsive than at present to the needs and concerns of the majority of the people—the workers, farmers and fishermen" (Wurfel 1998: 1). But unlike the LGC, getting a party-list law involved a drawn-out struggle between those who hoped to open up the political process to unrepresented groups and those who sought to ensure that this did not happen. With the passage of the Party-List Act (RA 7941) in 1995, a complicated (some say deliberately confusing) law introducing proportional representation came into being.[32] A slew of party-list organizations emerged to use it. Many did not embody the spirit of the law but were mere fronts for traditional political elites. A few did so, however, self-consciously straddling the line between civil society and political society in the process. Strict definitions of civil society tend to exclude such groups.[33] Yet the Philippine case suggests that it is worth considering them to the extent that they try to reverse the usual flow of influence between these two spheres.

The party-list group Akbayan, for example, began as an innovative attempt to counteract traditional elite political culture and win elections. Launched in 1997, Aksyon ng Sambayan (Akbayan; Citizen's Action Party) was the joint party-building project of four left-of-center political blocs: BISIG; Pandayan Para sa Sosyalistang Pilipinas (Pandayan); the Movement for Popular Democracy (MPD); and Siglo ng Paglaya (Siglaya).[34] Each of these "nonparty political formations" had deep roots in the antidictatorship struggle, reflected a mass movement bias, and had gained numerous practical insights into post-Marcos electoral politics.[35] Akbayan was the by-product of parallel rethinking on "the relevance and necessity of struggling within the state, not just challenging it from the outside" (Abao 1997: 275). It reflected a need "for a political vehicle that will carry a progressive reform agenda into the heart of the national electoral arena" (ibid.). What this meant to Carmela Abao, who went on to serve as Akbayan's first secretary-general, is that "instead of the traditional 'seizure of state power' strategy, the new concept proposes that the state be strengthened, particularly in terms of orientation and capability necessary to implement redistributive measures" (ibid.: 276). For Akbayan, its founders reasoned, building a political party with serious electoral machinery and governing capability necessarily required a shift in focus from the replacement of policies (emphasized by social movements) to the replacement of powerholders (emphasized by political parties). But if one challenge was "how to deal with mass movement dynamics that get in the way of the party-building process" (ibid.: 285), perhaps another was how to build a party capable of complementing rather than competing with its social movement constituencies, something that later proved to be easier said than done.

On the whole, the 1992–98 period, coinciding with the Ramos presidency, saw deepening investments within civil society in both the redistributive reform stream (anchored by the broad agrarian reform movement) and the political-electoral reform stream (anchored by groups focusing on changing the legal parameters of local governance and electoral politics work). Both spawned important innovations in the technology of change-oriented collective citizen engagement. But as the redistributive reform stream evolved, it moved deeper into the everyday politics of effecting policy and institutional reform from below via a complex program, well into ground-level implementation, building up an impressive output in terms of the amount of land redistributed to rightful farmer-beneficiaries. This may have been "everyday politics," but that it was fraught with serious contention inside the halls of state and risky conflict inside landlords' local domains cannot be overstated. Landed elites also brought their "guns, goons, and gold" to bear in the effort to evade land reform, and in some places, even local CPP-NPA forces began actively working with landlords and against local autonomous peasant groups to undermine the latter's campaigns for redistribution. Still, between 1992 and 1998, the PEACE Foundation alone, for example, was involved in the redistribution of 196,873 hectares of agricultural land under CARP (Franco 2001b), a testament to daring and innovative legal and extralegal tactics. And as the political-electoral reform stream evolved, it moved deeper into the complexities of reforming local executive and national legislative politics. The two tracks were not mutually exclusive. There was much overlap between them organizationally and politically. But new national and local elections in 1998 again disrupted the fields in which these and other civil society groups had been operating—setting the stage for a new round of splits and realignments as they sought to establish, maintain, or expand their political relevance.

The 1998 Elections

The 1998 presidential election had an especially divisive effect on civil society in general, which extended deep into the redistributive reform current in particular as groups and political blocs lined up behind different candidates. Although just prior to the election, PARRDS won a major policy victory when it successfully lobbied congress for an increase in CARP funds and extension of the program past June 1998, groups allied in the everyday politics of CARP implementation did not unite electorally, revealing continuing weakness vis-à-vis the dominant traditional elite political culture, and the still limited pull of radical social reform issues in the national political arena. Faced with an apparent absence of choice between contending elite political factions (as opposed to a real choice between candidates standing on programmatic platforms), PARRDS member organizations simply agreed to endorse different candidates—pragmatically spreading their eggs across many baskets, perhaps, but at the cost of becoming invested in competing campaigns in a political process where influence and spoils are at stake. At the same time, the first party-list election produced some countervailing cohesive effects within the redistributive reform current, mainly through the Akbayan campaign, since it involved many of the same groups active in PARRDS. But it induced fragmentation as well, partly because of a three-nominee-cap-per-party rule that had prompted more groups to form their own party-list organizations (Wurfel 1998). Indeed, a section of the MPD bolted from Akbayan to form the Pinatubo Party, while a section of Pandayan opted to stay away from Akbayan and form its own parties.

Election-related political competition within civil society is not necessarily detrimental to democratization, particularly if it is based on real choices. But in the absence of programmatic party competition, civil society fragmentation tends to reinforce elite democracy and undermine the building up of a reform-oriented political pole capable of attracting popular support. Indeed, the especially divisive effect that the 1998 elections wrought on the broad agrarian reform and rural development (ARRD) movement can be traced in large part to the unique way in which personalistic links between civil society and political society played out. Specifically, the electoral machinery of Joseph Estrada, the controversial actor-turned-politician who ended up winning the election, overlapped with part of the broad ARRD movement. In the division of political spoils after winning office, Estrada appointed the PARRDS board chair, Edicio de la Torre, to head the Technical Education and Skills Development Authority (TESDA) and, more important, chose the Philippine Rural Reconstruction Movement president, Horacio Morales, to head the DAR. Both men had been prominent figures in the national democratic wing of the antidictatorship movement, and from there they had gone on to help establish the "popular democracy" bloc in the mid-1980s. Their efforts to build a movement for popular democracy had spawned a small network of civil society institutions that sought to help ordinary people "gain power without getting into power," as Oscar Francisco (1994) has put it. Popular democrats had played key roles in coalition building in different sectors in the post-Marcos period, particularly on the ARRD front in the formation of CPAR in 1987 and later PARRDS in 1994. Their progressive credentials were solid. But their acceptance of appointments in the Estrada government—especially Morales's at the DAR—was an extremely risky political challenge given the inherently contentious nature of agrarian reform.

Although initially welcomed, Morales soon drew fire from both the social democratic AR Now network (a regrouping of ex-CPAR social democratic organizations formed in the late 1990s) and part of the PARRDS network, beginning with his failure to appoint their nominee to the key post of undersecretary of the Field Operations and Support Services Office (FOSSO). More clashes followed, against the larger backdrop of increasing polarization. From the start, Estrada was both much loathed and much loved, largely along class lines. Estrada's candidacy had, as Randolf David (2001: 149) puts it, been "jeered by educated voters"; his votes came mostly from the lower strata of society.[36] Once he was in office, numerous incidents revealing a corrupt and authoritarian side increasingly brought opposition. In the matter of agrarian reform, the antireform lobby made up of powerful regional landed elite families, such as the Lorenzos, Floirendos, and Cojuangcos, found a friend in Malacañang—leading, for example, to Estrada's ironic description of the agribusiness tycoon and former Marcos crony Eduardo "Danding" Cojuangco as the "godfather of land reform" in late 1998, a notion that was vehemently rejected by all agrarian reform groups across the board.

Nonetheless, some PARRDS members thought there was still room for land reform regardless of these developments and proceeded to operate on that basis, achieving important gains in terms of actually redistributing land under hostile conditions. The PEACE Foundation alone, for example, was able to facilitate the redistribution of another 11,082 hectares between 1998 and 2000 (Franco 2001b). In retrospect, though, the yearly land redistribution of the Morales DAR failed to match the peak years of DAR accomplishment under his predecessor, Ernesto Garilao. The Morales DAR redistributed an average of 133,355 hectares per year, compared to the Garilao DAR's 314,896 per year. But it is relevant to note that private agricultural land accounted for three-fourths of the Morales DAR's output, whereas such land made up only about half of the output under Garilao. The CARP scope that Morales was tasked to implement already involved the most politically contentious components, dominated mainly by large private lands, compared to that part covered under previous administrations. Under such circumstances, some groups argued, it would be difficult to expect a similar yearly output as in previous years—an argument that critics dismissed as being soft on the administration. Although its reduced output was much maligned by many anti-Estrada groups who had already opted to disengage from the Morales DAR, these groups would help put into power an administration that would fail to match even the land redistribution of the Morales DAR.

Half Full Versus Half Empty

As early as the eleventh CARP anniversary mobilizations in June 1999, however, the writing appeared on the wall. Historically the June 10 anniversary of the passage of CARL has provided civil society groups with an opportunity to mobilize either for or against CARP and the president's point person at the DAR (and, by implication, the president). On that day in 1999, it revealed a sharp "people power" parallax on the agrarian reform front. Three successive and competing mobilizations took place in the national capital—evincing a deepening political rift within the broad ARRD movement between the social democratic AR Now network and the multibloc PARRDS network. The "outright rejectionist" forces, led by the national democratic KMP, went first, shouting "IBASURA ANG CARP!" or "Discard CARP!" as they passed the gates of the DAR central office in Quezon City. Next came AR Now, which posted a report card at the same gates giving Morales a "poor" grade, claiming (quite disingenuously, given the DAR's famously dismal track record during the Aquino administration) that his was the worst DAR administration ever. Last came PARRDS, which rallied outside the gates before proceeding inside to confront local DAR officials (who were required to be at the national office on that day) on problems involving specific land conflicts.

The next year and a half were marked by intensifying conflict within the agrarian reform movement over how to view the Morales administration. They also saw a deepening rift within organizations that might have bridged the divide. As Ferrer (1997b: 13) has pointed out, in the Philippines some groups, usually those with "considerable resources," serve as mediators or facilitators within civil society by "bridging gaps between unfriendly groups, creating venues for dialogue, encouraging networking among groups, and helping weak groups to strengthen their capability." One group, Akbayan, might have played this role but in the end was unable to do so. Many PARRDS organizations were fraternally related to Akbayan.[37] PARRDS and its member organizations broadly and to varying degrees subscribed to the *bibingka* strategy, if not fully in practice, at least in principle. At the same time, many rural-based NGOs and POs that were not members of PARRDS were nonetheless fraternally related to Akbayan. In particular, many social democrats belonging to the AR Now network had joined Akbayan after their own party-list organizations had failed to reach the golden circle in 1998.

Such growth was certainly positive for Akbayan as a political party, since one of its main concerns from the start had been "building up not just a mass base but also an electoral base—the largest possible constituency within and beyond the progressive circle" (Abao 1997: 276). But it also brought deep antagonisms on the agrarian reform front right into its own ranks. It is useful to recall the dramatically different trajectories pursued by different CPAR member organizations since 1993—since in effect Akbayan now hosted a reconvening of most of them (less the Maoists), only this time in a political party association. Now the *bibingka* strategy activists were pursuing an increasingly conflictual line vis-à-vis the Morales DAR, while the tripartite activists had already denounced the Morales DAR and begun to lay the groundwork for the eventual emergence of an "Erap Resign" ("Erap" being the popular nickname of Joseph Ejercito Estrada) movement. The result was incoherence and inconsistency in Akbayan's positioning on agrarian reform, even as the party moved steadily into the anti-Estrada political movement.

Turning Point

Civil society opposition to the Estrada government received a big boost when Karina Constantino-David, a well-known professor at UP-Diliman and NGO activist on urban poor housing issues who had accepted an appointment as head of the Housing and Urban Development Coordinating Council (HUDCC), resigned in October 1999. The immediate cause of her resignation had been the issuance of an executive order, without her knowledge, creating a Commission on Mass Housing, with Estrada as cochair, along with presidential buddy Jose Luis "Sel" Yulo, duplicating the functions of her office (Constantino-David 2001: 225–26). But the reasons go deeper. In her brief time in office, Constantino-David had made some modest but important steps toward making the agency more responsive to the needs of the poor. Her actions had earned her the ire of the Chamber of Real Estate and Business Associations (CREBA), "an organization known for having an outlook that is pro-developer and anti-poor," which got the ear of the president through Yulo (Karaos 1999a). Yet she had also run afoul of progressive NGOs/POs, which should have been her most natural allies in civil society but, in her words, "seemed more comfortable dealing with promises rather than being told the facts" (Constantino-David 2001: 221). As she explains: "There were two basic sources of tension: the micro nature of their demands, coupled with a lack of appreciation of policy, and the judgemental, even self-righteous, reactions to decisions that they did not completely agree with" (221).

Constantino-David's resignation had a wide but varied political impact. Indeed, it offered contending lessons to different civil society groups then in the process of negotiating the roiling political waters from their respective corners. For those focused on Estrada, it offered the first clear proof of the antireform and corrupt tendencies of his administration (Karaos 1999b).[38] Constantino-David's account of her experience at HUDCC left no doubt as to the highly problematic nature of the Estrada administration from a "good governance" point of view. But for many of those struggling to actually implement a specific program such as CARP, the case also raised the intriguing possibility that perhaps what had been lacking was better synergy between the newly resigned Constantino-David and the pro-socialized-housing NGO/PO community, and, perhaps most important, stronger social reform pressure on the agency from below to counter the expected antireform pressures. In the uproar over her resignation, however, this latter theory was soon pushed to the margins.

Throughout late 1999 and early 2000, the situation grew more intense as a line between "pro-Erap" and "anti-Erap" began to be drawn with increasing vigor within civil society. In some cases, this one-dimensional view was stridently imposed by self-declared anti-Estrada groups on complex developments that were unfolding in specific issue areas, most notably agrarian reform, which simply did not fit into such facile categories. Indeed, partly as a result of the evolving political context and partly because of the birth of a new national peasant organization, the agrarian reform front virtually exploded in the last quarter of 2000.

Struggle for Land and Democracy

On June 10, 2000, the twelfth anniversary of CARP, representatives of local peasant organizations from different regions across the country came together to formally launch a new national peasant coalition called Pambansang Ugnayan ng Nagsasariling mga Lokal na Samahang Mamamayan sa Kanayunan (UNORKA; National Coordination of Autonomous Local Rural People's Organizations). The group's immediate goal was active pursuit of land reform using the *bibingka* strategy.[39] At the founding, newly elected UNORKA leaders presented DAR secretary Morales with a catalog of UNORKA-related land reform cases still pending at the department. Morales in turn promised to act on them within a month.

It was a dramatic promise, but one the besieged secretary failed to fulfill. The mistake would come back to haunt him. The lack of response had sparked a debate within PARRDS and PEACE over why and how to proceed. Agreeing that one weakness on their part had been the prominent role that NGO leaders close to the Morales team had been playing in facilitating and mediating the case follow-up, the group decided to try a new tack. The idea was to establish an alternative vehicle for pressuring the secretary to increase the fire "from above" on those members of the bureaucracy responsible for delays. In September 2000, the assembly proceeded on the calculation that the deepening executive crisis afforded an opening for making strides in consummating the reform in big landholdings that had been held hostage to landlord influence under the current and past administrations.

As a result, APLA leaders requested a meeting with top DAR officials, led by the secretary himself, by which time specific cases were to be resolved and presented. In preparation for the meeting, APLA and PARRDS set about consolidating their list of pending cases and highlighting those requiring a response from the department in order to move forward in the implementation process. Joint workshops with assigned DAR employees from the relevant department divisions were held to document the cases properly in order to speed up the processing. A list of nearly 500 pending cases was compiled—including, on UNORKA's part, 200 cases that had been compiled jointly with DAR employees and another 230 that the organization had compiled on its own.[40] After that, it was up to the DAR to take the appropriate action.

In mid-October 2000, the long-anticipated meeting with the DAR secretary took place, but it went badly. Morales, who was in a meeting with the president, failed to appear and sent several assistants in his stead. The assembled peasant leaders were irritated by the DAR chief's absence, and Morales's aides tried unsuccessfully to appease them, explaining it as a simple scheduling mishap. But the leaders retorted with "that's not our problem" and refused to leave the meeting hall until Morales arrived. In fact, they ended up sleeping there overnight—partly as an act of defiance and partly in case the secretary ever did show up. When Morales arrived at the meeting hall the next morning, the peasants quickly maneuvered him and his aides to the back of it, where there was no exit. In effect, they had taken him hostage. But the DAR chief and his aides were clearly unprepared for the task at hand. Even more irritated, but still adamant, the peasants refused to let the secretary leave until he pledged in writing that all the cases would be resolved and presented to the group by DAR officials on November 17.

"Erap Resign!"

In the meantime, the "Erap Resign!" movement had burst into full view in the wake of former Estrada crony Chavit Singson's allegations on October 2, 2000 of the president's involvement in a massive *jueteng* gambling racket. Singson's revelations sparked a huge public outcry and prompted the opening of formal impeachment proceedings against the president. The scandal became known as "*jueteng*-gate." One of the groups spearheading the protest movement was the Kongreso ng Mamamayang Pilipino II (KOMPIL II), a national coalition of different civil society groups that was formally launched to consolidate political support for an Estrada impeachment. In fact, among those most deeply involved in discussions months earlier on how to get rid of Estrada were the groups that eventually initiated the formation of KOMPIL II. As the group's name suggests, many of its most prominent members had been active in the antidictatorship movement in the 1980s, specifically in the group KOMPIL. Indeed the launching of KOMPIL II was billed as a reconvening of the Marcos-era "civil society coalition which consolidated support from the basic sectors, the churches, business and political blocs" prior to the overthrow of Marcos through a "people power" uprising in 1986 (Karaos 2001).

Some two thousand people, representing about two hundred groups, including Akbayan, attended the founding of KOMPIL II in October 2000.[41] KOMPIL II's membership ranged from right-of-center and center-right to center-left and left-of-center groups. It brought together the usual mix of basic-sector groups (women, urban poor, labor, and peasants) and other sectoral formations (Roman Catholic and business). Thus it was a "broad, pluralist anti-Estrada coalition" (Reyes 2001: 17). Notably, KOMPIL II members were careful to define themselves as part of a "civil society opposition movement distinct from the political opposition formed by traditional opposition political parties." Although members of the traditional political elite were formally excluded, several party-list political parties (including Akbayan) were permitted to join the coalition "in recognition of their grassroots nature and transformative politics" (Reyes 2001: 21). Because of this profile, KOMPIL II quickly became one of the most prominent groups in the anti-Estrada campaign, one that self-consciously saw itself as the democratic civil society core of a broader movement to oust Estrada.

Curiously, KOMPIL II failed to gain the formal support of UNORKA or PEACE, even though both organizations had close ties with groups and individuals active in KOMPIL II and the coalition's agenda included a declared commitment to agrarian reform. Indeed, in addition to the most obvious immediate objective—to rid the country of a corrupt and (according to KOMPIL II) immoral president—the coalition also stated its intent to send a strong anticorruption message to the rest of elite political society and to pursue needed social reforms as well, including "asset reforms" such as agrarian reform. But at least two obstacles, one having to do with the emerging class character of the anti-Estrada movement and the other having to do with the political process the peasant groups and their allies were undergoing at the time, stood in the way of these two groups declaring themselves "anti-Estrada" and officially joining the "Erap Resign!" movement.

First, KOMPIL II became closely allied with Vice-President Gloria Macapagal-Arroyo in spite of "conflicting attitudes" inside the coalition. Although many KOMPIL II activists were wary of her, she was nonetheless recognized as the "only legal alternative to Erap" (Karaos 2001: 16). Macapagal-Arroyo herself did not have a good track record on agrarian reform so far as UNORKA was concerned, and her husband Mike Arroyo was the scion of an influential antireform sugar baron family on the island of Negros. Moreover, the elite opposition that KOMPIL II was aligning itself with in the push to oust Estrada was steadily expanding to include many of the biggest anti–land reform interests. This elite opposition included former Estrada allies who were opportunistically jumping off the president's sinking ship—such as the real estate developer-turned-congressman Manuel Villar (who broke with the ruling party in early November 2000), and more pointedly, numerous despotic regional landed elites with whom UNORKA was currently engaged in land conflicts—such as the country's biggest banana plantation owner, Antonio Floirendo, a former Marcos crony.[42] From the vantage of serious redistributive reform, so far as UNORKA was concerned, the prospects for positive change under a new administration led by Macapagal-Arroyo were becoming increasingly grim (UNORKA Press Statement, November 22, 2000).

Second, UNORKA (and PEACE) had moved slowly but steadily into a contentious struggle with the top DAR leadership over certain unresolved land reform cases. The two organizations were highly mobilized both on the ground in local areas and in the national political arena, trying to exploit the larger political conflict in order to gain important concessions in the form of positive decisions on specific cases and reversals of antireform decisions that had already been made. One of the most contentious cases was the Worldwide Agricultural Development Corporation (WADECOR) case involving the huge southern Mindanao banana plantation owned by Antonio Floirendo, who was in the process of dumping President Estrada for Vice President Gloria Macapagal-Arroyo. UNORKA leaders and PEACE organizers—expecting at least respectful tolerance, if not understanding, of their efforts from allies in the anti-Estrada movement—were puzzled and frustrated when they did not get it. Instead, KOMPIL II activists repeatedly told them that their struggle for reform was futile and "would have to wait for the new administration," a position that did not sit well with the peasants, given the accelerating flow of antireform elites and despotic landlords into the opposition.[43] According to the UNORKA leader and veteran peasant organizer Evangeline Mendoza, such advice was misplaced and recalled the time when the CPP-led underground peasant organization PKM was being organized and "the framework of organizing was purely political and didn't touch on social reform issues like agrarian reform." Mendoza recalled:

> The point of organizing then was to change the state. But then [the peasants] eventually realized that they were not making any concrete gains in the process of struggling to seize the state power. That was the start of turning toward a claim-making/taking strategy—claiming resources from the state based on a belief that this approach can strengthen the organization and achieve concrete gains now and you can still criticize the government for policies that run counter to your interests. [By November 2000] we already knew of UNORKA areas where gains had been made and developed positively, even though there was no change in the configuration of state power.[44]

Yet this perspective was lost on activists in KOMPIL II, who were unable to grasp or appreciate the difficult dilemma confronting their erstwhile comrades. In the months leading up to EDSA 2, UNORKA and PEACE were dismissively labeled as "pro-Erap" and, with not a small dose of self-righteousness, diagnosed as lacking "proper political education" or "enough political education."

Endgame

By November 2000, the heat had been turned up on the Estrada camp with a series of mass protests—including a coordinated Welga ng Mamamayan (Citizens' Strike) on November 14, which drew people from many walks of life out into the streets for a day of protest. One sympathetic newspaper editorial breathlessly claimed that the event "redrew the map of the political protest movement in this country. For the first time, a broad spectrum of protesters from all social classes and sectors marched in the streets to demand the resignation of President Estrada."[45] The nationwide anti-Estrada demonstration was an opportune response to a massive pro-Estrada prayer rally that had been held a few days earlier in Manila's historic Luneta Park. In a taste of things to come, the estimated one-million-strong prayer rally was scornfully portrayed by one commentator as a show of force by "the legions of the ignorant whose idea of law is at best primitive and who mistake democracy for the rule of the uninformed mob" (Teodoro 2000).[46]

In this increasingly charged political environment, the endgame between UNORKA and the Morales DAR began in earnest. With UNORKA and PEACE desperate to lock in as many positive land reform decisions and overturn as many antireform decisions as possible before the new landlord-heavy opposition coalition seized power, the two sides met again in yet another meeting, which had been scheduled as a result of the October "hostage-taking" incident in which the DAR chief failed to deliver on a promise to resolve nearly five hundred pending land reform cases. The tense November 17 meeting was attended by some two hundred local peasant leaders, community organizers, and policy advocates on the civil society side and on the state side by the secretary, his undersecretary for field operations, several assistant secretaries, numerous regional directors, and sundry national office employees. UNORKA leaders opened the meeting by reading aloud a statement demanding a full accounting of the cases and promising to hold the department leadership accountable for its actions. But as they were soon to discover, apart from some fifty-four cases that had been resolved, the vast majority had not moved an inch. Even worse, the dismayed peasant leaders quickly realized that the meeting was being controlled by the DAR facilitators to prevent discussion of the most urgent cases, including the WADECOR case, where the FOSSO undersecretary had recently decided against the farmworkers in favor of the Floirendos.

The WADECOR decision had unjustly disqualified 154 farmworker families from the reform and at the same time had unfairly bound the rest to the Floirendos via an onerous sixty-year growers' contract with no exit option. When the case was finally forced onto the table for discussion, the situation quickly escalated into a near-brawl after DAR officials insisted on defending a decision that clearly constituted the worst kind of betrayal of rural poor people's rights by the government. A heated exchange between the two sides led to a walkout by UNORKA and the other groups. UNORKA and PEACE learned later that the "DAR management had approached the meeting with the attitude that a walkout was being orchestrated because the peasants were pro-GMA [Gloria Macapagal-Arroyo]."[47] In the context of a quickly unraveling Estrada camp, the November 17 meeting proved to be a small but significant turning point for UNORKA, which unexpectedly ended up giving new room for maneuver to dissidents in the Morales DAR, previously critical of the numerous antireform decisions that had been rammed through but now emboldened by the dramatic stand that had been made by UNORKA and its allies at the meeting. With the Estrada political edifice now crumbling fast in the rapidly rising tidal wave of public protest, these two groups now jointly made every effort to push through reform before it was too late. While UNORKA turned up the heat from below with rallies that flirted with an anti-Estrada line outside the DAR central office, its allies inside succeeded in engineering a reversal of the WADECOR decision and release of several other key decisions in favor of UNORKA later that month—none too soon in fact.

Just two months later, Estrada and those who had stuck with him (including Horacio Morales and Edicio de la Torre) were ousted from office by a combined civilian-military uprising known as EDSA 2, which lasted for four days (January 16–20, 2001). In terms of prospects for agrarian reform, the change seemed promising at first. Numerous KOMPIL II leaders with roots in the world of development NGOs went on to supply the new administration of Gloria Macapagal-Arroyo with several of its top appointees, including a former AR Now leader, Corazon "Dinky" Soliman.[48] Yet it soon became clear that UNORKA and PEACE's concerns had indeed been well-founded. The uprising did not create space or new momentum for social reform, especially land reform, despite earlier assurances. The agrarian reform department was turned over to a brash young former congressman and nephew of former president Fidel Ramos, Hernani Braganza, who had little prior experience of or interest in agrarian reform, and, as it turns out, precious little tolerance for a highly engaged and well-informed autonomous peasant movement. As EDSA 2's urban middle class civil society leaders stood silently by, Braganza proceeded to oversee a lowering of yearly land acquisition and distribution targets, a shift in emphasis to nonexpropriative modes of acquisition, and a reduction in the CARP fund, all the while arrogantly brushing aside efforts by affected rural poor civil society groups such as UNORKA to engage with the new department leadership, even to the point of using military force to disperse the rallies and demonstrations that such policy changes inevitably provoked. After two years in office, the new administration had averaged just 104,000 hectares of land moved per year—the lowest yearly land redistribution output in CARP history.

Civil Society and the Future of Reform

After numerous national political regime changes and in-between political transformations, the Philippines has still not yet crossed the minimum threshold for democracy, while its relatively free civil society remains colonized to a significant extent by an elite-dominated, status quo–oriented political society. If democratization involves something more than restoring less-than-democratic elite political competition and the periodic purging of corrupt government officials, then civil society groups concerned with pushing the process clearly have a long way to go. To be sure, a plethora of formidable obstacles continue to block the way to a more profound democracy than exists in the country today, including still widespread poverty, an unrepresentative party system, and all manner of government corruption, to name just a few of them. However, at least part of the difficulty can be traced back to civil society's own internal character and, relatedly, to how contending civil society groups have hitherto approached the challenge of democratization.

Looking back, a multilayered, fractious civil society has been both bane and boon to democratization in the Philippines. To be sure, civil society interactions have helped to extend the reach of democratic rights and freedoms to previously excluded populations and have expanded political competition. But as the previous discussion suggests, they have also served (unintentionally) to revive or reinforce the political influence of antireform elite interests. Indeed, Philippine civil society has as often as not been an arena of contestation, where the very meaning of democracy and the mechanics of democratization are disputed, its highly porous boundaries having opened the sphere to the intensity of socioeconomic class-based conflict, on the one hand, and vicissitudes of elite-dominated political-electoral conflict, on the other. Philippine civil society has long absorbed a variety of social antagonisms that civil society organizing has sharpened or blurred. Meanwhile, internal political conflict over the fundamentals of collective action and its potential impact on democracy is at least as important a feature of Philippine civil society today as its strength and innovativeness.

Certainly EDSA 1—and, upon closer inspection, EDSA 2—demonstrated the existence of distinct, even diametrically opposed understandings of democracy and what the challenge of democratization entails. Elite opposition promises of social and political reform, made before Marcos's overthrow, were left to languish after EDSA 1 in the rush to restore elite democracy based on unrepresentative political party competition and actively restricted popular participation. But the unfulfilled promises of the 1986 national uprising, in some cases strengthened on paper by legislation and programs, remained a motivating force in civil society, prompting land reform advocates from both the rural poor and urban middle class to organize and mobilize to pressure the new government to effect real redistribution, starting with the passage of a pro-peasant agrarian reform law. "Promises unkept keep movements alive," as Ronald Herring (1999) has put it. The same aspirations continued to go unfulfilled even after the passage by a landed elite-dominated legislature of an only partially redistributive law, and so, despite the persistence of localized authoritarian obstacles to democratic political change, affected groups at different levels continued to organize and mobilize for change through various forms of collective citizen engagement.[49] But the implications of this activity for democratization, which has been discussed here in terms of the extension to all citizens systemwide of effective access to the most basic political rights and civil liberties, generally associated with democracy but all too often taken for granted, have been mixed. The persistence of various contending reform movements may have kept the democratization process alive, but their inability to promote a redistributive social reform agenda during EDSA 2 was a missed opportunity to turbocharge this process and take it much further.

Even within the broad proreform movement, one person's progress in pushing forward the democratization process has sometimes meant another's setback. The post-1986 expansion of civil society proved to be no guarantee that redistributive social reform would be taken equally seriously by all civil society non–status quo associations. As time has passed since the uprising in 1986, many civil society actors, particularly those most tied to urban middle class leaderships and less driven by lower-class constituencies, have moved from their original social reform aims to no less important but perhaps less immediately urgent agendas. The fact that, in the absence of land reform, many potential political reform constituencies among the rural poor remain locked up inside unreformed local authoritarian enclaves does not seem to be viewed widely as a pressing problem that must be dealt with now rather than sometime in the future. Yet the results of this perennial failure seriously to address the concerns and problems confronting the rural poor have been disastrous, not just for the rural poor, but for Philippine democracy overall as well.

In the end, such problems reflect the continued influence of traditional elite political society on civil society and the still limited (if not diminishing) weight of strategic coalitions within civil society organized around social reform. Recent events suggest the need to intensify efforts within civil society to build an integrated radical reform pole—one capable of widening the area of overlap between these two reform currents and extending their influence systemwide in order to reach these captive communities. This in turn may require coming up with more effective ways to combine "seizing state power" with "exercising citizen power" agendas that are capable of prioritizing long-standing and still much needed social reforms. Yet recent events also suggest that movement in this direction is unlikely to occur anytime soon. Social reform groups may well be forced to draw on their own resources and find new ways to push their way back from the periphery into the center of Philippine civil society and politics.

Notes

1. The EDSA Shrine, located at a major intersection on the main thoroughfare running through Metro Manila, called the Epifiano Delos Santos Avenue (for which EDSA is the acronym), was built by the Catholic Church to commemorate the first "people power" uprising, which led to the collapse of the Marcos dictatorship in February 1986.

2. This is how the event was characterized by one EDSA 2 activist. See Reyes 2001: 14.

3. This interpretation was put forward by Eric Gutierrez, a political analyst, in an e-mail communication.

4. One text joke quoted by Ina Arriola (2002: 20) concerned the "different theme songs of EDSAs 1, 2 and 3. The joke runs thus: The theme song of EDSA 1 was 'Magkaisa' [Unite]; EDSA 2, 'Heal Our Land'; and . . . EDSA 3, 'Who Let the Dogs Out.'" Another was: "They are paying differential rates to people who go to EDSA: P300 for those who go there daily, P500 for those who come from the provinces, P700 for those who bring lead pipes, and P300 for the toothless and ugly" (quoted by the columnist Conrado de Quiros, *Philippine Daily Inquirer*, Apr. 30, 2001). As de Quiros pointed out at the time, the "darker side to this snobbery" was "the attitude of despair and the scorn for the masa [masses] as being hopelessly stupid."

5. The term *silenced majority* comes from an article by La Liga Policy Institute dated Apr. 29, 2001.

6. As the university professor and media commentator Randolf S. David remarked: "[Estrada] had walked into the presidency with an electoral mandate that exceeded the record of all previous presidents of the republic except Ramon Magsaysay. In a field of 11 candidates, he won 39% of all the votes cast, more than twice the number of votes obtained by his closest rival, the administration's anointed candidate [Jose de Venecia]" (2001: 149).

7. According to one Philippine social scientist: "Even more striking than persistent poverty, gross inequality characterizes the late 1990s, as it did in earlier decades. The Philippine social structure during the 1998 presidential election reflected class cleavages that had undergone very little transformation since the country's independence from colonial rule. Although the class structure had become far more complex than the two-tiered model of rich patrons and poor clients, its shape, nevertheless, remained pyramidal. A small pro-

portion of rich citizens formed the apex, while a huge mass who are poor or on the brink of poverty constituted the broad base. Although the middle class has expanded in size and political significance since World War II, it still made up a relatively narrow segment between the apex and the base" (Bautista 2001: 1).

8. According to one group of Filipino economists, based on their reading of the government's 1997 Family Income and Expenditure Survey, a low 25 percent of the total population of the Philippines was poor (Balisacan et al. 2000: 162). At the other extreme, the IBON Foundation, a research NGO on the extreme left of the political spectrum, places the figure much higher, at 87.5 percent in 2002 (IBON Foundation 2002). The government's National Statistical Coordination Board placed the figure at 33.7 percent in the year 2000. The National Antipoverty Commission recently sounded an alarm on the poverty situation, saying that "40 percent or 30.6 million Filipinos live below the poverty line; 15.3 million wake up every morning without food on the table; and the number of absolute poor families continue to increase by almost 2 percent every year" (quoted from *Today*, Dec. 6, 2002).

9. The obstacles to building issue-based citizen engagement, such as widespread ignorance of basic rights, difficulty of mass assembly, and diverse economic activities, among others, may be "internal to the process of articulating and defending interests" (Fox 1990: 3). They may also be external to civil society and lie in the interaction between civil society actors and the state at different levels. Here the degree of respect for basic political freedoms and the extent of access to political and other kinds of information are important (ibid.). But the obstacles to building citizen engagement may also be internal to civil society—stemming from competition between groups for financial resources, political legitimacy, and organized followers (Zald and McCarthy 1980).

10. Those who do not try to build such citizen engagement are not considered part of civil society.

11. This is a key point made by the American political scientist Terry Karl (1986) in her insightful study about El Salvador in the 1980s.

12. These uprisings included the Dagohoy rebellion (1744–1829), the Cofradia and Colorum movements in the nineteenth century, which crystallized around the Catholic Church's refusal to admit Filipinos to the clergy, and the Guardia de Honor movement, which combined religious and socioeconomic grievances in its advocacy of a "division of lands among the righteous."

13. Rizal satirized Spanish colonial authorities and collaborators in two novels, *Noli me tangere* and *El Filibusterismo*. He was arrested in 1892, and his execution four years later fanned the flames of revolt (Constantino 1975: 157–58).

14. Peasant mobilizations in Central Luzon put socioeconomic and political reform on the agenda. Boosting the clout of this regional peasant movement were individuals from outside the peasantry, especially sympathetic lawyers and left-wing political activists who pleaded land cases in court, spoke at demonstrations in Manila, and lobbied for tenancy reform in Congress (Kerkvliet 1977: 49–50). The transitional commonwealth government of Manuel Quezon initially responded with a conservative reform program. But the elite in areas targeted for reform refused to compromise, resisting the program in the legislature and fielding private armies to suppress peasant support. Undeterred, organized peasants joined with fledgling socialist and communist movements to form a popular front to challenge landlord candidates in the 1940 local elections, making some gains (Crippen 1946: 357–58).

15. Mary Racelis (2000) says the FFF (and its labor counterpart the FFW) was founded by Jesuit priests from the Institute of Social Order as part of a larger strategy to "counteract the atheistic elements of Communism while fostering social justice."

16. The earliest signs of student unrest were the anti–Vietnam War demonstrations held

during U.S. president Lyndon Johnson's 1965 state visit to Manila. But antiwar demonstrations became an arena for criticizing the status quo inside the Philippines as well.

17. The founding of the Communist Party of the Philippines (CPP) had captured the imagination of Manila's student population, but national democratic (ND) and student groups such as Kabataang Makabayan (KM; Patriotic Youth) and Samahang Demokratikong Kabataan (SDK; Democratic Youth Organization) were soon locked in a fierce rivalry with other groups for control of the rising student movement. Social democratic (SD) groups such as Lakasdiwa, the Catholic youth organization Kilusang Khi Rho ng Pilipinas (or simply Khi Rho), the youth arm of the FFF, and the National Union of Students in the Philippines (NUSP) were militantly anticommunist and distinguished themselves from the CPP by an avowed commitment to a nonviolent and reformist political strategy.

18. The best discussions of the student movement on the eve of martial law are Lacaba 1982, Daroy 1988, and Pimentel 1991.

19. At the convention, anti-Marcos delegates authored a "ban the Marcoses" resolution. But Marcos defeated the resolution by using bribery and coercion and pushed through the adoption of a parliamentary system (Wurfel 1988: 110–11).

20. For example, the CPP-led "national democratic" stream spawned two offspring. The first involved building guerrilla zones in hinterlands where state presence was weakest. The second involved organizing support for the revolution in the "white areas" between guerrilla zones and state power centers, as well as in urban centers nationwide. Although siblings, the two coexisted uneasily. While "white area" work was deemed necessary, it tended to be viewed instrumentally and as reformist by central and territorial party leaders. By contrast, many "white area" cadres saw a need for a truly open mass movement with real autonomy vis-à-vis the party that could protect members from "anti-red" repression. The underground movement thus produced the earliest open opposition force, but one tethered to a rope held by party leaders, who feared its potential. At times the rope that tied the aboveground democracy movement to the underground revolutionary movement lay slack, allowing cadres to respond creatively to situations. But when reformism fears kicked in, the rope tightened, pulling them back at inopportune moments.

21. The term *rightful resistance* comes from Kevin O'Brien's (1996) study of peasant mobilization in the 1990s in rural China.

22. Three organizations were instrumental in internationally publicizing the grave human rights situation prevailing in the Philippines after September 1972: the Catholic-sponsored Association of Major Religious Superiors in the Philippines (AMRSP); an AMRSP creation called Task Force Detainees (TFD); and the human rights lawyers' Free Legal Assistance Group (FLAG).

23. Widening of aboveground civil society space was promoted by church-sponsored groups such as PECCO and the human rights group TFD, by elite opposition-linked groups such as FLAG, and by national-democratic-initiated sectoral groups such as the League of Filipino Students (LFS) and Kilusang Mayo Uno (KMU; May First Movement).

24. By the mid–1990s, according to Karina Constantino-David (1997), some 58,000 "nonstock, nonprofit organizations" were officially registered. Regarding the use of SEC registration records as the yardstick for measuring growth of the NGO sector of civil society, Sidney Silliman and Lela Noble point out: "While government permission is not required to establish an NGO in the Philippines, registration with the Securities and Exchange Commission (SEC) does provide the best index as to the total number of NGOs in the country" (1998: 10). They use the term *NGO* to refer broadly to "any voluntary organization that is independent of both the government and private business sectors" (6). Even though SEC registration does provide the best recorded index available, one can still safely assume that many more volun-

tary, nonprofit associations of various types actually exist in the Philippines today, since many cannot or will not register.

25. National formations tend to be thicker in some regions than in others, and coalitions often exist more in theory than in reality after the initial political environment that gave birth to them shifts. Likewise, civil society organizational muscle is not spread uniformly across issues areas (or even within issue areas) and often ebbs and flows in relation to the rhythms of the larger political environment.

26. The PARCode was founded on the principle of an effective "zero retention" limit for landlords and a "selective and progressive" scheme to compensate expropriated landlords that depended on farm size and production capacity.

27. According to James Putzel, the initiative involved a campaign "to collect 2.5 million signatures to call for a referendum with the objective of rejecting the government's agrarian reform law and adopting PARCODE in its place" (1998: 96).

28. The program officially aimed to "form a harmonious and productive working relationship; a relationship where there is close coordination and complementarity of roles among the GOs, NGOs, and ARB organizations" (PHILDHRRA 1997: xiii). In 1989, the program was launched in three provinces (Antique, Bukidnon, and Camarines Sur) with three components: land tenure improvement, social infrastructure building and strengthening, and productivity systems development. By 1996, TriPARRD had spread to four provinces, and it eventually "was able to move close to two thousand hectares of which 59 percent were covered by the VOS scheme" (Quitoriano 2000: 16).

29. Indeed, it can be argued that once the new law had been passed and its implementing Comprehensive Agrarian Reform Program (CARP) came into existence, the coalition's chief reason for being had disappeared, unleashing centrifugal energies and making a formal parting of the ways simply a matter of time. For a deeper political analysis of CPAR's demise, see Putzel 1995.

30. Applied to health, agriculture, social services, and tourism, however, the code gave local governments control over budgets, equipment, projects, and personnel, expanded their financial resources by increasing their take from internal revenue collection, and institutionalized civil society participation in local governance in various ways (Cariño 1992).

31. They mobilized on this new frontier in numerous ways—from the mundane project basis to the comprehensive "full-blown effort to put forth an NGO agenda for local governance and development" (Gonzales 2000).

32. According to David Wurfel (1998: 1): "Some critical observers assume that a certain amount of this 'confusion' in the law is deliberate—to confuse COMELEC [Commission on Elections] and voters, so that the new law will be difficult to implement."

33. "Civil society, which is voluntary and self-generating, is a domain independent of the state, although it does seek benefits, policy changes, or accountability from the state. It does not seek to gain formal power or to overthrow the state, yet it is concerned with public rather than private ends" (Silliman and Noble 1998: 13).

34. Siglaya was a coalition of former national democrats. After the coalition was discontinued, only the group known as PADAYON chose to remain in Akbayan.

35. Siglaya and MPD had participated in the Partido ng Bayan (PnB) experiment during the first post-Marcos legislative elections in 1987; Bisig, Pandayan, and MPD had participated in another experiment, also called Akbayan, during the 1992 "synchronized" elections. While the former experience showed that it was possible (although difficult) for progressive reformists to win elections under certain conditions, the latter taught that "even the most progressive mainstream political parties were bastions of traditional politics" (Abao 1997: 276–77).

36. According to Cynthia Bautista (2001: 4), exit polls showed that "almost half of the

poorest E population and 40% of the D class across different regions nationwide elected him to office. Their votes, in turn, made up 25% and 63% of the total, respectively." In the ABCDE classification system used by polling agencies in the Philippines, Bautista explains, "AB constitutes the upper class while C corresponds to the middle class. The D and E groups make up the lower classes. D is further subdivided into D1 and D2, with the former owning the lots on which their houses are built" (2).

37. The overlap between PARRDS and Akbayan exemplifies Abao's observation that many practitioners of development work had found their way into the Akbayan party-building project. According to Carmela Abao (1997: 278): "Many Aksyon members are NGO workers or PO leaders. Almost all the organizers (mostly pol-bloc leaders), in fact, are full-time NGO workers. Over the years, political blocs have intersected with NGOs and POs in the areas of organizing, advocacy and agenda-building with the latter concentrating more on servicing and mobilizing local communities and the former providing the national advocacy for such local initiatives. Recently, however, NGOs and POs have started building coalitions which have enabled them to participate in political discourse and activity as distinct blocs."

38. As Annamarie Karaos (1999b) writes: "All in all, the Estrada administration has exposed its biggest flaws in the events surrounding the demotion and then the resignation of Karina David. What happened proved to be a classic example of the kind of wheeling and dealing that goes on inside Malacañang, the cavalier way in which important and serious decisions are made, the disregard for the informed opinions of Cabinet officials and in its place the influence wielded by the President's drinking and karaoke buddies. Until David's resignation, all these just seemed like tales we only heard about and for which we had no concrete proof. Now the proof is so real one finds it too painful to believe."

39. Some of the grassroots leaders involved in UNORKA's founding had started out in the CPP-led underground revolutionary movement but left during the 1992–93 split. Most of the local organizations that joined were products of PEACE Foundation community organizing around CARP using the *bibingka* approach.

40. The compilation process is tedious and technically involved. Among other steps, it requires specifying exactly where a given case is in the formal implementation process and explaining how it got stuck there.

41. Other well-known founding members were the national development NGO network called CODE-NGO (which became KOMPIL II's national secretariat) and the issue-based formations National Peace Conference (NPC), Women's Action Network for Development, Urban Land Reform Task Force, and Freedom from Debt Coalition (FDC). Numerous sectoral organizations joined too, including PAKISAMA (peasant federation), the Labor Solidarity Movement (composed of the Federation of Free Workers, Trade Union Congress of the Philippines, and Alliance of Progressive Labor), the Catholic Church's Couples for Christ, and the Makati Business Club (MBC). Several nonparty political formations were there as well, including the Social Democratic Caucus, Padayon, Pandayan, BISIG, and Sanlakas (various center-left and left-wing political blocs).

42. Landed elites that UNORKA identified as being part of the "pro-Gloria elite" include Corazon Cojuangco Aquino, Jose "Peping" Cojuangco, Heherson Alvarez, Roberto Sebastian, Paul Dominguez, the Ayalas, the Fajardos, Manny Villar, and Mike Arroyo. High-profile anti-CARP political elites closely identified with the "Gloria camp" include Teofisto Guingona and Manny Villar.

43. Interview with the UNORKA leader Evangeline Mendoza, Nov. 2001.

44. Ibid.

45. *Philippine Daily Inquirer*, Nov. 16, 2000.

46. Such comments certainly helped to cultivate the perspective that EDSA 2 was an elitist uprising and, moreover, betray the two assumptions that Peter Bachrach (1967: 2) once observed form the basis of any elite theory of politics—"first, that the masses are inherently incompetent, and second, that they are, at best, pliable, inert stuff or, at worst, aroused, unruly creatures possessing an insatiable proclivity to undermine both culture and liberty."

47. Interview with the UNORKA leader Evangeline Mendoza, Nov. 2001.

48. Of the top KOMPIL II leadership, the following were the most prominent political appointments under the new administration: CODE-NGO Chair Corazon "Dinky" Soliman was appointed secretary of the Department of Social Welfare and Development (DSWD); Ayala Foundation Executive Director and CODE-NGO Council Member Vicky Garchitorena was appointed head of the Presidential Management Staff (PMS) before resigning in December 2001; CODE-NGO National Coordinator Dan Siongco was appointed to the Board of the Development Bank of the Philippines; National Peace Conference and Gaston Ortigas Peace Foundation representative to CODE-NGO Teresita "Ging" Deles was appointed vice-chair (with cabinet rank) of the National Antipoverty Commission.

49. Francisco Lara and Horacio Morales (1990) stress the role of patronage networks, electoral machines, officialist socioeconomic organizations, conservative local churches, and private armies in facilitating authoritarian elite efforts to control the political process and its outcomes by restricting access to it at regional and district levels of the political system. Others have stressed "guns, goons, and gold" during national elections, regional clans, land-based elites in the national legislature, and entrenched government corruption as obstacles to post-Marcos democratization.

Works Cited

Abao, Carmela. 1997. "Dynamics Among Political Blocs in the Formation of a Political Party." In M. C. Ferrer, ed., *Philippine Democracy Agenda: Civil Society Making Civil Society*. Quezon City: Third World Studies Center.

Agoncillo, Teodoro A. 2002. *The Revolt of the Masses: The Story of Bonifacio and the Katipunan*. Quezon City: University of the Philippines Press.

Arriola, Ina. 2002. "The Mendiola Riot and the Masa Phenomenon." In *EDSA 3: Uncensored Perspectives. A Compilation of the Friends of EDSA 3*, 20-34. Quezon City: La Liga Policy Institute.

Bachrach, Peter. 1967. *The Democratic Theory of Elitism*. Boston: Little, Brown.

Balisacan, Arsenio, Rosemarie Edillon, Alex Brillantes, and Dante Canlas. 2000. *Approaches to Targeting the Poor*. Quezon City: School of Economics, University of the Philippines / United Nations Development Programme; Pasig: National Economic and Development Authority.

Bautista, Maria Cynthia Rose Banzon. 2001. "People Power 2: 'The Revenge of the Elite on the Masses'?" In A. Doronila, ed., *Between Fires: Fifteen Perspectives on the Estrada Crisis*. Pasig City: Anvil Publishing.

Borras, Saturnino, Jr. 1999. *The Bibingka Strategy in Land Reform Implementation: Autonomous Peasant Movements and State Reformists in the Philippines*. Quezon City: Institute for Popular Democracy.

Cameron, Maxwell. 1992. "Rational Resignations: Coalition Building in Peru and the Philippines." *Comparative Political Studies* 25(2) (July): 229–50.

Cariño, Jessica. 1992. *The Local Government Code of 1991 and People's Organizations and Nongovernment Organizations in Northern Luzon*. Working Paper 20. Baguio City: University of the Philippines, Cordillera Studies Center.

Constantino, Renato. 1975. *The Philippines: A Continuing Past.* Vol. 1. Quezon City: Foundation for Nationalist Studies.

Constantino-David, Karina. 1995. "Community Organizing in the Philippines: The Experience of Development NGOs." In G. Craig and M. Mayo, eds., *Community Empowerment: A Reader in Participation and Development.* Atlantic Highlands, N.J.: Zed Books.

———. 1997. "Intra-Civil Society Relations." In M. C. Ferrer, ed., *Philippine Democracy Agenda: Civil Society Making Civil Society.* Quezon City: Third World Studies Center.

———. 2001. "Surviving Erap." In A. Doronila, ed., *Between Fires: Fifteen Perspectives on the Estrada Crisis.* Manila: Anvil Publishing and Philippine Daily Inquirer.

Crippen, Harlan. 1946. "Philippine Agrarian Unrest: Historical Backgrounds." *Science and Society* 10(4) (Fall).

Daroy, Petronilo. 1988. "On the Eve of the Dictatorship and Revolution." In A. Javate-De Dios et al., eds., *Dictatorship and Revolution: Roots of People Power.* Manila: Conspectus Foundation.

David, Randolf S. 2001. "Erap: A Diary of Disenchantment." In A. Doronila, ed., *Between Fires: Fifteen Perspectives on the Estrada Crisis.* Manila: Anvil Publishing and Philippine Daily Inquirer.

Diokno, M. S. I. 1988. "Unity and Struggle." In A. Javate-De Dios et al., eds., *Dictatorship and Revolution: Roots of People Power.* Manila: Conspectus Foundation.

Ferrer, Miriam Coronel. 1997a. "Civil Society: An Operational Definition." In M. S. I. Diokno, ed., *Democracy and Citizenship in Filipino Political Culture: Philippine Democracy Agenda.* Quezon City: Third World Studies Center.

———. 1997b. "Civil Society Making Civil Society." In M. C. Ferrer, ed., *Philippine Democracy Agenda: Civil Society Making Civil Society.* Quezon City: Third World Studies Center.

Fox, Jonathan. 1990. "Editor's Introduction." In id., ed., *The Challenge of Rural Democratisation: Perspectives from Latin America and the Philippines.* Portland, Or.: Frank Cass.

———. 1996. "Does Civil Society Thicken? The Political Construction of Social Capital in Rural Mexico." *World Development* 24(6): 1089–1103.

Francisco, Oscar D. 1994. "The Politics of Civil Society." *PEACE Foundation Discussion Papers,* June: 7–21.

Franco, Jennifer C. 1998. "Between 'Uncritical Collaboration' and 'Outright Opposition': An Evaluation Report on the Partnership for Agrarian Reform and Rural Development Services (PARRDS) and the Struggle for Agrarian Reform and Rural Development in the 1990s." *Work in Progress.* Quezon City: Institute for Popular Democracy.

———. 2001a. *Elections and Democratization in the Philippines.* New York: Routledge.

———. 2001b. "Building Alternatives, Harvesting Change: PEACE Network and the Institutionalization of Bibingka Strategy." Quezon City: PEACE Foundation. Unpublished study.

Gonzales, Eleanor M. 2000. "Decentralization and Political Participation in the Philippines: Experiences and Issues in Societal Transformation." *Work in Progress.* Quezon City: Institute for Popular Democracy. www.ipd.ph/pub/wip/decentralization-e_gonzales.shtml.

Harvey, Neil. 1998. *The Chiapas Rebellion: The Struggle for Land and Democracy.* Durham, N.C.: Duke University Press.

Hedman, Eva-Lotta. 1997. "Constructing Civil Society: Election Watch Movements in the Philippines." In S. Lindberg and A. Sverrisson, eds., *Social Movements in Development: The Challenge of Globalization and Democratization.* New York: St. Martin's Press.

Herring, Ronald J. 1999. "Political Conditions for Agrarian Reform and Poverty Alleviation." Paper prepared for the DFID Conference on 2001 World Development Report on Poverty, Birmingham, England.

Huntington, Samuel P. 1968. *Political Order in Changing Societies*. New Haven: Yale University Press.

IBON Foundation. 2002. "Nearly 88% of Filipino Families Live in Poverty." www.ibon.org/news/pr/02/08.htm. Accessed 2/25/2004.

Ileto, Reynaldo Clemeña. 1979. *Pasyon and Revolution: Popular Movements in the Philippines, 1840–1910*. Quezon City: Ateneo de Manila University Press.

Institute for Popular Democracy (IPD). 1987. *Political Clans*. Quezon City: Institute for Popular Democracy.

Karaos, Annamarie A. 1999a. "Does Socialized Housing Have a Chance?" *Political Brief* (Nov.). www.ipd.ph/pub/polbrief/1999/november/socializedhousing.shtml.

———. 1999b. "After Karina, a Black Hole in Housing." *Political Brief* (Nov.). www.ipd.ph/pub/polbrief/1999/november/afterkarina.shtml.

———. 2001. "Not Mob Rule." *Intersect* 16(2) (Feb.): 12–19.

Karl, Terry. 1986. "Imposing Consent? Electoralism vs. Democratization in El Salvador." In P. Drake and E. Silva, eds., *Elections and Democratization in Latin America, 1980–1985*. San Diego: CILAS.

———. 1990. "Dilemmas of Democratization in Latin America." *Comparative Politics* 23(1) (Oct.): 1–21.

Kerkvliet, Benedict. 1977. *The Huk Rebellion: A Study of Peasant Revolt in the Philippines*. Berkeley: University of California Press.

———. 2001. "Political Ironies in the Philippines." Foreword in J. Franco, *Elections and Democratization in the Philippines*. New York: Routledge.

Lacaba, Jose. 1982. *Days of Disquiet, Nights of Rage: The First Quarter Storm and Related Events*. Manila: Salinlahi Publishing House.

Lane, Max. 1990. *The Urban Mass Movement in the Philippines, 1983–87*. Political and Social Change Monograph 10. Canberra: Australian National University.

Lara, Francisco, Jr., and Horacio Morales, Jr. 1990. "The Peasant Movement and the Challenge of Democratisation in the Philippines." In Jonathan Fox, ed., *The Challenge of Rural Democratisation: Perspectives from Latin America and the Philippines*. Portland, Or.: Frank Cass.

Mackenzie, Anne. 1987. "People Power or Palace Coup: The Fall of Marcos." In M. Turner, ed., *Regime Change in the Philippines: The Legitimation of the Aquino Government*. Political and Social Change Monograph 7. Canberra: Australian National University.

O'Brien, Kevin. 1996. "Rightful Resistance." *World Politics* 49 (Oct.): 31–55.

Philippine Partnership for the Development of Human Resources in Rural Areas (PHILDHRRA). 1997. "Making Agrarian Reform Work: Securing the Gains in Land Tenure Improvement." TriPARRD Series, no. 1. Quezon City: Center for Community Services.

Pimentel, Benjamin. 1991. *Rebolusyon: A Generation of Struggle in the Philippines*. New York: Monthly Review Press.

Putzel, James. 1992. *A Captive Land*. Quezon City: Ateneo de Manila University Press.

———. 1995. "Managing the 'Main Force': The Communist Party and the Peasantry in the Philippines." *Journal of Peasant Studies* 22(4): 645–71.

———. 1998. "Non-Governmental Organizations and Rural Poverty." In G. S. Silliman and L. G. Noble, eds., *Organizing for Democracy: NGOs, Civil Society, and the Philippine State*. Quezon City: Ateneo de Manila University Press.

Quitoriano, Ed. 2000. "Agrarian Struggles and Institutional Change: The Mapalad Case for Land." *MODE Research Paper* 1(2). Quezon City: Management and Organizational Development for Empowerment.

Racelis, Mary. 2000. "New Visions and Strong Actions: Civil Society in the Philippines." In M. Ottaway and T. Carothers, eds., *Funding Virtue: Civil Society Aid and Democracy Promotion*. Washington, D.C.: Carnegie Endowment for International Peace. www.codengo.org/main.php3?action=displayarticle&articleid=67.

Reidinger, Jeffrey. 1999. "Caciques and Coups: The Challenges of Democratic Consolidation in the Philippines." In H. Handelman and M. Tessler, eds., *Democracy and Its Limits: Lessons from Asia, Latin America, and the Middle East*. Notre Dame, Ind.: University of Notre Dame Press.

Reyes, Ricardo B. 2001. "A People-Powered Entry to the New Millennium." *Human Rights Forum* 10(2) (Jan.-June): 12–36.

Rocamora, Joel. 1994. *Breaking Through: The Struggle Within the Communist Party of the Philippines*. Manila: Anvil.

Silliman, G. Sidney, and Lela Garner Noble. 1998. "Introduction." In G. S. Silliman and L. G. Noble, eds., *Organizing for Democracy: NGOs, Civil Society, and the Philippine State*. Quezon City: Ateneo de Manila University Press.

Teodoro, Luis. 2000. "The Government They Deserve," *Today*, Nov. 14, 9.

Thompson, Mark. 1995. *The Anti-Marcos Struggle: Personalistic Rule and Democratic Transition in the Philippines*. New Haven: Yale University Press.

Tiglao, Rigoberto. 1988. "The Consolidation of the Dictatorship." In A. Javate-De Dios et al., eds., *Dictatorship and Revolution: Roots of People Power*. Manila: Conspectus Foundation.

———. 2001. "Big Lesson of People Power 2." *Philippine Daily Inquirer*, Jan. 26, 9.

Villanueva, Pi. 1997. "The Influence of the Congress for a People's Agrarian Reform (CPAR) on the Legislative Process." In M. A. Wui and M. G. S. Lopez, eds., *State-Civil Society Relations in Policy-Making: Philippine Democracy Agenda*. Quezon City: Third World Studies Center.

Workshop Report of the Tripartite Dialogue on Agrarian Reform. 1988. Photocopy of proceedings. N.p.

World Bank. 2000. *World Bank Development Report, 2000/1: Attacking Poverty*. Oxford: Oxford University Press.

Wurfel, David. 1988. *Filipino Politics: Development and Decay*. Quezon City: Ateneo de Manila University Press.

———. 1998. "The Party-List Election: Sectoral Failure or National Success?" *Political Brief* 6(2) (Feb.): 1–5.

Zald, Mayer N., and John D. McCarthy. 1980. "Social Movement Industries: Competition and Cooperation Among Social Movement Organizations." *Research in Social Movements, Conflict and Change* 3: 1–20.

Zinn, Howard. 1995. *A People's History of the United States, 1492–Present*. New York: HarperPerennial.

CHAPTER FOUR

South Korea

Confrontational Legacy and Democratic Contributions

SUNHYUK KIM

Democracy in the Republic of Korea (South Korea) is both old and new. The republic commenced as a liberal democracy in 1948, three years after Korea's liberation from Japanese colonial rule. The required elements of liberal democracy—a constitution, three branches of government, universal suffrage, elections, political parties, interest groups, media, and so forth—all existed at the beginning of the republic. Yet the realities of South Korean politics during the subsequent four decades were far from liberal democracy, which long prevented most Korea-watchers from unreservedly placing South Korea in the category of "liberal democracy." Up to the mid-1980s, in fact, South Korea was not a democracy: The constitution was frequently amended to eliminate term limits for presidents; the executive—especially the presidency—routinely predominated over the legislature and the judiciary; elections were rarely free and fair; political parties were created and disbanded at the caprice of individual leaders; interest groups functioned primarily as quasi-governmental institutions; and the mass media were monitored and controlled by the state. Despite the procedural façade and official rhetoric, liberal democracy was nowhere to be found in South Korea during the four decades after the republic's inauguration.

It was only in the mid-1980s that the elements of liberal democracy began to assume new and real meanings. In June 1987, the ruling party chairman Roh Tae Woo proposed an eight-point democratization package that incorporated most of the demands of the opposition party and social movement groups. As a result, a number of significant changes have occurred in South Korean politics since 1987. Political contestation has become much fairer, visibly increasing opposition party candidates' chances of getting elected. Press censorship has been abandoned.

Restrictive labor laws have been overhauled. Many political prisoners and prisoners of conscience have been released. Overall, civil liberties have been significantly expanded. Civilian control over the military, which is integral to the survival and protection of liberal democracy, has also been considerably augmented. A military faction whose members had intruded in politics under earlier authoritarian regimes was dissolved. With increased fairness in political contestation, expanded civil liberties, and strengthened civilian control over the military, South Korea has accomplished its transition from authoritarian rule to democracy and is now one of the most prominent consolidating democracies in Asia.

What brought about democratization in South Korea—indisputably the most momentous political change in the postwar history of the country? Several explanations have been offered. Some analysts have highlighted the role of external factors—particularly the posture and policies of the United States—in facilitating South Korea's democratic transition. Others have argued that the democratic transition in 1987 was chiefly—if not entirely—driven by a series of elite calculations and interactions. But most scholars of South Korean democratization concur that the country's democratic transition was driven primarily by movements (Choi 2002). According to this explanation, it was principally groups in civil society that significantly facilitated, if not directly caused, various phases of democratization in Korea. (For an explication of civil society, see Chapter 1.) In particular, analysts have emphasized that student groups, labor unions, and religious organizations had waged intense prodemocracy struggles since the early 1970s (S. Kim 2000a, 2000c; Choi 1993a, 1993b, 2002; Song 1994; Sin 1995). United under the leadership of several national umbrella organizations, these civil society groups mobilized a formidable democratic alliance against the authoritarian regime in 1987.

Placed in comparative perspective, therefore, South Korea's democratic transition differed from certain cases in southern Europe and Latin America because conflicts, negotiations, and pacts among political elites were not the primary determinants of democratization. Rather, as in the cases of Taiwan and the Philippines, described in this volume, and some eastern European and African countries, it was civil society groups that initiated and directed the process of democratization by forming a prodemocracy alliance within civil society, creating a grand coalition with the opposition political party, and eventually pressuring the authoritarian regime to yield to the "popular upsurge" from below. An oppositional, resistant, and rebellious civil society was one of the most significant reasons behind the most prominent political change in South Korea's postwar history, namely, democratization.

An oppositional and highly militant civil society in South Korea has its origins in the resistance to Japanese colonial rule and the authoritarian system of government in the first four decades of the republic. South Korean civil society has comprised diverse organizations whose democratic visions significantly differ—progressive "people's movement" groups were in the forefront of the struggle for democracy during the transition, whereas more moderate "citizens' movement" groups and transformed (formerly progovernment) organizations emerged in the wake of the transition to play an increasingly active role in consolidating democracy, calling for political and economic reform. The alliance of oppositional civil society and dissident political society was crucial in ousting the authoritarian government of Chun Doo Hwan and initiating the new democratic era. In the politics of democratic consolidation too, civil society groups in South Korea are campaigning for the cleansing and remaking of the country's traditionally weak and underinstitutionalized political society. Meanwhile, civil society's relationship with the state is also undergoing substantive change from outright confrontation to issue-based cooperation and policy-oriented coordination.

The main focus of my analysis of South Korea in this chapter is the many crucial contributions civil society groups have made to South Korea's democratization—democratic transition and democratic consolidation. Since the civil society that promoted South Korea's democratization was both resistant and rebellious, I first examine the origins of oppositional civil society. After analyzing its contributions to democratization, I reflect on the legacies of the oppositional civil society and their impact on further consolidation and deepening of South Korean democracy.

Historical Origins

A highly oppositional civil society in South Korea originated in the period of Japanese colonialism from 1910 to 1945. One of the most consequential legacies of Japanese colonialism in Korea was the formation and consolidation of a mode of "conflictual engagement" between the state and civil society.[1] Japanese imperialism imposed a powerful colonial state on the Korean peninsula. The colonial government of Korea had unlimited power over legislative, judicial, administrative, and military affairs, subject only to directions from the Japanese metropole, and was stronger and far better organized than the indigenous precolonial monarchy had been.

At the same time, Japanese imperialism gave rise to a highly resistant, militant, and oppositional civil society. The influx of Japanese capital brought about significant changes in the class composition of Korea. Whereas domestic capitalists and landlords were weakened and marginalized, the working and peasant classes increased in numbers. In the mid-1920s, strengthened labor and peasant classes successfully organized several national organizations, such as the Korean Federation of Workers and the Korean Federation of Peasants. Through these national associations, Korean workers and peasants waged not only their class struggles for workers' and peasants' rights but also a nationalist independence struggle against

Japanese imperialism. Mostly outlawed, these underground revolutionary labor and peasant unions symbolized the Korean people's untiring battle against Japanese colonialism. Due to the extensive network of police and security forces, however, as well as the collaboration of pro-Japanese groups of Koreans, the Japanese colonial state was to a large extent able to suppress the rebellious civil society during the colonial period.

Following Japan's surrender in August 1945, the Japanese colonial state in Korea rapidly unraveled. Japanese authorities transferred power to Yo Un Hyong, a centrist with close ties to leftists. Yo organized the Preparatory Committee for Establishing a New State (Konjun) to replace the Japanese state apparatus. Within two weeks, the Preparatory Committee had established 145 local offices. On September 8, 1945, it inaugurated the People's Republic of Korea (In'gong) and existing local offices were converted into people's committees (Inmin Wiwonhoe), which were quite effective in ensuring order, security, and the food supply (Choi 1993a: 157–58).[2]

In creating various organizations to replace the colonial state structures, the Preparatory Committee for Establishing a New State recognized and accommodated the explosive expansion of Korean civil society at the time. The expansion of civil society was most pronounced in the unprecedented proliferation of labor and peasant organizations. After a long period of suppression under Japanese colonialism, during which unions were completely outlawed, laborers and peasants vigorously formed their organizations. Moreover, numerous social groups representing youth, students, women, cultural activities, and religious sects were also created.

Communists played an instrumental role in the emergence and proliferation of these various social organizations. Korean communists, who had led a number of illegal and underground struggles against Japanese imperialism in and out of prison during the colonial period, reestablished the Korean Communist Party (Choson Kongsandang) on September 11, 1945. Capitalizing on the spontaneous grassroots activism of laborers and peasants, the Korean Communist Party helped organize the National Council of Labor Unions (Chonp'yong) and the National Federation of Peasant Unions (Chonnong) in late 1945. The Korean Communist Party also took the initiative in organizing the Korean Democratic Youth Federation (Minch'ong), the National Women's Union (Puch'ong), the Communist Youth Federation (Kongch'ong), the Writers' Alliance (Munhakka Tongmaeng), and the Scientists' Alliance (Kwahakcha Tongmaeng). By February 15, 1946, the number of diverse social organizations had reached thirty-five (Yang 1990: 86).

Yet these civil society groups were not entirely under the influence and control of communists. Such groups during this period were characterized by their high degree of functionality and autonomy. What might be called an "associational explosion" was already under way, and the communists simply took advantage of the popular demand for organization and representation. Largely in reaction to these "procommunist" organizations, rightist elements in civil society (which in many cases had also been pro-Japanese during the colonial period) organized their own groups, such as the Korean Patriotic Women's Association (Han'guk Aeguk Puinhoe), the Korean Youth Association (Taehan Ch'ongnyondan), and the Women's Alliance for Independence (Kon'guk Punyo Tongmaeng). As a result, Korea in the aftermath of its liberation witnessed two sharply opposing trends—aggressive proliferation and expansion of bottom-up "leftist" organizations, on the one hand, and reactive but expeditious construction of top-down rightist organizations, on the other. Overall, Korean civil society immediately after national independence in August 1945 was dominated by the former trend.

The arrival of the U.S. Army Military Government in Korea (Migunjong) in September 1945, however, ended the dominance of the bottom-up organizations and dramatically transformed Korea's political landscape. Alarmed by the close connection between diverse civil society groups and communists in Korea, the U.S. Military Government decided to stem the explosion of civil society. The newly created groups in civil society were systematically suppressed and depoliticized. On October 10, the U.S. Military Government completely denied the status of the People's Republic of Korea, and it subsequently promulgated laws prohibiting labor and peasant movements. It also forcibly dismantled grassroots organizations in both cities and the countryside. Groups in civil society, led by the National Council of Labor Unions and the National Federation of Peasant Unions, responded to the oppressive policies of the U.S. Military Government with violent strikes and demonstrations. Despite these protests, the U.S. Military Government continued its Cold War policies by disbanding leftist parties, closing and suspending leftist newspapers, and imprisoning leftist leaders. At the same time, it encouraged formerly pro-Japanese and rightist elements in Korean society to organize a range of social organizations. Rightists swiftly rallied around the flag of anticommunism and anti-Sovietism raised by the U.S. Military Government (Choi 1993a; W. Kim 1996).

When the Republic of Korea (South Korea) was officially inaugurated in August 1948, therefore, its predetermined regime type was liberal democracy. Civil society groups that had emerged in the immediate aftermath of Korea's liberation were considered a threat to the new liberal democracy and were either disbanded or forced underground. The National Security Law (Kukka Poanbop), passed shortly after the inauguration of the republic, was frequently used to suppress antigovernment civil society groups. Indeed, the measure defined sedition so broadly and vaguely that the law could easily be used as a political tool by the authorities to suppress virtually any kind of opposition (Eckert et al. 1990: 348). But as the gap between the official "liberal democracy" and the authoritarian realities of South Korean politics was beginning to widen toward the late 1950s, the country's highly militant and oppositional civil society reemerged as the spearhead of a protracted and intensive prodemocracy movement.

Civil Society and Democratic Transition

There have been three "democratic junctures" (periods in which an authoritarian regime collapses and a transition to democracy occurs or could have occurred but for a military coup) in the history of South Korea since 1948: 1956 to 1961, 1973 to 1980, and 1984 to 1987. In South Korea's three democratic junctures, diverse groups in civil society—particularly student groups, labor unions, and faith-based organizations—contributed to authoritarian breakdown and democratic transition. In the first democratic juncture (1956–61), students and urban intellectuals revolted against the repression and corruption of Syngman Rhee's authoritarian regime. Subsequently, during the phase of democratic transition under Chang Myon, student groups aligned with progressive opposition parties in their campaigns for democracy, self-assertive diplomacy, and reunification. In the second democratic juncture (1973–80), numerous national associations of dissident intellectuals, journalists, professionals, and religious leaders played an important role in galvanizing the anti-Yusin movement against Park Chung Hee's authoritarian regime (Yusin, which literally means "revitalizing reform," was the name of the highly authoritarian political system Park installed in October 1972). These national associations, called Chaeya, formed a prodemocracy coalition with the opposition New Democratic Party (Sinmindang) and waged intense prodemocracy struggles that generated a fatal split between hard-liners and soft-liners within the ruling bloc and ultimately brought about an implosion of the authoritarian regime. In the third democratic juncture (1984–87), the prodemocracy alliance of civil society incorporated the threefold solidarity of students, workers, and churches and furthermore encompassed the middle class. Civil society groups were effectively united and led by national associations that consisted of numerous sectoral and regional organizations, and civil groups also coordinated with the opposition party through numerous joint organizations. Over the three democratic junctures, the scope, power, and mobilization of civil society groups expanded considerably, and the concerted efforts of these groups and the opposition party pressured the ruling authoritarian regime to concede to the popular demand for democratization (S. Kim 1996, 2000a). In this section I want to focus on the third democratic juncture and probe how civil society contributed to the latest democratic transition in South Korea.

Severe state repression of civil society characterized the first four years (1980–83) of the Chun Doo Hwan regime. Following the multiphased coup and the subsequent violent suppression of the prodemocracy movement in Kwangju in May 1980, the authoritarian regime carried out a series of coercive campaigns to "cleanse" (*chonghwa*) the entire society by arresting thousands of public officials, politicians, professors, teachers, pastors, journalists, and students on various charges of corruption, instigation of antigovernment demonstrations, and attempted insurrection. Meanwhile a legislature pro tempore, called the Legislative Council for National Security (Kukpowi), passed numerous antidemocratic laws curtailing political competition, restricting basic democratic freedoms, establishing an elaborate system of press censorship, and suppressing the labor movement.

Starting in late 1983, however, Chun's suppression of civil society abated significantly. The authoritarian regime decided to liberalize the polity by allowing antigovernment university professors and students to return to their schools, withdrawing the military police from university campuses, pardoning or rehabilitating political prisoners, and lifting the ban on political activities of hundreds of former politicians. What the government intended through these liberalization measures was to make the ruling Democratic Justice Party popular and therefore electorally competitive. Contrary to what the authoritarian regime expected, however, the consequence of the liberalization was a "resurrection of civil society" (O'Donnell and Schmitter 1986: 48–56). Various groups in South Korean civil society, particularly the movements that had been decimated by the authoritarian regime's severe repression between 1980 and 1983, were rapidly resurrected.

In February and March of 1984, for example, students who had just returned to their campuses reorganized antigovernment groups. In November 1984, students from forty-two universities and colleges organized the National Student Coalition for Prodemocracy Struggle (Chonhangnyon)—the first nationwide student organization since the student uprising of April 1960. As in the cases of Myanmar and Indonesia, discussed in this volume, university students played a crucial role in initiating a prodemocracy movement against the authoritarian regime.

Moreover, the Korean Council for Labor Welfare (Han'guk Nohyop) was organized in March 1984. Composed of various labor unions that had spearheaded anti-Yusin prodemocracy struggles in the 1970s, the Korean Council for Labor Welfare tried to strengthen unity and solidarity among labor movement groups. In April 1984, the Chonggye apparel labor union, which had been prominent in the labor movement of the 1970s but was dissolved by the authoritarian regime in 1981, was also restored. The Korean Council for Labor Welfare and Chonggye jointly launched a massive campaign against the arbitrary labor laws enacted by the Legislative Council for National Security. The old student-labor alliance was resurrected, and students actively supported the restored labor unions. Church groups such as the National Catholic Priests' Corps for the Realization of Justice (K'atollik Chongui Kuhyon Chon'guk Sajedan) also assisted the labor movement by waging a petition campaign for the revision of objectionable labor laws.

Above all, the resurrected student groups, youth organizations, labor unions, religious organizations, and other civil society groups were coordinated under the unified leadership of a national umbrella organization, the People's Movement Coalition for Democracy and Reunification (Mint'ongryon). This coalition, established in March 1985, encompassed not only urban labor, landless peasants, and leading intellectuals but also most of the country's Buddhist, Protestant, and Roman Catholic clergy and lay groups (Harrison 1987). Unlike numerous national movement associations during the 1970s, this organization was not just a group of dissident dignitaries but was quite reflective of the alliance of students, laborers, and religious leaders.

As various prodemocracy movement groups were being resurrected in civil society, a genuine opposition reemerged in political society.[3] Between 1980 and 1983, there was no real opposition in South Korean politics. Opposition parties like the Democratic Korea Party (Minhandang) and Korean Nationalist Party (Kungmindang), created and controlled by the authoritarian regime, had been unwilling to challenge the regime's political legitimacy. What the authoritarian regime had in mind in implementing a series of liberalization measures in 1983–84 was further fragmentation of the opposition. Contrary to the regime's intent, however, the liberalization resulted in the dramatic expansion of a real opposition. Many of the reinstated opposition politicians formed the New Korea Democratic Party (NKDP; Sinhan Minjudang) in January 1985, immediately before the National Assembly elections in February.

The politics of authoritarian breakdown and democratic transition began in earnest with the formation of the NKDP and its electoral alignment with civil society groups. Many of these groups, particularly youth and student organizations, openly supported and vigorously campaigned for the NKDP—the first time since the early 1960s that university students supported a particular political party. The turnout in the National Assembly elections on February 12, 1985, was 85 percent, the highest since the 1950s. The NKDP emerged as the leading opposition party, unexpectedly winning 29 percent of the votes, compared to 35 percent for the ruling Democratic Justice Party. After the elections, the strategy of the civil society groups and the NKDP was to focus on the most important political issue: the legitimacy question (Cotton 1989: 251). The coalition between civil society groups and the opposition NKDP outlived the National Assembly elections and later developed into a grand democracy coalition against the authoritarian regime.

The prodemocracy movement in South Korea during 1986–87 took three different forms. First, starting in early 1986, religious activists issued a series of declarations reprimanding the authoritarian regime and demanding an immediate constitutional revision. Protestant pastors argued in a statement of March 1986, for instance, that a new constitution that would provide for direct presidential elections and address basic human rights and economic equality should be drafted immediately—and that the next government should be elected according to the new constitution. Cardinal Kim Su Hwan declared in early March 1986 that "democratization is the best way to make peace with God. The sooner the constitutional revision, the better" (KCSRC 1986: 40). Moreover, beginning with a statement at Korea University on March 28, 1986, some 783 professors at twenty-nine colleges and universities nationwide publicly announced "Statements on the Current Situation" (Siguk sonon), a peaceful nonconfidence campaign against the authoritarian regime.

Second, the opposition NKDP launched a popular campaign to collect ten million signatures nationwide in support of constitutional revision. This number—ten million—represented almost half of the electorate and a quarter of the entire population of South Korea at the time. The campaign started on February 12, 1986, the first anniversary of the 1985 National Assembly elections, and rapidly spread across the country. The size and ferocity of the petition drive astonished the authoritarian regime (Nam 1989: 302). The police carried out a series of harsh crackdowns on the campaign, raiding NKDP headquarters and the offices of civil society groups and arresting numerous activists. But the regime could not stem the tide.

And third, concurrently with the petition campaign, civil society groups and the NKDP jointly sponsored a number of mass rallies in support of democratization. The People's Movement Coalition for Democracy and Reunification and the NKDP set up the National Coalition for Democracy Movement (Min'gungnyon) and coordinated, organized, mobilized, and led mass rallies in major cities of the country—Kwangju on March 30, Taegu on April 5, Taejon on April 19, Chongju on April 4, Inch'on on May 3, Masan on May 10, and Chonju on May 31. International diffusion of the democracy movement was evident as well, because civil society groups and the opposition party were particularly encouraged by the February revolution in the Philippines in which the Marcos regime was at last expelled by "people's power." In Korea, the number of participants in the mass rallies exceeded 700,000 in total. Such a level of mass mobilization, except during election campaigns, was the highest since the April uprising of 1960. The grand democracy coalition of civil society groups and the opposition party succeeded in mobilizing South Koreans from all walks of life—students, workers, peasants, urban service industry employees, religious leaders, and other citizens—behind the slogan "Down with the Military Authoritarian Regime and up with a Democratic Government."

Two events were singularly instrumental in bolstering the power of the prodemocracy coalition and maintaining the high level of mass mobilization. First, at the dawn of 1987, Pak Chong Ch'ol, a Seoul National University student, was tortured to death during a police interrogation. Initially, the police announced that Pak had died of a heart attack. On May 18, however, the National Catholic Priests' Corps for the Realization of Justice disclosed that Pak had died under torture and that the police and the regime had attempted to conceal the fact. Pak Chong Ch'ol's murder and the revelation of the regime's conspiracy to cover up the crime put the authoritarian regime and the ruling party on the defensive and dramatically augmented the position and power of the prodemocracy coalition.

Second, Chun Doo Hwan declared on April 13, 1987, that he could no longer tolerate discussion of constitutional revision. This unilateral decision to terminate the public discourse on constitutional revision intensified mass mobilization. University professors initiated a public statement campaign challenging Chun's decision. Artists, writers, and actors followed suit. Religious leaders and priests waged a series of hunger strikes. Cardinal Kim Su Hwan and many religious organizations, including the National Catholic Priests' Corps for the Realization of Justice, the National Council of Protestant Pastors for Justice and Peace, and the Korean Christian Council (Han'guk Kidokkyo Hyobuihoe), also expressed their strong opposition to Chun's decision. Violent antigovernment protests by students and labor unions and other civil society groups spread across the country, and tens of thousands of South Koreans in major cities demonstrated against the decision.

In May 1987, civil society groups established the National Movement Headquarters for a Democratic Constitution (Kungmin Undong Ponbu). This organization, consisting of the People's Movement Coalition for Democracy and Reunification and twenty-five other major groups, covered all the major sectors and regions. Organizing local branches throughout the country, the National Movement Headquarters mobilized a series of massive prodemocracy demonstrations against the authoritarian regime in June 1987. The mobilization escalated particularly after Yi Han Yol, a Yonsei University student, was hit by tear gas bomb fragments on June 9 and injured critically. On June 10, the National Movement Headquarters organized an "Uprising to Defeat the April 13 Decision and End Dictatorship." On June 26, it held a "peace parade" in which one million people participated nationwide. Not only the prodemocracy movement groups but also many middle-class citizens joined in these mass rallies. Pak Chong Ch'ol's murder and Yi Han Yol's injury (and subsequent death) particularly angered middle-class citizens, because these two incidents vividly demonstrated the illegitimate, violent, and repressive nature of the authoritarian regime. Just like the deaths of the high school student Kim Chu Yol in 1960 and of a female labor striker, Kim Kyong Suk, in 1979, the deaths of Pak Chong Ch'ol and Yi Han Yol brought to the minds of ordinary citizens the image of "democratic martyr," a recurrent theme in the checkered history of South Korean democratization.

Finally, on June 29, 1987, cornered by the unprecedented mass mobilization, the authoritarian regime announced dramatic and unexpected concessions to the demands of civil society groups and the opposition party, adopting a direct presidential election system. As was the case in Taiwan and the Philippines, also discussed in this volume, diverse civil society organizations in South Korea played a crucial role in compelling the authoritarian regime to accept a transition to democracy.

Civil Society and Democratic Consolidation

The latest democratic transition in South Korea represents an excellent example of what is called a "mass-ascendant" mode of democratization (Karl 1990). What is even more distinctive about the case of South Korea is that civil society groups continue to play important roles in the politics of democratic consolidation. Since 1988 they have pressured Korean governments to launch various democratic changes. For example, civil society groups have persistently demanded the prosecution and punishment of those involved in past military coups, repression of the prodemocracy movement, and corruption scandals—culminating in 1996 with the high-profile imprisonment of two former generals-turned-president, Chun Doo Hwan and Roh Tae Woo. (For details, see S. Kim 2000a: chap. 6.) Civil society's push toward a clear break with the country's authoritarian past contributed considerably to making democracy the only game in town in Korea. Studies of democratic transition and consolidation generally agree that civil society, if it plays any role at all in democratic transition, is rapidly demobilized after the transition and significantly marginalized in the politics of democratic consolidation (Fish 1994: 34). As the political arena becomes more institutionalized and the fledgling democracy more consolidated, the locus and focus of politics incrementally but significantly shift to political society. South Korea's democratization has resisted this general trajectory. In this section, focusing on the activism of civil society during the Kim Dae Jung government (1998–2003), I analyze the contributions of civil society to the ongoing consolidation of democracy in South Korea.

One of the most notable trends in South Korean civil society since 1988 has been the proliferation of new "citizens' movement groups" (*simin undong tanch'e*). United nationally under the Korean Council of Citizens' Movements (Han'guk Simin Tanch'e Hyobuihoe), prominent examples include the Citizens' Coalition for Economic Justice (CCEJ; Kyongje Chongui Silch'on Simin Yonhap) and the Korean Federation of Environmental Movements (KFEM; Han'guk Hwan'gyong Undong Yonhap). The Korean Council of Citizens' Movements was created on September 12, 1994, by thirty-eight citizens' groups. Initially, the membership encompassed a wide variety of social groups: religious groups (Buddhist, Protestant, Tonghak, Won Buddhist), environmental organizations (KFEM, church-environmental institutes, green associations), women's groups, the consumer movement, the reunification movement, the movement for educational reform, and organizations for the handicapped. Leading members of the Korean Council of Citizens' Movements, particularly CCEJ and KFEM, had consistently emphasized that they would lead a new generation of social activism in Korea, different from the class-based and confrontational campaigns of the past. The formation of the Korean Council of Citizens' Movements constituted an official proclamation of the dawn at last of this new era.

The people's movement groups (*minjung undong tanch'e*), which played a crucial role in the authoritarian breakdown and democratic transition of 1987, have been striving to find a new identity in the politics of democratic consolidation. Many people's movement groups, however, such as the Korean Coalition for National Democracy Movement (1989) and its 1992 successor, the National Alliance for Democracy and Unification of Korea (Chon'guk Yonhap), have been far less influential in South Korean politics. Some people's movement groups decided to distance themselves from their old image as activists who almost reflexively castigated the ruling regime and criticized the status quo. Groups such as the Korean Trade Union Council, the Korean Teachers' and Educational Workers' Union, and the Korean Peasant Movement Coalition, whose leaders spearheaded the prodemocracy movement in 1987, announced that they would abandon their militant style of the past and adopt a softer style, promoting public policy debates and waging peaceful campaigns instead of violent demonstrations. Other groups are leaving the people's movement camp altogether and trying to repackage themselves as part of the citizens' movement.

There is one civil society group that has uniquely tried to bridge the gap between the citizens' movement groups and the people's movement groups. This organization, People's Solidarity for Participatory Democracy (PSPD; Ch'amyo Minju Sahoe Simin Yondae), has received much public and media attention since the economic crisis of 1997. Established on September 10, 1994, by approximately two hundred young professionals (such as professors, lawyers, and doctors), PSPD has tried to combine the old and new groups in a unified "progressive citizens' movement" (*Han'gyore 21*, September 15, 1994). Since its inauguration, it has consistently worked to remedy the bifurcation that has left Korean civil society in two separate, and to some degree competing, camps. Owing partly to the efforts of PSPD, citizens' movement groups and people's movement groups cooperated, for example, in the movement for the prosecution and imprisonment of the two former presidents in 1994 and 1995.

The activities of civil society groups during the Kim Dae Jung government focused primarily on various campaigns for social reform. Considering the past activism of civil society in effecting political change in South Korea, the fact that civil groups campaign for social reform is hardly new. The breadth and vigor of the movement, however, are notable. Civil society groups aimed at a complete transformation of South Korean society, concurrently calling for political, economic, and media reforms. In pushing for these various measures, civil society groups have also tried to present viable policy alternatives, thereby forging a constructive engagement with the state. Above all, civil society groups have monitored the performance of legislators and demanded the restructuring of the political system. Political reform has been a catchword since the inauguration of the Kim Dae Jung government. Yet political parties have repeatedly failed to arrive at a viable consensus and have therefore delayed implementation of comprehensive political reforms. Civil society groups, by contrast, spearheaded a movement to reform political society as a whole and render politicians more accountable.

Moreover, civil society groups have demanded a complete economic restructuring. From the outset, the Kim Dae Jung government knew that its survival would depend principally on the success or failure of its economic programs. This is why the regime was so serious about financial, enterprise, and labor reforms. Of these various economic measures, enterprise reform—in particular, reform of *chaebol,* South Korea's big family-owned business conglomerates—is considered vital because they are believed to have contributed to the economic crisis by overborrowing and misinvesting bank loans guaranteed by the government. In this respect, civil society groups like PSPD and CCEJ have devoted their main energy to economic reform campaigns, underscoring the urgency of a comprehensive *chaebol* reform. Indeed, PSPD is leading a movement for the right of minority stockholders to hold the owner families and the management of *chaebol* groups accountable. Civil society groups also successfully pressured the ruling parties to initiate National Assembly hearings to investigate the causes of the economic crisis, summoning public officials of the previous Kim Young Sam government as witnesses.

Lastly, civil society groups like Citizens' Solidarity for Media Reform (On'gaeryon) are actively addressing the long-overdue media reform. Since the democratic transition of 1987, the mass media in South Korea have become extremely powerful, and they now constitute what is called the fourth branch of government. Augmented by the largely Confucian South Korean political culture, in which reputation is exceptionally important, the mass media have grown—or even overgrown—into a potent institution, swaying public opinion, influencing politicians and bureaucrats, and amassing vast wealth. Citizens' Solidarity for Media Reform, composed of journalists' labor unions, reporters' clubs, citizens' movement organizations, and academics, is working vigorously to establish a citizens' network to monitor the mass media and protect ordinary people from the media's misuse of power.

Under the Kim Dae Jung government, civil society organizations in South Korea have focused primarily on two movements for political reform. The first is a campaign to monitor the National Assembly's inspection of government offices (*kukchong kamsa*). The second is the Nakch'on/Nakson movement to prevent the election of unfit or disqualified candidates in the 2000 National Assembly elections.

Monitoring the National Assembly's Inspection Process

On September 8, 1999, forty civil society groups, including CCEJ, PSPD, and KFEM, created Citizens' Solidarity for Monitoring the National Assembly Inspection of Government Offices (CSMNAIGO; Kukchong Kamsa Monito Simin Yondae). This organization set two main goals for the monitoring campaign. The first goal was to record the attendance of individual lawmakers in various committees and to evaluate their performance. Civil society groups tried to enhance fairness and objectivity in this process by agreeing in advance on a set of basic criteria for evaluation (*Han'gyore sinmun*, September 28, 1999).

As for the second goal, the participating groups of CSMNAIGO also agreed in advance on a list of 166 crucial "reform tasks" and decided to monitor whether these tasks were addressed adequately in committee (*Han'gyore sinmun*, September 6, 1999). The reform tasks included, for example, devising policy measures to end corruption in private schools and to deal with problems resulting from expanded implementation of the national pension system (*Han'gyore sinmun*, September 17, 1999). KFEM also planned to raise, in the Construction and Transportation Committee, issues related to the removal of green belts, environment-unfriendly land planning, dam construction, and drinking water policies (*Han'gyore sinmun*, September 14, 1999). Those charged with monitoring were civil society activists, lawyers, professors, and accountants who had been involved in their areas of expertise for years and were knowledgeable about policy, which considerably increased CSMNAIGO's credibility (*Han'gyore sinmun*, September 17, 1999). CSMNAIGO ran a website (www.ngokorea.org), and its activities were favorably covered by newspapers.

The National Assembly's inspection of 352 government offices officially began on September 28, 1999. In response to a vigorous civil campaign to monitor committee activities, however, some committees decided not to admit monitors to their sessions. The Unification and International Relations and Trade Committee, the National Defense Committee, and the Construction and Transportation Committee, for example, all prohibited CSMNAIGO attendance, claiming that monitoring activities might disturb the meetings, and that in any case, the rooms would be too small to accommodate all the monitors (*Han'gyore sinmun*, September 29, 1999). The Public Health and Welfare Committee similarly decided not to admit CSMNAIGO workers, arguing that evaluations by civil society groups lacking professional knowledge of policy matters would undermine the National Assembly's investigation. The Finance and Economy Committee followed suit (*Han'gyore sinmun*, October 1, 1999). But the real reason behind these decisions to block the monitoring campaign was that most committee members were afraid that CSMNAIGO's critical evaluation of lawmakers would damage their reputations back home and reduce their chances of reelection.

Decisions by a number of National Assembly committees to obstruct the CSMNAIGO monitoring campaign led to a direct confrontation between civil society groups and legislators. CSMNAIGO organized street demonstrations in front of the government ministries and waged phone, fax, and e-mail campaigns to protest the decision to block monitoring (*Han'gyore sinmun*, October 3, 1999). On October 11, 1999, CSMNAIGO sent a questionnaire to all nine standing committees of the National Assembly asking lawmakers to clarify their position on whether to allow CSMNAIGO workers to monitor their sessions. At the conclusion of their campaign, on October 20, 1999, CSMNAIGO released a report ranking the legislators in terms of performance—along with stinging criticism of the National Assembly committees that barred CSMNAIGO monitoring activities (*Han'gyore sinmun*, October 20, 1999). Overall, because of the resistance of major standing committees, CSMNAIGO's monitoring campaign proved only partially successful. Throughout the monitoring campaign, civil society groups were frustrated by the politicians' lack of cooperation—which provided a primary motive for the Nakch'on/Nakson campaign in the National Assembly elections of April 2000.

The Nakch'on/Nakson Campaign

One of the goals of civil society groups since the democratic transition in 1987 has been to increase the overall fairness of elections (S. Kim 2000a: 120). Led by the Citizens' Council for Fair Elections (Kongmyong Son'go Silch'on Simin Undong Hyobuihoe), the movement has contributed significantly to changing the election climate (*son'go p'ungt'o*) in Korea. At the same time, however, civil society groups began to realize that guaranteeing fair elections would not really change the fundamental psychology of Korean politicians. Hence they decided to switch to a new strategy of endorsing specific policies and candidates during elections. Many civil society groups were frustrated in late 1999 when National Assembly committees refused to cooperate with CSMNAIGO in order to protect their vested interests. These groups concluded that for any legislative monitoring to be effective, a campaign must be waged during elections and focus on affecting their actual outcome (*Sin Tonga*, March 2000).

On January 13, 2000, about three months before the National Assembly elections, 412 civil society groups, including PSPD and KFEM, established Citizens' Solidarity for the General Elections (CSGE; Ch'ongson Simin Yondae). At its inauguration, this organization envisioned two different stages of its campaign. The first was to create a list of politicians who should not be nominated by political parties to run for the National Assembly and then to campaign against their nomination (the Nakch'on movement). Second, if some of these blacklisted candidates were nominated anyway, the organization would campaign against them in the elections (the Nakson movement) (*Choson ilbo*, January 25, 2000).

From the very beginning of the campaign, there were mixed signals from the Kim Dae Jung government. On the one hand, Kim Dae Jung himself seemed sympathetic to the movement. He ordered the repeal of Article 87 of the election laws, which prohibited the intervention of civil society groups in elections.[4] On the other hand, the National Election Commission determined, on January 18, 2000, that CSGE's release of the list of "unfit" candidates was illegal and would violate Article 87.[5] Taking the latter signal from Kim Dae Jung more seriously, CSGE decided to go ahead with the Nakch'on/Nakson campaign in a movement it characterized as civil disobedience (*Choson ilbo*, January 19, 2000).

On January 24, 2000, CSGE disclosed a list of sixty-six politicians who should not be nominated as candidates for the National Assembly in April. The selection criteria included involvement in bribery and corruption scandals, violation of election laws, lack of legislative activity (too many absences in National Assembly sessions, for example), undermining of constitutional order (cooperation with Chun Doo Hwan's authoritarian regime in the early 1980s, for instance, or involvement in military coups), failure or refusal to sign anticorruption laws, instigation of regionalism, and more.[6] Reactions to this list varied greatly: the ruling National Congress for New Politics was supportive; the opposition Grand National Party (GNP) was ambivalent; the United Liberal Democrats (ULD), a partner in the ruling coalition, was enraged by the list's inclusion of its leader, Kim Jong Pil (*Choson ilbo*, January 25, 2000). Several days later, both the GNP and the ULD alleged that there had been collusion between the Kim Dae Jung government and the participating groups of CSGE, pointing to the fact that many civil leaders had joined the ruling party and even received financial support from the government. An intense debate erupted between CSGE and the two opposition parties on the question of collusion between civil society and the government (*Choson ilbo*, February 4, 2000).[7] According to polls taken at the time, the public was more sympathetic to CSGE. In a survey taken in late February 2000, some 54 percent of the respondents believed that civil society groups were more credible than the politicians in the two opposition parties who alleged collaboration between the ruling party and CSGE (*Han'gyore 21*, February 24, 2000).

On January 24, 2000, too, various faith-based groups, including Episcopal, Catholic, Protestant, and Buddhist organizations, openly expressed their support for CSGE's Nakch'on/Nakson campaign, stating that they completely endorsed the movement's aim to expel corrupt politicians from the political arena and restore the people's right of political participation (*Han'guk kyongje sinmun*, January 24, 2000). Furthermore, on January 28, some 232 members of Lawyers for a Democratic Society (Minbyon) created a support team to give legal advice to CSGE's campaign. Participating lawyers said that the main goal of the Nakch'on/Nakson campaign was to protect the people's constitutional right of political participation (*Choson ilbo*, January 29, 2000).

On February 9, 2000, revised election laws were passed in the National Assembly. Article 87 was amended to allow civil society groups to engage in election activities (either opposing or supporting candidates) on the Internet or at press conferences. Holding mass gatherings or waging petition campaigns remained illegal, however, as was the announcement of a list of "unfit" or "disqualified" candidates before the election campaign (it would be legal only during the sixteen days between the final day for candidacy registration and election day) (*Choson ilbo*, February 10, 2000). Within CSGE, there was heated discussion on whether to comply with the new election laws or continue their civil disobedience. Ultimately,

CSGE decided to pursue its Nakch'on/Nakson campaign within the time frame permitted by the new election laws—that is, announcing the list of unfit candidates on April 3 during the legal election campaign period.

CSGE's initial list of unfit politicians, released on January 24, did not entirely prevent political parties from nominating these problematic politicians. After parties made their nominations, CSGE filed several lawsuits to annul or suspend nominations; these lawsuits were later rejected by the Seoul district court on the grounds that voters have no legal interest in the nomination process of political parties. The court argued that, if necessary, voters should express their political preferences through votes, not by intervening in the nomination process (*Han'gyore sinmun*, March 10, 2000). On April 3, CSGE announced the final Nakson list of eighty-six unfit candidates. This list included sixty-four candidates who had been on the original Nakch'on list but were nevertheless nominated by parties, along with twenty-two more candidates selected according to the criteria of anti–human rights background, tax evasion, inappropriate remarks and behavior in the National Assembly, and the like. CSGE focused particularly on twenty-two candidates and announced that it would carry out individual Nakson campaigns in local electoral districts (*Choson ilbo*, April 4, 2000). After the announcement of the final Nakson list, on April 5–6, 2000, there were physical confrontations between CSGE activists and supporters of the involved candidates at several campaign sites. CSGE announced that it would consistently adhere to the principles of nonviolence and nonresistance in response to the violent actions of National Election Commission officials and supporters of candidates (*Choson ilbo*, April 7, 2000).

CSGE and its Nakch'on/Nakson campaign were covered sympathetically in the news media and well received by the public. Most of the newspapers closely followed CSGE's activities and the political developments surrounding them. In a survey of a sample of 1,000 people nationwide on March 8, 2000, some 59 percent of the respondents said they would not support candidates who were on CSGE's list, 67 percent agreed that those who incited regionalism should be on the list, and 57 percent believed that the criteria for selecting unfit candidates had been fair (*Han'gyore sinmun*, March 14, 2000). In another survey of 2,200 people conducted by *Han'gyore 21*, some 80 percent of the respondents thought CSGE's list of unfit candidates should be followed (*Han'gyore 21*, February 24, 2000). In a live Internet poll of "netizens," 78 percent of the respondents replied that they would not vote for candidates on CSGE's list, and 88 percent supported the inclusion of Kim Jong Pil—leader of United Liberal Democrats and a conservative politician who had staged a military coup and established the Korean Central Intelligence Agency in the early 1960s—on the list (*Han'gyore sinmun*, January 25, 2000).

In the National Assembly elections on April 13, 2000, fifty-nine out of eighty-six candidates listed by CSGE failed to be elected. In a ceremony one week after the elections, CSGE judged that its Nakch'on/Nakson campaign, in which 975 civil society groups and 1,000 activists had participated in one way or another, had contributed significantly to the increase of voters' political consciousness and efficacy, to the emergence of a new generation of young politicians, and to the partial revision of election laws. Scholars and political analysts in Korea generally acclaimed CSGE's Nakch'on/Nakson campaign as the first of its kind in Korean history. One political scientist characterized the movement as a serious "conflict between civil society and political society" (*Choson ilbo*, April 21, 2000). Another argued that civil society groups were an important force in the "imaginary political space" (*kasang chongch'i konggan*) between the old political order, characterized by military dictatorship and the *chaebol* economy, and the slowly emerging new political order (Chong 2000: 61).

The Nakch'on/Nakson campaign achieved several notable things. First, the movement demonstrated the great potential of civil society in effecting changes in political society. It provided strong testimony that civil society is critical not only in bringing down an authoritarian regime and ushering in a democratic government but also in enhancing the quality of democracy by promoting the exit of incompetent and immoral politicians from the political arena. Second, the movement helped create alliances among civil society groups: more than 900 organizations and 1,000 citizens participated actively in the campaign under the leadership of CSGE (*Choson ilbo*, April 21, 2000). And third, the Nakch'on/Nakson campaign greatly increased the sense of political efficacy and reduced the sense of political apathy, particularly among young people in their twenties and thirties (*Han'gyore 21*, April 20, 2000).

But CSGE's Nakch'on/Nakson campaign also revealed a number of weaknesses. First, the movement was in large part a negative campaign against those who should not be elected rather than a positive campaign for those who should. It underscored what Korean voters had to do to avoid further deterioration of their political society but failed to present an alternative vision of a better political society. Second, the movement was led primarily by the citizens' movement—one of the two main camps in the consolidational politics of Korean democracy—to the exclusion of the people's movement. As clearly indicated by CSGE's decision to abide by the new election laws, the participating organizations of CSGE, in their efforts to appear moderate to the news media, consciously tried to distance themselves from the radical image of the people's movement groups that spearheaded the campaign for democratization in the 1980s. As a result, CSGE's Nakch'on/Nakson campaign failed to develop alliances with labor unions, peasant groups, and other people's movement groups. In this respect, CSGE is reminiscent of the Chaeya movement of the 1970s, headed by a number of intellectuals and religious dignitaries who were united through their personal networks and commitments (Chu 2000: 110–11). And third, CSGE's campaign was unable to overcome regionalism. The movement was most effective in Seoul and its vicinity; in other regions where regionalism was strong (as in Yongnam or Honam), the Nakch'on/Nakson campaign was not very successful. Although the public was generally supportive of the movement's goals, most people actually voted according to their regional allegiance. Clearly, there are certain limits to civil society's power to reform political society.

In addition to these various movements for political reform, civil society groups in Korea have also campaigned for economic reform. Since the late 1980s, economic reform and economic justice have been the major goals of one of the leading citizens' organizations, CCEJ. Since the economic crisis of 1997, many other civil society groups have begun to focus on economic reform. There have been two major movements for economic reform: the campaign to monitor National Assembly hearings on the causes of the financial crisis and the minority shareholders' rights movement, led principally by PSPD.

Hearings on the Financial Crisis

Due largely to pressure from civil society groups, the Kim Dae Jung government agreed in December 1998 to hold public hearings on the causes of the financial crisis of 1997. PSPD, along with people's movement groups like the National Alliance for Democracy and Unification of Korea and the Korean Confederation of Trade Unions, waged a popular movement for National Assembly hearings on the crisis and punishment of those responsible. Immediately after the decision to hold public hearings, PSPD established the Citizens' Monitoring Group for the National Assembly Hearings, which was composed of twenty people. PSPD also announced that it would publish a daily assessment of the hearings to be released to the press (*Choson ilbo*, January 19, 1999). On January 18, 1999, the hearings on the economic crisis officially began. Closely evaluating all sessions of the public hearings, the Citizens' Monitoring Group critically commented on February 1, 1999: "The hearings are rapidly degenerating into an enormous waste of time, primarily due to the lack of knowledge and professionalism on the part of the questioning legislators. The public hearings look more like closing arguments by a defense attorney for those responsible for the financial crisis" (*Choson ilbo*, February 1, 1999).

On March 8, 1999, the National Assembly concluded the public hearings and the Special Committee on the Financial Crisis submitted an official report to Kim Dae Jung. PSPD released an overall evaluation of the hearings, titled "A Hearing on the National Assembly Hearings," which concluded: "The National Assembly hearings cannot receive more than 50 points out of 100. Legislators asked similar questions repetitively. Some of them asked rudimentary and commonsensical questions. Legislators completely lacked professionalism" (*Choson ilbo*, March 9, 1999).

The Minority Shareholders' Movement

Korean civil society groups widely agree that, in contrast to the significant advances in political democratization, there has been no notable progress in "economic democratization." Economic democratization, according to civil activists, has two dimensions: the overall market structure and the internal structure of companies. In terms of the overall market structure, scholars have long demanded that the enormous power and influence of *chaebol* groups must be reduced to level the economic playing field. In terms of the second dimension, it has long been pointed out that the internal structures of all major *chaebol* groups are too authoritarian, hindering managerial accountability and transparency (E. Kim 2000). These two issues became particularly prominent because it was believed that lack of progress in economic democratization was the essential cause of the economic crisis of 1997 (S. Kim 2000b). Civil society groups in Korea, especially PSPD and CCEJ, have concentrated on the minority shareholders' movement as a strategy to achieve economic democratization. They have used lawsuits and physical presence at shareholders' general meetings to promote minority shareholders' rights and contest the dominance of *chaebol* owner-chairpersons and their families.

On December 12, 1997, PSPD represented 100 minority shareholders of the First Bank (Cheil Bank) in a lawsuit to annul a decision passed at the March 1997 stockholders' general meeting, The Seoul district court ruled in favor of PSPD, saying it was unlawful for the bank to ignore the right of expression of minority shareholders and to proceed with revising statutes and electing board members and auditors without voting (*Choson ilbo*, December 13, 1997).

On February 19, 1998, CCEJ questioned the responsibility of officers of major commercial banks during their general shareholders' meetings. Furthermore, PSPD's Committee for Economic Democratization, led by Chang Ha Song, a Korea University professor, decided to align with foreign investors to promote the rights and interests of minority shareholders (*Choson ilbo*, February 19, 1998). On March 4, 1998, PSPD submitted a proposal to revise corporate statutes in order to appoint external auditors, strengthen the power of the board of directors, and prevent internal transfer of funds among *chaebol* companies of the same group (*Choson ilbo*, March 5, 1998). PSPD's requests closely matched the goals and core elements of the government's corporate restructuring plan.

In response to the vigorous efforts of PSPD and other civil society groups for *chaebol* reform and increased accountability, some *chaebol* groups began to cooperate. On March 26, 1998, for example, SK Group decided to accept PSPD's call for transparent management by increasing the number of external auditors and allowing shareholders to review internal transfers of funds (*Choson ilbo*, March 27, 1998). Encouraged by SK's cooperation, PSPD continued with its campaign for *chaebol* reform by targeting other conglomerates. At the shareholders' general meeting of

Samsung Electronics on March 27, 1998, PSPD minority shareholders scrutinized various issues for more than thirteen hours, inquiring about internal transfers of funds, problematic appointments of auditors, illegal support for the newspaper *Joongang ilbo*, and more (*Choson ilbo*, March 28, 1998). On September 10, 1998, PSPD launched a campaign to acquire ownership of ten shares of stock of each of the five *chaebol* group companies: Samsung Electronics, SK Telecom, Daewoo, LG Semiconductors, and Hyundai Heavy Industry. After acquiring the stocks, PSPD's plan was to inquire about the responsibility of management and demand effective *chaebol* reform (*Choson ilbo*, September 10, 1998). On September 16, PSPD filed a lawsuit against eleven directors of Samsung Electronics, including the company's CEO, Lee Kon Hui, for compensation for damages incurred by Samsung's bribes to former president Roh Tae Woo (*Choson ilbo*, September 17, 1998).

In the 1999 and 2000 sessions of shareholders' general meetings, PSPD continued its minority shareholders' campaign by releasing lists of demands to the five biggest *chaebol* groups and insisting on managerial transparency and accountability. In April 1999, Samsung Electronics and SK Telecom at last accepted some of PSPD's demands. In March 2000, PSPD and Dacom reached a landmark agreement on selecting external auditors and requiring the approval of an audit committee, composed of external auditors, for any major company decisions regarding internal fund transfers or major management changes (*Choson ilbo*, March 8, 2000).

In summary, civil society groups continue to play a pivotal role in the politics of democratic consolidation in South Korea. Compared with their role in the democratic transition, though, two characteristics are notable with respect to democratic consolidation. First, civil society organizations in South Korea, similarly to those in Japan analyzed in this volume, are now trying to effect specific policy changes rather than broad regime changes such as democratization. In this regard, more and more civil organizations are trying to engage the democratic government constructively by emphasizing legal, nonviolent, and popular methods of social protest. And second, especially after the financial crisis of 1997, civil society groups in South Korea, like those in the Philippines discussed in this volume, have paid greater attention to economic reform and restructuring. Unlike in the transition, when political issues were paramount and economic issues were held to be secondary, South Korea's civil society groups are increasingly interested in pursuing various economic issues related to financial reform and corporate restructuring.

Legacies of an Oppositional Civil Society

As we have seen, civil society groups have made a number of crucial contributions to the recent democratic transition and the ongoing democratic consolidation in South Korea. An oppositional civil society, originally formed during the Japanese colonial period, played important roles in all three democratic junctures. Furthermore, civil society remains strong and vibrant even in the politics of democratic consolidation—refuting one of the major observations in the literature on democratic transition and consolidation. Civil society groups are vigorously addressing important issues of political and economic reform, actively engaging and confronting the state. South Koreans are fortunate to have such an unusually robust civil society help their nascent democracy deepen and enrich itself. In fact, civil society in South Korea is fulfilling many of the beneficial roles envisioned in the literature on democratic transition and consolidation (Schmitter 1997: 247; Diamond 1994). During the transition, for example, civil society groups in South Korea represented reservoirs of popular resistance to arbitrary action by authoritarian rulers. Moreover, they also recruited and trained new leaders who would later become prominent in political and economic reform. In this regard, civil society organizations during the transition performed a primarily systemic role. During the consolidation phase, in contrast, these groups have disseminated information and empowered citizens in the collective pursuit and defense of their interests and values, stabilized expectations within social groups, and created multiple channels for the identification, articulation, expression, and representation of interests (Schmitter 1997). Civil society groups are gradually in this respect shifting their focus from systemic roles to socialization and public sphere roles, thus beginning to closely approximate the neo-Tocquevillean framework outlined in Chapter 1 of this volume.

Yet as Philippe Schmitter cogently cautions us and Muthiah Alagappa contends in Chapter 1, a robust civil society is "not an unmitigated blessing for democracy" (1997: 247–48). This is particularly true when political society remains underinstitutionalized, dichotomized, paralyzed, and immobilized. And South Korean democracy seems to fit this description. No significant changes have been registered in Korean party politics over the past decade of democratic consolidation. Above all, the dynamics between the ruling and opposition parties remain hostile, confrontational, uncompromising, and uncivil (S. Kim 2002). During the authoritarian regimes, there was a clear-cut distinction between the authoritarian ruling party and the prodemocracy opposition party. But today there is no environmental or institutional factor that encourages such a dichotomous outlook. The persistence of a black-and-white outlook in Korean party politics makes one suspect there may be deeper cultural factors behind the conflictual relationship between the ruling and the opposition parties. For example, Confucianism, which is still dominant in Korean cultural and ethnical systems, appreciates and encourages theoretical orthodoxy and ideological purity (Steinberg 1997). Values such as compromise, negotiation, bargaining, and accommodation are all alien, if not antithetical, to the Confucian Weltanschauung. Rather, a clearly hierarchical relationship between the superior and the inferior is the hallmark of Confucian social order. The only possible relationship between who is "right" and who is "wrong" is for the "wrong" party to acknowledge error and surrender unconditionally, hoping for generous and benevolent acceptance of the "right" party.

Furthermore, party politics in Korea is still firmly predicated on regionalism. Various parties have emerged and expanded, based largely on regional electoral support. Despite Kim Dae Jung's well-intended efforts to transform his party into a "national" party, the ruling party today remains a regional party heavily supported by Honam voters and staffed by Honam politicians. Other political parties—all vaunting and eager to protect their regional spheres of influence—are not very different. Party politics based on regionalism reinforces political bossism by increasing the premium of political leaders who can mobilize regional votes and thus determine the fate of candidates running for electoral office in the region. At the same time, regionalism discourages the emergence of a new generation of politicians geared toward professional knowledge of policy issues and hands-on experience with policymaking processes.

South Korean civil society is not entirely free of the problems associated with party politics, but it is generally perceived as substantially more credible, clean, public-minded, democratic, rational, and civil than political parties. As civil society bypasses the polarized, petrified, and problem-ridden political society, the principal locus of politics continues to consist of direct—sometimes conflictual, sometimes cooperative—interactions between civil society and the state. In principle, there is nothing intrinsically wrong with this direct engagement between civil society and the state, but if it continues to circumvent and ultimately replaces party politics, this may pose a threat to the consolidation of democracy in Korea. Key issues of politics will continue to be addressed in the midst of direct confrontation between civil society groups and the state. When direct confrontation between the state and civil society dominates political discussion, political parties are considered peripheral at best and irrelevant at worst. Yet democratic consolidation can seldom succeed without the development of a highly institutionalized and viable party system. Virtually all the consolidated democracies in the contemporary world are predicated on the balance of two elements: a robust civil society and a functional political society. This balance between a strong civil society and a strong political society represents an effective antidote to the abuse of power by the state. So long as the imbalance between an energetic civil society and a lethargic political society drags on, Korean democracy is likely to remain uninstitutionalized, unconsolidated, and unstable. In other words, one of the most prominent and urgent challenges South Korean politics faces today is to develop a robust political society that can synergistically collaborate with the vibrant civil society in furthering various reform agendas to enhance the quality of democracy.

Notes

1. On the concept of conflictual engagement between state and civil society, see Bratton 1989. The intense confrontation between state and civil society is a perennial theme in the study of Korean democratization. On the framework of strong state versus contentious civil society, see Koo 1993. On the framework of strong state versus strong society, see Song 1994. On the legacy of Japanese colonialism in Korea in general, see Cumings 1974, 1984.

2. For a thorough analysis of domestic and international political dynamics in Korea in 1945–50, see Cumings 1981, 1990.

3. Political society is defined as the "arena in which the polity specifically arranges itself for political contestation to gain control over public power and the state apparatus." It includes "political parties, elections, electoral rules, political leadership, intraparty alliances, and legislatures" (Stepan 1988: 4).

4. Article 87 states: "Organizations, regardless of their types and names, may not support or oppose any specific political parties or candidates. Nor may they encourage others to support or oppose any specific parties or candidates" (www.nec.go.kr. [accessed 3/7/2004]).

5. In mid-February 2000, the Public Prosecutors Office summoned a number of civil leaders involved in the Nakch'on/Nakson movement and investigated their motivations as well as the process of drafting the list of politicians.

6. The specific process of producing the list was as follows. First, civil society groups constituted an investigative team to collect background material on politicians. Second, the groups conducted surveys to generate seven criteria for opposing the nomination of a specific candidate. Third, a standing executive committee of civil leaders produced a list of ninety-five politicians. Fourth, a committee of a hundred voters reviewed and approved the selection criteria. And fifth, an advisory group of professors and scholars checked the list for factual errors. Although CSGE originally planned to release a list of seventy-seven politicians on January 20, 2000, it gave those seventy-seven politicians a chance to clarify the allegations. After reviewing the explanatory statements from those listed in the preliminary list, CSGE ultimately disclosed a list of sixty-six politicians on January 24, 2000. See *Choson ilbo*, Jan. 25, 2000.

7. ULD had been a coalition partner of the ruling party until this moment. But because of CSGE's inclusion of Kim Jong Pil on its list, Kim Dae Jung's support for the campaign, and the launching of the new Millennium Democratic Party, ULD declared in February 2000 that it would become an opposition party.

Works Cited

Bratton, Michael. 1989. "Beyond the State: Civil Society and Associational Life in Africa." *World Politics* 41(3): 407–30.

Choi, Jang Jip. 1993a. *Han'guk minjujuuiui iron* (Theory of Korean democracy). Seoul: Han'gilsa.

———. 1993b. "Han'gugui minjuhwa: Ihaenggwa kaehyok" (Korean democratization: Transition and reform). In Jang Jip Choi and Hyon Chin Im, eds., *Siminsahoeui tojon: Han'guk minjuhwawa kukka, chabon, nodong* (Challenge from civil society: State, capital, and labor in Korean democratization). Seoul: Nanam.

———. 2000. "50 nyon chongch'i tokchom punggoesik'in siminui him" (Citizens' power that brought down a 50-year-old monopoly of politics). *Sin Tonga* (Tonga monthly), March, 170–82.

———. 2002. *Minjuhwa ihuui minjujuui* (Democracy after democratization). Seoul: Humanitas.

Chong, Tae Hwa. 2000. "Che 16-dae kukhoe uiwon ch'ongson'gwa simin undong tanch'eui chongch'i kaeip" (The 16th National Assembly elections and political intervention of civil society groups). *Tonghyanggwa chonmang* (Trends and prospects) 45: 35–70.

Chu, Chong Hwan. 2000. "Hyondan'gye han'guk sahoeui songgyokkwa sahoe undongui kwaje" (The nature of Korean society at the current stage and tasks of social movement). *Tonghyanggwa chonmang* (Trends and prospects) 45: 100–20.

Cotton, James. 1989. "From Authoritarianism to Democracy in South Korea." *Political Studies* 37: 244–59.

Cumings, Bruce. 1974. "American Policy and Korean Liberation." In Frank Baldwin, ed., *Without Parallel*. New York: Pantheon Books.

———. 1981. *The Origins of the Korean War*, Vol. 1: *Liberation and the Emergence of Separate Regimes, 1945–1947*. Princeton: Princeton University Press.

———. 1984. "The Legacy of Japanese Colonialism in Korea." In Ramon H. Myers and Mark R. Peattie, eds., *The Japanese Colonial Empire, 1895–1945*. Princeton: Princeton University Press.

———. 1990. *The Origins of the Korean War*, Vol. 2: *The Roaring of the Cataract, 1947–1950*. Princeton: Princeton University Press.

Diamond, Larry. 1994. "Rethinking Civil Society: Toward Democratic Consolidation." *Journal of Democracy* 5(3): 4–17.

Eckert, Carter J., Ki-baik Lee, Young Ick Lew, Michael Robinson, and Edward W. Wagner. 1990. *Korea, Old and New: A History*. Cambridge, Mass.: Harvard University Press.

Fish, Steven. 1994. "Rethinking Civil Society: Russia's Fourth Transition." *Journal of Democracy* 5: 31–42.

Harrison, Selig S. 1987. "Dateline from South Korea: A Divided Seoul." *Foreign Policy* 67: 154–75.

Karl, Terry. 1990. "Dilemmas of Democratization in Latin America." *Comparative Politics* 23(1): 1–21.

Kim, Eun Mee. 2000. "Reforming the *Chaebol*." In Larry Diamond and Doh Chull Shin, eds., *Institutional Reform and Democratic Consolidation in Korea*. Stanford: Hoover Institution.

Kim, Sunhyuk. 1996. "Civil Society in South Korea: From Grand Democracy Movements to Petty Interest Groups?" *Journal of Northeast Asian Studies* 15(2): 81–97.

———. 2000a. *The Politics of Democratization in Korea: The Role of Civil Society*. Pittsburgh: University of Pittsburgh Press.

———. 2000b. "The Political Origins of South Korea's Economic Crisis: Is Democratization to Blame?" *Democratization* 7: 81–103.

———. 2000c. "Civic Mobilization for Democratic Reform." In Larry Diamond and Doh Chull Shin, eds., *Institutional Reform and Democratic Consolidation in Korea*. Stanford: Hoover Institution.

———. 2002. "Party Politics in South Korea." In Chung-in Moon and David I. Steinberg, eds., *Korea in Transition: Three Years Under the Kim Dae-jung Government*. Seoul: Yonsei University Press.

Kim, Wang Sik. 1996. "Migunjong kyongch'arui chongch'ijok wising" (The political status of the police under the U.S. Army Military Government in Korea). In Korean Political Science Association, ed., *Han'guk hyondae chongch'isa* (Contemporary Korean political history). Seoul: Pommunsa.

Kong, Tat Yan. 2000. "Power Alternation in South Korea." *Government and Opposition* 35: 370–91.

Koo, Hagen. 1993. "Strong State and Contentious Society." In Hagen Koo, ed., *State and Society in Contemporary Korea*. Ithaca, N.Y.: Cornell University Press.

Korean Christian Social Research Center (KCSRC), ed. 1986. *Kaehon'gwa minjuhwa undong* (Constitutional revision and democracy movement). Seoul: Minjungsa.

Nam, Koon Woo. 1989. *South Korean Politics: The Search for Political Consensus and Stability.* Lanham, Md.: University Press of America.

O'Donnell, Guillermo, and Philippe Schmitter. 1986. *Transitions from Authoritarian Rule: Tentative Conclusions about Uncertain Democracies*. Baltimore: Johns Hopkins University Press.

Schmitter, Philippe. 1997. "Civil Society East and West." In Larry Diamond et al., eds., *Consolidating the Third Wave Democracies: Themes and Perspectives*. Baltimore: Johns Hopkins University Press.

Sin, Myong Sun. 1995. "Han'gugesoui simin sahoe hyongsonggwa minjuhwa kwajongesoui yokhal" (The formation of civil society in Korea and its role in democratization). In Byong Jun An, ed., *Kukka, simin sahoe, chongch'i minjuhwa* (The state, civil society, and political democratization). Seoul: Hanul.

Song, Kyong Ryung. 1994. "Han'guk chongch'i minjuhwaui sahoejok kiwon" (Social origins of Korean democratization: A social movement approach). In Institute for Far Eastern Studies, ed., *Han'guk chongch'i sahoeui sae hurum* (New currents in Korean politics and society). Seoul: Nanam.

Steinberg, David. 1997. "Civil Society and Human Rights in Korea: On Contemporary and Classical Orthodoxy and Ideology." *Korea Journal* 37: 145–65.

Stepan, Alfred. 1988. *Rethinking Military Politics: Brazil and the Southern Cone*. Princeton: Princeton University Press.

Yang, Tong An. 1990. "Hollan sogui kukka hyongsong" (State building in the midst of turmoil). In Tong An Yang, ed., *Hyondae han'guk chongch'isa* (Contemporary Korean political history). Seoul: Han'guk chongsin munhwa yon'guwon.

CHAPTER FIVE

Taiwan

No Civil Society, No Democracy

YUN FAN

Taiwan has long been known for its economic miracle and political stability. Most works have described the Nationalist Kuomingtang (KMT) regime between 1950 and the mid-1980s as authoritarian. And ever since the transition from authoritarianism to democracy over the past twenty years, scholars have searched for explanations to account for this impressive transformation of Taiwanese politics.[1] Unlike in the case of South Korea, the democratic transition in Taiwan has either been regarded as predominantly elite-dominated or mainly attributed to ethno-nationalist sentiments. This does not mean that observers have completely overlooked the role of civil society in the process of democratization. Nevertheless, very few have examined democratic transition from the perspective of civil society.[2]

In Taiwan's experience, electoral competition is a necessary but not a sufficient condition for democratic transition. Not all elections are free and fair; nor do they all lead to civilian rule or a respect for social rights. Thus there also must be more to democratization than just a transition to elections. Since its arrival in 1949, the Nationalist émigré regime ruling Taiwan has been defined by authoritarian clientelism.[3] As Jonathan Fox (1994) has pointed out, the transition from authoritarian client status to freedom of association is an important dimension of democratization, which unfolds unevenly through cycles of conflict and negotiation among authoritarian rulers, opposition elites, and autonomous social movements. However, it still remains unclear as to how Taiwanese society made the transition from authoritarian clientelism to civil society, and how subordinated people made the transition from clients to citizens. What resources and ideologies did they use to organize themselves, defend their right to autonomous association, and then pursue the social rights and identities to which they are entitled? This process does not always follow electoral competition. Despite the vast body of literature on the emergence of electoral competition in Taiwan, the dynamics of the political transition toward respect for other fundamental democratic rights is still not well understood.

My aim here is to investigate the role of civil society in Taiwan's political change. In the first section of this chapter, I argue that civil society has contributed greatly to democratic transition—mainly by mobilizing political resistance, constructing counternarratives and ideologies, and marshaling international support for alternative elites. In the late 1970s, civil society started to delegitimate the nation-state and the incumbent government through resistance and mass mobilization. The opposition movement not only mobilized its supporters in electoral campaigns and on the streets but also generated counternarratives by publishing numerous illegal magazines. And with the growth of the domestic movement in the 1980s, overseas Taiwanese immigrants' organizations served as important conduits for international resources.

By investigating efforts by women's groups and community movements, the second part of this chapter aims to analyze the potential contribution of civil society to Taiwan's democratic consolidation. We shall see how women's groups learned to use legislative lobbying tactics with a nonpartisan strategy, as well as public education, to influence the public agenda, and we shall see how community movements helped to transform clients into citizens and empower civil society—in short, we shall see how civil society has furthered socialization by promoting public participation, providing education for democracy, and developing political skills, identities, and civic virtues. In sum, this chapter argues that the self-empowerment of civil society played a fundamental role in creating the necessary condition for the consolidation of democracy.

Let us begin with a little history. During the 1970s, the Nationalist regime lost its membership in the United Nations and then faced a diplomatic crisis when the United States normalized its relations with the People's Republic of China (PRC). This setback saw the creation and rapid rise of a political opposition movement known as *tangwai* (literally, "outside the party"), a grassroots coalition of ethnic Taiwanese and pro-independence activists for whom democracy was the means for national self-determination. In response to the opposition movement, as well as the external pressure, the KMT began a slow process of political liberalization—allowing non-KMT candidates to run for a limited number of seats in local and provincial assemblies, on the one hand, and recruiting Taiwanese elites into the ranks of the ruling party and the government, on the other (Cheng and Haggard 1992; Rigger 1999; Cheng 1989; Tien 1989).

The transition to democracy began in the 1980s. Since then Taiwan has experienced unprecedented social change. There were thousands of social protests and numerous social movements all over the island. The issues ranged across a broad spectrum: farmers' interests, religious rights, workers' rights, environmental concerns, women's rights, campus democracy, consumers' rights, and the right of old mainlander soldiers to go home. These organized as well as unorganized social protests triggered a process of gradual liberalization, coinciding with an increasingly emboldened political opposition (Chu 1988; Chang 1989; Fang 1991; Gian 1998; Gu 1992; Guo 1997; Lin 1998; Zhang 1995). In 1986, the opposition movement announced the founding of the Democratic Progressive Party (DPP) with the aim of democratizing the state—illegally yet forcefully challenging the legitimacy of the ruling regime. In July 1987, martial law was lifted and Taiwanese society witnessed the uncertain beginning of democracy. From 1988 until Taiwan's first change of government in March 2000, the country underwent a political transition from authoritarianism to democratic rule. Accounting for this transition, recent studies have emphasized the role of the ruling elite. I, however, want to call attention to the role of civil society, which has been central throughout the entire process of Taiwan's democratic transition.

Taiwan's Democratic Transition

As Alfred Stepan (1988) has pointed out, a critical question for democratization is how to bridge the gap between new movements based in the civil arena and organized opposition in the political arena. Certainly, the strategic alliance of social movements with the dissident opposition movement was crucial to Taiwan's democratic transition. A formidable political alliance between the opposition movement, later led by the Democratic Progressive Party, and the social movements started to emerge in the 1980s. This socially progressive force had its roots in civil society—primarily in the form of social movements and periodic episodes of broad-based coalition building. As shown in Table 5.1, the incidences of social protest increased from 143 in 1983 to 676 in 1987. Social protest as a means of pressing collective demands had proliferated into all kinds of issue areas and spread across the island within a very short time. Most notably, four major types of social protest emerged in these years: political, environmental, economic, and labor. These social resistances signal an emerging assertive civil society.

What are the social origins of Taiwan's civil society? Who were the leaders who took an active part in the movements for social and political democracy? The democratic transition in Taiwan has unfolded under conditions of prosperity rather than of economic hardship, as has been the case for many third wave democracies (Tien and Cheng 1997). Rapid industrialization and economic prosperity changed the composition of the social fabric, giving rise to a prominent and increasingly vocal middle class. The dynamic capitalist economy simply outgrew the regime's political capacity.[4]

TABLE 5.1
Social Protests Reported in Taiwan by Number, 1983–87

	1983	1984	1985	1986	1987	Total
Frequency	143	183	243	271	676	1,516
Increase		28%	33%	12%	149%	

SOURCE: Chu 1994.

TABLE 5.2
Social Protests Reported in Taiwan by Issue, 1983–87

Issue	1983	1984	1985	1986	1987	Total	Proportion of all issues
Political							
Frequency	5	4	20	35	106	170	11.2%
Increase		–20%	400%	75%	203%		
Environmental							
Frequency	43	61	34	78	167	383	25.3%
Increase		42%	–44%	129%	114%		
Economic							
Frequency	57	72	89	101	257	576	38.0%
Increase		26%	24%	14%	155%		
Labor							
Frequency	20	37	85	38	63	243	16.0%
Increase		85%	130%	–55%	66%		
Other							
Frequency	18	9	15	19	83	144	9.5%
Increase		–50%	67%	27%	337%		

SOURCE: Chu 1994.

It was during the 1970s that the first postwar generation became politically active and began to intervene in Taiwan's historical development. This particular decade's political generation was historically significant because it was the first native-born segment of the population to receive a modern education without seeing it interrupted by warfare.[5] Prior to the 1970s, the opposition movement was led either by local politicians or by mainlander intellectuals. Born in Taiwan and educated by the Nationalist Party, these opposition elites emerged in the new generation not only to further the organizational skills of the opposition but also to refine the counter-narratives of the island's democracy movement (Hsiao 2003). As shown in Table 5.3 and Table 5.4, the leaders of social movements in the 1980s and 1990s were also from the postwar generation and mainly from middle-class backgrounds (Fan 2000). The postwar generation of the middle class, including liberal intellectuals and professionals, either took the lead in persuading the authoritarian regime to opt for liberalization as an alternative to repression or constituted the vanguard of the democracy movement. In short, politicized segments of the middle class actively participated in the struggle against the regime, while the broader middle class provided solid support (Hsiao and Koo 1997).

TABLE 5.3
Social Movement Activists' Class Background

Class	All activists	All population
Highest	18.5%	2.9%
Second highest	19.2%	9.2%
Low white-collar	27.4%	20.6%
Petty bourgeois	7.5%	19.6%
Farmer	2.1%	11.2%
Blue-collar worker	10.3%	36.5%
Students	13%	—
Unemployed	0.7%	—
Homemaker	1.4%	—
TOTAL	100% (N=146)	100%

SOURCE: Yun Fan 2000.

TABLE 5.4
Social Movement Activists' Generational Background

Which year was s/he born	All activists	All population
Before 1953	8.8%	33.8%
1954–1963	61.2%	21.7%
After 1964	29.9%	44.5%
TOTAL	100% (N=147)	100%

SOURCE: Yun Fan 2000.

If the postwar political generation and middle class, both of which were shaped by postwar economic growth, became the principal agents of emerging civil society, the electoral mechanism turned out to be the structural feature that facilitated such change. The KMT party-state introduced electoral contests at the local level in the early 1950s. Direct elections were subsequently extended to cover the provincial assembly as well. Around 1970, supplementary elections for the National Assembly and the Legislative Yuan were experimented with and then regularized. They quickly became a funnel through which local elites could enter politics and join the ruling system, a process that generated pressures for the loosening of controls from above. Without the electoral system, the democratic transition in Taiwan probably would have taken a different route (Tian and Cheng 1997).

Mobilizing Political Resistance

The regime jailed most of the leaders of the *Formosa* magazine group in 1979. The following year, the mother and twin daughters of Lin Yi-hsiung, one of the jailed opposition leaders, were murdered at home. These terror tactics, meant to suppress the democratic movement, instead galvanized more Taiwanese into action. Not only did more and more people become involved in the opposition movement but society as a whole showed its support. All the family members of jailed political activists who decided to seek justice by running for office were elected, as were their defense lawyers.

In the post-*Formosa* era (1978–86), the continuing mobilization of the opposition movement was the most critical force pushing for Taiwan's democratization. These activists, in addition to organizing a Public Policy Research Association composed of editors and writers and calling for the formation of a democratic movement, published their magazines virtually underground in order to advocate liberty, democracy, and progressive social ideals. The group called New Tide initiated a series of strategy debates by calling for mass mobilization as the main tactic to show opposition to the elections. As a result, the streets became an alternative arena for the KMT regime to deal with, in addition to the legislature, which they dominated.

Deciding to found a new party, opposition activists announced the birth of the Democratic Progressive Party (DPP) on September 28, 1986. The founding of this opposition party can be viewed as the first step in Taiwan's democratic transition. In the following year, the regime lifted martial law, which had long suspended freedom of speech, freedom of the mass media, freedom of association, and freedom to pursue political activities. As Robert Dahl has argued, once a repressive regime abandons the premise of total control and allows some opposition, there is no natural stopping point until full-scale political competition is either reached or total control is reimposed (cited in Cheng 1989: 495). At any rate, a regime finds it extremely costly to reverse the trend toward liberalization and democracy once it has started. If the crackdown on the *Formosa* magazine group in 1979 had indeed deterred the efforts of the democratic movement as the regime expected, then Taiwan might not have undergone the democratic transition we have witnessed over the past twenty years. If the family members of the jailed leaders of the *Formosa* magazine group and their defense lawyers had not decided to continue their commitment to the movement, the democratic movement might have faltered. If society had not wholeheartedly supported the activists who ran in the election, thereby allowing them to win, these activists might have become discouraged and frustrated. Naiteh Wu (2000: 92–93) has pointed out the central role of people's moral support during Taiwan's democratic transition:

> The political "criminals" and their families have suffered terribly, not only from the years they were imprisoned, but also from the social isolation, which often was even harder to bear: they were isolated in a corner of society. Instead of being praised and respected, they were treated like patients with a deadly virus that everybody wanted to escape. After the *Formosa* [magazine] incident, however, all that was changed. The political "criminals" became the heroes of Taiwanese society, and many people sympathized deeply [with them] and supported their families. People gave political dissidents social and political support, which may be one of the main reasons the ruler and the ruling group recognized that the society was changing.

The formation of the opposition party, DPP, is a good window through which to examine the fabric and texture of the emerging civil society. When the democratic movement announced the founding of the DPP in 1986, without knowing whether or not there would be another crackdown, many people in society reacted with enthusiastic support. Some donated money; others joined as members. Although mainly human right lawyers and middle-class intellectuals spearheaded the movement, those who joined the DPP as members in the initial stage came from all walks of life and all levels of society. When asked why they joined, their answers were simple:

> At the time we joined the DPP, our primary intention was *to protect the DPP, to prevent another crackdown*. The more people like us joined the DPP, the less likely it was that the KMT would dare to touch the party. So, many people joined the DPP directly at street gatherings. We did not hesitate. (Fan 1994: 103; emphasis added)

> I joined the party in 1987. We as a group can be considered the party's founding members. The main reason I decided to become a party member was because I felt that a mouth [that is, talking] was useless. Someone had to sacrifice something. (Ibid., 102)

> I joined the party because I felt the founding of the party resulted from a lot of hard work. Although I knew it was not good for a schoolteacher to be a party member, I felt that we should support this party. So it was I who went to the DPP bookstore at Chung-li to join as a member. (Ibid., 106)

These people did not choose to become members because of their desire for political participation in a democratic society. They took the risk simply because they believed that by joining, they could protect the new party. For them, the DPP was a political movement. And the best way to protect a movement is to join it.

After its founding in September 1986, the DPP focused on mass demonstrations. Indeed most of the political demonstrations in the streets during the late 1980s were initiated by the DPP.

Chiang Chingkuo (CCK), the son of Chiang Kai-shek (CKS), died in 1988, and a succession crisis erupted within the KMT. Lee Denhuei, who was then vice president, won an internal political struggle between the mainstream and non-mainstream factions of the KMT. In March 1990, at a time when Lee Denhuei was supposed to be reelected by the "long congress," tens of thousands of angry students gathered in the CKS Memorial Hall—which symbolized the political core of the authoritarian regime—and sat for days to protest the nondemocratic presidential election. These students were not there to ask for educational reform or to demand democracy on campus. They were there to protest the fact that a president of Taiwan was going to be elected by a few old congressmen who had never been elected by the Taiwanese people in the first place. Nevertheless, Lee was safely elected by the congress. The first thing Lee did after his election was to meet with student representatives and promise political reform. This student demonstration of 1990, later called the March Student Movement or the "Lily Student Movement," was the first time in Taiwan's postwar history that a social movement group had emerged as the main negotiator for the opposition to the ruling government.

After that, political resistance became increasingly popular. Social activists, scholars, and liberal intellectuals all took to the streets. In May 1990, there was a mass demonstration protesting President Lee's appointment of a general as prime minister. In 1991, more than fifty thousand students, professors, and social activists gathered to rescue a group studying Taiwanese history from being illegally detained by the regime's Central Intelligence Agency. In 1992, a series of political street demonstrations was organized on the Nation's Birthday to protest military parades and demand revision of the Criminal Code, which was often used to imprison political dissidents. These demonstrations mobilized numerous social groups.

In the 1980s, the alliance between social movements and the democratic movement was viewed as a public secret. Some activists in the social movements wanted to make use of the DPP's resources, yet did not want to be labeled DPP members (Ho 2000). At the same time, the efforts of opposition movement activists to mobilize social groups were not always successful. Only after 1990 can the strategic alliance between certain social movements and the political opposition be said to have been consolidated. On many of these occasions, however, officials of the DPP and other political organizations were asked to position themselves at the tail of a demonstration because social movement activists were committed to self-organization both in appearance and in reality. Certainly, the idea of a self-constrained civil society was less threatening and thus had a better chance of success in the drive for democratization.

Constructing Counternarratives and Norms

The ultimate control of an authoritarian regime is to control the way people think. A society that is incapable of allowing for different voices cannot generate any political resistance. And, even if a different voice were to emerge on the political horizon, it would fail to evolve into resistance action. In order to preserve itself, difference in thought that leads to transformative action needs to be openly circulated and discussed if it is to be enriched. However, no public sphere in an authoritarian society exists for deliberative discussion, because all media, which are supposed to serve as the main channel of the public sphere, are controlled by the acting regime.

In criticizing Jürgen Habermas's normative concept of an overarching public sphere, Nancy Fraser speaks of "subaltern counterpublics" as "parallel discursive arenas where members of subordinated social groups invent and circulate counter discourses to formulate oppositional interpretations of their identities, interests, and needs" (Fraser 1992a: 123; Fraser 1992b: 610–12). In Taiwan, where before the 1980s, the Nationalist Party's monopoly on public discourse was obvious, civil society not only supported a counterpublic sphere but also constructed counternarratives, two things that are essential for the effective mobilization of political resistance. To understand the dominant narrative and counternarratives, we therefore need to observe both public and counterpublic spheres. The ideology underlying the counterpublic sphere was mainly disseminated by "outside-the-party" magazines, in which counternarratives grew and circulated. In the 1970s and 1980s, many Taiwanese got their wake-up calls from reading these magazines.

Democracy is the central element in these counternarratives. It was also the core of the new norms being advocated in the 1950s, 1960s, and 1970s. According to Wang Fuchang (1996: 133–88), ideology accounts for the failure of *Formosa* magazine in 1979 and the successful founding of the DPP in 1986. Before 1978, the political narratives of the opposition movement can be traced back to the publications *Free China* and *University Magazine* in the 1970s. Democracy was the main theme running through different instances of resistance and mobilization aimed at challenging the undemocratic political structure under the KMT regime. This structure, however, was supported by a powerful set of ideologies:

The KMT regime is the only legitimate regime on Chinese territory.
Since China was facing an emergency, the legal government was forced to move to Taiwan temporarily.
To maintain legitimacy (*fa tung*) during its temporary stay in Taiwan, the congress should not have to face elections until the day the regime returns to mainland China.

Taiwan's undemocratic political structure was thus justified in terms of Chinese nationalism and explained as merely a temporary phenomenon, an extension of the domestic war in China. As a result of this appeal to Chinese nationalist sentiment, prior to 1979, no democratic movement was able to challenge the core ideology of the ruling regime.

The crushing of the *Formosa* magazine group had a deep impact on the opposition movement. In terms of organization, there was serious strategy debate about whether to use street demonstrations or elections. In terms of ideology, Taiwanese consciousness became more pronounced in outside-the-party magazines.[6] Topics like the February 28, 1947, atrocity,[7] the heroes of Taiwan's political resistance, and the honor of being Taiwanese have been covered intensively in some of the more radical magazines. By calling upon the collective memories of the ethnic Taiwanese, they eventually led to the construction of an indigenous Taiwanese nationalism. Redefining the meaning of Taiwan's past and envisioning its future constitute successful counternarratives to Chinese nationalism. Basically, Taiwanese nationalism challenged the principle of Chinese nationalism as a pillar of the ruling KMT regime. Citing Chinese nationalism, the KMT regime was able to sustain martial law, the war mobilization system, and the undemocratic political structure that allowed it to maintain the "long congress" supposedly representing "all China." Taiwanese consciousness, broadly defined, can be seen as a native-land consciousness, grounded in Taiwan, which demands that the political, economic, cultural, and educational infrastructure should be designed for those who are currently living in Taiwan. In a narrower sense, Taiwanese consciousness relates to the suffering of the ethnic Taiwanese under the KMT regime, viewed as an immigrant regime worse than the colonial Japanese government.

The opposition movement was radicalized in 1979 because of the *Formosa* event. In a supplementary legislative election in 1983, the central issue of the opposition movement was the demand that the future of Taiwan should be determined collectively by all the residents of Taiwan. This call for self-determination can be viewed as a combination of democratization and Taiwanization, as opposed to Chinese nationalism. Later, this call for self-determination even led to the demand for Taiwan's independence, a demand that challenged both the domestic and the external legitimacy of the KMT regime.

Social justice is the third element in counternarratives. Socially progressive ideals such as human rights, environmentalism, labor consciousness, consumer rights, and gender equality were advocated in these magazines as well. These ideals do not necessarily attach to any specific ideology—rather, their chief appeal derives from a social concern founded on humanistic values—and many educated Taiwanese reacted to them and were ready to apply them at home (Bendix 1978). However, such ideas exist, not only as abstract values, but also as political strategies, and it is clear that the opposition intentionally set out to mobilize different segments of society by advocating progressive social values. "Socialize Political Movements, Politicize Social Movements" was the slogan proposed by the New Tide faction within the opposition movement, articulating a widespread desire to build a broad alliance between political movements and social movements to pursue democratic reform.

After the lifting of martial law, social movements gained strength; no longer was the opposition the sole bearer of these ideals. Thus, social movements gradually replaced the opposition in advocating social ideals and attacking the social foundations of the KMT regime by broadening the democratic vision of the Taiwanese people.

Marshaling International Support

Civil society during Taiwan's democratic transition not only mobilized domestic support for these alternative elites but also marshaled international support. Owing to the regime's imposition of martial law, most people in Taiwan dared not voice their opinions publicly. Beyond the country's national borders, however, especially in the United States and Japan, overseas students and immigrant Taiwanese spent considerable energy, time, and money mobilizing support to monitor Taiwan, while lobbying foreign governments and legislatures to press the KMT regime to relent on human rights issues and political liberation.[8] Even though they were being watched by the KMT's overseas intelligence system and ran the risk of being blacklisted, their political mobilization contributed greatly to the domestic opposition movement.

The main theme of this overseas mobilization has been Taiwan's independence, although human rights issues and democracy also rank highly on the list of concerns. In the 1950s and 1960s, Japan was the center of the overseas Taiwanese independence movement.[9] As increasing numbers of Taiwanese students turned to the United States and Canada for higher education in the 1970s, however, the center of activism shifted to North America. Among the various overseas Taiwanese organizations in the United States, World United Formosans for Independence (WUFI) became the most significant. Its history can be traced back to January 1956, when three students studying in the United States secretly founded Formosans for a Free Formosa (FFF) in Philadelphia. In 1959, the society was renamed United Formosans for Independence in order to recruit students on other campuses. In 1966, it was reorganized as United Formosans in America for Independence in order to include immigrant Taiwanese. In 1970, the organization emerged as WUFI, with overseas independence groups in several countries, including Japan. There were also several other overseas Taiwanese organizations, including the Formosan Clubs and the World Federation of Taiwanese Associations.

In addition to fostering the growth of domestic opposition in the 1980s, these overseas organizations became important channels for international support. In 1982, a few prominent leaders of the opposition movement visited the U.S. Congress, and the opposition strengthened its diplomatic relations after this trip according to Tunjen Cheng (1989: 487). Previously, the *Formosa* magazine group had maintained only loose contacts with human rights organizations. Since then, they have helped domestic leaders to arrange lectures and meetings with American politicians, media, and scholars.

Indeed, since 1982, the influence of these overseas Taiwanese has expanded from the promotion of political consciousness within the Taiwanese immigrant community and offering moral and material support to the domestic democratic movement to targeting American congressional legislation and public debates. A turning point came with the establishment, by a group of overseas Taiwanese scholars and entrepreneurs, of the Formosan Association for Public Affairs (FAPA), which is specifically dedicated to public policy research and congressional lobbying. With growing numbers of Taiwanese immigrants settled in the United States as professionals, FAPA has successfully mobilized grassroots support to set up more than fifty chapters in different states. There are only two or three full-time staff members in its Washington office, but, as an official of Taiwan's Ministry of Foreign Affairs commented, "Actually, FAPA has a staff of thousands, because its members, from New York to Ohio, can demand the assistance of members of Congress in their respective electoral districts." FAPA's activities range from lobbying Congress to pressure the KMT to release political prisoners and to respect human rights before the lifting of martial law to congressional passage of Taiwan-friendly resolutions and the establishment of the Taiwan Caucus. The achievement of this grassroots movement in promoting Taiwan's human rights, democracy, national security, and international status can be analyzed in four domains:

First, it lobbies the U.S. Congress to pass Taiwan-friendly resolutions. In the 104th and 105th congresses, ten Taiwan-related resolutions were successfully passed, including two congratulating Taiwan's first democratically elected president and welcoming Lee Deng-huei on his private visit to the United States, five assuring Taiwan's national security and American's commitment to a peaceful resolution of the Taiwan Strait conflict, and three supporting the inclusion of Taiwan in international organizations such as the United Nations, the International Monetary Fund, and the World Health Organization.

Second, it facilitates the establishment of Taiwan-friendly subgroups in both houses of Congress. Educating members of Congress about Taiwan's situation and winning their sympathy has been the major goal of organizations like FAPA. Since the first Taiwan Democracy Committee was established in the U.S. House in 1986, the number of congressional members enrolled has grown rapidly. Recently, the Taiwan Caucus has become one of the largest organizations in the U.S. House. The U.S. Senate also had a Taiwan Caucus in 2003. Although a caucus does not have any formal authority over its members, the Taiwan Caucus constitutes a channel through which those concerned about Taiwan issues can make themselves heard in Congress. Overseas Taiwanese groups can also use this leverage to communicate with the U.S. administration to promote Taiwan's democratic aspirations and international status more effectively and efficiently.

Third, it promotes political consciousness and public participation throughout the Taiwanese-American community. Realizing that it represents not only overseas Taiwanese but also Taiwanese Americans, FAPA cooperated with other Taiwanese-American groups in pressing for the use of "Taiwan" and "Taiwanese" designations in their passports, census classification, and other official U.S. documents. In order to highlight the contributions of Taiwanese Americans to the United States, FAPA has worked to obtain presidential and congressional endorsement of an annual Taiwanese-American Heritage Week. These groups also work to promote the public participation of their second generation by supporting second-generation organizations and leadership training programs.

Fourth, it facilitates mutual understanding between Taiwanese domestic opposition leaders and the U.S. Congress, as well as think tanks and the media. Because international relations are always monopolized by the ruling party, the opposition party usually lacks an effective outlet for its message. FAPA and other overseas groups have offered invaluable international resources to the democratic movement at home. The U.S. visit of Taipei's mayor, Chen Shui-bian, and his subsequent tour of the United States prior to his presidential campaign served to demonstrate his skill in dealing with foreign affairs, an attribute essential to a national leader. The annual exchange between Taiwanese congressional members and the Taiwan Caucus in the U.S. Congress now serves as an institutionally facilitated nonpartisan event promoting mutual understanding.

These activities by Taiwanese immigrants in American civil society can be regarded as part of the transnational civil society of Taiwan. International support, especially U.S. support, has been crucial to building Taiwanese confidence in democratic political change in the face of the military threat from the PRC, even though U.S. security objectives frequently conflict with and may even override liberal democratic goals in determining foreign policy, as Muthiah Alagappa (Chapter 1) and Laurence Whitehead (1988) point out. The international mobilization of overseas Taiwanese associations has encouraged the opposition and indirectly promoted the growth of political resistance, thus furthering Taiwan's transition to democracy.

In sum, then, Taiwan's civil society has made invaluable contributions to its democratic transition by mobilizing political resistance and social protests, by constructing counternarratives and ideologies, and by marshaling international support for alternative elites. Civil society has now grown to the point where it can challenge the long-standing imbalance between the island's strong state and weak society.

Taiwan's Democratic Consolidation: Citizens in the Making

The growth of civil society after the lifting of martial law in 1987 was remarkable in terms of the density of civic organizations. As Figure 5.1 shows, the number of

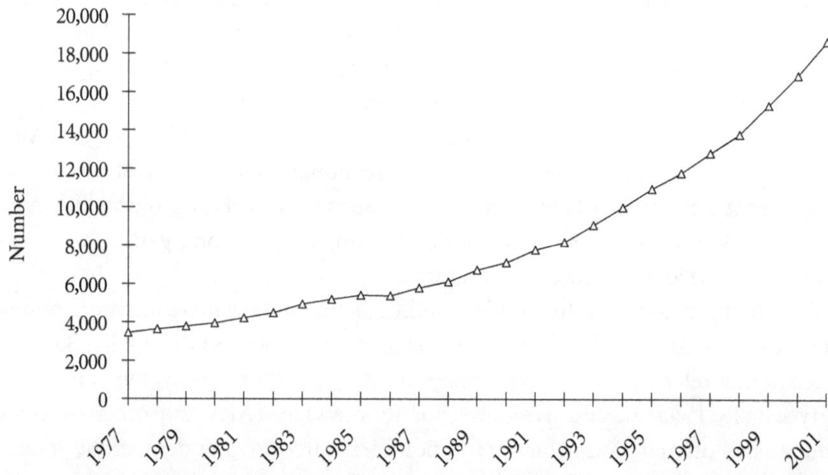

Figure 5.1. Number of National and Local Associations Registered in Taiwan, 1977–2001. Source: Ministry of Internal Affairs.

TABLE 5.5
Growth of Civil Society Groups in Taiwan, 1980–2001

Type of group	1980		2001	
	Number of groups	%	Number of groups	%
Education and culture	541	13.7	2,801	15.2
Medicine and public health	48	1.2	526	2.8
Religious	64	1.6	725	3.9
Sports	50	1.3	2,098	11.4
Social welfare and charity	2,471	62.4	5,794	31.4
International	51	1.3	2,055	11.1
Business	—	—	1,943	10.5
Other[a]	735	18.6	2,523	13.7
TOTAL	3,960	100	18,465	100

SOURCE: Ministry of Internal Affairs.
[a]Other civic groups include women's groups, neighborhood associations, alumni associations, and the like.

new associations increased dramatically in twenty years. Indeed, the number of registered associations, both national and local, increased fourfold—from 3,960 in 1980 to 18,465 in 2001. Although this number does not include all the organizations founded in the same period or any of the unregistered civil society organizations, the pattern still paints a clear picture of the growth of civil society.

As the density of Taiwan's civil society organizations increased, so too did their diversity: as shown in Table 5.5, they today operate in a variety of areas, from education, culture, business, and sports to social welfare and charity; in 1980, their activity was limited to the latter two fields. According to Robert Putnam (1993), associations can contribute to stocks of social capital and perhaps even to the performance of government, insofar as civic engagement through participation in associations supports democracy by nurturing democratic habits, creating forums for public deliberation, and encouraging active participation in public life.

How does a society make the transition from clientelism to civil society? How do subordinated people make the transition from clients to citizens? What resources and ideologies do they use to organize themselves, defend their right to autonomous association, and then pursue the social rights and identities to which they are entitled? By investigating efforts by women's groups, as well as community movements, this section aims to shed light on the process of civil society's self-empowerment. I chose women's groups and community movements as cases for investigation because the former constitute a center-oriented national movement intervening in Taiwan's national policy decision-making process, whereas the latter are local and work for change from within communities. An examination of both national and local-level movements can give us a better sense of the relationship between civil society and sociopolitical change in Taiwan. In contrast to those in Japan, advocacy groups in Taiwan are quite strong and have exercised considerable influence over public debate related to policy issues. Exemplifying this trend is the

Awakening Foundation, the leading feminist organization in Taiwan. This and other women's movement groups have successfully lobbied legislators on behalf of legal change over the past twenty years. To some extent, these social groups have been successful in changing attitudes and in raising the profile of socially progressive issues. After examining how the women's movement in Taiwan has employed legislative lobbying tactics with a nonpartisan strategy, as well as a policy of public education, to influence the public agenda, we shall see how community movements have helped to transform clients into citizens and to empower civil society. In the case of Taiwan, this article argues that the self-empowerment of civil society has played a fundamental role in creating the necessary conditions for the consolidation of democracy.

Learning to Lobby: The Women's Movement

The political accomplishments of the democratic transition involved not only a change of electoral rules and liberalization but also the emergence of new means by which organized groups learned to influence policy. Although it may be difficult today to appreciate the emergence of legal lobbying as innovative political participation, its role in Taiwan's political transition should not be taken for granted. Legal lobbying, as a way to influence public policy, was not a natural by-product of the transition to democracy. On the contrary, it was the unique historical result of the efforts of many groups in civil society. Since elected representatives in Taiwan are highly individual, and political parties do not compete on socioeconomic issues, citizens' interests and values will never be reflected directly by representative institutions without autonomous collective efforts on their part.[10] Legal lobbying required mastery of legal procedure, legal expertise, and the ability to influence public opinion. And it was during Taiwan's democratic transition that civil society groups learned this new form of political participation.

Since the early 1980s, the Taiwanese women's movement has united women who are privileged in terms of education and class but limited in terms of political experience compared to their counterparts in the labor and environmental movements (Fan 2000). These middle- and upper-class women formed an impressive array of volunteer organizations, such as the Awakening Foundation, the Taipei Women's Rescue Foundation (TWRF), the Garden of Hope Foundation (GHF), and the Modern Women's Foundation (MWF), to name just a few. Surprisingly, despite their limited political experience, they have made great strides in legislative lobbying, while maintaining a nonpartisan strategy. Indeed, these women's groups achieved an impressive amount of change through legislative lobbying compared to their counterparts in other social movements. Women's groups have initiated at least eight important bills since the early 1980s, four of which are entirely new legal proposals. All of these measures won the approval of the legislature, although the Equal Employment for Men and Women Act had to face strong opposition from industrial organizations (see "Big Events" 1995). It is worth noting that some of these successes predated the lifting of martial law.

Women's groups first exerted their influence on the legislative process in 1984. During the early stages of the Eugenic Protection Act in 1984, the Awakening Foundation called upon other women's groups to demand that the articles relating to legalized abortion be retained. Although the securing of legalized abortion came as the result of the state having a parallel interest in population control, the action nevertheless established a pattern: women's groups were capable of intervening in the legislative process and making changes to protect women's rights.[11] In 1987, activists in the Awakening Foundation began drafting an act aimed at improving gender equality in employment. This set a precedent, not only in the history of the women's movement, but in the history of Taiwan by capitalizing on an innovative legislative process that allowed civic associations to draft a law themselves and submit it to the Legislative Yuan. Although the act later faced opposition from corporations, a researcher on the contemporary Taiwanese women's movement has observed: "Collective action in proposing the 'Equal Employment Act' has helped to reshape the movement's actions. The women's movement has since moved onto a different stage to pursue gender equality through structural changes, and in particular *through legal reforms*," thus changing the major tactical thrust of the contemporary women's movement (Wang 1997: 224; emphasis added).

Why did a women's organization like the Awakening Foundation, with limited resources and little political experience, decide to invest such enormous effort in drafting laws and lobbying legislators—a process that was not only time-consuming but also unpredictable in the early stages of Taiwan's political transition? An activist in the Awakening Foundation recalls the following:

> [The] 1987 age-clause and pregnancy-free clause revealed that there was gender inequality in employment. . . . Therefore, while giving our sincere support to these working women, we decided to draft and petition for an equal employment law. Together with several lawyers, we outlined the draft. We wanted to reveal the difficulties facing working women, and we hoped that the government would eventually step in to address these problems. . . . Although it was extra work for all of us, the belief that "we were making history" encouraged us to continue with the job. (Quoted in Wang 1997: 210)

A sense of "making history" motivated these activists. Yet drafting a law and lobbying the legislature require more than hard work. As one activist said: "Amending the law requires expertise." Legal knowledge is indispensable in drafting and amending a law. But expertise and knowledge were traits that an organization like Awakening had never lacked. A committee comprising many female lawyers was organized, which spent a year and a half drafting and then introducing the Equal Employment for Men and Women Act.[12] From that point on, legislative change became the main tactic of the Awakening Foundation, as well as of many other women's groups in the 1980s and 1990s.[13] It was precisely because these women initially pursued their political goals with limited political experience and without direct access to either party that they developed methods of wielding influence that were quite distinct from partisan politics. The Equal Employment Act was not only the first bill ever to come out of nowhere; it was also the first one endorsed by Taiwanese legislators across party lines. It set a milestone by breaking through the steadfast refusal of legislators from the two major parties to promote the same bill (Wang 1997: 213). It became a model for the women's movement in developing a sensitive, party-neutral, legislative lobbying process.

Why did the women's groups choose a nonpartisan strategy and, more important, how were they able to succeed? Women's influence on politicians during the transition reflected the distinctive cultural and political dimensions of their demographic profile. With limited political activism and accustomed to being attacked by the ruling regime, the women's movement reinforced the opposition between women and the existing partisan organization of political participation (Wang Reishiang cited in Chang 1995). While its official policy declared the women's movement to be nonpartisan, individual women were sometimes purged for excessive partisanship.[14] Ironically, their low degree of politicization and their exclusion from both ruling and opposition parties helped account for their success in legislative lobbying. In short, even though these women were not strong political activists prior to participation in the movement, they not only established a public role through their social service but even developed a party-neutral lobbying strategy that proved to be very successful in passing a law.

Nevertheless, cross-party endorsement does not imply acceptance by politicians. Even though women went to the legislature and lobbied, they had no leverage over elected legislators—no votes to deliver and little money to contribute for campaigns.[15] Reflecting on their experiences working on the Equal Employment Act, they thought the ignorance of the masses was a major reason for the measure's defeat.[16] Therefore, as in the case of its American counterpart, observed by Elisabeth Clemens, "the women's movement drew on the symbolic resources of its activists, particularly its overwhelmingly educational style" (1997: 215). One activist noted: "[Only] when people understand the essential elements of a new law can they take it seriously, and only then will the law make sense and be actually followed. . . . Thus we must . . . inform women of legal issues. . . . Therefore, education becomes significant" (quoted in Wang 1997: 261). These women's groups therefore worked hard to educate the general public, especially women. As one activist commented: "Updating family provisions [in the legal code] challenges a patriarchal system that has existed in Chinese society for thousands of years" (ibid.). It takes enormous effort to change people's ideas on marriage and the family, especially in the legal realm.

The women's efforts in public education included establishing a hot line to answer legal questions, holding innumerable seminars, holding islandwide law classes, gathering thirty thousand signatures on petitions, organizing a "PoPoMaMa [Grandmoms and Moms] Legislative Observation Group" to monitor the legislative process, and even mounting a campaign to abolish gender inequality on constitutional grounds, an idea that gained the support of the chief justice. As one activist at the Awakening Foundation said: "The purpose of requiring a constitutional brief is to stop injustice immediately, before the final revision of the family provisions is completed. Requesting a judicial interpretation has a social and educational function, which lets both the judiciary and the public know exactly what women need" (*Awakening* 148 [Sept. 1994]: 12). In short, education and the cultivation of public opinion gave women the leverage they needed to become a convincing lobby.

In a society in which social groups had never exercised influence on public policy, the emergence of lobbying in the 1980s was rather remarkable and must be attributed to the effort of these civil society groups. But the women's groups were not the only ones to seize this opportunity. Environmentalists, workers, farmers, the physically challenged, students, and elders, among many others, have all to some extent learned to use the legal lobbying process in Taiwan's democratic transition.[17] This transition, according to Clemens, invoked "multiple mechanisms for the consolidation of patterns of social life: cultural elaboration, increasing returns, and shared strategies" (1997: 323). All of these processes were evident in the development of lobbying in Taiwan.

The Community Movement

Traditional communities in Taiwan at the time of the democratic transition were penetrated by local factions—which, many researchers agree, have occupied an important position in Taiwan's authoritarian history. They not only helped the KMT regime to consolidate its authoritarian rule but at the same time held a monopoly on economic resources (Wu 1987; Chu 1989). In Taiwan's political history, the relationship between local factions and the KMT can be said to have formed the core of the authoritarian-client system. "It is a system in which the regime as a patron distributes on an extensive scale material goods on a particularistic basis to the individuals in exchange of their political support and at the same time to insulate them from other political forces" (Wu 1987: 13). This vertical asymmetric network, embedded in interests, has worked against good democratic governance. Taiwan has sometimes been called an island of factions, and according to Mingtung Chen (1991) there are at least two in every town. Given that there are 365 towns in Taiwan, town-level factions thus number more than 700. Since most of the island's economically disadvantaged communities needed government investment, local elections became the channel by which different factions competed for budget resources. But most of the money ended up where the interests of local politicians were best served. Even worse, the system of patron-client politics grew into a corrupt, vote-buying culture.

The community movement that developed within civil society in the 1990s proved itself to have the potential to break this deadlock. When street protests started to decline in the 1990s, many activists, recognizing that democracy had to be developed from the bottom up, shifted their involvement to community building. Thus new faces and new organizations emerged in communities. Unlike the traditional organizations at the local level, these new groups tended to stress the spirit of public participation. Beginning with work on local cultural history and local environmental issues, they later turned to local landscape, crime prevention, community security, and youth education. The emergence of this trend certainly had something to do with the government policy of President Lee Teng-hui, who initiated a community renaissance program led by the Ministry of Culture with the political aim of resolving Taiwan's identity crisis. The growing number of local cultural history workshops can be said to have been influenced by this new policy. But the policy had a strong social impact as well. As one professor who devoted himself to a local history project said: "I am not a historian. Cultural history is just a tool, and my goal is to awaken Hualien's people's collective memories" (Lin 2002). He added that he was simply providing the nutrition needed to build a community.

In fact, many community groups started their work even before the new government policy. Many of them began with environmental issues. The Blue East Port River Protection Association (BEPRPA), founded by a group of environmental activists and residents, is a good example. The main purpose of this new organization was to revitalize the river and bring it back into the lives of the residents. These activists had sensed from the very beginning that it was useless to count on the government: only through the participation of community residents could the river be saved. The association therefore held a series of events and activities: a river seminar, a residents' river-consciousness survey, an "I Love the River" painting competition, an Old Pictures of the River exhibition, rowing on the river, and more. In this way, they invited residents to exchange views on the river and induced them to see not only the river's beauty but its pollution.

Within a few years, many residents, including local teachers and professors, had become involved as volunteers and activists. These teachers have not only helped with further research on the river and the community but, having learned through experience, have brought local cultural history, the environment, and the river into their classrooms and ignited the energy of the community. Through participation and discussion, they then got residents with different backgrounds involved in the process of public policy and helped residents to form their own community's identity and solidarity. One activist said that after working in the community movement for three years, their candidate won the local election without any vote buying—a breakthrough that many found encouraging (Lin 2002). In Taiwan's transitional period in the 1990s, BEPRPA was only one case among many.

Among the emerging social forces of the community movement, the community college program was another prime example. It was initiated by a group of educational reform activists who wished to build an autonomous civil society through civic education. The first community college was founded in 1998 in the Wenshan area of Taipei City. Within a few years, more than fifty community colleges had been established, more than three thousand courses had been taught, and more than one hundred thousand adults had enrolled.[18] Although community college does not offer official diplomas, the enrollment figures and the growing number of new colleges all over Taiwan demonstrate that there is a huge demand for adult education.

The goal, however, is not only adult education. The leader of the community college movement, Huang Wu-shiung, believes that the aim of community colleges should be to lay the foundations of a robust civil society.[19] One director of the program, Tsai Chuan-huei, stated their vision clearly:

> The founding of community colleges is not meant to copy a traditional university or college but to build a new sphere of higher education belonging to laypeople and welcome the arrival of a citizens' society. The community college has two dimensions: it is a general citizens' college and a community college with local elements. It must simultaneously deliver the contents of a formal college education and fill the needs of informal education. We must push for the founding of community colleges in order to vitalize these communities, to liberate social forces, and to cultivate citizens' abilities for public participation. (*School Begins,* no. 1)

The community college curriculum ranges from art, literature, sociology, feminism, social reform, and social movements to ecology, English, life philosophy, gardening, community newspapers, and even investment. The core of the curriculum, however, is humanism, public participation, and social reform. Adult students are encouraged to form clubs and associations around their hobbies and interests. Housewives, retired elders, workers, executives, young professionals—all sit together to learn and discuss. The focus of community colleges varies from location to location. Shin-yi Community College in downtown Taipei, for example, is famous for its parental education and community management training program. Wenshan Community College, located in suburban east Taipei, has a strong atmosphere of artistic creativity. Students of Beito Community College successfully organized a protest against air pollution caused by the local waste incinerator.[20] A recently established community college in southern Taiwan aims at agricultural renewal. All the adult students in these programs are encouraged to engage in public discussion of issues and public participation.[21]

One community college located in a residential complex managed to create a collective identity for the alienated residents by teaching them Japanese, English, and even computer skills. Now they run a community newspaper and have even established a community history museum. Today, this community college has become the community's public forum, just as at other community colleges. They not only discuss local issues but also debate national questions from educational reform to nuclear power plants. Many believe that the community college's public-spirited clubs and adult students are likely to supply the future organizational base and human resources for the community movement. By cultivating civic virtues, practicing democratic norms, and spreading democracy to more and more domains of life, community colleges have become a "public participation classroom" that will help to deepen democracy in Taiwan.

In a society in which social groups have never exercised their influence on public policy, the emergence of legal lobbying techniques was rather remarkable, and it must be attributed to the efforts of these civic-minded organizations. The women's groups did not act alone in their efforts to seize on a politically and socially inspired opportunity. Environmentalists, workers, farmers' groups, the physically challenged, students' groups, and elders' groups, among many others, have all to some extent learned to profit from the legal lobbying process in Taiwan's democratic transition.[22] Democratic transition as an institutional change invoked "multiple mechanisms for the consolidation of patterns of social life: cultural elaboration, increasing returns, and shared strategies" (Clemens 1997: 323). All of these processes were evident in the development of legal lobbying in Taiwan. The case of women's legal lobbying illustrates how a civic organization can, through the cultivation and implementation of political skills, further the viability of a politics based on pluralism.

Jon Shefner (2001) points out that if coalitions of social movement organizations are unable to obtain the resources to satisfy their needs, they may be as attracted to clientelism as are individual organizations. Judith Hellman (1994) is also pessimistic about social movements' ability to replace the old clientelistic networks. However, in the case of Taiwan, we have found that community movements may at least have weakened clientelism. As Jonathan Fox observed in Mexico, although authoritarian clientelism does not necessarily erode in a linear process toward citizenship, "social movements can gnaw at small cracks in the system and try to open them further" (Fox 1994: 183). By serving as a local channel for public actions, community movements habituate ordinary people to democratic practices and civic virtues through educational programs and public deliberation.

As Muthiah Alagappa points out elsewhere in this volume, not all civil society groups enhance democracy; some obstruct democratic development. Furthermore, not all aspects of civil society groups' activities are compatible with democratic values. However, fortunately, many civil society groups in Taiwan have been focusing their efforts on advocating policy change, demanding democratic accountability in political society and the state, and transforming clients into "citizens." As the women's movement and community movement demonstrate, the growth and self-empowerment of civil society played a significant role in deepening democracy by promoting public participation, providing education for democracy, and developing political skills, identities, and civic virtues. In short, "civil society" in Taiwan has proved to be critical for democratic consolidation.

Conclusion

This chapter has attempted to build an analytical bridge between civil society and political change in the case of Taiwan. As we have seen, civil society has grown enormously and has been a key ingredient in promoting Taiwan's democratic political change. The democratic change in Taiwan cannot be comprehended without reference to civil society. Without an assertive and robust civil society, democracy might not have emerged and taken root in Taiwan.

The relationship of civil society to the state during Taiwan's democratic transition has been confrontational. Civil society has served an instrumental function in delegitimating the state by constructing counternarratives against the ruling regime. The emerging civil society of the 1980s successfully mobilized political resistance and social protests and then formed strategic alliances pushing for democratization. Taiwan's civil society proved to have the capacity to generate a political alternative and to marshal international support to maintain a balance of power in favor of democratic forces that sustained the momentum of democratic transition. Since 1987, civil society has become more diversified in terms of issues and more populated in terms of associational density. Although Taiwanese civil society does not yet show an ability to monitor the government, there are several reasons to believe that the development of civil society has made it impossible for a democratically elected government to suspend democracy. Women's groups, by influencing policymaking, demonstrate the civil society's strength; additionally, community movements have proved to have the potential to overcome local factions and promote a new civic culture. Both cases imply that Taiwan's civil society is in the process of deepening democracy by habituating citizens to democratic practices and civic virtues.

This is not to say that there are no weaknesses in Taiwan's civil society. Internally, its membership base is still not strong enough, and most associations are themselves still learning to practice democracy. According to Hai-yuan Chu (2002), some 56 percent of the surveyed associations did not hold membership meetings and executive meetings as required by their charters. Most associations are controlled by a small group of active members. As a result, the accountability and membership base of these civic associations remain questionable.[23]

Externally, the constraining legal framework is still an issue. The Ministry of Internal Affairs did not allow associations to call themselves Taiwanese until 1999, when the supreme court ruled that this restriction violated people's freedom of association, and that their right to do so was therefore be protected by the constitution. Prior to that time, many associations that called themselves Taiwanese—such as the Taiwanese Political Science Association or the Taiwanese Environmental Alliance—chose not to register with the government. Today, the law still holds that the government has the right to grant legal status to associations. Regulations regarding frequency of meetings, content of minutes, and number of members remain unchanged.

Yet, as John Keane (1988) asserts, the global spread of civil society is not just talk.[24] After the presidential election in 2000, the concept of "civil society" in Taiwan became a normative ideal, guiding the reconfiguration of state-society relations in the postdemocratic transition period.[25] The relation between civil society and the state is no longer viewed as a zero-sum game. Both sides have a clearer understanding of the interface and interdependence between society and government. Over the past thirty years, a robust civil society has been a blessing for democracy in Taiwan.

Notes

1. Political democracy is defined here in classic procedural terms: free and fair electoral contests for governing offices based on universal suffrage, guaranteed freedoms of association and expression, accountability through the rule of law, and civilian control of the military. Democratization is defined as the process of movement toward these conditions; consolidation of a democratic regime requires fulfilling all of them.

2. Tunjen Cheng (1989) and Larry Diamond (1999) are among the few exceptions.

3. Naiteh Wu (1987: 14–15), who first described the Nationalist regime's status as authoritarian clientelism, points out: "In the political scientists' clientelism, the patron politicians offer material and non-material goods to the client supports. . . . In return for these benefits, the clients offer patron politicians political support in election. With the support from the former, the partner gains political power so that more benefits can be distributed to the supporter."

4. Tunjen Cheng (1989: 482) points out that the "ever-expanding civic and economic associations are simply beyond the capacity of the KMT to monitor, much less to control. Moreover, there is a limit to which the regime can penetrate internationally-oriented organizations, such as the Junior Chambers of Commerce, the Lions Clubs, and the Rotary Clubs."

5. A famous democracy movement leader at that time referred to his comrades in the following terms: "they are the first cohorts to have received the most complete modern education during the longest stretch of peacetime in China's one hundred years of history" (quoted in Hsiao 2003).

6. Based on the research of O-yang Sheng-en, who studied *Taiwan Political Forum*, *Formosa*, *The Eighties*, and *Deep Roots*, four "outside-the-party" magazines (Wang 1996).

7. On February 28, 1947, about two thousand people gathered in front of the Bureau of Monopoly in Taipei to protest the brutal beating on a woman cigarette peddler and the killing of a bystander by the police on the previous evening. The Chinese governor, Chen Yi, responded with machine guns, killing several people on the spot. Uprisings erupted. What

ensued was a series of massacres on the island by the troops sent from China by Chiang Kai-Shek, resulting in the deaths of more than 30,000 Taiwanese people, followed by an era of white terror (arrests and mysterious disappearances of countless additional people) by the military police for decades.

8. Sometimes they were even more successful than the ROC's foreign office in mobilizing support in the U.S. Congress.

9. After the KMT moved to Taiwan, Liao Wenyi, who was forced to flee to Japan in 1950 for advocating Taiwan's independence, became active in Tokyo and claimed to have founded a new party and a provisional government. Subsequently, Wang Yude, a Taiwanese in Japan, founded a new magazine called *Taiwan Youth Bimonthly* and initiated the Taiwan Youth Association, actively campaigning and raising funds on campuses. In 1967, Shih Ming founded the Independent Taiwan Association and issued the magazine *Independent Taiwan.*

10. Under the current electoral rule, politicians tend to compete with other candidates in the same party—which means the elections are rooted in the exchange of individual interests and patronage instead of bargaining of collective interests. For a detailed discussion of how representation constrains the public deliberation of policy see Kuo-Ming Lin (1997: 383–90) and Jihwen Lin (1998).

11. For a detailed analysis of the ideological dimension of the abortion debate, see Gu 1992.

12. The draft is full of innovative concepts, such as paternity leave for men, maternity leave for women (a maximum of one year's unpaid leave to care for newborns), and prohibiting discrimination relating to women's marriage, pregnancy, giving birth, or childrearing (*Awakening* 83 [1983]: 2, 16; *Awakening* 160 [1995]: 3–14).

13. Four of the five main organizers behind these impressive lobbying efforts—Awakening, GHF, TWRF, and MWF—are foundations. The exception is the Warm Life Association for Women (WLAW).

14. From interviews conducted in 1998, Taipei.

15. Although mobilizing female voters was considered during elections in the late 1980s, it failed to mobilize women voters.

16. The bill had been pending for many years. It was not passed until 2002.

17. See Hsiao and Sun 1998 and Lin 1998 for a detailed history of the impact of social groups on social welfare policies.

18. See editor's words in *School Begins*, no. 1, published by the National Association for the Promotion of Community University (NAPCU).

19. See the interview with Huang Wu-shiung in *School Begins*, no. 1, published by NAPCU.

20. Beito is located in the northern part of Taipei City.

21. For example: a conference organized by I-lan Community College had panels on three topics: community college and lifelong learning; local culture at I-lan; and social movements and intellectuals. More than three hundred students who had never attended a conference came to participate in this three-day discussion.

22. For a detailed history of social groups' influence on socia-welfare-related policies, see Hsiao 1998 and Lin 1998.

23. For a detailed discussion of the legal framework of NPOs, see Ku 1999, 2000.

24. Taiwan's democratic government, which aspires to international recognition and standing, has started to implement new policies protecting civil rights in many areas in order to adhere to the international human rights code. See Tseng 2004.

25. See Fan 2003.

Works Cited

Bendix, Reinhard. 1978. *Kings or People: Power and the Mandate to Rule*. Berkeley: University of California Press.

"The Big Events in the Legislation of the Equal Employment Bill." 1995. *Awakening* 160: 23–25.

Chang, Huei-tan. 1995. "Taiwan dang dai fun yu yueng tueng yo nyu xieng zhu i sh jian chu i ger li sh der guan dian" (Contemporary Taiwanese women's movement and feminist practice: A historical perspective). Photocopy. Taipei: National Tsing Hua University.

Chang Maukuei. 1989. *She huei yudong yu cheng zhi chuan xin* (Social movements and political transformation). Taipei: Institute for National Policy Research.

Chen, Ming-tung. 1990. "Uei qyuan zheng zi xia Taiwan zheng zh jieng jeng de deliou dueng (1945–1986): Sheng can i yuan ji sheng i yuan liou dueng de fen xi" (The mobility of local political elites under an authoritarian regime [1945–1986]). Taipei: National Taiwan University.

———. 1991. "Local Factions and Taiwan's Democratization." Paper presented at the Conference on Democracy in China and Taiwan—Prospects for National Unification, Center for East Asian Studies, Pennsylvania State University.

Cheng, Tunjen. 1989. "Democratizing the Quasi-Leninist Regime in Taiwan." *World Politics* 41: 471–99.

Cheng, Tunjen, and Stephen Haggard, eds. 1992. *Political Change in Taiwan*. Boulder: Lynne Rienner.

Chu, Hai-yuan. 2002. "Jie sher z iou, tuan ti tzan yu, yu mien zhu" (Associational freedom, group participation, and democracy). In Chu, Hai-yuan, Gu, Chung-hua, Chien Yung-shian, eds., *Fa zh, ren qyuan yu gueng mien sher huei* (Legal governance, human rights and civil society). Taipei: Laureate Book Co.

Chu, Yunhan. 1988. *Cong congti shehui jiegou de bianquan kan zili quiji jieto yuntong de zhuxian* (Investigating the emergence of self-help protests by looking at macrostructural change). Taipei: Min-de Foundation.

———. 1989. "Qua-chan chin-gi yu we-chua ti-chih" (Authoritarianism and economic oligopoly in Taiwan). In Chung-chi Wu, ed., *Lun-duan yu po-shiue: Wei-chua ti-chih de cheng-chi chin-gi fen-shi* (Monopoly and exploitation: The political economy of authoritarianism). Taipei: Taiwan Research Fund.

———. 1994. "Social Protests and Political Democratization in Taiwan." In Murray A. Rubinstein, ed., *The Other Taiwan: 1945 to the Present*. Armonk, N.Y.: M. E. Sharpe.

Clemens, Elisabeth. 1997. *The People's Lobby: Organizational Innovation and the Rise of Interest Group Politics in the United States, 1890–1925*. Chicago: University of Chicago Press.

Diamond, Larry. 1999. *Developing Democracy: Toward Consolidation*. Baltimore: Johns Hopkins University Press.

Fan, Yun. 1994. "Min zhu jien bu dang di fang dang bu de cu zh yu dueng yu uang luo de fen xi" (Organization and mobilization: A case study of local branch of democratic progressive party). MA thesis, National Taiwan University.

———. 2000. "Activists in Political Environment: A Microfoundational Study of Social Movements in Taiwan's Democratic Transition." Ph.D. diss., Yale University.

———. 2003. "Changing State-Society Relations." MS.

Fang Xiaoding. 1991. *Gonghui yuntong yu gongchang zhengquan zhi zhuznxing* (The transformation of union movement and factory regime). Taizhong: Donghai University.

Fisherman, Robert M. 1990. *Working-Class Organization and the Return to Democracy in Spain*. Ithaca, N.Y.: Cornell University Press.

Fox, Jonathan, 1994. "The Difficult Transition from Clientelism to Citizenship: Lessons from Mexico." *World Politics* 46(2): 151–84.

Fraser, Nancy. 1992a. "Rethinking the Public Sphere: A Contribution to the Critique of Actually Emerging Democracy." In Craig Calhoun, ed., *Habermas and the Public Sphere*, 109–42. Cambridge, Mass.: MIT Press.

———. 1992b. "Sex, Lies and the Public Sphere: Some Reflections on the Confirmation of Clarence Thomas." *Critical Inquiry* 18 (Spring 1992): 595–612.

Gian Jiashin. 1998. "Jiuning niandai Taiwan nutongzhi de rentong jiangou yu yundong jijie: Zhai kanwu wanglou wanglou shang xingzheng de nutong zhi xinshequn" (Taiwanese lesbians' identification under the queer politics since 1990). *Taiwan shehui yenjiu jikan* 30: 63–115.

Gu Yenling. 1992. "Funu yundong yu gonggong zhengce de hudong guanxi: Duotai hefahua han pingdeng gongzuoquan celue fenxi" (The interaction between the women's movement and public policy: The analysis of strategies toward legal abortion and worker's equal rights). Paper presented at conference on the State and Society in Taiwan's Democratization (Taiwan minzhuhua guozheng de guojia yu shehui), Qinghua University, Xinchu.

Guo Huiying. 1997. *Taiwan sizhu gonghui de yunzuo* (The operation of Taiwan's independent union movement). Taipei: National Taiwan University.

Haberson, John W. 1994. "Civil Society and Political Renaissance in Africa." In Donald Rothchild, John W. Harbeson, and Naomi Chazan, eds., *Civil Society and the State in Africa*. Boulder: Lynne Rienner.

Hellman, Judith A. 1994. "Mexican Popular Movements, Clientelism, and the Process of Democratization." *Latin American Perspective* 21(2): 124–42.

Ho, Ming-Hsiu. 2000. "Mien zhu zhuan xieng guo cheng zhueng der gu jia yu mien zhu sher huei" (State and civil society in democratic transition: A case study of environmental movement). Ph.D. diss., National Taiwan University.

Hsiao, A-Chin. 2003. "Ren-tung, hsiu-shih, yu shin-ton" (Identity, narratives, and action). *Taiwanese Sociology* 5: 195–250.

Hsiao Hsinhung Michael, and Sun Zhihui. 1998. *Shinian Taiwan shehui fuli yundong de fazhi: Chuangcheng yu bianquin* (A decade of development in Taiwan's social welfare movements). Taipei: National Taiwan University.

Hsiao, Michael, and Robert Weller. 1998. "Culture, Gender, and Community in Taiwan's Environmental Movement." In Arne Kalland and Gerard Persoon, eds., *Environmental Movements in Asia*. Richmond, Surrey: Curzon Press.

Hsiao, Hsin-Huang Michael, and Hagen Koo. 1997. "The Middle Classes and Democratization." In Larry Diamond et al., eds., *Consolidating the Third Wave Democracies: Themes and Perspectives*, 311–33. Baltimore: Johns Hopkins University Press.

Hsiao, Hsin-Huang Michael, and Robert Weller. 1997. "Culture, Gender, and Community in Taiwan's Environmental Movement." In Arne Kalland and Gerard Persoon, eds., *Environmental Movements in Asia*. Richmond, Surrey: Curzon Press.

Keane, John. 1998. *Civil Society: Old Imagines, New Vision*. Stanford: Stanford University Press.

Ku, Chung-hwa. 1999. "Gon min jen-she de jen go bian chian" (The structural transformation of civic association and the development of NPOs in Taiwan). *Taiwan: A Radical Quarterly in Social Studies* 36: 123–46.

———. 2000. "Taiwan gon min she-huei de gon gong shin yu tsz tsu shin" (The autonomy and publicness of NPO in Taiwan). *Taiwanese Sociological Research* 4: 145–89.

Lin, Jihwen. 1998. "Vote Buying Versus Noise-Making: Two Models of Electoral Competition

Under the Single Non-Transferable Vote Multi-Member District System." *Chinese Political Science Review* 30: 93–122.

Lin, Kuo-Ming. 1997. "From Authoritarianism to Statism: The Politics of National Health Insurance in Taiwan." Ph.D. diss., Yale University.

Lin Wanyi. 1998. *Shehui kanzhen, zhengzhi quanli ziyuan yu shehui fuli zhengce de fazhan: Yijiu baling naindai yilai de Taiwan jingyen* (Social protests, political power, and the development of social welfare policy). Taipei: National Taiwan University.

Lin, Zhao-zhen. 2002. "Report on Community Movement." *China Times*, Oct. 24.

Putnam, Robert D., Robert Leonardi, and Raffaella Y. Nanetti. 1993. *Making Democracy Work: Civic Traditions on Modern Italy*. Princeton: Princeton University Press.

Rigger, Shelly. 1999. *Politics in Taiwan: Voting for Democracy*. London: Routledge.

Shefner, Jon. 2001. "Coalitions and Clientelism in Mexico." *Theory and Society* 30: 593–628.

Stepan, Alfred. 1988. *Rethinking Military Politics: Brazil and The Southern*. Princeton: Princeton University Press.

Tien, Hungmao. 1989. *The Great Transition: Political and Social Change in the Republic of China*. Stanford: Hoover Institution.

Tien, Hung-Mao, and T. J. Cheng. 1997. "Crafting Democratic Institutions in Taiwan." *The China Quarterly* 37 (Jan.).Tseng, Yen-fen. 2004. "Politics of Importing Foreigners: Foreign Labor Policy in Taiwan." In Catherine Wihtol de Wenden, ed., *Migration Between States and Markets*. London: Ashgate Publishers.

Wang Fuchang. 1996. "Taiwan fan duei yueng dueng de gueng sh dueng yuan: 1979–1989 liang c tiaozhan gao feng de bi jiao" (Consensus mobilization of the political opposition in Taiwan: Comparing two waves of challenges, 1979–1989). *Taiwanese Political Science Review* 1: 129–210.

Wang Ginso. 2003. "Ua jie zhueng de di feng pai xi" (Disappearing factions). MS.

Wang, Tsaiwei. 1997. "Feminism and the Formation of Collective Identity Within the Women's Movement in Contemporary Taiwan." Ph.D. diss., University of Pittsburgh.

Whitehead, Laurence. 1988. "International Aspects of Democratization." In Philippe C. Schmitter, Guillermo O'Donnell, and Laurence Whitehead, eds., *Transitions from Authoritarian Rule: Comparative Perspectives*. Baltimore: Johns Hopkins University Press.

Wu, Naiteh. 1987. "The Politics of a Regime Patronage: Mobilization and Control Within an Authoritarian Regime." Ph.D. diss., University of Chicago.

———. 1993. "Ren kou liou dueng, di feng pai xi yu zheng zh zh ch: Jian sh i ger chuan tueng ger zheng zh zh huei" (Migration, local factions, and political support: Examining a traditional wisdom). In Michael Hsiao, ed., *Immigrant Population in Taipei County*. Taipei: Taipei County Cultural Center.

———. 2000. "Run de yiing shun li nian zai li sh bian ger zhueng de zuo yueng: Meu li dao sh jian han Taiwan miun zhu hua" (The role of moral value in political change: Explaining democratic transition in Taiwan). *Taiwanese Political Science Review* 4: 57–104.

Zhang Huitan. 1995. "Taiwan gangdai funu yundong yu nunxing zhuyi shijian: Yige lishi de guandian" (A preliminary study of the contemporary women's movement and feminist practice in Taiwan). MA thesis, Qinghua University.

CHAPTER SIX

India

Expanding and Contracting Democratic Space

AMITABH BEHAR

ASEEM PRAKASH

India has a robust civil society that occupies a significant space in the dynamic political landscape of the country. The civil society sphere is dynamic too, and its objectives, strategies, and influence are constantly being shaped and reshaped by a complex interplay of state, society, and the evolving processes of democracy in the country. In this fluid context, the role of civil society in political change has increasingly become dominant—leading to two simultaneous but contradictory processes.

On the one hand, the uncivil elements occupying the civil society space have successfully communalized Indian politics at the macro and meso levels to further their agenda of establishing India as a Hindu nation. This project of "Hindutva," led by a section of civil society, is steadily reducing the democratic space in the country, communalizing state institutions, and threatening the fundamental building blocks of secularism and the universal criterion of citizenship in the Indian republic, supporting the claim in the introduction that "antidemocratic forces in civil society may be working to limit and even reverse certain democratic developments." On the other hand, a large section of civil society, working primarily at the micro level, presents an alternative vision of justice and development that is embedded in the discourse of empowerment, rights, and democracy. This section has deepened and furthered certain dimensions of progressive political change and in the process has enlarged its own operating space at the local level. This civil society is attempting to foster and consolidate political change, not only by making the state more democratic, but also by employing various strategies to democratize the society. Its role in fostering political change can broadly be viewed as threefold. First, civil society plays an important role in contesting the state, the society, and its institutions from the perspective of the poor and marginalized to further a discourse of rights and democracy. Second, it is engaged in building alternative strategies, mechanisms, and visions of development, society, and politics in the country for democratic, decentralized, sustainable, people-oriented development. And third, it plays the critical role of trying to bridge the chasm between institutional and substantive democracy, particularly from the perspective of poor, ordinary, and marginalized citizens.

Our aim here is to sum up the impact of civil society on political change by analyzing, with the help of case studies, the two contradictory but significant processes initiated by civil society that are transforming Indian politics—first, by narrowing democratic and secular spaces at the macro and meso levels and, second, by opening new spaces at the micro level for democratic action for and by the poor and disempowered.

The Paradox of India

India today has a population of more than one billion people, speaking eighteen major languages and sixteen hundred minor languages and dialects, practicing more than six major religions, from six main ethnic groups, divided into 6,400 castes and subcastes and fifty-two major tribes (*India Today*, Aug. 19, 2002). India has twenty-eight states and seven union territories. More than five hundred principalities and British India, with different histories, language, culture, and resources, came together to form the Republic of India in 1950. Indeed, the country's plurality and diversity are strongly reflected in the multiplicity of the experiences of different communities, regions, and classes in independent India. It would be futile to search for homogeneous sociopolitical trends in India leading to a uniform trajectory of change and development. But certain broad developments and processes can be identified that have had serious implications for the country's sociopolitical and economic spheres.

Its immense diversity, plurality, size, and experience of sustained multiparty democracy, despite high levels of poverty and low human development, make India unique. A great deal has been achieved in the past fifty-two years in science and technology and certain sectors of the economy (expansion and diversification of production; the adoption of new technologies and modern management; advances in medicine, engineering, and software development), but there is nonetheless widespread inequality in India—across states, between rural and urban areas, within communities and castes, and between women and men. In 1992–93, for example, infant mortality was 59 per 1,000 in urban areas and 94 in rural areas; life expectancy at birth among women in Madhya Pradesh was fifty-seven years, which is eighteen years less than the life expectancy of women in Kerala, and infant mortality was 107 and 91 per 1,000 among the scheduled castes and scheduled tribes respectively, substantially higher than the infant mortality rate for the rest of the population. India's economic growth has been impressive—it is one of the few developing countries to have enjoyed sustained growth in per capita income since 1950—but levels of human development remain very low. Some 55 percent of children under the age of five remain malnourished—nearly twice levels reported in many parts of sub-Saharan Africa. India's maternal mortality rate, 410 per 100,000 live births, is almost 100 times the level found in the West. Close to two million infants die every year. Adult literacy in 1991 was only about 52 percent, and close to two-thirds of India's women could not read or write. Considerations of gender, caste, and class continue to affect access to basic social services. Despite India's many achievements, some 34 percent of the country's total population continues to live below the poverty line (Census of India 1991).

The progress of postcolonial India thus presents a mixed picture. The country has made striking achievements in some sectors but has failed massively in many dimensions of human development. Certainly, the fruits of India's economic development have not reached the poor, the marginalized, and the deprived. This failure highlights the persistence of widespread inequality and reflects the extent of human deprivation. Illiteracy, ill health, malnutrition, insufficient earnings, social exclusion, lack of say in decision making—all must be viewed as a "set of un-freedoms constituting human poverty" (Sen 1999: 15–17).

The Journey of the Indian State

Under British colonial rule, the state was an instrument used by the imperial Raj for aggressively pursuing its economic and political interests by developing elaborate sets of rules and laws to be implemented through bureaucratic mechanisms or the coercive state apparatus if required. The inherent principle of governance was to secure the economic agenda of the British Raj; the people were viewed primarily as a law and order issue (Sharma 1992: 32–35). All this changed, however, when India achieved its independence on August 15, 1947, through a mass-based, nonviolent independence movement led by Mahatma Gandhi and the Indian National Congress. The newly independent Indian Union enacted the constitution of India on January 26, 1950. Clearly stating the philosophy of the newly created state, the amended preamble of the constitution says: "We the people of India, having solemnly resolved to constitute India into a sovereign socialist secular democratic republic . . ." (Basu 1994: 20). With this vision India embarked on the path of postcolonial nation building with enthusiasm and optimism, despite the tragic and violent partition of the country.

To achieve these lofty ideals, India adopted the path of economic growth through planned development emphasizing technological advancement and heavy industry. One of the assumptions was that the benefits of economic growth would trickle down to the poor and eradicate poverty. Simultaneously, endeavors were undertaken to create modern institutions for democratic governance: a parliament, election commission, autonomous judiciary, and the like. But the rewards of economic growth failed to reach the poor and marginalized, and the prerequisite conditions for social and economic democracy failed to materialize. The political democracy guaranteed by the constitution to every Indian citizen was constrained by the lack of social and economic democracy (Pylee 1998: 14).

By the mid-1970s, the enthusiasm for nation building had given way to agitation against the prevailing corruption, food scarcity, unemployment, and a worsening economic situation after the India-Pakistan war. The energies unleashed by the protests and mobilization on these issues were channeled by the veteran socialist leader J. P. Narayan into political mass movements for *sampoorn kranti* (total revolution) and *navnirman* (reconstruction), directly confronting the authoritarian rule of Prime Minister Indira Gandhi. In June 1975, Indira Gandhi's election to the parliament was declared invalid by a state high court—prompting her to declare a state of emergency that meant the end of democratic governance and led to a suspension of fundamental rights and civil liberties for two years. In 1977, democratic rule was restored.

In postcolonial India, responsibility for nation building, social justice, and economic growth was entrusted to the state. It attempted to achieve these objectives through a combination of strategies: a mixed economy, planned development, social legislation, public welfare policies, and federal governance. This policy led to a maximalist role for the state, which entered all spheres of public and civic life. The state has not been able to achieve these objectives in five decades, however, and the Indian experience has been uneven. Economic growth has been slow, and its fruits continue to be distributed unequally among individuals, communities, and regions; social divisions and hierarchies have not been reduced; human development remains low. The factors responsible for the lack of human, economic, social, and political development are manifold and complex and beyond the scope of this study. Some scholars, however, cite the lack of development of a democratic polity, state, and society—notwithstanding regular elections, representative parliamentary democracy, elected governments (except for a brief spell of less than two years), and a vigorous multiparty system—as one of the significant reasons for this developmental failure.

The brief period of emergency and the emerging notion of state erosion changed the discourse of the Indian polity and irreversibly changed the character and trajectory of the Indian state. In 1980, Indira Gandhi returned to power after three years in the opposition, and her new priorities signaled the changing character of the Indian state and its slide from the "commanding heights." By the mid-1980s, the state had become open to working with outside agencies and initiated significant moves for decentralization of governance. The first shift was forcefully articulated by the seventh five-year plan, which accorded formal recognition to the role of

NGOs in fulfilling the plan's objectives, and since then the recognition has steadily grown. This shift was further consolidated in March 1994 when, at the behest of the prime minister, the Planning Commission organized a meeting of over a hundred NGOs, cabinet ministers, government of India officials, and several state government officials, which drafted an "action plan" to create a collaborative relationship between NGOs and the government. The second significant shift was to initiate the process of democratic decentralization by providing a constitutional mandate to institutions of local self-governance in both rural and urban areas. Two constitutional amendments gave uniformity and formal structure to the institutions of self-governance necessary for effective functioning. Above all, the seventy-third amendment formally recognized the traditional *panchayat*s as institutions of local self-governance in rural India—a fundamental restructuring of the country's governance and administrative system based on the philosophy of decentralization and power to the people. Many view the new *panchayati* system as having the potential to usher in an era of change in accord with people's needs and priorities and the power to revitalize a deeply troubled democracy (Behar and Kumar 2002).

Another watershed in the history of the Indian state after Indira Gandhi's emergency decree came in 1991 when—owing to depleted foreign reserves, growing foreign debt, a worsening economic situation, and the growing realization of the state's limited potential for social and economic transformation—India adopted the path of liberalization and structural adjustment, paving the way for a greater role of market forces and globalization. It was expected that this retreat of the state from the economic sphere (and gradually from other spheres) would unleash the process of growth and development. But the benefits of these changes, if any, have not reached the majority of a population that remains poor, vulnerable, and disadvantaged.

The most significant political change, however, has been the rise of communal and majoritarian politics in the 1980s and 1990s led by the Rashtriya Swamsewak Sangh (RSS) and its affiliate organizations—a change that has led to the killing of thousands of people in communal riots over the past decade, culminating in the genocide against the Muslim community in Gujarat in early 2002. The RSS and affiliates succeeded with communal mobilization by initiating the Ayodhya movement to build a Hindu temple in place of the Babri mosque. (The RSS believes the mosque was built by a Moghul ruler who destroyed a temple on the site marking the birthplace of the Hindu god-king Rama.) This movement gathered enormous support for the RSS from the majority of Hindus in northern India, resulting in electoral victories in several states for its political wing: the Bharitya Janata Party (BJP). The RSS and its affiliate organizations used the strategy of communal mobilization along religious lines for majoritarian politics—leading to the rise to power of BJP, which formed the national government in 1998. The polity is now so strongly dominated by RSS and its affiliates that the country's sociopolitical agenda is being set by these organizations, to which secular forces are simply responding. The state and its institutions under the BJP government are becoming increasingly communal as well, posing the biggest threat to the secular and democratic foundations of the Indian republic since independence.

In this overall context of liberalization, privatization, globalization, growing partnerships between state and market and state and civil society, democratic decentralization, the failure of the state as an agent for development and change, and the phenomenal rise of communalism, it is becoming clear that the revitalization of civil society discourse and space in India has generated contradictory trends of regression and hope for democracy in the country.

Mapping India's Civil Society

The process of democratization of society and polity has varied from region to region. The Indian state's federal structure has also encouraged diverse levels of democratization in different regions of the country. As a corollary, the development of civil society also varies, depending on the federal unit of state, the level of development of traditional political institutions, and the prevailing conditions for democracy and political mobilization. Thus civil society is vigorous and fairly well developed in some regions, whereas in others, its space is shrinking. Despite these differences across time and space, mapping the civil society terrain offers insights into the civil society space in India.

The Wide Spectrum of Key Players: From Missionaries to Identity Movements

In the mid-to-late colonial period, India witnessed extensive civil activity of three kinds. The first was the philanthropy of Christian missionaries, who built schools, colleges, dispensaries, and orphanages. The second category was initiated by an Indian bourgeoisie that was greatly influenced by Western liberal thought—leading to the building of schools, colleges, and hospitals, as well as issue-based social reform regarding widow remarriage, improvement of women's social status, women's education, the practice of suttee, and so on (Sen 1997: 30–32). These initiatives found very fertile ground in Bengal but soon traveled to the western coast in Mumbai (Bombay) and spread across the country. Mahatma Gandhi gave impetus to the third kind of civil society: activity based on voluntary action and movements such as Harijan Sevak Sangh, Buniyadi Talim, and the All-India Spinners Association. Gandhi believed that voluntary action and constructive work leading to the self-reliance of villages was essential to free India of its problems of poverty, inequality, and exploitation. Often these organizations were led by people who were also involved in the national freedom struggle as members of the Congress Party under Gandhi's leadership. By the time of independence, the entire civil society arena was occupied by the Congress Party and its affiliate organizations inspired by Gandhian ideals (Jayal 2000: 129).

After independence, the civil society landscape was occupied by religious and Gandhian organizations working on a variety of welfare and development issues: health, education, village industries, handicrafts, training of government officials. The religious organizations focused their attention on health and nutrition, famine relief, relief for refugees, and the like. The Gandhian groups, which still occupied most of the civil society space, started getting government support and funding and a few even became organs of the state such as the Khadi and Village Industries Commission. Many of the Gandhian organizations across the country not seeking government support were under the umbrella of Sarva Seva Sangh training volunteers for social action from ashrams based in remote areas of the country. These workers, called *sarvodayi,* constituted an important part of the civil society spectrum. Many other Gandhians did not believe in institutional structures and preferred individual and group social action (Mahajan 2002: 107). The most prominent among these Gandhians was Acharya Vinoba Bhave, who led a movement called Bhoodan, which urged voluntary donation of land by wealthy landlords for redistribution among the rural landless poor.

The 1970s were a volatile period for India. The country witnessed the end of a romantic armed revolutionary movement in rural West Bengal, unemployment and worsening economic conditions leading to mass political mobilization and nationwide strikes, and suspension of democracy for two years under a national emergency declared by an authoritarian regime, leading to a complete transformation of the civil society space. The emergency was used by Indira Gandhi, the prime minister, to suspend civil liberties, introduce censorship and curbs on the freedom of the press, and use arbitrary detention laws to muzzle any form of opposition. Although the experience of a national emergency during which democratic rule was suspended came as a rude shock, it rekindled interest in civil society—in fact, the opposition to emergency rule came substantially from civil society. Under different names, strands, and umbrellas, civil society was galvanized to act against the authoritarian regime. In fact, many activists regard the emergency as a watershed that led to the present proactive phase of civil society in India.[1] This experience transformed and revitalized India's civil society. For the first time in the country's postindependence history, civil society "emerged in response and resistance to the state" (Jayal 2000: 132).

This sociopolitical scenario provided fertile ground for the emergence of organizations and initiatives that would reshape the concept of civil society and shift the focus from welfare and charity to development, empowerment, and social change. Many of these organizations were a curious mixture of Gandhian and Marxist idealism. Notable among these pioneering initiatives were the Social Work and

Research Center (SWRC) established in Tilonia, Rajasthan, by Bunker Roy after his work in the villages of Bihar. Kishore Bharati (the Association for Indian Youth) in Hosangabad, Madhya Pradesh, was established to undertake education programs. The founder of Kishore Bharati was Anil Sadgopal, a trained molecular biologist, who believed that "education makes all the difference and it is the most important tool for change."[2] Similarly, Dunu Roy, a trained engineer from the elite Indian Institute of Technology, established Vidushak Karkhana (Fun Factory) in Shahdol district of Madhya Pradesh for economic advancement through appropriate technology. A young doctor couple, Rajnikant and Mabel Arole, set out to improve the rural health system at Jamkhed in Ahmednagar district of Maharahstra.

By the early 1980s, the civil society arena had grown big and diverse. Here we can only suggest the broad trends representing different dimensions of the complex and nuanced civil society space in India. Certainly, the emergence of nongovernmental organizations (NGOs) has significantly altered the civil society space over the past two decades. This shift is strongly reflected in the changing terminology used to define civil society organizations—from "voluntary sector" in the 1970s to the present "development sector," or NGOs, clearly indicating the changing character of the civil society institutions that now work as professional organizations instead of the Gandhi-inspired voluntary efforts for social and developmental work. Some think that voluntary social action has serious structural and institutional limitations in meeting sustainable development objectives and contend that professionalism is required to achieve the objective of NGOs. The experiences of the milk cooperative movement led by Dr. Kurien in establishing a highly successful Amul dairy cooperative gave a further fillip to this trend. The government too supported the growth of professional NGOs. The Institute of Rural Management in Anand was established in 1980 to build the capacities of young people for professional management of rural development programs, policies, and institutions. Later, in 1986, the Council for Advancement of People's Action and Rural Technology (CAPART) was set up by the government of India to provide financial and technical support to NGOs as a nexus coordinating the emerging partnership between voluntary organizations and the government for sustainable development of rural areas. Other noteworthy initiatives included Pradan, set up in 1982 to attract, support, and train young professionals for rural development; Ekalavaya, set up in the early 1980s in Bhopal for improving education; and the Center for Science and Environment (CSE), established in 1980 in New Delhi as a public interest research and advocacy organization promoting environmentally sound, equitable, and sustainable development strategies. This trend was responsible for the increasing number of professional NGOs working in diverse geographical regions and such diverse fields as community health, education, tribal development, women's issues, and the environment. The 1990s saw the growth of professional intermediary organizations focusing on issues like capacity building, research, advocacy, and networking. The

Society for Participatory Research in Asia (PRIA) in Delhi, with its wide, strong network in more than twelve states, and the National Center for Advocacy Studies in Pune (Poona) are good examples of this trend.

The NGOs have become key players in the field of development. Indeed, the government recognizes their contribution and is working with these agencies to achieve its development objectives. Several donor agencies, multilateral organizations, and international organizations, too, have realized the potential of NGOs in facilitating people-centered development and are working in close collaboration with these agencies. Despite the enthusiasm in the development sector for the potential of NGOs as a significant force for achieving people-centered development, there are questions concerning their role, ability, and efficacy. These issues emerge from the evident weaknesses of NGOs. Their success has been limited to dimensions of development that are soft and operate only at the micro level. (The NGOs are primarily working to improve the service delivery system and have neglected their role as catalyst for social, economic, and political changes favoring the poor, marginalized, and disadvantaged.) Most important, these agencies have been unable to induce sustainable development.

A parallel trend in the civil society arena was the development of sociopolitical action groups and social movements. In India, these are referred to as grassroots movements or "nonparty political formations," as classified by the eminent social scientists Rajni Kothari and Harsh Sethi. Such movements do not have party affiliations and work largely through political mobilization of disadvantaged communities, often occupying the antistate space, criticizing the dominant mainstream paradigms and strategies of development from the perspective of ordinary people. Despite their localized support base and local character, these movements have often been able to affect policy at the macro level, in some instances altering the country's development thinking. Some parallels can be drawn with social movements in Taiwan, which play a significant role in building and consolidating democracy in that country (see Chapter 5). To protect their autonomy, these grassroots movements usually do not accept financial support from the government or other agencies and employ only peaceful means, such as civil disobedience, for mobilizing support and sociopolitical action.

Various examples of grassroots movements can be cited to illustrate their issues, strategies, and nature. The Chipko movement led by Chandi Prasad Bhat in the hills of Uttaranchal galvanized local villagers to protest the felling of trees until an acceptable solution was worked out with the government. Nalini Nayak and Fr. Thomas Kocherry have mobilized coastal fish workers to protect their traditional rights and livelihood. In Madhya Pradesh, the Narmada Bachao Andolan led by Medha Patkar has resulted in sustained peaceful protest by tribals and peasants living in the Narmada Valley—primarily against displacement of tribal people and flooding of their land by a large dam project. The Self-Employed Women's

Association (SEWA), a union of women workers in Gujarat, responds to the specific needs of poor self-employed women by providing access to credit and so forth; unlike the other movements, it is not operating in the antistate space and often "practices a politics of part autonomy from, part engagement with, the state" (Katzenstein et al. 2001: 247). Like the NGOs, these struggle-oriented grassroots movements also form networks to enhance their efficacy. The National Alliance for People's Movements was formed as an umbrella group of more than a hundred grassroots organizations to intervene in the process of economic and political decision making from the perspective of poor and ordinary people. The National Front for Tribal Self-Rule (NFTSR) represents tribal movements and communities from across the country and successfully spearheaded the movement for extension of self-rule to tribal areas (ibid.: 250). In addition to these large alliances, activist organizations like the People's Union for Democratic Rights (PUDR) and People's Union for Civil Liberties (PUCL), mostly made up of educated urban progressives, have also played a significant role in supporting grassroots movements through media advocacy and judicial intervention.

We turn now to the politics of identity movements, which often operate in the civil society arena initially but are not shy of using violence as a strategy for mobilization and protest, later entering the mainstream political arena through electoral politics. These identity-based movements have significantly affected the contours of politics, democracy, and social change in the country. Movements initially occupying the civil space can be broadly divided into four categories in postindependence India. The first category comprises linguistic movements of the 1950s and 1960s leading to demands of federal reorganization of the Indian union. These movements—the Tamil, Telgu, and Punjabi movements, for example—were highly successful and the Indian union was reorganized on linguistic lines based on the recommendations of the State Reorganization Commission (1956). In the second category are caste movements, which have often entered the political arena as political parties representing the interests of a particular caste. The third class of identity-based movements has focused on regional autonomy and protonationalism, leading to violent struggles in Kashmir, Punjab, and Assam. The fourth and most successful identity movement with a pan-Indian appeal has been the Hindu nationalist movement, which has reaped rich political dividends and altered the political discourse in the country.

Unlike the social movements, which have remained largely localized, these identity-based forces have been able to establish themselves as regional and national movements, as their electoral successes indicate (Katzenstein et al. 2001: 245). The identity movements mobilize and consolidate support around identity issues and enter the electoral arena—influencing the country's political discourse to such an extent that election agendas have become limited to identity issues, leaving little space for politics concerning governance. And unlike the social movements rooted in a "transformative vision of social change" that have largely operated in the antistate space, these identity movements have shown their willingness to engage and capture state institutions when the opportunity arises. In this context of their electoral success and serious impact on the political discourse in India, civil society becomes the key arena for opposing identity-based movements and, more important, advancing an alternative democratic and secular vision of India—clearly reflecting the brimming conflicts and tensions within the civil society space.

Civil Society Discourse

The worldwide discourse on rethinking civil society in the context of enhancing citizen participation in the Western democracies as well as the totalitarian regimes of socialist societies created the environment for much of the interest in civil society in India (Mahajan 1999a; Alagappa, Introduction, above). The failure of the Indian state in achieving socioeconomic and political democracy and development further heightened the country's interest in civil society. A growing nonprofit sector, international development and aid agencies, the media, and certain academics started suggesting civil society as the site for solving the problems of India. Implicit in this suggestion was the idea that civil society could take on several functions where the state had failed to deliver. At this juncture, it is important to take note of a significant debate on civil society vis-à-vis the state. Rajni Kothari (1988: 134), citing the declining legitimacy of a postcolonial state that is unable to protect rights in a socioculturally plural society, posits civil society as an alternative to the state and equates it with nonstate, nongovernmental organizations (Dhanagare 2001). This comes closer to the view of Robert Cox (1999), as described in Chapter 1, in which civil society is a site for struggle and construction of a counternarrative for an alternative version of democracy that will cater to the needs of excluded classes. Gurpreet Mahajan, in contrast, suggests that such a nonstatist conception of civil society, especially in the Indian context, rests on a flawed assumption that all institutions and associations are necessarily agencies of democratization and would safeguard liberty, equal access to citizenship and resources, and political participation (Mahajan 1999a). But there is a third conception of civil society, offered by activists and radicals, that is closer to Kothari's version. This alternative conception locates it in a nonstate (or even antistate) domain of challenge to the establishment in the form of new social movements (Dhanagare 2001). Here we should enter a caveat suggested by Neera Chandhoke (1995: 9), who says: "Existence of civil society does not mean that it will always challenge the state, or that it will transgress the boundaries of the political as constructed by the state."

This renewed focus on civil society led to serious debates about the role, functions, character, and potential of civil society in India. Its relationship to the state came under substantial scrutiny. In one conception, civil society is "another name for voluntary associations of all types from sports associations and theater groups to trade unions, churches and caste *panchayats*, irrespective of the goals that these associations pursue and without consideration to the way they impact upon the freedom and rights of all citizens" (Mahajan 1999a: 1). Despite this broad definition, the concept of civil society in India is largely limited to NGOs, donor and aid organizations, development banks, bilateral and international agencies, and academia. The print and electronic media, which have an extensive reach throughout the country via English and vernacular newspapers and journals and television channels, do not commonly use the concept of civil society, unlike in Japan, where *civil society* was a widely used term in the post–World War II period. Indeed, its usage in the Indian media is restricted to stories regarding the development sector in the country—indicating that the concept has not spread to the public domain.

In fact, the notion of civil society has not even percolated down to the local NGOs and voluntary agencies in the development sector that coined the phrase in the first place. This lack of penetration is evident from the fact that no standard term for civil society has emerged in vernacular languages, just as translations of this English phrase into other European languages, such as German, do not convey the same meaning (see Introduction). In Hindi, the national language of India, literature and organizations use two phrases to denote the concept. The first is *sabhya samaj* (literally, "civilized society") and the second is *nagrik samaj* (literally, "citizen society"). Both notions have sparked debate at the local level, and failure to use these phrases can be attributed to the discomfort of organizations with the concept of civil society.[3]

Their discomfort is due also to the flabby definition of civil society devoid of a normative component. India today has a host of associations that are organized around the principles of primordial and ascriptive identities, such as caste, religion, and ethnicity, and that are pursuing an agenda that challenges the postindependence secular, modernist, democratic, and progressive consensus on nation building. Situating these groups in the discourse of civil society remains problematic. Given the normatively loaded context of India, *uncivil society* or *counter civil society* (Chandhoke 1995: 243) might describe these organizations more precisely. Certainly, the immense impact of uncivil society on the social, political, and state sphere cannot be denied—particularly since the rise of Hindu nationalism in the early 1990s. In this canvas, which includes the state, political society, and civil society, it is important to underscore the significance of the uncivil society (groups that espouse totalizing goals and resort to the use of violence to achieve those ends) and view it as an important factor to be studied while exploring the relationship between political change and civil society in India.

Civil Society and the State

Civil society in India has different strands, as we have seen, and its relationship to the state depends on the relationship it seeks. Four models of civil society-state relations can be identified in the country. The first is a partnership that encompasses a range of civil society organizations including the professional NGOs and service delivery organizations. The Society for Participatory Research in Asia, for example, has developed partnerships with the union government and several state governments to strengthen the institutions of rural self-governance (PRIA 2001). Similarly, the Center for Science and Environment was part of the official government of India delegation at the 2002 Global Summit on Sustainable Development in Johannesburg to represent the country's environmental concerns. The second model of the civil-state relationship is that of part partnership and part opposition, a category that includes many of the activist NGOs, grassroots organizations, and some social movements. In this model the organization develops a partnership with the state in several spheres of its work by joining government-appointed committees, facilitating the implementation of government programs acceptable to it, and so forth, nevertheless retaining its autonomy to criticize government programs and policies. Ekta Parishad (Unity Forum), a mass-based people's organization, has formed a joint task force with the government of Madhya Pradesh to help resolve the demands for land by landless farmers and tribals but through mass mobilization strongly opposes the forest policies being implemented by the state government and its partner, the World Bank. The third model is one of opposition and negotiation with the state, a category that includes many of the radical grassroots and social movements discussed earlier. The Narmada Bachao Andolan (NBA; Save Narmada Movement) rejects the state's development paradigm based on construction of large dams; it also criticizes the government's policies but is negotiating with it for compensation and rehabilitation through institutional and informal channels. The flexibility available to the Indian civil society in developing a relationship with the state suggests the strength of democratic institutions and culture in the country. In the fourth model, the new paradigm since the 1990s, civil society is able to steer the state's agenda in line with its own objectives. This model is taking shape under the guidance of RSS and affiliate organizations, which often dictate the agenda and policies of the state through the union government led by BJP. The union government's ordering the rewriting of history textbooks for schools across the country to suit RSS's communal historiography is a strong sign of this trend.

Despite the presence of vigorous institutions and a culture of democracy, the state often tries to curtail the flexibility of civil society through its repressive apparatus and extraconstitutional methods. Its attempts have been largely unsuccessful, however, and the guarantees in the constitution of India regarding civil and political rights, coupled with the democratic energies of the Indian polity, uphold the robustness of civil society's space. Nevertheless, the state has been able to narrow the space for the civil society organizations that seek legitimacy through state recognition. As discussed by Alagappa in Chapter 1, this would be justified by some on the basis of the Hegelian concept in which the state has to order, guide, and govern civil society. Most NGOs and voluntary agencies (apart from the social and grassroots movements) seek government recognition by registering with the government in order to gain the benefits and resources provided by the state. Two control mechanisms have been developed by the state. The first is the registration of organizations under the Societies Registration Act 1860, the Indian Trusts Act 1882, the Charitable and Religious Trusts Act 1920, or the nonprofit clause under Section 25 of the Companies Act 1956, which binds organizations under the laws of the act and gives the state the right to scrutinize an agency's work (Accountaid 2001: 1–4). Unless it is registered under one of these acts, an NGO cannot apply for institutional funding—seriously hampering its capacity to sustain itself. The second control mechanism concerns the other source of NGO funding: international donor agencies. To control the access of NGOs to international funds, the government of India introduced the Foreign Contribution Regulation Act (FCRA) 1976 (Accountaid 2001). Foreign institutional funds in India can be obtained only by organizations that are certified under the FCRA, for which it is essential to be registered with the government. Through the FCRA, therefore, the government is able to control the autonomy of NGOs.

In sum, then, the state–civil society relationship is dynamic. Its status depends on the interplay between the objectives pursued by civil society and the compulsions of the government of the day. In this dynamic relationship, no clear boundaries can be fixed; only a broad, ever-changing picture of civil society in the constitutionally mandated democratic space can be sketched.

Civil Society and Political Change

Civil society in India is contributing significantly to political change—but in two diametrically opposite directions, generating tensions within civil society and creating a highly dynamic polity. To describe the comprehensive impact of civil society on political change would be a daunting task and would in any case overshadow the significant political change taking place at the local level. Thus to gain a comprehensive understanding of the relationship between civil society and political change, we shall deal separately with the two divergent trends of civil society: one path leading to the opening of democratic space for the poor and marginalized and the other leading to the communalization of politics and state at the macro and meso levels.

One trend of political change promoted by the civil society is toward democratization in which the primary objective of the civil society is to secure the basic entitlements and rights guaranteed in the constitution to individuals and groups from marginalized and disadvantaged sections of society. Today, these entitlements and rights are respected neither by the agencies of the state nor by the dominant elements of society. Although India's constitution and laws have a well-developed notion of citizenship, in practice the rights of citizenship are not realized by the majority but remain confined to social and economic stratification. André Beteille (1999) would view this as a defeat of constitutional democracy. Significantly, civil society advances this agenda by undertaking the construction of the rights of poor and marginalized communities—leading to political processes that sharply question the status quo. In essence, civil society strives to ensure effective implementation of the spirit of the constitution, which has become an important reference point for a wide range of civil society actors in the country.

Another significant feature of civil society is its further democratization of its own space and institutions. Some Indian civil society organizations are pursuing interesting initiatives to democratize their functioning by making organizational management transparent and accountable, ensuring that decision making is more inclusive and participatory, and inculcating democratic practices within the organization.[4] Although there is not much discussion about the functioning of these organizations in the public domain, the idea is to induce change and instill the ethos of transparency and accountability by building a moral climate for it. As discussed in Chapter 1, the scope and vigor of governance within civil society can be viewed as useful indicators of emancipation of society from state domination, decentralization, and democratization of governance. Despite these sincere attempts to introduce progressive political change, their impact, according to many critics, is local and limited. Some of the factors responsible for limiting the impact have already been discussed. But there is another factor with serious implications that must be examined: the difference in membership and representation among the broad categories of political parties, uncivil society, and civil society.

The leadership of all these categories draws largely from the elite elements of society (see the discussion on elite domination of civil society organizations in new democracies in Chapter 1). In the case of political parties, the process of sustained democracy has led to a rearrangement of the power matrix that provides at least token representation to socially marginalized groups. In civil society, however, the leadership is almost exclusively elite; most of the leaders are highly educated members of the urban elite, motivated by ideologies of change, working to set up civil society institutions in rural areas. Despite this common ground of an elite leadership, there is a considerable difference in membership: the political parties and uncivil society draw their members from the elite, the middle classes, and the poor, whereas the membership of civil society is largely (in fact, almost exclusively) drawn from among the poor, marginalized, and disempowered. Above all, there is a sharp contrast in the representation of interests, with civil society on one side and political parties and uncivil society on the other. The political parties and uncivil society in practice represent the agenda of an elite interest, whereas civil society seeks to articulate the needs, aspirations, and interests of the poor and marginalized—often leading to a conflict of interest as the uncivil society and the political parties strive to restrict the efficacy of civil society groups. In this scenario, the civil society groups directly contribute to the debate in a settled democracy on elite versus participatory democracy. For example, the success of Narmada Bachao Andolan in mobilizing the local community against the construction of a big dam on the Narmada River has led to a situation in which the leaders of the ruling party in the state, who often have a nexus with the construction lobby, have organized fronts and platforms, pumping in personal resources to orchestrate opposition to NBA. By employing such tactics, the political parties and uncivil society with access to money and muscle are often successful in blocking civil society's efforts to induce political change. This clash of interests plays a critical role in limiting the impact of civil society on progressive political change.

But civil society faces its most serious threat in the postindependence era from the rise of Hindu fundamentalist forces, with their agenda of establishing a Hindu nation based on exclusivist principles, directly contradicting civil society's primary agenda of pursuing the "collective common good." The challenge to civil society became especially sharp during the recent communal violence in the state of Gujarat abetted by the state government led by the Bharitya Janata Party. For the past several decades, Gujarat has been fertile ground for civil society work, leading to significant political change.[5] During the recent communal carnage, however, the impact of this work was weakened. Indeed, several critics saw the occurrence of violence and riots as a clear sign of the ineffectiveness of civil society work in these communities.

Nevertheless, civil society has a bright opportunity to initiate far-reaching political change by proactively engaging with and strengthening the institutions of local self-governance. Certainly, the seventy-third amendment has institutionalized the *panchayat* system with progressive provisions for women and the scheduled castes and tribes. Several political commentators think the amendment will usher in profound institutional and political change. In the ten years since the inception of the amendment, however, the *panchayat*s have remained weak. Civil society can play a significant role in strengthening the *panchayat* system, leading to vigorous democracy at the grass roots. Indeed, many civil society organizations are playing exactly this role and have introduced changes in the development planning and prioritization process at the local level through their intervention in the *panchayat* system. The interesting attempt to institutionalize direct democracy through the Gram Sabha of the *panchayat* system in Madhya Pradesh demonstrates the potential of *panchayat*s for civil society and political change.[6] According to the framers of this system, however, this idea has not been understood and the Gram Sabha continues to be seen as an institution of the state, not of the people (Behar 2001). Even so, civil society can use such opportunities to further its agenda of democratic progressive political change.

Toward Democratization: Two Case Studies

To address the basic project of investigating civil society and political change, we offer two case studies that demonstrate the role, strategies, and efficacy of civil society in deepening progressive political change in India. The first case, Ekta Parishad, highlights the struggle for entitlements and rights of tribals and forest-dependent communities. The second, Majdoor Kisan Shakti Sangathan, underlines the struggle to make the state accountable and transparent. Both cases have furthered two critical dimensions of democracy—namely, rights and transparency—giving us a fair sense of civil society's role in affecting political change in contemporary India. But these case studies reflecting the successes of civil society should be read in conjunction with the limitations cited earlier. These two case studies would closely correspond to the categorization of "system transformation and within system change including policy change" as enumerated in the Introduction.

Ekta Parishad

Ekta Parishad (Unity Forum) is a mass-based people's organization working in many parts of Madhya Pradesh, with a membership of over a hundred thousand people.[7] The support base of Ekta Parishad is fairly well spread out in Madhya Pradesh and Chhattisgarh, with a clear concentration in the tribal and forest areas. Outside Madhya Pradesh, it has a strong presence in the states of Bihar and Orissa as well. Although Ekta Parishad is not a registered society, it has strong links with other NGOs at the state, national, and international levels.

Ekta Parishad mobilizes people (especially the poor) on the issue of proper and just utilization of resources for people-centered development. It demands that control of livelihood resources should be in the hands of local communities. This claim is articulated as a demand for ownership, control, and access to "*jal,* jungle, and *jamin*" (water, forest, and land). The primary objective of the movement is to achieve social, political, and economic change through peaceful and democratic means—in the process empowering marginalized people and putting them at the center of the development process. Reorganizing the village economy is another aim. Ekta Parishad seeks to achieve land redistribution and access to forest for forest dwellers (the tribals) and bases its efforts to regain control of local communities on local resources. It also presses for implementation of social legislation regarding minimum wages, release of bonded laborers, decentralization of decision making, and building a system more accountable to the people. Other key objectives are to promote the participation of women in change processes, to support local leadership in catering to the needs and aspirations of the poor and the marginalized, and to protect the tribal culture and way of life—especially the primitive tribes, which are increasingly threatened under the contemporary "mainstream" model of development.

Ekta Parishad presents a strong example of a mass-based civil movement working to ensure the rights of marginalized communities (particularly the tribals) guaranteed in the laws and constitution of India. Through its intervention, it has been able to influence several state policies and programs in favor of the tribals. More important, it has made significant contributions to changing the political climate and pressing the state to incorporate the interests of the tribals and marginalized. For example:

Fishing rights have been given to fisherfolk all over Madhya Pradesh owing to the pressure of organizations led by Ekta Parishad.

Nistaar rights (traditional rights) for villagers in protected areas were accepted owing to the systematic pressure of Ekta Parishad and other groups.

Certain cultural rights of the tribals (such as cutting a particular tree for religious reasons during the festival season) were restored only after Ekta Parishad put pressure on the government.

Control of land encroachment prior to 1980 is another success story of Ekta Parishad's sustained campaign (although Ekta Parishad recognizes the role played by other organizations and such factors as the involvement of the World Bank in the forestry sector of Madhya Pradesh).

Owing to pressure mounted by Ekta Parishad and other people's organizations, the second "antipeople" phase of the World Bank's forestry project has been continuously deferred for the past four years.

Ekta Parishad can clearly take credit for exposing the Malik Makbooja scam and the Supreme Court of India's consequent ban on all logging in Bastar district.[8]

Majdoor Kisan Shakti Sangathan (MKSS)

Majdoor Kisan Shakti Sangathan (MKSS; Organization for the Empowerment of Workers and Peasants) is a successful experiment that has been able to bring the issue of the state's transparency and accountability to the forefront—clearly demonstrating civil society's impact on progressive political change.[9] Its compelling struggle for transparency makes it an interesting case for analyzing civil society and democracy in India. But it is also interesting to note two significant implications of the movement: its initiation of progressive sociopolitical change in the communities where it works and its impact on making the state more transparent and accountable.

MKSS is a people's movement active in the rural areas of southern Rajasthan. Although the movement started as a struggle for the rights of workers and peasants, it soon realized that to secure the rights of the poor and marginalized, a battle had to be waged against government corruption. It also learned that to expose a corrupt system, access to information is essential. This understanding led MKSS to push for the right to information. Indian governance has borrowed heavily from the systems developed by colonial rule, however, which did not give common citizens access to information. Over the past fifty years, a nexus of vested interests has emerged that siphons off the state's resources. This nexus, in alliance with an inert bureaucracy, has denied information to the people and developed a corrupt and nontransparent system of governance. It was this well-entrenched system that the MKSS had to confront in its struggle for information.

The people's movement led by MKSS is completely participatory. The movement remained local and evolved from the experiences of its supporters—primarily poor peasants and workers. People's power gave strength to the movement and enabled it to launch successful local campaigns for land and minimum wages. All these campaigns converged in the MKSS struggle against corrupt governance. Through a few successful local battles, people realized that information holds the key to transparency and accountable governance; therefore, the right to information became the focal point of the movement.

Adopting a multipronged strategy, MKSS started using all possible channels to gain the right to information for common citizens. At the macro level, a strong network was built that was to play a key role in furthering the movement's cause. Locally, MKSS used people power through agitation and campaigns to pressure the government to grant the right to information, taking advantage of the democratic spaces in the system to expose cases of corruption and demonstrate the pertinence of transparency and accountability to the people. Through an extremely innovative method known as *jan sunwai* (public hearings), MKSS was able to channel people's power to expose corruption and make the system accountable. Pressure from MKSS led the chief minister of Rajasthan to announce in the state assembly on April 5, 1995, that citizens would be granted the right to obtain photocopies of government documents pertaining to development work. The ensuing government order was a major milestone: for the first time common citizens were given the legal right to obtain such information. Later, a comprehensive right-to-information bill (with several limitations) was passed by the state legislature, giving citizens the right to information and photocopies from all departments, not just for development work in *panchayat*s. It was a remarkable victory for MKSS. After a grassroots campaign lasting ten years, it had been able to force the issue onto the political agenda and then achieve its goals through continuous mass political action.

The impact of the MKSS struggle transcended geographical boundaries. Today, the right to information has become central to the debate on accountable and transparent governance all over the country. In other parts of India, experiments have begun to implement the government's order. In the Bilaspur division of Madhya Pradesh, for example, the right to information was given to citizens through an executive order in 1996 on the initiative of the division commissioner, Harsh Mandar. A few other states have already adopted the citizen's right to information as law. The eastern state of Goa has made the right to information an act; significantly, this measure is being used very effectively by citizens' forums opposing the construction of industrial housing that threatens to damage the environment. Another state, Tamil Nadu in southern India, has passed a bill on the right to information in its state assembly. Madhya Pradesh, a state neighboring Rajasthan, has approved a similar bill in its state assembly.

The MKSS campaign for the right to information has affected the immediate context in an interesting way. SWRC, one of the leading NGOs in the country, has, for example, strongly supported MKSS. Indeed, the MKSS campaign led to the demand for a right to information within the organization itself. Eventually, SWRC shared organizational and financial information with all the workers of Tilonia and organized a transparency meeting. This is an extremely significant development for India's NGOs, which are often accountable only to their donors. In the state of Goa, the right to information is being used against certain multinational corporations and their polluting industries. Although MKSS has no direct influence on Goa and its citizens' struggle against pollution, in many ways its campaign inspired the movement. Through its energetic and innovative struggle for the right to information, MKSS has been able to expand the democratic space for people against unaccountable and nontransparent systems. As seen in the examples of SWRC and Goa, the creation of this space in sectors other than government indicates the serious implications of this movement. Clearly, then, the movement has gained significant ground in the space of a few years. Several states (including Rajasthan) have passed laws to ensure the citizen's right to information, and the union government is working on similar legislation. MKSS has profoundly influenced the national agenda, and debates on governance now focus on transparency and accountability. The movement is substantially responsible for the changes taking place in the governance systems.

The two case studies demonstrate the impact of civil society on furthering progressive political change in the country. Even so, civil society faces serious challenges in its project of expanding the space for the discourse of people-centered development, individual and group rights, and democracy. Barring a few local successes, civil society has failed to initiate widespread progressive change in the sociopolitical dynamics of the country. And given the growing strength of uncivil society, this failure has serious implications for political change in India. Despite these limitations, civil society has initiated significant political change at the local level that sometimes translates into changes at the macro level:

Civil society has had an impact on policymaking (at both the state and union level) by making policies and programs more sensitive to the needs of the poor and marginalized.

By demonstrating the efficacy of new ideas at the local level and creating a political climate through strong advocacy, civil society is able to influence the state's planning and development paradigm.

The most significant contribution of civil society in India has been to further the discourse of democracy, not only at the level of public discourse (where institutions like the media play a key role), but at the local level where often democracy is not practiced despite the reasonably robust democratic tradition at the regional and national levels.

Toward Communalization: The Rise of Hindu Fundamentalism

The most significant shift in India's political landscape has been the rise of the Hindu right, leading to the formation of a BJP-led union government and the decline of the Indian National Congress in the 1990s. This rise of Hindutva has radically altered the political discourse of India by challenging the country's secular structure as enshrined in the Indian constitution, and as in Sri Lanka (see Chapter 9), these uncivil groups are contributing to the development of an illiberal democracy.

As we have seen, not all civil society organizations promote a universal criterion of citizenship and development. Marginalization and exclusion are not only the by-product of state policies, however; often their roots lie in the domain of civil society as well. One source of exclusion is the uncivil society that excludes people on the basis of ethnicity and religion. In India, RSS and its affiliate organizations, popularly known as the Sangh Parivar (hereafter Sangh), representing the Hindu right, are the most prominent example. The Sangh is a family of organizations comprising cultural, religious, political, militant, and social service wings. The social and political dimensions emanate from the Sangh's ideological commitment to challenge the present conception of an Indian nation and to reimagine it in terms of culture (read Hindu culture).[10] Culture in their ideological worldview is the basis for carving out a Hindu nation (*rashtra*), just as groups in Indonesia advocate an Islamic state (see Chapter 2). This Hindu nation by definition accepts as full citizens only those who are racially and culturally Hindu and castigates those who adhere to different faiths or religions.[11] This reimagination of the state has come to be known as Hindutva.[12] Through selective interpretation and self-serving historiography, Hindutva seeks to reorganize the Indian nation around the Hindu religion. It should be noted, however, that invoking such a history—largely mythological—has never entailed the rejection of modern science and technology or the modern nation-state, which Nehru himself saw as instruments to be employed for the secular nation-building project. To redefine the nation in exclusivist terms means winning state power, not through violence, but through the rules laid down by the constitution and through the ballot. This strategy requires general acceptance of the Sangh's ideological worldview—a crucial task to be performed by numerous social collectives representing the Sangh and operating in the civil society arena.

The Sangh Family of Organizations

The Sangh family has a number of wings (Table 6.1). All these social collectives devote their energy to mobilizing the popular consciousness around the Hindu nation. Accordingly, they push cultural exclusivity as a political model for rearranging social life in reaction to those who wish to draw them into a multicultural or nonreligious milieu. These collectives work at several levels. Rashtriya Swamsewak Sangh (RSS) is the core institution of the Sangh. Its members are exclusively male and primarily upper-caste. It imparts ideological and physical training to its members organized in *shakas* (cells) at the local level. These members are later expected to carry out a similar exercise through various affiliates of the Sangh. BJP, the parliamentary wing of the Sangh, participates in electoral politics.

Vishwa Hindu Parishad (VHP) is apparently the religious face of the Sangh, although it does not fall far behind Bajrang Dal (BD) in organizing and undertaking militant, often violent, agitation supporting the Sangh's raison d'être. VHP draws its members primarily from holy men as well as traders, small entrepreneurs, and professionals in the urban areas and large and midsized farmers in the countryside. It regularly organizes religious *yatras* (processions),[13] religious discourses, street-corner meetings, and fund-raising for construction of Hindu temples all over the country, especially in rural and tribal areas. VHP is the most fearsome mobilizational arm of the Sangh. Its role in demolishing the Babri mosque and involvement in the recent Gujarat carnage is well documented. Bajrang Dal is explicitly a militant wing, and its members are often foot soldiers in right-wing militant activism. BD regularly organizes training camps for its members—who are drawn mainly from the lower castes—where they are taught to use firearms and *trishuls* (tridents).

The social service wing, apparently formed to undertake social service and relief, is known to indulge in sectarian activities (Sabrang 2002b). Hundreds of other organizations, many of them registered as NGOs, claim independent status but in practical terms are working all over the country to promote the Hindu nation. These groups provide an entry point for RSS members to carry out their ideological work among the people while playing an important socialization function and role of civil society, as discussed in Chapter 1. Education often provides an effective cover for these ideological operations. Ekal Vidayalaya, for instance, tries to stop conversion to Christianity and promotes reconversion to Hinduism through teaching the values of Hindu culture; the Vikas Foundation claims to promote Indian culture but in practice promotes Hindutva by negating syncretic cultural traditions through *gurukuls* (residential schools teaching all aspects of life); Sewa Bharti works for the consolidation of Hindu society through celebrating Hindu festivals such as Holi, Raksha Bandhan, Sankranti, and Yugadi. Often invoking cultural symbols, they aim to construct a Hindu identity cutting across caste, class, and gender. Some

TABLE 6.1
The Sangh Family

Category	Role
Cultural wing	
Rashtriya Swamsewak Sangh (National Volunteer Corps)	Source of Sangh ideology; inculcates Hindutva ideology by organizing *shakas* (cells)
Political/parliamentary wing	
Bharitya Janata Party	Political party participating in electoral politics
Religious wing	
Vishwa Hindu Parishad (World Hindu Council)	Performs aggressive and agitational role in promoting Hindutva
Militant wing	
Bajrang Dal	Paramilitary wing of VHP; established to provide muscle and manpower for VHP's agitation
Social service wing	
Sewa Vibhag Sewa International Sewa Bharti Vanwasi Kalyan Parishad Ekal Vidayalaya Vikas Foundation Sanskrit Bharti	Apparently formed to carry out social service to the community; in practice, they provide an entry point for ideological volunteers.

organizations inculcate the philosophy of Hindutva through education of the young. Others have built temples in the name of rural development. Still others have issued historically inaccurate propaganda against Christians and Muslims—thereby creating their image as "adversarial others" in the eyes of the target community (Sabrang 2002b: 28–64).

Gujarat: Carnage and Elections

In early 2002, the western state of Gujarat witnessed a pogrom against the Muslims. This systematic violence, led by the Sangh and its affiliate organizations, spread across the state and continued for several months, often in tacit alliance with the police forces and the BJP state government, resulting in the brutal murder of thousands of Muslims, the rape of Muslim women, and the looting of Muslim property. Muslims in the affected areas were forced to become refugees in their own land, living in subhuman conditions in refugee camps with negligible support from the state and little hope of returning to their homes, given the looming threat of more violence. Here we want to analyze the Sangh's role in this genocide in order to gain insight into the role of civil society in political change.

Gujarat, often called a laboratory of Hindutva by the media, is a glaring example of the Sangh's influence in remolding the popular consciousness to accept Hindutva. The Sangh's preeminent status in Gujarat was achieved, moreover, while inclusive and secular civil institutions were collapsing. Trade unions, for example, which used to bring the working class together through class identity, have completely collapsed in the face of globalization (Mahadevia 2002: 4853–54). The Dalit Panther movement did react against oppression of their community in the 1980s but failed to acquire any institutional dimension (Yagnik 2002b: 36). Although Gujarat has a significant marginalized tribal population, there is no cohesive struggle mobilizing various strata of tribals to protect their rights and resources. Numerous localized struggles against the state's oppression and systematic exclusion from developmental processes were initiated but failed to give tribals a powerful political voice (Shah 2002b: 96–116). At first, the cooperative movement showed much promise, but it soon turned out to be a hybrid coalition of rich peasants, intermediary peasant castes, and small landholders, the clientele of the welfare state under the control of a single political party (the Congress Party), guiding a passive revolution (in the Gramscian sense). It is currently controlled by entrenched interests. NGOs have failed miserably to spread nonsectarian, secular values.

In this social and political vacuum, the reimagination project of Hindutva developed its roots. In this endeavor, the Sangh has not only created and sustained numerous organizations (Vishwa Hindu Parishad, Bajrang Dal, Vanwasi Kalyan Parishad, and several of their formal and informal affiliates) but also influenced and captured numerous other collectives in Gujarat (business associations,[14] neighborhood associations,[15] and others). Although the organizations representing the Sangh have memberships cutting across class, caste, and gender, their economic strength derives from upper-caste businessmen and upwardly mobile middle-class professionals.[16] The objective of these collectives is to "manufacture consent" for the success of the reimagination project.[17]

Consent is manufactured through a program that one might call "discipline, hate, and punish." Discipline implies enlisting the support of Hindus, activating them in campaigns, and organizing them under their leadership—in other words, inculcating the values of Hinduism while constructing the image of Muslims and others as culturally and socially alien, aggressive, antinational, pro-Pakistan, and favored at the expense of Hindus. (See Yagnik 2002a; Iyer et al. 2002; Lobo 2002; Sabrang 2002a.) The popular consciousness is "disciplined" by reworking the mindset of children and adults alike through textbooks, lectures, mass circulation of selected literature, public meetings, street theater, and films.[18] The network of schools started by the Sangh (Gyan Bharti, Vanwasi Kalyan Parishad, Hedegwar Chhatrayalaya) diligently works to reshape the consciousness of students by disseminating "knowledge" and "facts" colored by their ideological preferences and self-serving historiography. Fifteen hundred RSS cells in Gujarat—a figure quoted by one Sangh leader in Ahmedabad—give their members a rationale for Hindu-centric public and political life, try to inculcate a sense of religious devotion, create a sense of heroism and enthusiasm, and teach them to be fanatical.

Religious commitments are also harnessed and mobilized with the help of a series of religious *yatras*.[19] Seeking to construct a Hindu nationality, Sangh affiliates have carefully orchestrated the involvement in these processions of all the major and minor sects and different castes, including Dalits (former untouchables of the caste system) and Adivasis (Yagnik 2002b; Nandy et al. 1995: 107–10). Similarly, other Sangh outfits, such as Samajik Samarsta Mach, Bharat Sewashram, and Hindu Milan Mandir, work to develop unity between upper and lower castes by insisting that exploitation of Dalits by Brahmins is not the fault of the Hindu religion but of individuals, and denying that Sudras (lowest in the caste hierarchy) occupy an inferior position. In practice, however, none of these agencies reject the caste system (Shah 2002a). Furthermore, many other Sangh organizations disguised as NGOs receive funds from abroad through the Indian Development Relief Fund. A report titled *The Foreign Exchange of Hate* details the sectarian use of these funds, especially in tribal areas (Sabrang 2002b). Then there are numerous religious sects and individual saints—Swadhya, Swaminarayan, Murari Bapu, Sitaram Bapu, and the like—with a large following among Dalits, tribals, and other lower castes, who implicitly discipline people to the idea of a Hindu nation (Shah 2002a; Joshi 2002: 380; Mukta 2002: 61).[20]

This cultural and political disciplining has two goals. First, it tries to consolidate a Hindu social bloc vis-à-vis minorities, while also seeking to obscure the socioeconomic and cultural differences within the Hindu community itself. Second, it constructs a Muslim identity that owes fidelity only to Islam and not to the Indian nation-state and its majority population—hence suggesting that Muslims are culturally and socially unacceptable and, as a consequence, deserving of intense hatred. Once the mass hatred has been created, the Sangh simply needs an excuse to demonstrate its sentiments physically. And in Gujarat in 2002, the Godhra incident, where Hindu activists were allegedly burned alive by Muslim fundamentalists, became the trigger. In this outburst of genocide to punish the "culturally and socially unacceptable community," the Sangh—especially VHP and BD, with the active support of the Gujarat state government—was instrumental in planning, mobilizing, and leading the killing of Muslims, as well as destruction of their property and assets during the post-Godhra riots. (For details of these riots, see PUCL 2002; JFFTR 2002; Sabrang 2002a; Iyer et al. 2002; NHRC 2002; Human Rights Watch 2002.)

Another dimension of the work of the Sangh and affiliates is to ensure that their cultural and religious disciplining of the masses does not go to waste and voters are sufficiently polarized along religious lines during the elections to vote in favor of its political arm: BJP. VHP not only mobilized people for the chief minister's Gaurav *yatra* but also planned a Padpadshahi *yatra* in Gujarat during the campaign phase of the 2002 state assembly elections.[21] The aim of this procession was to mobilize people to vote for the party and its Hindu nation project. When the election commission banned this *yatra* because of its communal nature, VHP was forced to organize rallies in different parts of Gujarat. Thus all the Sangh's elements contributed to the polarization of votes along religious lines and the communalization of politics in the state—resulting in BJP's clean sweep in the December 2002 elections.

The Growth of the Sangh and Political Change

The Sangh and its affiliates, over the years, have grown in strength both organizationally (increasing membership) and geographically (forming bases in new areas). One can safely call them cadre-based organizations with the organizational structure, ideological discipline, and coherence normally associated with communist parties. The increase in the Sangh's social presence is directly proportional to the growing preeminence of its political arm, BJP. BJP's gradual rise, in turn, reflects the growing strength of the Hindu right. One can divide the growth of the Sangh's political arm into four phases: dormant, moderate/militant, moderate Hindutva, and extremist.

The Dormant Phase. The inauguration of the Indian republic and a strong political commitment to the modernist discourse—coupled with the poor performance of the Bhartiya Jana Sangh (an earlier incarnation of BJP) and Hindu Mahasabha (another right-wing political formation with the Sangh's ideology) in the first three general elections—gave reason to expect secular and democratic socioeconomic development. Yet Hindu nationalism was not completely absent from the political discourse of the country. Bhartiya Jana Sangh did manage to win thirty-five seats (9.4 percent of the total votes) in the 1957 parliamentary election and captured forty-one of forty-eight seats in the Madhya Pradesh state assembly in 1962. Stuart Corbridge and John Harriss think that the Hindu nationalist discourse of Bhartiya Jana Sangh was founded on its understanding of secularism (its manifesto insisted that "so-called secularism or composite nationalism is neither nationalism nor secularism but only a compromise with communalism of those who demand a price even for lip service to this country"), opposition to the special status of Kashmir,[22] use of Hindi as a national language, partial opposition to the Hindu Code Bill, and economic policies that supported the entrepreneurial class (Corbridge and Harriss 2002: 185–86). The national emergency gave crucial space and legitimacy to the Sangh's political arm and allowed it to expand its social support, at least in states like Gujarat. But with the collapse of the Bhartiya Jana Sangh following the lifting of the emergency, its politically active members and RSS regrouped themselves as BJP in 1980. BJP performed poorly in the 1984 general election, however, capturing merely two seats and leaving party ideologues to rethink their political strategy.

The Moderate/Militant Phase. The Sangh's new strategy required a moderate political arm and a militant social movement.[23] This strategy would allow its moderate political wing to join coalitions in various state governments while its militant wing could pursue aggressive mobilization (Basu 2001: 169). BJP thus started looking for coalition partners and in 1987 formed a coalition government in Haryana in alliance with Janta Dal. The 1990 state assembly elections resulted in BJP coming to power in Haryana, Madhya Pradesh, Rajasthan, and Gujarat (in a coalition led by Janta Dal).

Meanwhile, the Sangh's militant wing was engaged in aggressive mobilization through religious processions. In 1983, three major pilgrimages were organized for the whole of India—a systematic effort to involve all the social groups within the Hindu fold. In 1984, there were three major *yatras*. In 1989, VHP undertook yet another great procession at Ayodhya. All these *yatras* were meant to forge a symbolic unity between all Hindus by using mythological history and infusing it with new political meanings. In 1990, came the exercise that would change the entire course of Indian polity: the procession that started at Somanath in Gujarat and culminated in the destruction of the Babri mosque at Ayodhya on December 6, 1992—a train of events that completely polarized the polity and left behind a blaze of communal riots throughout the country.[24] This militant phase of Hindu nationalism was characterized by three significant developments: the emergence of Bajrang Dal (BD) as a paramilitary arm of the Sangh capable of indulging in violence; the reinvention of history in order to mobilize Hindus to correct perceived historical wrongs through violence; and the appeal to women that it is their historical duty to help their male counterparts in their endeavor to establish the Hindu nation.

The Moderate Hindutva Phase. The destruction of the Babri mosque through militant social activism did not translate into rich political dividends for BJP, however. The state assembly elections in Uttar Pradesh brought BJP to power, but a careful analysis of the election results shows that BJP was helped by a fractured mandate. Since then, Uttar Pradesh has been irreversibly split by caste politics. In the 1993 state elections, a referendum on BJP's Hindu nationalism, BJP fared poorly. And its losses were greatest in those areas where Sangh activism was most intense (Madhya Pradesh and Uttar Pradesh). The same story unfolded in the 1995 assembly elections: BJP lost in all the states except Maharashtra (in alliance with Shiv Sena) and Gujarat. Even so, this moderate phase allowed BJP to make inroads into West Bengal and Tamil Nadu (reflected in their share of votes). During this phase, BJP continuously shifted its identity between a moderate political party and a chauvinistic movement. BJP's election manifesto in 1998 referred to building a temple at Ayodhya, abolishing Article 370, and banning cow slaughter, but as leader of the National Democratic coalition in 1999, it dropped all such ambitions, although it continued to further the Hindu nation agenda through oblique means. For example, it embarked on a project to rewrite the history textbooks in line with its reimagination of the state.

The Extremist Phase. The Sangh's extremist phase can be seen in the recent happenings in Gujarat. The Gujarat riots of 2002 were triggered by the killing of *kar sewaks* (voluntary workers) who had gone to help build the new temple at Ayodhya. When the *kar sewaks* were burned to death in a train, allegedly by Muslims over a minor skirmish, more than thirteen districts of the state were engulfed in the ensuing violence. BJP, the state's ruling party, not only colluded with rioters but at times engineered the communal holocaust. Members of VHP and BD openly led the violent Hindu mobs that killed Muslims, indulged in sex crimes against Muslim women, destroyed Muslim property, and organized the desecration of Islamic symbols. This was a new face of communalism in India. No longer was it a violent clash between two communities for political benefits, while the state acted as neutral arbitrator. In this new scenario, it was the ruling political party in alliance with the other Sangh affiliates that actively planned and executed the violence against one community—and in this situation BJP as ruling party often used the state machinery and the police to perpetrate this genocide.

Despite substantial evidence, the state administration was given a clean report card. In fact, the country's deputy prime minister, L. K. Advani (senior leader of BJP), and the prime minister at BJP's national convention in 2002 placed the blame on Muslims. Ashok Singhal, a VHP leader, called Gujarat a "successful experiment" and warned that it would be "repeated all over India."[25] In December 2002, the ensuing elections for the Gujarat state assembly returned BJP with 121 seats out 182 (with 51 percent of the votes). Fresh from the success of Gujarat, VHP has resumed campaigning for construction of the Hindu temple at Ayodhya, organized a Dharma Sansad (religious parliament) in Delhi, and prepared the ground for militant agitation. For the time being, however, the constraints of coalition politics have kept the Sangh from taking a militant posture. Despite the momentary calm, the Sangh seems poised to invoke Hindu nation politics in future elections. Thus the political impact of the Sangh and its affiliates, primarily operating in the civil society space, has been enormous. According to the strategies used by the Sangh in its different phases, this impact has resulted in changes of government, communal riots, revision of history texts, demolition of mosques, even genocide. In all this, the primary objective of the Sangh has been to establish India as a Hindu nation. Many commentators view the growth of this ideology as the most momentous watershed in the country's politics since independence—and the most ominous.

Two Contradictory Projects

With its rich history, dating back to the precolonial era, and a tradition of playing a noteworthy role in the country's sociopolitical landscape, India's civil society is robust. Its relationship with the Indian state has been flexible and is constantly being reshaped with changing boundaries and roles in response to evolving conditions. The civil society arena itself is a space for contestation among groups and collectives adhering to divergent ideologies and objectives. In this complex milieu, civil society has a profound impact on political processes in the country. Hindu fundamentalists have effectively utilized the space provided to civil society within the country's democratic structure for communal mobilization and capturing state power. These chauvinist forces continue to use this space innovatively to manufacture consent and further their ideas of establishing India as a Hindu nation. In this grim scenario, the progressive and secular sections of civil society offer a glimmer of hope as they continue to work at the grass roots with the vision of democratizing a deeply divided hierarchical society and a state that is still largely colonial in character. Although the project of these secular groups in promoting progressive political change has significant potential, it has been overshadowed by the phenomenal rise of the Hindutva forces.

Notes

1. Interview with Ajay Mehta, a civil society leader, currently executive director of the National Foundation for India.

2. Personal communication.

3. Amitabh Singh, executive director, Debate, Bhopal, in a personal communication.

4. For example, an NGO in Rajasthan, the SWRC, organized a *jan sunwai* (public hearing) to make its financial systems transparent and accountable.

5. The impact of SEWA and the cooperative milk movement in Anand, Gujarat, has already been discussed in earlier sections.

6. The Gram Sabha, the general assembly of all adult villagers, is the lowest-tier institution of the *panchayat* system.

7. The authors have spent time working and researching the activities of Ekta Parishad in the field. This case study is based on our research and the literature available to us.

8. Using loopholes in government policy, the timber mafia was cutting thousands of trees for high-quality wood.

9. MKSS and its struggle have been documented. A research study has been completed by IDS (Sussex) on this movement, and the authors have personally interviewed MKSS activists and leaders and lived with them for a field research project. See Jenkins and Goetz 1999a, 1999b, and Harsh 1999.

10. Nandy and colleagues give an excellent description of what constitutes the Hindu nation (Nandy et al. 1995: 56–64). For another good work that juxtaposes Hindutva understanding of the state with mainstream Indian and Western understanding, see Jaffrelot 1993: 11–75.

11. The ideological basis for the present notion of a Hindu nation springs from the writings of V. D. Savarkar (1923) and M. S. Golwalkar (1939). These two writers positioned themselves against the predominant Western ideas of the nation-state and argued for moving beyond the concept of nation defined in terms of territory to a conception understood in terms of culture (read Hindu culture). It is a common culture—rituals, social rules, religious festivals, mythology, language—instead of some vague "social contract" that provides an organic unity that allows every individual to become a living limb of the society's corporate personality. In other words, Savarkar's and Golwalkar's efforts to conceptualize the basis for a Hindu nation derived their strength from weaving a matrix of all castes into a single organic social block. This organic unity is not, however, to be achieved by challenging the hierarchy from within. Instead, hierarchy is to be preserved and legitimized through invoking the dharma (universal law) that governs Hindu social rituals and customs—the bedrock of social hierarchy.

12. We use the word *Hindutva* to indicate a planned process that feeds into the reimagination project of the Sangh and derives its basis from the writings of Savarkar and Golwalkar.

13. For good descriptions of the role of religious *yatras* (processions) in creating communal division in the polity, see Nandy et al. 1995: 107–10, and Corbridge and Harriss 2000: 188.

14. Many of the business organizations and groups represented by the Sangh have overlapping memberships. There are also many documented instances of business organizations contributing money to the Sangh and its affiliates.

15. During the recent elections, many housing cooperatives in Vadodra organized private dinners and cultural functions that also provided a platform for BJP candidates to speak about their election promises and in the process evade the election commission's deadline. This tactic was immediately adopted by the Congress Party in its area of influence, but with far less success.

16. The members are big businessmen, traders, small entrepreneurs, professionals, farmers, workers, and peasants, including tribal sharecroppers and farm laborers.

17. The phrase "manufacture consent" comes from the title of Edward S. Herman and Noam Chomsky's seminal work *Manufactured Consent* (New York: Pantheon Books, 1988).

18. A college principal in one of the tribal blocks informed us that Hindu passion is incited not only by narrating and distributing literature on invented history with regard to the purported excesses inflicted by Muslims on Hindus but also through fictitious characters enacting the same. Films are regularly shown in this block depicting bearded men (read Muslims) exploiting tribal labor and raping their women.

19. For instance, the Ekatama *yatra* or the Ganga Jal (1983), the Janki Dharma *yatra* (1987), the Ram Jyoti *yatra* (1990), the Vijay Dashmi Vijay *yatras*, and the Ram *yatra* to collect bricks for the planned Ram Mandir in Ayodhya, which came to be known as Ram Shila Pujan. On September 16, 1990, the VHP announced a program of hundreds of local Rath *yatras*, along with eighteen thousand religious conferences across Gujarat to mobilize *kar sewaks* for the Ayodhya agitation (Nandy et al. 1995: 108–9).

20. We say "implicitly" because all the sects mentioned maintain their distance from electoral politics and do not support the Ayodhya movement. Although they have begun to praise the RSS for raising Hindu consciousness, none of them have expressed grief over the genocide in the state (Shah 2002a).

21. In Gujarat, Chief Minister Modi undertook the Gaurav *yatra* ostensibly for "restoring the pride of the state and the self-respect of its five crore people," which he claimed had been tarnished by pseudosecularists and their adverse and biased publicity of the riots. The real aim of the *yatra* was to unite within the Hindu fold all the voters belonging to different castes and social groups. By shrewdly invoking political, religious, and cultural symbols, the *yatra* persuaded the people that the Congress Party had refused to respect and protect these revered symbols of Gujaratis and Hindus.

22. Article 370 of the constitution of India confers a special status on Kashmir—a predominantly Muslim state.

23. Does the Hindu nationalist movement have parallels with social movements with regards to approaches and mobilization strategies? On this question see Basu 2001: 164–69.

24. The Sangh claims that the Babri mosque stood at the birthplace of the Hindu god Rama. Allegedly a Muslim emperor destroyed the temple to Rama and erected a mosque at the same site. At present the dispute is sub judice.

25. *Indian Express*, Sept. 4, 2002.

Works Cited

Accountaid. 2001. *Accounting and Legal Issues for NGOs: Accountaid Kit.* New Delhi: Accountaid.

Basu, Amrita. 2001. "The Dialectics of Hindu Nationalism." In Atul Kohli, ed., *The Success of India's Democracy.* Cambridge: Cambridge University Press.

Basu, D. D. 1994. *Introduction to the Constitution of India.* Delhi: Prentice-Hall of India.Behar, Amitabh, and Yogesh Kumar. 2002. *Decentralisation in Madhya Pradesh: Panchayati Raj to Gram Swaraj (1995 to 2001).* Working Paper 170. London: Overseas Development Institute.

Behar, Amitabh. 2001. "Gram Swaraj—Experiment in Direct Democracy." *Economic and Political Weekly,* Mar. 10–16.

Behar, Amitabh, and Yogesh Kumar. 2002. *Decentralisation in Madhya Pradesh: Panchayati Raj to Gram Swaraj (1995 to 2001).* Working Paper 170. London: Overseas Development Institute.

Beteille, André. 1999. "Citizenship, State, and Civil Society." *Economic and Political Weekly,* Sept. 4.

Chandhoke, Neera. 1995. *State and Civil Society: Explorations in Political Theory.* New Delhi: Sage.

Corbridge, Stuart, and John Harriss. 2002. *Reinventing India: Liberalisation, Hindu Nationalism, and Popular Democracy.* New Delhi: Oxford University Press.

Dhanagare, D. N. 2001. "Civil Society, State, and Democracy: Contextualising a Discourse." *Sociological Bulletin* 50(2) (Sept.): 167–91.

Golwalkar, M. S. 1939. *We Are Nationhood Defined.* Nagpur: Bharat Prakashan.

Harsh, Mander. 1999. *The Movement for the Right to Information in India.* Working Paper 14. Pune: National Center for Advocacy Studies.

Human Rights Watch. 2002. "We Have No Orders to Save You": State Participation and Complicity in Communal Violence in Gujarat. www.hrw.org/reports/2002/india/. Vol. 14, no. 3C (April). Accessed 2/15/2004.

Iyer, V. R. Krishna, et al. 2002. *Crime Against Humanity.* 2 vols. www.sabrang.com/tribunal/index.html. Accessed 2/15/2004.

Jaffrelot, Christophe. 1993. *The Hindu Nationalist Movement in India.* New Delhi: Viking.

Jayal, Niraja Gopal. 2000. "India." In Yamamoto Tadashi, ed., *Governance and Civil Society in a Global Age.* New York: Japan Center for International Exchange.

———. 2001. "Democracy and Social Capital in Central Himalayas: Tale of Two Villages." *Economic and Political Weekly,* Feb. 24.

Jenkins, Rob, and Anne Marie Goetz. 1999a. "Constraints on Civil Society to Curb Corruption: Lessons from the Indian Experience." *IDS Bulletin* 29 (4) (Oct.).

———. 1999b. "Theoretical Implications of the Right to Information Movement in India. *Third World Quarterly* 20(3): 603–22.

Joint Fact Finding Team Report (JFFTR). 2002. *A Continuing Crime: The Relief Rehabilitation Measures, the Attitude of Judiciary, and the Police Investigation and Arrests with Regard to Genocide in Gujarat.* Mumbai: Joint Fact Finding Team.

Joshi, Vidyut. 2002. "The Cultural Context of Development in Gujarat." In Indira Hirway et al., eds., *Dynamics of Development in Gujarat.* Ahmedabad: CFDA.

Katzenstein, Mary, Smitu Kothari, and Uday Mehta. 2001. "Social Movement Politics in India: Institutions, Interests, and Identities." In Atul Kohli, ed., *The Success of Indian Democracy.* Cambridge: Cambridge University Press.

Kothari, Rajni. 1970. *Politics in India.* New Delhi: Orient Longman.

———. 1987. "Voluntary Organisations in a Plural Society." *Indian Journal of Public Administration* (July–Sept.).
———. 1988. *State Against Democracy*. Delhi: Ajanta.
———. 1989. *Politics and the People*. Delhi: Ajanta.
———. 1991. *Human Rights: A Movement in Search of a Theory*. In S. Kothari and H. Sethi, eds., *Human Rights: Challenges for Theory and Action*. New York: New Horizons.
Lobo, Lancy. 2002. "Adivasis, Hindutava, and Post Godhra Riots in Gujarat." *Economic and Political Weekly*, Nov. 30–Dec. 6.
Mahadevia, Darshani. 2002. "Communal Space over Life Space: Saga of Increasing Vulnerability in Ahmedabad." *Economic and Political Weekly*, Nov. 30–Dec. 6.
Mahajan, Gurpreet. 1999a. "Civil Society and Its Avatars: What Happened to Freedom and Democracy?" *Economic and Political Weekly*, May 15–21.
———. 1999b. "Civil Society, State, and Democracy." *Economic and Political Weekly*, Dec. 4.
Mahajan, Vijay. 2002. *Voluntary Action in India in a Common Cause: NGOs and Civil Society*. Delhi: National Foundation for India.
Mukta, Parita. 2002. "On the Political Culture of Authoritarianism." In Ghanshyam Shah et al., eds., *Development and Deprivation in Gujarat*. New Delhi: Sage.
Nandy, Ashish, et al. 1995. *Creating a Nationality: The Ramjanambhumi Movement and the Fear of Self*. New Delhi: Oxford University Press.
National Human Rights Commission (NHRC). 2002. Report on the Visit of NHRC Team Headed by Chairperson, NHRC, to Ahmedabad, Vadodra, and Godhra from 19–22 March 2002. www.nhrc.nic.in/guj_annex_1.htm. Accessed 2/15/2004.
People's Union for Civil Liberties (PUCL). 2002. "A Communal Carnage? No, It's a Case of Genocide." www.sabrang.com/gujarat/statement/puclreport.htm. Accessed 2/15/2004.
Pylee, M. V. 1998. *Emerging Trends of Indian Polity*. New Delhi: Regency.
Sabrang Communications. 1999. "Caste Is a Precious Gift." *Communalism Combat*, Oct.
———. 2002a. *Genocide Gujarat*. Special issue of *Communalism Combat*, Mar.–Apr. www.sabrang.com/cc/archive/2002/marapril/index.html. Accessed 2/15/2004.
———. 2002b. The Foreign Exchange of Hate: IDRF and American Funding of Hindutva. www.stopfundinghate.org.
Savarkar, V. D. 1923. *Who Is a Hindu?* Bombay: Savarkar.
Sen, Amartya. 1999. *Development as Freedom*. Oxford: Oxford University Press.
Sen, Siddhartha. 1997. *Voluntary Organizations in India: Historical Development, Institutional Genesis, Institutional Development*. Vol. 4. Delhi: PRIA.
Shah, Ghanshyam. 2002a. "Caste, Hindutava, and Hideousness." *Economic and Political Weekly*, Apr. 13.
———. 2002b. "Unrest Among Adivasis and Their Struggle." In Takashi Shinoda, ed., *The Other Gujarat*. Mumbai: Popular Prakashan.
Sharma, B. D. 1992. *Web of Poverty*. New Delhi: Sahyog Pustak Kutir.
Society for Participatory Research in Asia (PRIA). 2001–2. *Annual Report*. New Delhi: PRIA http://www.pria.org/cgi-bin/reportold.htm. Accessed 2/15/2004.
Yagnik, Achyut. 2002a. "The Pathology of Gujarat." *Seminar*. Web edition at http://www.india-seminar.com/2002/513/513%20achyut%20yagnik.htm. Accessed 2/15/2004.
———. 2002b. "Search for Dalit Self Identity in Gujarat." In Takashi Shinoda, ed., *The Other Gujarat*. Mumbai: Popular Prakashan.

CHAPTER SEVEN

Japan

Social Capital Without Advocacy

ROBERT PEKKANEN

A chapter on Japan plays an important role in many edited volumes on civil society. Often it is the only chapter on a non-Western nation or non-Western industrialized democracy. Accordingly, the inclusion of Japan contributes a wider perspective and allows us some leverage in assessing otherwise culture-bound claims. In this volume, however, there are chapters covering states all across Asia, and the chapter on Japan consequently plays a slightly different role. Studies of contemporary Japan are not particularly well positioned to investigate the importance of civil society in bringing about a democratic transition, for example, but can illuminate the role of civil society in an advanced industrialized consolidated democracy. This chapter therefore examines political change, not as regime transition or democratic consolidation, but as policy change. Although returning to civil society and its role in shaping the public debate also returns civil society to the conceptual roots of a "public sphere," the investigation here is grounded in empirical data.

I begin by addressing the definition of civil society, before reviewing some of the central questions guiding the study of civil society in consolidated democracies. These questions must deal with the dual role of civil society groups: On the one hand, such groups are thought to produce social capital, which famously contributes to the performance of democracies (Putnam 1993; 2000); on the other hand, the rise of advocacy groups seems to portend an increasingly uncompromising and conflictual politics that might impair or at least skew the performance of a democracy (Skocpol 1999; see also Crozier, Huntington, and Watanuki 1975). Contending analysts present plausible arguments that civil society both sustains and undermines democracy; the relationship between democratic performance and civil society is being tugged at both theoretical ends. Japan's civil society, reviewed next, seems uniquely positioned for an investigation of this dichotomy. Japan has an abundance of small local groups but a striking dearth of large independent advocacy groups. What are the implications of this pattern of civil society for political change in Japan's democracy? Such a configuration should provide a high level of social capital—with local groups facilitating government performance—but at the same time, it means that fewer civil society voices are heard in public policy debates. In fact, in its conclusion, this chapter raises the provocative possibility that Japan (rather than the United States, which is often held up as a model) might have "gotten civil society right" in supporting groups that sustain social capital, while limiting advocacy groups. Before that, the chapter clarifies the definition of civil society employed, then traces out the pattern of Japan's civil society with descriptive statistics. An argument follows about the historical legacies and political institutions that account for this pattern. This is intimately connected to the "high social capital, low advocacy" nature of civil society in Japan today.

Let us begin with the issue of definition. Too often, vagueness plagues discussions of civil society. The definition employed here is this: civil society is the organized nonstate, nonmarket sector. This definition encompasses voluntary groups of all kinds, such as nonprofit foundations, charities, think tanks, and choral societies. It includes nonprofit organizations (NPOs), nongovernmental organizations (NGOs), and other voluntary associations. It is larger in scope than the category of civic groups, which comprises participatory organizations. It is also broader than the nonprofit sector, which excludes unincorporated voluntary groups and is sometimes limited to groups with public purposes (Hall 1987). Labor unions, companies, and other profit-oriented groups are not included.[1] The definition also excludes government bureaucracies, parastatal organizations, and political parties, as well as the family. This definition is consistent with that advanced in the introductory chapter by Muthiah Alagappa, which elaborates on features of the definition (depiction of civil society as a space, membership of civil society, and the relationship of civil society to the state) that I examine closely here. This chapter traces out these relationships in Japan's civil society. We see how the membership of civil society (the population of groups) affects the nature of the space that civil society occupies (in terms of public discourse). The relationship of the state to civil society is very much at the heart of things. The state's influence on the membership of civil society is delineated here, but equally important is the examination of how civil society might affect government policies.

Civil society is not a dichotomous variable. Attention should be paid to the *types* of organizations that exist, as well as to participation in organizations and their numbers. Civil society may vary in level and composition from time to time and from place to place. Because civil society comprises a motley crew, there should be theoretical gains from disaggregating the concept. This chapter adopts such a perspective on the pattern of development of civil society organizations in Japan before tracing its implications for democracy.

Japan's Dual Civil Society

The most striking aspect of Japan's civil society is its dual structure: Japan has a plethora of small local groups and a paucity of large professionalized groups. Neighborhood associations (NHAs) are especially plentiful in Japan, for example, but large advocacy groups are especially scarce. These dimensions are made clear by an overview of Japan's civil society. Table 7.1 and Figures 7.1 and 7.2 illustrate that Japan certainly does have many civil society groups; what Japan does not have, in comparative perspective, is many employees working in civil society groups. This means there are many groups with few or no employees and few groups with many employees. Many groups, but not many employees, is a defining feature of Japan's dual civil society.

Figure 7.1 shows the proportion of the total workforce employed by civil society organizations. (These figures exclude workers in education, health, and social services, whose figures vary widely because of state policies, but they do include workers in all other civil society groups.) This indicates the degree of professionalization of civil society organizations. Proportionally, Japan's 73,500 civil society professionals are fewer than half the number of the next lowest nation (Germany) and less

TABLE 7.1
Civil Society Groups in Japan

Type of group	Number of groups
With legal status	
Education legal persons	16,155
Social welfare legal persons	13,000
Public-interest legal persons (*zaidan*)	13,476
Public-interest legal persons (*shadan*)	12,451
Religious legal persons	183,894
Medical legal persons	22,838
PIP subtotal (broad definition)[a]	(261,814)
Cooperatives	23,718
Political groups	72,796
Think tanks (not counted elsewhere)	449
Neighborhood associations	8,691
Legal status subtotal	404,678
Without legal status	
Neighborhood associations	292,227
Children's groups	130,000
Elderly people's groups	150,000
Other civic groups	598,000
Voluntary groups with offices	42,000
Without legal status subtotal	1,212,227
TOTAL	1,616,905

SOURCES: Tsujinaka and Mori 1998: 298; Yamauchi 1997: 218, 227; Japanese government documents.

[a]All groups legally incorporated under Article 34 provisions and attached special laws.

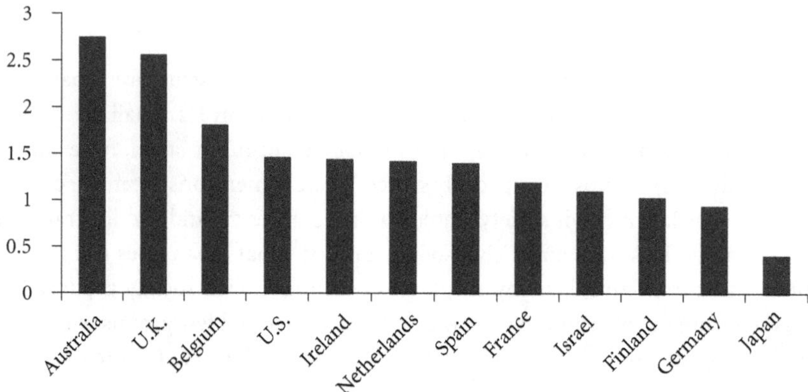

Figure 7.1. Civil society employment as a percentage of total employment. Based on data from Johns Hopkins Comparative Nonprofit Sector Project.

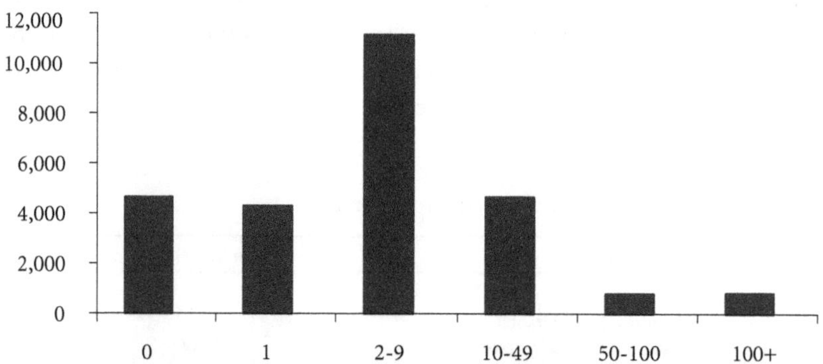

Figure 7.2. PIPs ("public-interest legal persons") by number of employees. Data from Prime Minister's Office 2000: 361.

than a third of the average for the developed nations in the figure. Figure 7.2 shows the number of employees working in "public-interest legal persons" (PIPs)—the legal category of civil society groups that includes the largest and wealthiest civil society groups. This is the category in which we would expect to find Japanese civil society's largest employers. Most groups, though, have only a handful of employees. Only a few thousand civil society groups in Japan employ more than ten people.

Besides the small size of the professional civil society sector in general, another factor intrudes in our consideration of civil society and democracy in Japan. Many groups face constrained independence from the state owing to institutional factors such as legal regulations and bureaucratic practices, including *amakudari* (literally, "descent from heaven"), the employment of retired bureaucrats in new posts, typically in areas they once regulated. Put simply, it is hard for independent groups to grow large in Japan and just as hard for large groups to remain independent.

The mechanics of this pattern can be traced to an institutional arrangement that places significant monitoring (reporting and investigating) and sanctioning powers (various punishments, including dissolution of the group) in the hands of a single bureaucratic ministry or agency. Even in the abstract, it is easy to see that if a single agency grants a group permission to form, monitors it, has the ability to punish it, and can even dissolve the group entirely, often without effective legal challenge, that agency holds significant power over the group. In Japan, the public-interest legal person has reporting duties to the competent ministry, which retains the power to investigate the group or even to revoke the PIP's legal status. Moreover, the concomitant tax benefits are not so generous as in other industrialized democracies. Even worse, the bureaucrats have insisted on continuing "administrative guidance."[2] Backed by sanctioning power, this administrative guidance forces licensees to comply with bureaucratic demands and impairs the independence of the civil society sector. It has been employed in such a heavy-handed way that many observers regard the social-welfare legal persons, for example, as little more than cheap subcontractors for the government, without the independence necessary to qualify them as true NPOs. The director of the Sasakawa Peace Foundation (a PIP), Iriyama Akira, puts it well when he says: "Even those like us who make it through and get permission have to suffer from very severe control and guidance from authorities. If I start to talk about the notorious administrative guidance, it'll take days." Despite the great logistical problems it creates, foreign groups such as the Asia Foundation sometimes choose not to become PIPs precisely to avoid bureaucratic interference. In a nationwide Economic Planning Agency survey of Japanese NPOs, the most common reason cited for not applying for legal status was that accounting and finance reporting requirements were too onerous (61 percent of the groups listed this reason); the third most common reason was the fear that the objective of the NPO, or the content of its activities, might come to be controlled by the bureaucrats (45 percent) (Noumi 1997). A PIP must submit a report of its annual activity, list of assets, accounts of changes of membership, and financial statements for the past year, as well as planned activity reports and budget estimates for the coming year.

It is the permitting agency that is empowered to investigate the PIP. Moreover, the permitting agency can conduct on-site inspections and audits and issue directives to the PIP that, if not obeyed, can result in the PIP's dissolution. Civil Code Article 68(1)(iv) provides that a PIP is to be dissolved if the authorizing agency cancels its authorization for the establishment of the corporation. Article 71 states that the authorizing agency may cancel its approval if the PIP has engaged in activities outside its purposes as defined in the articles of association, has violated the conditions under which it received approval for establishment, or violates supervisory orders issued by the authorizing agency. The Civil Code Enforcement Law, Article 25, requires an inquiry by the authorizing agency and also requires the agency to

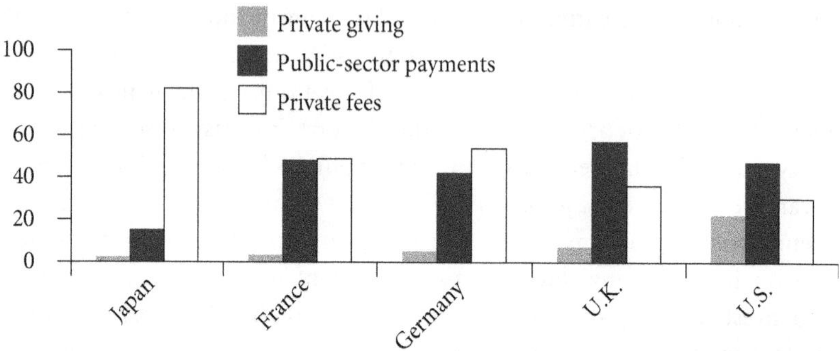

Figure 7.3. Revenue sources for civil and advocacy groups. Data from Salamon and Anheier 1996.

indicate the reasons for the cancellation to affected parties, who then have the right to a legal proceeding and appeal. One notes that a cancellation of authorization is interpreted as a response to changed circumstances, not as a mistake by the authorizers as to whether the PIP was in the public interest to start with. Despite the possibility of appeal, the legal deck is stacked in favor of the authorizing agency—in part because of the considerable discretion attached to defining the public interest (Hayashi 1972: 192–93).[3] It is not surprising, then, that advocacy groups are particularly small in Japan. They average only 3.4 employees and expenditures of 36.12 million yen ($361,200) a year (Salamon and Anheier 1997), only 22.7 percent of the average for all nonprofits in Japan (Atoda, Amenomori, and Ōta 1998: 105). Figure 7.3 shows the revenue sources for civil and advocacy groups in Japan and four other countries.

Citizen groups emphasize their independence. Yet the price of gaining legal status is often a de facto agreement to employ ex-bureaucrats of the approving ministry. Besides providing a cozy spot for these erstwhile denizens of Kasumigaseki (the part of Tokyo that houses Japan's bureaucracy), this practice also gives them substantial influence over the group's operations—especially when the bureaucrats assume posts on the board of directors. This latter practice occurs in about one-sixth of the PIPs supervised by the national bureaucracy; the former occurs in over one-third of them (Prime Minister's Office 1999: 124). The flip side of cutting off resource flows to challenging groups is that the state often seeks to co-opt, or supervise, the groups that do get legal status. Intense supervision and personnel transfers are further methods that compromise the independence of many groups.

The status of independent groups formed by citizen activists provides another example. These groups typify what Americans would regard as "real" civil society groups. They engage in a wide range of activities, from social welfare to the environment, and from women's rights to community issues such as crime prevention. The very category implies independence from the state. Citizen groups are small;

TABLE 7.2

Relationship Between the Bureaucracy and Permitted Groups in Japan

Category	Administrative guidance (%)	Seconding of staff (%)	Postretirement employment (%)	Exchange of opinions (%)
Agricultural	74.3	22.9	17.1	48.6
Economic	57.9	22.0	9.5	57.1
Specialist	42.9	18.0	6.8	33.8
Education	37.4	13.0	5.7	23.6
Welfare	52.4	4.9	6.1	18.3
Citizens	24.6	5.3	0	15.8
All groups	45.8	13.3	8.6	35.9

SOURCE: Adapted from Dantai Kiso Kōzō Kenkyūkai 1998.

very few have large staffs. A recent survey of several thousand such groups found that only 1.6 percent of them have more than five full-time paid employees; as a category, they average only 0.5 full-time paid employees (Yamauchi 1997: 220). As might be expected, very few of these groups have legal status. Tokyo-area citizen groups, for example, are almost all (82 percent) voluntary associations without legal status (Tsujinaka 1997: 19).[4] Small, unsupported by the state, strictly regulated—such terms sum up the status of professionalized civil society groups in general, and advocacy groups in particular. Table 7.2 illustrates the relationship between permitting bureaucracies and permitted groups. The close relationship between agricultural groups and the bureaucracy is underscored by the levels of staff seconding from the bureaucracy to the group, as well as the levels of postretirement employment of bureaucrats (*amakudari*). Citizens' groups are the most independent. They take no retired bureaucrats as employees and seldom accept administrative guidance. They even consult, or exchange opinions, with the bureaucracy less than any other group.

In the drafting of Japan's Civil Code—thirty years after the Meiji Restoration (1868) put Japan on the path to modernization—the framers made clear choices about legal frameworks to regulate civil society organizations. Legal documents, including the framers' notes and a comparison with the original German and Swiss laws that served as models, support a contention that the Civil Code was written with the intent of creating high hurdles for the organization of civil groups. This conclusion is corroborated by evidence from the explanatory notes attached to Article 35 of the Civil Code and to an earlier draft of the code. There is, for example, a conscious shift from nonprofit to public-interest legal persons—part of the Meiji oligarchy's effort to place strict limits on the formation of civil society groups. I hasten to add that this was done not so much to cripple civil society as to prevent the people from frittering away their energy in civil society organizations and steer them instead to the state goals of nation building under the slogan "Rich nation, strong army." Regulating civil society has always been part of the political process.

The Civil Code provisions drafted in 1896 have had considerable influence. The Meiji period (1868–1912) was pivotal to the creation of the modern Japanese state. Institutional shortcomings in the integration of the military with the parliamentary system contributed to the rise of militarism and the Pacific War itself. The institutions designed at that time to regulate civil society have also had serious consequences. Core provisions of the Civil Code in Japan seldom change. The framing of the Civil Code constitutes a critical juncture for the development of Japanese civil society. The framers intentionally inhibited the growth of civil society organizations in order to promote militarization and industrialization in the Meiji era. In the postwar period, however, the same regulatory framework continued, but with lower barriers for social welfare, religious, medical, and educational groups. Although the regulatory framework may have promoted economic recovery by inhibiting the growth of large civil groups, in recent decades, the framework has been unsatisfactory for increasing numbers of Japanese. Change has been slow to come. This is where the consequences of the Meiji framing become unintended.

Along the same lines, consider evidence from Craig Jenkins's (1998) study of foundations and social movements in the United States. He found that "overall, the foundations have been moderate reformers, funneling most of their support to the moderate wing of the movements and the professionalized groups. But, rather than co-opting these movements, they have channeled them into professionalized structures. In many respects, this has been a benefit to the movements, allowing them to consolidate their gains and protect themselves against attack" (Jenkins 1998: 215; for a critical view, see Dowie 2001). Thus regulation has implications, not only for the foundations themselves, but also for a host of other organizations. The small size of Japanese foundations—the largest Japanese foundation would not even rank among the top fifty U.S. foundations in terms of assets—has a secondary effect in retarding the institutionalization and growth of succeeding generations of Japanese civil society organizations (Pekkanen 2002a). Although there are too many factors involved in determining the life cycle of groups to examine here, it is clear that many groups grow larger and more professionalized over time. The United States has also experienced this phenomenon over the past fifty years. It takes time for groups to grow; most large groups have been around for a while. Even though the regulatory framework in Japan could change overnight, it will take time for large civil society organizations to develop. Besides simply amassing assets and staff, such groups need to accumulate legitimacy both for themselves and for the role of civil organizations in society as a whole.

The Meiji Civil Code profoundly affected the evolution of Japanese civil society. It is striking how difficult it is to alter this pattern. Despite Japan's high education and income levels, the country has very few large civil society groups. The empirical puzzle of a "weak" Japanese civil society has obscured the vitality of local civil society; in fact, both aspects are explained in large part by state action. This histor-

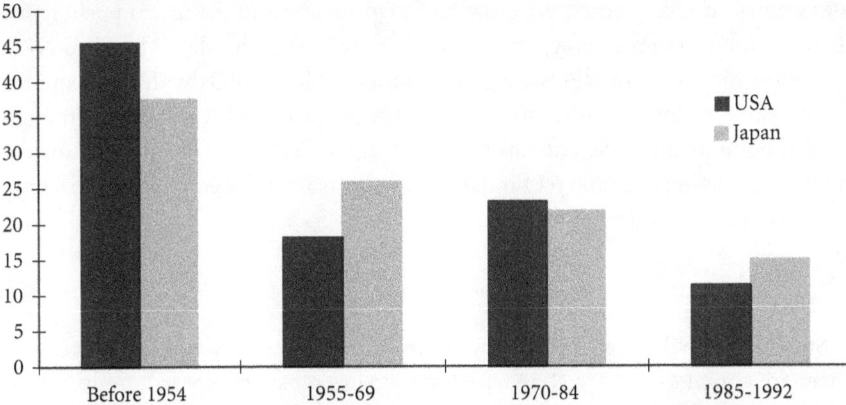

Figure 7.4. Large Japanese and U.S. Civil Society Groups by Founding Date and Percentage. U.S. data adapted from Independent Sector 1996, 241. Data are from 1993. Japanese data from JIGS survey (author's data analysis).

ical legacy will not easily be altered. This is not to say that Japan's civil society has been static for a century. The 1960s witnessed both growth and extreme polarization, and there has been even greater development since the early 1980s.[5] In time, legal and institutional developments like the NPO law will take further effect. The fact that it took Japan 100 years to enact a major change in the regulation of civil society highlights the importance of institutional choice.

Figure 7.4 shows how most large groups were founded decades ago. The groups featured here are all U.S. civil society groups with expenses over $10 million annually and Japanese groups with expenses over $1 million (100,000,000 yen) annually, broken down by when the group opened its doors.[6] The comparison could also be made for groups with equivalent budgets, that is, looking only at Japanese groups with expenses over $10 million annually. In fact, that comparison reveals almost identical results (author's data analysis). Given the generally smaller scale of Japanese groups, detailed at length above, the comparison of different budget sizes, however, seems more apt. Of course, the breakdown in dates is to a degree arbitrary (chosen to make the comparison with the U.S. data). The immediate postwar period saw many groups form in Japan, as did the period of hyperliquidity at the end of the 1980s. The central point, however, is that groups amass resources over time, and there is a relationship between age and resources. For the Japanese data, my analysis confirms a positive correlation between age and budget size (significance level $p < 0.01$), although I could not conduct a similar analysis on the U.S. data. The absolute number of groups is also different in the U.S. and Japanese data in Figure 7.3. However, the general relationship holds for both countries. Groups grow in size over time, amassing resources. Most large groups were founded many years ago.

Critical junctures matter disproportionately, because they influence the flow of later events. In recent years, the growth of civil society and the forces pushing for liberalization of the regulatory framework have fed off each other. More pro-NPO legislation means more NPOs with more money. More NPOs with more money means more incentives for lawmakers to push for pro-NPO legislation. Although the end point of this cycle remains to be seen, the trajectory of Japan's civil society might be changing in subtle yet fundamental ways from a low equilibrium to a high equilibrium.[7]

Neighborhood Associations

Small local civil society groups, by contrast, have been very successful in Japan. There are a total of 292,227 NHAs, perhaps Japan's most widespread group, which enjoy high participation rates (Pekkanen 2001a, 2002b, 2003a, 2003c, 2003d). Unlike its response to other civil society organizations, the government has actively promoted these groups. Local governments often directly subsidize neighborhood associations with grants, although the amounts are quite small.[8] Although they are independent entities, they often work with branches of local government in disseminating information or maintaining public facilities. Government funds flow to NHAs for these and other purposes. The services are provided quite cheaply, yet the money is important in holding these local groups together and may also create social capital. When the government pays a neighborhood association to clean a local park, for example, the work is done more cheaply and better than if professionals were employed. At the same time, civic community is strengthened as local people work together to maintain the area. Despite strong efforts at co-optation, however, it is the state's support for the NHAs that stands out in contrast to its treatment of other civil society organizations. Definitionally limited to small geographic areas, NHAs cannot challenge the state (in providing alternative sources of information such as policy analysis or policy proposals, for example). Instead, they support the state by providing services more efficiently.

The level of participation in neighborhood associations is remarkably high. Nominal membership levels are over 90 percent nationwide, making NHAs by far Japan's leading voluntary association. Actual participation rates are lower, of course, and vary widely across the many NHAs in Japan. Yet tens of millions of Japanese do participate in NHAs (participation was 72 percent in 2000, according to a national survey discussed below). A substantial number of Japanese are not only active in the NHA but spend a great deal of time in it. Leadership positions within NHAs can be quite time-consuming.

The NHAs engage in a diverse variety of activities. Typically, however, they center on local functions. Table 7.3 shows the proportion of NHAs in a typical small city, Ueda in Nagano Prefecture, that engage in various activities. The table goes a step further and also shows the percentage of NHAs that consider this activity to be

TABLE 7.3
What Japanese Neighborhood Associations Do

Activity	NHAs that do it (%)	NHAs that consider it a priority (%)
Festivals	85.5	32.3
Athletic meets, sports events	79.0	21.7
Construction and maintenance of parks	39.5	6.5
Publishing newsletters	26.6	5.6
Building or maintaining a community center	83.9	13.7
Distribution of government notices	89.5	16.1
Cleaning of gutters, rivers and streams, roads	91.1	45.2
Preventing illegal dumping	81.5	28.2
Crime prevention, fire prevention	84.7	32.3
Traffic management, traffic safety	69.4	12.9
Travel	31.5	1.6
Funerals and weddings	54.0	3.2
Club activities	75.8	24.2
Study groups	39.5	0.8
Support for children's groups	89.5	26.6
Support for elderly people's groups	83.1	11.3
Support for women's groups	51.6	0.0
Support for youth groups	24.2	3.2
Cooperating with government collections	87.1	10.5
Presenting petitions from residents to local government	84.7	31.5
Support of politicians	25.0	2.4

SOURCE: Yasui 1985: chart 4-2-2; data from NHAs in Ueda, Nagano prefecture.

one of their priorities. Although the data are only from one city, they are typical of NHAs throughout Japan (see, e.g., Bestor 1989: 165–66). Quintessential activities include facilitating communication among residents; hosting events such as athletic meets for local children; transmitting local requests for new streetlights, pothole repair, and the like to local government; forming neighborhood watch patrols; and organizing what is often the cultural heart of the local community, the festival. Neighborhood associations also serve as an organizational nucleus for elderly persons' groups, the women's auxiliary, and other local groups. The elderly persons' groups and women's auxiliaries are often subgroups of the NHA, and in any case membership is usually overlapping. However, these groups do have separate existences, including separate meetings, separate dues, and, often, separate (smaller) subsidies from the local governments. Typical activities for the elderly persons' groups include visiting local health facilities, studying history, traffic safety, and trips to hot springs.

The Origin of the NHA

The origin and development of NHAs shed light on their role as civil society organizations with a strong relationship to the state. This review emphasizes their mixed heritage as a spontaneous form of social organization, but one that was spread through the workings of the state. The spontaneous origin of NHAs helps to establish their credentials as civil society organizations. At the start of the Meiji period, these organizations existed only in certain parts of Japan, however, by estimates covering less than 10 percent of the population. It is the role of the state in the 1920s that was crucial in the spread of NHAs throughout all of contemporary Japan—demonstrating the power of the state, not merely to inhibit the development of civil society organizations, but to promote it as well. This dual role gives the Japanese state its influence in shaping civil society.

Conventional wisdom traces the origins of NHAs to Japan's medieval period. Certainly, informal, quasi-governmental, or compulsory neighborhood associations have played a significant role at different times in Japanese history. Moreover, many Japanese scholars' accounts seem to support this view by portraying the self-governing urban area, or *chou* (*chō*), as the forerunner of the neighborhood association. Korekazu Ueda, for example, traces the origins of NHAs to mutual defense and fire prevention groups begun in Kyoto by neighboring households (Ueda 1985). These groups may have been similar to the Tower Societies linked to the high-social-capital areas of northern Italy in Robert Putnam's *Making Democracy Work*. While the *chou* no doubt had an impact on local administration and perhaps serve as a cultural template, they are not the direct ancestors of the neighborhood association. In fact, the urban NHA emerged spontaneously in the early part of the twentieth century. The reasons for its origin and spread may be differentiated, however. It spread for social reasons, such as a response to the Kanto Earthquake, but also because of the state (Hastings 1995; Tanaka 1990; see also Pekkanen 2002a).

The Rise of the NHA

Whatever its historical origins, the modern NHA developed in the twentieth century. After the turn of the century, small numbers of neighborhood associations formed spontaneously. The growth period for NHAs was the 1920s, however, spurred by government introduction of sanitary associations. Seven out of ten NHAs extant in 1940 had formed in the Showa period (1926–89), 23 percent in the Taishō period (1912–26), and only 7 percent in the Meiji period (1868–1912) (Akimoto 1990). Membership in NHAs grew dramatically in the 1920s, and by 1933, some 77 percent of Tokyo households were enrolled in neighborhood associations. Even in budgetary terms, the total budget of Tokyo's NHAs in 1935 was equivalent to one-eighth of the city's tax revenue (Hastings 1995: 72).

The NHA evolved from these various voluntary associations, as well as from organizations centered on local shrines, whose activities included organizing the festivals. The key to their rapid spread, however, was the adoption of a government-created form, the sanitation association. While not aimed directly at creating NHAs, the sanitation associations provided the institutional form NHAs assumed.

The development of the NHA is a curious mixture of spontaneous and autonomous local impulses for association with government-inspired organizational templates. As Sally Ann Hastings puts it: "Although the government directive on sanitation unions provided their form, and the government relief policy at the time of the earthquake hastened their proliferation, the initiative for the founding of the neighborhood associations and the commitment to their perpetuation came from local residents" (1995: 79).

Many analysts see the establishment of neighborhood associations as an aspect of Taishō democracy. Tanaka Shigeyoshi rejects the view that NHAs were all imposed from above: "If anything, the administrative response came somewhat later than the general movement [for the formation of NHAs in the period]." Still, without the administrative push, NHAs would not have covered Tokyo so quickly. In Tokyo's Kanda ward in this period, 61 of the 112 NHAs were converted voluntary associations. Most of these voluntary associations had formed between 1890 and 1914. Of the 112 NHAs, 22 had formed before 1919, and 70 were formed between 1920 and 1924. Even of these 70, however, all but 4 were formalized from some preexisting organization (Tanaka 1990: 33, 40). Hastings's view is that the neighborhood associations emerged in Tokyo from the interaction between the state and a variety of local voluntary organizations that had specialized and limited functions (1995: 76).

Hastings contends that while "the relationship between Shinto shrine associations and the neighborhood associations was complex . . . the evidence suggests that the neighborhood associations absorbed the shrine organizations rather than that the shrines begat the neighborhood associations" (1995: 76). Hastings emphasizes the somewhat indirect role the government played in spurring the spread of the NHA:

> In a law that went into effect on July 1, 1900, Tokyo prefecture prescribed the establishment of sanitation unions in each city and village to prevent the spread of disease and to disseminate knowledge of sanitation. . . . The significance of the regulation of 1900 for the future of local organizations in Tokyo was that it designated the *chou* as the basic unit of organization within the cities and required the head of every household to join. Many of these sanitation unions eventually withered away for lack of funds. . . . Nevertheless, their creation established the form that the neighborhood associations would take: an organization composed of all household heads in the officially designated *chou*. . . . By the 1920s, most sanitation unions had become part of a neighborhood association. . . . Gradually, the functions of the various shrine and friendship associations were assumed by organizations having the form of the sanitation union. (Hastings 1995: 77–78)

The importance of sanitary associations as templates for the spread of neighborhood associations is also noted by Ronald Dore (1958: 272).

Another spur to the proliferation of the NHA was the Kanto Earthquake of 1923. In the aftermath of the disaster, NHAs proved their worth by helping assemble residents for fire fighting and evacuations, as well as subsequently in the administration of relief (Hastings 1995: 78–79; see also Steiner 1965: 219). Tanaka and Dore agree that the earthquake proved the NHA's value to local residents, especially in organizing help for the police and rescue work, and, at the same time, stimulated government interest in promoting and utilizing the NHA (Tanaka 1990: 42; Dore 1958: 272). Many local officials believe that areas with strong NHAs fare much better after earthquakes and other disasters than those without them even today.

Tanaka also emphasizes the establishment of sanitary associations under Government Order 16 of 1900, highlighting the significance of this regulation, which specifically included all residents, not just landowners. Tanaka thinks the government was taking the position that all residents in an area would be organized, and not just for sanitation (Tanaka 1990: 33). Documents from the time make it clear that while the formal sanitary associations covered the entire city, only about half the areas in the city had active associations (Tanaka 1990: 34). Still, by the beginning of the 1930s, NHAs existed in every ward, and over a third of all NHAs had been founded in the years 1923–27 (Dore 1958: 272).

Commenting on the later spread of the NHA, Tanaka writes that "in the background, it cannot be denied that the central government's intentions were at work" but concedes that neighborhoods exist as units, and that this is why the voluntary associations formed there (Tanaka 1990: 27). Tanaka finds multiple reasons for the rapid spread of the NHA in the 1920s, including government encouragement and internal spontaneous organization. Tanaka sees in government documents of October 1924 (including sample constitutions and membership fees) an indirect attempt to foster (*ikusei*) NHAs. The second, political, reason for the spread was the passage of universal manhood suffrage in 1925. Politicians tried to use the NHA to mobilize voters. While a few NHAs supported specific candidates, 77 percent of ward representatives had previously been president or vice president of an NHA (Tanaka 1990: 38–40). In other words, NHAs were more effective at training leaders than at serving as bases for electoral mobilization.

The NHA under Militarism

In some quarters, the image of the NHA as a branch of government—one characterized by spying on neighbors—still persists. It may owe much to the transformation of the NHA during Japan's militarist period, when NHAs were subsumed under the national mobilization of Japan and later incorporated into local government for use as a means of social control. After the 1931 Manchurian Incident, as Japan's war in China expanded, the government used NHAs for air raid training and similar tasks. In 1940, the NHAs were made part of the local administration—that is, wholly swallowed up into government. Participation was made compulsory. Responsibilities included rationing, civil defense, and propaganda. The *tonarigumi* (neighbor groups) system brought together units of ten to fifteen households for allocating government bonds, public health, rationing, civil defense, and fire fighting. Used for transmitting information and securing public cooperation, they were also an effective means of social control.

The Abolition and Revival of the NHA

After the war, the Allied Occupation forces, or SCAP, were determined to abolish Japan's neighborhood associations (see, e.g., Norbeck 1967; Masland 1946; and Braibianti 1948). They were seen as the means by which the militarist government had imposed such tight control over the populace. To the "policy makers of the American Occupation, *chōkai* were fundamentally undemocratic—John Embree compared them to the German Nazis' party organization—and they were marked for abolition" (Bestor 1989: 75). Kurt Steiner observes: "When the [NHAs], uniformly established throughout Japanese cities in 1940, engaged in rationing goods, digging shelters, fighting fires, or even in propagating patriotism, their activities were accepted and approved of by many as necessary for a nation at war. But many others chafed under the pressures of regimentation and were glad to be rid of them" (1965: 228). However, there was no grassroots movement among Japanese to abolish the neighborhood associations, and most people welcomed their return when they were revived, Tanaka Shigeyoshi notes (1990: 47).

In 1947, SCAP abolished Japan's 210,000 neighborhood associations and wrote regulations to ensure that they did not continue under other names. In 1952, however, the Japanese government reversed the ban and allowed neighborhood associations to form as voluntary, independent organizations.[9] Despite SCAP's efforts, NHAs quickly resurfaced, and by 1956, they were to be found in 98 percent of Japan's municipalities (Bestor 1989: 75).

Neighborhood Associations Today

One of the most remarkable things about NHAs is that participation seems to be increasing. Surveys in the 1970s found participation levels lower (60% in 1976, 55% in 1979) than more recent surveys (71% in 1997, 72% in 2000) (Pekkanen 2003b; 2003e). Although more detailed studies are needed to be certain of this trend, we can at least be sure that NHAs continue to be quite active and enjoy widespread participation. This might surprise those who have seen social changes such as the rise of single person households, apartment buildings, and weakening social ties (sometimes interpreted as moral decay) challenge organizations such as the NHAs. The dedication of millions of Japanese to the local communities and to the NHA must surely be the most important factor standing in the way of this predicted decline in NHA participation. However, the state has also been lively in its defense of the NHAs. Many local officials see the great benefits to local government and community of the NHAs and have worked actively to maintain membership and participation. These activities include distributing pamphlets that encourage participation and visits by city officials to NHAs. New apartment buildings where an NHA has not yet been established are frequently visited by local officials, who do their best to encourage the formation of NHAs there.

The relationship between state and NHAs today is mutually beneficial. A few NHAs prefer to stand aloof from the government. However, most accept small sums of money in the form of subsidies and grants, typically no more than 5 to 30 percent of the NHA budget. NHAs also serve as vehicles of demand articulation, voicing local concerns and desires to local governments. On the other hand, the most common task that NHAs perform for city governments is to liaise with citizens. Typically, this means disseminating information from the local government to the residents. This is done via the *kairanban*, or rotating message board. This is a clipboard with documents attached, which neighbors pass from house to house, affixing their seal after having viewed the contents. There might be a dozen or so requests a month from the local government to place items on the rotating message board, not all of which the local NHAs will grant. The tension between the local government, which seeks to get the organizations to disseminate as much information as possible, and the NHA, which selects which government requests it will accept, reveals the independence of the groups, as well as their close cooperation with the government. This productive tension characterizes the NHA-government relationship. Cooperation with the local governments is integral to the NHAs. The privileged relationship with local government serves to legitimate the organization itself. However, NHAs retain their independence in terms of budget, leadership selection, and operations.[10]

As we have seen, Japan's civil society is distinguished by its dual structure. Local civil society is vital, and the neighborhood association epitomizes a plethora of small local groups. At the other end of the spectrum, professional civil society is small by international standards. Advocacy groups are particularly weak. Recent debates on civil society in consolidated democracies, especially the United States, are reviewed in the next section. As it turns out, the distinctive pattern of Japan's civil society makes it peculiarly well positioned to shed new light on these debates.

Civil Society in Consolidated Democracies

Much of the theoretical writing on civil society has examined the case of the United States. Accordingly, this brief review will look at the contentions of scholars concerning the role of civil society groups in the United States. Jeffrey Berry has traced the rise of new public-interest advocacy groups and defines them as "a political interest group whose basis of organization is not built on the vocational or professional aspirations of its members or financial supporters" (Berry 1998: 369).[11] These groups include AARP, NRA, NOW, Public Citizen, Eagle Forum, and the Environmental Defense Fund. Such groups sometimes offer selective benefits, but

TABLE 7.4
Press Coverage of Interest Groups as a Proportion of All Interest Groups Mentioned in U.S. Print Media in 1991

Interest groups	Proportion of coverage (%)
Advocacy groups	40.2
Corporations	1.8
Trade associations	23.7
Professional associations	26.7
Labor unions	5.6
Think tanks	—
Other (veterans' organizations, nonprofits, churches, etc.)	2.1

SOURCE: Adapted from Berry 1998: 387.

their main function is advocacy. The success of these advocacy groups "in mobilizing large numbers of supporters has worked to make our national interest group system more representative of the interest of the American population" (Berry 1998: 370). These groups require large professional staffs in order to be effective. It is precisely this type of group that faces such stiff legal and practical hurdles in Japan. If the intent of the Japanese framework was to prevent such groups from forming, lest they become influential in the policy process, evidence from the United States suggests that such fears are well grounded.

Berry presents convincing evidence of the effectiveness of these groups in influencing public discourse. Such groups are the most common type of interest group to be called for testimony at congressional hearings, for example. Advocacy groups testify before Congress even more than trade associations and labor unions combined and appear about twice as often as professional associations (Berry 1998: 376). Although this pattern might reflect the desire of legislators to summon an extreme witness, more likely it demonstrates the considerable expertise developed by these professionalized groups. Aside from influencing congressional proceedings, advocacy groups are mentioned in media much more than any other type of group in the United States (Table 7.4).

Advocacy groups are effective in getting their message out through newspapers. Not only are they subjects of coverage themselves, but their findings are considered newsworthy. Research conducted by advocacy groups gets more media play than any other research except for the government's own—even more than that originating in academia (see Figure 7.5). Getting research into the public debate through the media is perhaps the most effective way to influence public debate. Even if their research is objective, advocacy groups are able to influence agendas and the framing of issues simply by covering new areas they wish to highlight. Professional staff are essential to independent research. It is only because of the development of this capability that advocacy groups have become so prominent in debates. Looking at specific cases, environmental groups such as Earth Action Network, the Environmental Defense Fund, and the Public Interest Research Group created pressure that forced tuna companies to give up drift nets, forced McDonald's to abandon foam containers, and forced apple growers to cease using Alar. From a broader perspective, these groups have been conspicuously successful in changing attitudes and raising the profile of environmental issues. In 1970, for example, only one in ten Canadians even considered the environment worthy of being on the national agenda. Twenty years later, one in three thought the environment was the most pressing issue facing Canada (Wapner 1995: 323–27).

In the same year that Robert Putnam chronicled the decline of social-capital-producing groups in the United States (Putnam 2000), David Horton Smith took nonprofit scholars to task for a "flat-earth paradigm" that "overemphasizes the larger, wealthier, older, more visible nonprofits in which most of the work is done by paid staff rather than by volunteers" and ignores small, nonprofessionalized, grassroots associations (Smith 2000: xiv).[12] Although the smaller groups are clearly more difficult to research, there are some reliable examinations of neighborhood associations in the United States. An intensive survey of fifteen American cities found that a city with NHAs in 20 to 40 percent of its area (regardless of their participation rates) was exceptional. Moreover, participation was often weak, with only 6 percent participating in the NHA on a monthly basis and only 40 percent participating at all.[13] Although it would be premature to conclude that local civil society is indisputably more vital in Japan than in the United States, we do have some basis for plausibly suggesting this is true. At the least, neighborhood associations are much more prevalent and active in Japan than they are in the United States.[14]

Japan's Dual Civil Society and Democracy

What is distinctive about Japan's civil society, as we have seen, is a pattern of many small, local groups and few large, professionalized groups. This pattern holds important implications for democracy. Small local groups and large professionalized groups, particularly advocacy groups, make distinct contributions to a consolidated democracy, as shown by the review of recent work by Robert Putnam (2000) and Theda Skocpol (1999). Small local groups can contribute to stocks of social capital and perhaps to the performance of local governments. They form a crucial basis of social life. These groups lack professional staff, however. Unlike small local groups without full-time employees, professionalized groups that have a large core of full-time employees can develop expertise, institutionalize movements, and influence policies and other outcomes down the road; they change the political landscape.

Compare the many old people's clubs in Japan with the American Association of

Retired Persons (AARP) in the United States. AARP claims thirty million members, 160,000 volunteers, 1,837 employees, and, through its dozens of registered lobbyists and more than 150 policy and legislative staffers, an important influence on policymaking.[15] Although Japanese old people's clubs might improve the quality of life of many aged people by giving them opportunities to socialize, they are neighborhood affairs with a limited membership, no professional staff, and no impact on policymaking. The distinction is not in the number of members or volunteers but in the concentration, in the United States, of membership in one organization with professional staff.[16] Original research made a crucial contribution to the success of the Nobel Prize-winning International Campaign to Ban Land Mines, which compiled gruesome statistics such as the fact that one in every 236 Cambodians is an amputee, compared with one in every 22,000 Americans (Price 1998: 620). Beyond research, however, the message must be put out. Greenpeace, for example, has its own media facilities and can distribute photographs to newspapers and circulate video news spots to television stations in eighty-eight countries within hours (Wapner 1995: 320). The point is not that one organizational configuration is more effective than the other, but rather that these institutional forms have many implications for politics, policy formation, and government performance.[17] Japan has many small groups of the neighborhood watch type and few large, independent groups like AARP. Let us explore how each type relates to Japanese democracy.[18]

NHAs and Democracy

A number of NHA activities have implications for government performance. Through their cooperation with local government, NHAs can improve government performance while lowering costs. At the same time, NHAs can contribute to social capital directly and indirectly. More generally, the state's making requests of groups does not necessarily diminish participation in them. For example, one fairly common task that Japanese NHAs perform is cleaning local parks. The state could subcontract this task out, and pay for it out of the residents' taxes. When the residents band together to clean their own local park (usually small in area), however, it is likely to be cleaned more thoroughly. Moreover, the experience of working together to clean a public area reinforces community spirit and promotes social capital.[19] When NHAs are available and willing to perform this service, efficiency is increased and social capital is also generated.

In this way, the NHA contributes to building social capital, simultaneously with improving government performance. NHAs build social capital indirectly as well. They form the nucleus for many other local organizations, such as women's clubs, youth clubs, and elderly persons' groups. The organizational infrastructure of the NHA facilitates the formation and operation of these groups. Although AARP provides aggressive advocacy, the elderly persons' groups in Japan might serve their members even better by creating social capital. Frequent interaction with others is not only enjoyable; for many elderly people, it also has important health benefits. The trips to local health facilities familiarize the elderly with the available health resources and how to access them. They also provide a chance for both health professionals and peers to observe the health of the group members, giving an opportunity for early detection of health concerns. Putnam has argued that group membership correlates with better health for the elderly in the United States, and these arguments apply in full measure to Japanese NHAs and elderly persons' groups (Putnam 2000).

Recalling the NHA activities listed in Table 7.3, it would be hard to imagine a group that contributes more directly to social capital. The NHA's informational role is surely also crucial. NHAs provide a superb environment for social capital, as high levels of information flow through embedded networks that provide multiple opportunities for sanctions. Besides providing information networks, NHAs contribute directly to the dissemination of information by local governments. One of the most important tools for this is the circulating message board (*kairanban*) system alluded to above. Often the actual passing of the clipboard from neighbor to neighbor presents an additional opportunity to share information and discuss issues. Besides internal issues such as festivals, children's outings, and death notices, NHAs sometimes consent to circulate notices from local government offices. Disseminating information in this way is much cheaper and more effective than mailing it directly. The prefecture of Saitama, adjacent to Tokyo, for example, mails documents such as national health insurance forms and election forms but attempts to circulate most other public notices through the NHAs (Nakata 1996: 209). In short, messages circulated on the rotating message board are cheaper to disseminate than other forms of public notice, more likely to be read, promote contact among neighbors, and stimulate discussion of local issues among neighbors. Some kinds of state demands may actually contribute to social capital (see Pekkanen and Read 2003).

Survey data also present some interesting findings about NHA participation and levels of generalized trust at the individual level. It is not surprising that NHA participants are more than twice as likely as nonparticipants to say that they can rely on their neighbors (Nihon Sōgō Kenkyuujyō 2003, 171). More important, the survey reveals that individuals who participate in NHAs have higher levels of trust of *anyone*: they are more likely than nonparticipants to agree with the statement that most people can be trusted. This is one indication that NHA participation directly increases levels of generalized trust, and thus contributes directly to building stocks of social capital.

It seems impossible to understand the remarkably high rates of participation in NHAs without considering social capital. Many Japanese participate in NHAs less out of an intrinsic desire to engage in their activities than because they feel that to do otherwise would affect their reputation with neighbors. Naturally, widespread participation in NHA activities also reinforces the norm of participation and increases the visibility (and thus potential consequences) of deviance. If a resident chooses to defect from NHA activities in Japan, there will be no storming of his or her house by enraged neighbors or other physical coercion. Rather, residents typically say that they fear being insufficiently engaged in the social network, which could prove inconvenient in daily life. To take a mundane example, a resident expecting an important package, but who cannot be at home when it arrives, will feel more confident in relying on neighbors to receive it. By participating in the NHA, residents signal that they are trustworthy and will reciprocate favors, thus meriting help and consideration. In this way, the NHA sustains and is sustained by the social network of the community.

Advocates and Democracy

Jeffrey Berry has demonstrated the influence on public debate in the United States of advocacy groups, which can employ a variety of means, ranging from appearance before Congress to publication of a group's own research. Although it is a step further to show how this influence can translate into influence over policy outcomes, the link is widely accepted. Here I shall focus on directly establishing only the footprint of Japan's civil society groups in policy debates.

Characterizing Japan's civil society as "members without advocates" highlights how ineffective civil society groups have been as advocates (Pekkanen 2002a). This is not to claim, of course, that certain interest groups, such as Nōkyō or the Japan Medical Association, have been powerless, but rather to stress the dearth of effective advocacy groups beyond a limited number of industry or professional organizations. Nevertheless, by and large, Japanese civil society groups do not figure prominently in public debates. According to my calculations, for example, a sample of *Asahi Shimbun* articles on politics or political issues in 2001 showed that nearly twice as many articles mentioned individual corporations by name as mentioned any civil society organization. In other words, in media discussions of politics, corporations overshadow civil society groups. Figure 7.5, which directly compares the sources of research covered in newspapers in the United States and Japan over a few key categories, is even more telling. As we have seen, newspapers cover and use research published by civil society groups in the United States more than that provided by any other source. In Japan, however, the government is the most prominent source of research. The relative contributions of academia are the same in the two countries. What is striking is that Japanese civil society groups are so subdued. Newspapers hardly ever cover their research. In large part, this is because the meager professional staffs of Japanese civil society groups simply do not produce much research to cover.

Japanese civil society groups are not prominent in public debates. Although this does not necessarily mean they are not powerful in shaping public opinion or affect-

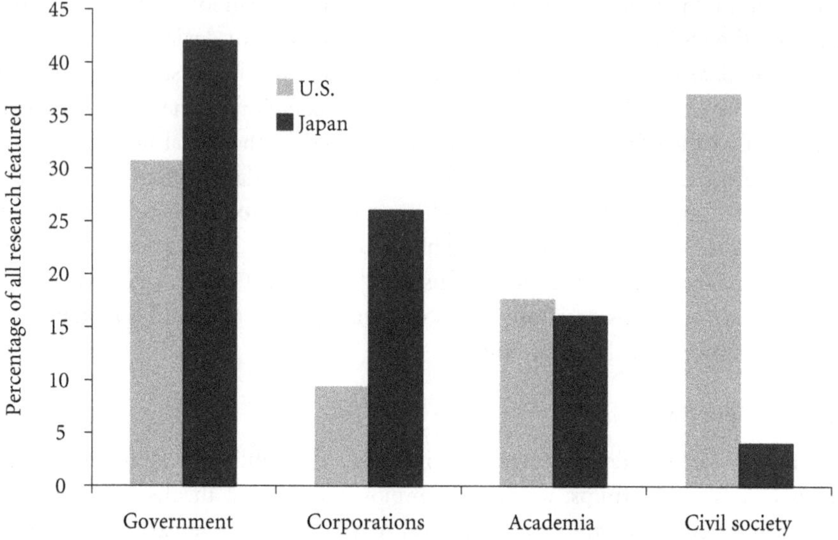

Figure 7.5. Research in newspapers in Japan and the United States by source. U.S. data for 1995 adapted from Berry 1998: 379; Japan data sampled from *Asahi Shimbun* and *Nihon Keizai Shimbun* in 2001–2.

ing policy outcomes, I do contend that this is the case (and much evidence supports this view).[20] Consider policy debates on moral issues. In many countries, including the United States, civil society groups, in the form of religious groups, heavily influence the public debate on issues seen as having a moral dimension, such as abortion or euthanasia (Hardacre 1991, 2003). This is not true in Japan despite the large number of religious groups (see Table 7.1). Another example is policy change on women's issues. Although essentially toothless, the Equal Employment Opportunity Law (EEOL) of 1986 guaranteed gender equality in the workplace. Although one might have expected women's groups to have taken the lead in forcing this measure onto the policy agenda, it was in fact elements of the bureaucracy that pushed the issue in order to bring Japan into compliance with the UN's antidiscrimination pledge, signed by Japan during the 1975 Year of the Woman (Pharr 1990; Upham 1987). For an environmental example, consider the sweeping package of antipollution measures that gave the 1971 Diet the label "the Pollution Diet." Although thousands of environmental groups sprang up between 1965 and 1975 in Japan, they did not play a role in getting the antipollution measures on the agenda. These groups remained local and disaggregated (Pharr and Badaracco 1986; Upham 1987). Similarly, it was not Japanese environmental groups but the bureaucracy that took the lead in the passage of the Kyoto Accords (Reimann 2001a; 2001b; 2001c; 2002; 2003). Japanese civil society groups have also been weak on issues ranging from whaling to human rights (fingerprinting of Korean residents, for example) (see Shipper 2002).

Has Japan Got Civil Society Right?

In recent works, both Putnam and Skocpol concur with Berry's empirical findings on the growth of advocacy groups. Neither, however, shares any sense of optimism about this development (Putnam 2000; Skocpol 1999). For Putnam, the issue is acute, because it parallels the atrophy of civic engagement. He cautions that the "vigor of the new Washington-based organizations . . . is an unreliable guide to the vitality of social connectedness and civic engagement in American communities" (Putnam 2000: 52). In this context, he cites the example of Greenpeace using aggressive direct-mail solicitations to become the largest environmental group in the United States in 1990 and then scaling back on these techniques. By 1998, Greenpeace membership had plummeted 85 percent (Putnam 2000: 53). Putnam argues that civic engagement through participation in associations supports democracy by inculcating democratic habits, by serving as forums for deliberation over public issues, and by instilling civic virtues such as active participation in public life. But he contends that advocacy groups in which members do not participate, but simply write a check, do not constitute civic engagement in the sense that active participation in civic or other groups does. In other words, membership without participation in an advocacy group does not sustain democracy per se. Putnam goes further, however, in arguing that it might in fact undermine democracy. He admits there might be more bang-for-the-buck from advocacy groups. Writing a check to a group such as the NAACP might be a time-efficient way to advance one's political agenda—and more effective in that sense than one's own participation in a civic group. But the explosion of advocacy groups in Washington, D.C., does not nurture many desirable traits. Putnam cautions that "Americans at the political poles are more engaged in civic life, whereas moderates have tended to drop out" (Putnam 2000: 342). The civic disengagement of the moderates is a frightening price to pay and could lead to highly polarized debates without compromise.

Skocpol too notes the proliferation of Washington-based advocacy groups. Coupled with the decline of large cross-class voluntary associations, she terms this development "advocates without members" (Skocpol 1999). Like Putnam, she sees a number of troubling consequences. For one thing, people from privileged backgrounds used to have to interact with those from humbler circumstances as they rose in these organizations. That process has been short-circuited by the new model of organization building. Even more troubling, this development "magnifies polarized voices" in politics. Advocacy groups need visibility, and clashes with sharply opposed groups are good fodder for media coverage. Foundations are active in promoting groups clearly on one side or the other of divisive issues. Skocpol seems to share Putnam's misgivings that the proliferation of advocacy groups means that the middle is dropping out of American politics.

What, then, are we to make of Japan? Long viewed as a poor imitation of

America's powerful civil society, has Japan in fact got it right? Observers have complained about the rise of special interest groups in the United States at the same time as they have effused over the benefits of social capital. Neighborhood associations enhance Japanese government performance, and the dearth of advocacy groups avoids the troublesome consequences of the American proliferation. In Japan, the polarization of political debate feared by Skocpol and Putnam alike is not a menace.[21] One might argue, of course, that Japan avoids a cacophonous polarization at the cost of silence from certain members of the choir. For the purposes of this volume, the important consequence is that civil society does not have much influence over the course of political change in Japan. In some ways, Japan's civil society presents a striking contrast to South Korea's (Chapter 4; see also Tsujinaka and Yeom, forthcoming; Pekkanen 2003a). Japan's professional organizations can in general be characterized as much more timid and less contentious than those of South Korea. At the same time, South Korea's local civil society groups are weaker than Japan's. In Chapter 4 in this volume, Kim carefully analyzes the political consequences of Korea's civil society configuration and development.

Although we have found Japan's civil society to exert negligible influence over policy, caution is advised in analyzing the other states surveyed in this volume. The Japanese case suggests that we must reject any simplistic equation of economic development and democratization with the development of a strong civil society in the American mold. "Civil society modernization" theory is not tenable. Historical legacies and institutional arrangements have a critical influence on the configuration of civil society.

Notes

1. See Cohen and Arato 1992 on the exclusion of market organizations from definitions of civil society. See also Suzuki 2003 on the weak social functions of Japanese unions in particular.

2. This supervision is established by Civil Code Article 67. Paragraph 2 establishes a supervision system (*kanshi seido*) by the competent supervising ministry (*shumu kanchou*). Article 84 makes further provisions for fines of PIP directors who violate directions by the competent ministry.

3. Two recent changes have improved the legal environment: the 1998 "NPO Law" (Law for the Promotion of Specified Nonprofit Activities) and the 2001 granting of tax privileges (in the fiscal year 2001 tax reform). The 1998 NPO Law created a new category of PIP (through a special law attached to Article 34) and was designed to limit administrative guidance and bureaucratic discretion in the granting of legal status, while allowing many more civil society groups to gain legal status (Pekkanen 2000a; 2000b). There is evidence, however, that administrative guidance continues. A survey of the 1,034 groups granted NPO legal person status by November 1999 (to which 463 responded) found only 5.2 percent "satisfied" with the law. As of April 27, 2001, by contrast, 4,626 groups had applied for and 3,933 had been granted NPO legal person status. The 2001 tax changes created a subcategory of NPO legal persons—tax-deductible (*nintei*) specified nonprofit activities legal persons—to which indi-

viduals or corporations can make a contribution that is deductible from their income tax. Implementation had not occurred at the time of this writing, but the change will not lower tax rates for NPOs and only allows certain NPO legal persons to receive charitable contributions. These groups must be certified by the commissioner of the National Tax Administration of the Ministry of Finance as meeting a number of stringent criteria—for example, one-third of the organization's budget must come from donations. This "public support test" alone could disqualify as many as 90 percent of NPO legal persons (Pekkanen 2001b).

4. Not all civil society groups in Japan are starved for resources, but the most independent ones are. The pattern of tax benefits also supports the political-institutional hypothesis. In general, charitable contributions by individuals or corporations are not tax deductible in Japan. There is a subcategory of special PIPs, however, to which contributions are deductible. Given its civil code system, Japan's tax laws differ in many respects from those of the United States. PIPs are taxed at a lower rate than corporations on activities subject to taxation; the United States uses a system of "related activities" instead. Donations are not tax deductible in Japan, however, except for those made to a select and numerically small group of "special public interest increasing legal persons" (*tokutei kōeki zōshin hōjin*, commonly called *tokuzō*). Differences in tax privileges are more complex and include deductible contributions, reduced taxation, and tax-free activities for PIPs. Of the 232,776 PIPs incorporated in 1997, only 17,000 held this status. In contrast, the government has been promoting social-welfare legal persons in an effort to deal with such social issues as the aging society; not surprisingly, every one of the 14,832 social-welfare legal persons held special PIP status (Yamauchi 1997: 198).

5. Indeed, Japan's leading scholar of civil society, Yutaka Tsujinaka, has examined changes over time in Japan's civil society. See Tsujinaka 2003 for the best introduction, although Tsujinaka 2002a and especially Tsujinaka 1988 are much more comprehensive. See also Pharr 2003 for a historical and comparative analysis.

6. These Japanese groups are all the groups in the Japan Interest Group Survey (JIGS) survey. The JIGS data set was collected by the Cross-National Survey on Civil Society Organizations and Interest Groups, a team of six researchers led by Yutaka Tsujinaka and based at Tsukuba University in Japan. The team conducted an extensive survey of more than 1600 associations in Tokyo and also in Ibaraki Prefecture in 1997, involving 36 questions and 260 sub-questions. The team utilized random sampling of telephone book directories (the NTT telephone book). Not all groups necessarily have their own telephone line, but this allows the team to also sample groups without legal status. In this way, the JIGS survey is more comprehensive than government data and catches many groups that would otherwise be uncounted. I am indebted to Yutaka Tsujinaka for sharing this data set with me.

7. This development is best analyzed by Tsujinaka (1996, 1997, 2002a, 2002b, 2002c, 2003).

8. These amounts vary over time and location. For example, though, in Marugame City in Kagawa Prefecture (a city of 81,176), the subsidy (*hojokin*) is a nominal 280 yen per household. (Kimura Yoichi, section chief, Marugame City Municipal Government, Living and Environment Section, personal interview, Oct. 17, 2003, Marugame City, Kagawa Prefecture, Japan.)

9. However, this legacy makes a few government officials skittish. At the least, in some interviews, both city and national (Ministry of Home Affairs) officials have quoted Occupation Era regulations and shrilly disavowed excessive influence over NHAs at some length—as a preamble lest the American interviewer think NHAs today were the same as in the 1930s—before proceeding to more substantive discussions of the issues. This behavior is

unusual, though, and most officials simply discussed their relationships with the NHAs without such a preamble.

10. Politicians also attempt to use NHAs for electoral mobilization. Interviews with many national and local (prefectural and city/town/village level) politicians and NHA leaders confirm this. My impression is that NHAs are most effective, however, at mobilization for the city level of political office, rather than the national level. Moreover, NHAs because of their nature encompass a range of political views, and risk alienating members or brutal internecine strife if political support becomes overt. Aware of the risks, NHAs generally avoid co-optation by politicians.

11. Jeffrey Berry calls these groups "citizens groups," but to avoid confusion with the citizens groups of Japan, I shall refer to them as advocacy groups.

12. David Horton Smith criticizes American researchers for focusing on the nonprofit organizations for which there are good data and thus seeing only the tip of the iceberg (Smith 1994, 1997a, 1997b, 2000). Robert Wuthnow too finds a vast proliferation of small "support groups" in the United States (Wuthnow 1991, 1998, 1999). The first systematic effort to investigate the proportion of large and small groups in the United States is by Michael Foley and Bob Edwards (2003), who examine the population of peace groups.

13. Berry, Portnoy, and Thomson 1993; Thomson 2001. See also Markus 2002 for a study of civic participation (including neighborhood associations) and its influence on local governance.

14. Neighborhood associations exist in many other states, but nowhere are they so widespread and important a part of civil society as in Japan. Although several observers have analyzed NHAs in various countries, the only comparative analyses I am aware of are Pekkanen and Read 2003 and Nakata 2000a. China has Residents Committees (RC) in urban areas; see Read 2000, 2001, 2002, and Kokubun and Kojima 2002. Significantly, Benjamin Read cites recent changes in residents' committees that could revitalize these organizations or even transform them from appendages of the state into something like modern Japanese NHAs. For a cogent analysis of Korea's neighborhood associations, see Seo 2003. I owe an intellectual debt also to Ben Read, because our work together (Pekkanen and Read 2003) greatly sharpened my comparative understanding of NHAs.

15. Telephone interview with Karen Stewart, AARP staff, July 31, 2000.

16. Although volunteers are a higher percentage of the population in the United States than in Japan (48.8 percent in 1995 versus 26.9 percent in 1996), they are numerous in Japan too (Yamauchi 1999: 59).

17. With a focus on the organizational level, Shimizu Hiroko (2000) demonstrates the importance of the distinction between paid staff and volunteers. She argues that paid staff are crucial to the development of organizational capacity in the nonprofit sector and cannot be replaced by volunteers. Compared to the United States, however, few Japanese organizations have paid staff.

18. There is little to suggest that NHAs did not facilitate governmental effectiveness and efficiency under authoritarianism. However, after 1940 at the latest, they likely did not produce as much social capital because of (1) subsumption by the state, clearly removing NHAs from civil society and at the same time rendering participation obligatory and not voluntary; and (2) the use of these groups for social control (i.e., surveillance of neighbors), which probably impaired the groups as vehicles for spreading trust and generalized reciprocity. Japan's authoritarian period began in 1931, however, and from then until 1940, it is possible that NHAs helped in "Making Dictatorship Work." Without further research, it is impossible

to say whether NHAs (or social capital) improve democratic governance or all governance. Even if the latter, however, the point that social capital producing groups also make democracies function more smoothly would be untarnished. For a general discussion of these issues, see Pekkanen and Read 2003.

19. Many Japanese feel that having to clean the park is bothersome and do so only out of social obligation, but many others feel pride in working together and keeping their local park pristine. Because most Japanese are involved in NHAs to some degree, I have had many conversations about NHAs with a wide variety of participants that do not necessarily constitute interviews (although many did). Here I summarize such views. They represent my characterizations based on these conversations and I do not directly attribute them to any particular individual.

20. My thanks to Susan Pharr for her suggestions on this point.

21. And the troublesome consequences of a highly contentious South Korean civil society are perhaps also avoided. For work on South Korea's neighborhood associations, see Seo 2003. For a rigorous empirical comparison of Japanese and South Korean civil society organizations, see Tsujinaka et al. 1998 and Tsujinaka and Yeom forthcoming.

Works Cited

Akimoto Ritsuo. 1990. "Chūkan shūdan toshite no chōnaikai" (Neighborhood associations as intermediate organizations). In Kurasawa Susumu and Akimoto Ritsuo, eds., *Chōnaikai to chiiki shūdan* (Neighborhood associations and local groups). Tokyo: Minerva Shobō.

Amemiya Takako. 1994. *Kōeki hōjin no setsuritsu-un'ei* (Setting up and running public-interest legal persons). Tokyo: Kanki.

———. 1995. "Nonprofit Public Interest Corporations in Japan." MS.

———. 1996. "Comparative Nonprofit Law Project: Conference and Workshop for Legal Specialists. Country Paper: Japan." Manila: Asia Pacific Philanthropy Consortium.

———. 1999. "Japan." In Thomas Silk, ed., *Philanthropy and Law in Asia.* San Francisco: Jossey-Bass.

Amenomori Takayoshi. 1997. "Japan." In Lester M. Salamon and Helmut K. Anheier, eds., *Defining the Nonprofit Sector: A Cross-National Analysis.* New York: St. Martin's Press.

Atoda, Naosumi, Takayoshi Amenomori, and Mio Ohta. 1998. "The Scale of the Japanese Nonprofit Sector." In Tadashi Yamamoto, ed., *The Nonprofit Sector in Japan.* New York: Manchester University Press.

Berry, Jeffrey M. 1998. "The Rise of Citizens Groups." In Theda Skocpol and Morris P. Fiorina, eds., *Civic Engagement in American Democracy.* Washington, D.C.: Brookings Institution.

———. 1999. *The New Liberalism: The Rising Power of Citizen Groups.* Washington, D.C.: Brookings Institution.

Berry, Jeffrey M., Kent E. Portnoy, and Ken Thompson. 1993. *The Rebirth of Urban Democracy.* Washington, D.C.: Brookings Institution.

Bestor, Theodore. 1989. *Neighborhood Tokyo.* Stanford: Stanford University Press.

Braibanti, Ralph J. O. 1948. "Neighborhood Associations in Japan and Their Democratic Potentialities." *Far Eastern Quarterly* 7: 136–64.

Cohen, Jean L., and Andrew Arato. 1992. *Civil Society and Political Theory.* Cambridge, Mass.: MIT Press.

Crozier, Michael, Samuel Huntington, and Joji Watanuki. 1975. *The Crisis of Democracy; Report on the Governability of Democracies to the Trilateral Commission*. New York: New York University Press.
Dantai Kiso Kouzou Kenkyuukai. 1998. *Dantai no kiso kōzō ni kan suru chōsa: Chūkan hōkokusho* (Survey: Interim report of the basic structure of groups). Tsukuba: Tsukuba Law Faculty.
Dore, Ronald. 1958. *City Life in Japan*. Berkeley: University of California Press.
———. 1967. *Aspects of Social Change in Modern Japan*. Princeton: Princeton University Press.
Dowie, Mark. 2001. *American Foundations: An Investigative History*. Cambridge, Mass.: MIT Press.
Fagen, Richard R. 1969. *The Transformation of Political Culture in Cuba*. Stanford: Stanford University Press.
Foley, Michael, and Bob Edwards. 2003. "Social Movements Beyond the Beltway: Understanding the Diversity of Social Movement Organizations." *Mobilization* 8: 85–107.
Hall, Peter Dobkin. 1987. "A Historical Overview of the Private Nonprofit Sector." In Walter W. Powell, ed., *The Nonprofit Sector: A Research Handbook*. New Haven: Yale University Press.
Hansmann, Henry. 1980. "The Role of Nonprofit Enterprise." *Yale Law Journal* 91: 54–100.
———. 1987. "Economic Theories of Nonprofit Organization." In Walter W. Powell, ed., *The Nonprofit Sector: A Research Handbook*. New Haven: Yale University Press.
Hardacre, Helen. 1991. "Japan: The Public Sphere in a Non-Western Setting." In Robert Wuthnow, ed., *Between States and Markets: The Voluntary Sphere in Comparative Perspective*. Princeton: Princeton University Press.
———. 2003. In Frank J. Schwartz and Susan J. Pharr, eds., *The State of Civil Society in Japan*. Cambridge: Cambridge University Press.
Hastings, Sally Ann. 1995. *Neighborhood and Nation in Tokyo, 1905–1937*. Pittsburgh: University of Pittsburgh Press.
Hayashi Shigeo. 1972. *Kōeki hōjin kenkyū nyūmon* (Introduction to public-interest legal person research). Tokyo: Public-Interest Legal Person Association.
Independent Sector. 1996. *Nonprofit Almanac 1996-1997*. Washington D.C.: Independent Sector.
Iwasaki Nobuhiko. 1985. "Chōnaikai wo dono yō ni toraeru ka" (How to treat neighborhood associations). In Iwasaki Nobuhiko et al., eds., *Chōnaikai no kenkyū* (Research on neighborhood associations). Tokyo: Ochanomizu Shōbō.
Iwasaki Nobuhiko, et al., eds., 1985. *Chōnaikai no kenkyū* (Research on neighborhood associations). Tokyo: Ochanomizu Shōbō.
Jenkins, Craig J. 1998. "Channeling Social Protest: Foundation Patronage of Contemporary Social Movements." In Walter W. Powell and Elisabeth S. Clemens, eds., *Private Action and the Public Good*. New Haven: Yale University Press.
Kodansha. 1993. *Japan: An Illustrated Encyclopedia*. Tokyo: Kodansha.
Kokubun, Ryosei, and Kazuko Kojima. 2002. "The 'Shequ Construction' Programme and the Chinese Communist Party." *Copenhagen Journal of Asian Studies* 16: 86–105.
Markus, Greg. 2002. "Civic Participation in America." MS.
Masland, John W. 1946. "Neighborhood Associations in Japan." *Far Eastern Survey* XV.
Nakata H., et al. 1997. "Kōekiteki dantai no zaisan NPO Finance" (Finance of public interest groups). *Juristo* 1105: 56–64.
Nakata Minoru. 1993. *Chiiki kyōdō kanri no shakaigaku* (The sociology of local joint management). Tokyo: Toshindo.

———, ed. 1995. *Korekara no chōnaikai jichikai* (Neighborhood associations now). Tokyo: Jichitai Kenkyūsha. Originally published in 1981.

———. 1996. *Chōnaikai jichikai no shintenkai* (New developments in neighborhood associations). Tokyo: Jichitai Kenkyūsha.

———. 1997a. "Chiiki bunken to komyūniti" (Devolution and community). In *Jichi dayori* (Local autonomy tidings). Tokyo: Jichitai Kenkyūsha.

———. 1997b. "Jyumin jichi soshiki no kokusai hikaku kenkyū jyosetsu" (Introduction to the comparative study of neighborhood associations). *Jyōhō bunka kenkyū*: 157–71.

———. 2000a. "Kenkyuu no mokuteki, houhou, kadai" (Themes, methods, and aims of the research). In Minoru Nakata, ed., *Sekai no jyuumin soshiki* (Residents' associations around the world). Tokyo: Jichitai kenkyuusha.

———, ed. 2000b. *Sekai no jyuumin soshiki* (Residents' associations around the world). Tokyo: Jichitai kenkyuusha.

Nihon Sōugōu Kenkyuujyō. 2003. *Sousharu kyapitaru: yutaka na ningenkankei to shimin-katsudou no koujyunkanwo motomete.* (Social Capital: For a Virtuous Circle of Rich Human Relationships and Citizen Activities). Tokyo: Nihon Sōugōu Kenkyuujyō.

Norbeck, Edward. 1967. "Associations and Democracy in Japan." In Ronald P. Dore, ed., *Aspects of Social Change in Modern Japan.* Princeton: Princeton University Press.

Noumi, Yasushi. 1997. "Kouekiteki dantai ni okeru kouekisei to hieirisei." (Public interest and nonprofit in public interest groups). *Juristo* 1105: 50-55.

Pekkanen, Robert. 2000a. "Hou, kokka, shimin shakai" (Law, the state, and civil society). *Leviathan* 27: 73–108.

———. 2000b. "Japan's New Politics: The Case of the NPO Law." *Journal of Japanese Studies* 26: 111–43.

———. 2001a. *An Analytical Framework for the Development of the Nonprofit Sector and Civil Society in Japan.* Washington, D.C.: Aspen Institute.

———. 2001b. *Civil Society and Its Regulators: Non-Profit Organizations in Japan.* Washington, D.C.: Japan Information Access Project.

———. 2001c. "A Less-Taxing Woman?: New Regulations on Tax Treatment of Nonprofits in Japan." *International Journal of Not-for-Profit Law* 3(2).

———. 2002a. "Japan's Dual Civil Society: Advocates Without Members." Ph.D. diss., Harvard University.

———. 2002b. "Nihon no shimin shakai to Nihon NPO Sentaa" (The NPO Center and Japan's civil society). *Hiroba* (Sept.): 6–7.

———. 2003a. "Civil Society and Political Change in Japan and Korea." Paper prepared for presentation at the International Political Science Association Congress, Durban, South Africa (June).

———. 2003b. "Local Civil Society and the State: The Case of Japan's Neighborhood Associations." Presentation at Association for Asian Studies Annual Meeting, New York City.

———. 2003c. "Molding Japanese Civil Society: State-Structured Incentives and the Patterning of Civil Society." In Frank J. Schwartz and Susan J. Pharr, eds., *The State of Civil Society in Japan.* Cambridge: Cambridge University Press.

———. 2003d. "The Politics of Nonprofit Regulation." In Stephen Osborne, ed., *The Voluntary and Non-profit Sector in Japan: An Emerging Response to a Changing Society.* London: Routledge.

———. 2003e. "State and Society in Japan's Neighborhoods." Paper prepared for the annual meeting of the American Political Science Association, Philadelphia.

———. 2004. "Sources of Policy Innovation in Japanese Democracy." In Woodrow Wilson Center, Asia Program, Special Report 117.

Pekkanen, Robert, and Ben Read. 2003. "Explaining Cross-National Patterns in State-Fostered Local Associations." Paper prepared for the annual meeting of the American Political Science Association, Philadelphia.

Pekkanen, Robert, and Karla Simon. 2003. "The Legal Framework for Voluntary and Not-for-Profit Activity." In Stephen Osborne, ed., *The Voluntary and Non-profit Sector in Japan: An Emerging Response to a Changing Society*. London: Routledge.

Pharr, Susan J. 1990. *Losing Face: Status Politics in Japan*. Berkeley: University of California Press.

———. 2003. "Conclusion." In Frank J. Schwartz and Susan J. Pharr, eds., *The State of Civil Society in Japan*. Cambridge: Cambridge University Press.

Pharr, Susan J., and Joseph L. Badaracco. 1986. "Coping with Crisis: Environmental Regulation." In Thomas K. McCraw, ed., *America Versus Japan*. Boston: Harvard Business School Press.

Price, Richard. 1998. "Reversing the Gun Sights: Transnational Civil Society Targets Land Mines." *International Organization* 52: 613–44.

Prime Minister's Office of Japan. 1999. *Kōeki hōjin hakusho heisei 9nen* (White paper on public-interest legal persons 1998). Tokyo: Ministry of Finance.

———. 2000. "Tokutei hieiri katsudō hōjin no katsudō un'ei no jittai ni kan suru chōsa yōshi" (Overview of the survey of NPO legal persons). Tokyo: Ministry of Finance.

———. 2001. "Shimin katsudō dantainado kihon chōsa yōshi" (Overview of the basic survey of citizens' groups). Tokyo: Ministry of Finance.

Putnam, Robert. 1993. *Making Democracy Work*. Princeton: Princeton University Press.

———. 1998. "Democracy in America at the End of the Twentieth Century." In Dietrich Rueschemeyer, Marilyn Rueschemeyer, and Bjorn Wittrock, eds., *Participation and Democracy East and West: Comparisons and Interpretations*. Armonk, N.Y.: M. E. Sharpe.

———. 2000. *Bowling Alone: The Collapse and Revival of American Community*. New York: Simon & Schuster.

Read, Benjamin L. 2000. "Revitalizing the State's Urban 'Nerve Tips.'" *China Quarterly* 163 (Sept.): 806–20.

———. 2001. "Democratizing the Neighborhood? New Private Housing and Homeowner Self-Organization in Urban China." Paper presented at the annual meeting of the American Political Science Association, San Francisco.

———. 2002. "China's Urban Residents' Committees as a Crucial Case of State-Fostered Grassroots Association." Paper presented at the annual convention of the International Studies Association, New Orleans.

Reimann, Kim. 2001a. "Building Networks from the Outside In: International Movements, Japanese NGOs, and the Kyoto Climate Change Conference." *Mobilization* 6(1): 69–82.

———. 2001b. *Global Citizens in a Borderless World? States, International Politics, and the Delayed Appearance of Environmental Advocacy NGOs in Japan*. Civil Society in the Asia-Pacific Monograph Series. Cambridge, Mass.: Program on U.S.–Japan Relations, Harvard University.

———. 2001c. "Late Developers in Global Civil Society: Domestic Barriers, International Socialization, and the Emergence of International NGOs in Japan." Ph.D. diss., Harvard University.

———. 2002. "International Politics, Norms, and the Worldwide Growth of NGOs." Paper presented at the American Political Science Association, Boston.

———. 2003. "Building Networks from the Outside In." In Frank Schwartz and Susan Pharr, eds., *The State of Civil Society in Japan*. Cambridge: Cambridge University Press.

Robertson, Jennifer. 1991. *Native and Newcomer*. Berkeley: University of California Press.

Salamon, Lester M. 1994. "The Rise of the Nonprofit Sector." *Foreign Affairs* 73: 109–22.

———. 1997. *The International Guide to Nonprofit Law*. New York: Wiley.

Salamon, Lester M., and Helmut K. Anheier. 1996. *The Emerging Nonprofit Sector: An Overview*. New York: St. Martin's Press.

———. 1997. *Defining the Nonprofit Sector: A Cross-National Analysis*. New York: St. Martin's Press.

Salamon, Lester M., et al. 1999. *Global Civil Society: Dimensions of the Nonprofit Sector*. Baltimore: Johns Hopkins University Press.

Seo, Jungmin. 2003. "Rethinking the Yushin Regime (1972–79): Bansanghoe and the role of the Korean State." Paper presented at the annual meeting of the Association for Asian Studies, Washington, D.C.

Shimizu Hiroko. 2000. "Strategies for Expanding the Nonprofit Sector in Japan—An Assessment of the Potential and Constraints on Nonprofit Organization Use of Volunteers and Paid Staff." Paper presented at the Johns Hopkins Comparative Nonprofit Sector workshop, Baltimore.

Shipper, Apichai. 2002. "The Political Construction of Foreign Workers in Japan." *Critical Asian Studies* 34(1) (Mar.).

Skocpol, Theda. 1985. "Bringing the State Back In: Strategies of Analysis in Current Research." In Peter Evans et al., eds., *Bringing the State Back In*. Cambridge: Cambridge University Press.

———. 1993. *Protecting Soldiers and Mothers: The Political Origins of Social Policy in the United States*. Cambridge, Mass.: Harvard University Press.

———. 1997. "America's Voluntary Groups Thrive in a National Network." *Brookings Review* 15(4): 16–19.

———. 1999. "Advocates Without Members: The Recent Transformation of American Civic Life." In Theda Skocpol and Morris P. Fiorina, eds., *Civic Engagement in American Democracy*. Washington, D.C.: Brookings Institution.

Skocpol, Theda, and Morris P. Fiorina, eds. 1998a. *Civic Engagement in American Democracy*. Washington, D.C.: Brookings Institution.

———. 1998b. "Making Sense of the Civic Engagement Debate." In Theda Skocpol and Morris P. Fiorina, eds., *Civic Engagement in American Democracy*. Washington, D.C.: Brookings Institution.

Skocpol, Theda, Marshall Ganz, and Ziad Munson. 2000. "A Nation of Organizers: The Institutional Origins of Civic Voluntarism in the United States." *American Political Science Review* 94(3): 527–46.

Skocpol, Theda, et al. 1998. "How Americans Became Civic." In Theda Skocpol and Morris P. Fiorina, eds., *Civic Engagement in American Democracy*. Washington, D.C.: Brookings Institution.

Smith, David Horton. 1994. "The Rest of the Nonprofit Sector: The Nature, Magnitude, and Impact of Grassroots Associations in America." Paper presented at the annual conference of the Association of Researchers on Nonprofit Organizations and Voluntary Action, Berkeley, California.

———. 1997a. "Grassroots Associations Are Important: Some Theory and a Review of the Impact Literature." *Nonprofit and Voluntary Sector Quarterly* 26: 269–306.

———. 1997b. "The Rest of the Nonprofit Sector: Grassroots Associations as the Dark Matter Ignored in Prevailing 'Flat-Earth' Maps of the Sector." *Nonprofit and Voluntary Sector Quarterly* 26: 114–31.

———. 2000. *Grassroots Associations*. London: Sage.

Steiner, Kurt. 1965. *Local Government in Japan*. Stanford: Stanford University Press.

Suzuki, Akira. 2003. "The Death of Unions' Associational Life? Political and Cultural Aspects of Enterprise Unions." In Frank J. Schwartz and Susan J. Pharr, eds. *The State of Civil Society in Japan*. Cambridge: Cambridge University Press.

Tanaka Shigeyoshi. 1990. "Chōnaikai no rekishi to bunseki shikaku" (Neighborhood associations: History and analytical perspectives). In Kurasawa Susumu and Akimoto Ritsuo, eds., *Chōnaikai to chiiki shūdan* (Neighborhood associations and local groups). Tokyo: Minerva Shōbō.

Thompson, Ken. 2001. *From Neighborhood to Nation*. Hanover, N.H.: University Press of New England (Tufts).

Tsujinaka Yutaka. 1988. *Rieki Shūdan* (Interest groups). Tokyo: University of Tokyo Press.

———. 1996. *Interest Group Structure and Regime Change in Japan*. College Park: Center for International and Security Studies, University of Maryland.

———. 1997. "Nihon no seiji taisei no bekutoru tenkan: kooporatizumuka kara tagenshugika he" (Vector change of Japan's political system: From corporatism to pluralism). *Leviathan* 20: 130–50.

———, ed. 2002a. *Gendai nihon no shimin shakai—rieki dantai* (Civil society in modern Japan: Interest groups). Tokyo: Bokutakusha.

———. 2002b. "Hikaku no tame no bunseki wakugumi" (A comparative framework). In Tsujinaka Yutaka, ed., *Gendai nihon no shimin shakai—rieki dantai* (Civil society in modern Japan: Interest groups). Tokyo: Bokutakusha.

———. 2002c. "Seidoka—soshikika—katsuodotai" (Systematization–institutionalization–groups). In Tsujinaka Yutaka, ed., *Gendai nihon no shimin shakai—rieki dantai* (Civil society in modern Japan: Interest groups). Tokyo: Bokutakusha.

———. 2003. "Japan's Civil Society Organizations in Comparative Perspective." In Frank J. Schwartz and Susan J. Pharr, eds., *The State of Civil Society in Japan*. Cambridge: Cambridge Univ. Press.

———. N.d. "A Comparison of Interest Groups in Korea and Japan: With Special Emphasis on Korea's Political Regime and Its Interest Group Situation Since 1987 Democratization." MS.

Tsujinaka Yutaka and Mori Hiroki. 1998. "Gendai nihon no rieki dantai: Katsudō kūkan betsu ni mita rieki dantai no zonritsu kōdō yōshiki" (Modern Japan's interest groups: Patterns of formal actions by sphere of activities). *Senkyo* 51(4): 4–15.

Tsujinaka, Yutaka, and Jaeho Yeom, eds. N.d. *Gendai kankoku no shimin shakai—rieki dantai—nikkan hikaku ni yoru taisei ikou no shougeki no kenkyuu* (Contemporary Korean civil society and interest groups—Research on the impact on system change through a Japan-Korea Comparison). Tokyo: Bokutakusha (2004).

Tsujinaka Yutaka, Mori Hiroki, and Hirai Yukiko. 2002. "Dantai no purofiiru" (Groups' profiles). In Tsujinaka Yutaka, ed., *Gendai nihon no shimin shakai—rieki dantai* (Civil society in modern Japan: Interest groups). Tokyo: Bokutakusha.

Tsujinaka Yutaka et al. 1998. "A Comparative Analysis of Korean and Japanese Interest Associations: Korean Civil Society and Its Political Regime since 1987." *Leviathan* 24: 19–50.

Ueda Korekazu. 1985. "Gyōsei, seiji, shūkyō to chōnaikai" (Local government, politics, religion, and neighborhood associations). In Iwasaki Nobuhiko, et al., eds., *Chōnaikai no kenkyū*. Tokyo: Ochanomizu Shōbō.

Upham, Frank K. 1987. *Law and Social Change in Postwar Japan.* Cambridge, Mass.: Harvard University Press.

Wapner, Paul. 1995. "Politics Beyond the State: Environmental Activism and World Civic Politics." *World Politics* 47: 311–40.

———. 1996. *Environmental Activism and World Civic Politics.* New York: State University of New York Press.

Wuthnow, Robert. 1991. *Acts of Compassion: Caring for Others and Helping Ourselves.* Princeton: Princeton University Press.

———. 1998. *Loose Connections: Joining Together in America's Fragmented Communities.* Cambridge, Mass.: Harvard University Press.

———. 1999. "Mobilizing Civic Engagement: The Changing Impact of Religious Involvement." In Theda Skocpol and Morris P. Fiorina, eds., *Civic Engagement in American Democracy.* Washington, D.C.: Brookings Institution Press.

Yamamoto, Tadashi, ed. 1998. *The Nonprofit Sector in Japan.* New York: Manchester University Press.

Yamauchi Naoto. 1997. *Za nonpurofitto ekonomii* (The nonprofit economy). Tokyo: Nippon Hyouronsha.

———. 1999. *NPO deetabukku* (NPO databook). Tokyo: Yuhikaku.

Yasui Kouji. 1985. "Seibi sareta zenchiteki chōnaikai taisei" (Citywide neighborhood association system). In Iwasaki Nobuhiko et al., eds., *Chōnaikai no kenkyū*. Tokyo: Ochanomizu Shōbō.

PART III

Controlled and Communalized Civil Society

Challenging and Reinforcing the State

CHAPTER EIGHT

Malaysia

Construction of Counterhegemonic Narratives and Agendas

MEREDITH L. WEISS

Despite the strength and centralization of the Malaysian state, forces from civil society have exercised substantial, if sometimes indirect, influence over policy agendas, popular demands, the currency of certain political ideas, and the shape of political contests at least since the 1970s. Some of these efforts are best understood in Gramscian or New Left terms; others resonate more clearly with the neo-Tocquevillean liberal-democratic view of civil society, outlined by Muthiah Alagappa in Chapter 1. In fact, most activism traverses both of these two conceptions. Activists from Malaysian civil society simultaneously proffer an alternative ideological grounding for politics—countering the state's communitarian or quasi-authoritarian, "Asian democratic" discourse—and work within the prevailing framework to alter policies or throw support behind or against certain institutional actors. Thus the political changes recommended by the diverse array of civil society's actors run the gamut from the transformational to the relatively trivial. All, however, call for resourcefulness and persistence in working around, against, or through the semidemocratic state. The case of Malaysia offers a particularly useful lens on the sorts of political change that civil society agitation can influence or encourage and on the varied means available to prospective reformers—a useful contrast to other states in Asia.

Malaysia is fundamentally defined by its racial and religious pluralism: its population of approximately 23 million is 66 percent *bumiputera* ("princes/sons of the soil," or Malays and smaller indigenous groups); 25 percent Chinese; and 7 percent Indian. The remainder is about equally divided between "others" and noncitizens (Government of Malaysia 2001). By law, all Malays are required to be Muslim, and some Indians, Chinese, and "others" (for instance, Arabs and Thais) are also Muslim. Among the non-Muslim minority are Buddhists, Hindus, Christians (both Catholic and Protestant), Chinese religionists, Sikhs, and others. Unlike many other states in the region, Malaysia has little recent experience of political or ethnic violence and an only moderately repressive regime. There is space for dissent, but the legal infrastructure is in place to crack down if criticisms go too far. Democratic institutions are well entrenched. And while opportunities for popular participation in decision making are limited, the state has allowed more scope for an autonomous civil society than in, for instance, Singapore or New Order Indonesia. Not surprisingly—given Malaysia's diversity and long history with political Islam—political changes proposed from below are hardly unidirectional. Regardless of intent (whether prodemocratic or not) and however indirect it may be, the impact of nongovernmental activism is apparent in state policies and programs, as well as in the discursive and ideational bent of society. In fact, one of the most significant contributions of civil society actors to the Malaysian polity is the provision of alternative national narratives or ideologies to counter or supplement those of the state.

As suggested by Muthiah Alagappa's introduction to this volume, civil society activists may engage at various levels and with a multitude of strategies and objectives (see especially Table 1.1). In Malaysia, there are four main paths by which activism in civil society can effect political change. First, pressure from within civil society may encourage top-down change, including the government's acceptance or co-optation of agendas or leaders from civil society. These efforts represent engagement primarily at the level of political society as civil society activists develop an alternative vision of the polity and express it via party politics and the state. Although the shape and aims of the incumbent regime may be substantially transformed as a result, civil society may be significantly enfeebled in the process. Second, civil society actors may pursue policy advocacy—what Alagappa categorizes as state-level engagement. Such efforts may have an impact on state policies and may have a multiplicative effect by encouraging yet more activism, but they are unlikely to succeed if the changes pressed are not aligned with a preexisting government agenda. Third, civil society actors may pursue normative changes to counter or subvert government discourse with both immediate and long-term implications for foreign and domestic policy. These initiatives exemplify individual and group-level socialization in Alagappa's matrix. And, fourth, activists—particularly when allied in broad coalitions—may pursue systemic reforms targeting the state's institutions and bases of legitimacy. Although such system-level initiatives are likely to shift the political ground and could well bring radical change, they are more prone to yield a combination of concessions and counterstrikes. All these paths—except, perhaps, policy advocacy—also represent ways in which civil society organizations construct and present counterhegemonic narratives, for instance, for a more liberal democratic, Islamic, or racially stratified state. Such narratives affect political competition in both the short and long terms by contesting the foundational ideological premises of the state.

In this discussion of the breadth, depth, and nature of Malaysian civil society, together with a consideration of initiatives that have followed each of these four paths, we shall discover the several directions political reform may take and the prospects for political change in Malaysia. This examination reveals the complexity, nuance, and fluidity of political engagement in Malaysia, the extent to which the Malaysian state delimits the scope of activism, and the means by which popular engagement may open up and alter political space, even if it fails fundamentally to change the polity.

Mapping Malaysia's Public Sphere

Malaysia's political system is generally classified as semidemocratic, pseudodemocratic, or, somewhat more disparagingly, semiauthoritarian. As William Case explains: "Pseudodemocracies have few of the protections associated with liberal democracy, but also lack the more systematic repression associated with hard authoritarianism" (2001b: 43). This subtype, he argues, seems stable and resilient in Malaysia.[1] Power has alternated among parties at least at the state level in Malaysia's federal system; opposition parties are allowed to operate aboveground and pose a genuine challenge at both state and national levels; and the public has faith in elections and other democratic institutions, even though it knows that the odds are stacked in favor of the incumbent regime. Much as in Singapore, state, government, and party are largely fused in practice in Malaysia. And given that the United Malays National Organization (UMNO) has dominated a coalition government since independence from the British in 1957, an attack on the party is likely to be maligned as a challenge to the state.

The remainder of Malaysia's public sphere, though, is far more institutionally and ideologically diverse than Singapore's. In Malaysia, a range of legally sanctioned opposition parties operate alongside government parties in political society, and there is a wide array of nongovernmental organizations (NGOs) in civil society.[2] In December 1998, a total of 29,574 societies were registered under the Societies Act (Registrar of Societies n.d.). This number, however, says little about civil society per se. The majority of these organizations are recreational, religious, or otherwise apolitical, and some politically oriented groups register as businesses or companies to circumvent the intrusive regulations, cumbersome paperwork, and legal liability entailed by the Societies Act. Also, many groups have been denied registration as societies. A well-known example is the Malaysian chapter of Amnesty International, which has been trying unsuccessfully to register for well over a decade.

Although the reach of the state is limited rather than all-pervasive, the nature of political society does color civil society. Above all, historical predilections and the communal basis of most political parties have left ascriptive identities the most common basis for affiliation with specific groups or issues. Moreover, activism tends to be remarkably civil rather than feisty—perhaps reflecting not just the possibility of repression but also the pervasive official discourse on purported nonconfrontational Malaysian values, as well as the regime's habit of bringing dissenters into the fold to avoid messy fights. Indeed, UMNO now has a dozen partners in the ruling National Front (Barisan Nasional) coalition.

The government bases its claims to legitimacy on the outcome of regular elections (interrupted only by emergency rule in 1969–71) and, when elected, opposition parties have been allowed to take control of state governments. Even though the state makes no pretense of full or liberal democracy and places serious limits on democratic praxis, democratic institutions carry at least significant symbolic weight in Malaysia, however subverted in practice. Opposition parties face significant handicaps; elections fall short of generally accepted standards for fairness; and freedoms of expression, association, and the press are curtailed by a series of periodically reinforced laws. Moreover, institutional changes, such as the elimination of local elections in the 1970s (see Saravanamuttu 2000), have contributed to a trend of executive centralization and diminution of democracy in the country.

Malaysian civil society may usefully be mapped spatially, not just in terms of organizations, but also in terms of ideas or potentialities. Some borders with other parts of the public sphere (political society and economic society) are permeable; others are fixed. For instance: a segment of civil society aligns itself with the Islamist formal opposition and another segment with secular, generally prodemocratic parties, including members of the ruling coalition; a number of organizations advocate for policy issues largely ignored by political parties; and sections of civil society ally themselves on an ad hoc basis with a range of political or economic actors, depending on the issue at hand. Indeed, contests within civil society may be as divisive and important as contests between civil society and the state. Complicating the picture are long-term or impromptu networks, generally either advocacy-oriented or prodemocratic, linking groups and actors from all these different camps.

Hence civil society in Malaysia does not look quite like its counterparts anywhere else, and its influence is not always in the direction of liberal democracy. Because of the arena's fluidity and polycentrism, the influence of nonstate actors on political decision making may be obscured. Moreover, except in rare moments of cataclysmic change, civil society's pressure may have the greatest impact when channeled through institutions of the state such that the provenance of an initiative is not always clear. It is hard to pinpoint why in Malaysia—unlike, for instance, in Sri Lanka or Indonesia—civil society activism so often operates within state-supported, even if oppositional, frameworks and so rarely veers toward violence. The most likely reasons are these: stiff legal prohibitions on weapons; the high probability of a quick and severe regime crackdown on any sort of militancy (especially given international support since September 2001 for suppression of anything that looks remotely like terrorism); the largely urban, middle-class base of activism in Malaysia; and, not least, the scope for political influence through NGOs and opposition parties. Indeed, long experience of networking and a legacy of advocacy work have prepared civil society organizations to help galvanize the political opposition when opportunities appear propitious for political change, including greater democratization.

Locating Malaysia's Civil Society

The most useful definition of civil society in Malaysia is a loose one: the space in which political engagement outside of state and party institutions occurs.[3] Even this definition is problematic, though, given the extent of overlap in agendas, approaches, and personnel between opposition political parties and nongovernmental organizations. Stipulating that actors from civil society—unlike those from opposition parties or apolitical groups—seek to influence state policies but not to lead the state clarifies the distinction between civil society and other spheres. But there is an important caveat: activists may switch back and forth among civil society, political society, and truly apolitical activities or act in multiple arenas simultaneously. Moreover, to say that a Malaysian activist operates within civil society says little about that person's strategies or orientations, because Malaysian civil society is a highly diverse realm.

Islamic-oriented organizations are a key component of civil society in Malaysia, in contrast to many other polities. These groups themselves represent a range of foci and degrees of orthodoxy.[4] While Islamic-oriented groups may pursue political changes different from those pursued by secular groups, there tends to be a significant overlap in policy preferences (in favor of enhanced civil liberties, judicial autonomy, and the like), and both the religious and secular groups considered here generally seek to improve rather than overturn the democratic state. As Vidhu Verma (2002) points out, however, if carried too far, Islamic revival—which doubles as a representation of Malay nationalism—could dangerously enfeeble the multicultural balance and individual liberties necessary to Malaysian democracy. The term *masyarakat madani* has been used to describe an Islamic-inspired vision of civil society in Malaysia modeled after Medina society in the time of the Prophet Muhammad.[5] In this framework, civic-minded citizens debate issues such as ethnic pluralism and social justice, resolving conflicts in nonadversarial ways. Moreover, civil groups hold the state to a specifically moral rather than performance-based standard, stressing accountability, good governance, and similar indicators. In a *masyarakat madani*, the emphasis is on informed debate, civic consciousness, accountability, and constructive engagement rather than contention—much as in a "civic society" (see MINDS 1997). Although the term *masyarakat madani* per se is seldom used in general parlance and remains more of an academic concept, the concepts informing it may play into some groups' or individuals' ideas about the roles, potential, and obligations of civil society.

Gradual Evolution

The roots of contemporary Malaysian civil society may be traced to the burgeoning of associational life in the early twentieth century. Faced with urbanization, intercommunal disparities, and the prospect of independent sovereignty on the horizon, a range of groups oriented around communal progress, religion, minority rights, and more began to populate a newly invented public sphere (see Milner 1991). These associations tended to follow the lines of ascriptive—racial or religious—identities. An array of clubs for sports, recreation, literature, and so on proliferated alongside politically significant associations. In the latter category were groups that made representations to the British colonial government on specific issues, as well as groups that focused on cultivating race consciousness and nationalism, especially among Malays, or on community development, self-determination, labor, and group rights among the Chinese and, to a lesser extent, Indian communities. Complemented by exhortations in newly developed nationalist newspapers and journals, these associations played a notable role in cementing political identification and organization—still along racial lines but, for the first time, on a panpeninsular rather than state level. Moreover, these groups encouraged a higher degree of popular engagement by both women and men in politics.[6]

After World War II, many associations shifted in focus or form. With the promulgation of blueprints for independence, most notably the controversial Malayan Union Plan of the mid-1940s, elites of all communities were encouraged to form political parties, drawing largely on existing organizations and networks. As a group, Malays were the most prone to turn to parties for political influence once these became an option. The United Malays National Organization and Pan-Malayan Islamic Party (Parti Islam seMalaysia, or PAS) are still the most significant political parties for Malays. These two parties have historically relied heavily on patronage-based ties with the Malay community; in fact, PAS developed out of a wing of UMNO in the 1950s. Moreover, both parties have used Islam as a way to win Malay votes, although religion has been more central to the PAS platform (especially in recent years) than that of UMNO.

Among the other communities, both non-Malays and radical, leftist Malays, however, such a shift toward political society was less pronounced and less legally sanctioned. While UMNO formed in 1946 to rally the community behind a pro-Malay plan for self-government as a party, for instance, the left-wing Malay Nationalist Party (Partai Kebangsaan Melayu Malaya) joined with the illegal Malayan Communist Party, fledgling Malayan Indian Congress (now part of the ruling coalition), and a range of civil society organizations, many of them non-

Malay, in the All-Malaya Council of Joint Action and Center of People's Power (Pusat Tenaga Rakyat) to propose an alternative strategy. Overall—not least since vernacular education remained largely a community affair—Chinese Malaysians in particular retained significant scope for a politically engaged, highly significant civil society, which functioned alongside and often in coordination with largely communal political parties.

Even though the state has grown strong since independence and most decisions are made in political society, Malaysian civil society has been growing and deepening, particularly since the 1970s. Today, the sphere includes not just NGOs but also "public intellectuals," mass-based religious movements, trade unions, and sometimes political parties—since some Malaysian opposition parties for whom winning power is simply not feasible tend to function like NGOs by providing welfare services (generally targeting marginalized communities), fostering critical debate, and aligning themselves with the ranks of NGOs.[7] The impact of civil society on the political order has been substantial, although not always prodemocratic or obvious. As we shall see, for example, it is largely due to championship of Islamist values and policies in civil society that Islam has become so deeply politicized and so central an element of state policies and certain parties' platforms. Similarly, advocacy efforts by voluntary associations have kept issues of Chinese education and minorities' cultural rights alive. The United Chinese Schoolteachers' and School Committees' Association (Dong Jiao Zong) has been especially important to this effort (see Tan 1997). The regime's establishment of a National Human Rights Commission and enactment or fortification of legislation on issues such as domestic violence and consumer protection may also be traced to civil society's agitation on these concerns. In other words, even if a repressive legal apparatus (Weiss 2003b) deters civil society activists from excessive stridency, and executive centralization has minimized outside influence on decision-making processes, elements from civil society have been quite successful at least in getting issues onto policy agendas.

Moreover, the regime is aware of the expertise and social services that NGOs have to offer and takes advantage of these resources. Representatives from NGOs serve on a range of government boards related to the environment, consumer protection, health, women's issues, and the like. These activists are aware of the danger of co-optation and take steps to safeguard their independence. Most notable in this regard is the Federation of Malaysian Consumers' Organizations; although it is careful to maintain its autonomy from state control, it serves on more government bodies than any other Malaysian NGO. Even though the state has the final say after considering these contributions, such opportunities do grant a degree of legitimacy to NGOs—at least to moderate, "professional" groups that the state does not find too threatening—and do allow activists genuine access to policymakers (Lim 1995: 167–68; Tan and Bishan 1994: 16–23). Moreover, the state has been content to leave certain social services in the hands of NGOs. Providing shelters for battered women, for instance, remains primarily the purview of women's groups such as the Women's Aid Organization; support services for people with HIV/AIDS and concerted efforts at prevention are largely the domain of NGOs such as Pink Triangle and Community AIDS Services Penang; and Ikhlas, an NGO, runs a safe house for intravenous drug users, including needle exchanges and special services for transvestites—services the government itself would never touch, however warranted.

The strengthening of Malaysia's civil society over the past few decades is in large part an artifact of constraints on other sorts of political activity and the availability of at least some space for NGO-based mobilization.[8] Joining an advocacy group is one way of engaging in opposition politics. The government would prefer that activists organize in parties, rather than in NGOs, since these challengers could then be legitimately defeated in elections—and however suspect some of its methods may be, the regime is very skilled at winning votes. In 1981, to encourage a clear distinction between politically engaged and so-called friendly NGOs, the government introduced amendments to the Societies Act (under which all NGOs are supposed to be registered) that would require all "political" societies—defined as those that issued public statements—to register as such within a specified period and be subject to special constraints. A mass movement among NGOs, however, forced repeal of these amendments (see Gurmit 1984). In an oblique nod to the political influence of NGOs, the regime famously labeled several of these groups (along with two opposition parties) "thorns in the flesh" in a 1986 attack. Prime Minister Mahathir Mohamad complained at the time that "intellectual elites" under the sway of foreign powers were sabotaging democracy by their activism (Gurmit 1990; Means 1991: 194, 198–99).

Keeping Activism in Check

As these jibes suggest, however significant the scope of advocacy work and lobbying, activism is hardly risk-free. The regime periodically cracks down on activists from both civil society and political parties when they get too critical. Laws such as the Internal Security Act (ISA), which allows detention without trial, may be employed in such cases. Dozens of academics, students, religious leaders, and youth leaders were arrested in the early 1970s under the ISA and other legislation following a spate of agitation in defense of the poor. Similarly, 1987's Operation Lalang saw the detention of over one hundred activists and politicians under the ISA. These political party and NGO leaders, Chinese educationists, academics, Muslim and Christian activists, and environmentalists were charged with inciting racial animosity or showing Marxist tendencies (Fan 1988: 238–55). Since then dozens of activists have been detained under the ISA or charged with illegal assembly and the like for their participation in prodemocracy protests and campaigns. The ISA has also been wielded—especially forcefully of late—against suspected Islamic militants, many of them linked with Islamist NGOs or parties. In each of these periods of crackdown, students and lecturers have proved especially vulnerable. The Universities and University Colleges Act and related legislation have been progressively tightened since the mid-1970s; suitability certificates and pledges of loyalty or good conduct have been introduced (most recently in January 2002);[9] and students have been suspended or expelled for their extracurricular efforts. Civil servants outside academia have been similarly targeted for known or suspected opposition proclivities.

Despite the regime's periodic insinuations (presumably to divert attention from the state's own foibles), international actors have played a marginal role in Malaysian civil society agitation, at least in terms of concrete assistance. Although international agencies do donate funds to local NGOs, generally via offices elsewhere in the region, such philanthropy has been dwindling as Malaysia's economic status has increased vis-à-vis that of its neighbors. Amnesty International and other groups regularly wage campaigns in support of local groups, but Amnesty has not been allowed to register an official local office in Malaysia, and these international solidarity campaigns have limited impact. The regime's tendency to operate on sharply divergent keys when dealing with "the West" probably undercuts international sympathy campaigns as well. Mahathir in particular is known for his unabashedly anti-Western (especially anti-American) rhetoric, yet the state's realpolitik remains quite favorable to these important trading and strategic partners. In other words: the regime can dismiss criticism from foreign activists as "meddling" and evidence of ill will toward Malaysia, yet still work closely with the business and government elites of the states from which these activists hail.

All the same, the Malaysian regime undoubtedly finds itself constrained to at least some extent by the threat of international censure. Foreign opinion almost certainly played a role, for instance, when the government revoked the ISA charge against a prominent politician in 1998 to avoid having to produce him for trial (since he had been beaten in custody).[10] Conversely, Mahathir's government has been able to claim that its recent ISA detentions of a large number of purported Islamic militants, some of them linked with PAS, demonstrate the country's commitment to the global "war on terrorism." Such claims not only obviate American intervention but put these human rights violations purportedly beyond international censure.

Certainly, international backing for human rights, women's rights, environmental conservation, or other causes provides Malaysian activists with ideological support, campaign ideas, and materials. Such assistance, though, is largely generic, as Malaysians may simply piggyback on sympathetic global regimes and merely adapt borrowed ideas or tools to the local context. More significant in galvanizing local campaigns have been demonstration effects from nearby states: student activism spread in waves across Southeast Asia in the 1970s and again in the 1990s; calls for systemic "Reformasi" migrated from Indonesia to Malaysia; and so forth. Increasingly, formally constituted regional networks centered on sustainable development, human rights, labor, health, media, and more—not to mention the recognition that problems such as air pollution and illegal immigration are inherently transnational concerns—are making these links more consistent and less opportunistic.

The Impact of Modernization

Particularly significant for the development of civil society in recent years are changes in communication media, as well as demographic shifts in Malaysia. The rapid diffusion of the Internet and e-mail have radically altered the ability of NGOs and activists to reach a broader public. This advantage is especially relevant for groups allied with opposition parties and thus unlikely to gain favorable coverage in the state-controlled mass media.[11] Electronic mailing lists have proved fruitful sites for discussion and debate. Campaigns and events have been coordinated via e-mail and websites. Widespread availability of cellular phones and fax machines has helped in these efforts, too, especially in terms of staging demonstrations or other sorts of protests and in collecting signatures for petitions and appeals. Such tools were essential, for instance, in disseminating information and expanding the pool of engaged activists in large-scale street protests in the late 1990s.

At the same time, urbanization, rising education levels, and the expansion of the middle class have transformed the capacity and reach of all sectors of civil society. In particular, *dakwah* (Islamic proselytization and revival) groups have flourished on university campuses among Malays brought there largely under the aegis of government-sponsored affirmative action programs since the early 1970s (see Zainah 1987). Quotas to increase Malays' education levels have been accompanied by programs to erase the identification of race with occupational category—primarily by increasing Malays' stake in the modern, capitalist, urban-based economy. Such programs have fostered a growing Malay middle class with a range of interests and preferences in common with its non-Malay counterparts. Moreover, these middle-class Malays are as susceptible as anyone else to downturns in the economy and hence are aggravated with the state when their degrees are insufficient to gain them adequate employment. And often they are acutely aware of the simultaneous creation of a class of Malay crony capitalists of which they are not a part—much as many non-Malays feel similarly excluded from the top echelons of wealth and power within their communities. Not surprisingly, then, the "postmaterialist" concerns traditionally associated with Chinese and Indian activists (social justice, human rights, women's rights, environmentalism) have increasingly been taken up by Malays, as well, although often through Islamic-oriented rather than secular NGOs.[12] The increasing scope of common interests across communities, however, has created new possibilities for cross-racial coalitions.

How Activism Contributes to Political Change

Indeed, while Malaysian civil society remains segmented along racial and religious lines, its demonstrated ability to cut across these lines to collaborate on certain issues presents a uniquely valuable, if not yet fully realized, contribution to the possibilities for political change in Malaysia. The governing coalition is oriented primarily along racial lines, so communalism has become the dominant model. What has kept the opposition fragmented and largely ineffective in the past has been its organization along such vertical cleavages. Even parties that are ideologically noncommunal tend to be closely linked with one ethnic group and have found it difficult to sustain cooperation with parties primarily representing other groups. The growing political significance of Islam—and regime rhetoric to discourage support for PAS, the preeminent Islamic party—has exacerbated these problems. The regime dissuades Islamist and secular parties from collaborating, for instance, by insisting that PAS is abusing the trust of its partners and hopes to foist an Islamic state on the multireligious populace. It has used similar tactics to discredit cross-party alliances including majority-Christian and majority-Chinese parties, warning Malays against trusting these "chauvinist" parties. Civil society campaigns uniting Islamic, Christian, secular, and other groups, by contrast, have not drawn the same sort of fire—probably because these coalitions do not seek state power themselves and their policy recommendations are just that: recommendations rather than enforceable edicts.

Activists from civil society have aided political reform less by being bold and destructive—although demonstrations and the like do figure prominently in activists' repertoires at critical junctures—than by providing ideas, information, and public education. Such reticence is greater than one finds in comparable settings (the Philippines, for instance) and is due, not just to the deterrent effect of the regime's repressive power, but also to the significance attached to democratic institutions in Malaysia—in particular, the belief that political change should come through elections confirms a necessary role for parties. Hence Malaysian civil society operates on a cultural or normative level in promoting political liberalization, leaving institutional changes largely to political parties, or may focus more on limited policy goals than broad political concerns. With this overview of the position and potential of Malaysia's politically oriented civil society, we turn to a consideration of the paths by which civil society activism may yield political or policy change.

Four Paths to Political Reform

Civil society activism may wield significant influence over state agendas and policies, but such influence, as we have seen, may traverse different paths and reflect different perspectives. Even when activists challenge the legitimacy or mandate of

TABLE 8.1
Four Paths for Civil Society's Influence

Primary level/arena of engagement	Principal processes	Example
Political society	Top-down change through co-optation of leaders, agendas, or both	*Dakwah* activism
State	Policy advocacy including aggregation of opinions and representation of alternative approaches to issues	Activism around violence against women
Individual/group	Socialization toward new political norms or priorities	Human rights activism
Political system	Comprehensive system reform including changes in political norms, legislation, and leadership	Reformasi movement

the government, they may still petition the regime for desired reforms. Few within civil society contest the priority of democratic institutions in Malaysia, even if they criticize Malaysian democracy as too shallow or unresponsive. The difficulty in measuring the contribution of civil society activism to political change comes from recognizing precisely where such initiatives have had an impact. Some of these effects are subtle—such as civic education to promote alternative ideas about governance among the public, while implicitly challenging the legitimacy of the incumbent regime in the process. Other effects are more clearly visible—issue-advocacy campaigns that bring previously disregarded issues onto policy agendas, for example, or the training of new political leaders in civil society who bring innovative ideas with them when they enter government or join opposition parties.

There are four principal routes through which civil society activism may further political change in Malaysia (see Table 8.1). The distinctions among these routes reflect the various levels and functions of civil society activism laid out by Alagappa in Table 1.1. First, pressure from below may translate into top-down changes. Seeing the popularity of a particular grassroots leader or proposed new agenda, the government may co-opt the leader into its own ranks or claim the agenda as its own. The progress of the *dakwah* movement since the early 1970s exemplifies this path to reform. Second, activists may lobby for the introduction or amendment of certain policies. Policy advocacy may yield substantial results if a policy is introduced that would not have occurred to most legislators but for civil society activism. Such initiatives are frequently unsuccessful, however, especially if the desired enactments contravene some element of the government's agenda. A prime example of this path to reform is the campaign among Malaysian women's groups for legislation proscribing domestic violence. Third, civil society groups may proceed along normative lines, countering government discourse by advancing alternative priorities. Campaigns to improve human rights in Malaysia may be seen to follow this path.

And fourth, civil society activists may pursue broad, systemic change, forming inclusive coalitions to press simultaneously for institutional and ideological reform. The Reformasi movement of the late 1990s illustrates this route to reform.

Not all initiatives fit neatly into this typology. Some campaigns may span more than one path, for instance, obliging the government to implement immediate policy changes even as it co-opts key civil society agendas or leaders to preempt future challenges. Also, activism along several of these paths may have a counterhegemonic effect by shifting the bases of legitimacy of the regime—which in itself suggests how potent a political force civil society activism may be, at least in the long run. Nevertheless, thinking in terms of these four paths reinforces several ideas—that civil society activism may have substantial but indirect effects on policies; that the state's response may be reactionary as well as progressive; that the lines between political and civil society are more often fluid than fixed; and that civil society, as a realm, is far from monochromatic in ideology and priorities such that activists are about as likely to work at cross-purposes with one another as to collaborate.

Top-Down Change

Popular support for initiatives originating outside the state poses a threat to the regime. Claiming a mandate to rule, granted through elections, the state would like to be seen as the source of all things good. This preference reflects an electoral imperative: if large numbers of citizens support an agenda different from that of the incumbent regime, those citizens may vote for a party more in line with their preferences. So long as an alternative agenda being advanced in civil society (or even in an opposition party) does not contravene other priorities of the state, but can be integrated into state institutions and priorities, the regime may seek to co-opt initiatives that promise to bolster its popular support—in the process defanging worrisome challenges.

Not all initiatives may be co-opted in this manner. Civil society activists may resist the state's takeover of their initiatives—by phrasing their demands in such a way as to require a change of regime, for instance, or through prominent leaders' refusing to join the regime. In such cases, though, the government may react harshly. In 1994, for example, the government banned Darul Arqam, a movement that sought to establish self-sustaining communities based on Islamic law. Initially, the regime did not see Darul Arqam as problematic, because it prioritized social rather than political development. In time, however, the group appeared more threatening, given its disdain for the too-secular state. As Ahmad Fauzi Abdul Hamid (2000) explains, the government could not simply "out-Islam" Darul Arqam. Not wanting other citizens to get any ideas about stepping outside the aegis of the state, the regime banned this challenger (see Kamarulnizam 2002: 98–112, 168–77).

This crackdown notwithstanding, perhaps the most significant civil society initiative in Malaysia in terms of its effect on the government has been the drive for

Islamization of state and society. What gave this movement so strong and durable an influence was the regime's decision in the early 1980s to adopt an agenda of controlled Islamization rather than contesting it. A largely secular state—above all, Mahathir Mohamad's increasingly dominant UMNO—began to recast its image and programs to appeal to an Islamist (and by extension, given Malaysia's demographics, Malay rather than multiracial) audience. Thus a popular movement has come to pervade and fundamentally reshape the state apparatus.

Example: Islamic Activism. The *dakwah* movement in Malaysia refers to a broad Islamic revival that swept the country in the 1970s and 1980s.[13] Along with greater attention to Islamic rituals and identity came a range of Islamic NGOs—most notably among students, but also among the broad Muslim public.[14] Among the chief factors in the spread of *dakwah* activism was the phenomenon of Malay students' studying abroad on government scholarships, especially in the United Kingdom, where displaced and uncomfortable students sought out fellow Muslims. In the process, they picked up on the Islamic revival spreading elsewhere in the world—for instance, from Pakistani fellow students.[15] Back in Malaysia, groups such as the Malaysian Islamic Youth Movement (Angkatan Belia Islam Malaysia; ABIM)—by far Malaysia's largest NGO—formed with the aim not so much of proselytizing as making Muslims better Muslims (Zainah 1987; Chandra 1987; Verma 2002: 99–102).

Many *dakwah* groups had a clear and significant political import. More than simply promoting ethical, religiously observant behavior among their adherents, these groups criticized the government for being insufficiently Islamic. They also mobilized around democracy, civil rights, and morally just social policies, such as advocating on behalf of beleaguered peasants (Chandra 1987; Zainah 1987). Over the years, a variety of Islamic NGOs have sustained a focus on policy advocacy and spreading awareness in support of political liberalization and good governance, human rights, and Muslim women's rights.[16] Rather than representing a nondemocratic or extremist fringe, as Saliha Hassan explains, the bulk of Islamic NGOs enjoy some protection from state censure because "the government continues to perceive Islamic organisations and movements as reliable indicators of the feelings, aspirations and concerns of its Malay Muslim–majority electorate" and hopes that being in tune with the demands of these groups will help it preempt challenges (Saliha 2003: 98).

Sensing a shift in the Malay Muslim ground and wishing to counter the influence of Islamic NGOs in the *dakwah* movement, the government took steps to co-opt or counterbalance nongovernmental mobilization. The state already sponsored a number of Islamic welfare organizations. Now it stepped up the scale of its efforts to establish *dakwah*, Islamic research, and related organizations as Islamic NGOs proliferated in the 1970s. Some of these state-established groups, such as the Council for the Welfare of Muslim Women (Lembaga Kebajikan Perempuan Islam) with its attention to women's legal rights, could be considered politicized. While government-sanctioned groups may enjoy favored access to government decision makers and resources, they are constrained in what they can demand (Saliha 2003).

The government's adoption of *dakwah* goals went beyond the establishment of *dakwah* organizations.[17] In 1982, Anwar Ibrahim, leader of ABIM since 1972, resigned in order to join UMNO and enter politics. A flow of ABIM members followed Anwar into the government, ultimately wielding significant influence on policies from within the regime. Saliha observes: "Partly due to the influx of Anwar and his fellow ABIM members, UMNO soon changed its image from that of a 'secular Malay-nationalist political party' to that of a progressive, modern, Islamic Malay national movement" (2003: 106). The state has also co-opted Islamic religious leaders—augmenting the state's Islamic credentials and gaining an apparent endorsement from religious authorities (Saliha 2003). Islamic activists that the state cannot co-opt or control (e.g., participants in Darul Arqam and followers of other Islamic sects, such as Shiites), it deals with more harshly.[18]

Fundamentally, the movement pervaded government agendas—as epitomized by the Policy for the Absorption of Islamic Values (Dasar Penyerapan Nilai-nilai Islam), introduced in 1982. The policy was targeted both at balancing Malays' material and spiritual development and at furthering national development more broadly. Implementation of the policy began with the encouragement of universal values such as reliability, honesty, responsibility, and fair and accountable leadership, all promoted as essential to Islam. The policy also included the establishment of Islamic institutions—particularly in the financial sector but extending also to a new Islamic university, grandiose mosques, revised media policies, enhanced ties with Muslim states, and more. At the same time, practices such as the recitation of Islamic prayers, strict observance of Muslim dietary laws, and granting time for all Malay civil servants to attend Friday prayers became institutionalized within government agencies and for functions organized by Malay-dominated organizations. Discursively, too, with this change in approach has come a new imperative of justifying state policies in terms of Islam to counter Islamic NGOs' charges of rampant materialism and westernization in Malaysia (Saliha 2003; Verma 2002: esp. chap. 4).

There is no single "Islamic agenda," however, and what the government has implemented is a more moderate program than many Islamic activists would prefer, even if marking a significant drift from the state's secular orientation. The government has resisted implementation of Islamic criminal law, for instance, even though a significant proportion of Islamic activists clamor for enforcement of *hudud* penalties; has instituted Islamic banking alongside, rather than instead of, the standard capitalist fare; has cracked down on things like male cross-dressing but has never mandated that women veil; and has highlighted the rituals of Islam (prayer, fasting) without dramatically changing the functioning of economy and state. Given these varying agendas, the state's efforts have failed to stifle nongovernmental Islamic activism. The movement has not remained static, moreover, but has shifted to occupy ground not controlled by the state, at times collaborating with PAS or other Islamic parties. Indeed, 1982 saw not only the accession of Anwar to UMNO but also the rise of a younger, more radical cohort of leaders in PAS who ensured that their party outpaced UMNO in Islamization. Inspired by the Iranian revolution, the new PAS leaders sought a system of governance under which Islam would no longer be "subordinated to Malay culture and nationalism" (Alias 1994: 182).

Hence the Islamization of society and politics has not all been controlled from the top. Tension remains between the state's vision of Islam's place in a multireligious polity and more radical visions articulated by civil society and other challengers. PAS has grown in popularity in recent years and posted substantial gains in the 1999 elections. Overall, though, while co-optation of the broad, ever-changing Islamization movement will remain an incomplete project, the political terrain has shifted over the past two decades such that the Islamic-secular dimension has become the preeminent axis for political conflict. The regime's top-down endeavors to co-opt *dakwah* activism thus present a hugely significant example of civil society's influence on state policies and, indeed, on the very character and legitimizing mission of the polity.

Policy Advocacy

A more straightforward approach to influencing policies is issue advocacy: lobbying for the adoption, abrogation, or amendment of government policies. Malaysian NGOs have lobbied over the years—especially since the 1970s—for a variety of issues. This approach, which focuses on the state level, includes gaining intermediation in state decision making, enforcing government accountability, and supplementing the state in developing and delivering services. Partly because activists are aware of the threat of repression, they may couch their initiatives, discursively and tactically, in such a way as to validate the government's democratic credentials—for instance, seeking to hold the state accountable to its own constitution or claims to multiethnic accommodation—rather than proposing dramatic legislative overhauls. Activists may also capitalize on a favorable international climate (for instance, for gender-sensitive, environmental, or other policies) that may generate moral and material support from abroad, push the state toward accommodation, or at least deter a stiff crackdown in response.

That some advocacy efforts yield results and others do not highlights the limits to democracy in Malaysia. Like the Singapore state, the Malaysian regime recognizes the need to appear responsive to outside input but deems itself the ultimate arbiter of what is good for the country. The state is thus "democratic" in the sense that it is open to suggestions that are palatable to the government, do not menace the institutional order, and further the regime's long-term goals for Malaysia and its own longevity. If these conditions are not met, the state may reveal its authoritarian side by stifling untenable initiatives. The low popular profile of advocacy-oriented NGOs—which tend to be small, urban, middle-class, and often "academic" groups—makes it easier for the state to dismiss their demands. For this reason, much of policy advocacy work in Malaysia, as in neighboring Singapore, consists of staking out and gradually extending the boundaries of what is considered acceptable.

Some of the earliest advocacy efforts centered on education. Chinese NGOs have been especially active in petitioning the government for policies friendly to vernacular education since the 1950s; these efforts persist today.[19] Education policies would have been on the government's agenda regardless, even if less sensitive to non-Malays' concerns, had communally based NGOs not gotten involved. These efforts invoked a tension between the state's acknowledgment of the needs of Malaysia's non-Malay communities—as expressed regularly at elections—and its predilection for pro-Malay policies. The Chinese education movement has never gained much new ground. But it has, for example, preserved existing institutions, especially vernacular schools, from eradication; encouraged the introduction of English-medium foreign universities in Malaysia; and pressed the state to honor a long-neglected electoral promise of a Chinese-medium university. Other agenda items too have been pressed onto the government's plate with some success by civil society activism. Among the most notable, as we shall see, are "women's issues" such as reviews of rape and divorce laws, sexual harassment policies, and domestic violence legislation. Similarly, the state has adopted elements of an environmentalist agenda. The preservation of Penang Hill and Endau-Rompin State Park in response to massive lobbying efforts by environmental and consumers' NGOs undoubtedly earned the regime significant symbolic capital at home and abroad without incurring excessive costs.[20]

Other policy advocacy efforts have been fruitless, or even counterproductive, as the demands fall outside the bounds of what the state will tolerate. Massive coalitions to combat the tightening of the already restrictive Official Secrets Act or the continuing use of the Internal Security Act have been unsuccessful, because loosening these laws would diminish the government's power to respond to political or security threats (Gurmit 1987; Weiss 2003a). Moreover, issue advocacy may evoke a reactionary response if, after considering an issue, the regime decides to tighten restrictions beyond the status quo. Demonstrations among indigenous peoples in Sabah and Sarawak, for instance, have prompted crackdowns—the reverse of the policies demanded.[21] These considerations notwithstanding, NGOs are unlikely to give up on advocacy as a first line of attack in pursuing their policy goals. Such work may allow civil society activists to induce some degree of political change, affecting the content, parameters, and pace of enactment of new laws, even if it is the state that really determines the scope of that influence.

Example: The Women's Movement. Activism around the issue of violence against women in the 1980s and 1990s, most notably by politically engaged women's NGOs, exemplifies this path to policy influence by civil society. The initiative first developed as a group of women (and eventually several men) came together in the early 1980s to educate the public about endemic violence against women. The movement soon took shape organizationally and programmatically. Five NGOs and various individuals allied in the Joint Action Group Against Violence Against Women (JAG), launched in October 1984.[22] This coalition then joined forces with the National Council of Women's Organizations (NCWO) (Lai 2003). Although it was the newly formed feminist-oriented women's organizations that agitated most stridently against violence to women, the issue was "readily accepted as a common social concern of all women." Once a domestic violence bill was mooted in 1985, it drew support from a panoply of women's organizations, even though many Muslim women, for instance, had preferred to stick with Islamic-oriented organizations rather than join the JAG (Maznah 2002: 232).

Activism around violence against women not only targeted the state directly in lobbying for appropriate legislation but also devoted significant attention to public education in order to raise awareness of the magnitude of the issue. For International Women's Day in March 1985, for instance, activists organized a two-day exhibition and workshop focusing on domestic violence, rape, sexual harassment, prostitution, and the portrayal of women in the media. The event drew significant media attention and well over a thousand participants, both male and female. It was subsequently replicated in other Malaysian cities. A few months later, the JAG and NCWO organized a national workshop on laws that discriminate on gender lines, the results of which were then presented in a memorandum to the government. NGOs, sometimes with the help of the media, also held a workshop and exhibition for the Chinese community, conducted a survey on domestic violence, developed outreach programs (including shelters), and held public forums. These events raised awareness about issues (including the linked issues of rape, sexual harassment, and so forth) and also spawned progressive new women's organizations. A sweeping crackdown on activism in 1987 set matters back, however, particularly since four prominent women were among the activists arrested.[23]

Even so, civil society activists were involved in negotiations with the bar, the attorney general, the Ministry of Justice, and the Women's Affairs Department, resulting in the amendment of rape laws in 1989. The amendments stiffened the penalties for convicted rapists, prohibited questioning the defendant's sexual history in most cases, and expanded the provisions for abortions for rape victims. The definition of "rape" remained narrow, however, disappointing activists seeking a more comprehensive statute. Women's rights activists remained engaged in the implementation phase of government policies on rape, too. Women's NGOs ran gender-sensitization training programs for police, set up one-stop crisis centers, and conducted research to determine the effectiveness of legislation (Lai 2003: 62–63).

Various member organizations of the JAG next turned their sights on lobbying for a Domestic Violence Act (DVA). These NGOs held an awareness-raising seminar in May 1989 and then collected a remarkable fourteen thousand signatures for a petition supporting the proposed DVA. A significant focus of the campaign was ensuring that the DVA would cover both Muslims and non-Muslims—a sticky issue given Malaysia's dual legal code in which Muslims are covered by sharia'ah law and non-Muslims by common law for civil offenses. Women's activists thus made the case that, contrary to popular interpretation, the Qur'an does not condone domestic violence. As part of the campaign, for instance, Sisters in Islam, an NGO, published a concise, cogent booklet, "Are Muslim Men Allowed to Beat Their Wives?" (Sisters in Islam 1991), distributing it also through other women's groups. Placing the DVA within the legal codes remained a core concern. Representatives of women's NGOs, the NCWO, several government departments, and the police met in a joint committee that submitted a revised DVA proposal to the government in early 1992. NGO activists lobbied both government and opposition politicians to support the DVA. Pursuing such dialogue with government officials marked a change in NGOs' strategy. They now hoped to have more of an impact on government agendas and policies through engagement than through ideologically informed aloofness.[24]

Although the DVA was finally passed in 1994, the act did not completely satisfy all activists—marital rape is still not recognized as a crime, for example, and the law stands apart from the rest of the criminal code, although it covers both Muslims and non-Muslims. But the DVA was not officially implemented until June 1996, after further lobbying by women's groups, and effective enforcement remains an issue, because the government has never prioritized combating domestic violence.[25] Indeed, it is highly unlikely that either the revision of rape laws or the issue of domestic violence would have made it onto the policy agenda at all if not for this decade-long advocacy campaign by women's NGOs.

Normative Change

A more abstract path to influencing politics and policy is by promoting a normative shift among the public and within the regime, socializing citizens toward a reorientation of politics. This approach counters government discourse by suggesting alternative grounds for legitimacy or for the evaluation of government effectiveness. Such a normative shift is likely to be more gradual than, for instance, passage of a legislative enactment in response to a civil societal campaign, yet it carries implications for a panoply of foreign and domestic policies. This sort of approach among activists is best understood in terms of a New Left framework (see Chapter 1) in which the primary function of civil society is discursive: undermining prevailing values and inculcating new ones. All the same, a normative shift becomes apparent when it results in policy change. Thus activism around norms or political ideas is likely to be paired with issue advocacy.[26] Successful pursuit of this sort of political reform is likely to require a long-term effort by a broad coalition of activists and organizations. Sustained effort from many sectors of Malaysian civil society in support of human rights, as we shall see, represents an attempt to bring political change through endorsement of a normative shift—a change in the basis of politics.

Example: Human Rights Activism. The human rights movement in Malaysia is hard to pin down. It has included nearly all NGOs at one time or another, could be said to include most issues around which activists organize, and has accomplished remarkably little in tangible terms, despite truly massive efforts. The root of this ambiguity lies in the sort of influence the movement seeks. Human rights activism is not just about policy advocacy but aims to change Malaysians' expectations of the state and the state's definition of democracy. In other words: the human rights movement seeks to influence the state by advancing a normative shift.

The Malaysian government—particularly Mahathir, prime minister from 1981 to 2003—consistently argues that universal standards of human rights are not suitable for Malaysia, given the country's level of development and cultural makeup.[27] An NGO-produced human rights report explains: "This argument prioritises economic development over civil and political rights because, it is argued, as a developing nation Malaysia has not yet reached the desired economic status to allow full realization of human rights. An extension of the argument is that 'Asian values' place greater importance on the community and hence collective rights should be given precedence over civil and political rights" (Suaram 1998: 4). The report goes on to assert, however, that the government routinely violates the collective rights of indigenous peoples to their land, culture, and identity; the right of Malaysian society to clean air and water; and the right of urban settlers to housing (4–5). Thus the report advocates a rethinking of how human rights are treated in Malaysia and, moreover, how they should be regarded.

Malaysian activists have codified this normative challenge to the regime in the "Malaysian Charter on Human Rights," developed through the 1990s out of consultations among fifty NGOs. The charter accepts the premise of Malaysian exceptionalism as "multicultural" and "developing," yet it insists that "recognition and respect of the right to political, social, cultural and economic self-determination of all peoples are fundamental to the protection of our dignity and equality; and to justice, peace and freedom in our country. . . . The promotion of human rights is indivisible to the pursuit of a holistic and just development" (MNGO 1999: ii). The charter does present specific policy demands—such as ratifying and implementing a range of UN covenants and conventions, recasting economic development to guarantee environmental rights, and satisfying the right of all to food, shelter, and other basic needs. But the fundamental project embodied in a document such as this is discursive rather than policy-oriented. Setting forth a comprehensive statement of the rights Malaysians do—or ought to—enjoy provides an ideological foundation upon which to base more concrete claims.[28] Part of this project is historical: uncovering the derivation of repressive laws not just to oppose those laws but to challenge the regime's depiction of the status quo as natural and beyond reproach. As the long-time activist Kua Kia Soong insists: "The bald fact is that these basic human rights and freedoms denied Malaysians today are by no means new but were enjoyed by Malaysians in the Fifties and Sixties" (Kua 1998: 6)—that is, before laws such as the Internal Security Act (1968) or Universities and University Colleges Act (1971) were promulgated and incrementally enhanced (see Weiss 2003a).

Accepting the state's stance on the rights to which Malaysians are entitled—especially the sort of individual freedoms appropriate to the local context—would undercut efforts at policy advocacy. Redefining the standards to which the state should be held opens up new discursive ground for civil society advocacy. A whole range of issues have accordingly been cast by civil society activists as human rights concerns worth addressing, not just on pragmatic grounds or because of observed disparities, but based on a normative imperative to safeguard rights—at least as defined by these activists.[29] In the state's eyes, its rights-related policies are already sufficient to meet its definition of human rights in Malaysia. Indeed, the state has to some extent acceded to this contest on discursive grounds. In response to statements from civil society about universal rights and liberties (whether as promulgated in the Universal Declaration of Human Rights or, for some activists, in the Qur'an), the government has promoted a counterdiscourse of "Asian values." Moreover, the government has labeled civil society and opposition party opponents an "internal Other," such that "alternative political ideas were rendered subversive and deviant" (Nair 1999: 92), rather than simply discarded as infeasible. This tactic has been made especially visible in the ISA detentions of a number of human rights activists (most recently from the Reformasi movement, described below) on vague charges of plotting the overthrow of the state.

It is difficult to measure the extent of political change brought about by this long-term discursive campaign. The state has felt compelled to spell out its conception of human rights, for instance, as embodied in the mandate of the National Human Rights Commission (SUHAKAM), established in July 1999—but this conception has not been much altered by civil society's pressure. As Verma (2002: 172–73) details, SUHAKAM's mandate "defines 'human rights' as those fundamental liberties enshrined in Part 2 of the federal constitution," a definition deemed too limited by a collection of thirty-four NGOs that argue for a definition that "embodies universal standards." As this contest implies, the language of individual freedoms—freedoms of the press, of association, to a fair trial, and so forth—pervades much of Malaysian society. At least a significant proportion of the voting public (particularly among the educated urbanites who tend to populate advocacy NGOs, but also among *dakwah* activists and others) has come to debate whether the limitations placed on such freedoms are necessary or just. Mahathir himself insisted in a December 1998 speech (at a time of intense popular agitation over issues of justice and democracy): "Our country truly has available various spaces or places or institutions for voicing opinions or expressing feelings. From the ballot box, to association meetings, to NGO activities, to television, newspapers (including opposition party papers), political parties, elected representatives, and all the way to parliament, each member of the public has the opportunity to voice their views to anyone, including the Government." He clarified, though, that these rights had to be constrained lest minority voices overwhelm those of a less strident majority (Mahathir 1999: 7).

Mahathir's remarks, however carefully couched, indicate acknowledgment that his regime's legitimacy was being judged, not just in terms of his own choosing, but also on the basis of human rights standards enumerated by nonstate voices. In meeting this challenge—explaining how his government did in fact meet the new standard—Mahathir signified, however grudgingly, a shift in the discursive terrain in favor of counterhegemonic human rights language and norms. The state may yet refuse to yield ground, in policy terms, to bring laws and institutions in line with its rhetoric. In that case, though, it risks alienating voters who apply human rights standards in evaluating regime performance. Hence while some of Malaysia's most egregious human rights violations have yet to be corrected—such targets of human rights activism as the continuing use of detention without trial and tight restrictions on speech and assembly—greater progress seems to have been made at the discursive level. Ultimately, this normative shift could lead to concrete political change.

Systemic Change

The final path by which civil society activists may pursue political change combines elements of the other three routes but as part of a comprehensive program. This path seeks drastic change, not just of specific policies or normative commitments, but of the institutions and outputs of the political system broadly and all at once. The timbre of such reforms is not a given. Depending on the groups involved and their specific preferences, the systemic changes sought may be prodemocratic, may be pro-Islamic, or may assume some other cast. In any case, a drive to bring systemic change will almost certainly require a coalition effort, as the changes involved are too sweeping and complex for one organization to handle. Given the nature of the initiative, partial success is more likely than complete systemic change.

The government may institute top-down changes to meet or to stifle civil society's demands, and the normative ground may shift irrespective of what becomes of state policies and institutions.

Contemporary Malaysian political history has few examples of activism at this level. Islamic activism may be seen in this light inasmuch as it seeks to reorient the polity around Islam instead of around economic development and maintenance of racial and religious harmony, the twin linchpins of the current order. But "Islamic activism," which defines a direction of change more than a specific set of policies,[30] may or may not require the sort of systemic overhaul detailed here. Indeed, Malaysian demographics mandate that any attempt at systemic change must appeal both to Muslim and non-Muslim constituencies if it is ever to be implemented. Islamic activism is therefore unlikely to bring installation of an Islamic order, even if it forces modifications to the present regime.

The Reformasi movement that began in late 1998, as we shall see, exemplifies such a system-level initiative. Reformasi activists sought not only policy change in the form of repeal or revision of various laws but also a normative shift in the substitution of prodemocratic, noncommunal norms, justified equally well in secular and Islamic terms, for the quasi-authoritarian, communally oriented status quo. Although the movement as a whole cannot be declared a success, the state did institute a series of top-down reforms in an attempt to defuse civil society's pressure, and conventional wisdom suggests that Malaysians' expectations of democratic institutions have changed. In short, the Reformasi movement represents the pursuit of systemic change, inasmuch as it sought to alter both the ideological basis and specific features of the state through a single, reasonably coherent, coordinated campaign.

Example: The Reformasi Movement. The Reformasi movement was sparked by the removal of a popular government leader in September 1998, coupled with severe economic disgruntlement. Reformasi came to encompass most contemporary Malaysian social movements. From late 1998 through the general elections of November 1999, then less consistently for at least a year thereafter, civil society leaders and opposition party activists, usually organized around different causes, came together for frequent, vociferous street protests, dialogue sessions, and more. Reformasi activists pressed for a change of policies, state leadership, and political orientation. The movement, which included both Islamic and secular groups and parties, campaigned for everything from women's rights to sustainable urban development to protection for workers and ethnic minorities. Eventually, the movement fizzled out for a number of reasons—a combination of electoral defeat (despite some notable gains in the polls); a government crackdown including the prolonged ISA detentions of a number of Reformasi activists; tensions between Islamic and secular components of the movement; the failure of movement protagonists to articulate clear, convincing positions on key issues like Islamization policies in PAS-controlled states; and general burnout after so long a period of sustained mobilization.

Reformasi marked the apex of prodemocratic activism in Malaysia in several ways. First, it represented a real mix between civil society-based and party-based activism and showed the deep connections between the two. Second, the movement crossed social cleavages such as race more gracefully and meaningfully than previous initiatives had done, although still without striking a truly stable racial and religious balance. Third, the movement elucidates how prodemocratic goals (or any other set of goals) may come to represent a common denominator uniting activists. And fourth, the regime's responses to Reformasi demands indicate the balance between repression and granting concessions to quell discontent, whereas shifts in political discourse indicate the extent of normative or ideological change that has occurred within civil society, the state, and the mass public.

Malaysia's Reformasi movement built upon years of more or less atomized agitation by civil society and opposition parties for political change. What caused mobilization and coordination suddenly to mount was the sacking of Deputy Prime Minister Anwar Ibrahim (a charismatic leader and former *dakwah* activist). Many saw Mahathir's treatment of Anwar as going too far in his quest to preclude challenges and centralize power in his own hands. Moreover, Malaysia's poor economic situation in light of the Asian economic crisis gave NGOs grounds to criticize state policies and led opposition parties to hope that voters might give up on the ruling National Front coalition. Both NGOs and opposition parties of all ideological and demographic stripes, supplemented by a range of unaffiliated individuals, promptly came together in formal and informal institutions to discuss how best to take advantage of this propitious opportunity for change. These networks soon developed into an opposition electoral coalition. Although political parties then assumed the initiative, the Alternative Front (Barisan Alternatif) clearly and openly drew upon the experience, advice, and material support of civil society.[31]

The changes pursued by the Reformasi movement and the coalitions involved constituted systemic reform, including both normative and institutional dimensions. Reformers hoped to instill a noncommunal, more participatory, less clientelistic political sensibility among the mass public and governing elites. They hoped also to improve the transparency and independence of the various branches of government, abolish a series of laws curbing free association and criticism, and bring a new slate of leaders into office. The issues raised by the movement echoed prior civil society campaigns, some of which included the formation of large, cross-sectoral coalitions (for instance, the coalitions of women's groups described above, or even broader coalitions around amendments to the Societies Act and Official Secrets Act). The experience of these campaigns had shown that, if only by dint of years of practice, groups from civil society seemed better poised than opposition parties to coordinate their efforts around issues—despite significant differences (religion, central focus, and the like) among the groups. The opposition parties, stymied particularly by the division between Islamic and secular parties, had been unable to maintain the sort of unity necessary to oust the current regime and overhaul the political order. Opposition parties had formed coalitions in the past—from before independence to the early 1990s—but these had been limited in breadth and duration (Weiss 2001: chaps. 3–4).

Ultimately, these "NGO issues"—many of them espoused in the past by parties such as the leftist Democratic Action Party, as well as by NGOs—formed the basis of a prodemocratic opposition electoral platform. Political parties were able to build on the experience of networking in civil society and past coalition-building efforts among parties to facilitate cooperation in political society toward the goal of systemic political change, with "justice," good government, and sustainable development as common denominators. Given the different comparative advantages of parties and NGOs in pursuing reform, reformists from civil society were encouraged to focus on civic education and bringing out the vote and to help draft an electoral platform. For their part, parties were encouraged to foster enduring ties with civil society groups for the legitimacy, the human and material (including media) resources, and the creative ideas they could provide. This interplay was expected to continue past the polls.[32]

While perhaps the most impressive coalition-building venture in Malaysian history (apart from the solidification of the National Front, itself a multiracial but communally oriented and party-based coalition) and a watershed in its rallying of popular discontent with the status quo, the Reformasi movement achieved only limited progress. The incumbent regime fared less well than usual in the November 1999 polls, but it still retained power overall.[33] It is impossible to say whether a successful opposition would have reconfigured political institutions as much as promised or how much influence nonparty actors would have retained over setting agendas and implementing policy.

Still, the Reformasi movement did induce at least limited, and apparently sustainable, political change.[34] Most observers and participants seem to agree that at least some degree of normative shift occurred—leaving communalism and patronage politics less dominant than previously, especially among younger and urban voters, even if far from overcome. And in response to the movement's demands, government leaders have taken steps at least to appear more accessible and accountable—by setting up a (relatively ineffective) National Human Rights Commission; revamping the ruling party (for instance, establishing Puteri UMNO to attract younger Malay women) to appeal to disillusioned voters; and establishing new feedback channels as a sign of openness. The opposition—the Islamic party, PAS, far more than the Alternative Front as a coalition—has introduced top-down reforms in the two states it controls, but some of these have been in the direction of

Islamization, in contravention of the Alternative Front's platform.[35] The fact remains, though, that on account of the collaboration between civil-society and party-based actors, coalition building went further than it otherwise could have done; that a significant proportion of the voting public is now more supportive of institutional reforms than previously; that at least some degree of normative and institutional change has occurred; and that the experience of Reformasi will inform future coalition-building, reformist ventures. If civil society activism failed to secure the systemic change it sought, the effort did have some effect on the polity, and it may yet prove to have been a first step toward more radical reform.

A New Approach to Democracy?

As Malaysian civil society has evolved over the years, many individuals and groups have come to play increasingly apparent and varied roles in the polity. Such engagement has not brought about—or even necessarily sought to achieve—liberal democracy or revolutionary transformation. Civil society activists and campaigns have promoted political change, but this change has been neither cataclysmic nor unidirectional. Part of the effect of nonstate activism has been to change the timbre of the state—most notably by magnifying the place of Islam in Malaysian politics. Part has been to counteract centrifugal tendencies by keeping some services outside the aegis of the state, forcing new issues onto policy agendas, and monitoring policy implementation. Part has been to change what citizens expect of the state. And part has been to deepen and strengthen broad-based democratic engagement and to make even substantial reform seem possible. Overall the effect has been to refine rather than overturn state institutions and to challenge the regime's ability to dictate the criteria on which it should be judged. Furthermore, activists recognize that their critiques are sometimes more appropriately directed at individual leaders than at the system at large. Trends suggest that this sort of influence will continue as elements from civil society become better equipped to mobilize across social cleavages and more deeply enmeshed in opposition politics and processes of political reform.

Despite their increasing involvement with electoral politics, the fact that civil society activists continue to agitate well beyond elections implicitly advises a new approach to democracy. The regime claims that its mandate, given through successive elections, trumps other claims in the interim. Many NGOs, together with several opposition parties, propose instead that voters presume scope for more consistent input. The usual tendency is to form broad coalitions of NGOs around particular goals. Experience has shown that the regime is more likely to respond to a campaign with broad support, at least within the urban or Malay middle class, since such demands can less easily be written off as the carping of westernized academics. That recent high-profile campaigns have focused more on prodemocratic goals than, for instance, Islamization has more to do with Malaysia's multicultural make-up and the imperative of finding common ground to unite groups in a working coalition than with any preference for full-fledged liberal democracy. Although the same ends may be pursued by opposition parties, civil society activists may have more room to maneuver: they are not constrained by the need to pursue votes (unless they opt to shift their efforts to political society);[36] they have no pretense of aiming to establish a state; and they may in fact have very fluid links with other NGOs or even with parties. All the same, the threat of NGOs' throwing their weight—or at least their ideas and resources—behind opposition parties and facilitating opposition coalition building at elections may lend their demands more clout—encouraging the state to address and thus defuse their claims.

Political reform that results from civil society agitation, whether through the state's co-opting of agendas and leaders or through policy change, reinforces the fact of the regime's fallibility and permeability to outside influence. It also affirms the need for citizens to take seriously their own role in the polity and to monitor and judge the state's performance despite the government's "Asian values" discourse. Thus the four paths to civil society's influence feed into one another in significant ways. The impact of nongovernmental activism may be indirect or obscured. It may be filtered through government or opposition parties. It may be more effective at a normative than a policy level. It may be muted or convoluted by significant differences in ideology, goals, and preferred tactics across groups in civil society. Still, this influence is apparent and mandates a nuanced, multifaceted understanding of the role of individuals and groups from civil society in working within, around, or despite the semidemocratic state to foster political change in Malaysia.

Notes

1. Among scholars of Malaysia, William Case (2001a, 2001b) makes the argument for "consolidated and high-quality semidemocracy," or alternatively "pseudodemocracy," most cogently. See also Zakaria 1989; Crouch 1996; von Vorys 1975; Milne and Mauzy 1999.

2. In line with usual Malaysian usage, I employ the term *NGO* loosely here.

3. Moreover, "civil society" refers here only to its politically oriented portions—rather than to groups and individuals engaged in the space between family and state (the classic definition of civil society) but clearly and consciously apolitical in orientation. As Garry Rodan clarifies: "A distinction must be drawn between civic and civil society, the latter involving regular attempts to advance the interests of members through overt political action" (1996: 28). For instance, sports clubs, social welfare organizations, and other groups may build social capital (Putnam 2000) and perform socially useful functions but make no effort to influence politics or policy.

4. Only a marginal fringe of Malaysian Islamic activists would ever be likely to employ violent tactics. As defined in Chapter 1, such groups would not be considered part of civil society and hence are excluded from this analysis.

5. In Indonesia, the term *masyarakat madani* is as likely to be used as just one of several translations of "civil society."

6. See esp. Roff 1994; Tham 1977; Firdaus 1985; Khadijah n.d.; Tan 1997; Heng 1996.

7. These endeavors may generate goodwill and name recognition for the party among voters but are likely to cultivate too narrow a constituency to yield electoral victory. Chua Beng-Huat suggests a similar implication for Singaporean opposition parties: "Without the ability to unseat the PAP [People's Action Party] as the government," he explains, "opposition parties have in fact to campaign primarily on issues with identifiable constituencies, such as the poor, rather than with the generalized interests of seizing state power" (Chua 1995: 197).

8. Where lack (or "shallowness") of democracy imposes more serious constraints on the space available for autonomous organization, NGOs tend to fare little better than opposition parties at carving out an aboveground, influential niche. New Order Indonesia provides a good example of such a situation. See, e.g., Aristides 2000; Eldridge 1996; Walker 1996.

9. See Rosli 2002 for a trenchant critique of this "Pledge of Loyalty" by an affected academic.

10. The inspector-general of police at the time was eventually convicted for the beating of former Deputy Prime Minister Anwar Ibrahim—the marks from which, especially a notorious black eye, caused the regime much embarrassment.

11. Most mainstream media in Malaysia are owned or controlled (directly or indirectly through holding companies) by the state. All media are constrained, too, by the Printing Presses and Publications Act, stringent official secrets and sedition acts, and other legislation. Self-censorship based on fear of reprisals is common, although a small number of independent publications (more commonly on-line than in print nowadays) persist in presenting alternative news. Some of these sources strive to avoid bias; others are more concerned to counter the bias of the mainstream media. For more on the structure and political bent of the media, see Zaharom 2002, Mustafa 2002, or the website of Charter 2000, a local initiative for freedom of the press, www.malaysia.net/aliran/charter/ (accessed 2/26/2004).

12. Verma 2002, for instance, makes a strong case for the ways in which rapid modernization has increased the space for Islamism, especially as represented in PAS, to restructure Malays' political and cultural identity more firmly around religion. This orientation does gloss over class and other striations in the Malay community, but emphasizes the difference between Malays and other ethnic groups and in privileging Islam, asserts the superiority of the former.

13. See Hamayotsu 1999 for a succinct overview of politicized Islam prior to Malaysia's Islamic revival of the 1970s. See Kamarulnizam 2002 for a broader treatment of Malaysian Islam, with particular attention to more recent developments.

14. Along with politicized *dakwah* organizations, there have been a wide array of apolitical Islamic welfare organizations old and new. These groups buttress the framework for Islamist activism in Malaysia but are otherwise beyond the scope of this chapter. See Saliha 2003 or Jomo and Ahmad Shabery 1992 for a more complete picture.

15. Highlighting the diversity of activism thus encouraged is the shadowy Malaysian Mujahideen Group (Kumpulan Mujahideen Malaysia), linked with the better-known Jemaah Islamiah. The group purportedly consists of graduates of Pakistani universities who, as students, came to support the Afghan resistance to the Soviet Union and then took their radical stance back home to Malaysia (interviews, Kuala Lumpur, Dec. 2002).

16. Syed Ahmad 1999 describes the provenance and spread of prodemocratic ideas

among Muslims in Malaysia, including the importance of discourses from other Muslim societies.

17. For details on the government's Islamization program see (among others) Saliha 2003, Jomo and Ahmad Shabery 1992, or Hamayotsu 1999.

18. In the mid-1980s, the government revisited a previously proposed constitutional amendment establishing the Sunnah wal Jamaah sect (which follows the teachings of the Prophet Muhammad, the Qur'an, and the Sunnah) as the only sect to which Malaysian Muslims may subscribe (Saliha 2003).

19. See esp. Tan 1997 for a historical perspective, and the contributions to Kua 1985 for an array of more contemporary arguments.

20. Not all conservationist demands have been so well received, however. See Ramakrishna 2003 for details on these and other environmental campaigns.

21. Interview with Colin Nicholas (Centre for Orang Asli Concerns), July 22, 1997, Kuala Lumpur.

22. The five NGOs were the Women's Aid Organization, the Association of Women Lawyers, the University Women's Association, the Malaysian Trades Union Congress (Women's Section), and the Selangor and Federal Territory Consumers' Association.

23. Lai 2003: 60–63; interview with Zaitun Kasim (All-Women's Action Society), Aug. 1, 1997, Petaling Jaya.

24. Interview with Maria Chin Abdullah (Asia-Pacific Development Centre, All-Women's Action Society, and Sisters in Islam), July 25, 1997, Kuala Lumpur; Lai 2003: 63–65. Indeed, women's NGOs have taken engagement a step further since then. In 1999, a coalition of organizations and individuals launched the Women's Agenda for Change (WAC), a comprehensive overview of changes in policies and in the broader political climate sought by women's movement activists, as well as the Women's Candidacy Initiative (WCI), through which a prominent women's NGO activist ran for office on a platform including the issues in the WAC. See Martinez 2003 for details.

25. Lai 2003: 63–65; interview with Zaitun Kasim, Aug. 1, 1997, Petaling Jaya; interview with Maria Chin Abdullah, July 25, 1997, Kuala Lumpur.

26. As described above, various sorts of engagement by civil society activists in Malaysia may work to counter the regime's efforts at ideological hegemony and thus promote normative change. I identify normative change as a distinct path as well, however, primarily to refer to efforts for which a shift in the discursive orientation of the regime is considered an end in itself rather than just an externality.

27. For the full argument, see Rodan 1997.

28. For various approaches—nationalist, communitarian, and traditionalist—to normative justifications for human rights in Malaysia, suggesting the breadth of this debate, see Verma 2002: 176–84.

29. For detailed analysis and overview of the issues and justifications involved, see Milne and Mauzy 1999: 103–21; Weiss 2003a.

30. Kamarulnizam 2002, for instance, makes a case for the complexity of Islamic activism in Malaysia, describing the pursuit of varying Islamist goals through both moderate and more radical Islamic NGOs, as well as through both government and opposition political parties.

31. Elsewhere I have written extensively about the Reformasi movement and the coalitions it engendered. See, e.g., Weiss 2001: chaps. 5–6.

32. These summary conclusions draw on observation of Reformasi events, as well as con-

temporaneous discussions in "alternative" media such as Malaysiakini.com, the *Aliran Monthly*, *Harakah*, and the sangkancil listserv, www.malaysia.net/lists/sangkancil (accessed 3/7/2004). Reformasi protests in Malaysia, unlike those in neighboring Indonesia at around the same time, remained almost exclusively nonviolent (at least on the part of the protesters). This distinction is probably due to a combination of factors: the general tendency in Malaysia for "civil" engagement with the state; the primacy of the middle class in Malaysian Reformasi, as opposed to the increasingly more desperate urban poor in Indonesia; the deeper financial and moral bankruptcy of the Indonesian state; the far more prevalent and obvious use of institutionalized state violence against challengers in Indonesia; and the greater scope in Malaysia since independence for aboveground and sometimes influential political opposition, social activism, and networking.

33. See Funston 2000 or Weiss 2000 for details.

34. The extent and nature of these changes are probed in the contributions to Loh and Saravanamuttu 2003. The volume as a whole proposes that a "new politics" is indeed in the offing in Malaysia, characterized by a new role for civil society actors in electoral politics and political affairs more broadly, as well as by cracks in the Malay hegemony that underlies the long-dominant consociational order.

35. PAS's pursuit of such policies and subsequent pro-Taliban statements after September 11 threw the Alternative Front into disarray. One of the four constituent parties had already withdrawn by then. The remainder contested the March 2004 elections as the Alternative Front; the Democratic Action Party campaigned on its own. Concern over PAS's perceived radicalism contributed to the front's stunning decline in those polls.

36. Some NGO activists *do* shift toward political society, and this tendency may become more pronounced in future. The government has said that NGO activists may be allowed to contest elections—but this has in fact already happened. The WCI was to institutionalize just such a process. Similar efforts have been proposed to develop a "Rainbow Coalition" consisting of representatives of NGOs concerned with the environment, human rights, and so forth, who would negotiate with the BA or even the BN for seats they might contest (see, e.g., Saravanamuttu 2003).

Works Cited

Ahmad Fauzi Abdul Hamid. 2000. "Political Dimensions of Religious Conflict in Malaysia: State Response to an Islamic Movement." *Indonesia and the Malay World* 28(80): 32–65.

Alias Mohamed. 1994. *PAS' Platform: Development and Change 1951–1986*. Petaling Jaya: Gateway.

Aristides Katoppo. 2000. "The Role of Community Groups in the Environment Movement." In C. Manning and P. v. Diermen, eds., *Indonesia in Transition: Social Aspects of Reformasi and Crisis*. Singapore: Institute of Southeast Asian Studies.

Case, William. 2001a. "Malaysia's General Elections in 1999: A Consolidated and High-Quality Semi-Democracy." *Asian Studies Review* 25(1): 35–55.

———. 2001b. "Malaysia's Resilient Pseudodemocracy." *Journal of Democracy* 12(1): 43–57.

Chandra Muzaffar. 1987. *Islamic Resurgence in Malaysia*. Petaling Jaya: Penerbit Fajar Bakti.

Chua Beng-Huat. 1995. *Communitarian Ideology and Democracy in Singapore*. New York: Routledge.

Crouch, Harold A. 1996. *Government and Society in Malaysia*. Ithaca, N.Y.: Cornell University Press.

Eldridge, Philip. 1996. "Development, Democracy, and Non-Government Organisations in Indonesia." *Asian Journal of Political Science* 4(1): 17–35.

Fan Yew Teng. [1983] 1988. *Oppressors and Apologists*. Kuala Lumpur: Egret.

Firdaus Haji Abdullah. 1985. *Radical Malay Politics: Its Origins and Early Development*. Petaling Jaya: Pelanduk.

Funston, John. 2000. "Malaysia's Tenth Elections: Status Quo, Reformasi, or Islamization?" *Contemporary Southeast Asia* 22(1): 23–59.

Government of Malaysia. 2001. *Census 2000 Preliminary Data Published in the Eighth Malaysia Plan* 2001. Available from www.statistics.gov.my/English/pageDatawalC.htm.

Gurmit Singh, K. S. 1984. *Malaysian Societies: Friendly or Political?* Petaling Jaya: Environmental Protection Society Malaysia and Selangor Graduates Society.

———, ed. 1987. *No to Secrecy: The Campaign Against 1986's Amendments to the OSA*. Kuala Lumpur: Aliran.

———. 1990. *A Thorn in the Flesh*. Petaling Jaya: Gurmit Singh K. S.

Hamayotsu, Kikue. 1999. "Reformist Islam, Mahathir, and the Making of Malaysian Nationalism." Paper read at the second International Malaysian Studies Conference, Aug. 2–4, Kuala Lumpur.

Heng Pek Koon. 1996. "Chinese Responses to Malay Hegemony in Peninsular Malaysia 1957–96." *Tonan Ajia Kenkyu* 34(3): 32–55.

Jomo Kwame Sundaram and Ahmad Shabery Cheek. 1992. "Malaysia's Islamic Movements." In J. S. Kahn and F. Loh Kok Wah, eds., *Fragmented Vision: Culture and Politics in Contemporary Malaysia*. North Sydney: Asian Studies Association of Australia and Allen & Unwin.

Kamarulnizam Abdullah. 2002. *The Politics of Islam in Contemporary Malaysia*. Bangi: Penerbit Universiti Kebangsaan Malaysia.

Khadijah Md. Khalid. N.d. "Continuity and Change in Women's Political Participation in West Malaysia." MS.

Kua Kia Soong, ed. 1985. *National Culture and Democracy*. Petaling Jaya: Kersani Penerbit for Selangor Chinese Assembly Hall.

———. 1998. "The Struggle for Human Rights in Malaysia." Paper read at the Asia-Pacific People's Assembly Human Rights Forum, Nov. 9, Kuala Lumpur.

Lai Suat Yan. 2003. "The Women's Movement in Peninsular Malaysia from 1900–99: A Historical Analysis." In M. L. Weiss and Saliha Hassan, eds., *Social Movements in Malaysia: From Moral Communities to NGOs*. London: RoutledgeCurzon.

Lim Teck Ghee. 1995. "Nongovernmental Organizations in Malaysia and Regional Networking." In Tadashi Yamamoto, ed., *Emerging Civil Society in the Asia Pacific Community*. Singapore: Institute of Southeast Asian Studies and Japan Center for International Exchange.

Loh, Francis Kok Wah, and Johan Saravanamuttu, eds. 2003. *New Politics in Malaysia*. Singapore: Institute of Southeast Asian Studies.

Mahathir Mohamad. 1999. *Perlembagaan Negara Menjamin Hak Rakyat*. Kuala Lumpur: Jabatan Penerangan Malaysia.

Malaysian Non-Governmental Organizations (MNGO). 1999. *Malaysian Charter on Human Rights*. Petaling Jaya: ERA Consumer Malaysia. [1994]

Martinez, Patricia. 2003. "Complex Configurations: The Women's Agenda for Change and the Women's Candidacy Initiative." In M. L. Weiss and Saliha Hassan, eds., *Social Movements in Malaysia: From Moral Communities to NGOs*. London: RoutledgeCurzon.

Maznah Mohamad. 2002. "At the Centre and the Periphery: The Contribution of Women's Movements to Democratization." In F. Loh K. W. and Khoo B. T., eds., *Democracy in Malaysia: Discourses and Practices*. Richmond, Surrey: Curzon.

Means, Gordon P. 1991. *Malaysian Politics: The Second Generation*. Singapore: Oxford University Press.

Milne, R. S., and Diane K. Mauzy. 1999. *Malaysian Politics under Mahathir*. New York: Routledge.

Milner, A. C. 1991. "Inventing Politics: The Case of Malaysia." *Past and Present* 132: 104–29.

MINDS, ed. 1997. *Masyarakat Madani: Satu Tinjauan Awal*. Ampang: Malaysian Institute of Development Strategies.

Mustafa K. Anuar. 2002. "Defining Democratic Discourses: The Mainstream Malaysian Press." In F. Loh K. W. and Khoo B. T., eds., *Democracy in Malaysia: Discourses and Practices*. Richmond, Surrey: Curzon.

Nair, Sheila. 1999. "Constructing Civil Society in Malaysia: Nationalism, Hegemony, and Resistance." In Jomo K. S., ed., *Rethinking Malaysia*. Hong Kong: Asia 2000 for Malaysian Social Science Association.

Putnam, Robert. 2000. *Bowling Alone: The Collapse and Revival of American Community*. New York: Simon & Schuster.

Ramakrishna, Sundari. 2003. "The Environmental Movement in Malaysia." In M. L. Weiss and Saliha Hassan, eds., *Social Movements in Malaysia: From Moral Communities to NGOs*. London: RoutledgeCurzon.

Registrar of Societies. N.d. *Message from the Registrar of Societies, Dato' Ismail Bin Dolah Harun*. Available from www.jppmros.gov.my/speech01.htm.

Rodan, Garry. 1996. "Theorising Political Opposition in East and Southeast Asia." In G. Rodan, ed., *Political Oppositions in Industrialising Asia*. New York: Routledge.

———. 1997. "Civil Society and Other Political Possibilities in Southeast Asia." *Journal of Contemporary Asia* 27(2): 156–78.

Roff, William R. [1967] 1994. *The Origins of Malay Nationalism*. 2d ed. Kuala Lumpur: Oxford University Press.

Rosli Omar. 2002. "An Anti-Democratic Pledge." *Aliran Monthly* 22(2): 35–38.

Saliha Hassan. 2003. "Islamic Non-governmental Organisations." In M. L. Weiss and Saliha Hassan, eds., *Social Movements in Malaysia: From Moral Communities to NGOs*. London: RoutledgeCurzon.

Saravanamuttu, Johan. 2000. "Act of Betrayal: The Snuffing Out of Local Democracy in Malaysia." *Aliran Monthly* 20(4): 23–25.

———. 2003. "NGO Candidates for the Election." *Aliran Monthly* 23: 6.

Sisters in Islam. 1991. *Are Muslim Men Allowed to Beat Their Wives?* Kelana Jaya: SIS Forum.

Suaram. 1998. *Malaysian Human Rights Report*. Petaling Jaya: Suaram Komunikasi.

Syed Ahmad Hussein. 1999. "Politik Muslim dan Demokrasi di Malaysia: Anjakan, Pertemuan dan Landasan Baru Persaingan Politik." Paper read at professional lecture (*perlantikan profesor*), Nov. 8, Penang.

Tan Boon Kean and Bishan Singh. 1994. *Uneasy Relations: The State and NGOs in Malaysia*. Kuala Lumpur: Gender and Development Programme, Asian and Pacific Development Centre.

Tan Liok Ee. 1997. *The Politics of Chinese Education in Malaya, 1945–1961*. Kuala Lumpur: Oxford University Press.

Tham Seong Chee. 1977. *The Role and Impact of Formal Associations on the Development of Malaysia*. Bangkok: Friedrich-Ebert-Stiftung.

Verma, Vidhu. 2002. *Malaysia: State and Civil Society in Transition*. Boulder: Lynne Rienner.

Von Vorys, Karl. 1975. *Democracy Without Consensus: Communalism and Political Stability in Malaysia*. Princeton: Princeton University Press.

Walker, Millidge. 1996. *NGO Participation in a Corporatist State: The Example of Indonesia*. Berkeley: Institute of Urban and Regional Development, University of California.

Weiss, Meredith L. 2000. "The 1999 Malaysian General Elections: Issues, Insults, and Irregularities." *Asian Survey* 40(3): 413–35.

———. 2001. "The Politics of Protest: Civil Society, Coalition-Building, and Political Change in Malaysia." Ph.D. diss., Yale University.

———. 2003a. "The Malaysian Human Rights Movement." In M. L. Weiss and Saliha Hassan, eds., *Social Movements in Malaysia: From Moral Communities to NGOs*. London: RoutledgeCurzon.

———. 2003b. "Malaysian NGOs: History, Legal Framework, and Characteristics." In M. L. Weiss and Saliha Hassan, eds., *Social Movements in Malaysia: From Moral Communities to NGOs*. London: RoutledgeCurzon.

Zaharom Nain. 2002. "The Structure of the Media Industry: Implications for Democracy." In F. Loh K. W. and Khoo B. T., eds., *Democracy in Malaysia: Discourses and Practices*. Richmond, Surrey: Curzon.

Zainah Anwar. 1987. *Islamic Revivalism in Malaysia: Dakwah Among the Students*. Petaling Jaya: Pelanduk.

Zakaria Haji Ahmad. 1989. "Malaysia: Quasi Democracy in a Divided Society." In L. Diamond, J. J. Linz, and S. M. Lipset, eds., *Democracy in Developing Countries*, vol. 3: *Asia*. Boulder: Lynne Rienner.

CHAPTER NINE

Sri Lanka

Ethnic Domination, Violence, and Illiberal Democracy

NEIL DEVOTTA

> Ceylon amongst all countries of Asia is best fitted to make a success of democracy. In doing so we can not only benefit ourselves but [also] encourage the whole democratic movement in Asia, and in fact prove to be a valuable link between East and West.
>
> —S. W. R. D. Bandaranaike
> addressing the Sinhala Maha Sabha in 1948

Sri Lanka attained universal suffrage in 1931, merely three years after its British colonizer mandated likewise in the United Kingdom. The island gained independence in 1948 in perhaps the most orderly transfer of power in the post–World War II era. If two turnovers of power between opposition parties represent a consolidated democracy (Huntington 1991: 266–67), Sri Lanka, which saw parliamentary control switch between the dominant parties in 1956, March and July 1960, 1965, 1970, 1977, 1994, 2001, and 2004, also achieved such august status more than forty years ago. The country's literacy rate has long remained over 90 percent. Voter turnout at elections typically hovers between 70 and 75 percent. Although the island did not produce an independence movement like its Indian neighbor, nineteenth- and twentieth-century Sri Lanka nevertheless evidenced commendable associational life. But this in turn raises a puzzle: Why, despite such positive precedents and conditions, has Sri Lanka's civil society failed to preclude illiberal democracy and enable positive political change?[1]

In seeking to answer this question, this chapter argues that a state's political structure can influence what civil society groups demand and how they go about making those demands. Sri Lanka's political structure has enabled particularistic and ethnic-based groups to hold sway—leading to ethnocentric groups triumphing over interethnic and inclusive groups to generate adverse political change and illiberal governance. Thus one may say that ethnocentric groups have promoted illiberal democracy in Sri Lanka. Merely seeking to further an ethnic group's interests does not make an organization "ethnocentric," for pursuing such preferences peacefully is a fundamental right in a liberal democracy. Consequently, a group may peacefully propose ethnocentric policies and still be a part of civil society. It is only when it tolerates or supports totalizing goals or perpetrates violence that it leaves the civil society arena and enters political society. In short, one may be ethnocentric and be a part of civil society, just as one may encourage ethnic accommodation yet endorse or threaten violence and move beyond civil society.[2]

The fact remains that groups that seek to further their interests through illiberal means (intimidation, threats, harassment, voting fraud, rioting, violence) counter the civil society agenda and undermine liberal democracy. In this sense, the Liberation Tigers of Tamil Eelam (LTTE), which has fought to create a separate state and is currently proscribed as a terrorist organization in some countries, would be regarded as the most ethnocentric and violent group on the island, although the account provided here will make clear that it was Sinhalese ethnocentrism and its attendant violence that provoked LTTE terrorism. Thus certain groups in Sri Lanka are branded ethnocentric, not merely because they are pro-Sinhalese or pro-Tamil, but because they have, in the main, facilitated interethnic violence.

It is necessary to distinguish political associations from civic associations. While the former polarize and politicize interaction between societal interests, the latter engender crosscutting cleavages that promote social capital and civic engagement. The distinction is thus made between "bonding" (exclusive) and "bridging" (inclusive) social capital (Putnam 2000: 22). Distinguishing between political and civic associations when both promote significant social interests can, however, be difficult (Foley and Edwards 1996), since both groups operate within one polity. Furthermore, certain groups sometimes alternate between civility and incivility, and their protean nature makes it hard to compartmentalize their activities neatly. This noted, it is clear that in Sri Lanka, the ethnic "bonding" social capital that was generated by political societies has triumphed over the interethnic "bridging" social capital generated by multiethnic and liberal groups, thereby engendering communalism, sectarianism, insecurity, and institutional decay (DeVotta 2004).

Groups that resort to intraethnic violence must also be located within political society. In almost all instances, such violence erupts over political differences, the distribution of scarce resources, and the attempt to gain and maintain political power. Incorporating groups into a space that is compartmentalized between civil society and political society, even while recognizing that many groups keep switching between them, is consistent with the analytical framework adopted in Chapter 1.

Since 1983, Sri Lanka has experienced a bloody civil war between the majority Sinhalese-led government and LTTE. This essay does not seek to explain the civil war, but it is impossible to separate the precipitating events from illiberal democracy. If ethnocentric and hence illiberal Sinhalese practices legitimated the Tamil separatist movement, this violent quest has in turn justified even more illiberal practices to maintain the island's territorial integrity. It is important to understand this invidious relationship in order to grasp why the island's robust civil society has hitherto failed to reassert the rule of law and preclude illiberal governance. Sri Lanka's Sinhalese and Tamils lived in relative harmony until the Sinhalese sought to make Sinhala the island's only official language.[3] Later in this chapter, I shall explain how postindependence associations generating "bonding" social capital enabled such an ethnocentric agenda, detail how the constitutional structure coupled with the country's demographics allowed such associations to triumph over the island's "bridging" civil society groups, and show how their demands influenced politicians to adopt ethnocentric policies and practice ethnic outbidding.[4] The predominance of these ethnocentric groups ultimately undermined liberal democracy and, over time, embedded illiberal democracy. Ultimately, the reactive Tamil nationalism unleashed even more violence, which spiraled into a gruesome ethnic conflict. In conclusion, I indicate how Sri Lanka's civil society, the numerous challenges notwithstanding, is seeking to generate "bridging" social capital so as to promote peace and reform the current illiberal milieu.

Main Arguments

In analyzing why civil society in Sri Lanka has not been more effective in precluding illiberal democracy, this chapter makes three arguments that connect civil society and democracy. First, I contend that the governmental structure and institutions representing the state influence the types of associations that spring up (Pharr 2003). This suggests that the opportunities and constraints the political structure enables will influence what groups demand and how they go about making these demands. Thus, for example, racist organizations that once thrived in America could not produce the same odious results today, because the rules, norms, laws, and conventions that have gradually, but effectively, restructured institutional relations between state and polity now discourage a racist mentality. This also means that a rich associational life does not necessarily guarantee a stable polity—for increased mobilization could easily be correlated with institutional decay (Huntington 1968; DeVotta 2004). Without strong, efficient, and impartial institutions, therefore, "an increasingly active civil society may serve to undermine, rather than strengthen, a political regime" (Berman 1997: 402). This argument does not dismiss civil society's importance; it merely suggests that the degree of civility can be broadened and circumscribed depending on the state's institutions. It does, however, operate from the premises that civil society is more a prophylactic rather than a panacea, and that the more stable the state apparatus within a democracy, the more likely civil groups are to thrive. Civil society does not operate in a vacuum; on the contrary, its performance may depend on the state's institutions and the confidence the polity reposes in them (Encarnacion 2001).

The fact remains that even well-designed institutions may fail to function properly. It should therefore come as no surprise that badly designed institutions can create incivility. States whose institutions function efficiently and impartially negate the need for alternative sources to substitute public goods that would most likely also promote negative externalities. A state that guarantees public safety and property rights, for example, not only exudes confidence among the public but also precludes others from trying to take on these responsibilities. A state that fails to provide such public goods, by contrast, may see unsavory groups rise to provide alternative services, as is the case with the Sicilian Mafia in some parts of Italy (Gambetta 1993). Thus, institutions, when they act properly and impartially, also guarantee social capital, engender trust, and influence the organizational demands being made. As Margaret Levi has noted, "state institutions can, under certain circumstances, lay the basis for generalized trust," for "the absence of an effective state leads us to the Hobbesian world of nature" (Levi 1996: 50). An effective state does not, however, guarantee that civil society organizations will thrive. The Sri Lankan state during the 1980s and early 1990s was highly effective and clearly had no qualms about trying to control civil society groups. This was especially the case between 1989 and 1993 when President Ranasinghe Premadasa's government unscrupulously and ham-handedly opposed civil society groups it believed challenged the state as a provider of scarce resources and services. It specifically harassed the Sarvodaya Shramadana Movement, a local NGO focusing on rural development, by closing down the group's press, blackguarding the group and its leader in the state media, manipulating state agencies to investigate, interrogate, and imprison group members, and proscribing government departments from collaborating with Sarvodaya as it sought to improve health and social conditions in villages (Bond 2004: 82–83). Thus the Voluntary Social Service Organizations (Registration and Supervision) Act passed in 1980 allowed government officials to search the offices of any organization and dictate when and where groups convened their meetings (Saravanamuttu 1998: 119). And in 1993, upon the recommendations made by the Commission of Inquiry in Respect of Non-Governmental Organizations, a different government utilized an emergency regulation to introduce "The Monitoring of Receipts and Disbursements of Non-Governmental Organizations Regulation No. 1," which required all NGOs with annual budgets over 50,000 rupees to register with the state and make known their funding sources and expenditures (Wickramasinghe 2001: 84). While such monitoring only lasted a year, it shows how the nature of the state and its institutions influence the effectiveness of civil society organizations.

Second, I contend that Sri Lanka's problem is not that it lacks associational life but that it has allowed ethnocentric associations to dominate the island's sociopolitical networks. Put differently, associations generating "bonding" social capital have triumphed over associations generating "bridging" social capital, especially since the mid-1950s, and this has led to institutional decay and an illiberal democracy (DeVotta 2002). Around the early 1950s, politicians in the opposition realized they could commingle language with nationalism to catapult themselves to power, and they consequently pandered to the demands of jingoistic associations that clamored for a Sinhala-only language policy. Many Sinhalese associations may have initially operated in a civil fashion, but once the language issue was introduced into the political arena, they resorted to ethnocentric demands. If one accepts (notwithstanding the debate on how exactly social capital ought to be defined) that social capital represents norms, networks, values, and actions that generate trust and promote civic engagement, then these nationalist associations and the politicians who supported their radical demands undermined trust and civic engagement between the ethnic communities.[5]

The fact remains that ethnocentric associations generate "bonding" social capital, which everyone in a polity must deal with, and this mandates that their impact on civil society be analyzed as well. As Michael Foley and Bob Edwards have argued: "Individual and collective actors get things done better thanks to social capital; society as a whole may or may not be better off as a result" (Foley and Edwards 1997: 552). In other words, individuals and groups may generate social capital to further their ends, even as they generate negative externalities for society at large. Furthermore, as Francis Fukuyama has observed: "One person's civic engagement is another's rent-seeking; much of what constitutes civil society can be described as interest groups trying to divert public resources to their favored causes" (Fukuyama 2001: 12). This is especially the case in polyethnic societies, where one group's social capital may come at the expense of other ethnic groups. This is all the more reason to pay close attention to political society and the way it often constrains civil society.

Indeed, in Sri Lanka's case, it is argued that "all institutions and interests outside political society (i.e., those that should strictly belong to the civil society) draw their power, usually to a greater and sometimes lesser extent, not from their own social bases but from political society itself. Civil society organizations and formations deriving the bulk of their power from sources independent of political society are by and large not a feature of the Sri Lankan social scene" (Fernando 1997: 2). In Sri Lanka, for example, the United Coordinating Council of Muslims (UCCM) brings together over eighty Muslim organizations to lobby for Muslim preferences. While this umbrella organization operates as a political force, it often engages in activities that strengthen civil society. At the same time, the organization can sympathize with radical groups that resort to illiberal practices when opposing devolution (because it believes the Muslim community in the Eastern Province will be marginalized if Tamils are allowed autonomy over the northeast region). In the latter instance, elements within UCCM could be said to encourage these radical groups, but to brand the organization "ethnocentric" or "violence-prone" is to disregard its complex nature. To use another example, while labor unions would be widely considered part of civil society, many unions in Sri Lanka are very much part of political society as well. In fact, the most prominent labor unions are allied with the leading political parties. Thus while the Nidahas Sevaka Sangamaya (Free Workers' Union) is allied with the Sri Lanka Freedom Party, the Jathika Sevaka Sangamaya (National Workers' Union) is allied with the United National Party. Indeed, party leaders often use their union members to beat up opponents and crush strikes initiated by opposing unions. The Jathika Sevaka Sangamaya (JSS) also played a major role in organizing and carrying out anti-Tamil riots between 1977 and 1983. The same holds true of student unions on campuses, which means that student groups can rally either for or against government and university policies, depending on what their respective political parties advocate. Thus, the Inter-University Students' Federation, a group affiliated with the once Maoist and now hypernationalist Janatha Vimukthi Peramuna (JVP; People's Liberation Front), is notorious for attacking its rivals, typically by using clubs and iron rods, so that university students have been killed and some universities have been forced to close down during the mayhem. The chapters on South Korea and Burma in this book also discuss violent student movements; what is so starkly apparent about Sri Lanka's student groups is the degree to which many of them take their cue from political parties.

There are at least two major reasons why Sri Lanka's civil society organizations are so often linked with political society. Historically, the country lacked an independent civil society ethic, thus forcing independent associations to depend on political parties, and this has led to the masses waiting for the state and political parties to solve problems.[6] Consequently, many groups have supported initiatives taken by the state, which in turn has sometimes used civil society opportunistically to legitimize its agenda. This pattern was evidenced after the People's Alliance (PA) under Chandrika Kumaratunga came to power in 1994 promoting a peace platform—and civil society groups, many promoting peace to begin with, jumped on the government's peace bandwagon. These groups more or less campaigned for the government but were soon discredited once the cease-fire between the government and LTTE broke down and the PA pursued a vicious "war for peace" campaign.

The confrontation and co-optation strategies practiced by the state are a second, and more important, reason why civil society in Sri Lanka often draws its power from political society. In the confrontation strategy, the state, by passing laws and resorting to intimidation, has at times made it difficult for civil society to function; in the co-optation strategy, politicians and their parties have opportunistically embraced popular initiatives pioneered by civil society. Thus a movement organized by women seeking information on their children who had disappeared (after the JVP sought to violently topple the government between 1988 and 1990 and the government retaliated by brutally cracking down against supposedly pro-JVP youth) was, for example, effectively co-opted and divested of its nongovernmental credentials by a southern politician.[7] Civil society groups enable such co-optation because they believe that joining forces with politicians will allow their preferences to be implemented expeditiously. But doing so merely undermines these groups' status as civil society organizations and sometimes even converts them into service delivery organizations overseen by politicians.

Finally, the chapter claims that illiberal democracy in Sri Lanka, to a large extent, was both the cause and a consequence of the civil war. If ethnocentric and illiberal practices marginalized the Tamil minority and influenced the quest for separatism, then the civil war has also promoted illiberal governance and further weakened civil society's influence. It should be axiomatic that a democracy at peace is likely to be a country where civil society operates relatively unfettered. A country at war, by contrast, whether a democracy or autocracy, enables its rulers to institute draconian restrictions on civil liberties, which hinder civil society's effectiveness. This is especially so if the country is polyethnic and those being targeted belong to a particular ethnic or religious group. Thus, in Sri Lanka's case, the Prevention of Terrorism Act of 1979 allowed the security forces to arrest, imprison, and hold incommunicado for eighteen months without trial anyone suspected of unlawful activity—a measure that led to thousands of Tamil youths being tortured and killed. The law may have been designed to eradicate terrorism, but the egregious practices it encouraged undermined civil liberties and human rights and broadened illiberal governance. There is no reason to assume that demands being made by a particular group, especially within a polyethnic setting, will always be liberal and egalitarian. More often than not, certainly in Sri Lanka, the demands of religious and ethnic groups have been provincial, particularistic, and promoted violence—which in turn has marginalized interethnic groups, emboldened ethnocentric groups, and undermined democracy (Hardin 1995).

Civil society operates most effectively by functioning as an intermediary between society and the state, while guaranteeing individuals' rights against excessive state control. This assumes that the state views all society as a single entity to be accommodated or subordinated. Yet what often ensues in polyethnic societies is that the state can accommodate certain groups' interests by subordinating other groups, to the point where civil society itself may become politicized. This is especially true during ethnic conflicts or civil wars. Thus, for example, a Sinhalese civil society group calling for interethnic comity during peacetime could easily adopt a jingoistic prowar agenda during ethnic conflict and thereby enter political society. Civil society thrives only when it enjoys the space "to conduct advocacy activities, develop better channels of communication with the executive and legislative branches of government, and provide input into the governing process" (Fomunyoh 2001: 44). This, however, is best achieved within a stable state. A state in crisis, especially a separatist crisis, may be a state that emasculates a robust civil society. Such has been the case in Sri Lanka.

Civil Society Before Independence

Sri Lanka, called Ceylon until 1972, gained independence in 1948. The Portuguese and Dutch colonized the island before the British supplanted the latter in 1796. The country was divided into two Sinhalese kingdoms and a northern Tamil kingdom when the Portuguese arrived in 1505, although by 1597, the Portuguese controlled the entire littoral. The Portuguese and Dutch never conquered the whole island. The British accomplished this when they defeated the Kandyan kingdom in 1815 and administratively unified the island in 1832.

According to the last all-island census, conducted in 1981, the island's ethnic groups were as follows: Sinhalese 73.95 percent, Sri Lankan Tamils 12.7 percent, Indian Tamils 5.52 percent, Sri Lankan Moors 7.05 percent, Burghers and Eurasians 0.26 percent, Malays 0.32 percent, and Veddhas (indigenous peoples) 0.19 percent (Sri Lanka Department of Census and Statistics 1996: 16). The Indian Tamils, descended from indentured laborers who came mainly to work on tea plantations, have not been involved in the separatist violence that has engulfed the country since 1983. The Sinhalese are mostly Buddhists (69.3 percent) and the Tamils mainly Hindu (15.5 percent). The Moors, in the main, also speak Tamil, but their ethnic identity is tied to their Muslim faith. While the Christian population (7.6 percent) includes both Sinhalese and Tamils (14), it is rare for Sinhalese to be Hindu or Tamils to be Buddhist. This means that while organizations like the Young Men's Christian Association and Young Women's Christian Association usually include both Sinhalese and Tamils, explicitly Sinhalese Buddhist and Tamil Hindu associations almost never include members from other ethnicities and religions. This, of course, is not true of secular associations like the Leo's Club, Lion's Club, Jay Cees, and Rotary Club, which typically include members from all ethnic and religious backgrounds.

Most Sinhalese claim an Aryan and North Indian pedigree and argue that they were the first to settle the island, around 600 B.C.E. The Tamils, by contrast, are of South Indian provenance and claim always to have lived on the island. This is plausible given that only twenty-two miles separate South India and the northernmost Tamil areas in Sri Lanka. The Tamils consequently claim the north and east as their historic homeland, while the Sinhalese claim that the entire island is Sihadipa (the island of the Sinhalese) and Dhammadipa (the island ennobled to preserve and propagate Buddhism). These contradictory claims and the politicking they have influenced are partly why Sinhalese "bonding" social groups have long triumphed over the island's "bridging" social groups.

Associational life in Sri Lanka predates colonialism and was centered on religion, culture, and the economy. Colonialism and its attendant centralized governance, especially under the British, gradually vitiated civil society's influence in the economic realm, although associational life remained vigorous in the religious and cultural realms. Consequently, Buddhist, Hindu, and Muslim organizations were created to propagate their respective religions and promote Sinhalese and Tamil culture, although at times organizations were also created to mediate intrareligious and intracommunity disputes. An apt example in this regard is the Jaffna Youth Congress (JYC). When this idealistic and anticolonial Tamil organization encouraged equal seating and equal dining practices with lower-caste Tamils, their upper-caste Tamil elders organized the Young Men's Hindu Association (YMHA) "to teach young men not only discipline and healthy habits, but also respect for their elders' customs and beliefs and conformity in every aspect of life" (Hellmann-Rajanayagam 1994: 31). The YMHA exemplifies how even peaceful organizations can support antidemocratic and antiegalitarian practices.

When Christian missionaries and their organizations sought to undermine Buddhism in the nineteenth century, anti-Christian feelings were aroused, and local religious elites used the religio-cultural infrastructure to oppose the missionaries. In the nineteenth century, the leading Christian organizations included the Church Missionary Society, Salvation Army, Wesleyan Missionary Society, Society for the Propagation of the Gospel, Young Men's Christian Association, and Young Women's Christian Association. These groups produced pamphlets and tracts to spread their faith and denounce local religions. In time, the local religions retaliated by adeptly copying their colonial masters' tactics. They not only used printing presses to produce Buddhist and Hindu literature but also created associations that mirrored the missionary organizations. Prominent among these were the Society for the Propagation of Buddhism, the Young Men's Buddhist Association, the Buddhist Theosophical Society, the All-Ceylon Buddhist Congress, the Muslim Education Society, the Ramakrishna Mission, the Vivekanda Society, the Young Men's Hindu Association, and the Maha Bodhi Society (Saravanamuttu 1998: 105).

These associations not only blocked the missionaries' influence; they also bolstered the local religions. Many created schools and cultural centers to promote Sinhalese and Tamil identity and heritage. The Theosophical Society, for example, under the influence of Henry Steel Olcott and Helena Petrovna Blavatsky, denounced the British authorities' discriminatory practices against non-Christians and founded numerous Buddhist schools to rival the Christian schools created by the missionaries. One of Olcott's and Blavatsky's followers, Anagarika Dharmapala, founded the Maha Bodhi Society and was at the forefront in producing anti-Hindu and anti-Christian agitprop (DeVotta 2001: 77–79). Dharmapala voiced the fears and frustrations of Buddhist elites. Yet his rhetoric exemplifies how Sri Lanka's preindependence associational life was mostly oppositional in nature and tinged with communalism. Sinhalese Buddhist associations opposed the pro-Christian colonial administration, Christian missionary organizations, and (eventually) non-Buddhists in general, whom they considered less adversely affected by colonial malpractice. It is not surprising that this was all combined into an anti-Western and pro-Buddhist mind-set, which was carried over into the postindependence period.

It is instructive that while organizations like the Ceylon National Congress were initially polyethnic in nature, most associations in the country were created around religion or language or both. Certainly, the country's population was concentrated along religio-linguistic lines, although this was most likely exacerbated by the divide-and-rule colonial policies and classificatory practices of the British, expressed through such instruments as the census (Anderson 1991). The upshot was that by the twentieth century, the country's masses identified themselves primarily along religio-linguistic lines, reflected even in the names of sports clubs (e.g., Sinhalese Sports Club; Moors Sports Club; Tamil Union Cricket and Athletic Club; Colombo Malay Cricket Club; Burgher Recreation Club).

Especially ominous were the numerous Buddhist societies that sprang up two decades prior to independence, because their appearance indicated that the majority community had realized that it could use the franchise and superior numbers to lobby for particularistic preferences along religious lines. Prominent among these associations were the Sri Sasandhara Society (Society for the Support of the Buddhist Priesthood), Sri Lankadhara Society (Society for Preserving Lanka), Dhamma Deepthi Sisyaya Samitiya (Students of the Light of the Dharma Society), Buddhagaya Defense League, Kandy Union of Buddhist Societies, Servants of the Buddha Society, and All-Ceylon Buddhist Congress (Russell 1982a: 139–40). Clearly, then, preindependence Sri Lanka's associational life was heavily influenced by communal attachments, which meant that the civil society these associations promoted could also turn ethnocentric and violent at critical moments, as happened less than a decade after independence.

The transfer of power that led to independence was such an elite affair that many in the countryside were unaware of the event's significance. As Sir Ivor Jennings, adviser to Sri Lanka's first prime minister, D. S. Senanayake, noted: "The transfer of power took place so efficiently that the ordinary citizen did not even realize that it had happened" (Jennings 1950: 202). Another observer has noted: "Compared to the sturm und drang of the Indian movement, the Ceylon independence movement in the 1920's and 1930's appears staid and dull, even phlegmatic" (Russell 1982b: 64). A major reason for this was that the island, despite allowing the franchise to be gradually broadened from communal representation in the late nineteenth century to universal suffrage in 1931, lacked a party system. The government was instead run by an executive committee system, in which legislators belonging to seven committees oversaw the business conducted by the State Council and the executive. Each committee chair held a ministerial position and the seven chairmen made up the Board of Ministers, which in turn ran the government. This arrangement enabled politicians to operate in a manner consistent with the country's feudal heritage. With no "government" and "opposition" as such, it also shielded the politicians from taking responsibility for their actions. Most important from a civil society standpoint, it minimized grassroots mobilization seeking radical change during the first two decades following the introduction of universal franchise. Although the Lanka Sama Samaja Party (Lanka Equal Society Party) and the Communist Party were created in 1935 and 1943, respectively, leftists did not command sufficiently widespread support to be a political threat in the preindependence era. The first mainstream political party, the United National Party (UNP), was organized only two years or so before independence and was not seriously opposed until September 1951, when S. W. R. D. Bandaranaike left the party and formed the Sri Lanka Freedom Party (SLFP).

This is not to suggest that the country was devoid of associations that combined sociopolitical issues and sought more representation and even independence from the British. The Young Lanka League was organized in 1915, for example, and many other such associations soon followed. Tamil youth played an important role in the Tamil Maha Jana Sabhai, which became the Jaffna Youth Congress (JYC) in 1924. JYC and the Colombo Youth League were both influenced by Indian nationalists, and the former worked hard in the Northern Province to uplift those marginalized along caste lines. The JYC competed ideationally and sociopolitically with the All-Ceylon Tamil League and its constituent partner the Jaffna Association. The All-Ceylon Tamil League and the Jaffna Association were dominated by the upper-caste Vellalas (farmers) who supported the rigid caste structure and opposed universal franchise. JYC and Catholic organizations like the North Ceylon National League worked, in contrast, to create a more liberal and egalitarian society. These groups consequently supported creating the Depressed Tamil Service League, a non-Vellala group, which went on to establish schools, open libraries, and educate the lower castes. It also helped create the Jaffna Diocesan Union, North Ceylon Workmen's Union, and the North Ceylon Vehicleman's Union to mobilize laborers (Russell 1982b).

Thus, by the time independence came, the island had a rich associational life and, thanks to universal franchise, democracy was already in situ. Yet it is clear that the country experienced nothing like the grassroots movements witnessed in Latin America and eastern Europe when those countries transited from authoritarianism to democracy. If, by democratic consolidation, we mean two turnovers of power between opposition parties, Sri Lanka was a consolidated democracy by 1960. Gauged against the classical definition, however, whereby the rules governing formal democratic processes are institutionalized and observed by all parties so as to preclude democratic erosion and authoritarian regression (Diamond 1994; Schedler 1998), it becomes clear that the ethnic particularism and ethnic outbidding that dominated the country's politics after the mid-1950s undermined democratic consolidation. Ethnocentric groups played a major role in this regression.

The Sinhala-Only Movement: The Genesis of Illiberal Democracy

Despite their competing historiographies and intermittent South Indian invasions, the country's Sinhalese and Tamils cohabited peacefully for nearly two millennia until the Tamils realized that the Sinhalese could dominate the electoral process using universal suffrage. They thereupon consequently sought equal representation for the minorities and Sinhalese, which created ethnic tensions during the 1920s and 1930s. Interethnic confraternity among elites nevertheless enabled the Tamils to disregard their reservations and join their Sinhalese counterparts in seeking independence. Soon thereafter, Sinhalese elites, assisted by caste-conscious Tamil politicians, disenfranchised the country's Indian Tamils, signaling the potential for ethnocentrism and illiberal governance. The realization that the island's ethnic demographics, the first-past-the-post electoral system, the unitary state structure, and the absence of substantive minority guarantees were conducive to fashioning a Sinhalese-centric political order soon influenced Sinhalese elites to pursue ethnocentric policies. In this, they were fully assisted by Sinhalese associations that realized that a Sinhala-only policy stood to benefit their community at the Tamils' expense.

American missionaries had started some excellent schools in the Northern Province, which taught many Tamils English. This, coupled with the north's arid and inhospitable terrain and the prestige associated with government employment, encouraged Tamils to seek jobs with the state. In any case, the state was the largest employer, and there were few opportunities for employment in the private sector. Furthermore, Britain's divide-and-rule policy, which promoted the notion that the majority community had to be kept in a weakened state, ensured that the Tamils became disproportionately represented in the civil service. Their English qualifications likewise led to their becoming overrepresented in professions associated with higher education. Although they were just 13 percent of the population in 1956, Tamils made up 30 percent of the Ceylon Administrative Service, 50 percent of the clerical service, 60 percent of engineers and doctors, and 40 percent of the armed forces (Phadnis 1979: 348). These statistics were wormwood for most Sinhalese, who soon mobilized to reverse the situation. The mechanism used to do so was the Sinhala language, although the role of ethnocentric groups in this process was equally important.

Toward the Sinhala-Only Policy

The *swabasha* (self-language) movement initially included Sinhalese and Tamils who wanted their respective languages—Sinhala and Tamil—to replace English as the country's only official language. Thus the Southern Province Teachers' Association, which primarily represented Sinhala-speakers, and the Northern Province Teachers' Association, which primarily represented Tamil-speakers, lobbied the All-Ceylon English Teachers' Association to incorporate both Sinhala and Tamil into school curricula. In this effort, they were assisted by organizations like the Ceylon Social Reform Society. Realizing that Sinhala was bound to play an important role in postindependence Sri Lanka, the Hindu Board of Education, which framed the curricula for the Hindu schools in the Northern Province, made Sinhala a compulsory language in their school system (Russell 1982c). But when Sinhalese nationalists began clamoring in the mid-1950s for Sinhala to be made the sole national language, the Tamils discontinued teaching Sinhala.

When politicians in the opposition, led by S. W. R. D. Bandaranaike, realized that the Sinhala-only demand could be used for political gain, they introduced the language issue into the political arena in 1955. Soon those in the governing party were embracing the Sinhala-only policy, which led to ethnic outbidding as politicians and their respective parties tried to convince the majority Sinhalese that they were best suited to institute Sinhalese preferences and marginalize the Tamils. The Sinhala-only movement accentuates two arguments. First, it highlights the nature and influence of those associations that used language and nationalism to institute ethnocentric policies to the extent that they coerced politicians to follow through on demands that all knew were inimical to the country's unity and democracy. Second, it shows how the island's constitutional structure enabled these groups to succeed and thereby marginalize the Tamils, who consequently had little choice but to mobilize politically and militarily. The language movement demonstrates how groups that had once been civil and might have generated "bridging" social capital transformed themselves and generated "bonding" social capital, how they thereby moved from civil society to political society, and the extent to which they contributed to illiberal democracy. It also highlights how Tamil civil society was radicalized to the point of resorting to terrorism (Thangarajah 2003).

Ethnic Outbidding and Illiberal Democracy

The first-past-the-post electoral system introduced by the British ensured that the Sinhalese would control over 80 percent of the electorate. The state's unitary nature and the lack of any substantial minority guarantees also ensured that ethnic entrepreneurs could merely cater to Sinhalese preferences and disregard minority aspirations. The grassroots demand to make Sinhala the official language thus allowed aspiring politicians to politicize the language issue—although eventually both major parties, the United National Party and the Sri Lanka Freedom Party, sought to corral the Sinhalese vote by outbidding each other on the pro-Sinhalese and anti-Tamil stance.

According to Ghia Nodia, "nationalism is usually championed by *alternative* rather than *ruling* elites" (2000: 171). Certainly this was so in postindependence Sri Lanka, with S. W. R. D. Bandaranaike's SLFP manipulating the language issue to capture power in the 1956 elections. Bandaranaike had left the UNP when he realized that D. S. Senanayake was grooming his son, Dudley, to succeed him. Eager to become prime minister, Bandaranaike formed the SLFP in September 1951, although the party fared poorly in the 1952 elections. At that time, Bandaranaike had supported linguistic parity. When a motion was debated in the State Council in May 1944 on making Sinhala the only official language, he noted that it "would be ungenerous on our part as Sinhalese not to give due recognition to the Tamil language." He further argued that many states were functioning well despite having more than two official languages and said: "I have no personal objection to both these languages [Sinhala and Tamil] being considered official languages; nor do I see any particular harm or danger or real difficulty arising from it" (Ceylon, State Council, *Debates*, May 25, 1944: 810–11). He maintained this position until 1955, when he decided to champion the Sinhala-only position. Thereafter Bandaranaike argued that the Sinhalese were engaged in a life-and-death struggle to maintain their language and culture, and that to grant "parity to both Sinhalese and Tamil would only lead to the deterioration of Sinhalese which may disappear from Ceylon within 25 years."[8]

The country's prime minister, Sir John Kotelawala, had long advocated linguistic parity. As late as June 1955, he stated: "I can assure you—and I have said it not once but many times—that the U.N.P., of which I am the head, have accepted the principle that both Sinhalese and Tamil will be the languages of this country. We have said so, and we propose to put it into practice" (Ceylon, House of Representatives, *Debates*, vol. 21: col. 485). Soon thereafter, he further argued that "bilingualism, and even trilingualism [Sinhala, Tamil, and English], should therefore be encouraged as far as possible if the communal harmony which we pride ourselves in having today is to be preserved for the future" (House, *Debates*, vol. 22: cols. 1753–54). Yet after he and the UNP realized they would lose the upcoming election if they did not embrace a Sinhala-only platform, Kotelawala thundered: "I want Sinhalese to be the official language of the country as long as the sun and moon shall last."[9] Both the UNP and SLFP thereafter went about trying to outbid the other on who could best ensure Sinhalese superordination and Tamil subordination (DeVotta 2004).

The political structure was a major reason why such outbidding took root. There were no serious minority guarantees in the constitution, for example, and the first-past-the-post electoral system encouraged political candidates to disregard minority sentiments in predominantly Sinhalese districts. Had the SLFP and UNP decided not to embrace the Sinhala-only movement, therefore, some extremist group could easily have organized a party and incorporated the ethnocentric Sinhalese demands into its platform. Certainly, the quest to make Sinhala the state's official language was a bottom-up affair, and there was much support for it among postindependence Sinhalese grassroots organizations. Pro-Sinhala and ethnocentric groups were not the only associations in Sri Lanka at the time. What is striking is how the groups that were truly civil refused to become intermediaries and instead used their associations as social venues to preserve their organizational interests.[10] It is hardly surprising, then, that the only political change that ensued was the one championed by ethnocentric groups.

Writing in the mid-1950s, the vice-chancellor of the University of Colombo referred to "an undercurrent of opinion," which he described as follows:

> It is aggressively nationalist and aggressively Buddhist. In language policy it is anti-English; in religion it is anti-Christian; in foreign policy it is anti-Western; and in economic policy it is both anti-capitalist and anti-socialist. Socially, it might be described as anti-Colombo, because it consists primarily of English-educated young men from the provinces, the sons of small cultivators, minor officials, shop-keepers, and the lower middle-class groups generally. It dislikes the cosmopolitan airs of the products of the big Colombo schools, who dominate Colombo society. It is not a political movement, but it is politically important because it has the support of the Buddhist *Sangha*, or priesthood, of the teachers in the Sinhalese schools, and of the *vedarala* or practitioners of indigenous medicine, all of whom have strong political influence in the villages. (Jennings 1954: 344)

Sir Ivor Jennings described what came to be identified as the Pancha Maha Balavegaya (Five Great Forces): Sinhalese laborers, teachers, farmers, *ayurveda* physicians, and Buddhist monks. These groups operated under a number of associations. Among the more prominent were the Young Men's Buddhist Association, the Theosophical Society, the Ayurveda Sangamaya (Congress of Indigenous Medical Practitioners), the Sinhala Bhasa Arakshaka Mandalaya (Sinhala Language Protection Council), the Bhasa Peramuna (Language Front), and the Lanka Jatika Guru Sangamaya (Sinhalese Teachers' Association), with especially the latter two incorporating Sinhalese educators, poets, writers, and language teachers. Many in these associations threatened violence against the state and Tamils if Sinhala were not made the sole official language. Buddhist monks in Sri Lanka command enormous influence, and they too were organized under the Eksath Bhikkhu Peramuna (United Buddhist Front), which operated as an umbrella organization, uniting a clergy divided along caste lines. Many monks were also associated with numerous *sangha sabhas* (Buddhist clergy associations), and they in turn joined with the other groups in organizing massive rallies and processions demanding a Sinhala-only policy. Despite some reservations over Bandaranaike, all these groups supported him and the SLFP over the UNP. They did so for at least three reasons. First, the SLFP had from the outset appealed to rural, Buddhist voters and promised to unleash a social revolution; second, the SLFP was the first major political party to adopt a Sinhala-only platform; and third, John Kotelawala was seen as pro-Western and insensitive to Sinhalese/Buddhist sensibilities. As one observer noted: "Here were the best election agents any politician could wish for—12,000 men whose words were holy to over 5,000,000 people, campaigning for the downfall of the Government, zealously and, what is more, gratis" (Vittachi 1958: 19).

While some *bhikkhus* (Buddhist monks) called for tolerance, accommodation, and conciliation, the majority embraced an exclusivist and radical position on the language issue. These "political *bhikkhus*" vilified the Sinhalese Marxist politicians who preferred linguistic parity and warned that the failure to adopt a Sinhala-only policy would signal the death knell of the Sinhalese. They also anathematized the Tamils as "parasites" and threatened to chase them back to the Northern Province. In doing so, they and their extremist lay acolytes made clear that the minorities lived under the majority community's sufferance. Although their associations may once have contributed to civil discourse encouraging an inclusive Ceylonese identity, these very same associations were now utilizing the one person, one vote principle to promote ethnocentrism and threaten violence. The pro-Buddhist, pro-Sinhalese advocates thus championed democracy because Sri Lanka's ethnic demographics ensured that majority rule would mean Sinhalese Buddhist rule. That the latter would inevitably facilitate illiberalism hardly bothered them, because they viewed an ethnocentric, illiberal democracy as consistent with the principles of majority rule.

The Mahajana Eksath Peramuna (People's United Front)—the coalition Bandaranaike had put together—won the 1956 election in a landslide. Bandaranaike had promised to adopt a Sinhala-only policy in twenty-four hours, but soon after coming to power, the new prime minister began to hint that it was imperative for the Tamil language to be accommodated in some fashion. In groping for a compromise, Bandaranaike angered the Sinhalese extremists, who went on hunger strikes and organized protests against the delay in instituting a Sinhala-only policy. Such pressure forced Bandaranaike to introduce a Sinhala-only bill on June 5, 1956, leading to the first ever anti-Tamil riots.

The Sinhala-Only Act of 1956

The 1956 elections saw S. J. V. Chelvanayakam's Federal Party (FP) become the Tamils' major representative, and from here on, most Tamils clamored for a federal arrangement that provided the Northern and Eastern Provinces with autonomy. Sinhalese radicals and their organizations claimed, however, that autonomy would lead to the island's dismemberment and demanded that the unitary state be maintained intact. The FP had organized a satyagraha (peaceful protest) on the day the Sinhala-only bill was presented, and some two hundred Tamils gathered outside parliament to fast and meditate from sundown to sunrise. The Sinhala Language Protection Council had threatened to mobilize to counter the FP's protest, and their members and supporters attacked the Tamils soon after the satyagraha had started. A junior minister in the SLFP led the rioters, while the police merely looked on. Among those injured were a number of Tamil parliamentarians. Soon the violence spread to areas beyond Colombo and led to the death of some 150 Tamils.

This was the first ever anti-Tamil riot, and it was inflamed by the illiberal politicking both major parties had embraced. It is instructive that excepting the Marxists and some clergy, hardly any Sinhalese civil society group lobbied for linguistic parity. This was partly because most associations were created along religious-linguistic lines and were therefore exclusivist in nature. There was also widespread support for the Sinhala-only policy. Thus pro-Sinhalese and pro-Buddhist groups dominated the process with no opposition. Tamil groups understandably protested and organized against the Sinhala-only bill, but Sinhalese politicians easily disregarded their entreaties (DeVotta 2004, 42–91).

The Official Language Act, No. 33 of 1956, or Sinhala-Only Act, was passed on June 15, 1956, although the government indicated that it wanted to accommodate the Tamil language. The Tamils were also aggrieved that the Sinhalese had colonized Tamil lands—another reason why they demanded autonomy for the northeast. This dispute led to an agreement in July between Bandaranaike and the FP's leader, S. J. V. Chelvanayakam, whereby the Tamils agreed to cease demanding linguistic parity and the government agreed to recognize Tamil as a minority language and create regional councils to deal with agriculture, education, and Sinhalese colonization of Tamil areas. The B-C Pact, as it was called, would have satisfied most Tamils, while ensuring that Sinhalese enjoyed the dominant position in the island's sociopolitical and economic spheres. But the UNP decided to scuttle the pact, and its leaders claimed that Bandaranaike was selling out to the Tamils. Insisting the B-C Pact would ensure that Sinhalese would become a minority in their own land, the UNP's leader, Dudley Senanayake, proclaimed: "I am prepared to sacrifice my life to prevent the implementation of the Bandaranaike-Chelvanayakam Agreement, which is a racial division of Ceylon under the guise of the Regional Council System and is an act of treachery on the part of the Prime Minister."[11] J. R. Jayewardene, a future UNP prime minister and president, who was eager to dethrone Senanayake as party leader, embarked on a march from Colombo to Kandy to protest against the B-C Pact. The UNP opposed the pact not only to prove its pro-Sinhalese credentials but also because the party recognized it could undermine the government by allying with the very same associations that had catapulted Bandaranaike to power. Consequently, the Eksath Bhikkhu Peramuna (United Buddhist Front), Sinhala Jatika Sangamaya (Sinhala National Association), Sinhala Bhasa Peramuna (Sinhala Language Front), Tri Sinhala Peramuna (Tri Sinhala Front), and Sri Lanka Sangha Sabha (Sri Lanka Sangha Association) joined forces with the UNP and organized protests demanding that the prime minister abrogate the pact.

Around this time the minister of transport and works issued a directive calling for the Sinhala letter *sri* to be included on all vehicle number plates, and in March 1958, the Bandaranaike government dispatched forty buses with the *sri* lettering to the Northern Province. When the Tamils started replacing the Sinhala *sri* with the Tamil *shri*, many Sinhalese protested by smearing tar over Tamil lettering on buses, public buildings, commercial buildings, and street signs. Numerous Sinhalese organizations that had demanded the Sinhala-Only Act and wanted Bandaranaike to abrogate the B-C Pact participated in these protests, and the All-Ceylon United Bhikkhu Association played a prominent role in leading the anti-Tamil crowds. A beleaguered Bandaranaike used the commotion surrounding the *sri* protests to jettison the B-C Pact, and soon thereafter anti-Tamil riots spread throughout the island for a second time (Vittachi 1958).

Some years later, Chelvanayakam and the UNP's Dudley Senanayake sought to create district councils and recognize the Tamil language in the northeast. But the very organizations that had coalesced to undermine the B-C Pact now banded together with the SLFP and again undermined the so-called Senanayake-Chelvanayakam Pact of 1965. In the 1950s and 1960s, civil society groups, as we think of them today, were limited. And in any case, the language controversy was an emotive issue that obliged most organizations to support their ethnic group's preferences. Yet it is also clear that the great influence wielded by ethnocentric associations was a major reason why ethnic accommodation and reconciliation failed. On the one hand, the political structure was such that the major Sinhalese parties had no choice but to go along with the ethnocentric groups' demands. On the other hand, accommodating these demands marginalized the Tamil minority and, even more important, consolidated illiberalism.

A Buddhist monk assassinated Bandaranaike in September 1959, and his widow, Sirimavo, took over the SLFP. It was clear that S. W. R. D. Bandaranaike had resorted to ethnic outbidding and embraced the island's ethnocentric associations for opportunistic reasons. Although he continued to show some concern for Tamil grievances even after Sinhala was made the only official language, he failed to pacify the aggrieved Tamils, because he underestimated the degree to which pro-Sinhala groups could constrain and oppose him. Mrs. Bandaranaike's two governments (1960–65; 1970–77), by contrast, marginalized the Tamils in the most insouciant fashion. In doing so, she fully heeded the demands made by various Sinhalese Buddhist associations, although these groups did not have to exert themselves unduly, given Mrs. Bandaranaike's ethnocentric proclivities. Consequently, in 1972 the SLFP-led coalition promulgated a new constitution declaring that Sri Lanka was a unitary state and that Buddhism was to have the foremost place in the country. A standardization system and a subsequent district quota system for higher education were also designed to lower the number of Tamil students gaining access to higher education. Policies were implemented to ensure that the government hired only Sinhalese for the civil service. Pro-Buddhist and pro-Sinhalese groups had made such demands since the mid-1950s, and Mrs. Bandaranaike's second government responded to them with alacrity. All this further marginalized Tamil youth. And as ethnocentric groups influenced the Sinhalese-led state, the state's subsequent discriminatory policies radicalized these young Tamils, who moved out of civil society into an increasingly restive, and soon to be violent, political society (Thangarajah 2003).

Although the constitutional structure was a major reason why ethnocentric groups in Sri Lanka were able to stoke a radical agenda and influence politicians to embrace ethnic outbidding, the Sri Lankan case also shows how civil society can cease to be effective when pitted against a powerful state apparatus prone to illiberal governance. This was best evidenced in the post-1977 era after J. R. Jayewardene's UNP came to power.

Illiberal Governance and Ethnic Conflict

Jayewardene had promised to accommodate Tamil concerns and revamp the SLFP's highly unpopular dirigiste and autarkic policies. Many Tamils therefore voted enthusiastically for the UNP, and the more than two-thirds parliamentary majority it garnered enabled Jayewardene to replace the May 1972 constitution with the August 1978 constitution. While the new constitution made Tamil a national language, it failed to accommodate Tamil demands for autonomy—despite the northern insurgency turning restive and radical.

Jayewardene's government instituted structural reforms soon after coming to power, and the regime's legitimacy became tied to the success of these reforms (DeVotta 1998). As stability became an overarching requisite, the government resorted to ham-handed practices to silence its critics and rein in the growing Tamil rebel movement. Consequently, the government passed the draconian Prevention of Terrorism Act of 1979, which merely exacerbated Tamil grievances and undermined the rule of law. The government's thugs were also given a free hand early on and retaliated against the Tamil insurgency by inciting the August 1977, June 1981, and July 1983 anti-Tamil riots. The 1983 riots killed between four hundred and two thousand Tamils, forced tens of thousands to flee Sinhalese areas, and plunged the country into ethnic conflict. Prominent among the Sinhalese who perpetrated the riots were members of the Jathika Sevaka Sangamaya—a UNP labor union headed by a notoriously anti-Tamil minister of trade and industries. The security forces too played a major role in contributing to the mayhem. The UNP goondas and the security forces, for example, torched the Jaffna Public Library, forever destroying many rare South Asian manuscripts and convincing Tamils that some Sinhalese were bent on annihilating their culture. All this contributed to the numbers mobilizing to fight for separatism (Wilson 2000). Although it is debatable whether J. R. Jayewardene approved of such violence, it is indisputable that he coddled certain government ministers who directed and supported the thugs. Jayewardene had bragged that the only thing he could not do was turn a man into a woman and vice versa—thereby implying that the government could ride roughshod over the opposition, courts, and civil society and institute its preferences—and he conveniently disregarded the UNP goondas' actions, because the climate of fear was conducive to implementing his economic plans and illiberal designs.

Civil society operates at its zenith when citizens believe that the only game in town is a liberal democracy that they can influence. Thus the more citizens believe they can trust a state's institutions, the more likely it is that civil society will thrive. In polyethnic societies, where many associations are bound to be organized along ethnic lines, all groups must feel they have access to the state's institutions and are not discriminated against when trying to influence the way institutions operate. If an ethnic group is led to believe that its interests are not being considered while other groups' interests are being accommodated—or, worse, that ethnocentric associations calling for the group's marginalization are being coddled by the state, while their own demands are disregarded—then segments among the population will begin to lose confidence in the state. Ethnic riots, especially when well organized and abetted by politicians and institutions like the police and army, similarly undermine democracy and confidence in the state (particularly among those targeted by the state). In Sri Lanka's case, a focus on the way ethnic riots were incited and the organizations involved indicates the extent to which ethnocentric groups have dominated the political landscape. Often they have done so with the government's connivance, and this suggests two points. First, it indicates the degree to which "bonding" social groups in political society have triumphed over civil society; second, it proves that civil society does not operate in a vacuum, but depends on the institutions that represent the state. Furthermore, both the Sinhala-only movement and the subsequent ethnic riots greatly influenced Tamil separatism, which successive governments have used to pursue illiberal policies.

It is instructive that most Sinhalese supported the anti-Tamil practices because their community benefited from such illiberal governance (DeVotta 2003). The ethnic outbidding that plagued the elections conducted between 1956 and 1970, which usually saw the party espousing the most ethnocentric rhetoric capture power, especially evidenced this. What the Sinhalese did not realize was that illiberalism could not be compartmentalized to target just the Tamils—indeed the influence of ethnocentric associations and the attendant illiberal policies eventually affected all Sri Lankans. This blowback was best displayed during the UNP's reign from 1977 to 1994 (DeVotta 2004).

The 1978 constitution instituted by the UNP conferred on the president almost dictatorial powers, which Jayewardene and his successor, Ranasinghe Premadasa, baldly abused. The very same goondas who had led the anti-Tamil riots were now used to threaten and assault opponents and civil society activists of all ethnic backgrounds. JSS workers, for example, who were typically transported around in government vehicles, were encouraged to beat up those protesting structural adjustment policies. The police aided or abetted the thugs or just looked away, because they too had been threatened. Notable professors and supreme court justices were likewise harassed and beaten. Civil rights activists and civil society advocates were also harassed and assaulted by government thugs or the police force. When the supreme court ruled in favor of a prominent women's rights activist who was beaten for protesting outside the U.S. Embassy, for example, Jayewardene's government paid the requisite compensation but promoted the officer responsible for the assault. The government's thugs thereafter harassed the supreme court justices and vandalized their properties. Even Buddhist monks and Catholic priests belonging to a civil society group called Pavidi Handa (Voice of the Clergy) were harassed, and leaflets they were peacefully distributing were confiscated. Despite having engaged in an unconstitutional act, the government promoted the officer responsible and paid his fine as well (Obeyesekere 1984; Tambiah 1986).

Mrs. Bandaranaike's illiberal policies had targeted the Tamils; Jayewardene's illiberal policies targeted all of civil society. The government mandated, for example, that all nongovernmental and grassroots organizations had to register with the state and set up a so-called NGO Commission, which argued that NGOs had no business criticizing the government. Government thugs were used to harass and threaten NGOs that criticized the state, and NGO leaders were pilloried as parasites and marionettes controlled by foreign puppeteers. What the UNP government ultimately proved is that the state controls the space in which civil society operates and that the latter's effectiveness can, to a significant degree, be made dependent on the state. As indicated elsewhere in this volume, this is true of Malaysia, where the state has made clear the extent to which civil society groups can agitate; it is also true of Pakistan, which, despite its well-developed civil society, has been unable to institute positive political change. Sri Lanka, however, has proved that the state can control civil society and impose its preferences violently.

In trying to distance its goondas and supporters from the 1983 anti-Tamil riots, the government falsely claimed that a Naxalite (Marxist) group was responsible for the mayhem. It then banned three leftist parties, among them the Janatha Vimukthi Peramuna. Driven underground, the JVP eventually resorted to a terror campaign that sought to topple the government. Jayewardene's successor, Ranasinghe Premadasa, retaliated by creating paramilitary groups that went on a killing spree. Their efficiency was such that between forty thousand and sixty thousand young Sinhalese died or "disappeared" between 1988 and 1990: human rights organizations categorized Sri Lanka as the country with the most "disappeared" persons during the late 1980s. Given that the leftist JVP was trying to topple the government, the state hinted that the extrajudicial killings were necessary in order to maintain democracy. None of the security personnel responsible for these murders were brought to trial. On the contrary, many were promoted. Indeed, when Amnesty International lobbied the government to incorporate a number of human rights policies, it agreed to nearly all suggestions except bringing to justice those who had committed extrajudicial killings. The upshot is that the state's autocratic practices made it impossible for civil society groups working to promote ethnic reconciliation, human rights, and liberal democracy to exert any serious influence.

Ethnic Conflict and Its Impact on Civil Society

When a new People's Alliance coalition, headed by the Bandaranaikes' daughter, Chandrika Kumaratunga, came to power in 1994, there was much optimism among the war-weary public that a peaceful settlement to the conflict was in the offing. The war had led to a proliferation of civil society groups (including foreign NGOs) that embraced the new government and prodded it to negotiate with the LTTE rebels. The rebels violated the cease-fire, however, and the war reignited. The government's new "war for peace" strategy not only led to the most savage stage of the conflict but also marginalized civil society. As noted earlier, almost all the leading civil society organizations had supported the PA during the prelude to the elections. This was perhaps understandable given that the governing UNP had committed horrendous acts of malpractice during the previous seventeen years and the PA appeared to favor a political solution to the conflict. Yet civil society groups had little to show for all their involvement—and indeed were totally discarded by the PA—when the government embraced its "war for peace" strategy. That the PA government could use civil society groups to bolster its pacific credentials but then cavalierly dump them and wage the most violent phase of the war indicates the limited influence of civil society in generating political change. Consequently, civil society groups calling for a cessation to hostilities and a peaceful resolution to the conflict were lambasted as unpatriotic. Ethnocentric groups and extremist political parties attacked those organizations encouraging the majority community to compromise with the Tamils, claiming that these organizations were living off sinecures provided by foreign NGOs. In this way, civil society organizations dependent on funds from foreign entities were branded corrupt and accused of threatening the island's sovereignty. Thus, in November 2003, an editorial in the *Island* newspaper thundered:

> Today there are far too many cooks in this peace soup. Notable are those "academics" and NGO activists, most of whom have failed to enter our Sri Lankan Universities, qualified abroad and arrived here to head heavily funded NGOs who dance to the tune of their governments or sponsors. These people under the cover of "civil society" do not represent the people—only a miniscule anglicised Colombo society. Our negotiators [who engage in peace talks] should be persons of the calibre who can tell these "elitists" to get lost with their offers of free junkets and research funding.[12]

In a different article the newspaper argued that "the 'peace process' is another attractive vehicle [through which] to make money. It is being well milked not only by the so-called civil society but also by many prestigious international organizations that are said to have boarded the gravy train."[13]

There no doubt are individuals who manipulate foreign NGOs and thereby operate in a parasitic fashion. That noted, and as the introduction to this volume indicates, foreign-funded NGOs do play a major role in strengthening civil society and in alleviating people's mundane burdens, which government often refuses to tackle. In the Sri Lankan case, the aversion to foreign-funded NGOs, especially those associated with promoting peace between the Sinhalese and Tamils, seems to be influenced by "an ideology of xenophobia" not uncommon among ethnocentric and jingoistic Sinhalese elements. As Jayadeva Uyangoda notes, the antipathy to members of foreign-funded NGOs who work as activists and scholars to bring about a peaceful resolution to the ethnic conflict

> has a strong Sinhala chauvinistic and anti-intellectual dimension. The only genuine intellectual or political activity in this stream of thinking is that which defines itself within the national—meaning narrowly and parochially understood Sinhala Buddhist—tradition. In this "tradition," to be genuine is to say that there is no ethnic question in Sri Lanka and that all minority communities should live under the hegemony of the majority community. To be genuinely intellectual is also to say that our "Sinhalese" forefathers had developed thousands of years ago all the foundations of science, technology, mathematics and engineering. To derive intellectual legitimacy for one's research work is to defend the state's right to violate human rights of the minority communities and to advocate the theory that rebellious minorities should be brought under control by military means alone. Such theories, . . . however inane they may be, are an integral part of the Sinhalese intellectual culture today. It defies dissent and difference, resists alternative points of view and analyses and brands any deviation as anti-national. Actually, fascism as an ideology is made of such stuff. (Uyangoda 1996b: 7)

If the ethnic conflict enabled the government to disregard civil society, it also found that these anti-NGO ethnocentric groups supported its intransigent "war for peace" strategy with alacrity. Some in the Buddhist clergy have been at the forefront in legitimating these groups, and certain extremist monks threatened to go door to door lobbying for war (Seneviratne 1999; Tambiah 1992). All this enabled the government to disregard civil society's demands even when government forces committed the most egregious violations. Thus, in most instances, military personnel who raped, tortured, and murdered Tamil civilians were not brought to trial even when they were identified. Instead, the officers were transferred, promoted, or given diplomatic postings.

The ethnic conflict has inadvertently led to the proliferation of arms throughout the island, contributing further to a violent society (Uyangoda 1996a). While Sri Lanka's civil society was now much more conspicuous and composed of many more local and international organizations than during any previous period (Wickramasinghe 2001), it was also unable to force the state to alter its illiberal behavior. This indicates an important point: a high density of associations does not necessarily correlate with an effective civil society.[14] Certainly, the civil war overrode all other considerations, and the Kumaratunga government adeptly used it to disregard civil society's entreaties. But civil society's limited influence in the 1980s and 1990s was also related to successive governments being more interested in staying in power than in facilitating a civil society. Despite pressure brought to bear by civil society groups, the state resorted to violence, intimidation, and fraud to rig successive elections. Consequently, almost all elections conducted under the PA government were less than free and fair. The October 2000 and December 2001 parliamentary elections—which saw fraud, intimidation, ballot-box stuffing, violence, and murder perpetrated by politicians, their gangs, and even the police and security forces—were arguably the worst the island has experienced (DeVotta 2003).

Repeated violence among rival political candidates and their campaign organizations does not ensue if civil society is wholly effective in influencing a liberal milieu. This is not to suggest that civil society organizations that are promoting "bridging" social capital are ineffective by choice. On the contrary, such groups may do their utmost to proscribe or reduce election-related violence, but they can only succeed if the state's institutions are willing to uphold the rule of law. Sri Lankan elections over the past decade indicate how ruling politicians especially have used the state apparatus to intimidate, harass, and murder opponents in order to maintain power. Organizations, including the media, that have tried to report on such activities have been threatened or attacked as well, and a politicized police force has had little choice but to assist the perpetrators or disregard the victims' complaints.[15] While media associations on the island (such as the Editors' Guild of Sri Lanka) and outside (Reporters Without Borders, the International Committee to Protect Journalists, the National Union of Journalists, the International Federation of Journalists) have lobbied forcefully, they have enjoyed little success against progovernment forces. This suggests that civil society is most effective when it has the capacity to restrain the state by utilizing constitutional checks and balances. If those controlling the levers of power are determined to attain and maintain power at any cost, however, so that violence, ballot-box stuffing, election fraud, and murder are tolerated—and there are no built-in constraints to prevent those in power from riding roughshod over their opposition—the impact of civil society will be vitiated. Indeed, this is one major reason for civil society's limited impact in Sri Lanka.

The civil war has further poisoned interethnic and intraethnic relations. In the latter instance, Sinhalese groups willing to give the Tamils autonomy clash with Sinhalese groups determined to maintain a unitary state. Many protagonists in these radical groups, it must be noted, locate themselves in different organizations, depending on which group is in the limelight. In any event, they pose a potent challenge to ensuring an effective civil society that is capable of generating democratic political change (Matthews 1988–89).

Toward Peace and Reform?

In January 2002, the newly elected United National Front (UNF) coalition and the LTTE agreed to a cease-fire, which in turn led to peace talks between the groups. Many felt that battle fatigue, a bankrupt government, the rebels' recruiting problems—and especially the post–September 11, 2001, antiterrorism campaign waged by the United States and its allies—provided a sufficient impetus for both parties to reach a comprehensive and permanent peace agreement. And civil society groups in Sri Lanka sought to ensure that this happened. What is striking, however, is the way the UNF government completely disregarded civil society in its quest for peace. Indeed, civil society was, in the main, denied a watchdog role in the peace process.[16] There could be at least three major reasons for this behavior. The first is perhaps the government's realization that peace can only be achieved provided the state comes to an understanding with the LTTE, and hence there was no reason to complicate matters by involving civil society. The second reason may have had to do with civil society's limited reach, especially among the country's rural population. The fact remains that the nationalist parties and ethnocentric groups are more adept at mobilizing the masses than civil society, and the government was understandably more worried about the former than the latter. Finally, the government may have disregarded civil society because it did not believe civil society groups had the capacity to generate significant political change. If history is a gauge, the UNF government cannot be blamed for thinking so.

Despite being sidelined, civil society groups fully realize the disastrous effect the ethnic conflict has had on democracy and on all Sri Lankans' human rights, civil liberties, and civil rights, and they are determined to deepen, broaden, and consolidate the now tenuous peace. Ethnocentric associations, however, have also mobilized to advocate hard-line policies. The December 2001 elections were seen as a vote for peace, and the results temporarily defanged the ethnocentric groups that might otherwise have pressured the government into refusing to sign the memorandum of understanding with the LTTE. Although jingoistic and ethnocentric elements in the south have consistently called for a war to the finish, the military stalemate reached between the government and the LTTE blunted their message. The nationalist political parties have joined with groups such as the University Teachers' Solidarity for a Unitary Nation, All-Ceylon Trade Union Federation, All-Ceylon Farmers' Federation, Intercompany Employees' Union, Student Movement for the Protection of the Motherland, and National Bhikkhu Front to protest against the cease-fire and peace talks. And in a sign that ethnic outbidding continues to be practiced, President Kumaratunga—despite having initiated the peace process soon after coming to power in 1994 and having proposed to turn over the northern peninsula to the LTTE for ten years as a precursor to a settlement—claimed that the prime minister and his government were giving away too much to the LTTE and thereby fostering conditions for the country's eventual dismemberment. In November 2003, just four days after the LTTE responded to the government's proposals for an interim administration with its counterproposals, the president fired three UNF ministers overseeing the Defence, Interior, and Communication Ministries, suspended parliament for two weeks, and briefly imposed a state of emergency by claiming that the UNF government was undermining the country's national security. While the LTTE's proposals were extraconstitutional and would, if adhered to, create a de facto separate state, the president's actions were deemed crassly opportunistic. As the *Financial Times* observed, "It is hard to escape the conclusion that Mrs. Kumaratunga could not bear to see her bitter rival Ranil Wickremesinghe, the prime minister, succeeding where she had failed."[17]

Chandrika Kumaratunga, who was first elected president in November 1994, was reelected to the presidency in December 1999 a few days after an LTTE suicide bomber sought to assassinate her. Despite losing the sight of one eye in the bombing, the president took her oath of office before the country soon thereafter, and the expectation was that her second six-year term—Sri Lanka's 1978 constitution disallows more than two presidential terms—would end in December 2005. However, in January 2004, Kumaratunga announced that her initial term was not due to end until November 2000, and that she had only taken the oath of office soon after her second presidential victory to pacify a grieving nation distraught over her near-death experience, that she had subsequently taken a "secret" oath of office in November 2000 before the country's pro-president chief justice, and that her second term would not end, and thus the next presidential election would not be held, until December 2006. Sri Lanka's leaders are notorious for pursuing power by any means, which is one major reason for the country's illiberal democracy and ethnic conflict, yet many considered the president's claims surrounding the secret swearing-in ceremony to be opportunistic, unprincipled, undemocratic, and corrupt.[18]

In January 2004, the president's People's Alliance joined forces with the JVP to form the United People's Freedom Alliance (UPFA). The parties disagree on many fronts—for example, the PA favors some devolution for the northeast, but the JVP adamantly opposes any arrangement that vitiates the extant unitary state structure; and the PA supports limited open market policies while the JVP opposes privatization and demands import restriction—and it was clear that the alliance was primarily designed to capture parliamentary power from the UNF as quickly as possible. Just over two weeks later, on February 7, 2004, the president sacked the UNF parliament nearly four years before its term ended and called for new elections on April 2. With the president now controlling the communications ministry, the UPFA resorted to egregious propaganda against the UNF alliance, even going so far as to have its members supervise the daily coverage in the state media.[19] The UPFA also vilified local election monitoring organizations, claiming that they were biased against the UPFA and were supported by Western governments determined to ensure the promarket UNF was victorious. This occurred even as the elections commissioner allowed these monitoring organizations and other civil society groups to get involved to ensure that the upcoming election was nonviolent, free, and fair. Indeed, these elections saw monitors in every polling booth, and this was one reason the April 2004 parliamentary elections were arguably the freest and most fair to be held in the past decade.[20] The elections commissioner's support for civil society during this campaign and the UPFA's opposition to such involvement led a leading civil society activist to argue: "Those politicians, who see the state as being vested with supreme powers, to both abuse and to coerce, would quite possibly be unhappy at this turn of events. Politicians of a Marxist and socialist orientation in particular, who believe that the state should control the commanding heights of the economy, and other areas of social life, would wish to reverse this strengthening of civil society."[21] The PA-JVP alliance won the most seats in the elections (garnering 105 out of 225 seats), and it is highly likely that the new government will ignore civil society or seek to restrict civil society's involvement, especially when dealing with the peace process.

The April 2004 elections also saw a party comprised of Buddhist monks win nine votes. Some argued that the clergy's spectacular success, despite senior clergy members and the laity strongly disapproving of monks seeking political office, was due mainly to the island's leading civil society groups pandering to Western interests and disregarding Buddhist preferences. Thus a citizen wrote to the *Island* complaining: "These days the print and electronic media are swamped by 'sermons' from many foreign-funded NGOs. . . . Their leaders have one thing in common, [which is that] all are non-Buddhists. To . . . [parody] Winston Churchill 'Never in the field of political conflict have so few (non-Buddhists) had the temerity to hector, insult, and preach to so many (Buddhists).' No wonder our bhikkus have entered the fray!"[22] And the newspaper likewise argued: "The emergence of Buddhist monks as a political party is clear proof of the absence of genuine grassroots level organisations to represent various sections of society. Its manifestation has obviously been catalysed by the anti-national cabal that is posing as the sole representative of Sri Lankan civil society."[23] Such arguments reiterate that to be pro-devolution and pro-peace and to work with foreign organizations to achieve those goals is to be anti-Buddhist and anti-national. Overcoming such perceptions is a major challenge facing Sri Lanka's civil society organizations.

The vast majority of Sri Lanka's leading civil society groups operate out of the capital, Colombo, and one reason they have hitherto appeared ineffective is because their literature and reports have, in the main, been produced mostly in English—thereby cultivating an elitist image that disconnects them from grassroots elements. Thus, *Island*, despite being the bête noire of non-Buddhist anglicized civil society groups in the capital, may have had a point when it argued:

> Foreign governments are all for helping "civil society" but in Sri Lanka, the presently recognised "civil society" is not representative of Sri Lankan society as a whole. A group of academics and NGO organisations, comprising mainly foreign graduates from the elitist minority English speaking segment of society cannot represent "civil society." Our civil society should include well established and long recognised institutions . . . whose existence appears to be unknown to the "international community" ever willing to throw their largesse, at times, for very doubtful causes.[24]

Indeed, reports put out by certain prominent Colombo-based civil society organizations convey the impression that they were written for the donor community, not the grassroots public. In an effort to counter such perceptions, the National Peace Council (NPC) is now actively engaged in training grassroots politicians in the Sinhalese south to educate them about the peace process, and the Center for Policy Alternatives (a think tank) tries hard to publish nearly all its literature in Sinhala and Tamil as well.[25] The NPC, which views itself as a facilitator network and catalyst organization, has conducted workshops with Muslims and Tamils in the Northern and Eastern Provinces. This is especially important, given that Eastern Province Muslims suspect that the government and LTTE are seeking a peace deal while disregarding their concerns. The education efforts are especially necessary because politicians in district councils outside the capital are often left uninformed about major developments pertaining to the peace process. In Matara, a predominantly Sinhalese Buddhist town about 100 miles south of Colombo, for example, only eleven out of eighty participants at an NPC workshop had read the memorandum of understanding reached between the UNP government and the LTTE. Local UNP politicians claimed they had not done so because the party had failed to send them the document.[26]

The Sarvodaya Organization has also organized meetings between villages in the north and south so that Sinhalese and Tamils can commingle, and various other groups have organized rallies to promote the peace process. A new organization called the Initiative for Political and Conflict Transformation similarly works to bring together Sinhalese and Tamil politicians from all political parties—often through meetings held abroad with representatives from the African National Congress or those responsible for negotiating the Good Friday Agreement in Northern Ireland—to educate them about devolution and power sharing.[27] These groups are assisted by other prominent organizations such as Women for Peace, the Citizens' Committee for National Harmony, the Dharmavedi Institute for Communication and Peace, the Movement for the Defense of Democratic Rights, and the Movement for Inter-Racial Justice and Equality.

In March 2004, the leader of the LTTE's eastern wing broke away from the organization, claiming that eastern Tamils and cadres were being discriminated against by the northern leadership. At the time of writing (in early April 2004), the LTTE's northern rebels had attacked their eastern counterparts in order to ensure that the movement remained monolithic. This intra-LTTE fight may weaken the organization, but it will not eradicate it. And this means that the new Sri Lankan government will need to negotiate with the group if the peace process is to continue.

Assuming that the LTTE is sincere and will settle for significant devolution, Sri Lanka will ultimately need cross-party support to reform the political structure. Civil society groups can make a crucial difference by continuing to promote religious, economic, and cultural contacts among Sinhalese, Tamils, and Muslims and educating the public, especially the Sinhalese, about the benefits of widespread devolution. If institutions are in fact restructured, they should ensure that the new political structure incorporates checks and balances to prevent a governing party from riding roughshod over the opposition and civil society. Perhaps this would allow Sri Lanka's "bridging" social groups to triumph at last over the ethnocentric and radical elements.

Notes

1. Illiberal democracy ensues when the fundamental tenets of constitutional liberalism—limited government, the rule of law, free and fair elections, and the freedoms of religion, speech, and assembly—are perverted or negated (DeVotta 2002).

2. This is not to suggest that political society is devoid of civility, although it often has seemed that way to those studying Sri Lanka over the past two decades (DeVotta 2003).

3. Many writers use "Sinhala" and "Sinhalese" interchangeably. I use "Sinhala" to refer to the language and "Sinhalese" for the people who speak it.

4. Ethnic outbidding refers to the auctionlike process whereby political elites and parties seek to outbid their opponents in guaranteeing their ethnic community's preferences. See Rabushka and Shepsle 1972; Horowitz 1985; DeVotta 2002.

5. See the special issue devoted to "Social Capital, Civil Society, and Contemporary Democracy," *American Behavioral Scientist* 40(5) (Mar.–Apr. 1997).

6. Author interview with Sathivale Balakrishnan, program director for the National Peace Council of Sri Lanka, Colombo, Jan. 9, 2003.

7. Author interview with Paikiasothy Saravanamuttu, executive director of the Center for Policy Alternatives, Colombo, Jan. 6, 2003.

8. Quoted in "Sinhalese Fade-Out with Parity Predicted," *Ceylon Daily News*, Jan. 4, 1956, 5.

9. Quoted in "Sinhalese Only—If UNP Gets 68 Seats or Less," *Ceylon Daily News*, Mar. 15, 1956, 5.

10. Here I have in mind sports clubs and boys and girls clubs associated with various high schools, choral societies, and social organizations.

11. Quoted in "Pact a Racial Division of Ceylon, Says Dudley," *Ceylon Daily News*, Aug. 12, 1957, 7.

12. "Peace Talks: Wanted Negotiators Not Appeasers," *Island*, Nov. 4, 2003 (www.island.lk/2003/11/04/editorial.html [accessed 11/4/2003]).

13. "Foreign NGOs, the LTTE etc.," *Island*, Apr. 4, 2004 (www.island.lk/2004/04/04/featur10.html [accessed 4/8/2004]).

14. As Edward Aspinall notes in Chapter 2 of this volume, this is also true of Indonesia.

15. See Waruna Karunathilaka, "Sri Lanka: Lessons in Control from the West," *Guardian Unlimited Observer*, Apr. 29, 2001 (observer.co.uk/freepress/story/0,8224,479504,00.html [accessed 3/7/2004]).

16. Author interview with Jehan Perera, director of research and media for the National Peace Council of Sri Lanka, Colombo, Dec. 23, 2002.

17. "Crisis in Colombo," *Financial Times*, Nov. 6, 2003, 12.

18. Indeed, it is questionable whether the alleged secret oath-taking ceremony took place at all.

19. The UPFA insouciantly justified this bias by claiming that the pro-UPFA coverage in

the state media was a mere counterweight to the purported partiality the private media showed the UNF.

20. The northeast, however, saw massive voting fraud, because the LTTE rigged the elections to make certain the Tamil National Alliance, which the rebels controlled, was victorious.

21. See Jehan Perera, "Unfair Attack on Election Monitors," *Daily Mirror*, Mar. 30, 2004 (www.dailymirror.lk/2004/03/30/opinion/1.asp [accessed 3/30/2004]).

22. "Vultures?" *Island*, Mar. 28, 2004 (www.island.lk/2004/03/28/featur10.html [accessed 4/10/2004]).

23. "Elections, Democracy and Civil Society," *Island*, Mar. 31, 2004 (www.island.lk/2004/03/31/editorial.html [accessed 4/10/2004]).

24. "Monitor the Monitors," *Island*, Mar. 19, 2004 (www.island.lk/2004/03/19/editorial.html [accessed 4/10/2004]).

25. Author interview with Kethesh Loganathan, head of the Conflict and Peace Analysis Unit, Center for Policy Alternatives, Colombo, Jan. 3, 2003.

26. Author interview with Sathivale Balakrishnan.

27. Author interview with Tyrol Ferdinands, managing trustee of the Initiative for Political and Conflict Transformation (INPACT), Colombo, Jan. 2, 2003. It must be noted that the former general secretary of the National Peace Council of Sri Lanka was most responsible for bringing together politicians of different persuasions. The confidential nature of these gatherings and petty rivalries led to a few members leaving the NPC and forming INPACT. Some, however, question whether a civil society group like INPACT should be involved in coordinating political gatherings.

Works Cited

Anderson, Benedict. 1991. *Imagined Communities: Reflections on the Origin and Spread of Nationalism*. 2d rev. ed. London: Verso.

Berman, Sheri. 1997. "Civil Society and the Collapse of the Weimar Republic." *World Politics* 49(3) (Apr.): 401–29.

Bond, George D. 2004. *Buddhism at Work: Community Development, Social Empowerment and the Sarvodaya Movement*. Bloomfield, Conn.: Kumarian Press.

DeVotta, Neil. 1998. "Sri Lanka's Structural Adjustment Program and Its Impact on Indo-Lanka Relations." *Asian Survey* 38(5) (May): 457–73.

———. 2001. "The Utilisation of Religio-Linguistic Identities by the Sinhalese and Bengalis: Towards a General Explanation." *Commonwealth and Comparative Politics* 39(1) (Mar.): 66–95.

———. 2002. "Illiberalism and Ethnic Conflict in Sri Lanka." *Journal of Democracy* 13(1) (Jan.): 84–98.

———. 2003. "Sri Lanka's Political Decay: Comparing the October 2000 and December 2001 Parliamentary Elections." *Commonwealth and Comparative Politics* 41(2) (July): 115–42.

———. 2004. *Blowback: Linguistic Nationalism, Institutional Decay, and Ethnic Conflict in Sri Lanka*. Stanford: Stanford University Press.

Diamond, Larry. 1994. "Rethinking Civil Society: Towards Democratic Consolidation." *Journal of Democracy* 5(3) (July): 4–17.

Encarnacion, Omar G. 2001. "Civil Society and the Consolidation of Democracy in Spain." *Political Science Quarterly* 116(1) (Spring): 53–79.

Fernando, Sunimal. 1997. *Sri Lanka Country Profile*. Colombo: INASIA.

Foley, Michael W., and Bob Edwards. 1996. "The Paradox of Civil Society." *Journal of Democracy* 7(3) (July): 38–52.

———. 1997. "Escape from Politics? Social Theory and the Social Capital Debate." *American Behavioral Scientist* 40(5) (Mar./Apr.): 550–61.

Fomunyoh, Christopher. 2001. "Democratization in Fits and Starts." *Journal of Democracy* 12(3) (July): 37–50.

Fukuyama, Francis. 2001. "Social Capital, Civil Society, and Development." *Third World Quarterly* 22(1) (Feb.): 7–20.

Gambetta, Diego. 1993. *The Sicilian Mafia: The Business of Private Protection.* Cambridge, Mass.: Harvard University Press.

Hardin, Russell. 1995. *One for All: The Logic of Group Conflict.* Princeton: Princeton University Press.

Hellmann-Rajanayagam, Dagmar. 1994. *The Tamil Tigers: Armed Struggle for Identity.* Stuttgart: Franz Steiner Verlag.

Horowitz, Donald. 1985. *Ethnic Groups in Conflict.* Berkeley: University of California Press.

Huntington, Samuel P. 1968. *Political Order in Changing Societies.* New Haven: Yale University Press.

———. 1991. *The Third Wave: Democratization in the Late Twentieth Century.* Norman: University of Oklahoma Press.

Jennings, Ivor. 1950. *Nationalism and Political Development in Ceylon (3): The Background of Self Government.* New York: Institute of Pacific Relations.

———. 1954. "Politics in Ceylon Since 1952." *Pacific Affairs* 27(4) (Dec.): 338–52.

Levi, Margaret. 1996. "Social and Unsocial Capital: A Review Essay of Robert Putnam's *Making Democracy Work.*" *Politics and Society* 24(1) (Mar.): 45–55.

Matthews, Bruce. 1988–89. "Sinhala Cultural and Buddhist Patriotic Organizations in Contemporary Sri Lanka." *Pacific Affairs* 61(4) (Winter): 620–32.

Nodia, Ghia. 2000. "Nurturing Nationalism." *Journal of Democracy* 11(4) (Oct.): 169–73.

Obeyesekere, Gananath. 1984. "The Origins and Institutionalisation of Political Violence." In James Manor, ed., *Sri Lanka in Change and Crisis.* London: Croom Helm.

Phadnis, Urmila. 1979. "Ethnicity and Nation-Building in South Asia: A Case Study of Sri Lanka." *India Quarterly* 35(3) (July–Sept.): 329–50.

Pharr, Susan J. 2003. "Targeting by an Activist State: Japan as a Civil Society Model." In Frank J. Schwartz and Susan J. Pharr, eds., *The State of Civil Society in Japan.* Cambridge: Cambridge University Press.

Putnam, Robert D. 2000. *Bowling Alone: The Collapse and Revival of American Community.* New York: Simon & Schuster.

Rabushka, Alvin, and Kenneth A. Shepsle. 1972. *Politics in Plural Societies: A Theory of Democratic Instability.* Columbus: Merrill.

Russell, Jane. 1982a. *Communal Politics under the Donoughmore Constitution, 1931–47. Ceylon Historical Journal* 26. Dehiwala: Tisara Prakasakayo.

———. 1982b. "The Dance of the Turkey Cock—The Jaffna Boycott of 1931." *Ceylon Journal of Historical and Social Studies* 8(1): 47–67.

———. 1982c. "Language, Education, and Nationalism—The Language Debate of 1944." *Ceylon Journal of Historical and Social Studies* 8(2): 38–64.

Saravanamuttu, Paikiasothy. 1998. "Sri Lanka: Civil Society, the Nation, and the State-Building Challenge." In Alison Van Rooy, ed., *Civil Society and the Aid Industry: The Politics and Promise.* London: Earthscan.

Schedler, Andreas. 1998. "What Is Democratic Consolidation?" *Journal of Democracy* 9(2) (Apr.): 91–107.

Seneviratne, H. L. 1999. *The Work of Kings: The New Buddhism in Sri Lanka*. Chicago: University of Chicago Press.

Sri Lanka Department of Census and Statistics. 1996. *Statistical Pocket Book of the Democratic Socialist Republic of Sri Lanka*. Colombo: Department of Census and Statistics.

Tambiah, Stanley J. 1986. *Sri Lanka: Ethnic Fratricide and the Dismantling of Democracy*. Chicago: University of Chicago Press.

———. 1992. *Buddhism Betrayed? Religion, Politics, and Violence in Sri Lanka*. Chicago: University of Chicago Press.

Thangarajah, Yuvi. 2003. "Ethnicization of the Devolution Debate and the Militarization of Civil Society in North-Eastern Sri Lanka." In Markus Mayer, Darini Rajasingham-Senanayake, and Yuvi Thangarajah, eds., *Building Local Capacities for Peace: Rethinking Conflict and Development in Sri Lanka*. New Delhi: Macmillan India.

Uyangoda, Jayadeva. 1996a. "Militarization, Violent State, Violent Society: Sri Lanka." In Kumar Rupesinghe and Khawar Mumtaz, eds., *Internal Conflicts in South Asia*. London: Sage.

———. 1996b. "NGOs, Hate Politics and Questions of Democracy." *Pravada* 4(5–6): 6–9.

Vittachi, Tarzie. 1958. *Emergency '58: The Story of the Ceylon Race Riots*. London: André Deutsch.

Wickramasinghe, Nira. 2001. *Civil Society in Sri Lanka: New Circles of Power*. New Delhi: Sage.

Wilson, A. Jeyaratnam. 2000. *Sri Lankan Tamil Nationalism: Its Origins and Development in the Nineteenth and Twentieth Centuries*. Vancouver: University of British Columbia Press.

CHAPTER TEN

Singapore

Engagement and Autonomy Within the Political Status Quo

SUZAINA KADIR

Despite its small size and unique characteristics,[1] Singapore continues to attract scholarly attention. Political economists have been fascinated at the speed and effectiveness of the country's industrialization (Doner and Hawes 1995). Within a short span of time, Singapore has been able to transform itself from a regional trading post into Southeast Asia's premier financial services hub. In the process, the city-state has earned a place as the region's most developed country, with per capita income levels reaching U.S.$33,000 in 1997. There have been other accolades, as well, including the title of being perhaps Asia's most globalized city and least corrupt country. The success of Singapore's industrialization has led to a parallel fascination with the country's political development. Scholars consistently point out a paradox: despite Singapore's level of economic growth and a concomitant expansion of the middle class, its social forces have failed to exert much pressure for greater openness and democratic change (Lam 1999; Rodan 1996). In the context of Third Wave democratization that has swept Asia, this paradox becomes amplified. As other chapters in this volume show, various countries in Asia have undergone democratic transitions. Political analysts contend that Asia's Third Wave can be linked to an emerging middle class and an increasingly robust civil society.[2] Yet Singapore, the most developed country in Southeast Asia, remains a highly centralized, one-party-dominant, quasi-democracy (Lam Peng Er 1999; Mutalib 2000; Mauzy and Milne 2002).

Scholars point to a range of factors in explaining the anomaly. Some have argued that the excessive, if not repressive, mechanisms of the state prevent any serious challenge (Rodan 1996). Others point to a complex dynamic between state-led industrialization and the institutionalization of hegemonic control over Singapore society as explanatory variables (Chua 1994; Jesudason 1999). More recently, scholars have highlighted the intervening role of elites in understanding the persistence of Singapore's semidemocratic status. William Case (2001), for example, argues that the political status quo can be linked to the decision of the strongman Lee Kuan Yew and his chosen successor, Goh Chok Tong, to limit civil liberties and manage change in order to perpetuate development. The acquiescence of highly educated, middle-class Singaporeans is in turn attributed to a mixture of corporatist controls, legitimating mentalities, coercion, and the government's success in fulfilling the careerist and consumerist longings of the population.

This chapter acknowledges the paradox that exists when a country achieves such a rapid rate of industrialization yet experiences no pressure for greater openness and democratic change. But unlike some studies of Singapore, this chapter questions the extent to which this immunity has remained consistent. It challenges any overt assumption that the state is consistently protected from civil society. Instead, I make the case for greater care in conceptualizing the dynamics of interaction between civil society and the state in Singapore. While the constraints on civil society remain strong, the interaction between the government and civil society is growing increasingly complex. Rather than questioning the extent to which civil society in Singapore has the organizational space to transform the regime, I contend that we should be focusing on the *processes* of interaction and how they *define*, *bound*, or *transform* the two sides. Only then can we truly understand the prospects for political change in Singapore.

The chapter presents several case studies reflecting these interaction dynamics. These cases not only show that civil society is far from being a cohesive ideological force but also point out at least two distinct forms of interaction between civil society and the state in Singapore. Certain groups, as we shall see, have been able to confront and contest the state on issues pertaining to perceived public interest. Through a strategy of consistent *interest advocacy*, these groups have been able to successfully negotiate for space vis-à-vis the state. These groups also took advantage of close linkages with political society. In contrast, other groups discover that the government is unwilling to accommodate any direct challenge to its political dominance or its core values. When it comes to *identity politics*, for example, civil society groups face even tougher constraints and very little space for maneuverability. This raises interesting questions about the complexities involved in state-civil society interaction when identity issues like religion and race are being contested. The state's inflexibility in allowing for this space may not necessarily be a negative development in the push for democratic change in the long run. As the chapters on Sri Lanka and Pakistan show, autonomous space for civil society groups can be and is used for uncivil political action. Religious and ethnic clashes undermine the democratic process. Hence, state management of civil society space may be positive for ensuring democratic practice in the long run.

In the final analysis, I argue, the greater complexity of interactions between civil society and the state needs to be appreciated in its own right. Only then can we consider their impact on state, society, and political change. The constraints facing civil society in Singapore are real. Yet the state is not totally insulated from civil society in Singapore. The evolving interactions between the two sectors continuously push the state to face up to its own promises and positions and, I believe, can prevent an absolute turnabout on concessions already granted. Similarly, civil society adapts to and learns in its efforts to build autonomous democratic space in Singapore. The chapter clearly shows that these interactions do not, however, guarantee democratic change in Singapore. In some instances, civil society activity helps to sustain the status quo or, worse still, provides an avenue for the state to reinforce its authoritarian tendencies.

Delineating State and Civil Society

The difficulty in locating the boundaries of state, society, and civil society in Singapore reflects the complexities that prevail in the theoretical debate at large. It is important to make sense of the Singapore state, however, and conceptualize what we mean when we begin to address civil society—especially important when the state and the government appear to dominate almost every aspect of Singapore society, even at times intervening directly in the private realm of the family.[3] Because the state seems so pervasive, we must delineate its boundaries carefully. Only then can we understand the different identities and shifting forms of civil society in Singapore.

The Singapore State

Much of the literature on Singapore has focused on the state and the dominant political party. In the 1970s, Chan Heng Chee described Singapore as an "administrative state," where power rests in the hands of the bureaucracy and politicians are sidelined (Chan 1975). Those studying the newly industrializing economies classified Singapore as a "developmental state," where economic growth and development are almost entirely directed by the government (Haggard 1990). Still others have used terms like *corporatist state* to describe the extent to which the state manages its relations with society via a complex mechanism of top-down corporatist linkages (Rodan 1993; Lam 1999; Case 2001). Generally, though, there is agreement that the Singapore state is highly autonomous of other social formations.

The character of the Singapore state, however, cannot be understood separately from the dominant People's Action Party (PAP), which has been in power since the country was declared independent in 1965. Until the 1980s, PAP enjoyed an absolute majority in parliament. In the 2001 general elections, it won 75 percent of the votes, and it now occupies eighty-two of the eighty-four seats in parliament. For this reason, Singapore has been consistently described as having a one-party-dominant system of government. This label has led to blurred boundaries between state and political society. Indeed, one can say that while the state has been able to preserve its autonomy vis-à-vis other social forces, it has in fact been captured by the party (Khong 1995; Mauzy and Milne 2002). "In Singapore, the core of the state might be perceived as the party-cabinet-government complex. In orbit circling it are the two types of subordinate organizations. One consists of the civil servants and the government-linked companies (GLCs) . . . linked to the PAP. The second represents the forces of labor and capital," Diane Mauzy and R. S. Milne write (2002: 27). S. Rajaratnam, a former senior minister and one of PAP's founding members, describes the party's capture of the state: "It did not take long before we established a close link between us and the civil service . . . after the first two elections, the PAP really became an administration. It was no longer a party. And the civil service became part of that" (Khong 1995: 28). The links between the bureaucracy, the military, and the party are tight. Several PAP cabinet ministers are former military officers, for example, including the current deputy prime minister, Lee Hsien Loong, and the minister for education, Rear Admiral Teo Chee Hean.

The conflation of party and state is central to an understanding of state-society relations in Singapore. It has allowed for the establishment of corporatist-style linkages in which a powerful party has been able to control other societal actors—ensuring state autonomy but also guaranteeing a party stronghold in government. Through control of various state agencies, PAP has made it extremely difficult for opposition parties to gain ground. In 1988, for example, the PAP government instituted a plan called the Group Representative Constituencies (GRC) in electoral politics. The GRC scheme requires political parties to offer a package of six candidates together, one of which must represent an ethnic minority. With the opposition already facing problems recruiting people, the GRC scheme further weakened its capacity to challenge PAP. The opposition parties were reduced to challenging PAP in only a few select constituencies, thereby guaranteeing a PAP victory on nomination day.

The development and expansion of the Singapore state have been the result of historical circumstances as well as subsequent policies adopted by PAP. Faced with tough challenges in 1965, the government focused inward by concentrating on export-oriented manufacturing and attracting foreign investment as a means of increasing state capacity. To this end, government leaders worked on insulating the state from social forces and instilling discipline into the bureaucracy. Government leaders also sought to rein in labor unions and control the workforce. Hence, in the early 1970s, the government established the National Trades Union Congress (NTUC), an umbrella organization, to represent nearly every legitimate trade union in Singapore.[4] The NTUC proved to be a valuable resource that enabled the state to control errant labor unions and ensure acceptance of economic policies deemed necessary for the country's industrialization drive.

The Singapore state also made use of established mechanisms to extend its control over public space. The Societies Act; the Internal Security Act (ISA), which allowed for detention without trial of persons acting in any manner prejudicial to the security of Singapore or the maintenance of public order; and the Penal Code, which made it an offense to engage in unauthorized public demonstrations—all were legal instruments left behind by the British. As PAP consolidated its control over government, it was able to use such instruments to expand state power and redraw the boundary of political space in Singapore. In so doing, the party undercut the power of opposition parties and insulated itself from pressure from other societal forces, including civil society.

The extensive reach of the state is unlikely to diminish any time soon. Not only do the various mechanisms of state control remain in place, but new measures have been introduced to strengthen the state's grip on public space. The Newspaper and Printing Presses Act ensures substantial state control over the media in Singapore, thereby controlling, if not stifling, public debate. In addition, there is the Singapore Broadcasting Authority (SBA), which monitors the media and the arts, as well as the Public Entertainment and Licensing Unit (PELU), which grants the licenses needed for performances and public displays.[5] Such measures constrict the space within which organizations can maneuver independently of the state.

Corporate linkages are also intact. The umbrella trade union organization, NTUC, maintains organic links with various associations in society and effectively prevents them from becoming pressure groups. The Consumer's Association of Singapore (CASE), for example, was set up by the government in 1971 to look into consumer needs, but it is very closely tied to NTUC. Indeed, the officers of the association, including the current president and executive director, are seconded from NTUC. The recent public dispute between the volunteers and management of CASE reaffirms the state's level of control over potential pressure groups in Singapore.[6] When the volunteers sought an expanded advocacy role for the association, they were rebuked by CASE's president and deputy director. Frustrated and clearly unhappy at the constraints imposed on CASE, the volunteers resigned en masse.

Civil Society in Singapore

How do we locate civil society in an environment where the state has such an extensive reach? When trying to make sense of civil society activism in Singapore, we must always bear in mind the nature of the Singapore state. In a state where the autonomous space is severely curtailed by the ruling party, the extent to which civil society can effect political change is curtailed as well.

Scholars on Singapore seldom agree on where to locate civil society. Some take civil society to include all organizations that are nongovernmental or nonprofit in nature (Chua 2000). While political parties are defined as those in the realm of political society, entities that do not compete for power fall into the realm of civil society. This approach can be problematic, though, because there is little to distinguish between interest groups, government-sponsored organizations, civic voluntary activity, and autonomous social formations. Chua Beng Huat suggests drawing a careful distinction between groups that seek cooperation or even incorporation with the state and those that push for alternative constructions of social and political space in Singapore (ibid.). Because the reach of the Singapore state involves hegemonic ideological control, he argues, the delineation of an autonomous public space is critical in order for civil society to check the pervasive capacities of the state. Not all organizations in Singapore are pushing for greater autonomy vis-à-vis the state. Certain groups, in fact, help to entrench the state's hegemonic ideological control. Organizations that are either state-initiated or state-funded will most likely seek cooperation with the state. After all, their very existence hinges on state sponsorship and support.

To help delineate the boundaries of civil society in Singapore, a brief survey of its historical development may be useful. Inasmuch as it sought to address basic welfare needs of the city's various communities, civil society in colonial Singapore has been described as "vibrant" (Mauzy and Milne 2002). Malays, for example, had established self-help groups to aid impoverished Malays. The Chinese community had their various trade organizations and clan associations that were active in building temples and managing burial grounds. They also set up hospitals and clinics and built schools. While many of these associations were independent of the colonial state, some were closely linked to it, such as the Straits Chinese Association (ibid.).

When PAP came to power, it began to occupy much of the space originally occupied by these associations. It created its own community organizations and took over voluntary activity. It sought control over the various associations via the Registrar of Societies and monopolized many of their traditional functions. As PAP captured the state, it sought to control autonomous associations via the established legal mechanisms and would employ the coercive arm of the state when necessary. The Singapore police embarked on a successful campaign to rein in triads and secret societies, for example, many of which had important links to the various clan associations. Nevertheless, the state allowed the continued presence of functional organizations like the Chinese Chamber of Commerce, the National Council of Churches, various mosque and temple associations, and the Society for the Prevention of Cruelty to Animals, to name a few. The autonomy of these groups was curtailed, however, notably by regulations stipulated in the Societies Act, and civil society space shrank considerably.

Drawing on Alagappa's conceptualizations in Chapter 1, civil society in this chapter is defined as networks of voluntary organizations, residing in a space between family and the state, formed by citizens to pursue mutual interests or beliefs. Some level of autonomy vis-à-vis the state is therefore an essential component of civil society. The debate is over the nature and extent of this autonomous space, especially in Singapore, where the state is so pervasive.

Organizations that are directly promoted or established by the state are excluded here. Grassroots organizations such as the community centers (CC), citizen consultative committees (CCC), and resident committees (RC), for example, cannot be considered civil society organizations. These organizations act as channels of communication between the government and the people, provide welfare services and social services, and create opportunities for people to participate and interact directly with politicians. In addition, these organizations answer directly to the prime minister's office (PMO). In many ways, these parapolitical institutions perform key functions of political parties, and many aim at generating public support for government policies. Resident Committees (RC), for example, serve as an important avenue through which the PAP government can generate support for its campaigns and policies.

Similarly, ethnic self-help organizations such as Mendaki, Sinda, and CDAC (self-help organizations set up by the government in 1980 to raise the educational and living standards of the Malay, Indian, and Chinese communities respectively) are also excluded from analysis. These organizations, established by the state to look into the educational and welfare needs of the ethnic communities, depend on government support and financial resources and are overseen by a cabinet minister or member of parliament. Ethnic self-help groups do not enjoy any level of meaningful autonomy vis-à-vis the state. Such organizations tell us more about the state's corporatist linkages with society than about civil society activism in negotiations with the state.

But even if we exclude these groups, there are still a substantial number of organizations directed at volunteerism and civic participation in Singapore. A host of voluntary welfare organizations (VWOs) cater to specific cultural and social needs of the population. These nonprofit organizations provide basic social and welfare services to the elderly, youth, and the disabled. Examples include the Boys' Brigade, the Association for the Visually Handicapped, the Siglap Mosque Youth Council, and the Muhammadiyah Association.

Herein lies the problem of delineating the boundaries between civil society and the state in Singapore. Although these organizations are nonprofit and voluntary, the ties between such groups and the state remain close. These voluntary organizations are subsumed under a larger rubric that is state-initiated. Although the ties between these VWOs and the state are informal rather than formal, these organizations are likely to seek cooperation with and even incorporation into the state. All come under the management of the National Council of Social Services (NCSS), for example, which in turn answers to the minister of community development and sports (MCDS), a PAP politician.

VWOs reflect the complexity of roles that "civil society" can play vis-à-vis the state. Tisa Ng, former president of the Association of Women for Action and Research (AWARE), notes that these VWOs are an important partner in ensuring effective governance in Singapore.[7] She points out that they are increasingly at the forefront of providing basic welfare services to the public. Government grants for the homeless and elderly are channeled through VWOs, based on population size within the respective homes, for example. According to Ng, VWOs allow the government to look good without turning it into a welfare state. The VWO system does not lock the government into providing welfare services for everyone and at all times, but instead provides services flexibly, based on need, with effective control in the state's hands. In turn, the VWOs give the impression of a burgeoning nonprofit and voluntary sector in Singapore, much akin to growing civil society space in many parts of the world.

The Singapore government has, in fact, been championing VWOs as a critical component of "civic society" and an example of the synergistic partnership between civil society and the government.[8] Yet while we can include VWOs as part of civil society to the extent that they generate social trust among citizens, we must remember that such organizations do not necessarily engage with the state for the purposes of advocacy or extending the public space for citizens vis-à-vis the government in power. I have chosen to exclude any in-depth analysis of these VWOs in this chapter for precisely these reasons.

Some groups in Singapore do push for distance from the PAP government. These groups have an agenda that differs from the one propagated by PAP. They have never sought to turn away from the state but have instead opted to challenge and negotiate with the state when the opportunity arises. They enjoy some level of autonomy vis-à-vis the state and seek some leverage in policymaking. Such groups include women's organizations like AWARE, environmental groups like the Nature Society, AIDS advocacy groups like Action for AIDS, and minority rights/ethnic/religious groups like the Association of Malay Muslim Professionals (AMP). Then there are groups that guard their independence fiercely. Much like the groups in the preceding category, groups such as the Singapore Islamic Scholars and Religious Teachers Association (PERGAS) enjoy relative autonomy from the state and have consistently sought to maintain their distance. Their mode of engagement vis-à-vis the state is therefore different. Rather than pursuing the role of a policy advocacy group, these civil society organizations seek autonomous space vis-à-vis the state as a focal point of interaction. They simply want to be allowed the space to realize their vision of a just society based on religious ideals. They do not seek to establish leverage vis-à-vis the state but rather to expand public space for identity groups.

Recently, civil society activists have resorted to ad hoc gatherings as a means of strengthening informal networks within the restricted public space in Singapore. Their objective is not so much advocacy as strengthening ties between civil society groups in Singapore. There is no interaction with the government, and in so doing, these activists guard their distance from the state quite seriously. Instead, their activities center on enriching the public domain and developing citizenship networks. The Working Committee Network (TWC) I and II are examples. TWC I evolved because individual civil society activists recognized that they were working in isolation from one another. They therefore sought to build an informal network of civil society activism. No government official or politician was invited. Formed in November 1998, TWC I involved ad hoc gatherings of activists to discuss a range of issues, including feminism and the role of foreigners in Singapore. They sought to keep it informal so they could bypass registration under the Societies Act. In March 2003, a similar ad hoc grouping called TWC II was announced.[9] Led by a nominated member of parliament, Bretha Mathi, the group focused on the issue of mistreatment of maids in Singapore. Like its predecessor, TWC II's activities were ad hoc and informal, focusing on exhibits and small get-togethers in public housing estates to discuss the issue of maid abuse.

Additionally, cyberspace is becoming an important means for providing information and promoting diverse opinions. Despite government efforts, there is no mechanism for the state to completely control cyberspace. Although website owners have had some run-ins with government officials, cyberspace is a new arena for civil society that remains for the most part beyond the state's reach. These websites represent an emerging dynamic within the civil society space in Singapore (Ho, Baber, and Khondker 2002). Some may even argue that, although very small and nascent, they constitute the true civil society space. For example, Gillian Koh argues that the expansion of Internet technology in Singapore has opened up new spaces and possibilities for activism, alternate community building, and even resistance (Koh and Ling 2000). Additionally, K. C. Ho, Zaheer Baber, and Habibul Khondker recently documented the various types of Internet sites available in Singapore that push for alternative lifestyles, which, they argue, point to "the potential for the rise of a public sphere" free of state control and with the capability of resisting the dominant state agenda (Ho, Baber, and Khondker 2002).

In sum, then, the boundaries of civil society in Singapore remain a matter of debate. I argue here for the exclusion of groups with strong links to the state. VWOs sit on the margins precisely for this reason. The rest of the chapter focuses on groups with relative autonomy vis-à-vis the state. This autonomy stems from the extent to which these groups are financially independent of the government, as well as the degree to which they contest the state's agenda. Their mode of engagement and level of autonomy differ, however. Some strategize as pressure groups; others seek autonomy and suggest a form of identity politics vis-à-vis the state. Some employ a confrontational style; others are far more cooperative. Meanwhile, cyberspace represents a new open space for Singaporeans. Ultimately, this chapter points to how "civil society" in Singapore must be conceived of, not so much as organizations that seek to change or are successful in changing the government, but as citizenship and public space vis-à-vis the state. Only then can we understand the dynamics of interaction and negotiation between government and civil society and its impact on political change and the political status quo in Singapore.

Singapore's "Civic Society" Project

In 1991, the minister for information and the arts, Brigadier General George Yeo, addressed the issue of civil society in Singapore for the first time. Identifying the stratum of institutions between family and state as constituting "a core sphere of public activity" necessary for good governance, he described the PAP government as a "banyan tree" whose pervasive and overpowering reach into society had prevented the development of civil institutions crucial for Singapore's future.[10] The speech was in line with the promise by Prime Minister Goh Chok Tong that his administration was committed to a more open and consultative style of governance.

Goh Chok Tong took over at the helm of the Singapore government in 1990. Almost immediately he differentiated his administration from that of his predecessor, Lee Kuan Yew, by promising that the PAP government would work in greater consultation with its citizens and encourage more participation on matters pertaining to local governance. He was also responding to PAP's declining percentage of votes in the 1980s. The PAP monopoly of parliament was broken in the 1981 by-election, and by the 1984 general elections, PAP's share of the total votes had dropped by about 12.6 percent (Rodan 2002). The PAP leadership attributed their loss of votes to the emerging middle class, whom they perceived to be better educated and seeking greater participation in government. Hence, when Goh Chok Tong took over, the PAP government made a concerted effort to establish channels of communication. The government-initiated Feedback Unit, for example, was given a new boost to promote communication between the state and its citizens, while grassroots organizations were encouraged to comment on government proposals.[11] The government spoke openly about its intent to relax its grip on society and allow more space for the growth of what it called "civic society." It therefore sought to incorporate these new middle-class "interests."

In 1999, a new government manifesto called "Singapore 21" was launched. The Singapore 21 process spanned at least a year and involved numerous discussions among various subcommittees on issues pertaining to governance such as possible expansion of public space, citizenship, and censorship. The synergies of both state and society were emphasized in the group's final publication, although the report omitted certain politically sensitive ideas, such as changing the rules of the game to make electoral competition fairer.[12] Instead, the manifesto highlighted "active citizenship" and "volunteerism" as the cornerstones of "civic society" in Singapore. Civil society groups welcomed the government's statement that it was time to "trim the banyan tree." Many interpreted this to mean there would be more space for them vis-à-vis the state. Consequently, in the period immediately after General Yeo's speech, the activities of civil society groups like the Association of Women for Action and Research (AWARE) and the Nature Society (Singapore) became more pronounced.

For a variety of reasons, the Goh administration proved to be an opportunity for groups in civil society geared to interest advocacy, particularly those focused on the environment, health, and public safety. In the following pages, I highlight several major modes of interaction between the state and civil society groups, as well as the different contexts in which civil society operates in Singapore.

Advocacy Politics, Civil Society, and the State in Singapore: AWARE and the Nature Society (Singapore)

The Association of Women for Action and Research (AWARE) and the Nature Society Singapore (NSS) are two civil society associations that have maintained their autonomy and have successfully engaged in advocacy politics vis-à-vis the Singapore state. AWARE consistently advocates gender equality and persists in contesting the state's patriarchal framework. NSS focuses exclusively on protecting the environment. Both organizations have taken advantage of the opportunities for consultation and negotiation offered by the Goh administration and became more active in the 1980s and 1990s. Yet NSS is far more successful than AWARE. A careful look at the dynamics of the interaction between these two associations and the state reveals the persistent constraints facing civil society in Singapore and suggests the specific conditions under which civil society can achieve tangible results. The cases of both AWARE and NSS show, however, that there is room for civil society to engage the state, and in so doing, try to broaden the limited space for civil society to maneuver and grow in Singapore. In other words, although it continues to establish the boundaries within which civil society can maneuver, the state does not remain immune to pressures, including external ones. Civil society can also make use of the sometimes porous boundaries in Singapore—such as between civil society and political society—to broaden space for maneuverability. There are thus both opportunities and constraints for civil society engaged in advocacy politics in Singapore.

AWARE

The Association of Women for Action and Research (AWARE) is one among some forty women's organizations in Singapore.[13] AWARE was established in 1985 by a group of professional women wishing to take up the issue of sexism and gender equality across race and class lines. Its membership is estimated to be around seven hundred. AWARE's website states that its aim is to "achieve total gender equality so that women can develop their full potential [and] participate fully in both public and private life."[14] It seeks to do this by conducting research, publishing books, and organizing talks to raise awareness of women's rights. AWARE also monitors and highlight sexism in the public arena. The funding for AWARE comes mainly from members' subscriptions and donations from nonprofit organizations such as the Lee Foundation and the Shaw Foundation. AWARE does not accept direct funding from the government.[15] This policy reflects AWARE's decision to keep its distance from the state. This level of autonomy may have helped the organization to consistently engage in campaigns that have specifically targeted government policies that discriminate against women.

Since its formation, AWARE has undertaken a range of actions that have contested the state's conceptualization of Singapore society, which AWARE sees as patriarchal. In 1993, Prime Minister Goh openly acknowledged this patriarchalism when he asserted "minor areas where women are not accorded equal treatment should be expected so long as the welfare of women and of the family is protected. I would not regard them as pockets of discrimination or blemishes but as traditional areas of differential treatment" (Chan 2000). The government reiterated this point in its report to the Beijing Conference in 1995 and in its formal reservations about the Convention on the Elimination of All Forms of Discrimination Against Women (CEDAW), adopted in 1979 by the UN General Assembly. This patriarchalist framework explains various policies that discriminate against women, including the state's refusal to grant equal benefits to men and women working in the civil service and its refusal to grant automatic citizenship to foreign spouses of Singaporean women.

AWARE's activities focus on campaigns against domestic violence, raising awareness about rape, calling for constitutional amendments to the Women's Charter, and urging gender equality when it comes to national service and civil service benefits. The frequency and extent of these campaigns not only reflect AWARE's determination to fight for gender equality but, more important, point to the space for maneuvering that has opened up for the organization since Goh Chok Tong took over. They also reflect AWARE's strategy of concentrating on women's issues in a nonpartisan and nonconfrontational way.

Not all of AWARE's campaigns have been successful. The president of AWARE, Tisa Ng, recently complained of yet another government rejection of its calls to end unequal benefits for female civil servants.[16] Nor has it managed to get effective domestic violence legislation passed in parliament, even though its former president, Kanwaljit Soin, was a nominated member of parliament. Nevertheless, the interaction dynamics between AWARE and the government over this bill and other proposals are worthy of analysis. During her tenure as a nominated member of parliament, Soin introduced a private member's bill on domestic violence and AWARE began a concerted campaign to draw public support for the measure.[17] The group organized a public dialogue on family violence, sold "Stop Family Violence" T-shirts and bumper stickers, and sent letters to the press on the issue. Although the bill was eventually defeated in parliament, the campaign did generate substantial public support. Soin was also invited to sit on the select committee looking into amendments to the Women's Charter and succeeded in including a new section, titled "Protection of Family," allowing victims of domestic violence to apply for a protection order.

AWARE's strategy of interaction with the government over domestic violence can be described as successful insofar as it called attention to the problem of domestic violence and raised questions about the Women's Charter. By making careful use of an opportunity for organizations to have a spokesperson in parliament, AWARE and its issue gained substantial notice. In this sense, one could say that the PAP government was forced to acknowledge the problem of domestic violence. AWARE has been careful, as well, not to take a partisan view or adopt a strategy that could be construed as challenging the PAP government politically—a policy that has ensured the organization's survival. Having a member sit in parliament, albeit without voting powers, served AWARE well in enabling the organization to bring the matter to the government's attention without formally entering the "political" arena—there was no need for alignment with any single political party.

Recently, AWARE submitted a strongly worded and carefully researched set of proposals to the Remaking Singapore Committee (RSC), established in early 2002 to come up with proposals on how Singapore society and politics might be recast. Members of the public as well as civil society groups were encouraged to submit their proposals and suggestions to RSC. AWARE has consistently seized on such opportunities to advocate on behalf of gender equality in Singapore. Its proposal was aptly titled "Voices from the Other Half" and suggested a range of policy recommendations—allowing women to perform national service, removing the quota for women in medical school, supporting gender equality in the Women's Charter, providing equal benefits for female civil servants—all reflecting AWARE's persistent advocacy of gender equality in Singapore. In June 2002, the government announced its decision to review the quota of women entrants to medical school, a move Tisa Ng attributes in part to AWARE's persistence in advocating the issue to policymakers.

One can certainly not predict whether all these proposals will result in significant policy shifts. The point is that AWARE has been able to carve out a space for itself despite the constraints of the Singapore state. It does so by undertaking campaigns that do not overtly challenge PAP's dominance, yet it persistently questions the broad framework of state values. Under Prime Minister Goh's administration, there has been greater leeway for groups like AWARE to push their agenda and even to question state policies. The state's decision to allow for nominated members of parliament from civil society to debate issues of "public concern" has also been an opportunity for groups like AWARE to engage the state and protect their space. As a result of this space and through its interactions with the state, AWARE has been able to draw public attention to the issues it champions. In so doing, it has been able to maintain its leverage, however small, vis-à-vis the state.

Another Case of Advocacy: The Nature Society

Of the many nongovernmental organizations in Singapore, the Nature Society (NSS) has been the most successful in its negotiations with the state. At least three major development proposals were reconsidered, and eventually shelved, after extended NSS campaigns and open contestation with the state. Furthermore, the government has portrayed these three cases as evidence of its open, consultative style, and of scope for citizen advocacy in Singapore. In all likelihood, both of these claims are true. Despite the complaints of civil society activists that the Lower Pierce Reservoir and Chek Jawa decisions are being hijacked by the state to bolster its legitimacy, the cases do point to tangible results from interactions with the government.[18] But this success has only been possible because the Nature Society was able to show how the environment is a public issue of concern to all. It did not challenge the ruling party openly or embarrass government agencies. Moreover the autonomy, commitment, and passion of NSS volunteers lent it a credibility that many other civil society groups in Singapore lack. It has therefore been able to gain the trust of citizens as well as of the government.

The prominence of the Nature Society is a new phenomenon. Although the group traces its origin to 1954, membership grew significantly only in the late 1980s. Between 1954 and 1990, the group was known as the Malayan Nature Society and served as the Singapore branch of the parent organization. In 1991, the group severed its ties with its Malaysian counterpart and changed its name to the Nature Society (Singapore). As membership grew in the late 1980s, the organization's activities increased in quantity and scope. By 1999, membership stood at just over two thousand, most of them professionals, executives, senior administrators, and academics. According to the NSS constitution, its objectives include promoting awareness of nature and the environment, encouraging environmental conservation, and initiating and supporting research projects relating to the study and conservation of nature and the environment.[19]

Like AWARE, the Nature Society has been careful to keep its distance from the government. Its activities are based solely on the voluntary effort of its members, and funding is predominantly from donations and membership dues. The group's activities range from scientific and recreational activities like bird-watching and nature tours to organizing educational seminars for schoolchildren and the general public. The group also publishes a newsletter, *Nature News*, and its own quarterly magazine, *Nature Watch*. Among the research projects undertaken by NSS are the *Master Plan for the Conservation of Nature in Singapore* (published in 1990), the *Proposed Golf Course at Lower Pierce Reservoir: An Environmental Impact Assessment* (1999), and the *State of the Singapore Environment* (1999). Since the late 1980s, the group has been an active participant in discussion forums and events organized by the Housing and Development Board of Singapore (HDB), the Ministry of Environment, grassroots organizations, schools, polytechnics, and other institutions. In the latest round of discussions concerning the "Singapore Green Plan 2012," for example, NSS submitted its comments to the Ministry of Environment in January 2002 and held a forum on the plan in March of that year. Moreover, NSS writes regularly to the local media regarding the environment.

The prominence of NSS can be attributed to the commitment of its members. There can be little doubt that this group of volunteers is passionately involved in efforts to conserve the environment in Singapore. The number of activities organized and the amount of research produced by NSS are a reflection of this dedication. Additionally, the society has been able to make its case because it has presented its arguments in a manner understood by a very pragmatic government. Its arguments are well supported by scientific research and championed by the public; its reports are hardly "political"; and the society has proved itself willing to compromise for the sake of public interest. This, of course, raises interesting questions for civil society groups that are unable to engage with the state in a similarly rational scientific manner. It also points to serious constraints for groups that do not have the research capacity to build their case against the state. Civil society activists acknowledge their difficulty in matching the government's extensive research capacity. They point out that the state often harnesses the entire civil service when building its case on any particular policy. Despite this reality, groups like NSS have been able to engage with the government.

At the same time, NSS's strategy and tactics might not have succeeded if there had been no political opportunity to engage with the state. When the administration of Prime Minister Goh Chok Tong promised greater consultation and openness on policy matters, NSS took advantage of this, entering into consultations with the government and campaigning vigorously for its suggestions to be taken seriously. In light of the government's promise, as well as the changing global context, in which environmental issues could not be ignored, the state was under pressure to consider the NSS proposals. But NSS's strategy of allowing the state to backtrack without embarrassment proved to be a winning option for both: in the process, civil society space is expanded, while the government gains legitimacy.

Three examples testify to the complex dynamics of NSS-government interactions in Singapore: the plans for an industrial park at Sungei Buloh; the proposal to develop golf courses at the Lower Pierce Reservoir; and the intended development at Tanjung Chek Jawa. All three cases reflect a degree of success on the part of the group, which elicited a positive response from the state and even gained policy reversals of development plans. The first case involved government plans to build an agro-technology park on eighty-seven hectares of mangrove swamp in Sungei Buloh. NSS, however, wanted the area set aside for a bird sanctuary. Members had been asked to look at initial plans and site surveys and convey their opinions to the consultants hired for the project. In 1990, NSS submitted its *Master Plan for the Conservation of Nature in Singapore* to the government, suggesting that Sungei Buloh be set aside as a bird sanctuary. When the government's Green Plan was passed in the same year, it incorporated many recommendations of NSS's master plan, including those pertaining to Sungei Buloh. This was viewed as a victory for NSS.

The second case occurred some years later and involved a more direct contest between NSS and the government. In the early 1990s, the Public Utilities Board (PUB) drew up a proposal to develop two eighteen-hole golf courses on the northern banks of the Lower Pierce Reservoir and hired a consultant to conduct an independent study of the environmental impact.[20] Subsequently, the proposal was circulated internally among a few government agencies, including the Urban Redevelopment Authority (URA), the Ministry of National Development (MND), and the National Parks Board. When the Nature Society chanced on the proposal by accident, NSS volunteers worried that the project would have a negative impact on the environment at the reservoir and decided to undertake their own environmental assessment on plant and animal life in the vicinity. Their report was published in 1999.

NSS then launched a campaign to dissuade the government from moving forward with the project, sending letters to the MND and to the Forum page of the *Straits Times*.[21] When the *Straits Times* published a comparison of the two assessment studies,[22] this led to heated exchanges between NSS and the ministry in the local media, with both parties reluctant to negotiate. In the end, Professor Tommy Koh stepped in and suggested trying to find an amicable solution. A series of discussions was organized, and the Nature Society tried to marshal public support on the matter.[23] The report of the government-sponsored study, finalized in August 1992, argued that the golf courses could be built without unduly affecting the environment. Nevertheless, the PUB reduced the size of the project and suggested including forest corridors to facilitate movement of animals and birds. After consideration by the Urban Redevelopment Authority, the PUB proposal was rejected, and it did not pursue the matter further.

Government officials were somewhat embarrassed at the direct challenge they had to confront during the episode and believed it was unnecessary (Tan Tay Cheong 2000: 16–17). Convinced that the project would have been defeated as it went through the normal decision-making channels of the government, they did not think the environmentalists had anything to worry about. NSS, however, was not convinced that internal mechanisms were a sufficient guarantee and thought that the process should have been open to the public. But the wrangling over the Lower Pierce Reservoir, it must be noted, took place when Singapore was preparing to attend the UN Conference on Environment and Development in Rio. Various ministries were in the midst of preparing the first Singapore Green Plan, which was to be presented at the summit, and the government was anxious to establish its green credentials. Moreover, Professor Koh was chairing the preparatory committee for the conference. Clearly, then, the government was under some pressure to diffuse the controversy and was somewhat taken aback when NSS came out so strongly on the matter. For NSS, though, it was a rare opportunity. It seized upon it, pushed the issue, and by going public put even more pressure on the government.

Although the government may simply have acceded temporarily for the purpose of saving face at the Earth Summit, its apparent change of heart was a boost not only to NSS in particular but to civil society in general. It showed that there was room for maneuvering and contestation—even when done publicly. It was at the very least a symbolic win for NSS and for civil society space in Singapore. At the same time, having changed course with regard to the Lower Pierce Reservoir, the government would find it far more difficult in the future to renege without exposing itself to accusations of insincerity. This is not to say that the PAP government has never backtracked on a promise. But this incident certainly makes it more difficult for the government, while claiming to be consultative, to continue pushing its agenda forward without the participation of its citizens.

The third case involved a similar confrontation between NSS, environmentalists, and the government. The dispute occurred as the government prepared for the tenth anniversary of the Earth Summit. This time the issue concerned the intended development of Tanjung Chek Jawa, a beach on the small island of Pulau Ubin. The campaign to save Chek Jawa began in May 2001, when the Urban Redevelopment Authority held a public forum to discuss land use in Singapore. At this forum, a public plea was made by Joseph Lai to save the beach from the government's proposed reclamation.[24] At the time, NSS members were not even aware of the beach. After learning about the case, however, NSS members and other environmentalists worked in concert to conduct a site survey, take photographs, and prepare a report on preserving the area. They also decided to organize public field trips to the area over two weekends in September and October 2001. The response was overwhelming—about a thousand people visited the area. NSS also started writing to the *Straits Times* Forum page to publicize the cause.

Government officials suggested patience, pointing out that they were trying to sort out the various responses they had received from the public. In December 2001,

NSS and other environmentalists submitted their reports to the government on the impact of reclamation at Chek Jawa. They were then invited to a closed-door meeting with the national development minister, Mah Bow Tan, during which it was announced that the government had decided against reclaiming Chek Jawa. Environmentalists quickly applauded the government's move, pointing out that public involvement had been crucial in getting the government to change its mind.[25] The *Straits Times* hailed the move as "a day the government showed itself open to the merits of persuasive argument from its citizens."[26]

Civil society activists, however, are simply not uniformly pleased with the outcome. Some think the government is merely using Chek Jawa to pacify the public in a case in which it would have conceded anyway—especially in light of its preparations to attend the Earth Summit in June 2002. Hence they accuse the government of hijacking the efforts of civil society groups in order to bolster its own image and increase its legitimacy. To be fair, there were other clashes between the government and environmentalists that produced little concession. Although conservationists fought against the plan to demolish the National Library, for example, after much debate the government went ahead and razed it to make way for a downtown university campus. But the success of the NSS and other environmentalist groups in saving Chek Jawa does point to a space for contestation between civil society and the state—as long as it is enabling for both. Chek Jawa was a success because a political opportunity opened up for environmentalists, namely, that the government was once again under pressure to present its green credentials to the international community while facing fairly strong public reaction at home against the reclamation project. Ultimately, the process reaffirmed space for negotiation and made it harder for the government to renege on its promises without risking a loss of legitimacy and of face.

The Nature Society (Singapore) is another example of a civil society organization that has been able to build up its leverage vis-à-vis the state. It has been able to do so for a host of reasons including external pressure. NSS maintains its autonomy while at the same time continuing to work closely with the state on matters pertaining to the environment. Its leverage is possible precisely because of its advocacy role vis-à-vis the state. In the current political climate of engagement and consultation, such a mode of interaction serves groups like AWARE and NSS well. These examples show that interaction between the state and civil society is more dynamic than previously thought. The state is not entirely immune to pressures from civil society groups and does engage with them, even if only to legitimize its own position. This allows for civil society space, however minor, and a strategic interaction that can produce results, albeit not necessarily producing political change in the direction of greater democracy.

Identity Politics, Civil Society, and the State: AMP and PERGAS

While groups like AWARE and the NSS engage in advocacy politics vis-à-vis the state, others focus more specifically on identity issues. These include clan associations and literary and cultural groups, as well as religious associations. The Association of Malay Muslim Professionals (AMP) and Islamic Scholars Association (PERGAS), which practice what I call identity politics, focusing specifically on the Malay Muslim minority in Singapore, are two such organizations. The modes of interaction of these two associations vis-à-vis the state differ somewhat. AMP was far more willing to engage and, at times, openly confront the state on a spate of issues, including the issue of Malay Muslim political leadership and religious expression. The autonomy of AMP vis-à-vis the state is also open to question.

PERGAS, on the other hand, appeared initially unwilling to confront the state openly. It sought instead to protect the autonomy accorded to Islamic schools and religious teachers, while maintaining a position of autonomy and distance from the state. However, in the face of perceived threats of state interference in Islamic education, PERGAS indicated its willingness to confront the government directly, and its autonomy enabled it to do so effectively. The government's reaction reflected discomfort at engagement in identity politics and a quiet determination to maintain its position on the issue of Malay Muslim minorities. Efforts by these groups to embrace the language of civil society nevertheless proved futile in the end.

The Association of Malay Muslim Professionals (AMP)

The Association of Malay Muslim Professionals (AMP) was established in 1990 to provide leadership and advise the government on matters pertaining to the Malay Muslim community. More than five hundred Malay Muslim professionals, businesspeople, and executives attended the inaugural conference and declared their intent to form a "nonpartisan, community-oriented, civil society organization" that would focus on uplifting the Malay community to new heights. They also criticized government-linked Malay organizations, like Mendaki, and government-picked Malay members of parliament, pointing out that "many Malay MPs had failed to lead the Malay community and move it to be on par with the other communities."[27] In response, the government challenged the professionals to set up an alternative organization and offered to help it with dollar-for-dollar funding up to a million dollars. The result was AMP. At the inaugural conference, these leaders presented a set of proposals outlining their aims for the Malay community in the next decade. Their vision, they declared, was "to build a model Muslim community."[28]

The case of AMP offers insights into the constraints facing civil society space in Singapore. Unlike the two groups discussed earlier, AWARE and NSS, AMP speaks to a particular ethno-religious group in Singapore: the Malay Muslim community.

Malay Muslims comprise, at best, 14 percent of Singapore's population, but in the region as a whole, they are the majority ethnic community, so the PAP government has always felt a need to treat them with care.[29] For example, a minister was appointed specifically to handle Muslim affairs, who works with other agencies dealing with Malay Muslims, such as Mendaki and MUIS, the government Islamic body.

When AMP was formed, it was thought to be an alternative space for Malay Muslims vis-à-vis the government-sponsored Mendaki. However, it duplicated many of Mendaki's activities, especially its education, economic, and social welfare programs. AMP was careful to differentiate itself from Mendaki, however, by highlighting its identity as a nonpartisan and nongovernmental organization. Nonetheless, the fact remained that AMP was linked to the government in terms of its funding and basic infrastructure. For much of the 1980s, many of AMP's programs were similar to those of Mendaki, and the association was fairly dependent on government funding of its major projects.

Toward the end of the 1990s, however, AMP began to project its role as a critical voice within the Malay Muslim community. Increasingly, it began to champion the concerns of the Malay community. It also sought more space for Muslims to practice their religion. AMP revisited the issue of Malay leadership at its ten-year anniversary national convention in late 2000, saying that it wanted to concentrate its efforts on three issues: the economic and educational position of Malays vis-à-vis the rest of the population; the creation of a model Muslim society; and the formation of an alternative leadership for Malay Muslim Singaporeans that would be truly representative of Malay concerns and sentiments.[30] This was a direct challenge to PAP's style of leadership. It was also a strong criticism of the Malay PAP members of parliament. AMP had therefore departed sharply from its traditional focus on education and welfare programs. The participants at the convention also raised issues of racial and religious discrimination, especially with regard to education and the workplace. Some said the state was deliberately preventing Muslims from practicing their religion by not allowing Muslim women to wear the headscarf in public schools. Prime Minister Goh Chok Tong, guest of honor at this convention, reacted sharply to the proposals. It was very well for AMP to deal with socioeconomic programs for the Malay Muslim community, he said, but not acceptable for AMP to venture into "political areas" such as the establishment of an alternative leadership for the Malays. The PAP government rallied quickly around their Malay MPs, and the leadership issued strong warnings that AMP was trespassing into "the political arena," thereby risking deregistration.[31]

Shortly after its national convention, AMP found that its plans to move into a bigger and more centrally located headquarters were no longer feasible, since it was unable to secure a lease on the building. Then the government announced a review of its funding procedures. Funding for nongovernment or welfare organizations like AMP would now be disbursed on a case-by-case basis, it concluded, and proposals would have to be submitted for approval before funding would be released (rather than being given to the organizations in one lump sum). By some, this was seen as a clear sign that AMP had fallen out of favor with the government. With its funding affected by the government decision, AMP projects were in question. The association was forced to begin a massive funding drive to sustain its programs. To this date, it is unclear whether AMP can sustain itself in the long run. Additionally, its longtime president was recently appointed president of the Islamic Religious Council (MUIS), a move many interpreted as state co-optation of the association.

In the process of engaging with the state, AMP had chosen to question the government's position with regard to the Malay Muslim community. Its proposals on alternative leadership had directly challenged PAP's political dominance. And in highlighting the possibility of a marginalization of the Malay community, AMP was questioning PAP's commitment to building a meritocratic society with equal opportunities for all. In the face of such direct challenges to the government, the state's response was quick and harsh. The AMP example points to the existing constraints facing civil society in Singapore. Civil society groups that engage in identity politics or overtly challenge the dominant party are dealt with harshly and without compromise.

PERGAS

The government's reaction to AMP must be seen in the sociopolitical context of the time. Several developments within the Malay Muslim community proved troubling for the regime. For example, at a National Day rally in August 1999, Prime Minister Goh Chok Tong raised concerns about the increasing number of Malay Muslim parents sending their children to the semiautonomous Islamic religious schools known as madrasahs.[32] The government considered this trend worrisome, since there might be problems integrating these students back into the mainstream after their graduation. Moreover, it said there were high rates of madrasah dropouts. The response from the Malay Muslim community was initially mixed. Some did not regard the issue of madrasah education as a problem. For others, the government's points were suspect.[33] These skeptics came up with their own figures to dispute the government findings. Questioning the government's conclusion that the dropout rate was high, they also argued that graduates of these madrasahs often went on to further studies in universities in Malaysia, Indonesia, and the Middle East.[34]

Even as the madrasah issue was being debated, the Ministry of Education (MOE) proposed the introduction of compulsory education in Singapore.[35] Although the proposal had been under discussion prior to the speech on madrasah education, Malay Muslims reacted with skepticism when the announcement was made. Many saw it as a deliberate government move to undermine and eventually eradicate madrasah education in Singapore. These concerns were evident in Internet discussions. Cyber Ummah, a website of the Singapore Islamic Scholars and Religious Teachers Association (PERGAS), was especially vocal on the subject and quickly became a platform of support for madrasah education and for harsh criticism of the government and the PAP Malay MPs, who were described as government stooges unwilling to fight for Malay interests.[36] Finally, in April 2000, PERGAS released a press statement announcing that the organization was rejecting the government proposal for compulsory education in its present form if it meant the end of schooling in primary madrasahs.[37] In the same statement, PERGAS warned that the government's move would be seen by the Malay Muslim community as "another sinister" motive to eradicate madrasah education in Singapore. They warned that PERGAS members and the Muslim community would not be silenced on matters pertaining to their religion.[38]

PERGAS was registered in 1957 as an Islamic teachers' association acting as an informal body overseeing general Islamic education in Singapore. Its members are mainly teachers at the Islamic schools, who are called "asatizahs." Membership is voluntary and funding comes largely from public donations (*zakat*). PERGAS is also eligible for subsidized grants from the Ministry of Community Development and Sports (MCDS) for its training and educational programs. For much of its history, PERGAS focused almost exclusively on religious classes and discussion forums for Malay Muslims. Engagement with the state on community issues was minimal. More recently, however, PERGAS changed its name to better reflect its vision of "continuing the tradition of the Prophet through Islamic propagation."[39] PERGAS's leaders now emphasize that the organization must represent the interests of both teachers and Islamic scholars (*ulama*), and it has begun to recruit the latter.[40] The organization's newly stated objectives include "producing a religious elite" able to "uphold and expand Islam and Islamic ideals" and lead Malay Muslims to excel.[41]

The organization's recent activism reflects a shift in PERGAS's otherwise detached style of interaction vis-à-vis the Singapore government. PAP Malay MPs were taken by surprise when PERGAS launched its open protest against compulsory education. At this stage, it is unclear whether this newfound activism is a result of developments within the Malay Muslim community at large—such as a deepening level of religiosity among Muslims in Singapore. Nonetheless, there is evidence that the younger leaders of PERGAS are keen to transform the association into an advocacy group on behalf of Muslims in Singapore along the lines of AWARE and NSS. Of late, PERGAS has openly challenged the prevailing government stance on various issues affecting the Muslim community. Perhaps triggered by the need to protect autonomous Islamic education in Singapore following the government's decision to introduce compulsory education, PERGAS has issued public statements calling on the government to allow young girls to wear the headscarf to public schools, questioned the government's support for U.S.-led war in Iraq, and registered its dissatisfaction with the local media's portrayal of Muslims. In August 2003, PERGAS held its first Islamic scholars' conference and issued a statement refuting press reports that it advocated a secular outlook for Singaporean Muslims. It reaffirmed that all Muslims were obliged to uphold their religious principles and practices. In light of the overt attempts by state agencies, such as the Islamic Religious Council (MUIS), to encourage Muslims to adapt to the secular environment in Singapore, PERGAS's position is a direct challenge.

PERGAS's mode of interaction vis-à-vis the government can be differentiated from that of groups like AWARE. Rather than seeking leverage, PERGAS aims primarily at protecting the autonomy enjoyed by Islamic scholars and reserved for Islamic education in Singapore.[42] In seeking to maintain a traditionally autonomous space of the Muslim minority from intrusion by the state, therefore, PERGAS does not seek leverage over the government. PERGAS is not familiar with advocacy roles in national-level policies. Instead, it seeks disengagement to the extent of wanting to be left alone to pursue its vision of an Islamic society within the framework of a multireligious and multiracial Singapore. However, in doing so, PERGAS looks poised to engage more fully in identity politics vis-à-vis the state. Its prior position of independence, as compared to AMP for example, puts the association in a stronger place to challenge the moral authority of the state. In arguing against compulsory education, PERGAS leaders stated such a policy would lead to a closure of madrasahs and would mean that "the rights of Muslims to channel our children in accordance with our community's needs would be taken away."[43] PERGAS wanted the education and lifestyles of Malay Muslims to be allowed to proceed without further interference from the state. PERGAS sought distance from the state, not initially close engagement. In so doing, PERGAS seeks an expansion of the space for Muslims and, perhaps, a rejection of the current consultative framework offered by the Goh Chok Tong administration. Exactly one month after the PERGAS press statement, the prime minister announced that madrasahs would be exempt from compulsory education on the condition that they prepare their students to sit for national examinations at the end of six years.[44]

An interesting comparison can be made between PERGAS and AMP. Although PERGAS opted to confront the state directly (and through the Internet) over the madrasah issue, it framed the debate in religious terms and held the state accountable for its promises to respect the rights of minority communities. PERGAS emphasized its autonomy and called for the state to respect whatever space was allowed for religious communities. Facing a potential public dispute with the Muslim community, the state backed down, even if its retreat was meant to be temporary. PERGAS was able to do this because it was relatively autonomous and had strong community support. AMP, by contrast, had become far too intimate with the state to begin with, and it subsequently had problems establishing its legitimacy. Even though it had defined itself in contrast to Mendaki, AMP had worked closely with the state on matters pertaining to the education and social welfare needs of the community, and when it sought to broaden its advocacy role on behalf of the community, it was unable to mobilize based on its religious credentials. Fearing a state backlash, AMP backed down. In the end, AMP ended up with restricted space, while PERGAS's credibility increased among the Malay Muslim population. Although this may put PERGAS in a better position to challenge the state, the issue of identity politics raises serious questions for democratic development in the long run. Certainly, the state will not be predisposed to accommodate identity politics in any overt way, and further resistance may create opportunities for the state to retaliate with authoritarian measures, including depriving organizations such as PERGAS of autonomous space.

Evading the State: Cyberspace

Cyberspace remains the hardest space for the government to control. More and more Singaporeans are using the Internet in place of the government-controlled media and have been turning to it for alternative sources of information. The Internet has also become a haven for Singaporeans wanting to question government policies, poke fun at the political system, and suggest alternative lifestyles. The website Talkingcock.com presents satirical news reports, for example, while Mr.Brown.com ridicules the national education classes conducted in Singapore schools. Then there are websites and eforums that advocate alternative lifestyles, including SiGNeL (Singapore Gay NewsList) and People Like Us website, which promote gay/lesbian lifestyles, and The Club, which serves as a "social club" for "people in Singapore who enjoy sex." These websites have served as an effective medium to resist mainstream views advanced by the state (Ho, Baber, and Khondker 2002: 141).

Civil society activists also make use of cyberspace to broaden political discussion. The Think Center, founded by James Gomez, used its website to present alternative news reports and commentaries on censorship and other regulatory mechanisms of the state. The center also used the Internet to issue invitations to campaigns, forums, and rallies—thereby circumventing the requirement of an entertainment license. In 2001, however, the Think Center was designated a political organization by the government, which opened it to several restrictions, including making it subject to a law on foreign donations.[45]

Before the Think Center was established, another group of civil society activists had been using the Internet to encourage open political discussion. Around 1995, the Singapore Internet Community (SINTERCOM) was established with the aim of providing space for open and fair political discussions about Singapore. SINTERCOM opened chat rooms and discussion sites as well as a "Not-Published-by *Straits Times*" forum page. After a few years, its founder Tan Chong Kee was asked by the Singapore Broadcasting Authority (SBA) to register it as a "political site." In compliance, Tan submitted the Internet articles for vetting and then asked for guidelines on what was permitted on the Internet. When Tan complained that SBA refused to clarify the meanings of "objectionable content,"[46] SBA retorted that it did not pre-censor any objectionable material on the Internet. According to Tan, this policy would have exposed SINTERCOM to potential lawsuits, and it was simply impossible to monitor everything that would be circulated.

Frustrated and faced with a dead end, Tan decided to shut SINTERCOM down in April 2002.[47] The case of SINTERCOM reflected the state's apprehensions about political debate and indicated that the PAP government still had a very narrow conceptualization of political space in Singapore. Certainly, the Internet was the hardest space for the government to restrict. Recently, Senior Minister Lee Kuan Yew lamented in an interview with the *International Herald Tribune* that globalization and the Internet had made greater openness in society inevitable. The state was simply unable to monitor these spaces.[48] After a few months, SINTERCOM was revived under two new (and anonymous) editors. Again SBA requested that the new SINTERCOM register as a "political site." The editors responded that they would not register the site and challenged the SBA to block the site if it chose to. To this day, SINTERCOM (which subsequently changed its name to NEW SINTERCOM) has not been blocked.[49] There are also two virtual notice boards on Singapore in cyberspace. One is called the SG-Daily and the other is the Singapore Forum. SBA does not regulate either.

Cyberspace has also been used by the Malay Muslim community to discuss government policies when serious debate has been heavily circumscribed. During the height of the madrasah and compulsory education furor, websites like Cyber Ummah became active spaces in which to challenge the government and the Malay MPs. Later, attention shifted to another Muslim-oriented website, Fateha.com, set up and managed by a group of young Malay professionals. The leader of the group, Zulfikar, describes the website as a "monitor of government policies and pronouncements" affecting the Malay Muslim community.[50] (Fearing persecution by the Singapore authorities, Zulfikar left for Australia in 2002, and since then the website Fateha.com has not been accessible online.)

These examples show that while the state seems to want to manage cyberspace, especially in the realm of political debate, it has not been successful. Meanwhile, SBA continues to refine its regulations pertaining to the Internet, clearly reflecting its impulse to manage political discussions in cyberspace. Moreover, the issue of the Internet is being reviewed by the Censorship Review Committee (CRC) established by the Ministry of Information and the Arts (MITA).[51] Realistically, however, regulation of cyberspace is not easy. Compounding this difficulty is the fact that the state has been at the forefront of pushing Singapore society toward a highly globalized status. Despite its desire to control public space, the PAP government must therefore ultimately respond to the pressures of globalization—creating an opportunity for civil society groups to try to expand the space available to them. Indeed, some analysts think it is here, in this arena of cyberspace and the Internet, that the push for greater public space and public accountability can be most effective.

Prospects for Political Change

The report card on civil society in Singapore is clearly mixed. As we have seen, civil society in Singapore is hardly a cohesive force in society. While some groups guard their autonomous space vis-à-vis the government, there are hundreds of volunteer and welfare associations that function in partnership with the government and help in many ways to legitimize the regime. Even relatively autonomous groups are pursuing different modes of engagement with the state. While some focus on maintaining pressure on specific policies, others simply want to maintain autonomy from state intrusion. At the end of the day, civil society in Singapore must walk a fine line within a severely constricted space.

The Goh administration has lived up to its promise of becoming a more open and consultative government. It has established more channels of communication between the citizenry and the state. It has also increased resources, including funds, for what it calls "civic society." This policy has differentiated the Goh administration from its predecessor. But it also presents a challenge for civil society in Singapore. Civil society activists already complain about a culture of dependence in Singapore. They fear that civil society groups may be co-opted by the state in the current framework.[52] Despite efforts to "trim the banyan tree," the government remains unwilling to fully expand public space for civil society groups. To be fair, of course, the Goh administration never intended a radical redefinition of political space in Singapore. It was careful to use the term "civic society" rather than "civil society"—reflecting a careful interpretation of a "synergy" in its relationship with civil society groups (Koh and Ling 2000). The state understands the need to engage with civil society but wants to do so at a pace and scope that it finds agreeable. This means keeping control of the political space while loosening its grip in the realm of social and other welfare activities. This policy remains a fundamental constraint that undermines civil society's ability to bring about political change in Singapore.

But we have also seen the different modes of interaction and extent of autonomous space available for groups to maneuver vis-à-vis the state. In some instances, civil society groups have been able to get the state to acknowledge their agenda and even respond to it. Here the group's autonomous character and strategies become important. Groups that maintain their distance have been more successful in questioning the state. Groups that embrace a public issue and seek to assert consistent pressure on certain government policies via interest advocacy have been more successful than those that advocate particularistic (ethnic/religious) issues—what I describe here as identity politics. Some groups seek primarily to preserve their autonomy and focus on protecting their turf against an intrusive state. Rather than seeking leverage vis-à-vis the state, these groups, such as PERGAS, focus on maintaining autonomous space to conduct their activities, including the right of madrasahs to continue to operate in Singapore. PERGAS's religious credentials, coupled with its focus on minority rights, have enabled a degree of success in its dealings with the state. This success may only be temporary, but it raises an important distinction between groups that focus on advocacy and leverage versus those that seek primarily to defend autonomous space. Yet PERGAS also looks poised to shift its strategy toward advocacy, but in the realm of identity, which might be detrimental to its autonomy and maneuverability vis-à-vis the state.

In the final analysis, civil society in Singapore has played various roles—including helping to maintain the political status quo. Civil society activism in Singapore does not involve confronting the state or undermining it. On one level, it involves pressing the state to address broad citizenship concerns such as the environment and gender equality; on another, it involves protecting whatever autonomous space there is from further intrusion by the state. Civil society in Singapore cannot bring about fundamental or even substantial political change. It can only urge the state to trim the banyan tree further, thereby opening up space and light for civil society to thrive.

Certainly, the cases in this chapter show the importance of exploiting political opportunities when they arise. At the very least, such opportunities allow some room for civil society groups to push, however gradually, for greater space vis-à-vis the state in Singapore. And this brings us back to the issue of leadership. In 2001, Prime Minister Goh Chok Tong announced that he would transfer power to the "third generation" of PAP leaders by 2007. Will this transition present another opportunity for civil society groups in Singapore? Some activists worry that the new administration may take a tougher stance, restricting space for maneuver. In all likelihood, however, Singapore politics will sway between "politics as usual" and a "return to politics." In other words, PAP is unlikely to tighten control to the levels seen in the Lee Kuan Yew era. Changes in society and in the international arena make such a move difficult. Civil society groups must therefore be able to weigh this opportunity carefully. After all, a new administration in Singapore needs legitimation just as much as the Goh administration did in 1990. In this environment, civil society groups must walk a fine line between seeking an expansion of public space and protecting themselves from being co-opted or eradicated. And in Singapore, this is a tightrope walk.

Notes

1. Singapore is best described as a city-state—its main island is barely 30 miles across and its population amounts to roughly 3.5 million people. Compared to its immediate neighbors, Malaysia and Indonesia, Singapore's physical size and demography make the country appear

minuscule. Indonesia, for example, comprises thousands of islands and has a population that is at least fifty times larger. Singapore also lacks basic natural resources, buying the bulk of its water and gas supplies from Malaysia and Indonesia respectively. Singapore lacks an agricultural hinterland, too, thereby denying it a farmer population and the rice and plantation cultures so vital to the rest of Southeast Asia. Finally, the city-state stands out in the region for being the only country with an ethnic Chinese majority. These specifics factor heavily into the nature and development of the Singapore state.

2. Scholars disagree on the underlying causes of the democratic transitions in Asia. While some argue for the importance of the middle class, others point to state weaknesses that allowed the Asian financial crisis to undermine the authoritarian structures. Despite the disagreements, most acknowledge that civil society did play a role in the region's Third Wave democratization.

3. This conceptualization has led to descriptions of Singapore as a "nanny state" where the government intervenes actively in all aspects of life in defense of "the nation's interests." This system is reflected in the barrage of campaigns targeting private behavior such as family size, dating, marriage, and romance. The government conducts "Romancing Singapore" campaigns to encourage its citizens to be more romantic (see www.romancingsingapore.com/home/main.asp [accessed 3/7/2004]).

4. Of the eighty-two registered trade unions, only nine are not affiliated with NTUC (including the Airline Pilots' Association, Reuters Local Employees' Union, Film Industrial Employees' Union, and Singapore Tobacco Employees' Union).

5. Recently, the PELU banned a display of dolls to mark Children's Day organized by a civil society group called the Think Center. See *Straits Times*, Oct. 1, 2002.

6. The volunteers chose to resign en masse in the face of charges by the president and deputy director of CASE that they were dabbling in issues beyond their purview. See *Straits Times*, Oct. 7, 2002.

7. Interview with Tisa Ng, president of AWARE, Singapore, Mar. 11, 2003.

8. Parliamentary Debates Singapore, vol. 70, no. 15 (May 19, 1999).

9. *Straits Times*, Mar. 9, 2003.

10. See General Yeo's speech reported in *Straits Times*, Apr. 11, 1991.

11. For example, community development councils (CDCs) were formed to decentralize the management of welfare and other social programs—seen as a means to encourage more participation and interaction among citizens and parliamentarians.

12. Discussion with Tan Chi Chiu, president of the Singapore International Foundation (SIF), who had been involved in the Singapore 21 process. I had several opportunities to discuss these issues with Dr. Tan, since both of us sit on the Remaking Committee (RSC), another committee along the lines of Singapore 21. I am grateful to Dr. Tan and Tan Chong Kee for making available their time, despite busy schedules.

13. These forty women's organizations form a loose federation within the Singapore Council of Women's Organizations (SCWO). See Lim 2000.

14. See www.aware.org.sg (accessed 3/7/2004).

15. Interview with Tisa Ng, Singapore, Mar. 11, 2003.

16. Ibid.

17. *Straits Times*, Oct. 27 and Nov. 2, 1995.

18. Several civil society activists have voiced their concern that the government is taking credit for Chek Jawa and using it to its advantage. There is some truth in these allegations, since the government has repeatedly referred to its decision on Chek Jawa as an example of

its efforts to save the environment. Environmentalists fear that the government will change its mind when its economic calculations change.

19. See the Nature Society (Singapore) Constitution, Article 3.1. See also NSS's website, www.post1.com/home/naturesingapore (accessed 3/7/2004).

20. The Public Utilities Board then had statutory authority to regulate and manage Singapore's reservoirs, rivers, waterways, drainage systems, and water treatment facilities.

21. NSS sent its first letter to the minister in charge of national development, S. Dhanabalan, in July 1991. The minister replied that MND had deferred its decision on the golf courses until a government-sponsored study on the environmental impact was completed. S. Dhanabalan wrote that his chief planner would be unlikely to approve the project if the study indicated extensive damage to the nature reserve.

22. *Straits Times*, May 10, 1992.

23. Ibid.

24. In 1992, the government had approved plans to reclaim the beach and other parts of Pulau Ubin to create "reserve land" to be used for military training. Reclamation was to start in January 2002. Tanjung Chek Jawa embraces a collection of six distinct habitats, including mangrove, sandy beach, sand and mud flats, a coral bubble, and a small island.

25. *Straits Times*, Jan. 2, 2002.

26. Ibid.

27. *Straits Times*, Oct. 3, 1990.

28. See the AMP website, www.amp.org.sg (accessed 3/7/2004).

29. Malay Muslim Singaporeans make up about 14 percent of the population, while Chinese constitute about 76 percent. Malay Muslims are a more significant minority in Singapore than these figures would suggest, however, because Singapore's immediate neighbors, Indonesia and Malaysia, are Malay Muslim–majority countries: 88 percent of Indonesians and over 54 percent of Malaysians are Muslim.

30. Proceedings of the Second National Convention of Singapore Malay/Muslim Professionals, "Vision 2010: Setting the Community Agenda in 21st-Century Singapore," Nov. 4–5, 2000.

31. *Straits Times*, Nov. 7, 2000.

32. *Straits Times*, Sept. 1, 1999.

33. See *Berita Harian*, Sept. 1, 1999.

34. PERGAS press release, Jan. 14, 2000. See www.pergas.org.sg/cyber-press.html (accessed 3/7/2004).

35. The MOE proposal required all children to attend primary school until the age of ten, or the parents would be fined or jailed.

36. The website www.CyberUmmah.com.sg has, however, since closed down.

37. *Straits Times*, Apr. 7, 2000.

38. PERGAS press statement, Apr. 7, 2000.

39. *Berita Harian*, Mar. 16, 2003.

40. Discussion with Ustaz Hasbi, president of PERGAS, Feb. 22, 2003.

41. PERGAS website, www.pergas.org.sg (accessed 3/7/2004).

42. PERGAS press release, Feb. 8, 2002.

43. PERGAS press release, Jan. 14, 2000.

44. Prime Minister's Office press release, May 8, 2000.

45. *Economist*, May 24, 2001.

46. Interview and discussions with Tan Chong Kee.

47. *Straits Times*, Apr. 27, 2002.

48. See the interview reprinted in *Straits Times*, Sept. 25, 2002.

49. The site has not been maintained, however, since the search for a new editor was in vain.

50. Interview with Zulfikar, Oct. 16, 2001.

51. The SBA answers directly to MITA. The CRC was set up in early 2002 to review and recommend new guidelines on censorship. One important aspect of the committee's work concerns the question of censorship pertaining to political matters such as campaigns and political videos. The CRC also reviews SBA regulations on cyberspace and on Internet political discussions.

52. Interview with Chua Beng Huat, Sept. 24, 2002.

Works Cited

Brown, David. 1993. "The Corporatist Management of Ethnicity in Contemporary Singapore." In Garry Rodan, ed., *Singapore Changes Guard: Social, Political, and Economic Directions*. Melbourne: Longman-Cheshire.

Case, William. 2001. *Politics in Southeast Asia: Democracy or Less?* London: Curzon.

Chan Heng Chee. 1971. *Singapore: The Politics of Survival*. Singapore: Oxford University Press.

———. 1975. "Politics in an Administrative State: Where Has All the Politics Gone?" In Seah Chee Meow, ed., *Trends in Singapore*. Singapore: ISEAS.

Chan, Jasmine. 2000. "The Status of Women in a Patriarchal State: The Case of Singapore." In Louise Edwards and Mina Roces, eds., *Women in Asia: Tradition, Modernity and Globalisation*. St. Leonards, N.S.W.: Allen & Unwin.

Chua Beng Huat. 1994. "Arrested Development: Democratization in Singapore." *Third World Quarterly* 15(4): 655–68.

———. 1997. "Still Awaiting New Initiatives: Democratization in Singapore." *Asian Studies Review* 21(2–3): 99–107.

———. 2000. "The Relative Autonomies of State and Civil Society in Singapore." In Gillian Koh and Ooi Giok Ling, eds., *State-Society Relations in Singapore*. Singapore: Oxford University Press.

———. 2001. "Non-Transformative Politics: Civil Society in Singapore." Paper presented at the Conference on Civil Society in Asia, Griffith University, Brisbane, July.

———. 2002. "Constrained NGOs and Arrested Democratization in Singapore." Paper presented at the NGOs and the Nation in a Globalizing World conference, Academia Sinica, Taipei, June.

Chua Soo Sen. 2000. "The Singapore Government and Civil Society." In Gillian Koh and Ooi Giok Ling, eds., *State-Society Relations in Singapore*. Singapore: Oxford University Press.

Doner, Richard, and Gary Hawes. 1995. "The Political Economy of Growth in Southeast and Northeast Asia." In Manocher Dorraj, ed., *The Changing Political Economy of the 3rd World*. Boulder: Lynne Rienner.

George, Cherian. 2000. *The Air-Conditioned State*. Singapore: Land Mark.

"Globalization's Last Hurrah?" 2002. Second annual A. T. Kearney / Foreign Policy Magazine Globalization Index. *Foreign Policy*, Jan./Feb. http://www.foreignpolicy.com/story/cms.php?story_id=2484. Accessed 2/17/2004.

Haas, Michael. 1989. "The Politics of Singapore in the 1980s." *Journal of Contemporary Asia* 19(1): 48–77.

Haggard, Stephen. 1990. *Pathways from the Periphery: The Politics of Growth in the Newly Industrializing Countries*. Ithaca, N.Y.: Cornell University Press.

Ho, K. C., Zaheer Baber, and Habibul Khondker. 2002. "Sites of Resistance: Alternative Websites and State-Society Relations." *British Journal of Sociology* 53(1) (Mar.): 127–48.

Jesudason, James. 1999. "The Resilience of One-Party Dominance in Malaysia and Singapore." In Hermann Giliomee and Charles Simkins, eds., *The Awkward Embrace: One-Party Domination and Democracy*. Australia: Harwood Academic.

Khong, Cho-Oon. 1995. "Singapore: Political Legitimacy Through Managing Conformity." In Muthiah Alagappa, ed., *Political Legitimacy in Southeast Asia: The Quest for Moral Authority*. Stanford: Stanford University Press.

Koh, Gillian, and Ooi Giok Ling, eds. 2000. *State-Society Relations in Singapore*. Singapore: Oxford University Press.

Lam Peng Er. 1999. "Singapore: Rich State, Illiberal Regime." In James Morley, ed., *Driven by Growth: Political Change in the Asia-Pacific Region*. Armonk, N.Y.: M. E. Sharpe.

Lim U Wen. 2000. "Women NGOs in Patriarchal Singapore: Interaction Between State and Civil Society." In Gillian Koh and Ooi Giok Ling, eds., *State-Society Relations in Singapore*. Singapore: Oxford University Press.

Mauzy, Diane K., and R. S. Milne. 2002. *Singapore Politics under the People's Action Party*. London: Routledge.

Mutalib, Hussin. 2000. "Illiberal Democracy and the Future of Opposition in Singapore." *Third World Quarterly* 21(2): 313–42.

Rodan, Garry. 1993. "Elections Without Representation: The Singapore Experience Under the PAP." In R. H. Taylor, ed., *The Politics of Elections in Southeast Asia*. Cambridge: Cambridge University Press.

———. 1996. "State-Society Relations and Political Opposition in Singapore." In Garry Rodan, ed., *Political Oppositions in Industrializing Asia*. London: Routledge.

———. 2001. "Singapore: Emerging Tensions in the 'Dictatorship of the Middle Class.'" In Garry Rodan, ed., *Singapore*. Aldershot, U.K.: Ashgate.

Singam, Constance, Tan Chong Kee, Tisa Ng, and Leon Pereira, eds. 2001. *Building Social Space in Singapore: The Working Committee's Initiative in Civil Society Activism*. Singapore: Select Publishing.

Tan Tay Cheong. 2000. *Social Capital and State–Civil Society Relations in Singapore*. Working Paper 9. Singapore: Institute of Policy Studies.

PART IV

Repressed Civil Society

Penetrated, Co-opted, and Avoiding the State

CHAPTER ELEVEN

Pakistan

Civil Society in the Service of an Authoritarian State

AQIL SHAH

Repeated military interventions, prolonged suspension of the political process, and the concomitant weakness of democratic institutions and norms have distorted the development of civil society in Pakistan. With two-thirds of the country's population still rural in an overbearing military-bureaucratic state, powerful landed interests and armed extremist groups continue to restrict and curtail the activities of organizations operating in the nonstate public sphere, impeding their ability to develop and regulate norms of societal self-governance, as well as their potential to influence political change. A few vocal civil society groups demand inclusion and accountability from the state, but most wage their battles outside the political arena. Far from resisting autocratic rule or altering the political balance of power in favor of an open and accountable political system, large swathes of this depoliticized civil society typically derive privilege and benefits from the authoritarian state.

Muthiah Alagappa's assertion in Chapter 1 that civil society is a contested arena of power, struggle, and inequality, populated by diverse and often competing interests and groups, is supported by the example of Pakistan. The methods, functions, and purposes of civil society actors and organizations are heavily conditioned by the nature of their interaction with, and location in relation to, the state, political society, and the market. In theory, the role these actors and organizations can play in political liberalization is also closely linked to regime type, with the space for civil contestation most open in liberal and democratic states, and the least so in authoritarian ones. In Pakistan, where political democracy and authoritarian rule are too often poorly differentiated from each other, the actual role civil society plays in political change goes beyond regime type. Problematizing this role in such hybridized authoritarian contexts—autocratic military rule punctuated by periodic appeals to the electorate—rests ultimately on the peculiar political and constitutional context.

Since independence in 1947, the evolution of civil society has been marred by the structural dynamics of state formation, legitimation, and consolidation. With national security concerns dominating political decision making from the outset, the state has traditionally adopted centralized, authoritarian systems of governance. For the most part, these models of authority have remained deeply contested and lacked domestic legitimacy. The contested nature of state authority underscores the complexity of defining, locating, and denoting agency to the nonstate sector in Pakistan. While civil society has witnessed dramatic growth in its organizational diversity since the mid-1980s, the nonstate sector has yet to emerge as an independent, legally protected public realm of associational and civic activity. Although there is no inherent connection between civil society and democracy, as idealized in liberal democratic theory (see, e.g., Alagappa, Chapter 1 this volume), it is this author's contention that in comparison to overt military rule, as well as to the military-dominated pseudodemocratic regime in place since 2002, civil society organizations fared relatively better under elected governments in the 1990s (as well as the brief civilian interlude in the 1970s). During this failed transition to democracy, the development of civil society both as a distinct sphere in relation to state and political society and as a site for the construction of alternative political and normative discourses received an impetus from the broader democratic opening in the state. Admittedly, the impact of the nonstate sector (agency) on state policies and politics remained more circumscribed in the face of the structural constraints outlined above.

Developments within the realms of state and political society, as well as their interaction with each other and civil society, have informed the dialectic between democratic and antidemocratic impulses in civil society. In this chapter, two ways in which civil society's antidemocratic tendencies affect the prospects of political liberalization are discussed at length. First, amid widespread economic and social disparities, incentives for religious extremism remain strong. Rightist Islamist groups, often in alliance with powerful sections of the state, violently pursue exclusionary agendas that undermine the stability and legitimacy of democratic institutions. Second, liberal sections of Pakistani civil society have lent support to a military regime since it toppled a democratically elected government in 1999. For reasons analyzed in this discussion, instead of delegitimating and resisting the illegal assumption of power by the military, not only did influential civil society actors welcome the coup, but many of them joined the regime at the highest levels of state. Even when some civil society groups have pushed for political liberalization, their impact has been constrained by state repression, weak links with groups in political society, and unfavorable international conditions.

To explore civil society's role in political and democratic change in Pakistan, this chapter addresses four key questions. First, to what extent has an authoritarian state distorted and undermined the nature, development, and politics of civil society in Pakistan? Second, what are the implications of civil society's weaknesses for democracy and political change? In other words, does civil society really matter? Third, what role have rightist militant groups played in obstructing change in the direction of open democratic politics? And fourth, why have seemingly liberal sections of civil society supported military rule since 1999?

Historical Perspective

The nature, composition, and development of civil society in Pakistan have been shaped by several interrelated factors: a lingering legacy of colonial rule; the peculiar demands of postcolonial state formation, and the ruling elite's need for political legitimation; and long periods of military rule.

Civil Society at Independence

In British India, the colonial state followed a formal policy of noninterference in the religious and cultural affairs of its colonial subjects.[1] At the same time, the British were not averse to introducing legal and administrative policies that radically altered the political practices and discourse of India's religious communities. The decision to institute separate electorates for "Muslims" and "Hindus," for instance, injected the issue of "communalism" into the center of state-society interaction. A civil society "divided" along communal lines was well suited to the British view of governance that privileged the state as a nonpartisan force for social integration (Washbrook 1999).

In the decisive stages of the anticolonial resistance, the Muslim League mobilized a distinct "Muslim" identity to counter the professed secular nationalism of the Indian National Congress (Jalal 1997). When the British ceded power in 1947, reconciling an overtly communitarian ideology with the urgent demands of modern state building in an ethnically differentiated polity proved exceptionally difficult for the disparate Muslim League leadership. In the years to come, this dislocation informed an ideologically motivated state's uneasy interaction with democratic institutions and civil society. The postcolonial state, although it readily appropriated constitutional notions of parliamentary democracy, predictably worked at cross-purposes with it. The ruling Muslim League, with virtually no base of support in the areas that constituted the new state, knew only too well that electoral democracy would require the realignment of state-civil society relations. Instead of enacting a new constitution, it therefore adopted the Government of India Act 1935 as an interim constitution that provided a formal federal parliamentary system, but one that concentrated legal and administrative powers in an unelected governor-general and denied substantive autonomy to the provinces. Giving authoritarian centralization the veneer of a federal system—whether to assuage demands for provincial autonomy or to appropriate democratic rhetoric and symbols for legitimacy—was fraught with problems. In the coming decades, the state's legitimacy was to remain deeply contested, especially in the eastern wing of the country, over the unequal distribution of power and resources.

The nature and composition of a yet to be "decolonized" civil society hardly proved beneficial for the evolution of representative institutions. With the arbitrary appropriation of the public realm by the colonial state, notions of public interest and collective action had largely remained underdeveloped in a variegated Indian civil society (Jalal 1997). In the postcolonial setting, the ruling elite purposefully depoliticized the public sphere to make it subject to the exigencies of an authoritarian state. Individual rights; state accountability to the citizenry; freedoms of expression, dissent, and critical thinking; provincial autonomy and decentralization—all were conveniently banished under the overarching rubric of threats to national security posed by hostile neighbors: Afghanistan to the west, India to the east. The state's prioritization of defense over development combined with the external imperatives of the cold war to pave the way for the rise to power of the civil-military bureaucracies within its power structures. No other development would impede the development of democratic initiatives and civil society more than the dominance of the coercive arms of the state over parliamentary ones (Jalal 1990; Rizvi 2000).

Civil Society under Authoritarian Rule (1958–1988)

With the direct assumption of political power by the armed forces under General Muhammad Ayub Khan in 1958, the fate of both parliamentary democracy and civil society in Pakistan was sealed. Ayub moved quickly to ban political parties, disqualify politicians from seeking public office, suppress political dissent, and subordinate the judiciary. Threatened by the independence of the print media, the junta systematically targeted them. Empowered by a 1959 Martial Law Ordinance to take over newspapers that "published or contained matters likely to endanger the defense, external affairs, or security of Pakistan," the regime seized and nationalized many newspapers, including the progressive *Pakistan Times* and *Imroze*. To further curb press freedoms, the regime amended a 1960 Press and Publications Ordinance in 1963 to gain intrusive control over the inner workings of newspapers and periodicals. Publication of academic works critical of the government was also summarily banned, public-sector university employees were fired at the slightest sign of dissent, and many civic organizations, including the All-Pakistan Women's Association (APWA), were either disbanded or co-opted into supporting General Ayub's professed "modernist reform" agenda. "These measures collectively cordoned off and tamed the intelligentsia, which has had profound implications for cultural and social development in Pakistan," Omar Noman concludes (1990: 29).

Generous aid from the United States helped the military regime score impressive growth in the industrial and agricultural sectors, but economic wealth was concentrated in the hands of a small industrial and corporate elite in West Pakistan.[2] By the mid-1960s, widespread economic and political grievances had begun to fuel polarization along both regional and class lines. The disastrous fallout of the 1965 war with India, coupled with the unmitigated failure of Ayub's "developmental" state to fix economic inequalities, gave enough ammunition to political forces—such as Zulfiqar Ali Bhutto's Pakistan People's Party (PPP)—to mobilize large sections of civil society on a populist platform enabling them to openly and defiantly challenge the state's military-bureaucratic power structures. Students and labor unions were at the forefront of the anti-Ayub agitation. In March 1969, the port city of Karachi, which comprised 40 percent of Pakistan's industrial capacity, was brought to a standstill by labor strikes (Noman 1990).

Besieged by this growing, often violent, resistance to his authority, Ayub handed over power to General Yahya Khan, who called for Pakistan's first general elections in twenty-four years in 1970.[3] In East Pakistan, Sheikh Mujeeb's Awami League, now calling openly for secession from Pakistan, swept the polls, and Bhutto's PPP scored a majority in West Pakistan. The military, unaccustomed to the art of political bargaining and resistant to the transfer of power to the Awami League, decided to crush the opposition in East Pakistan with brute force, ultimately paving the way for the country's dismemberment in 1971. Ayub's era has been called a "watershed in defining relations between state and society in Pakistan," as its main political legacy was centralization of state authority by cementing many of the political distortions that arose in the first decade (Jalal 1995: 55).

Aware of the military's interventionist tendencies, Bhutto had quickly moved to dilute its political role by restructuring the high command, removing senior officers, making the abrogation of the constitution punishable by death, and creating the Federal Security Force (FSF) to impose law and order (Rizvi 2000). Far from subordinating an ambitious high command to elected authorities, these intrusions into what the military deemed its internal affairs only increased the contempt of the senior ranks for their civilian bosses. The PPP's rather weak organizational base, intraparty divisions over the nature and direction of socioeconomic reforms, and Bhutto's authoritarian tendencies meant, however, that he would come to rely excessively on the coercive arms of the state to preserve and enhance his power (Jalal 1995; Rizvi 2000). To deal with a tribal uprising in Baluchistan province, for instance, the prime minister preferred to send in the army to talk and mediate.

Was the brief elective interlude any different for civil society? Bhutto had staked his claim to political power on a populist platform. His program included ambitious land and labor reforms and the nationalization of key industrial and agricultural sectors. The Bhutto years were notable for encouraging trade union activities and women's rights advocacy groups (SPDC 2003). Being predisposed to centralizing power in his own hands, however, Bhutto had no qualms about suppressing his political opposition, gagging the press, and curtailing civil liberties. By the mid-1970s, Bhutto had all but alienated the urban intelligentsia and professional classes by curbing dissent within the PPP, suppressing freedom of expression, and making undue compromises to accommodate a restive religious lobby.[4] Business and industrial interests, visibly hurt by his nationalization program, were quick to forge an alliance with the political opposition to challenge his rule (Noman 1990; Jalal 1995). Rejecting the results of the general elections held in April 1977, the Pakistan National Alliance (PNA), an umbrella group of nine opposition parties spearheaded by Islamist factions, organized countrywide protests. As law and order deteriorated in the major urban centers, Bhutto leaned on the army to restore peace. By then, the military had decided to take matters into their own hands. Before the government and the PNA could resolve matters peacefully, the army under General Mohammad Zia-ul-Haq once again intervened and deposed Bhutto in July 1977.

Bhutto's capitulation to Islamist demands, and the success of the PNA's ideologically couched anti-Bhutto agitation, had placed Islamization at the center of public debates on legislation and political reforms.[5] General Zia, seeking political legitimacy, was quick to make a state-sponsored Islamization program the mainstay of his rule to co-opt sectarian and Islamist parties (see Nasr 1994; Rizvi 2000). Besides introducing Islamic norms and institutions in the economy, the judiciary, and the education system, he enacted discriminatory Islamic legislation targeting religious minorities and women (Alavi 1988). Zia even went a step further by enforcing a strict Islamic code of public morality on the electronic media, the performing arts, and cinema. Meanwhile, he deployed the army and paramilitary troops to crush political dissent. For instance, military authorities used brute force to deal with the Movement for Restoration of Democracy (MRD), a PPP-led opposition alliance, especially in the party's stronghold of Sindh province (Rizvi 2000). Lending the military ruler a helping hand in consolidating his grip on power was massive U.S. economic and military assistance in return for Pakistan's support in the anti-Soviet resistance in Afghanistan.

Zia's onslaught on civil society, targeting the country's intelligentsia, students, labor and trade unions, lawyers, and other professional associations, represented a systematic campaign to coerce and co-opt all possible arenas of contestation to military rule.[6] To stifle dissent, universities were purged of academics critical of the military and the press was gagged with repressive censorship (Rizvi 2000; Niazi 1986). As the military entrenched its institutional dominance of state and society under Zia, its wide-ranging political and social engineering further segmented civil society. Heightened state repression could not, however, completely curb opposition from within civil society. For instance, journalists and lawyers periodically protested against and challenged the military's hold on state power. Zia's attempt to distort the legal status and rights of women through the imposition of the repressive Hudood Laws spurred educated, urban middle-class women into militant action against the military regime (Mumtaz and Shaheed 1987).

Civil Society and the Failed Democratic Transition (1989–1999)

After Zia's death in a plane crash in August 1988, the military transferred power to elected politicians.[7] Given its entrenched position and power in the state structures, the transition to elective rule was trumped from the onset by the military's reluctance to loosen its grip on both domestic politics and the country's security and foreign policies. The elected government also had to contend with other menacing facets of the Zia legacy: weakened civilian institutions, a thriving culture of political and administrative corruption, the breakdown in the rule of law, a black economy of arms and drugs, and the concomitant militarization of society.

The tendency of civilian governments to flout democratic norms, the willingness of democratically "semiloyal" opposition groups to "knock on the garrison's door" for support,[8] and the frequent dismissals of elected governments by military-backed presidents thwarted the consolidation of the transition to civilian rule. Eleven years after the country's formal transition to civilian rule, the army intervened once again in October 1999 to depose the democratically elected government of Prime Minister Nawaz Sharif after his futile attempt to replace the army chief General Pervez Musharraf.

Despite the fragility of the transition and the authoritarian manner in which elected governments exercised power, however, the decade-long civilian interregnum had expanded the public realm in terms of the opportunities available to civil society actors and institutions to debate, pursue, and shape public policy agendas. Transition to civilian rule also gave a fillip to the growth of civil society organizations (mainly in the media and nonprofit sectors) on account of the broader political opening, the growing import of neoliberal emphasis on civil society in external aid regimes, and the continued deterioration of public capacity to deliver social services. Thus, civil society continued to develop as a *distinct sphere* in relation to the state and political society. Elected governments of both the Pakistan People's Party (1988–90 and 1993–96) and the Pakistan Muslim League Nawaz (PML-N; 1990–93 and 1997–99) had adopted a generally supportive attitude toward civil society organizations, especially those providing social welfare services. NGO leaders were often invited to sit on advisory committees and commissions set up by the government. A National Rural Support Program (NRSP) was established to mobilize support for social development at the community and village levels with an endowment of Rs. 500 million. The high point of government-NGO collaboration was the formulation of the National Conservation Strategy, approved by the federal cabinet in 1992, which was drafted after an exhaustive process of consultation between official agencies, NGOs, community-based organizations, environmental activists, and experts.

This is not to imply that the NGO-government interaction was wholly devoid of hostility. Although the government extended support at the policy level, it obstructed NGOs' activities at the operational level (SPDC 2002b). Foreign-funded organizations often aroused official suspicion on account of their growing role in traditionally state-led developmental activities and independent access to external resources. Many were deemed inimical to national security because of their espousal of sensitive issues such as human rights, prevention of violence against women, and nuclear disarmament (SPDC 2002b). State–civil society friction grew worse in 1996, when the second PPP government (1993–96) submitted an NGO bill to parliament.[9] This bill proposed intrusive regulation of nonprofits through mandatory registration, compulsory auditing, detailed information disclosure, and gave the government the power to seize assets and terminate operations. Two years later, the second PML-N government ordered intelligence inquiries and deregistration of a large number of NGOs in the wake of a growing tussle with the NGO sector.[10] Soon afterward, the government reintroduced the bill regulating NGOs, which had been pending in the senate since 1996.

Despite these periodic setbacks, civil society groups managed to articulate public interests, mobilize public opinion, and organize for collective action around legal and political issues, including reforms in the legal system, greater public representation for women, accountability in public office, and respect for human rights. Many of these groups were able to forge links, however tenuous, with other social and political actors to resist the government's antidemocratic actions. For instance, the proposed fifteenth amendment to the constitution, otherwise known as the Shariat bill—which sought sweeping powers for Prime Minister Nawaz Sharif—had galvanized strong opposition both inside and outside parliament, including opposition on the part of NGOs and sections of the print media. In moderate sections of political society, a growing consensus on the role of civil society organizations as legitimate actors in social and political development was also discernible. Democratization, although incomplete and prone to reversal, had also stimulated a vocal public debate on hitherto sensitive issues such as civil-military relations, nuclear policy, India-Pakistan relations, and accountability for defense expenditures. While limited in impact, citizen-led peace initiatives such as the Pakistan Peace Coalition and the India-Pakistan People's Forum for Peace and Democracy were able to organize for regional peace and dialogue. Policy research institutes, although few in number, capitalized on the democratic opening to carve out a niche for independent research. Frequent elections provided many NGOs with the opportunity to promote participation in the political process by developing voter education and awareness programs and imparting election-monitoring skills. In addition, the press was able to claw back the ground lost during decades of authoritarian censorship. Dissenting opinions and exposés often triggered political confrontations with the government of the day. During Sharif's second tenure (1997–99), for instance, senior editors and journalists critical of his administration's policies were systematically targeted, harassed, and even incarcerated under trumped-up charges. But the print media's regular exposure of corruption in high places, as well as their forceful criticism of economic and political mismanagement, had reinforced a strong public demand for accountability. In the absence of any organized capacity in civil society to effectively push for institutional reforms, however, incumbent governments were able to exploit that sentiment to use anticorruption drives for partisan purposes (Shah 2001).

Mapping Civil Society

Community welfare, philanthropic, and professional associations have existed in Pakistan since the early years of independence, but the growth of private, organized, nonprofit development and advocacy groups in civil society was coterminous, paradoxically enough, with the Zia years (1977–88). Many were formed, or became active, in response to the military regime's political repression, human rights violations, and the enactment of discriminatory legislation against women and minorities, as well as a general rise in religious and ethnically motivated violence. Moreover, the massive economic, military, and humanitarian assistance extended to Pakistan for allying with the United States against the Soviet occupation of Afghanistan provided the impetus for the proliferation of Islamic charities and seminaries. While these were ostensibly set up for providing relief assistance in Afghan refugee camps, many of them served as conduits for arms and manpower for the Afghan jihad (International Crisis Group 2002a).

Civil Society Organizations

The mid-1970s and early 1980s saw a phenomenal increase in the size and wealth of the lower and middle strata of Pakistani society, especially in Punjab. The availability of alternative sources of employment outside the state, especially in the Persian Gulf and in foreign-funded aid activities within Pakistan, the increased use of education as an instrument of social mobility, and growing urbanization led to a dramatic increase in public expectations and aspirations.[11] This complex process of social differentiation, according to Mustapha Pasha (1997), resulted in both the consolidation of the power of the existing elite and the emergence of new economic and social forces that articulate their social and political interests through nonprofit civil society organizations. Reliable data are scant, but one recent estimate has put the number of private, voluntary nonprofit organizations in Pakistan at 45,000 (SPDC 2002b).[12] These vary greatly in size, outreach, and focus. Some 46 percent are primarily focused on education, 18 percent are advocacy-oriented, 8 percent are providing social services other than education, and another 5 percent are characterized as "religious." The leading activity of the nonprofit sector is "religious education," which accounts for almost 30 percent of the sector's organizational share.

Nonprofit activity faces several legal and official constraints. Six different laws, most of them dating back to the colonial period, govern their registration: the Societies Registration Act (1860), the Trusts Act (1882), the Charitable Endowments Act (1890), the Cooperative Act (1925), the Voluntary Social Welfare Agencies Ordinance (1961), and the Companies Ordinance (1984).[13] Instead of providing a facilitative regulatory environment, the current legal framework is characterized by duplication, ambiguous administrative guidelines, arbitrary application of the law, and official discretion to refuse registration or even dissolve organizations without the right to appeal. Recent attempts to streamline the legislative environment for nonprofits have included a 2002 military-sponsored Non-Profit Public Benefit Organizations (Governance and Support) Draft Act.[14] Criticized by many NGOs as a thinly veiled attempt to extend government control over the financial and internal governance of nonprofits,[15] the bill stipulates the establishment of national and provincial Non-Profit Organizations Commissions to provide public oversight of NGOs. Registration is mandatory for nonprofits that apply for or receive any government or foreign funds in excess of 300,000 rupees (roughly U.S.$5,000) in a single financial year. The proposed act would make it obligatory for NGOs to provide such commissions with financial accounts, including the "identity of the donor, the amount and the purposes for which funds were received" in case of foreign funds. The bill also empowers the commission to initiate audits and liquidate registered NGOs if they are found to be in violation of the act or other relevant laws.

Trade union activity remains subject to repressive laws. The Industrial Relations Ordinance 2002 restricts the right to form unions, the right to organize collective bargaining, and the right to strike. Another law, the Essential Services Maintenance Act 1952, specifically curtails union activity in sectors associated with state administration. Besides, the country's eight thousand registered unions represent just over 5 percent of the total employed labor force as—partly because the agricultural and informal sectors, which employ the majority workforce—are excluded under current laws (NGORC 2002). Trade union numbers are also falling owing to privatization, public-sector downsizing, and a general decline in industrial activity (NGORC 2002).

Neat categorization of civil society organizations is neither possible nor desirable, given the wide-ranging and often overlapping functions and roles of these entities, but several broad types can be identified for the purpose of this discussion. First, there are the developmental NGOs, primarily concerned with the implementation of largely donor-driven development projects, capacity building of community-based organizations, and service delivery. Then there are groups that seek to reform public policy, push for civil and political rights, and pursue political liberalization. These include human rights and media watchdogs, bar associations, the private media, and policy research institutes. Falling somewhere between these two broad categories are grassroots groups, voluntary associations, philanthropic trusts, community-based organizations, panchayats (councils of elders), madrasahs (religious seminaries), and Islamic charities.

Civil society's organizational terrain is characterized by hierarchical and uneven development along geographic and social lines. In the perpetual absence of representative political mechanisms, this variegated civil society is often a deeply contested arena of competing social forces, with the competition often spilling over into open political conflict. Philippe Schmitter (1995) warns of the possibility of several societies occupying the civil society space but espousing countervailing interests and agendas. Social and geographic fragmentation, the unequal distribution of power between different groups, the pervasive militarization of society since the 1980s, and the associated breakdown of the rule of law have all retarded the scope for the development of civil society as a regulated, legally protected autonomous sphere. An authoritarian state's systematic attempts to co-opt and control civil society groups to suit its own interests have further pulverized the nonstate sphere.

Developmental NGOs

The development sector, by far the most active and visible section of civil society, comprises indigenously funded welfare organizations, externally financed NGOs, and large government-organized NGOs (GONGOs). The 1990s also saw the rise of the "third-generation" civil society organizations that seek to differentiate themselves from more conventional nonprofits by combining development activities with "strategic policy advocacy for broad socioeconomic change."[16] These organizations claim to "strengthen civil society by creating and expanding space for the non-elite by questioning decision-making institutions and systems in which the state and the power elite have occupied a dominant position leaving little space for the non-elite" (SUNGI 1999). Since their phenomenal growth in the 1990s, developmental NGOs have formed national and provincial structures to represent, articulate, and coordinate their own interests, as well as to protect the autonomy of the nonstate sector from state interference. The largest of them is the Pakistan NGO Forum (PNF), a coalition boasting a membership of 2,500 NGOs that acts as the collective voice for the sector. Formed in 1995, the PNF was instrumental in resisting the Sharif government's anti-NGO campaign and crafting its own alternative NGO bill in 1999 for the consideration of the senate.

The nonprofit development sector is highly differentiated along rural and urban as well as class lines. Although roughly 70 percent of Pakistan's population is rural, NGOs are concentrated largely in urban areas, reflecting a clear urban bias. Low levels of institutional development, weak organizational skills, and poor internal transparency and accountability characterize most of the prominent ones, owing partly to the larger-than-life role of well-known public figures who peddle their personal influence to promote these organizations at the obvious cost of professionalization. The easy availability of a large pool of semiskilled government officials, attracted to the nonprofit sector by lucrative remuneration, further removes the incentives for institutional capacity building. While their presence enhances the organization's chances of leveraging the state for funds and patronage, more often than not, these contracted officials facilitate the state's penetration of the nonprofit sector.

Crosscutting linkages with international NGOs and human rights bodies have increased the political and intellectual resources available to civil society organizations (Keck and Sikkink 1998). At the same time, growing dependence on external donors has not only tainted their public credibility but also distorted the organizational agendas of NGOs. With their portfolios determined largely by shifting and often competing donor priorities, the incentives for these civil society organizations to develop indigenous roots, build ownership for their programs, or reflect genuine public interests remain low. These structural constraints, coupled with their manifest unwillingness to link up their resources and influence with other civil constituencies (media, professional associations) for broader policy reforms, partially explain the failure of many prominent NGOs in affecting politics or state policies in the direction of open and accountable governance. This is not an indictment of the NGO sector as a whole, or of those funded by foreign aid in particular. Many well-meaning NGOs run issue-based advocacy programs to mobilize support for and influence state policies on various issues of public interest. A number of organizations, among them the Aurat Foundation, Shirkatgah, ASAR, Simorgh, and Rozan, to name but a few, are engaged in innovative projects that aim at meaningful social, economic, and political empowerment of disadvantaged strata of Pakistani society, especially women. Still others are providing valuable services in rural health, sanitation, education, and micro-credit.

Professional Associations, Think Tanks, and Human Rights Groups. In the absence of an organized democratic opposition, high court and supreme court bar associations have often assumed the role of the political opposition by defiantly protesting violations of constitutional norms. For instance, lawyers' groups have called countrywide strikes protesting against the 1999 military coup, the illegal incarceration of political leaders, the constitutional amendments introduced by the military regime, and General Musharraf's attempts to validate his stay in power through a public referendum. Professional media associations like the Council of Pakistan Newspaper Editors (CPNE) and All Pakistan Newspapers Society (APNS) articulate and communicate group interests to governments. These press organizations exert an indirect democratizing effect by openly protesting and opposing state policies that seek to curb press freedom. The promulgation of repressive press laws by

General Musharraf, for instance, has met with unanimous opposition from the APNS, CPNE, and other media bodies.[17]

A few human rights groups publicly highlight the state's human rights abuses and widely disseminate information to mobilize public opinion. Prominent among them is the Human Rights Commission of Pakistan (HRCP), a private nonprofit organization that has consistently pushed since it started functioning in 1986 for the protection of civil and political liberties and maintenance of the sanctity of the judicial and electoral machinery. Indeed, it has earned domestic and international recognition for monitoring human rights violations, investigating electoral malpractice, and reporting on electoral fraud. The HRCP was instrumental in pushing the Bonded Labor Act 1992 and catalyzing reforms in juvenile justice. Moreover, the HRCP publishes a well-researched and widely disseminated Annual State of Human Rights Report, an English quarterly, and an Urdu monthly, all documenting human rights violations, including extrajudicial killings and torture, incidents of political repression, sectarian killings, and violence against women and minorities. It also spearheads public advocacy campaigns pressing the government for the annulment of discriminatory legislation, such as the blasphemy law that carries a mandatory death penalty for those convicted of blasphemy.

Nongovernmental think tanks too have made modest contributions in articulating public policy reforms. The Sustainable Development Policy Institute (SDPI) conducts policy-oriented research on environmental policy, decentralization, and human development and provides advisory services to public and private organizations. The Mahbubul Haq Human Development Center in Islamabad publishes an Annual Human Development Report on South Asia that combines analysis with extensive data on human development indicators. The report has become a valuable source of reference for academics and policymakers alike. The Pakistan Institute for Labor Education and Research (PILER) works on labor policy and trade union issues. Fiscal reforms, tax administration, social service delivery, and poverty alleviation form the core of the policy research of the Social Policy Development Center (SPDC). The NGO Resource Center (NGORC), a project of the Agha Khan Foundation, aims to build the capacity of the NGO sector by conducting research and analysis on key sectoral issues such as legal and fiscal frameworks for NGOs, NGO registration, and NGO-corporate partnerships.

Grassroots Relief Groups. At the grassroots level, many self-organized groups work on health, housing rights, sanitation, community infrastructure, and the environment. The Orangi Pilot Project (OPP), in which Karachi slum dwellers, disappointed by the state's apathy about their squalid living conditions, developed extensive sanitation and housing infrastructure, has earned international acclaim.

Islamic Charities and Madrasahs. Islamic relief trusts and seminaries, often affiliated with religious political parties, as well as with sectarian militant groups, have generally exploited the state's inability to meet the material and security needs of its citizenry to broaden their social bases. While Pakistan-based madrasahs have come under renewed international scrutiny in the aftermath of 9/11, their activities and outreach received a major boost during the Afghan jihad, when both state patronage and external financial support were readily available. Although it is difficult to assess the exact magnitude of external assistance, strong transnational links forged during that period with state and nonstate actors in Saudi Arabia, Kuwait, UAE, and Iran, as well as contributions from nonresident Pakistanis, continue to fund them. Notably too, religious institutions and causes boast a 94 percent share of the contributions made by private indigenous philanthropists annually (AKDN 2000). The overwhelming majority are organized along sectarian lines and instill an insular worldview into their students. But not all madrasahs are involved in fomenting extremist violence. While there are no reliable estimates, Pakistani officials claim that only 10–15 percent might be linked to militancy or international terrorism (International Crisis Group 2002a: 2). There is no doubt that many well-known madrasah networks, especially those affiliated with the Sunni Deobandi sect,[18] provide cannon fodder for militancy in the region and beyond.[19] For instance, all the militant sectarian groups banned by the Musharraf regime in January 2002 "either originated in jihadi madrassas or developed their own chains" (International Crisis Group 2002a: 12). Often the lines between philanthropy and extremism can get blurred in practice. Still, many Islamic charities and madrasahs continue to serve an important social purpose by providing educational and welfare services to the poor strata of society who cannot afford to pay for food, education, and housing.[20]

Civil Society, Democracy, and Military Rule

Long episodes of autocratic rule characterized by the forceful suspension of the political process, suppression of opposition and dissent, and centralization of state authority have largely depoliticized "civil" society, stunting its evolution and its ability to influence political change. Since independence in 1947, military-dominated authoritarian governments have coerced, co-opted, and manipulated important vocal groups in civil society to suit their own agendas, including legitimizing and prolonging military rule. For their part, civilian-led governments have all too frequently exceeded the limits of democratic authority and violated parliamentary codes of conduct, making the task of institutionalizing democratic norms and values even more difficult. Given this peculiar pattern of historical development, civil society is weakly institutionalized and able neither to regulate nonstate governance effectively nor to articulate public interests independently and organize for collective action.

Military rule has been the bane of Pakistan, a country locked in a zero-sum conflict with a large, hostile neighbor, India. It is no surprise that many Pakistanis consider the military's political role as legitimate, if only as a remedial measure. But each military intervention is followed by the suspension of the political process at the national and provincial levels. Nonpartisan local bodies are created to circumvent aspirations to representative rule and undermine the existing party-based elite. These typical divide-and-rule tactics distort the political process, undermine political parties, and accentuate subnational loyalties (Shah 2003). At least theoretically, political parties and the larger political process in which they function provide the crucial intermediary link between civil society and the state. As Sunil Khilnani (2001: 31) notes, "Parties have an amphibious status, existing on both terrains: they represent each to the other." The mainstream moderate political parties in Pakistan—although centralized and undemocratic in many respects—offer the only viable political mechanisms for neutralizing and regulating diverse, and often conflicting, regional, ethnic, and linguistic interests in society.[21] To understand the role of civil society in fostering political change, as well as the larger problem of liberalization in Pakistan, one must also look for answers in the weakness of institutions in political society.[22] This weakness, as argued earlier, stems in large measure from the deliberate destruction of institutions and norms conducive to democracy by an interventionist military. In the absence of a clear determinate relationship between democracy and civil society, it might be the case that the emergence of a responsive and accountable political system will have to precede the emergence of a politically oriented civil society in Pakistan. In sum, what role civil society and its constituent units can play in political liberalization will depend crucially on the larger political setting: the responsiveness and strength of state institutions, the democratic vitality of political society, and the level of democratic institutionalization in state and society at large. In other words, a strong democratic state is crucial.

The prospects of political institutionalization remain grim, however. At present, Pakistan seems headed in the direction of a long period of military control over politics. Like his predecessors, General Musharraf has systematically curtailed the political and civil liberties of opposition groups and militarized civilian institutions in the name of reducing corruption. In an ostensible break with military-inspired local governments in the past,[23] the General has sponsored a new breed of devolution reforms which re-establish elected local councils at the *zilla* (district) and *tehsil* and union (subdistrict) levels.[24] But notwithstanding the military's rhetoric of local empowerment, local governments retain only nominal autonomy over the administrative and financial affairs of their respective jurisdictions. Moreover, Musharraf's decision to hold elections to local bodies on a nonparty basis further belies the military's claim to be building grassroots democracy. Widespread allegations of rigging and manipulation aside, the nonpartisan nature of local elections has exacerbated subnational (clan, ethnicity) divisions and undermined the organizational coherence of political parties. Since military-inspired devolution from the center to the local level bypassed the provinces, the scheme has undermined the very concept of federalism, exacerbated provincial grievances over reduced financial and administrative autonomy, and increased ethno-regional rifts (see International Crisis Group 2004).

The September 11, 2001, terrorist attacks on the United States proved a blessing in disguise for Pakistan's military ruler, catapulting the military into the front line of the U.S.-led war on terror in Afghanistan. General Musharraf, sensing an opportunity to acquire de facto international acceptance for his illegitimate hold on state power, swiftly joined America's antiterror coalition. International support emboldened Musharraf to revamp the country's political system to suit the army's corporate interests.

Responding to international sensitivities, and aware that appropriating democratic and civil society discourses and rhetoric cannot permanently legitimize the army's usurpation of political power, Musharraf held countrywide elections on October 10, 2002. As a hedge against an unfavorable outcome, the military instituted a series of legal and administrative measures aimed mainly at excluding two former premiers, Nawaz Sharif and Benazir Bhutto, from running, and thus marginalizing their parties.[25] To institutionalize its political dominance over elected authorities, General Musharraf reintroduced constitutional amendments under the Legal Framework Order 2002 (LFO) that empower him to arbitrarily dismiss the government and dissolve the national assembly. He also appoints the chiefs of the armed services and approves appointments to the superior judiciary. A supra-parliamentary National Security Council, headed by the general-president, is to oversee the performance of the civilian government.

In the wake of the largely rigged elections,[26] the pro-Musharraf Pakistan Muslim League Quaid-e-Azam (PML-Q), a faction of the PML-N created and sustained by the military's patronage, formed a coalition government at the center with a razor-thin parliamentary majority. The October 2002 polls were also notable for the unprecedented electoral gains of the Muttahida Majlis Amal (MMA), or United Action Forum, a broad alliance of six religious parties. This exclusively Islamist alliance secured over fort-five seats in the national assembly, besides sweeping the ballot in the Northwestern Frontier Province (NWFP) and Pashtun areas of Baluchistan. It now runs the provincial government in the NWFP and shares power with the PML-Q in Baluchistan. Facilitated both by the political vacuum created as a result of the military's systematic targeting of the moderate, secular parties, as well as the rising tide of anti-American public sentiment stoked by the U.S. military campaign in Afghanistan, the religious Right's political ascendancy augurs ill for the prospects of political liberalization. For instance, the MMA's agenda includes the Islamization of laws and educational texts, the creation of a Saudi-style ministry of vice and virtue, banning performing arts, ending co-education, and segregating women in public (Shah 2003).

In 2003, Musharraf's hybridized political order was precariously poised. Lacking the two-thirds majority in parliament required to validate constitutional amendments, Musharraf refused to seek parliamentary ratification for the LFO. He asserted instead that these changes were irreversible, citing a May 2000 Supreme Court judgment allowing him to amend the constitution. The opposition parties (the PPP, PML-N, and even the MMA) argued that the LFO had gone beyond the limits prescribed in the Supreme Court decision[27] and required parliamentary approval. The year-long government-opposition disagreement over the LFO stalemated parliament, raising concerns about the sustainability of the military-dominated regime as it grapples with intractable problems of economic revival, rising ethno-regional resentment over centralized rule, and growing intergovernmental tensions (center-province, province-local) over financial as well as administrative autonomy. By December 2003, however, the military had secured the MMA's consent to validate the LFO in parliament through a constitutional amendment bill.[28] As a concession to the MMA, Musharraf agreed to the separation of the office of the president from that of the chief of army staff by December 2004. Also, the National Security Council is to be set up through an act of parliament.

The Rise of the Armed Right Wing

In Pakistan, as elsewhere in Asia, the state often fails to mediate the competing social and political tensions among civil society groups, which often spill over into open conflict and violence. Michael Foley and Bob Edwards (1996) remind us of the dangers of glossing over the sharp divisions and conflicts that can, in the absence of political settlements, spill into societal anomie and violence.

Pakistan's military rulers, as well as their civilian counterparts, have traditionally appealed both to Islamic ideology and to the long-standing enmity with India to manipulate/manage ethnic, sectarian, and linguistic fissures in society. The military has continuously disrupted the political process (citing threats to national security posed by political corruption) to thwart any democratic or civil challenge to its dominance of state and society. In the process, extremist religious groups emboldened by the state's ideological posturing have gradually filled the resulting political vacuum. Since these groups share the military's hostility to India, as well as its aversion to moderate, secular political parties, they remain its closest allies in sustaining the antidemocratic status quo. Unsurprisingly, the military often uses the instability created by religious violence to pressure and destabilize noncompliant civilian governments (Ahmed 1997). Shielded by their alliance with the military, extremist groups openly preach and recruit for their parochial political agendas, breeding intolerance and extremism in the society at large.

Given the relative impunity with which extremist groups can inflict violence, as well as their symbiotic alliance with influential sections of the Pakistani national security elite, they continue to restrict the sociopolitical space available to weaker civil organizations. Moreover, they often actively try to replace, and even subvert, opponents in civil society. In parts of the Northwest Frontier Province, for instance, Islamic hard-liners have waged a violent anti-NGO campaign, calling for restrictions on women working for NGOs and the suspension of all women-related development work. In the wake of the U.S.-led military strikes in Afghanistan, armed extremists carried out a series of violent attacks on at least a dozen NGOs in the same areas. Fatwas (religious injunctions), threats of violence, and physical attacks are often part of regular campaigns to malign and intimidate NGOs accused of spreading un-Islamic cultural values, promoting Western ideas of development, and working against the national interest. "We will not let the government prop up NGOs in any future setup," says Qazi Hussain Ahmed, leader of the right-wing Jamaat-i-Islami, reacting to the Musharraf regime's plans to induct NGO professionals into government.[29]

Since they wield the ability to undermine both the nonstate sector, civilian political institutions, and often the state itself, these right-wing groups and the challenges arising from them are crucial to any analysis of political change in Pakistan. As Lawrence Whitehead (1997: 107–8) explains, "the quality and solidity of civil society is heavily conditioned by the nature and strength of the challenges arising from the uncivil interstices between state and civil society." Leigh Payne (2000) describes the armed right wing in Venezuela, Argentina, and Nicaragua, three countries undergoing transition from authoritarian rule, as "uncivil movements" (see also Whitehead 1997). This chapter draws on Payne's conceptualization of "uncivil movements" to examine extremist groups that use violence to advance their totalizing goals. As Payne explains, "uncivil movements resemble other political groups—for example, political parties, interest groups, social movements, counter movements and authoritarian movements. Indeed uncivil movements form, participate in, and evolve into and out of these other types of political groups at different times." And unlike these other groups, which may resort to violence in self-defense, uncivil movements employ violence as "a deliberate strategy to eliminate, intimidate and silence adversaries in other movements or in the government" (Payne 2000: 1). In Pakistan, not all Islamist groups qualify, although most remain motivated by, and continually resort to, organized violence. And many are not inherently opposed to parliamentary democracy. In fact, they often appropriate democratic practices and institutions to alter public policies and influence outcomes (Payne 2000). For the purposes of our analysis, it is important to emphasize that these groups exist and operate in the civil society space (see Chapter 1 in this volume).

The growth of militant right-wing groups and the associated rise of religiously motivated violence in Pakistan can be traced to the Zia period (1977–88). The Iranian revolution of 1979, Pakistan's active involvement in the U.S.-led anti-Soviet jihad in Afghanistan, and Zia's domestic Islamization program radicalized sectarian identities in Pakistan, fostering the growth of militant extremist groups (Nasr 2002). As the Afghan jihad gained momentum, jihadi madrasahs proliferated in the northwestern border areas and urban centers under Pakistani patronage and with Saudi funds. These published propaganda literature, mobilized public support, recruited, and trained mujahideen (International Crisis Group 2002a: 11).[30] Mosques and madrasahs with exclusionary sectarian affiliations provided the ideological polemic as well as the leadership for extremist groups (Zaman 1998). By the early 1990s, sectarian identities had become potent means of political expression for many rural and urban political constituencies. From time to time, these groups forged alliances of political convenience with other political actors to enhance their political power. With active support from the military's Inter-Services Intelligence Agency, many of these right-wing jihadi groups exploit the deep religiosity of the people to recruit fresh cadres for the army's "jihad" in Indian Kashmir.

Right-wing sectarian organizations like the Sipahe Sihaba Pakistan (SSP; Army of the Prophet's Companions) preach exclusionary and violent versions of the Sunni Islamic faith, often engaging in targeted violence against the minority Shias. The SSP's declared objectives are: to wage a war against Shias, have them declared non-Muslims,[31] ban their religious activities, and make Sunni Islam the official religion of the state. For the SSP, the ideal Islamic state is the one ruled by the *khulfa-e-rashideen* (rightly guided caliphs) who succeeded Prophet Mohammad. The group advocates the emulation of that state in Pakistan (see Zaman 1998).

The SSP derives support mainly from urban commercial interests in the Punjab's Jhang district, although its sectarian activities are by no means restricted to that area. Promoting a sectarian consciousness through marques, madrasahs, and polemical literature, it has projected itself as a potent tool for the urban Sunni middle classes with which to combat the powerful landed Shia elite (Zaman 1998). The top leadership of the SSP also uses electoral politics to achieve its exclusionary agenda. Maulana Azam Tariq, its former chief, was twice elected to the national assembly. In 1992, he tabled a bill in the lower house seeking the death penalty for those convicted of insulting the Prophet's companions.

After the founder of the SSP, Maulana Haq Nawaz Jhangvi, was allegedly assassinated by Shia terrorists in 1990, his close aides formed another splinter group, the Lashkar-e-Jhangvi (LeJ), to avenge his death.[32] In 1999, former Prime Minister Nawaz Sharif narrowly escaped an attempt on his life by the LeJ, believed to be a reprisal for Sharif's crackdown on sectarian extremists. LeJ has recently been implicated in a series of terrorist attacks on churches, as well as on Shia mosques and processions. American and Pakistani intelligence officials believe ties forged with al Qaeda during the Afghan jihad have facilitated the collaboration between LeJ and other terrorists and remnants of al Qaeda now hiding in Pakistan.

Amid international pressure to clamp down on terrorist outfits, Musharraf banned the SSP, along with other militant groups, in January 2002.[33] The curious yet deeply embedded nature of the military's political ties to Islamists was exposed once again when these groups resurfaced under different names. Maulana Azam Tariq, detained on terrorism charges, was allowed to contest the October 2002 elections and got himself reelected to the national assembly. Until his own murder in October 2003 by unknown assailants, the Maulana had supported General Musharraf and his PML-Q allies inside parliament.

Forging "Coup Coalitions"

The Pakistan Army's bloodless October 1999 coup was welcomed by prominent development NGOs and sections of the print media and the liberal intelligentsia. This apparent antidemocratic posturing of civil society actors is not unique to Pakistan. As noted in Chapter 1, civil society in Asia is a contested arena of power and competitive agendas, which contains both democratic and antidemocratic currents. In many Asian countries, some civil society groups have acquiesced in or embraced authoritarian rule, just as others have opposed it. Antidemocratic elements existed in civil society in the Philippines during the early years of the Marcos dictatorship, in Indonesia under Suharto, and in South Korea in the 1970s and 1980s (see the relevant country chapters in this volume). Even when groups have openly professed democratic ideals, definitions and conceptions of democracy have differed markedly across civil society organizations.

While state repression under both the military dictatorship of General Zia and the elected governments of the 1990s invoked opposition from disparate civil society groups, the purportedly liberal military regime that came to power in the wake of the October 1999 coup presented a different set of constraints and opportunities for civil society groups. One NGO activist captured the dilemma posed by the assumption of power by a "reform-oriented" army general, saying, "we were caught between principles and practicality. We have to deal with a military government, and we have to engage with it, but we cannot condone a military set-up. But there is also *a clear consensus* that the (democratically elected) government should not be restored."[34] Why did seemingly liberal sections of civil society acquiesce in the coup and forge antidemocratic alliances with the military?

Throughout the 1990s, the growing gap between public expectations of elective rule and the performance of civilian governments had fueled public disenchantment. Faced with a burgeoning debt burden and a shrinking revenue base, the country's civilian managers had consistently failed to bridge the growing gap between the state's military requirements and the economic needs of its populace.[35] In May 1998, when growing public and political pressures (not least from the military and Islamist quarters) forced Sharif to test atomic weapons in response to India's detonation of its own nuclear devices, Japan, the United States, and other Western donors slapped wide-ranging economic sanctions on Pakistan, exacerbating an already precarious economic situation. Widespread allegations of corruption at the highest levels of the state, violent sectarian conflict, a deteriorating law-and-order situation—all interacted in an overall milieu of political, economic, and social instability to undermine Sharif's public credibility.

By the time Musharraf deposed Sharif, therefore, the legitimacy of his government was already in decline. Sensitive to the domestic and international context in which it took power, the military cleverly attuned its reform agenda with the long-standing demands of vocal groups in civil society: accountability, decentralization of power, gender equity, and good governance. Disillusioned with politics and the traditional political elite, many prominent members of civil society misread in the military's ostensible reformist posture a genuine commitment to democratic reforms. For instance, a recent volume on *Power and Civil Society in Pakistan* (Gillani and Weiss 2001: ix), with contributions from prominent academics and NGO leaders, sanguinely asserts that "after a dozen years of floundering democracy, a new breed of military rule seems to have emerged, hindered not by the politics of selfishness but by the sentiment of love of country and compatriots . . . the military government seems breaking new ground by assigning capable, qualified people to hold key positions in government." The willingness of these members of civil society to engage the military was also driven in part by a broader intellectual skepticism about the efficacy and relevance of the ritual of electoral democracy to the country's governance woes. In that sense, influential voices in the media and NGO circles have sought to redefine the very conception of democracy and accepted, albeit grudgingly at times, the need for collaborating with the military as a way of gradually negotiating democratic space in an embedded authoritarian state. Thus, some privileged civil society elites have accepted military intervention as a "necessary evil" to cleanse politics and governance. This development is perhaps indicative of the expansion of the space available to civil society groups since the early 1990s for constructing alternative political discourses. But a less sympathetic view holds that this "antidemocratic" posturing on the part of many in civil society is reflective of their moral antipathy towards partisan politics. Such "antipolitics" poses peculiar dangers to democratic politics and institutions (Linz and Stepan 1996). It is not surprising that this antipolitical theme is eerily familiar to justifications of military intervention echoed by successive Pakistani dictators—namely, that Pakistan is not yet ready for Western-style democracy, and that the country's political system will have to be reconstructed to take into account local conditions. Musharraf has often used this argument to claim legitimacy for his regime's actions.[36] Arguably, support from these elements within civil society for its intended reform initiatives has been crucial to the military's ability to neutralize external concerns about its coercive actions and acquire a semblance of legitimacy otherwise missing in the domestic context.

While the boundaries between political and civil society can often get blurred in practice as individuals occupy more than one space, or periodically enter and exit these different spheres, the adoption of mutually antagonistic views and practices by actors in both has prevented the formation of strategic alliances. For instance, the widespread, and at times valid, fear among many civil society groups that collaborating with political parties will undermine their autonomy partly explains their inability or unwillingness to join ranks with parties for broader democratic goals.[37] There are a few exceptions, including the bar associations that work closely with parties along partisan lines. Groups like the Women's Action Forum (WAF) have cooperated with political parties on issues of common interest. Other forms of resistance to state repression or demands for group rights come from *katchiabadi* (slum) residents, peasant associations, fisherfolk, and professional media associations. The antipolitical stance of influential civil society groups has been further reinforced by the active depoliticization of society sought by authoritarian regimes. One manifestation of this policy is the systematic harping on the venality of politics by successive military regimes, which has brought into sharp focus the arbitrary division of politics into random degrees of "corruption" and "integrity"—integrity being personified by the military, and corruption by political leaders. Drama serials on state-controlled television, for instance, typically invoke a shabby image of the politician, whereas the military man is invariably portrayed as honest and patriotic. This defamation of politics is cleverly coupled with an anti-India siege mentality, perpetuated through a clever mix of images, symbols, and the fiction of military bravado transmitted via key means of socialization (school texts, radio, and television).

Restrictive structures of the political party system in Pakistan also play a part. In a situation of perpetual uncertainty created by frequent disruptions of the political process, political parties remain desperate to maintain their traditional bases of support, failing thereby in integrating new economic and social forces. "The failure of the mainstream political parties to respond to people's aspirations for socio-economic change has led to a general disillusionment with traditional forms of politics dominated by feudal and big business interests, and the lack of a political debate on issues of poverty, distributive justice, women's rights and environmental degradation," the late federal minister and NGO leader Omar Asghar Khan observed (2001: 283). "Civil society must work to empower people and not their leaders who symbolize traditional power structures that are oppressive and anti-people. Anybody who is investing in leaders and not people is not strengthening democracy, only weakening it," says Sarwar Bari, the head of an NGO, reacting to legislative training programs (Rizvi 2003).

In addition to a classic technocratic bias toward popular politics, the real and present threat presented by the armed religious Right helps explain the support of some prominent actors and organizations of civil society for Pakistan's seemingly liberal authoritarian regime, which they see as a rampart against Islamic fundamentalism. Dismissive of Pakistan's "narrow, corrupt and feudal" political elite, a former Pakistani vice president of the World Bank, Shahid Javed Burki, thinks, "General Musharraf is the man best equipped to ensure that Pakistan rids itself of jihadi groups."[38]

In Pakistan, a large majority of the public is still dependent on—and derives financial and social power from—the state. Hence the sharp dichotomy between state and civil society conceals complex political realities. Government employment and contracts constitute the biggest sources of economic security in the country. Professional associations, such as academia and trade unions, also remain beholden to a coercive state for their economic survival, as well as the fear of persecution. Civil society is thus embedded in the state via both co-optation and coercion.

And, finally, perennial authoritarianism has only further exacerbated the lack of any meaningful public articulation of the distinction between private interest and public good (Jalal 1997). Thus subnational loyalties such as those of tribe, culture, and language remain powerful markers of identity and political bargaining. These markers assume added significance in a state where access to privilege and authority is politically contested. Given the unmitigated failure of the state in managing the diverse ethnic, social, and political claims on it, as well as the absence of a pluralistic political process, the public has been forced to access the state and its resources through these subnational loyalties. A civil society terrain marked by this process of "privatization" in the sense of public withdrawal from public affairs is hardly conducive to the evolution of democratic institutions and norms that can augment the autonomy of the nonstate public realm.

A Tale of Two Development NGOs

Decentralization of power has become a critical part of civil society discourse in Pakistan, as elsewhere, not least because of its growing currency in international development circles. In early 1999, the SUNGI Development Foundation (SDF), a large and well-known social development organization,[39] organized a series of "people's assemblies," ostensibly to facilitate "creative engagement between the elite and the dispossessed at the grassroots level." People's assemblies were expected to generate "informed debate and mobilize collective action to remove inequities that marginalize large sections of the population." To its proponents, these "stakeholder" consultations presented a unique platform for discussing practical strategies and generating support for decentralization (SUNGI 1999).

When the military seized power, Western governments had moved quickly to censure the regime and freeze development aid. Keen to lure donors back and gain external legitimacy, General Musharraf wasted no time in co-opting certain leading civil society leaders into government. Those enjoying close ties with the establishment and donor agencies were the obvious first choice. Appointing the late Omar Asghar Khan, the son of a pro-Musharraf former air force chief and architect of the concept of people's assemblies, as federal minister for local government,[40] on the one hand, and creating a National Reconstruction Bureau under retired General Tanvir Naqvi, on the other, the military regime made "devolution of power" the linchpin of its reform program. As external donors rerouted their governance programs and enlisted prominent NGOs for the "bottom up reconstruction" of democracy, the military was dismantling the political system from the top. Political rallies were banned, parliament stood suspended, and the constitution was put in abeyance. In January 2000, the chief justice and half the bench of the Supreme Court were summarily dismissed for refusing to take oath under Musharraf's provisional constitution. None of this authoritarian centralization affected the pro-military policies of civil society groups, or their external donors, who continued to support the "devolution plan" even as Musharraf usurped almost all the attributes of executive power.

With help from the Asia Foundation and other Western donors, the regime's civilian reformers gave citizen participation a whole new meaning. Ironically, at a time when the "people's elected assemblies" had been dissolved, they organized "people's assemblies" around the country to help the military devolve power. Some 15,000 people participated in thirty-six of these assemblies at the district level, four at the provincial level, and one at the national level. Prominent civil society figures did not tire of publicizing this "devolution" revolution, which, they claimed, was going to radically transform Pakistan. While ostensibly radical in intent and nature, the main purpose of the scheme has been to acquire legitimacy, ensure regime survival, and create a pliant political elite that could help root the military's power in local politics and displace its traditional civilian adversaries (International Crisis Group 2004). It was therefore scarcely surprising that the military resorted to the time-tested strategy of manipulating the non-party-based local-government elections to obtain favorable results for mayoral (*nazim*) candidates affiliated with the Pakistan Muslim League Quaid-e-Azam in key districts of the vote-rich Punjab province.[41] In April 2002, when Musharraf held a fraudulent referendum to get public approval for a five-year extension of the presidential office, these local officials staged pro-Musharraf rallies mobilizing voters.[42] Again, in the run-up to the general elections held on October 10, 2002, these *nazim*s openly mobilized state resources to campaign for PML-Q candidates. With help like this from *nazim*s and military intelligence agencies, the party bagged the highest number of seats in the Punjab provincial assembly, as well as in the national assembly.[43]

Yet prominent civil society organizations have remained undeterred in the pursuit of Musharraf's "true" democracy. The Pattan Development Foundation (PDF), a flood relief NGO that has ventured into the lucrative business of electoral research, has to its discredit glossed over blatant violations of the electoral process by the military. A case in point is the April 2002 presidential referendum, the most controversial electoral exercise in Pakistan's history, with allegations of widespread irregularities.[44] Like the results of "all the previous elections held since 1988," the referendum results were "marred with controversy," the Pattan Development Foundation's referendum survey, funded by the UK's Department for International Development (DFID), declared (PDF 2002). Pattan's pro-Musharraf bias is evident in the way the survey downplays electoral abuses documented (inter alia by the Human Rights Commission of Pakistan) from all over the country, treating a dictator's flagrant abuse of state authority as a relatively fair electoral exercise.[45] Reluctantly attributing instances of irregularities to the "relaxed atmosphere of the polling stations" and the absence of voters' lists, which made the exercise "vulnerable to multiple and noneligible voting," the survey claimed notably that official pressure or intimidation was negligible, and that irregularities were limited to 26 percent of the polling stations covered. But not even a passing mention was made of Musharraf's state-financed propaganda campaign, the money doled out to local mayors to ensure that his rallies were well attended, the large number of captive votes of government officials used to ensure a high turnout, the open intimidation of polling staff by state functionaries, and more. In sum, the fact that a nongovernmental organization like Pattan felt constrained to legitimize the military's political machinations highlights the sad absence of alternative research on the referendum.

The two cases discussed above reflect the anti-political bias of "donor-financed" civil society. With their political ambitions stalled, first by General Zia's repressive dictatorship and later by a restrictive political party system, many politically oriented liberal professionals had opted instead to operate in the civil society space that helped them develop close links with influential aid agency officials, as well as the local civil-military bureaucracy—links that could be used for political gain when the opportunities were available. It is no coincidence that key members of the NGO community (including the late Omar Asghar Khan, the former head of SUNGI) first joined the Musharraf regime, and later in December 2001 formed the Qaumi Jamhoori (National Democratic) party, with the alleged backing of the military establishment.[46] Critics charge that with little political or electoral experience, the Jamhoori party was formed to reap the windfalls of the establishment's patronage—as well as the goodwill earned by the social welfare work of party members—to contest the October 2002 general elections.

Prospects

An overbearing Pakistani state has traditionally tried to relegate civil society to an appendage, appropriating the public sphere for itself and tolerating little dissent or opposition to its long-standing denial of the basic rights and needs of the populace. The prolonged absence of representative rule, the weakness of institutions in political society, and the political ascendancy of the military have all combined to obstruct the institutionalization of the public sphere as a legally protected domain outside the control of the state. The state-sponsored theocratization of public policy, notably under Zia, and the associated rise in the political clout of the Islamist right wing have further pulverized liberal forces and voices in society.

Since the mid-1980s, civil society organizations have proliferated, especially in the development sector. Largely urban-based and externally financed, many of these advocate and strive for the protection of minority and women's rights, accountability and transparency in public institutions, and reforms in specific policy areas like environmental and labor regulation laws. Still others openly seek to expand the arena of nonstate governance at the local and community levels through the provision of education, health, and sanitation services. Some also engage in important socialization functions, such as imparting voter education and disseminating information to citizens. While civil society's organizational diversity and its importance in the political and economic domains are growing, its institutionalization as a distinct sphere of self-governance outside the control of the state is still far from assured. The legal and policy framework required for constructing and strengthening a nonstate sector remains largely underdeveloped. Regulatory laws are archaic and open to abuse. Thus far, efforts to regulate the public sphere have mainly emanated from the state, engendering resistance from vocal NGO coalitions, which often rightly perceive them as attempts at control and manipulation.

The institutional foundations of civil society are likely to remain weak in Pakistan in the absence of a successful and sustained democratic transition that finally institutionalizes the principles of civilian supremacy, the rule of law, and constitutionalism. In the meanwhile, the extent to which civil society organizations can affect policy reform and political change will depend on both internal political dynamics and international factors.

For the time being, the military's coercive powers and international backing ensure General Musharraf's hold on state authority. But durable legitimacy continues to elude him, as it did his military predecessors. In a country where politicians have often forged alliances of convenience with the military in the past, the concerted opposition of the PPP and PML-N to Musharraf's authoritarian rule is an encouraging development. While the ongoing tussle is unlikely to alter the civil-military configuration in favor of civilian supremacy, the pressures generated by a defiant and loud parliamentary opposition, growing center-province tensions, and the problems of economic revival could ultimately push the military to modify the prevailing political arrangements to assuage domestic dissent.

The regional and external context also remains important. Short of a lasting resolution of the conflict over Kashmir with India, the Pakistani military is likely to retain its political dominance and, with it, the initiative to disrupt or manipulate the political process whenever it deems its corporate interests to be threatened. Clearly, representative government is not a luxury Pakistanis can afford to postpone until the time is ripe to resolve the Kashmir conflict. Periodic elections may not be a sufficient solution to the encroachment of authoritarianism on democracy in Pakistan, but they do stimulate political liberalization. Besides, even formally elective rule is preferable to a military dictatorship or a military-dominated hybrid regime in civilian guise, because it offers better prospects of fostering political stability in a multi-ethnic polity. Four years of centralized, arbitrary military rule under General Musharraf, with its all too predictable patterns of political repression, constitutional engineering, election rigging, and fraud disguised as "democratic reforms," have undermined the rule of law, weakened the moderate political parties, emasculated the judiciary, and exacerbated ethno-regional strife.

Without exaggerating the importance of international factors, it is worth noting that the scope and nature of the international community's engagement with Pakistan is also likely to affect the direction of political change. The military owes its dominance of state and society in no small part to the political, diplomatic, and economic support given it by the United States throughout the country's history. External linkages have been crucial to the ability of military dictators to prolong their stay in power. The military's calculations of retaining or transferring power are therefore a function at least in part of the incentives or disincentives in the prevailing international environment. So long as the United States needs Pakistan as a strategic ally in the war on terror, the Pakistani military's grip on the political system will continue. Amid the increasing international concerns about the "talibanization" of nuclear-armed Pakistan that have gained wider currency in Washington in light of the electoral prominence of right-wing Islamists since 2002, the military can also draw succor from its vaunted role as a bulwark against Islamic extremism.[47] If and when geopolitical conditions warrant a change of guard in Pakistan, the U.S.-led international community might look more favorably upon a democratic dispensation in which the military's political role was reduced, if only temporarily.

Notes

1. Muslim rule in India had been marked by a personalized form of sovereignty making no formal distinction between temporal and spiritual authority; see Ahmed 1941.

2. In 1955, the four provinces of Punjab, Northwest Frontier, Sindh, and Baluchistan were united under the One Unit system into West Pakistan to achieve parity with East Pakistan (Bengal).

3. In the eastern wing, resentment over two decades of biased economic and political policies of the West Pakistani establishment galvanized a popular movement for provincial autonomy under Sheikh Mujeeb's Awami League.

4. Bhutto's attempts to appease the Islamists included the banning of alcohol, nightclubs, and gambling. For details, see Nasr 1994.

5. The PNA's main catchphrase for enlisting the support of diverse societal groups opposed to Bhutto was the promise of "Nizame Mustafa" (the system of Prophet Muhammad).

6. See, e.g., Lawyers Committee for Human Rights 1985.

7. Earlier in 1985, Zia had lifted martial law and installed the elected government of Prime Minister Mohammad Khan Junejo in power, although he retained presidential powers to dismiss the civilian government. In May 1988, he used those powers to sack the Junejo government for failing to maintain law and order and for rampant corruption. The transition in 1988 represented only the military's formal withdrawal from politics.

8. According to Juan J. Linz (1978), a key test of loyalty to a democratic political system is the rejection of military support for gaining power.

9. On January 25, 1996, the bill was introduced as the Social Welfare Agencies (Registration and Regulation) Act, 1996.

10. Analysts attribute the government's hostile actions to NGO opposition to its decision to conduct nuclear tests. See, e.g., Khan 2001 and NGORC 2002.

11. The impact of labor migration to the Gulf on state and society in Pakistan is discussed in Addleton 1992 and Noman 1991.

12. The SDPC survey included the following criteria for selection of organizations: organized, private, self-governing, nonprofit, and voluntary. Thus nonvoluntary, professional associations (lawyers, doctors, engineers etc.) were excluded by definitional fiat. Also excluded are inactive organizations and privately run madrasahs that violate the "voluntary" and "organized" criteria.

13. Although registration is not mandatory in order to undertake charitable, welfare, and developmental activities, it confers legal status on the NGO to open a bank account in the name of the organization, sign contracts in the name of the organization, and offer personal indemnity to its members against the organization's liabilities. A registered NGO also qualifies for financial assistance from government agencies and local, national, and international donors.

14. The bill was encapsulated in a government-sponsored "Enabling Environment Initiative Report" prepared by the Pakistan Centre for Philanthropy (PCP), a nonprofit support organization based in Islamabad. An amended version of the law was presented to the national cabinet before the October 2002 general elections.

15. For some of these reactions, see Mudassir Rizvi, "Pakistani NGOs Fear Curb on Funds," *Asia Times*, August 9, 2002.

16. For a typology of NGOs, see Korten 1987.

17. These laws include the following: (1) the Press Council Ordinance, which seeks to establish a government-controlled Press Council to regulate the press; (2) the Registration Ordinance, which requires all media publications to be registered centrally and authorizes the government to refuse registration if applicants have been convicted of a criminal offence or, in the case of printers, of a crime involving "moral turpitude"; and (3) the Defamation Ordinance, which imposes criminal sanctions for defamation, including minimum compensatory damages of Rs. 50,000 (U.S.$ 860) and up to three months' imprisonment.

18. Sunni Islam has two major strands, Deobandi and Barelvi. The Deobandi School, established in Darul ulum Deoband in the United Provinces (now Uttar Pradesh), India, in 1867, is rigid and inward-looking. The Barelvi movement emerged as a countermovement to it, drawing its inspiration from Sufi saints.

19. The Taliban were mostly recruited from Deobandi madrasahs in the Northwest Frontier Province.

20. More notably, the Minhajul Qu'ran schools run by the Pakistan Awami Tehrik (People's Movement), a Barelvi party, combines modern education with the option of specializing in Islamic studies. For a comprehensive analysis of Pakistan's madrasah problem and the prospects of reform, see ICG 2002a.

21. Despite the military regime's concerted campaign to discredit the mainstream parties and their leadership, the results of the October 2002 general elections show they still remain popular. The PPP polled the highest number of votes, despite the fact that the electoral process was deeply flawed and stacked against the main opposition parties. See Human Rights Commission of Pakistan, "Election: Deeply Flawed," Oct. 20, 2002, www.hrcpelectoralwatch.org (accessed 4/1/2004).

22. The importance of strong political institutions for democracy is well known. See, e.g., Huntington 1968.

23. Both generals Ayub and Zia instituted local government schemes to cloak a centralized, authoritarian system of government under the garb of decentralization. See International Crisis Group 2004.

24. Musharraf's devolution plan promised extensive administrative and financial powers for elected governments. For the first time since independence, the plan formally vested executive authority over the district administration in the hands of the elected *nazim* (mayor). See "Local Government (Proposed Plan): Devolution of Power and Responsibility Establishing the Foundations for Genuine Democracy," Government of Pakistan, National Reconstruction Bureau (Islamabad: May 2000). See also Devolution Final Plan, August 2001.

25. For details, see Shah 2003.

26. The European Union Observer Mission to Pakistan called the electoral process "deeply flawed." See its report at www.eueom.org.pk/finalreport.asp (accessed 4/4/2004); Human Rights Commission of Pakistan, "Pre-Poll Rigging," at www.hrcpelectoralwatch org (accessed 4/4/2004).

27. In empowering General Musharraf to amend the constitution, the Supreme Court had declared off limits salient features of the 1973 constitution such as the federal and parliamentary structure of government.

28. The 17th Amendment to the 1973 constitution formalized the presidential powers that Musharraf had sought through the LFO. It also changed the constitutional procedure for presidential election, thus paving the way for a parliamentary endorsement of Musharraf's presidential tenure until 2007 by a vote of confidence.

29. Mudassir Rizvi, "Opposition Builds Up Against Devolution," *Asia Times Online*, Apr. 13, 2000.

30. Madrasahs specifically created for the Afghan jihad included the Jamaat-e-Islami's Rabita (contact) madrasahs. Others linked to the Jamiat Ulema Islam (JUI) served mainly as recruitment grounds.

31. The Sunni anti-Shia campaign received a stimulus from the state's declaration of Ahmedis—followers of a religious reformer who claimed to have received divine revelations as non-Muslims in 1974. On the radicalization of sectarian identities in Pakistan, see Zaman 1998.

32. The U.S. State Department added the Lashkar to its list of Designated Foreign Terrorist Organizations in January 2003.

33. Other militant groups proscribed were the Lashkare Taiba, Jaishe-e-Mohammad, Tehrike Nifaze Shariate Mohammadi, and Tehrike Jaffariya. The LeJ had been banned in August 2001.

34. Quoted in Beena Sarwar, "Pakistan: The Democracy Debate," Inter Press Service, November 28, 1999. Emphasis added.

35. In 1990, some 5.8 percent of the GDP was allocated for defense and 1.1 percent for health. See United NationsDevelopment Program 2003.

36. See, e.g., Musharraf's interview with *Time Magazine (Asia)*, October 6, 2003.

37. Although it deserves separate treatment, the "antipolitics" of the seemingly nonpartisan civil society organizations in Pakistan could make for an interesting comparison with cases where civil society organizations are polarized along partisan lines, as in Bangladesh.

38. Quoted in Luce and Bokhari 2002.

39. SUNGI claims to be an advocacy-oriented NGO with an integrated multisectoral approach to rural development. This approach involves a range of linked activities, such as community-based institutional development, gender-focus initiatives, natural resource management, small sustainable village-infrastructure projects, health and sanitation interventions, capacity building, and small rural enterprise development. See www.sungi.sdnpk.org (accessed 3/7/2004).

40. Omar Asghar Khan died in mysterious circumstances in Karachi on 25 June 2002.

41. See Azmat Abbass, "Old Habits Dies Hard," *Herald* (Karachi), Aug. 2001; see also Zahid Hussain, "An Engineered Order," special report, *Newsline* (Karachi), Sept. 2001.

42. See, e.g., Massoud Ansari, "How the Referendum was Won," cover story, *Newsline*, May 2002. Also, in the same issue, Shahzada Zulfiqar, "Constructing Consent."

43. For an analysis of the military's manipulation of the electoral process in the PML-Q's favor, see Shah 2003.

44. While the Election Commission claimed a voter turnout of 56 percent—with a 97 percent vote in Musharraf's favor, independent observers and political parties put the turnout at 10–15 percent.

45. HRCP Report on Referendum 2002. www.hrcpelectoralwatch.org (accessed 3/7/ 2004).

46. Author's interviews with senior officials of the Musharraf regime, Islamabad, June 2001.

47. For a critique of the bluwark thesis, see Stepan and Shah 2004..

Works Cited

Addleton, Jonathan. 1992. *Undermining the Center: The Gulf Migration and Pakistan*. Karachi: Oxford University Press.

Agha Khan Development Network (ADN). 2000. *Philanthropy in Pakistan: A Report of the Initiative on Indigenous Philanthropy in Pakistan*. Pakistan: ADN.

Ahmed, Muhammad Basheer. 1941. *The Administration of Justice in Medieval India*. Aligarh: Historical Research Institute.

Ahmed, Samina. 1997. "Centralization, Authoritarianism and the Mismanagement of Ethnic Relations in Pakistan." In Michael E. Brown and Sumit Ganguly, eds., *Government Policies and Ethnic Relations in the Asia and Pacific*. Cambridge, Mass.: MIT Press.

Alavi, Hamza. 1988. "Pakistan and Islam: Ethnicity and Ideology." In Fred Halliday and Hamza Alavi, eds., *State and Ideology in the Middle East and Pakistan*. New York: Monthly Review Press.

Foley, Michael, and Bob Edwards. 1996. "The Paradox of Civil Society." *Journal of Democracy* 7(3): 38–52.

Gillani, Zulfiqar, and Anita Weiss, eds. 2001. *Power and Civil Society in Pakistan*. Karachi: Oxford University Press.

Government of Pakistan. National Reconstruction Bureau. 2000. "Local Government (Proposed Plan): Devolution of Power and Responsibility Establishing the Foundations for Genuine Democracy." Islamabad: Government of Pakistan, National Reconstruction Bureau.

Human Rights Commission of Pakistan (HRCP). 2002. "Interim Report Election 2002: Pre-Poll Rigging." www.hrcpelectoralwatch.org (accessed 4/3/2004).

Huntington, Samuel P. 1968. *Political Order in Changing Societies.* New Haven: Yale University Press.

International Crisis Group (ICG). 2002a. *Pakistan: Madrassahs, Extremism, and the Military.* Asia Report 36. Brussels and Islamabad: ICG.

———. 2002b. *Pakistan: Transition to Democracy.* Asia Report 40. Brussels and Islamabad: ICG.

———. 2004. *Devolution in Pakistan: Reform or Regression.* Asia Report 77. Brussels and Islamabad.

Jalal, Ayesha. 1990. *The State of Martial Rule: The Origins of Pakistan's Political Economy of Defense.* Lahore: Sange Meel.

______. 1995. *Democracy and Authoritarianism in South Asia.* Lahore: Sange Meel.

———. 1997. "Ideology and the Struggle for Democratic Institutions." In Victoria Schofield, ed., *Old Roads, New Highways: Fifty Years of Pakistan.* Karachi: Oxford University Press.

Keck, Margaret E., and Kathryn Sikkink, eds. 1998. *Activists Beyond Borders: Advocacy Networks in International Politics.* Ithaca, N.Y.: Cornell University Press.

Khan, Omar Asghar. 2001. "Critical Engagements." In Anita Weiss and Zulfiqar Gillani, eds., *Power and Civil Society in Pakistan.* Karachi: Oxford University Press.

Khilnani, Sunil. 2001. "The Development of Civil Society." In Sunil Khilnani and Sudipta Kaviraj, eds., *Civil Society: History and Possibilities.* Cambridge: Cambridge University Press.

Korten, David. 1987. "Third Generation NGO Strategies: A Key to People-centered Development." *World Development* 15 (suppl.): 145–59.

Linz, Juan J. 1978. *The Breakdown of Democratic Regimes: Crisis, Breakdown and Reequilibration.* Baltimore: Johns Hopkins University Press.

Linz, Juan J., and Alfred Stepan. 1996. *Problems of Democratic Transition and Consolidation: Southern Europe, South America and Post-Communist Europe.* Baltimore: Johns Hopkins University Press.

Luce, Edward, and Farhan Bokhari. 2002. "An Undemocratic Friend." *Financial Times*, Apr. 28.

Mumtaz, Khawaz, and Farida Shaheed, eds. 1987. *Women of Pakistan: Two Steps Forward, One Step Back?* London: Zed Books.

Nasr, Syed Vali. 1994. *The Vanguard of the Islamic Revolution: The Jamaat e Islami of Pakistan.* London: I. B. Tauris.

———. 2002. "Islam, the State, and the Rise of Sectarian Militancy in Pakistan." In Christophe Jaffrelot, ed., *Pakistan: Nationalism Without a Nation.* London: Zed Books.

NGO Resource Center (NGORC). 2002. *Civil Society in Pakistan.* Karachi: NGORC.

Niazi, Zamir. 1986. *The Press in Chains.* Karachi: Royal Book Company.

Noman, Omar. 1990. *Pakistan: Political and Economic History since 1947.* Rev. 2d ed. New York: Kegan Paul International.

———. 1991. "The Impact of Migration on Pakistan's Economy and Society." In H. Donnan and P. Werbner, eds., *Economy and Culture in Pakistan: Migrants and Cities in a Muslim Society.* London: Macmillan.

Non-Profit Public Benefit Organizations (Governance and Support) Draft Act. 2003. Enabling Environment Initiative, Pakistan Centre for Philanthropy.

Pasha, Mustapha K. 1997. "The Hyper-Extended State: Civil Society and Democracy." In

Rasul B. Rais, ed., *State, Society and Democratic Change in Pakistan*. Karachi: Oxford University Press.

Pattan Development Foundation (PDF). 2002. *Interim Report: Presidential Referendum Study*. Islamabad: Pattan.

Payne, Leigh A. 2000. *Uncivil Movements: The Armed Right Wing and Democracy in Latin America*. Baltimore: Johns Hopkins University Press.

Rizvi, Hasan Askari. 2000. *Military, State and Society in Pakistan*. London: Macmillan.

Rizvi, Mudassir. 2000. "Opposition Builds Up Against Devolution." *Asia Times*, Apr. 13. www.atimes.com (accessed 4/3/2004).

______. 2002. "Pakistani NGOs Fear Curb on Funds." *Asia Times*, Aug. 9. www.atimes.com (accessed 4/3/2004).

———. 2003. "Pakistan: Aid Well Meant, Poorly Spent." *Asia Times*, Feb. 11. http://www.atimes.com (accessed 4/3/2004).

Schmitter, Philippe. 1995. "On Civil Society and Consolidation of Democracy: Ten Propositions." Mimeographed. Stanford University, Department of Political Science.

Shah, Aqil. 2001. "South Asia." In Robin Hodess, ed., *Global Corruption Report 2001*. Transparency International. Berlin, Germany.

______. 2002. "Democracy on Hold in Pakistan." *Journal of Democracy* 13(1): 67–75.

———. 2003. "Pakistan's 'Armored' Democracy." *Journal of Democracy* 14(1): 26–40.

SPDC. 2002a. *Dimensions of the Non-Profit Sector in Pakistan (Preliminary Estimates)*. Working Paper No. 1. Karachi: Social Policy and Development Center.

———. 2002b. *Nonprofit Sector in Pakistan: Government Policy and Future Issues*. Working paper No. 2. Karachi: Social Policy and Development Center.

Stepan, Alfred, and Aqil Shah. 2004. "Pakistan's Real Bulwark." *The Washington Post*, May 5.

SUNGI Development Foundation. 1999. "Public Interest Organizations: Responding to Challenges and Opportunities." People's Assemblies process report, Islamabad.

United Nations. Development Program. *Human Development Report 2003*. New York: Oxford University Press.

Washbrook, David. 1999. "The Rhetoric of Democracy and Development in Late Colonial India." In Sugata Bose and Ayesha Jalal, eds., *Nationalism, Democracy and Development: State and Politics in India*. New Delhi: Oxford University Press.

Weiss, Anita, and Zulfiqar Gilani, eds. 2001. *Power and Civil Society in Pakistan*. Karachi: Oxford University Press.

Whitehead, Lawrence. 1997. "Bowling in the Bronx: The Uncivil Interstices Between Civil and Political Society." In Robert Fine and Shirin Rai, eds., *Civil Society: Democratic Perspectives*. Portland, Or.: F. Cass.

Zaman, Muhammad Qasim. 1998. "Sectarianism in Pakistan: The Radicalization of Shia and Sunni Identities." *Modern Asian Studies* 32(3): 689–716.

CHAPTER TWELVE

Burma

Civil Society Skirting Regime Rules

KYAW YIN HLAING

In August 1988, taking advantage of relentless economic hardship brought about by government mismanagement, informal student and other societal organizations mobilized the people of Burma in a nationwide antigovernment protest calling for the replacement of the "Burmese Way to Socialism" with a multiparty system. Within two weeks after the onset of this social movement (known as the Four Eights democratic movement, because it started on the eighth day of the eighth month of 1988), hundreds of social movement organizations (SMOs) emerged throughout the country and joined student protesters. In most major cities, leaders of SMOs also formed strike committees to coordinate with the activities of various local SMOs.

Although the emergence of such a large number of SMOs in such a short time came as a surprise to most Burma-watchers, no one has thoroughly investigated how these SMOs came into existence. Most Burma-watchers regarded SMOs as an indication that civil society, an entity destroyed by the military after it took control of the country in March 1962, was reemerging (see Fink 2001; ICG 2001; Liddell 1999; Steinberg 2001.) They also attributed the reemergence of civil society to the breakdown of a repressive socialist regime. And when the military reasserted control over the country in September 1988, scholars and journalists alike trotted out the obituary of civil society organizations in Burma. For most Burma-watchers, civil society organizations came into being when there was an opening of political opportunity and ceased to exist when that opportunity disappeared. I take issue with such a perspective. Indeed, I contend that the military was never able to wipe out civil society organizations. Most of the SMOs that led the Four Eights democratic movement were not the organizations that emerged after the breakdown of the socialist government but the groups, formal and informal, that survived the military's cleansing campaign. Most Burma-watchers failed to acknowledge the existence of civil society organizations because they thought that only formal organizations could function within the limits set by the government. In their opinion, civil society could not exist if there was no legitimate official space for civil society organizations.

In authoritarian countries like Burma, as we shall see, politically conscious people did not accept that the state had the exclusive right to establish the parameters of civil society. In politically unfavorable circumstances, activists formed informal organizations. As explicated in Chapter 1, it is necessary to consider informal social groups as part of civil society, because their activities are very similar to those of civil society organizations in democratic countries. Similarly, we must not discount the contributions of local religious and social organizations. Whenever there was a political opportunity, civil society activists tried to appropriate these local organizations and turn them into SMOs or politically conscious civil society organizations. In the following pages, I explore the role of both legal and informal civil organizations in the emergence of the Four Eights democratic movement, as well as the state of civil society thereafter.

The Social Movement Model

Students of civil society usually employ the authoritarian corporatist model to examine the state of civil society in authoritarian countries. As Mary Gallagher illustrates in Chapter 13, in most authoritarian countries, the state creates social organizations to control society. This means that those who join government-sanctioned organizations can only bring about gradual political change. But the authoritarian corporatist model is not very useful in explaining the emergence of social movements—especially in questioning how such movements spread, even though the legal space for independent civil society organizations remains closed.

Three leading scholars of social movements, Doug McAdam, Charles Tilly, and Sidney Tarrow, have proposed an approach (which they call an interactive and dynamic framework for analyzing mobilization) that can help us understand how political activists might overcome their organizational deficits and launch nationwide political protests. In explaining the ebb and flow of a social movement, the interactive framework considers how broad processes of change affect the sociopolitical environment, how activists perceive and construct opportunity and threat, and how activists appropriate social and organizational bases (McAdam et al. 2001: 45). According to this framework, broad social and political change in a country brings about changes in the social, political, and economic environments, which in turn create opportunities for activists to engage in collective action. The framework does not, however, assume that collective action will automatically follow from changes in the environment. What the framework suggests is this: whether activists will engage in collective action depends on the reality of the opportunity, the threat of forceful retaliation from the regime, and how the activists and the general populace perceive the opportunities and threat (McAdam et al. 2001: 46–47).

As this framework suggests, activists must therefore convince others that the movement is worth joining. And this, in turn, can be done by constructing an injustice frame (underscoring "the seriousness and injustice of a social condition" or redefining "as unjust and immoral what was previously seen as unfortunate but perhaps tolerable"), an identity frame (defining a common identity of the movement in order to "define enemies by real or imagined attributes and evil"), and an agency frame (creating "consciousness that it is possible to alter conditions or policies through collective actions") (Gamson 1995: 87; Tarrow 1998: 109–12). This process, often referred to as collective action framing, involves "interactive reconstruction of disputes" among activists, their opponents, the state, and the media (McAdam et al. 2001: 48). So long as the movement continues, therefore, activists and their opponents try to frame and reframe identities, rituals, demands, and goals.

The framework also notes that in order to carry out the framing and actual mobilization, activists need resources and structure. These resources include money, labor, time, expertise, and access to media. The mobilization structure usually includes both formal organizations and informal social networks. In the face of organizational shortcomings, activists might appropriate existing networks, organizations, and collective identities and turn them into "vehicles of mobilization" (McAdam et al. 2001: 44–45; Boudreau 2001). Although informal networks can serve as a "common source of recruitment into social movements," they are not sufficiently organized to engage in "sustained challenges against powerful opponents." Since it is nearly impossible to achieve a sustained social movement without some form of organization, activists need to create formal organizations "that are sufficiently robust to structure sustained relations with opponents, but are flexible enough to permit the informal connections that link people and networks to one another to aggregate and coordinate contention" (Tarrow 1998: 124). When a movement's activities are launched, organizers must "invent, adapt, and combine various forms of contention" in an effort to mobilize bystanders. In so doing, activists should employ tactics within their current repertoire (such as forms of contention), create new ones, or adopt innovative actions—especially means that are banned by the regime in question.

Unlike the corporatist model, the innovative framework outlined here draws attention to the movement precisely because of its potential, through informal networks, to undertake a full-fledged social movement. Unlike the relative deprivation argument, the framework allows one to see the complexity in the process of mobilizing a social movement. Throughout the chapter, relying on the interactive model, we shall see how political activists in Burma tried to mobilize social movements through their informal networks.

Military Rule and the Fate of Civil Society

Although there were no formal civil society organizations in precolonial Burma, by the time the military took control of the country in 1962, there were a number of them. Thanks to Western education and the advent of print capitalism under the British, Burmese came to learn how formal associations could be formed and how people in other parts of the world, especially in the West, tried to achieve social and political objectives by forming associations. Burmese saw how Christian missionaries and European, Indian, and Chinese businesspeople formed religious, social, and business associations soon after their arrival in Burma. Making use of this knowledge themselves, they began to form trade and student unions as well as religious, social welfare, business, community, and native-place associations. The open parliamentary system bequeathed by the British after independence allowed the public to form both political and nonpolitical organizations freely. As a result, this period in Burma's political history saw the emergence of a host of new organizations. In the early 1950s, some civil society organizations were affiliated with political parties. As early as 1961, however, many such organizations began to establish autonomy from other political parties—most notably the ruling one.[1] This is the chief reason why the military had to deal with so many civil society organizations in establishing the Burma Socialist Program Party (BSPP) and launching *kkhit-pyone-taw-hlan-ye* (social revolution).

As in many socialist countries, the military-dominated government did not allow civil organizations to flourish freely. Within a few months after taking control of the country, the socialist government imposed a 9 P.M. curfew on all students staying at university hostels (Htun Aung Gyaw 1997: 20). When the Rangoon University student union rejected the new regulations by staging demonstrations on campus, the government responded by arresting student leaders and dynamiting the historic student union building. This act had a twofold purpose: to ensure that these student organizations disappeared and to demonstrate the government's willingness to deal forcefully with perceived threats. As a final move to curb the growth of civil society organizations, the government issued the National Solidarity Act of 1964 outlawing all political organizations and forbidding the formation of new political associations without government permission (Ba Kyaing 1983: 176–77). The law permitted only the government's own Burma Socialist Program Party and its affiliated organizations. And since the law did not define "political organization," it not only entrusted the government with the discretionary power to take action against any organization it targeted but also discouraged the general public from involving itself in politically controversial organizations.

Immediately after the National Solidarity Act was issued, the government outlawed all organizations that had the potential to mount challenges to it and arrested outspoken leaders of these banned organizations. Although the law did not outlaw business organizations, the anticapitalist campaigns carried out by the BSPP government drove a number of foreign businesspeople out of the country and made the existence of private business organizations irrelevant to the new political and economic systems. Furthermore, the government created the Workers' Asiayone (workers' organizing committee), the Peasants' Asiayone (peasants' organizing committee), the Lanzin Youth Organization, the War Veterans' Organization, the Literary Workers' Association, and the Actors', Artists', and Performers' Association, claiming that these were the proper channels for the public to make its needs known to the government (Kyaw Yin Hlaing 2001a: 141).

Just as in most socialist and communist countries, the state-sponsored organizations did not represent the interests of the social sectors whose names they bore. They were merely corporatist organizations utilized by the government to contain the demands of the public and keep watch over potential saboteurs of the party. The constitutions of all these organizations stated clearly that their members would participate in the construction of a socialist society under the tutelage of the BSPP. Therefore the social groups formed by the BSPP government by no means deserve to be called civil society organizations; they were merely tools of the government. The Literary Workers' Organization not only absorbed the formerly independent Journalists' Organization and Writers' Association but also required its members to write stories and articles in support of the party and its policies. Furthermore, its members were obliged to report to the government whenever they found fellow writers defaming the party in print (interviews, 1998).[2] The same responsibilities were imposed on members of other organizations as well—members of the Lanzin Youth Organization, for instance, were instructed by their respective township committees to keep an eye on the activities of suspicious youths (interviews, 1998).

Although the law did not forbid the formation of nonpolitical peasant, youth, worker, writer, journalist, and artist associations, neither the government nor its watchdog organizations would tolerate the existence of rivals to state-sponsored organizations. Whenever journalists, writers, and artists tried to form independent groups, the government, with the help of state-sponsored organizations and other state agencies, managed to outlaw them by finding fault with the way they functioned. In the mid-1970s, for instance, a group of writers and journalists in Mandalay formed an independent literary group known as the Saturday Literary Discussion Group (Khin Nyunt 1989: 73). The government's Literary Workers' Association, however, regarded it as a rival and scrutinized its activities. When members of the Saturday Group had a discussion on the literary work of a left-wing nationalist leader, a senior member of the Literary Workers' Association had the group banned by the government on the charge of spreading communist literature (interview, writer, January 2002). In view of such harsh government measures, scholars came to conclude that civil society in Burma was effectively dead.

This was only a partial truth. Although the government narrowed the space for autonomous political organizations and their activities, some room was left for social and religious associations. Thus a number of organizations remained intact, and some of the targeted groups managed to survive by keeping a low profile. The organizations that the socialist government tried to eradicate included political parties and their affiliates, such as student unions, business groups, and politically conscious religious organizations. Although all political parties and their affiliates, as well as peasant organizations and trade and student unions, ceased to exist, the Union of Burma Chamber of Commerce and Industry (UBCCI), the Mandalay Traders, Brokers, and Industrialists Association (MTBIA), hundreds of market associations, and the biggest politically conscious religious organization, Yahanpyo Aphwe (All-Burma Young Monks' Association), continued to exist throughout the socialist period (interview, retired politician, January 2002). On account of government surveillance, however, members of the Yahanpyo Aphwe stopped participating in political activities and devoted most of their time to the administration of Mandalay Hill (a prominence with several religious temples and statues of Buddha). The UBCCI continued to exist because some of its leading members kept the office open throughout the socialist period. The MTBIA managed to escape the socialist government's anticapitalist campaigns by disguising itself as a religious organization under the new name of the Traders, Brokers, and Industrialists Kahtina Association (interviews, senior member of the UBCCI, March 1998; interview, senior member of the Traders, Brokers, and Industrialists Kahtina Association, September 1998; Suu Hngyat 2001: 57). Under the guise of a religious association, the Traders, Brokers, and Industrialist Kahtina Association functioned as it had done in presocialist days.

The organizations that remained completely intact encompassed nonpolitical religious groups (including the Young Men's Buddhist Association),[3] monasteries, native-place societies, community organizations, and ethnic groups. Apart from community organizations, all these groups had the potential for social influence beyond a ward or village temple. The government also allowed the formation of new religious and native-place organizations, provided that they registered with the Home Ministry. A retired journalist estimates that the number of native-place organizations in Rangoon and Mandalay doubled during the socialist period (interview, December 2001). While the government tried to put party cadres on the boards of trustees of big temples serving as venues for political activities, it also kept certain ethnic organizations, especially the associations of ethnic minorities with insurgent wings, under surveillance, although allowing their religious and social wings to engage in nonpolitical activities freely. The Malun Rice Donation Association, for instance, formed by a group of Burmese businesspeople in the 1890s to support monks studying dharma, continued to operate as it had done during the colonial and parliamentary periods. All in all, the socialist government allowed civil society organizations to exist so long as they posed no challenge, direct or indirect, to it.

The socialist government was fully aware, of course, of the continued existence of the UBCCI and the tricks played by the MTIBA. Government officials condone their existence because they are not regarded as threats. Indeed, these two business organizations have not only assumed a nonthreatening posture but have formed amicable relations with local authorities by bribing them or donating to state functions (interview, former BSPP official, January 2002).

The narrowing of legal space for autonomous political activities did not, however, bring an end to autonomous political organizations. When there was no room for them within the civil society space set by the government, students, teachers, lawyers, and writers created informal discussion groups and engaged in illegal political activities. As a result of political constraints, membership in such organizations was strictly confined to the social networks of their initial founders (interview, former Burmese Community Party activist, June 2002). If the founder was a teacher, he would try to recruit politically conscious colleagues and students. If students were the founders, they would try to approach their peers. Informal study groups formed by lawyers and writers usually consisted of people from different social backgrounds, including monks and laborers. In the initial stage, those who wished to form an informal organization would try to recruit members by asking like-minded people to read books and articles on politics, history, and social analysis.[4] They then discussed the readings with potential members of their discussion group, sometimes individually and sometimes in small groups. Usually, they ended up inviting readers who expressed genuine enthusiasm about the books and exchanging views on them (interview, former BCP member, June 2002).

When the founders were teachers and the recruits were students, discussions were run more like political training sessions. The teachers tried to teach methods of analyzing domestic and international political developments. "Whenever we got together," a former member of an informal reading group organized by a private schoolteacher notes, "our teacher first gave a brief lecture on the book or article we planned to discuss that day. Then he would ask what we thought of the book. We also had to discuss how we thought we could use the knowledge we gained from the books in analyzing domestic and international political situations" (interview, August 2002). The discussion groups run by students "provided students with an opportunity to question and discuss rather than merely listen and repeat" (Fink 2001: 185). "The discussion sessions were very challenging," a former student leader said. "We had to talk about what we thought of the books we read and how we could apply the knowledge we gained from those books to the situation in our country. Although we did read banned books from time to time, most of the books were legal publications. In most cases, it was not the books that made our discussion groups illegal but the manner in which the discussions were conducted" (interview, August 2002). Since the subjects they discussed were politically sensitive, informal discussion groups held their meetings in monasteries, private homes, and other secret locations, rarely holding two meetings consecutively in the same place.

The size of informal organizations and the extent of their activities varied as well, depending on the connections of their leading members and their ambitions. Some organizations confined their membership to a small number of trusted people (five to eight) and dissolved whenever members became too busy to take an active part. This usually happened when members of small student study groups graduated. Some ambitious informal organizations, however, managed to establish networks with other informal groups in various parts of the country. Christina Fink summarizes the way such study groups functioned:

> The literature discussion groups expanded to several towns, and they were able to collect a number of books. The way the system worked was that no one could own a book permanently. Once a person had read it, he or she would write a short comment and the name of his or her hometown in the back and pass it on to another member. In this way, books traveled all over Burma. Sometimes a book would return to the original owner six months or a year later. (Fink 2001: 185)

Members of a discussion group were usually unacquainted with members of other groups, even if they belonged to the same network. In such a network, only representatives of the groups met occasionally and exchanged information about one another's activities (interviews, 2002). Study groups that belonged to the same network usually read the same books, however, printed the same kind of antigovernment brochures and pamphlets, and shouted the same antigovernment slogans whenever they engaged in protests. Thus whenever a member of a discussion group came across another group's antigovernment activities, he or she had to check the pamphlets they distributed and the slogans they shouted before getting involved. If their pamphlets and slogans were similar to those of his or her own group, it could safely be assumed that they were a "brother group" and therefore acceptable. In this way, one did not have to worry about getting tricked into sham antigovernment activities orchestrated by government agents.

Many ambitious informal organizations were loosely connected to illegal political groups, especially the Burma Communist Party (BCP). Some political activists, however, created informal organizations independently but later tried to contact either the BCP or right-wing political masterminds in search of leaders who could give them guidelines for their activities. Some of these groups became affiliates of illegal political organizations, while others simply remained sympathizers. The informal affiliates functioned according to the instructions received from their illegal political organization (interview, former SMO leader, September 2002). The sympathizer groups did not always follow instructions, however, although they did occasionally sound out advice on organizing certain activities. There is no way of knowing the exact number of affiliated informal groups or independent informal groups, but the independents appear to have outnumbered the groups that were connected to illegal political groups. Of the forty-two informal groups I was able to identify, only five were directly linked to the BCP, fifteen were sympathizer groups, and twenty-two were independent. Independent groups were generally smaller in size than the groups directly or indirectly connected to illegal political organizations.

Although discussion of books on politics and society and the country's political situation was the primary goal of most informal study groups, a number of them, especially student groups, also celebrated the anniversary of certain political events by secretly disseminating pamphlets with antigovernment messages and scrawling antigovernment slogans on the walls of classrooms. "In those days [during the socialist period]," notes a former Lanzin Youth leader, "you were sure to receive pamphlets with antigovernment messages around July 7. Antigovernment students usually did it to celebrate the anniversary of the government's demolition of the student building on the Rangoon University campus. Whenever July 7 drew near, university authorities asked students like me [Lanzin Youth leaders] to keep an eye on suspicious students" (interview, December 2001). Although the people who celebrated the anniversary of political events usually tried to conduct their activities secretly, their actions were akin to what James Scott has called hidden transcripts: they tried to hide their identities, but they always wanted the government to be aware of what they had done. They also wanted the government to know there were people like them who were unhappy with the regime. Informal study groups often mailed their antigovernment pamphlets to senior government officials as well.

Informal study groups also tried to organize overt demonstrations when they thought that public anger against the government was running high. Whenever people suffered from economic difficulties or some injustice at the hands of the government, informal reading groups often tried to increase the level of public discontent by urging the public to join in their antigovernment activities. Whether an informal reading group organized a successful demonstration depended largely on the political opportunity and the level of public grievance. Large-scale demonstrations were more likely to occur if the opportunity arose when public grievances were at a peak. Since it was not always easy to recognize a ripe opportunity under an opaque repressive regime, informal study groups usually placed more emphasis on the level of public rancor. Whenever they thought the level of public outrage was high, they tried to organize demonstrations against the government.

To be sure, not all informal study groups were equally active in organizing antigovernment activities. Of the forty-two informal groups I studied, twelve confined their activities mainly to political discussions. Of the remaining thirty, only eight played an active role in organizing protests and the rest merely participated in protests organized by other groups. Moreover, not all members of active informal groups were equally active in antigovernment work. According to three activists from three different groups, only 50 to 70 percent of the members took part in overt antigovernment activities. Members of BCP-connected study groups, however, participated in both covert and overt antigovernment activities more actively than right-wing-affiliated and independent groups. Because the BCP was one of the strongest antigovernment armed groups, association with it could earn one a long prison term, even if one did not participate actively. BCP-affiliated groups therefore tended to attract especially dedicated people as members. All the BCP-affiliated groups I studied were fifteen to twenty years old at the time they ceased to function, whereas independent and right-wing groups tended to break up within eight years.

All in all, then, despite the government's narrowing of the legal space for autonomous political organizations, a number of them remained intact throughout the socialist period. The government had the power—as Michael Mann would put it, the despotic power—to close down the legal space for autonomous political groups, but it did not have enough power—what Mann calls infrastructural power—to close down all the illegal spaces. Although the illegal spaces lay outside the parameters set by government, they were not totally beyond the government's control and manipulation, so the groups could not really function freely there. As we shall see, changes in the government and sociopolitical and economic developments would shape the way in which these informal groups functioned in illegal spaces.

The Four Eights Movement

Because the socialist government was prepared to do whatever was necessary to eliminate its foes, it was not easy for SMOs to organize overt protests. The government cracked down on all antigovernment demonstrations. Several members of the two major antisocialist movements—commonly known as the U Than movement and the Hmaing Centenary movement—were shot dead on the streets by government security forces. Others received long prison terms. One activist who played a leading role in both movements was hanged (Htun Aung Gyaw 1991: 1–2). Given such brutal actions on the government's part in the 1970s, no major antigovernment activities occurred in the first half of the 1980s. Most informal study groups confined their activities to discussing the country's political and economic problems and celebrating special anniversaries by distributing antigovernment brochures and pamphlets. In the latter half of the 1980s, however, sociopolitical and economic developments allowed these informal study groups to organize a nationwide democratic movement.

The 1980s were, in fact, bad years both for the socialist government and for the people. The country's economic growth had stalled and the cost of living was exorbitant. In 1985, some 40 percent of the population was living below the absolute poverty level (UNICEF 1988). Since the socialist government controlled the entire economy, it was responsible for the bad economic conditions. Public grievances against the government were heightened when people found out about their government's inept handling of the country's economic problems. Instead of correcting its mismanagement, the government laid the blame for the failing economy on the international economic situation (Yitri 1989: 543). Then, in an attempt to control the illegal money circulating in the black market, the government carried out demonetization in 1986 and 1987. As a result, the country's two largest banknotes became worthless in the first demonetization initiative and the next three banknotes followed in the second. In the first demonetization, people who had paid taxes on their income could convert all of their demonetized banknotes into legal tender; those who could not prove their tax payment could convert only 75 percent of their banknotes and the rest was confiscated by the government as a fine for presumed tax evasion (*Guardian Daily*, November 8, 1988). But in the second exercise, there was no systematic conversion of demonetized bills to legal tender.

Not only did the government's negligence have a negative impact on many people, but the Burmese banking system was so inefficient that most people chose to keep their money with them rather than depositing it in a bank. Many lower-middle-class families in fact lost their life savings owing to the inefficient banking system, and all business transactions came to a halt in the second demonetization exercise. The country was in shock. People's resentment intensified when they learned that the United Nations had given Burma the status of "least developed country." A retired government officer observed: "It was very embarrassing and upsetting to see our country on the list of the world's poorest countries. You know, our country used to be one of the most prosperous in Southeast Asia" (interview, 1999). The more the economic condition deteriorated, the more people resented the government. By 1988, the socialist government found itself in its most vulnerable position since it had come to power in 1962.

Taking advantage of this situation, BCP-affiliated student study groups in Rangoon and Mandalay distributed a series of pamphlets urging college students in Rangoon to rise up against the government. At the outset, most students tried to distance themselves from such activities—the cost of participating in antigovernment protest would be too high—but an unexpected development brought changes in favor of opposition groups. In the middle of March 1988, a minor off-campus brawl between some engineering students and some outsiders broke out near the Rangoon Institute of Technology (RIT). Initially, the incident was nonpolitical, but it grew into a violent riot because of mismanagement by local authorities. In the course of its suppression, a student was fatally wounded—infuriating students at Rangoon University and RIT. Taking advantage of the situation, leaders of informal study groups publicly urged students to express their unhappiness with the government's handling of the incident by participating in antigovernment rallies at the university. Although this development gave various study groups on university campuses an opportunity to cooperate, the BCP-affiliated and independent groups never managed to find a way to work together. Not only did they not trust each other, but no one could agree on who should lead a new coalition. "It was really bad," notes a former member of a study group. "Everybody wanted to be a leader. Everybody thought they deserved to be a leader. All these groups were fighting against the same enemy. But we were not united even in the presence of a common enemy" (interview, September 2002). Ordinary students were not aware of the existence of different SMOs on their campus. They simply supported whoever dared to lead them at the public assemblies. On March 17, when leaders of an independent group marched to RIT with five thousand Rangoon University students, they were stopped on the way by well-equipped riot police. When students refused to comply with their orders, the police crushed the demonstration by force. The cost of launching an antigovernment procession proved to be very high. A number of students were allegedly beaten or shot dead, hundreds of students were arrested, and forty-one students suffocated inside an overpacked police van (Yitri 1989: 545).

As people's resentment of the government mounted, study groups tried to arrange mass rallies at Rangoon University and RIT, and more antigovernment pamphlets began circulating on campus. To control the situation, the government closed down every university in the country. When universities were reopened in May, students at Rangoon University and RIT found many of their friends missing. By this point it was not difficult for opposition groups to provoke students into joining antigovernment rallies. Moreover, various study groups turned themselves into full-fledged SMOs. Many began recruiting new members into the inner circles of their organizations. Small independent study groups began joining bigger BCP-affiliated or independent groups. At this time, there were three major student-led groups: the communist sympathizers led by Min Ko Naing and two independent groups, led by Min Zaya and Than Win. Since no group was strong enough to attract all the students, the only viable option left was for these different groups to avoid confrontations among themselves by focusing on antigovernment rallies.

Because the BCP-affiliated SMOs appeared stronger and better organized than their independent counterparts at Rangoon University and RIT, they often managed to present their demands as the demands of all the students (interview, student leader, August 2002). In June 1988, for example, a BCP-affiliated SMO asked the government to take action against the officials responsible for the death of students in the March incident, to release all the arrested students, and to allow student unions to form in universities across the country (Htun Aung Gyaw 1997: 41). Although the government did not satisfy all these demands, it did release some students and take nominal action against a few officials supposedly responsible for the students' deaths. When student-led SMOs from Rangoon University and RIT undertook antigovernment activities on their respective campuses, the government again suspended classes at all universities. While informal study groups-turned-SMOs were pondering their next step, the BCP instructed its agents to organize nationwide antigovernment rallies with the help of its affiliated and sympathizer groups (interview, former BCP member, June 2002). Similarly, independent student groups started mobilizing for the BCP's nationwide movement when they learned about it from their friends (interviews, former student activists, 1998, 1999, 2000).

The public, meanwhile, held the government responsible for most of their suffering and called upon it to undertake radical political and economic reforms. When the government failed to carry out these reforms, the people called for the government to resign. Having witnessed the regime's brutal actions against its opponents, however, most Burmese thought of themselves as utterly powerless vis-à-vis the government. "The major problem we encountered," notes a movement leader, "was that most people we tried to mobilize did not think they could do much to change the situation" (interview, August 2002). SMOs therefore needed to convince the public that it was possible to alter conditions through collective action. Although they did not collaborate, this leader continued, BCP-affiliated and independent SMOs alike tried to rouse people out of their faintheartedness and bring them "into action in conflictual settings" by informing them of the "diagnosis and remedy for existing forms of suffering." Antigovernment pamphlets distributed by various SMOs blamed all the suffering of the people on government corruption. And, these pamphlets added, replacing the authoritarian government with a democratic one through collective action was a good way of eradicating all the suffering. The government, of course, responded harshly. A number of political activists who were arrested while engaging in antigovernment activities were not only jailed without trial but tortured. Given these political constraints, many people, among them several political activists, were not optimistic about the possibility of a nationwide antigovernment movement.

Political developments in the first half of 1988, however, gave activists the confidence they needed to persist in their antigovernment activities. At the special party congress held in July, Ne Win, chairman of the Burma Socialist Program Party, stepped down after proposing a referendum on whether Burma should adopt a multiparty system. To many people's surprise, the congress voted down Ne Win's proposal (Yitri 1989: 547). For the first time in the history of the BSPP, an irreconcilable split occurred between the party's chairman, Ne Win, and his comrades. Until then, the congress had been a mere rubber stamp, and party members had meekly followed Ne Win's instructions. Those who defied him were fired immediately. This is why Burma-watchers jokingly remarked that the BSPP did not have a chairman, the chairman had a party. This 1988 split was not a division between softliners and hard-liners, however, as in China or eastern Europe. Instead, it was due to the congress's fear of losing the privileges they had acquired. Although party delegates officially asked Ne Win to remain in power, he prudently chose not to stay.

Both the opposition and the general public sensed the opening up of opportunity. Burmese people found Ne Win's disappearance from active politics especially significant, because none of his potential successors seemed as capable as he. "The government at the time," says a leading member of an opposition group, "was very unstable. Most high-ranking officials did not know Ne Win would resign. Although they voted down Ne Win's proposal, they were not prepared to handle the ongoing political situation properly. People were very angry with them. It was impossible for the government to consolidate its position in one or two days or even a few months. It was in a most untenable position. We thought the time was right to organize a nationwide demonstration" (interview, June 1994). Furthermore, SMOs began receiving moral and even material support from major foreign embassies, including those of the United States, Japan, Germany, and Australia. A delegation from the Japanese government, for example, informed the opposition groups of its eagerness to work with them. "It was a great encouragement to learn," notes a student leader, "that all these leading democratic countries supported us. They were eager to work with us. Their support encouraged us to increase the momentum of our activities" (interview, November 1995).

Despite the new political opportunity and the support accorded by major foreign embassies, SMOs still had trouble disseminating information about a nationwide movement. It was too dangerous to transport antigovernment pamphlets freely, of course, and they had no access to the state-controlled media. Even late in July 1988, many people, especially in rural areas, did not know that opposition groups were trying to organize a nationwide democratic rally on August 8. A survey of 100 urbanites and 100 rural people conducted in 1999 indicated that only 15 of the rural people and 25 urbanites knew about the Four Eights movement two weeks before the rally began. The rest did not learn about it until the following week. The problem was resolved when members of an independent student SMO happened to run into the BBC correspondent Christopher Guiness. On August 6, 1988, an interview with a group of Rangoon University students was aired by the BBC. First, the student leaders described how students were tortured in prison:

> I will tell you what I know about the treatment of girls arrested. I was treated the same way. . . . They abused the girls: Some of them injected lethal drugs into some girls who were half-dead. . . . Some students got pregnant. Some of them tried to take their own lives. I am one of them but I did not try to commit suicide. I have to go on fighting. I have been very much hurt by the government. I will therefore fight the government up to my last breath. They hurt us inhumanly. (BBC broadcast, August 6, 1988)

Then they called for the whole nation to rise up for democracy:

> We of the Rangoon University democracy movement will consolidate students of thirty-two regional colleges. . . . This will be all over the country. We will then agitate the workers, farmers, and the poor people. . . . When the whole country rises up we will get democracy. What is required for national upheaval? First hardcore student organization, then worker organization, then farmer organization. When workers and farmers join the movement, soldiers who are the sons of workers and farmers will also join.

Finally they outlined the country's social, economic, and political problems and reminded people that these hardships would continue so long as the dictatorial government stayed in power.

Student activists listed the injustices in the society, attributed responsibility to the government, and proposed a democratic movement as a solution. Many Burmese people were deeply touched.[5] This BBC broadcast helped the movement turn bystanders into participants. Many student leaders I interviewed, people from the peripheral northern, eastern, and southern regions, decided to get involved in the movement after listening to the interview. A student leader recounted:

> Before [listening to the interview], I and many of my friends were just wavering. We did not know if we should get involved in the movement. We knew something was going on in Rangoon. But our town is far from Rangoon. We did not know what exactly students from Rangoon University were doing. When we heard about their plan to launch a democratic movement, we decided to follow their footsteps. We then formed a union and organized demonstrations in our town. Of course, people were nervous about the government's possible actions. Many people who were touched by the news about students being tortured and girls being raped supported us—some joined our union and worked with us; some people, especially those who were involved in student protests during the parliamentary period [1948–62], gave us good advice; and some donated money and food. At first they did it secretly. As the movement gained momentum, people came to show their support to our union and our movement more openly. . . . As a matter of fact, people were already aggrieved at the government for the economic and social difficulties it had heaped on them. This broadcast just alerted people to translate our grief into action. (interview, former student leader, November 1995)

At about the same time, the Voice of America (VOA) came to serve as a source of information about the movement. SMOs used both the BBC and VOA as a coordination mechanism between the summit and the base. It reminded people living in the peripheral areas to pay serious attention to the activities of SMOs at the center. In fact, student activists framed the BBC interview exactly in the way they wanted. Taking advantage of rumors circulating in Rangoon regarding students being tortured and raped in prison, they convincingly portrayed how they had suffered. In reality, none of the students involved in the interview had been tortured or raped (at least at the time of the interview).[6] They simply made it up "to provoke the whole country to rise up against the government" (interview, former SMO leader, August 1995). After all, there was no other source of information the BBC could use to verify the authenticity of what the student leaders said in their interview. Setting aside any ethical considerations, their tactics worked well. By co-opting an external resource, namely, the foreign media, the movement spread word of uprisings throughout the country.

The two broadcasting stations also helped the movement convince people that the cost of participation was not as high as they thought. Many people, although angry with the government, continued to remain bystanders. Most of these people believed that a nationwide movement would bring changes to the country, but what kind of changes would such a movement yield? The uncertainty led many potential participants to adopt "a wait and see attitude to determine if collective action is likely to be viable before tossing their own hats into the ring" (Chong 1991: 116). I myself, as a student protester, discovered that many activists would join the movement only when they thought enough people would take part "to make it viable." To mobilize these people into the movement, SMOs needed to furnish them with information about the opening up of an opportunity. Again the BBC and VOA removed this responsibility from the shoulders of the SMOs by highlighting in their broadcasts the state of political opportunity in the country. Through these broadcasts, people learned about the support of major democratic countries. Both stations reported in detail how U.S. senators had pressed the government to stop using force against peaceful demonstrators. Since many Burmese regard the United States as a model democratic country, American support for their movement meant a lot. Once they found out that leading democratic countries backed them, SMOs escalated the momentum. A prodemocracy activist recalls:

> You know, we motivated many nervous people by saying: "Hey, the VOA announced that the United States government has sided with us. And the BBC said the Japanese government is planning to suspend its aid unless the government agrees to negotiate with the opposition." Very effective. It works. We could convince many people. People did not trust the state media. At the same time, a lot of rumors were circulating in town. People did not really know what to believe. Often, many people we talked to were not sure whether they should believe us or not. They could check what we said to them with the BBC and VOA. (interview, SMO activist, December 1995)

Despite the wavering populace, by August 8, 1988, the SMOs in Rangoon and Mandalay had mobilized enough people to begin the movement. For the first few days, however, the government fired on demonstrators. If the security forces had kept shooting, the movement might have collapsed at once. Even today, those who follow political developments in Burma have yet to uncover the reason why the security forces stopped firing at demonstrators. In any case, their change of policy enabled SMOs to mobilize even more people into the movement.

SMOs, however, suffered from an "organizational deficit"—that is, the network of the BCP's affiliated study groups was not large enough to organize a nationwide movement. To make up for this deficit, SMOs tried to find a way to appropriate organizations that had been functioning within the narrow legal space allowed by the state. BCP-affiliated SMOs first tried to appropriate the associations in which members of their "brother reading groups" were involved. In such cases, the agents of SMOs tried to control the associations from behind the scenes and turn them into SMOs (interviews, 2002). In places where there were no affiliated reading groups, BCP-affiliated SMOs sent out their agents to establish contact with well-respected figures with the intent of using them as brokers who could help them turn local organizations into SMOs. Independent SMOs sent out their agents as well. Since they did not have brother study groups beyond Rangoon, agents of independent SMOs were usually sent where they had personal friends or relatives and through these personal connections tried to enlist the help of established organizations and social networks: bar associations, monasteries, the Sangha, community and alumni organizations, and local branches of Burma's Medical Association.

By the second week of the movement's inception, a number of conventional religious and social organizations had emerged as SMOs. By then the movement had spread to every corner of the country. At about the same time, popular figures like Aung San Suu Kyi and U Nu came to join the movement. BCP agents then tried to unite the movement by forming general strike committees in various parts of the country. In the meantime, the major student SMOs still had not learned to work together. Mutual distrust had prevented the development of esprit de corps between them. While the three student-led SMOs (headed by Min Ko Naing, Min Zaya, and Than Win) from Rangoon never managed to find a way to cooperate, nine student unions emerged at Mandalay University. BCP agents now paid more attention to the formation of a parallel government, however, and no longer tried to reconcile student-led SMOs.

In the last week of August 1988, the socialist government stopped functioning and the country found itself in a state of anarchy (Kyaw Yin Hlaing 2001a: 243). When it became abundantly clear that the socialist government could not reimpose its control over the country, the president, Maung Maung, promised to hold multiparty elections. He then asked the strike committees and SMOs to call off their demonstrations and start preparing for elections. SMOs did not trust the party-state, however, and along with strike committees throughout the country, they asked the BSPP government to hand over power to an interim government instead. When the SMOs persistently refused to accept his reassurances, Maung Maung handed power to the military. The military then formed an "interim" government called the State Law and Order Restoration Council (SLORC), which became the State Peace and Development Council (SPDC) in 1997.

Creating Civil Society Space Overseas

As soon as it took control of the country, the junta gave SMOs three options: dissolve; turn themselves into political parties by registering with the election commission; or turn themselves into nonpolitical organizations by registering with the Home Ministry and refraining from political activity (Associations Act, SLORC Law 6/88, September 30, 1988). Organizations that registered with the Home Ministry were allowed to continue provided they stayed out of politics. Immediately after the SLORC came to power, most community, professional, ethnic, and native-place organizations stopped all antigovernment activity. Several student and Sangha organizations, however, continued to engage in antigovernment activities both covertly and openly. In response, the junta arrested hundreds of members of antigovernment organizations and sentenced them to long prison terms. In 1990, the government formally issued the Sangha Organization Act outlawing all political Sangha organizations. The law explicitly states that any monk who remains a member of an outlawed Sangha organization or involves himself in political activities will cease to be regarded as a monk (Sangha Organization Act, SLORC Decree 6/90). After the arrest of many of its leaders, the Yahanpyo Aphwe (All-Burma Young Monks' Association), which had managed to survive the BSPP government's anticivil society, took measures to dismantle itself.

In addition to taking harsh action against SMOs, the junta also created new organizations such as the Union of Myanmar Chamber of Commerce and Industry (UMCCI), the Rice Millers' and the Rice Merchants' Association, the Border Trade Merchants' Association, the Association of Fishery Product Traders, the Women's Affairs Organization, and the Union Solidarity and Development Association (USDA) (Kyaw Yin Hlaing 2001a: 249). The junta also manipulated the way these associations functioned by installing its supporters as their leaders and using them as tools for controlling society. For instance, the USDA—an association led by senior government officials—and the Women's Affairs Organization—led by wives of senior government officials—were used to mobilize supporters and monitor the activities of opponents of the regime. Similarly, various business organizations were used to contain the demands of the business community, raise funds for state activities, and co-opt independent business organizations like the Mandalay Traders, Brokers, and Industrialists Association. The junta also tried to control artists', writers', and musicians' organizations by replacing their executive committees with people it trusted and, in turn, using them to recruit volunteers for its legitimating activities. It has to be borne in mind that not all so-called government-organized nongovernmental organizations function in a similar manner. While acting as government support groups, various business, professional, and women's organizations engage mainly in apolitical activities. The USDA, on the other hand, is often considered the junta's political tool, as it is widely believed to have orchestrated the violent clash between government supporters and NLD members that took place in central Burma on May 30, 2003. Despite the junta's actions, several civil society organizations survived. Community, professional, ethnic, native-place, and religious organizations continue to undertake nonpolitical social and religious activities. Moreover, new social, religious, ethnic, and native-place organizations have emerged. Although their exact number is unknown, local newspapers mention the names of fifteen new ethnic, native-place, and religious organizations formed after the SLORC came to power. Among new organizations, local environmental and social welfare organizations have done well as NGOs. They have engaged in several activities aimed at containing environmental degradation, alleviating poverty, and educating the public about HIV/AIDS. The Shalom Foundation, formed by peace negotiators between the government and ethnic insurgent groups, seeks to promote peace among minority communities across the country. Along with local NGOs, the government also allows foreign NGOs to undertake poverty alleviation and health education activities on their own or in cooperation with local NGOs. Although they have encountered a number of bureaucratic hassles in dealing with local state agencies, both local and foreign NGOs have successfully managed to undertake many of their projects. However, as in the socialist period, these new organizations have to abstain from activities that the government would deem as subversive to its rule.

Although they assumed a nonpolitical and nonthreatening posture, social, business, and religious organizations have resisted the junta's attempt to co-opt them. The Mandalay Traders, Brokers, and Industrialists Association, for instance, persistently shrugged off the junta's attempts to turn it into a branch of the UMCCI (interview, leading MTBIA member, August 2001). Similarly, Byamaso A-thin, which provides ambulances, hearses, and medical services for a nominal charge to the residents of Mandalay, especially the poor, managed to remain totally independent of the state. Because Byamaso A-thin was more popular than the government's Maternal and Child Care Association, which provided similar services to the public, the Mandalay regional commander and his wife, patrons of the Mandalay branch of the Maternal and Child Care Association, tried to control it by offering financial assistance and attempting to put government officials on its executive committees (interview, retired government official, December 2001). The leaders of Byamaso A-thin refused to accept either the financial assistance or the executives (interview, August 2001).

Associations that refused to comply with the demands of local authorities often ran the risk of being harassed by state agents. Although the government rarely inspected the accounts of noncontroversial independent social organizations, Byamaso A-thin found its accounts being checked by government accountants from time to time (interview, 2002). To keep their organization out of trouble, therefore, members of Byamaso A-thin must refrain from activities that are even remotely political. Thus they turn down all foreign donations and support their activities with donations from the general public. To be sure, government-owned business enterprises have sold paper and construction materials at subsidized rates to nonpolitical religious organizations promoting Buddhism. The junta did not bother to intervene in the affairs of these organizations, because they did not pose any challenge to the regime. Although it has announced a road map for democracy in Burma, the junta has yet to change its attitude toward politically conscious civil society organizations. Members of social, business, and religious organizations continue to believe that they have to assume a nonpolitical posture in order to escape long prison terms.

In the first three years of SLORC rule, some twenty SMOs are said to have remained active as informal organizations. The junta had learned from the past, however, and accordingly came down harshly on members of informal groups. To prevent student protests, it closed down all schools and universities for three years. Even after schools were reopened, the government shut them down again whenever student groups tried to organize protests. As a consequence, many politically conscious students fled to border areas to join overseas Burmese prodemocracy organizations; others worked for political parties.[7] Accordingly, the number of informal student organizations declined in the late 1990s.[8] The number and strength of overseas Burmese prodemocracy organizations, by contrast, have increased since the SLORC took control. This does not, however, suggest that the existing legal civil society organizations are unable to play any role in the democratization of Burma. As has been seen above, legal civil society organizations can easily be turned into social movement organizations when political opportunities permit. However, having learnt from the mistakes of its predecessor, the junta does not tolerate any challenge to its rule and always seeks to take preemptive action against its challengers. As a result, since late 1988, the political opportunity structure has been unfavorable for any legally constituted civil society organization to engage in meaningful autonomous political activity in the territory controlled by the government. Many politically conscious people tried to create a space for their activities in areas beyond the junta's control. If the socialist period can be called the era of informal political groups, then the SLORC/SPDC period must be labeled the era of overseas Burmese prodemocracy groups. In the 1990s, more than forty such groups emerged in North America, Europe, and Asia. Even though they existed in foreign countries and in insurgent-controlled areas (commonly known as liberated areas), overseas prodemocracy groups were still subject to external and internal constraints. Indeed, their success or failure depended on whether they could find a way to overcome these constraints. Consider, for example, the following case studies of the All-Burma Students' Democratic Front and the Free Burma Coalition.

The All-Burma Students' Democratic Front: A Militant Organization

The All-Burma Students' Democratic Front (ABSDF) was the first autonomous political organization formed by student leaders who fled to the border regions of Thailand and India. At the beginning, the organization had its headquarters in the Karen-controlled area, with branches in India as well as in the Kachin-controlled area in northern and northeastern Burma. The organization claimed to work for the liberation of "all nationalities under military dictatorship," restoration of democracy, human rights, internal peace, and the emergence of a federal union in Burma. To this end, the ABSDF engaged in both military action and political activities. After receiving rudimentary military training given by former Burmese soldiers and members of ethnic insurgent groups, a number of ABSDF members fought alongside their ethnic counterparts against Burmese government forces. As a result, the ABSDF was often referred to as "the most militant arm of Burma's student movement" (Hanlon 2002: 1).

Along with these military activities, the ABSDF—in collaboration with Amnesty International, Asia Watch, the International Human Rights Lawyers, the Lawyers' Committee for Human Rights, the International Human Rights Commission for Jurists, and the International Fellowship of Reconciliation—tried to expose the violation of human rights by the Burmese military government. In a bid to "educate students in the liberated areas [those who fled to border areas] in the concept of democracy" and professional journalism, the ABSDF also organized various training programs. The primary purpose of these programs was to produce activists who could raise the political consciousness of local people (those residing in border areas) and those who could gather "firsthand and accurate information in a systematic way" for the Democratic Voice of Burma, Radio Free Asia, the BBC, and VOA (Facts About the All-Burma Students' Democratic Front: 7). To "educate female members of ABSDF about the importance of women's roles in society with regard to social, educational, political, and economic aspects," the ABSDF created the Women's Empowerment Training program. To expand job opportunities for local people and refugees, the ABSDF offered training in teaching, medical aid, the English language, midwifery, tailoring, and communications (ibid.: 7–8).

In general, the ABSDF emerged out of SMO leaders' efforts to create a space for their activities beyond the reach of the state. Its members tried to topple the government because they believed that this was the only way that substantial political changes in Burma could materialize. Although the territories in which these activities were carried out were beyond the direct control of the government, the ABSDF was still subject to a number of constraints. Because all so-called liberated areas were controlled by ethnic insurgents, the ABSDF was in no position to challenge any of its hosts and thus was unable to pursue a course of action that did not interest its host. And because most ABSDF leaders were Burmese, insurgent groups generally did not trust them. Although they allowed the ABSDF to operate within their area of control, ethnic insurgents refused to provide them with anything more than outdated weapons. Even though the ABSDF could not do anything that might upset its hosts, insurgent groups rarely consulted with the ABSDF on major decisions affecting its fate. When Kachin and Mon insurgents signed their cease-fire agreements with the junta, for example, ABSDF members were not informed, and many of them who did not manage to escape to the Thai-Burma border were arrested by the government. Likewise, the space for ABSDF activities shrank as government forces occupied more and more insurgent-controlled areas.

Moreover, ABSDF tactics formulated in Thailand were seriously shaped by the Thai government's policies toward the junta. Whenever the Thai government wanted to improve its relations with the junta, it tended to adopt a tough policy stance toward Burmese prodemocracy movements. Whenever the Thai government moved the ABSDF camps operating on Thai soil from one place to another, ABSDF leaders had little choice but to comply. Thus the credibility of ABSDF leaders was often undermined. Whenever they were forced out of a place by the Thai government, grassroots members of the ABSDF tended to feel that their leaders were not making any effort to improve the lives of their followers. A former ABSDF member recounted in frustration:

> We were operating in the area controlled by them [ethnic insurgent groups]. They were more experienced and much stronger. Our actions were always constrained by their plans and programs. There were a lot of things we could not do freely. Whenever there was a clash of interest or a clash of opinions, we had to follow theirs. However, there were some very nice and understanding ethnic insurgent officers. Those people listened to us. It was the same with Thailand. We could organize training sessions quite freely, but we could not organize protests against visiting Burmese officers. They would arrest us. It also depended on who was in power. The Democrat Party was usually sympathetic to us and nicer to us. The current . . . government [of Prime Minister Thaksin Shinawarta] is not very friendly to us. What we could do in Thailand was always shaped by who was in power. (interview, July 12, 2002)

The ABSDF's activities were also constrained by infighting over leadership of the organization. Most ABSDF leaders came from different student-led SMOs—especially the Min Ko Naing and Min Zaya groups—and with them came all their old differences. The first chairman and founding member of the ABSDF, Tun Aung Kyaw, writes poignantly of this in his master's thesis:

> The power struggle among the student leaders . . . weakened the student movement. Vice-chairman Win Moe, Joint General Secretary I Aung Naintg, and Joint Secretary II Ko Ko Oo . . . resented me as chairman because they thought they were the ones who deserved to be chairman, not me, but I could work with them as their adviser. They also hated Than Win, general secretary of the ABSDF, because he had opposed [their former leader] Min Ko Naing. Because of disunity among the students, lack of food and medicine, malaria and tropical diseases, many students and some leaders returned home. . . . All these facts hampered the student movement on the border. (Htun Aung Gyaw 1997: 105)

The power struggles continued even after Htun Aung Gyaw and Than Win were replaced. In 1991, the power struggle contributed to the breakup of the ABSDF into two groups, one led by Chairman Naing Aung and the other by Vice-Chairman Moe Thee Zun. Although the two groups reunited in 1997, they were never able to cooperate fully again. Amid these bitter power struggles, leading members of ABSDF branches in northern Burma executed a number of people accused of spying for the military government. Sources close to the ABSDF later revealed that some of these people were executed merely because they did not get along with leading members. Once the news about the ABSDF executions became public, a number of Western foundations, including Médecins sans frontières and the International Rescue Committee, cut off funding. In the late 1990s, most grassroots members publicly revealed their unhappiness with their leaders' failure to meet their basic needs and began to question their credibility. Frustrated with such problems, a social worker who used to work closely with ABSDF members writes: "Now reduced in size, wracked by division . . . one might be forgiven for thinking they are a spent force" (Hanlon 2002: 1). Many former members confessed in interviews that they thought the ABSDF was on the verge of collapse at this point. Ultimately, Moe Thee Zun, Naing Aung, and some of their supporters left the ABSDF. Moe Thee Zun then (re)joined the Democratic Party for a New Society (DPNS), which he and some student leaders created as a legal political party in Yangon in late 1988. The DPNS became an overseas prodemocracy organization after it moved to Thailand in late 1990. Naing Aung, on the other hand, created his own organization, the Network for Democracy and Development (NDD). The remaining ABSDF members continue to engage in armed struggles under the tutelage of the new leader, Than Khe.

Paradoxically, the three groups began to cooperate soon after they decided to go their separate ways. This decision to collaborate can be attributed to the difficulty they faced individually in soliciting funds from Western governments and foundations. While the ABSDF was riddled with internal power struggles, Shan ethnic leaders formed a civil society group known as the National Reconciliation Program for Burma (NRP) (interview, prominent political activist, 2003). The funding organizations that were frustrated with the ABSDF ultimately came to grant significant funds to the NRP. Leaders of ABSDF, DPNS, and NDD understood that they could not keep their organizations functioning without sufficient resources. After trying to raise funds on their own, leaders of all three groups came to realize that they were in no position to compete with the NRP individually or win the confidence of the funding agencies. An analyst close to all three factions confirmed this in an interview: "The fact that NRP took away the donation they used to receive was a wake-up call for them. Seriously lacking in sufficient human and organizational resources to undertake any major political project on their own, they all tried, unsuccessfully, to solicit funds. Western funding agencies would not contribute to their cause unless they were convinced that the funds would be meaningfully and effectively spent."

In reality, however, the ABSDF was shrinking even before it broke up, as droves of members left the organization to resettle in Australia, North America, and Europe. To save themselves and their organizations, ABSDF, DPNS, and NDD leaders tried to reinvent their images. DPNS and NDD, for example, dissociated themselves from military activities and portrayed themselves as nonviolent prodemocracy organizations. The ABSDF, although it did not formally renounce armed struggle, stopped emphasizing it after reaching an agreement with the other two factions to work together for the democratization of Burma (interview, former ABSDF member, January 2003). Under the new arrangement, the three groups formed a loose alliance. Subsequently, the ABSDF, DPNS, and NDD were granted significant funding to jointly undertake a political capacity-building project. Since then, the three groups have jointly held several workshops on Burma's political future and civil disobedience training for political activists in Burma. The workshops gave Burmese political activists from Asia, North America, and Europe opportunities to exchange views on what measures ought to be adopted to bring democracy to Burma. Mainly, the participants discussed how they should advise the main opposition party in Burma—the National League for Democracy (NLD)—in its deadlock with the national reconciliation process. They also tried to bring the attention of the international community to the atrocities committed by the junta by sending information about human rights violations and forced labor to Amnesty International and the international media, especially Radio Free Asia and the Democratic Voice of Burma. In contrast to its previous tactics of armed struggle, the alliance's current activities do not require a sudden opening up of political opportunity. So long as they receive funding from Western foundations, they can hold workshops and send information to human rights organizations even when the Burmese military government enjoys good relations with its Thai counterpart.

Although the internal wrangling of the ABSDF continues, the loose alliance of ABSDF, DPNS, and NDD has revived the Burmese prodemocracy movement along the Thai-Burma border. Recognizing that they cannot survive without working together, none of the leaders of the three groups has done anything to jeopardize the alliance. "We were happily surprised to see that the political capacity-building project was going really well," a former ABSDF member said. "At workshops, members of different groups had intense discussions. They expressed their opinion freely but did not treat each other like rivals. The intense discussions at workshops looked more like a group of comrades exchanging views freely" (interview, January 2003). At this point, it is hard to measure the extent to which the ABSDF–DPNS–DNN alliance has influenced the interaction between the junta and the NLD or the junta's relations with Western countries. But its activities have certainly kept political developments in Burma in the international limelight.

The Free Burma Coalition: A Ghost Buster

The Free Burma Coalition (FBC) was formed in 1995 by Zar Ni, a Burmese graduate student at the University of Wisconsin-Madison, to "force international corporations out of Burma" (www.freeburmacoalition.org/frames/victories.htm: 1). On its own, the FBC was neither financially nor organizationally stable enough to confront international corporations. By "making good use of cyberspace," however, Zar Ni and his associates consolidated their position by forming an alliance with various student organizations and community groups around America (*Bangkok Post*, April 29, 1998) and networking with human rights and student organizations from twenty-eight Asian and European countries (interview, FBC member,

September 2002). On their website, they opened a discussion forum about Burmese politics and invited people to participate. High school, college, and graduate students around the world gathering information about Burmese politics for their research papers or class projects came to learn about the FBC, and many of them asked if there was anything they could do to help (personal communication, member of the FBC support group, Cornell University, January 2001). While disseminating information about Burmese politics via the Internet, FBC members also solicited the support of student and community organizations in the United States by giving talks at universities, colleges, and town halls. Within a year, the FBC had managed to organize support groups on 120 school and college campuses (interview, Zar Ni, January 2004). By 2002, the FBC had established charters at nearly 50 college campuses in the United States (*Sacramento Bee*, November 12, 2002).

Through its network of support groups, the FBC asked the American people to help it pressure multinational corporations not to do business with the Burmese military government. It also organized protests against international corporations that invested in Burma. And the FBC's strategy paid off. In 1996, for instance, Harvard University decided to give "a five-year $1 million contract to Coke due to FBC instigated student protests against Pepsi" (*Boston Globe*, May 27, 1996). From then on, the FBC gained one victory after another. By the end of 2001, with the assistance of its supporters, the FBC had forced more than fifty major international corporations, including Compaq, Pepsi, Eddie Bauer, Kodak, and Hewlett-Packard out of Burma (www.irrawaddy.org/res/outburma.html: 1–6). Furthermore, owing to protests and activities orchestrated by the FBC and its support groups, the United States and EU countries have imposed economic sanctions on Burma, which prohibit U.S. and EU business corporations from making new investments in Burma. Moreover, twenty-five American cities, including San Francisco and Los Angeles, have passed purchasing laws that "ban or restrict contracts with companies that do business in Burma" (Agence France Presse, May 24, 1996; *Los Angeles Times*, August 15, 2002). As in the case of the ABSDF, it is not easy to measure the extent to which the FBC's activities have contributed to political change in Burma, because they may have more long-term than short-term effects. In any case, the FBC has been more successful at drawing international attention to the Burmese democratic movement than any other overseas Burmese prodemocracy organization.

Why has the FBC been more successful than the ABSDF? The answer lies in the FBC's skillful appropriation of civil society organizations in the United States, as well as differences in their methods and the state of political opportunities. Because America's political system is more open than Thailand's, the FBC could mobilize supporters more easily than the ABSDF. Furthermore, growing American sentiment against multinationals and the U.S. government's consistent Burma policy have given the FBC ample opportunities to expand its activities through appropriate civil society organizations in the United States. ABSDF members, by contrast, could not make use of civil society organizations in their host regions: Thailand's civil society organizations were nowhere near as dynamic as their American counterparts, and most of them in any case did not care about Burmese political movements. The Thai organizations that did have some sympathy for Burmese students operating on Thai soil were not influential enough to shape their government's foreign policy or persuade Thai businesspeople not to do business with the Burmese military government.

Since the FBC was led by senior graduate students and those who understood Western norms, the FBC's tactics were always in resonance with the practices accepted by its support organizations. The FBC had always tried to present itself as a nonviolent organization and its members always avoided activities that might make them come across as terrorists. The ABSDF, by contrast, although it portrayed itself as a democratic organization, actively engaged in armed struggle and was often accused of human rights violations. As a result, it began losing the support of NGOs. And because most of its military operations ended in failure, it became increasingly difficult for the ABSDF to sustain the morale of its members. ABSDF leaders devoted more energy to the organization's internal power struggles than to convincing members that their goal of bringing down the military government was still attainable. In other words, the ABSDF leadership failed to develop a consistent agency frame. Consequently, a number of members left the organization to resettle in North America, Europe, and Australia. As a result, the ABSDF's membership shrank from over ten thousand in 1989 to about three hundred in 2004 (interview with a leading ABSDF member, January 2004). Unlike the ABSDF, the FBC experienced no major power struggle. Since Zar Ni had created the organization single-handedly, only those who were willing to work under his tutelage joined it. Thus the FBC's approach to decisions and activities was consistent and stable. In addition, the FBC did not have to support its members as the ABSDF did; it simply had to mobilize the support of people in Western countries who were sympathetic to its cause to begin with, which it did by highlighting the injustices inflicted on Burmese society by the military government and multinational corporations.

In sum, then, it is easier to sell the injustice frame to politically conscious Americans and Europeans than to sell the agency frame to dispirited Burmese students. All in all, it was the FBC's skillful appropriation of norms, symbols, civil society organizations, and civil society space in its host country that contributed to its emergence as the most successful overseas Burmese prodemocracy organization.

Beyond the Reach of the State

To understand the role of civil society organizations in authoritarian countries, we need to look beyond the legal space for civil society set by the state. In Burma, under two military regimes, many political activists did not passively accept the restrictions imposed on them. When they could not undertake meaningful activities within the space allotted civil society by the state, politically conscious people created underground spaces by forming informal study groups with like-minded citizens. Although some of these groups were affiliated with the Burma Communist Party and others with former right-wing politicians, many of them remained independent. The military governments were fully aware of the existence of these groups and their potential for mobilizing antigovernment activities, so government agents monitored the groups closely and detained members who engaged in "suspicious activities." Thus the informal study groups had to keep their activities secret.

The activities undertaken by informal study groups varied according to political opportunities and constraints. When constraints outweighed opportunities, these groups merely exchanged books on political science and occasionally got together to discuss them. Left-wing study groups distributed antigovernment pamphlets from time to time. When political opportunities arose, several reading groups tried to mobilize antigovernment activities by becoming social movement organizations. This was the case with Burma's Four Eights prodemocracy movement. In 1988, taking advantage of public grievances over government mismanagement of the economy and the split in the military-dominated socialist government, informal study groups transformed themselves into SMOs and organized antigovernment protests. By appropriating legal organizations and foreign radio stations, these groups expanded the movement throughout the country. But when the military council that replaced the socialist government failed to restore order in the country and started to suppress the movement by force, the window of opportunity slammed shut and the movement dispersed. Tens of thousands of students and movement leaders fled to border areas and tried to create a new civil society space on foreign soil by forming overseas Burmese prodemocracy organizations.

Although their civil society space lay beyond the reach of the state, their activity was conditioned by a number of external and internal constraints. As can be seen in the achievements of the two biggest overseas operations—the ABSDF and the Free Burma Coalition—these overseas groups needed to find a way to keep their members together and overcome their lack of resources and organizational weaknesses. Their ability to overcome these constraints was seriously shaped by the sociopolitical environments of their host countries and the internal structure of the organizations themselves. Because American society is more open, vital, and politically informed than that of Thailand, the American-based Free Burma Coalition experienced fewer constraints than the Thailand-based ABSDF. Furthermore, FBC leaders managed to present themselves and their goals to the international community more effectively and efficiently than their ABSDF counterparts. As a result, the FBC turned out to be more successful than the ABSDF.

Although they differed in terms of what they achieved, the activities of the

ABSDF and FBC have kept the Burmese prodemocracy movement in the international limelight. All in all, the activities undertaken by informal study groups and overseas prodemocracy organizations were not much different from those conducted by civil society organizations in other countries. To understand the impact of civil society on political change in Burma, one must, therefore, consider the informal study groups and overseas prodemocracy groups operating outside the legal space allocated for civil society by the state.

Notes

1. For a detailed discussion of the state of civil society in parliamentary Burma, see Kyaw Yin Hlaing, "Bring Out the Dead: A Study of the State of Civil Society in Burma" (paper presented at Workshop on Civil Society and Political Change in Asia, February 2002, Hawaii).

2. Most of my interviewees did not want to be cited by name. Some also asked me not to mention their job title or the exact interview date. I have, of course, respected these wishes and consequently offer the vague citation "interviews" from time to time.

3. The YMBA was formed by Western-educated young Burmese inspired by the Young Men's Christian Association. In the 1920s, it was involved in several political activities, but it came to focus mainly on religious activities in the 1940s.

4. The books, articles, novels, and journals read by informal reading groups ranged from Burmese translations of great works by Tolstoy, Chekhov, Dostoyevsky, Camus, Sartre, Hemingway, and Steinbeck to Francis Fukuyama's *The End of History* and Samuel Huntington's *The Clash of Civilizations*, as well as *Journal of Democracy*, *Foreign Affairs*, *Newsweek*, *Time*, and banned novels by local authors (Fink 2001: 185).

5. On the day this interview was aired, I was on my way back home after attending a conference in Pagan, an ancient capital of Burma. On the way back, our car broke down and while the driver was fixing the car, I walked to a nearby village. There I saw two dozen people listening to the BBC's interview with the student leaders. The whole crowd was moved. Some women cried. What they were hearing was not just a newscaster but the voices of students who had been tortured by their own government. Many young men angrily remarked: "It is time to do something. This government no longer deserves to be in power" (personal observation, August 6, 1988).

6. It is not this paper's intention to suggest that abuses of political prisoners in Burmese prisons did not occur; rather, the argument here will be confined to the participants of the BBC interviews aired on August 6, 1988.

7. Between 1988 and 2000 the junta closed down universities and colleges more than four times in an attempt to disperse antigovernment students. These shutdowns lasted from four months to three years.

8. When I was conducting research for this study in December 2001, I could not find a single student who was still active in informal student organizations.

Works Cited

All-Burma Students' Democratic Front (ABSDF). 1997. *Letters to a Dictator*. Bangkok: ABSDF.

Aung San Suu Kyi. 1991. *Freedom from Fear and Other Writings*. Edited by Michael Aris. London: Penguin Books.

Aye Saung. 1997. *Burma in the Back Row*. Hong Kong: Asia 2000.

Ba Kyaing, U. 1983. *A-htoo-nin-a-htwe-htwe-u-pa-de-pund-gyoke* (Compilation of special and general laws). Rangoon: Yi Yi Swe Sarpay.

Boudreau, Vincent. 2001. *Grass Roots and Cadre in the Protest Movement*. Quezon City: Ateneo de Manila University Press.

Burma. Government Press Committee. 1990. *Skyful of Lies: BBC and VOA*. Rangoon: News and Periodical Department.

Burma Muslim Chamber of Commerce (BMCC). 1959–61. *Annual Reports*. Rangoon: BMCC.

Chong, Dennis. 1991. *Collective Action and the Civil Rights Movement*. Chicago: University of Chicago Press.

Ergas, Zaki, ed. 1987. *The African State in Transition*. New York: St. Martin's Press.

Facts About the All Burma Students' Democratic Front (ABSDF). www.members.optushome.com.au/absdfau/factab.htm. Accessed 2/20/2004.

Fink, Christina. 2001. *Living Silence: Burma under Military Rule*. New York: Zed Books.

Foreign and Commonwealth Office. 1993. *Burma: Continued Repression*. London: Foreign and Commonwealth Office.

Gamson, William A. 1995. "Constructing Social Protest." In Hank Johnston and Bert Klandermans, eds., *Social Movements and Culture*. Minneapolis: University of Minnesota Press.

Hanlon, David. 2002. "Whatever Happened to the ABSDF?" www.irrawaddy.org/art/2002-1/01art03.html.

Htun Aung Gyaw. 1991. "Burma's Insein Prison: Punishment and Oppression." *Crime, Law, and Social Change* 15: 125–34.

———. 1997. "Student Movements and Civil Society in Burma." MA thesis, Cornell University.

International Crisis Group (ICG). 2001. *Myanmar: The Role of Civil Society*. Asia Report 7. Bangkok: ICG.

Khin Nyunt. 1989. *The Special Press Conference*. Rangoon: News and Periodical Enterprises.

———. 1991. *Bakaba ug dab nld gaungsaung acho nainggyandaw arna yayuye thaput-oo kalainchone zatlanzone* (How some leaders of the Burma Communist Party, the Democratic Alliance of Burma, and the NLD tried to take control of the country). Rangoon: News and Periodical Enterprises.

———. 1997a. *Ahtoo thatinsar shinlinpwe nite phyintpor nay thaw nainggyanye ache anaymya shinlin pyor kyar chat* (Clarification by Secretary-1 of the SLORC, Lt. Gen. Khin Nyunt, at the special press conference). Rangoon: News and Periodical Enterprises.

———. 1997b. *Anout nainggyangyi tachyo aa demokayesi ye hlu akhwint aye ayechone htar thi apweasi mya ar ngwekye nin phintsi mya kunyiputpopi aphyatamout lotengan mya ko arpaynaymumya akyaung shinlin pyankyarchat* (Clarification by Secretary-1 of the SLORC, Lt. Gen. Khin Nyunt, on how some Western powers have been aiding and abetting terrorism committed by certain organizations operating in the guise of democracy and human rights by giving them assistance in both cash and kind). Rangoon: News and Periodical Enterprises.

Kyaw Yin Hlaing. 1996a. "The Mobilization Process in the Four Eights Democratic Movement in Burma." MS.

———. 1996b. "The Politics of State-Youth Relations in Socialist Burma." MS.

———. 2001a. "The Politics of State-Business Relations in Post-Colonial Burma." Ph.D. diss., Cornell University.

———. 2001b. "Sangha in Burmese Politics: Friends or Foes of the State?" MS.

Lang, Hazel. 2002. *Fear and Sanctuary: Burmese Refugees in Thailand.* Ithaca, N.Y.: Cornell University Southeast Asia Program.
Liddell, Zunetta. 1999. "No Room to Move: Legal Constraints on Civil Society in Burma." In Burma Center Netherlands, ed., *Strengthening Civil Society in Burma: Possibilities and Dilemmas for International NGOs.* Chiang Mai, Thailand: Silkworm Books.
Mann, Michael. 1984. "The Autonomous Power of the State." *Archives europeénnes de sociologie* 25.
———. 1986. *The Sources of Social Power: A History of Power from the Beginning to A.D. 1760.* Vol. 1. New York: Cambridge University Press.
Maung Maung. 1999. *The 1988 Uprising in Burma.* New Haven: Yale University, Southeast Asian Studies.
McAdam, Doug, Sidney Tarrow, and Charles Tilly. 2001. *Dynamics of Contention.* New York: Cambridge University Press.
McCarthy, John, and Mayer Zald. 1977. "Resource Mobilization and Social Movements: A Partial Theory." *American Journal of Sociology* 82(6) (May): 1212–41.
Saw Maung. 1989. *SLORC Chairman and Commander-in-Chief of the Defense Services Senior General Saw Maung's Addresses.* Vol. 1. Rangoon: News and Periodical Enterprises.
———. 1990a. *Mainkhunmya* (Speeches of SLORC chairman General Saw Maung). Rangoon: News and Periodical Enterprises.
———. 1990b. *SLORC Chairman and Commander-in-Chief of the Defense Services Senior General Saw Maung's Addresses.* Vol. 2. Rangoon: News and Periodical Enterprises.
———. 1991. *SLORC Chairman and Commander-in-Chief of the Defense Services Senior General Saw Maung's Addresses.* Vol. 3. Rangoon: News and Periodical Enterprises.
Silverstein, Josef. 1968. "Burmese Student Politics in a Changing Society." *Daedalus* 97(1): 274–92.
———. 1974. *The Future of Burma in Perspective: A Symposium.* Athens: Ohio University Center for International Studies, Southeast Asia Program.
Smith, D. E. 1965. *Religion and Politics in Burma.* Princeton: Princeton University Press.
Smith, Martin. 1991. *Burma: Insurgency and Politics of Ethnicity.* London: Zed Books.
Steinberg, David. 1981. *Burma's Road Toward Development: Growth and Ideology Under Military Rule.* Boulder: Westview Press.
———. 2001. *Burma: The State of Myanmar.* Washington, D.C.: Georgetown University Press.
Suu Hngyat. 2001. *A-nay-shok-man-da-lay* (The slow walking mandalay). Yangon: Win Media.
Tarrow, Sidney. 1998. *Power in Movement.* 2d ed. New York: Cambridge University Press.
Taylor, Robert H. 1974. "The Relationship Between Burmese Social Classes and British-Indian Policy on the Behavior of the Burmese Political Elite, 1937–1942." Ph.D. diss., Cornell University.
———. 1987. *The State in Burma.* Honolulu: University of Hawai'i Press.
Tin Maung Maung Than. 1993. "Sangha and Reforms and Renewal of Sasana in Myanmar: Historical Trends and Contemporary Practice." In Trevor Ling, ed., *Buddhist Trends in Southeast Asia.* Singapore: Institute of Southeast Asian Studies.
UNICEF. 1988. *The State of the World's Children.* Geneva: UNICEF.
Yitri, Moksha. 1989. "The Crisis in Burma: Back from the Heart of Darkness?" *Asian Survey* 29(6) (June): 543–58.

CHAPTER THIRTEEN

China

The Limits of Civil Society in a Late Leninist State

MARY E. GALLAGHER

China was one of the few socialist countries to emerge from the 1990s with a dynamic, expanding economy and an intact ruling communist party. How has China's "economic transition without political liberalization" shaped state-society relations? Has civil society emerged? If so, what are its parameters and how is it affected by restrictive state regulations?

Since 1978, the People's Republic of China has experienced massive social and economic change. Political normalization following the Cultural Revolution, economic reform, and increased integration with the rest of the world have led to a great expansion in individual autonomy and a more diverse, open society. Rapid economic growth and extensive social change have not led to significant political liberalization, however. The Chinese Communist Party (CCP) continues to maintain its monopoly of political power and its leading position over other institutions, including the government, the legal system, and all social organizations. Associational life in China remains tightly constrained by this system, with the party-state employing corporatist regulations to achieve control and co-optation of social organizations (Brook and Frolic 1997).

The boundary separating state and society, especially organized groups, is extremely porous and in constant movement. The state is devolving institutions to society but maintaining control and influence through laws, structural affiliations, personnel, and financial measures. The state is also actively creating new groups and associations that are ostensibly social organizations but remain linked to their state creators.[1] Groups formed independently from within society are also affected by this control and influence; indeed, no social organization in China can register without a government sponsor. Other forms of civil society are therefore emerging outside the realm of the regulated, legal social organization: more fluid social networks, groups "virtually" organized on the Internet, and, finally, "unofficial civil society." "Unofficial civil" society includes groups with common interests or attributes that remain outside the sphere of state-sanctioned organizations either because the state refuses to recognize them or because these groups themselves studiously avoid organization in order to maintain their autonomy and independence from the state.

Future political change will be shaped by this split between official civil society (restricted through corporatist regulations and party domination) and its unofficial counterpart. Corporatist groups are likely to experience gradual liberalization and increasing strength and influence as the Chinese state continues with market reforms, "rule of law" projects, and bureaucratic reorganization. But given the benefits of close ties in the current period, it remains unclear whether such groups will become more autonomous from the state. In fact, given the degree of mutual penetration and dependence between social organizations and state institutions, future political change in China will decidedly not occur as a standoff between state and official civil society. It is groups and interests outside the legal, organized sphere that are more likely to clash directly, even violently, with the Chinese state. Civil society's future development, its direction, quality, and relationship to the state, are contingent, of course, on changes in China's political institutions, its legal infrastructure, and the economy.

Civil Society, Corporatism, and the Chinese Case

Two analytical frameworks have surfaced in the literature as ways to understand the effects that economic liberalization and growth have on state-society relations in China. Debates centering on the fit of these frameworks, civil society versus state corporatist, have dominated research into both historical and contemporary trends in Chinese state-society relations. The civil society framework looks for the rise of relatively autonomous groups as state power recedes to make way for the market. Its major underlying assumption is that the growth of societal associations limits the power of the state.[2] The state-corporatist framework also looks for the rise of interest associations at the societal level. The rise of associations is seen not as an indication of receding state power, however, but as an evolution away from direct state control to indirect state coordination. Loss of state power is not assumed to be a necessary result of greater market penetration.

Both of these approaches have been deployed in analysis of Chinese state-society relations under reform, with state corporatism being more dominant, because many researchers have remained skeptical about the application of civil society in the Chinese context.[3] Variants on the state-corporatist models, usually emerging due to problems in the application of corporatism to the Chinese case, have recently become more central to this discussion. They include Philip Huang's (1993) notion of a "third realm," Kenneth Foster's (2002a) "hybrid organizations," Margaret Pearson's (1994) "socialist corporatism," X. L. Ding's (1994) "institutional amphibiousness," Baogang He's "semi civil-society," Michael Frolic's state-led civil society (Brook and Frolic 1997), and many others. The central focus in this literature is the existence of a realm between society and the state that is constituted by both, but subsumed by neither. These variants of state corporatism are also rooted in China's history, drawing from the guilds of the late Qing era and the effects of socialist organization and ideology on current developments.

The corporatist paradigm and its China-specific applications set their sights, not only on the formation of associations, but on the role of the state in initiating, running, and controlling these groups, not necessarily through repression or violence but through mutual penetration, converging interests, and co-optation. Under state corporatism, associational life is strictly controlled by the state. Characteristics of state-led formation include a pre-emption of issues, co-optation of leaders, institutionalization of access, state planning and resource allocation, development of quasi-state agencies, a political culture stressing formalism, consensus, and continuous bargaining, and the periodic but systematic use of physical repression (Schmitter 1974). All of these characteristics fit, to varying degrees, the current relationship between the Chinese state and social organizations.

It is, however, inaccurate to cast the debate as a dichotomous choice between civil society and state corporatism. These models are quite different in what they seek to explain. The civil society model is an analytical model of social change, founded on the prediction that growth in autonomous social organizations leads to greater societal independence from the state and eventually, perhaps, to democratization. State corporatism, in contrast, is a descriptive model of state-society relations in nations where the state plays a central role in controlling the growth and development of societal actors. As Jonathan Unger and Anita Chan point out, corporatism is made up of a collection of "institutional mechanisms" and as such can be deployed by many different types of regimes (Unger and Chan 1995: 37). Pointing out that the Chinese government employs state-corporatist structures to reign in and control society does little to help us understand future political change. In this sense, the civil society model is overly teleological, while corporatism is not teleological enough.

Formulations of civil society in terms of neo-Tocquevillean and neo-Gramscian, or New Left, frameworks (see Introduction and Chapter 1 above) take care to avoid this teleological bias in which civil society is highly associated with democracy. One of the key contributions of this volume is to show that civil society's relationship to democratization is highly contingent. Unfortunately, even the more sophisticated frameworks presented in this volume have limited usefulness for our understanding of civil society in China. In both the neo-Tocquevillean and New Left schools, civil society is evaluated by its relative distance from state actors, with an implicit normative assumption that the ideal nature of civil society is independent and separate from the state. Chinese civil society can only come up short if this is the major focus of comparison. Moreover, a linear focus on movement away from the state (from no autonomy to more autonomy) will only capture one angle of China's associational life, and arguably not the most important aspect. One of the key arguments presented here is that state-civil society interaction is important because it is changing the nature of the Chinese state. This transformative effect of civil society is, however, a result of the close interdependence and mutual penetration of the state and social groups. My emphasis here echoes Suzaina Kadir's point in Chapter 10 that in Singapore as well, it is more important to study "the process of interaction and how it defines, bounds, or transforms the two sides," rather than measuring the degree of societal autonomy from the state.

State corporatism, however, also has profound limitations, because it is largely a descriptive model. Social organizations in China are indeed structured in state-corporatist fashion, but adopting state corporatism as a lens through which to try to view the full range of Chinese society would be a mistake, because it would provide an incomplete view and a static model. State corporatism cannot help us explain how authoritarian states deploying corporatist organizations to control and co-opt society (such as South Korea and Taiwan) suddenly democratize and become plural, open, competitive polities. These limitations lead me to consider other forms of civil society, above all, "unofficial civil society." In the final section of this chapter, I shall explore some of the ways in which political change may occur in China in the future in spite of the state-corporatist characteristics of social organizations.

Historical Perspective

Debates over the nature of state-society relations in late imperial times, the republican era, and contemporary China surfaced most visibly during the late 1980s, when China seemed at first to be going through a period of rapid social change and liberalization and then (after the suppression of the Tiananmen Square demonstration on June 4, 1989) to be going through a period of renewed authoritarian control and repression. The possibility of an emergent civil society during the spring protests of 1989 led to questions about the social and cultural foundations of such a phenomenon. Historians asked questions about the nature of associations in the Qing era, the pattern of life, commerce, and labor in imperial and republican urban China, the development of western-influenced associations and groups as colonialism encroached, and the effects of intellectual movements, such as the May Fourth and New Culture movements, on ordinary urban residents and the vast rural peasantry. Many of these historical debates employ the civil society model (in some cases only to criticize it), and comparisons with the post-Mao period are apparent if not explicit.[4]

Historical studies of Chinese state-society relations from the late Qing era to 1949 reveal several points. First, there seems to be a general consensus that Chinese civil society during the late imperial era interacted closely with state actors, leading some to argue that Chinese civil society differed in fundamental ways from that developing in Europe.[5] Although the commercialization and urbanization of the Chinese economy led to a rapid development in a variety of associations (such as guilds and native-place and temple associations), these were more closely tied to the state, in a distinctly hierarchical relationship, than their counterparts in Europe were. This hierarchy encompassed both political and moral qualities. Second, associational life diversified and societal power (in particular, the power of the merchant class) increased as the Qing state declined and stability broke down. With the arrival of the republican era, Chinese society changed rapidly and many new types of associations gathered strength, including labor unions, chambers of commerce, and student and intellectual groups. Third, the consolidation of state power, first by the Guomindang in 1927 and then by the CCP after 1949, led to the domination and absorption of these movements by the state apparatus. Harnessed by highly mobilized parties, this initial burst of postimperial activity had illiberal consequences both in mainland China and on Taiwan.

Party-state domination of society reached its apex during the rule of Mao Zedong. Associational life in Maoist China was organized through party-controlled mass organizations and strictly controlled. Social organizations apart from these CCP-created and controlled structures were either weeded out or co-opted. Other important characteristics of Chinese society in this period include the high degree of segmentation between the rural and urban populations, the "encapsulation" of society into hierarchical institutions (the *xitong* at the macro level, the *danwei* and the *jiti* at the micro),[6] and the relative homogeneity and egalitarianism of individual status (White et al. 1996: 22). This social structure was notable in the near total absence of horizontal links between individuals or groups. Informal relationships tended to be through personal connections and were often hierarchical too.

In the years since the end of the Cultural Revolution (1966–76), Chinese society has experienced a reawakening. The depoliticization of daily life, the decline of ideology, the expansion of the private and nonstate sectors in the economy, the opening to foreign trade, investment, and influence, the withdrawal of the state from key functions such as labor allocation and certain aspects of social welfare—all have radically changed the way Chinese people live, work, and interact with one another and with state and party authorities. Private space and leisure time have expanded and diversified (Davis et al. 1995). A consumer revolution has taken place among urban Chinese, leading to a rapid expansion in domestic tourism, fashion, the arts, and other interests that had been severely restricted in the late Maoist period (Davis 2000).

Official Civil Society

In tandem with these changes affecting Chinese as individuals, there have been dramatic changes in how Chinese interact in collectivities, including voluntary social associations. According to Tony Saich, by the beginning of 1998, there were more than 180,000 registered social associations in China, of which slightly fewer than 2,000 were national-level organizations. Shanghai alone has over 7,000 social organizations. Saich estimates that if "all kinds of citizen run organizations and economic associations" were included, the total number of social organizations would be around one million (Saich 2000: 126).

Generally speaking, China's social organizations have come into being in three different ways. First, many of these associations were created from scratch by the Chinese state, which has taken an active role, at both the central and local levels, in creating new entrepreneurial groups, industrial and trade associations, and groups representing different professions. Second, in order to reduce the size of the Chinese state and its budget, the government has also spun off associations from the bureaucracy. These associations may still have functions that involve public administration or regulation, however, and often the staff is simply transferred from the government institution. Frequently, these associations are housed in the same complex as the government bureaucracies that spawned them. And, third, some social organizations are created independently from within society by individuals or groups. Although reliable data are not available, it seems that this last category remains the smallest in number.

Chinese social organizations are tightly bound to the state through four major mechanisms. The first is the legal and administrative regulations that govern them. The second mechanism is their restricted financial autonomy. The third is the practice of "double-posting" government or party cadres to leadership positions within social organizations. And the fourth is the ideology of the CCP.

Legal and Administrative Guidelines

Chinese social organizations are constrained by a host of legal and administrative regulations that delineate the scope of each organization, establish the organization's crucial legal standing, and establish the proper hierarchical relationship between the organization and the relevant state or Communist Party institution.

Vertical and Horizontal Control. The State Council issued the main regulations guiding the establishment of social organizations in China in 1998.[7] The "Regulations for Registration and Management of Social Organizations" (*shehui tuanti dengjiguanli tiaoli*) set out the requirements that social organizations must meet, as well as the necessary steps that must be taken to ensure legal recognition. Requirements include fifty individual members or thirty unit members, a fixed domicile, and the possession of a full-time staff and adequate funding (the amount depends on the scope of the organization). It is difficult for small, poorly funded organizations to reach these basic requirements. More onerous for all social organizations, however, are the stipulations for proper registration and supervision. These regulations set out a system of hierarchical organization that ties the social organization to two supervising bodies: the professional business unit (*yewu zhuguan danwei*) and the authorizing government body (*dengji guanli jiguan*). Every social organization in China is vertically linked both to a guarantor and to the regulating government authority.

As stipulated in the regulations, a professional business unit (PBU) must be found to serve as guarantor of the social organization. This unit must be responsible "for the supervision and guidance over social organizations' activities being conducted in accordance with the law and the articles of organization" (Ge 2001).[8] Although most PBUs are departments of governments (local, provincial, national) or of the Chinese Communist Party, the PBU may be an enterprise or a higher-level social organization. The regulations do not specify what relevant documents must be submitted to the PBU for approval. Nor do they specify the time frame in which PBUs must decide the fate of a social organization. PBUs are not required to furnish reasons for declining an application of a social organization (Ge 2001).

After a social organization has found a PBU, it then makes an application to the registration and administration organs (*dengji guanli jiguan*), usually the local civil affairs department or, in the case of national social organizations, the Ministry of Civil Affairs. These government bodies are then responsible for annual inspection of the social organization, for the verification of any violation of the regulations, and for imposing administrative punishments on social organizations that violate regulations or any relevant laws (Ge 2001). These organs must make a decision within sixty days about any social organization; if an application is rejected, they must explain why. Reasons for rejection or dissolution include the vaguely worded clause that "social organizations shall abide by the Constitution, laws, administrative regulations, and state policies." During 1990–92, for example, the State Council reexamined and reverified all social organizations and dissolved those that were found to be "against the four fundamental principles of the constitution." From 1997 to 2000, the State Council again reinspected all social organizations and dissolved those found to be "spreading the thought of bourgeois liberalization" (Ge 2001).

The guidelines regulating the supervision of social organizations set high standards for membership, staffing, and funding. At the same time, these regulations set onerous standards for proper registration and authorization. Every social organization must find another work unit willing to take responsibility for it. Every social organization must also satisfy vague but broad measures of political correctness.

Overlap and Competition Among Organizations. Government regulations also require that organizations must not overlap one another significantly in scope or purpose. Competition and pluralist interaction between social organizations is discouraged. The 1989 regulations on the formation of social organizations proclaimed: "There is no need for the establishment of a social organization where there are other social organizations whose business scope is either identical or similar to that of the proposed social organization in the same administrative area" (Ge 2001). The restrictive corporatist framework is indicated by ministerial provisions aimed at preventing social organizations from "being excessive in number, developing without planning, overlapping of business among the organizations, enrolling members repeatedly, and making members suffer excessive economic burdens." The regulations also warn against "malicious competition among the organizations, which in turn leads to all kinds of shortcomings for society" (Ge 2001).

In sum, then, the legal and administrative regulations guiding the establishment of social organizations fit well into the state-corporatist framework. Social organizations are vertically and horizontally integrated into government and party structures—ensuring avenues for control, co-optation, and surveillance. Once established, they are permitted to have a monopoly of representation. Competition between them is discouraged.

Financial Autonomy, Political Dependence

Social organizations can be divided into three broad categories: organizations devolved from the socialist state (previously designated as bureaus or government departments or groups from one of the mass organizations); organizations created by the state (GONGOs); and organizations set up through the initiative of private individuals or groups. Groups devolved from or created by the party-state are top-down social organizations; groups initiated within society are from the bottom up (Kang 2001). Generally speaking, top-down social organizations receive some financial subsidization from the government, whereas bottom-up groups are expected to raise funds from society.[9] Expectations of financial autonomy combined with expectations of political correctness sometimes create problems for social organizations. As one Chinese analyst (Kang 2001) commented: "Their activities must not directly damage the governmental interests and go against its will, otherwise the government will directly stop their activities or ban them. At the same time, social organizations' activities must meet with the needs of society, otherwise they can't receive the approval and support of the society and lose their basis for existence." A case study of the Chinese Youth Development Foundation (CYDF), one of the best-known social organizations in China and responsible for Project Hope, a fund-raising initiative to send donations to impoverished rural youth and improve rural education, revealed the same problem. Social organizations suffer from a "paradox of legitimacy." They must get legitimacy from a branch of the Communist Party or government body and get legal authorization from the state.

At the same time, they must find legitimacy within market society. The case study concluded: "This latter legitimacy is even more important for their survival in the market and international environment" (Yuan and Sun 2001).

At this time, however, the avenues by which social organizations can achieve financial autonomy are narrow. The regulations of 1998 stipulate that social organizations should safeguard and increase their financial worth through measures that are "legal, safe, and effective" but do not clarify what these measures might be (Li 2001). Social organizations that attempt to provide social welfare to marginal groups often compete with private enterprises or, even worse, with state-owned enterprises that are the beneficiaries of state subsidies. Because social organizations are not permitted to participate in for-profit activities and receive scant government subsidization, they are often hard-pressed to compete in this environment (Yang 2001). There is also little official encouragement for private contributions—for example, tax policies that would encourage greater individual or corporate giving to domestic social organizations. This further limits the domestic resources of social organizations.

Double-Posting of Personnel

The rigorous registration and approval process for a social organization tends to have two effects. First, it privileges top-down social organizations—organizations that are being spun off or devolved from government or party institutions. These groups can rely on their prior government resources, including funding, expertise, staffing, and links to the government, enterprises, and the media. Second, even for the bottom-up organizations, the prerequisites for approval (finding a PBU and then applying for legal registration to another government office) draw the social groups into closer and more intimate contact with government and party institutions. The result is the penetration of the social organization by the state or party and the practice of double-posting—appointing government or party cadres to serve jointly as officials of the social organization.[10]

This interpenetration occurs at all levels of social organization, but it is most obvious within the large national-level groups. The Chinese Youth Development Foundation, for example, is an offshoot of the Communist Youth League (CYL), one of the mass organizations. CYDF's board of directors is drawn entirely from the leadership of the CYL. The CYL directs their appointment to CYDF and supervises their work (Yuan and Sun 2001). The highest honorary positions of the CYDF, moreover, are filled by former or present leaders of the CYL (Li et al. 2001). This penetration through double-posting is also seen in the major Chinese business associations, including the Young Entrepreneurs, the Shanghai Entrepreneurial Society, and the Chinese Association of Enterprise Directors.[11]

Double-posting is not only a national-level phenomenon. The evolution of the Shenzhen Voluntary Federation (Shenzhenshi Yiwugongzuo Lianhehui), a particularly activist and independent group, shows similar trends. It was first established as a division of the Shenzhen City Communist Youth League in 1989 to serve the needs and protect the rights of young migrant workers, and its development over the next decade demonstrates both the potential and the limitations of social organizations (Yi and Yong 2001). By 1990, the Shenzhen Voluntary Federation had broken off from the Shenzhen CYL and established itself as a social organization under the CYL's direction. Personnel are double-posted, but the Volunteers note that their methods are different from those of most other social associations in China: the Shenzhen Volunteers must give prior approval to any staff sent from the Shenzhen CYL. The Volunteers also choose their leaders in competitive elections. But even an independent and feisty organization such as the Shenzhen Voluntary Federation is bound to the state and party and penetrated by CCP personnel. CYL members sit on the Volunteers' Secretariat (Mishuchu) and "advise the Board of Supervisors on their daily work" (Yi and Yong 2001).[12]

Party-state penetration of social organizations through double-posting of personnel is not uniformly recognized as bad for the growth of social associations. It allowed the Shenzhen Voluntary Federation to develop from a group of 400 in 1993 to a group of 30,000 in 1999. Private business associations value high-profile cadres or former cadres in leadership positions because they lend credibility, prestige, and the powerful suggestion that the group enjoys good connections with officialdom. Given the degree of corruption and the continuing importance of personal connections (*guanxi*) in Chinese business circles, double-posting and penetration are likely to persist for some time.

Ideology and Interest Representation

A final constraint to the development of Chinese social organizations is the ideology of the CCP—in particular its ongoing commitment to serve as the encompassing group for all legitimate societal interests. This monopoly on interest representation reduces social organizations to a subordinate role and restricts their ability to speak for their members or their cause. The CCP conception of how interest representation should occur falls far short of a pluralist model of competition and even differs somewhat from the traditional state-corporatist model of interest representation by hierarchical, peak associations with heavy state control and mediation. In China, the Communist Party remains the final arbiter of society's interests and the sole legitimate representative of the interests of the entire Chinese people. The newest example of this encompassing impulse of the CCP is the "Three Represents" theory pushed by Jiang Zemin. The Three Represents extend the CCP's representation past its traditional constituents—workers and peasants—to the "advanced cultural and productive forces of society."[13] The most notable implication of this theory is high-level support for the inclusion of private entrepreneurs in the party's ranks, a phenomenon that has already occurred locally in many areas.

Two Case Studies: Labor and Capital

To demonstrate the effects of these constraints, two key cases of social organization are examined here: labor and capital. These cases are critical because they involve two of the most dramatically changed groups since the onset of the reform period in 1978. The state's attempts to regulate and control both labor and private capital reveal the way state intervention and state-led organization of civil groups shapes the direction of political change.

The All-China Federation of Trade Unions

The All-China Federation of Trade Unions (ACFTU) is the national association and sole legal representative of Chinese workers. The ACFTU was established in 1948, and the Trade Union Law of 1950 was one of the first laws to be promulgated by the new communist government under Mao Zedong. The ACFTU is a "mass organization" and, as such, under communism, was intended to act as a "transmission belt" relaying party edicts and government policies to workers, while conveying worker concerns and suggestions to the leadership. In practice, of course, the former function was fulfilled more effectively than the latter. Prior to 1978, the vast majority of Chinese enterprises had a trade union organization. With ownership limited to state or collective, however, the union's function within the enterprise was secondary to the factory's communist party organization. Its job was to harmonize labor relations, encourage worker efficiency, and perform certain welfare functions (To 1986).

Conflict between the CCP and the union was not unheard of—particularly in the early days before the dominance of the CCP was firmly established over all social organizations. But as Mao extended his power at the expense of other CCP officials who were more sympathetic to independent unions, the union was gradually weakened in the 1950s and early 1960s. Key union leaders were suppressed for promoting "economism" (advancing the narrow material interests of workers) over concern for the achievement of national communism. During the power struggles and chaos of the Cultural Revolution, disgruntled contract and temporary workers besieged enterprise unions. When radical Red Guard students invaded the central offices of the ACFTU in Beijing, the union ceased to exist, and it did not reappear as a coherent organization until the reforms of the late 1970s (To 1986).

The ACFTU is a corporatist body with the enterprise-level union as the base. Although industrial unions and local trade union bureaus exist, all are under the umbrella of the ACFTU. The higher level approves appointments at a lower level (Chan 1993; Howell 1990; Wilson 1990; White 1996). Since the end of the Cultural Revolution, the trade union has been revived and reformed somewhat to fit the demands of a marketizing economy. The government has revised the Trade Union Law twice, in 1992 and 2001, each time granting the ACFTU greater legal responsibilities and rights (Gallagher and Jiang 2002). Current union responsibilities include organizing an enterprise-level trade union in every enterprise with twenty-five or more workers, protecting and representing workers' legal rights and interests, and aiding workers during labor disputes. Union rights are more circumscribed. The union does not have the right to organize a strike or work actions. It must remain supportive of the Chinese Communist Party and the principles of its rule. And because the higher-level authorities of the ACFTU must approve all trade unions, independent trade union organizations are strictly forbidden.

The ACFTU (including its branches at the local and firm levels) is a highly constrained association. Of all the social organizations in China today, the trade union is perhaps the weakest as measured by autonomy from the state and CCP. In terms of policy influence and interest representation, too, the ACFTU is extremely weak. In light of the strong, developmentalist views of most central and local leaders, the union serves as middleman between enterprise managers and workers, an arrangement that severely compromises its role as the representative of workers. In a repressive political environment, the union enjoys a monopoly on representation but has little credibility among workers.[14] Moreover, the rapid diversification in enterprise ownership through foreign investment, stockholding conversions, mergers, bankruptcies, and factory leasing has led to a proliferation of enterprises without unions. In the most dynamic sectors of the Chinese economy, the entire trade union organization is marginalized—even though these sectors experience high rates of labor conflict and strikes.[15] Much of China's labor conflict thus falls outside the state-corporatist framework and trade unions play little role in worker protests and lawsuits against their employers.[16]

The constraints on the trade union are partly the result of its genesis as a mass organization in a communist political system. This is an important characteristic of Chinese state corporatism more generally. Unlike other regimes in which labor unions and social organizations are captured by the state and reined in by the state's control, Chinese trade unions have long been a part of the state apparatus. The current period is not one of capture but one in which the state is attempting to relax its overwhelming control and influence and devolve limited rights and responsibilities, all the while maintaining a monopoly on political power.

To focus only on the organization's genesis (as a mass organization) would be misleading, however, since some mass organizations have achieved greater autonomy and diversification. Both the Women's Federation (Zhonghua Quanguo Funu Lianhehui) and the All-China Youth Federation (Zhonghua Quanguo Qingnian Lianhe Hui) have become vibrant, diverse organizations with significant NGO-like activity. These organizations have more diffuse goals and wide policy arenas. Moreover, their growing autonomy does not threaten the Chinese party-state as much as a more activist, aggressive labor movement undoubtedly would.[17] It is not only the structure of mass organizations that restricts their autonomy; it is also how the state perceives the threat of autonomy. This perception dictates the degree to which the state actively controls the organization.

AFCTU leaders at the central and provincial levels at times do press for an enlarged union role and more effective representation of workers' interests. In the late 1980s, many of these issues were discussed with active encouragement by ACFTU officials. After the June 4, 1989, suppression of the Pro-Democracy Movement, however, union reform remained stalled. With the rapid expansion of the nonstate sector, layoffs, and restructuring in the state sectors that came in the 1990s, the union's role has been strengthened legislatively but not in reality. Pressure for change is beginning to emanate from other social organizations, however, which are beginning to usurp major duties and responsibilities of the trade union. Legal aid organizations, which are often under the jurisdiction of universities and therefore have less oversight than many registered social organizations, now operate in many Chinese cities and offer free or low-cost legal aid to workers involved in labor disputes and other work-related grievances. Despite the fact that the Trade Union Law of 2001 encourages trade union officials to serve as representatives of workers during the dispute resolution process, the union's role is usually minimal. There is growing conflict between the ACFTU, which feels that these new legal aid organizations are trespassing on its own territory, and legal aid activists, who feel that they are filling in for an illegitimate, malfunctioning labor union.[18]

Many theorists would argue that by definition Chinese trade unions should not included in civil society. Their historical identity as a mass organization under Communist Party leadership leaves them with little autonomy and probably less legitimacy in the eyes of most workers. However, as a study of how civil society develops in a late communist state, the union's problems and peculiarities are not uncharacteristic. They in fact highlight in the extreme some of the basic limitations of civil society's development in a repressive political environment. China's rapidly changing economy and social environment will, however, continue to pose new challenges related to labor that will affect the future of the trade union. As is already apparent in the legal realm, the trade union's inability to fulfill its legally mandated duties has led to the rapid development of new social organizations eager to serve as representatives of workers' interests.

Business Associations

Business associations have expanded rapidly under reform. Many have been created by the state, which seeks to incorporate entrepreneurial and business interests into structures that render them less dangerous and destabilizing to the government. These associations have been studied widely by scholars. Both qualitative and quantitative research methods have been employed. In general, the conclusions reached are overwhelmingly uniform and mutually reinforcing.[19] First, Chinese business associations are not necessarily weak, but their degree of effectiveness is not related to autonomy—in fact, high levels of autonomy may be inversely related to the association's effectiveness as a representative of the association's interests. Second, Chinese business associations are closely tied to the state, and associations of large firms are more embedded than associations made up of individual entrepreneurs and small business owners. Third, Chinese business associations increasingly represent the interests of their members, but many businesses continue to use vertical ties of clientelism to cultivate ties with officials. The existence of business associations and the continued importance of clientelism are not necessarily contradictory—in fact, as Margaret Pearson (1997) argues, they may be "consistent and complementary." And, fourth, researchers of Chinese business associations overwhelmingly employ state corporatism (or its variants) as a device to describe the structure of these associations and their relations to the government.

Pearson's study of business associations in the foreign and private sectors finds that these groups play limited but important roles in "the dual task of serving both control and co-optation functions, on the one hand, and advocacy for newly legitimized interests, on the other" (1997: 135). Pearson argues, however, that their real value to their members comes in the "vertical, informal clientelism embedded in these associations" (ibid.). Members find greater access to officialdom through the association, but the association itself does not play an active role in representing members' interests to the state. These associations instead seem to provide a space where government-business relations can deepen and thicken. There is little sense that these associations are growing away from the state.

Bruce Dickson employs two quantitative surveys to evaluate the characteristics of business associations in China (2002: 255–87). His study is particularly important because it encompasses greater regional variation than other studies, which tend to concentrate on one region.[20] Dickson finds that both officials and business association members believe that these organizations represent the interests of their members. Most members also believe that their association influences policymaking. But Dickson also finds that in economically developed regions, government and business views tend to converge rather than diverge. Businessmen in wealthy regions are also the least likely to believe that associations can influence government policy. Dickson concludes:

> In the areas that are most economically developed and where privatization has advanced furthest, the convergence of views between entrepreneurs and local officials is most pronounced. . . . Instead of seeking an officially recognized and protected autonomy, entrepreneurs seek to be embedded in the state, and the state in turn has created the institutional means for linking itself with private business interests. (ibid.: 286)

Dickson's quantitative study accords with David Wank's (1999) in-depth examination of government-business relations in Xiamen, Fujian province. Wank finds that as the market has penetrated China's southeastern coast, government-business ties have intensified and strengthened. China's emerging market economy is not taking shape along the lines of private property, increased social autonomy, and the expansion of contract-based commercial development. Instead, Wank sees a transformation from communism in which particularistic ties between private entrepreneurs and local officials increase—forming a "symbiotic clientelism." Business associations play a key role in granting private entrepreneurs access to government functionaries: "Participation in certain business associations can dramatically increase interaction with officialdom, personalizing relationships with them and increasing support" (Wank 1999: 137). Wank finds that business-government relations under advanced marketization do not proceed inexorably toward greater separation and declining use of *guanxi* and clientelist ties. In fact, private entrepreneurs may become increasingly more sophisticated and expansive in their cultivation of government officials.[21] Associations seem to play a role in this process as they offer routine and regular access to officialdom for even the least connected:

> Participation in most of the aforementioned associations also enhances renown because of the exclusivity of membership. One must be invited to join; therefore membership indicates that one is successful and prosperous and, in some way, approved by government officials. Less well-endowed entrepreneurs squeeze membership to maximize renown. One former worker listed all seventeen of his associational affiliations and positions on his name card. The list was so long it required a fold-over sheet, so his name card resembled a small booklet. (Wank 1999: 139)

These findings from Pearson, Dickson, and Wank all point to an increasingly symbiotic relationship between government and business, which is fortified by business associations. Models based on an oppositional logic do little to explain this relationship. Moreover, the massive extent of the corruption between officials and entrepreneurs makes it hard to determine who is in charge or who is controlling whom in the web of ties and interests that bind together public officials and private businessmen (Wank 2002).

One way to understand the role of business associations is to focus less on their relative autonomy and more on their organizational evolution. Kenneth Foster's comparison of two national-level sectoral associations reveals how business associations have evolved over the course of the reform period. He finds that certain associations (in this case the China Chain Store and Franchise Association), although initially founded by the state, may gradually grow more active and independent from the state sponsor, with activities and functions increasingly geared toward interest representation of their members and services. In the case of the Chain Store Association, the reasons for this switch seem to include the dissolution of its original government sponsor (and thus a reduction in government oversight), movement of the association's offices out of the original bureaucracy, and expanding private and nonstate membership.[22] Clearly, future research on business associations must pay attention to their organizational evolution, their changing relationship to the government bureaucracy (particularly at a time of a shrinking Chinese state), and their membership characteristics.

Chinese business associations are better at representing the interests of their members than Chinese trade unions. This does not mean, however, that they are a good example of a developing civil society. Indeed, these associations are tightly bound to state organizations and actors through the mechanisms specified here. Their power, in effect, derives not from their autonomy but from their close ties with officialdom and converging goals. Business associations reflect the changing nature of the Chinese state and are better understood in a state-centric framework. Even state corporatism, with its hierarchical logic between government and business, may miss crucial aspects of the government-business relationship in regions where the private economy is dominant and growing wealthier. The symbiotic relationship between government and private business is likely to increase as entrepreneurs "join the association" of the leaders—the Chinese Communist Party.

Labor unions and business associations are thus key institutions for exploring the changing nature of state-society relations in modern China. We might expect, given the leadership's current emphasis on economic growth, that labor unions would be the one of the most severely restricted types of social organization, while business associations would be given greater autonomy to pursue economic growth and prosperity.[23] This is not the case. In fact, both types of associations are encouraged to develop only in a limited and restricted fashion. Neither is allowed to drift away from the state's control. The development of both is geared toward strengthening the Chinese state and controlling new social forces that might arise to challenge the CCP's monopoly on political power. The CCP's decision in 2002 to allow private entrepreneurs to join the party is perhaps one more indication that the party-state would rather absorb China's new rich than allow private business associations to develop as autonomous social organizations.

Are these case studies unrepresentative, given the highly sensitive nature of the state's changing relationship to labor and capital? Even in areas with less political sensitivity, the state is intent on maintaining control over social organizations. Elizabeth Economy's study of environmental NGOs paints a realistic view of the extent to which these new groups can operate as activist organizations for the protection of the environment, scarce natural resources, and endangered wildlife (Economy 2004). The state has allowed these groups to flourish because they provide resources needed to solve some of the severe problems of environmental degradation caused by rapid economic growth. The Chinese state has also found that encouragement of domestic NGOs raises its international standing. Even so, Economy calls the relationship between NGOs and the state a "tightrope act." NGO leaders and activists must constantly worry about their relationship with state officials, and cultivating these relationships is an essential part of NGO work. In fact, the informal cultivation of state officials is far more important to NGO success than lobbying or public pressure. Moreover, environmental NGOs also face the same constraints as other NGOs when it comes to registration, finding personnel, and locating sources of financing.

Future Development

Despite the state's ability to maintain control of certain organizations—the trade union, for example—it is unlikely that this ability is all-encompassing. Tony Saich (2000: 124) argues that declining state capacity and growing societal complexity make for routine evasion of formal mechanisms of control: "There is a significant gap between rhetoric and practice and between the expressed intent of the party-state authorities, a system that is itself deeply conflicted, and what can actually be enforced for any significant period throughout the entire country." This trend is likely to continue in the light of consistent state withdrawal from social welfare functions, even as unemployment, layoffs, and (the related) economic inequality continue to grow. Social organizations are increasingly filling this gap left by the state's withdrawal. These organizations run the gamut: advocacy and service for the disabled, environmental protection, consumer protection, disaster relief, HIV/AIDS work, poverty alleviation, care for the elderly, and women's rights protection and services (Young 2001).

Although these social organizations seem unlikely to contribute to dramatic political change in the near future, their role in policy reform and implementation is important and growing. Groups pushing for greater awareness of HIV/AIDS have been critical in exposing the Henan Province blood scandal, in which thousands of peasants were infected when they sold their blood.[24] Environmental groups have also been important in increasing the environmental awareness of the government and the general public. Economy finds that some groups have also successfully lobbied for greater protection of some endangered animal species (Economy, forthcoming). Finally, groups formed to aid the integration of migrant workers into urban society have brought migrant issues to the forefront. Greater awareness of migrant issues may have played a role in the government's recent decision to pay more attention to migrant rights, including the problem of education for children of migrants and abuses of the custody and repatriation regulations (Rosenthal 2001; Xinhua News Report 2003).

From this survey of Chinese social organizations, it is clear that while autonomy from the state is extremely limited, there are other characteristics worth exploring that indicate the different ways social organizations and state institutions interact. To confine one's view to the relative degree of autonomy of Chinese social organizations is to miss many other key characteristics of these groups—including their organizational evolution and internal dynamics. And to see their evolution as a process either of growing autonomy or of continued dependence is to miss the way in which the constant interaction between the state and social groups can transform parts of the state itself. This is particularly true of business associations. Their members continue to grow richer and more powerful without, apparently, the expected push for greater autonomy and distance from local officials.

Unofficial Civil Society

In China's repressive political environment, much change is happening outside official civil society. Protest, contention, and social expression are occurring—often in ways that are unorganized and inarticulate (Thornton 2002).[25] Despite the unclear legal standing of these social actors, the existence of an unofficial civil society is important to our overall understanding of the Chinese case. It is, moreover, the declared aim of this volume to examine civil society "in the context of a country's prevailing circumstances" (see Introduction). In China, the growth of unofficial civil society is directly related to the state's unwillingness to deploy corporatist organizational tactics to capture, co-opt, and control new kinds of resistance and civil action. Corporatist incorporation necessarily entails the legitimation of these groups and at least some degree of recognition that their interests are justified and should be represented in policy debates. Such legitimation, however, remains anathema to the Chinese party-state.

The Floating Population

Estimates of the migrant labor force in China generally range from about 60 million to 100 million. Migrant workers are most often peasants who have left their rural homes to search for employment in the industrial or service sector. Although men make up the majority of the migrant workforce in China, female migrants predominate in many labor-intensive factories in the coastal developmental zones, where they are preferred for their obedient nature and "nimble fingers." Research also indicates that many migrants do not necessarily leave their region but rather simply relocate to urban or suburban areas within their home province. Nevertheless, this huge exodus of the rural population to the cities is one of the most striking changes of the reform era and is reshaping Chinese society in myriad ways.

The mobility of China's large peasant population (at the beginning of the reform period, well over 80 percent of the population still lived in the countryside) has long been restricted through the implementation of a residency permit (*hukou*) system, which strictly divided the population into rural and urban sections. Those classified as urban residents receive greater access to social welfare, education, and the like. In the past, urban residents were also allocated jobs, which were then generally kept for life. Rural residents did not enjoy these extensive benefits of socialism and in addition were not permitted to move freely into cities or other regions in search of employment. This system has been relaxed under reform, and certain boundaries have eroded. Migrant workers are now allowed to look for work in Chinese cities and establish temporary, even long-term, residence in Chinese cities. The residency permit system still remains in effect, however, with key welfare benefits and perquisites of urban life denied to most migrants (Solinger 1999).

Given their second-class status in urban areas and the lack of an infrastructure able to handle such massive movements of people, migrants face numerous hardships, including inadequate access to housing, social welfare, medical care, education for their children, and even basic daily amenities. At the workplace, migrants may face severe exploitation and abuse at the hand of managers who take advantage of their semilegal status and their dependence on the workplace for basic needs such as food and housing. In several ways, Chinese internal migration poses problems that other countries have faced when confronted with large-scale international immigration—how to provide basic social welfare, for example, and how to integrate these new groups into a society that is often discriminatory and unwelcoming.

The problems of migrants have not escaped the notice of the Chinese state and certain social groups. In fact, many social associations have formed to help migrants integrate into urban society: Rural Women Knowing All (national), the Migrant Women's Club (national), the Migrant Workers' Document Handling Service Center (Guangzhou), and the Center for the Protection of Migrant Workers' Rights (Shanghai). These associations (often in conjunction with the Women's Federation) address many of the problems cited here and offer legal aid, counseling, and literacy training. These associations also play a critical role in attracting greater media attention to the plight of migrants by publishing newspapers and magazines on migrant issues.

These groups all have one thing in common, however—they are groups to protect migrants but not groups made up of migrants. According to research, large city administrations resist the formation of autonomous associations of migrants (Solinger 1999: 170; Zhang 2001). In Beijing's Zhejiang village, for example, a collection of retired doctors were continually thwarted in their attempts to set up small clinics to serve the migrant population, who were excluded from most medical care in Beijing by its high cost and linguistic barriers (Li 2001). When migrants from Rui'an (also in Zhejiang province) formed a preparatory committee for the Rui'an Itinerant Merchants Society (Rui'an Xingshang Gonghui), they originally received some support from the Beijing Industry and Commercial Federation (Gongshanglian) and the United Front Department. Based on the principles of "voluntary membership, self-elected leadership, privately hired staff, self-management of internal affairs, and private fund-raising" (Li 2001), this group was one of the first to press for an association that would advocate for migrants, provide services to migrants, and also be initiated, run, and funded by migrants. The Beijing government ultimately refused its legal registration.[26]

Migrants continue to form informal, flexible networks, usually based on native place. These social networks allow migrants to navigate the difficulties of urban life, but they remain closed out of the corporatist framework. Although other groups may offer them charitable assistance, education, and legal aid, representation of their interests is not considered to be legitimate. Legitimation would likely lead to greater demands on the state from migrants for social welfare, education, and basic services. Moreover, such legitimation would also reduce the ability of city administrators to eject migrants. It would be the first step toward recognizing their status as increasingly permanent fixtures of urban China. As the *hukou* system is dismantled, as is planned, a major challenge for the Chinese state will be to integrate migrants into urban society, to recognize and protect their legal rights and interests, and to allow migrants themselves to represent migrants.

Popular Religion

The rise of popular and unorthodox religious groups is perhaps even more problematic for the state-society relationship in China. Renewed interest in religious matters is a widespread phenomenon in contemporary China, although it has manifested itself differently in rural and urban areas.[27] Rural China has experienced a great revival in popular religion—including local temple shrines, spirit mediums, syncretic sects of every kind, and underground "house churches." In urban China, the revival has been more subdued, owing to greater state control, but there is increased attendance at the official patriotic churches even here, as well as heightened interest in heterodox beliefs, including the "qigong craze" made famous by the Falungong movement, which has been banned and repressed since 1999 (Madsen 2000; Overmyer 2003).[28]

Analysis of these phenomena from the viewpoint of civil society has resulted in a generally pessimistic outlook on the contribution of religion to the development of a more autonomous and civil Chinese society.[29] Richard Madsen finds that the Catholic Church, split between its rural and urban roots and its official and unofficial organizations, is ill suited to contribute to China's civil society. Fragmented by its internal divisions, the Catholic Church and its members are unable to develop norms of interpersonal trust, reciprocity, and civil exchange. The CCP and the Religious Affairs Bureau continue to exploit this internal divide for their own benefit by generating suspicion between the official and unofficial church (Madsen 1998: 126–29).

The revival of traditional religions in China's rural areas demonstrates characteristics that build strong local ties and social networks (Dean 2000).[30] Often organized around the reconstruction of a temple, this new organizational activity strengthens local society and may even connect locals to an overseas community of emigrants (particularly in southeastern China where this revival has been most prominent) (Shue 2001). Robert Weller argues, however, that local religious associations under the current political regime will remain just that—extremely localized and fragmented:

> The Daoist Association and religious bureaucracy are attempts to control religion; occasional clampdowns on "superstition" or religious "charlatans," or forbidding temples from doing large public rituals of renewal, are attempts to repress. The state has eased up greatly on religion over the last decade, yet any larger kind of growth is clearly out of the question under the current regime. Temple religion will remain localist and communitarian, but it also remains an important point of concentration for social capital. (Weller 1999: 88)

Both Madsen and Weller, although examining quite different types of religious revival, find that religion's contribution to civil society is constrained by the political institutions created by the state to control and co-opt official religious organizations, while repressing religions that do not strictly respect the hierarchy of party over belief. Underground house churches and local temple associations alike build their own internal social capital, but the effects on the development of civil society are limited.

Popular religious groups outside the legal, corporatist apparatus can, however, be important loci of resistance to the Chinese state. This is no small point if one considers the crucial role that "syncretic popular religious sects and secret societies" have played in the weakening and overthrow of imperial rulers (Shue 2001: 20). As Vivienne Shue notes, these groups reject the party-state's claim to a monopoly on a "doctrine of truth," based, not on Confucian learning and morality, but on scientific rationalism and modernization, which serves to buttress the CCP's hold on power, despite the decline in socialist ideology and socialist practice (as evidenced by the smashing of the iron rice bowl and other socialist institutions).

Popular religious groups that subscribe to alternative truths and systems of belief face severe repression.[31] Such movements are not incorporated into the state's apparatus of social control through registration and penetration. Instead, they are condemned as unscientific and retrograde—evidence of the low quality of Chinese peasants, workers, and other marginalized groups. Their search for a higher truth and morality go directly against the state's own dogged insistence that whatever the differences between current ideology and practice, the CCP remains the only legitimate representative of and ruler of the Chinese nation. According to Shue (2001: 20): "Until and unless the Chinese state moves on to a newer repertoire of legitimation claims—one that does not include official knowledge of ultimate ethical truths—we can expect popular religious belief and practice to continue to be perceived always as a potential, and sometimes as an active, counterhegemonic danger to stability and order." Because these groups cannot be incorporated into the state's vision of Chinese society, they remain on the outside.

Given the high levels of state repression of unofficial religious groups, as well as other barriers, it is difficult to measure the extent of their membership and influence, not to mention the particular dynamics of this type of unofficial civil society. Influence also varies considerably by region—for example, most unofficial Chinese Catholics live in Hebei Province, while most Tibetan Buddhists live in Tibet or on its borders. External reports, however, find that the number of unofficial Chinese Catholics is at least equal to the official Patriotic Catholic Church and may be even twice as large. Likewise, registered Chinese Protestants are estimated to be between 0.8 and 1.2 percent of the total population, while an "estimated 2.4 to 6.5 percent worship in Protestant house churches that are independent of government control."[32] Falungong adherents were at one point believed to number in the tens of millions.[33] But given the dogged campaign to rout them out of Chinese society since 1999, the sect's numbers have fallen rapidly, perhaps to one million or less.

We have seen, then, how certain social organizations remain outside the state-corporatist framework of control through co-optation and penetration. Through analysis of two very different groups—migrants and followers of popular religions—we can observe how the state refuses to legitimate these groups, and how these groups respond to their marginalization. In the case of migrants, denied the right to organize, a vast number of informal networks, associations, gangs, and secret societies have arisen, most often based on native-place affiliation. Rural religious groups continue to build informal and highly fragmented associations. Given their local foundations and the resistance of the state, it is unlikely they will evolve into a broad-based rural civil society. And in the case of urban unorthodox religious movements and sects, in the wake of the Falungong movement, these groups currently bear the overwhelming repressive attention of the Chinese state (Chen 2003; Tong 2002).

China's Intellectuals

Any discussion of Chinese civil society would be incomplete without a discussion of Chinese intellectuals, who by historical tradition and cultural impulse tend to place themselves at the forefront of social change. The 1989 Pro-Democracy Movement was the most recent period of intellectual ferment and mobilization for political and social change. Since that time, most observers have become somewhat pessimistic about the role of Chinese intellectuals in future political change. As is rightly pointed out, Chinese intellectuals, broadly defined as those with higher education, have materially benefited from the past decade of economic reform. For those with technical or other advanced training, professional opportunities have widened and offer a level of material comfort that was heretofore unknown. Some of those formerly known as intellectuals in the traditional sense have now become professionalized as doctors, engineers, lawyers, and managers of private and foreign-invested companies. Intellectuals who have remained engaged in research and teaching have also felt their choices shift. Government- and university-supported research institutes have blossomed, allowing intellectuals some degree of policy influence and a relatively wide range of freedom to pursue research and writing.[34] Opportunities abroad have also attracted a large number of Chinese intellectuals, many of whom have been able to combine the academic freedom of the West with continued involvement in Chinese intellectual circles through academic collaboration and informal networks.

In addition to these institutional changes wrought by economic reform, Chinese intellectual discourse has become more varied and complex. While nationalistic writing has tended to gain the most attention in the West, Chinese intellectuals have wide-ranging views on the nature of their society and its relationship to the outside world, especially the United States.[35] The ability to debate and discuss has vastly expanded, although there are still limits on what the government allows to be openly debated or published.[36] The Internet and various other methods of electronic exchange of information have vastly improved this exchange, particularly informal modes of communication and debate. Access to external news outlets and other organizations also allows much more information about events, both internationally and within China, to be disseminated. Chinese dissident groups also continue to exist and operate externally, although their influence is somewhat limited by their distance and a good deal of fractious infighting. Chinese dissidents who have attempted to organize or disseminate information within China have, however, been dealt with very harshly, receiving long prison sentences or expulsion. Unlike South Korea and Taiwan in the 1980s, China has no viable internal political opposition.[37]

Intellectual contribution to civil society formation in China has certainly been critical. Many of the most dynamic organizations are situated within universities, where they enjoy some degree of protection and autonomy. Unlike in 1989, when student leaders actively resisted collaboration with other sectors of society, especially workers, student groups have begun to reach out to those who have not benefited from the market. This is apparent in the explosion of social organizations that offer help and aid to society's "weak groups" (*ruoshi qunti*). Weak groups in this definition include women, children, workers, especially the unemployed, the poor, the disabled, and the diseased.[38] In the event of some larger shock or political crisis, this growing concern for other social groups may indicate a new opportunity for intellectuals to cut across traditional boundaries and link up more effectively with other social groups.

The Chinese intelligentsia is not necessarily hampered as a force for political change by its somewhat fractured nature. The diffuse, informal networks and the lively debate that occurs spontaneously on the Internet are both good indications of the latent power of Chinese intellectual society. Organizationally speaking, Chinese intellectuals' associational life may be well controlled and monitored by the party-state,[39] but there is significant activity occurring beyond the bounds of organizations through informal channels, global linkages, and virtual public space on the Internet. The effects on government policy are difficult to measure under normal circumstances, but in the event of a larger political crisis, intellectual ferment would be difficult to ignore or control. As we learn in the Burma case study in this volume (Chapter 12), formal organization and government sanction are not always necessary for civil society to develop and to learn certain tactics of communication and interaction that become critical when the political winds shift.

Avenues of Future Political Change

The existence of a large "unofficial civil society" outside the realm of state control and management may indeed be evidence of a stronger civil society in China, but it is a civil society that is still hampered and constricted by the state's own activist policies in shaping, managing, and co-opting social organizations. The implications for political change are important but hard to specify. If the Chinese state continues to control social organizations so strictly, many of these unofficial groups will continue to operate behind the scenes, but with possibly frequent spontaneous eruptions onto the political scene. Political change wrought by these types of groups is most likely in the event of an economic crisis or severe downturn in which large numbers of people, especially the urban unemployed and the rural migrant population, confront increased economic deprivation. It is this type of political crisis that is also most likely to unleash the latent power of China's intellectuals by tapping informal networks and linkages home and abroad.

A second avenue of political change is more gradual but still significant. In fact, it seems already to have begun to occur. This type of change is best defined as a mutual penetration of the state and social groups that has a transformative effect on the state itself. One existing instance of this is the overlap between the party-state and wealthy entrepreneurs. Much of the research on the state-centric models (state corporatism and its variants) shows that in China's postsocialist reality, new organizations are often formed through the merging of state bureaucracy with social groups. The complex relationships that develop within organizations—and between organizations and the relevant state authorities—cannot be fully understood through models that posit an oppositional logic or even, as in the case of state corporatism, a hierarchical logic. Burdened by the legacy of state socialism, Chinese state-society relations are not proceeding in a linear fashion toward civil society's ever greater independence from the state. To understand future political change in China, therefore, one must pay attention to the shifting boundary between state and social groups—including those that may seek out a close, mutually beneficial relationship with state institutions and in doing so affect change within the state itself. This type of gradual political collaboration between the party and China's new economic elite does not necessarily bode well for liberal political change.

A third avenue of political change is civil society's capture of state-led associations or institutions, such as occurred during the prodemocracy movement of 1989. After the students in Beijing took over Tiananmen Square, organized groups and delegations began sending donations and other expressions of sympathy and support. Many of these groups were government-run or government-organized, including the ACFTU, state-run newspaper and television stations, and factory and bureaucratic "work units" (Walder 1991: 485).[40] Civil society's capture of such key organizations is very intriguing as a model for future political change. In this scenario, the dependent nature of Chinese civil society becomes far less important. In fact, the high level of state-led organization may be seen as a benefit to civil organizations, since it provides the structure necessary to mobilize individuals and groups.

In conclusion, then, it is necessary to emphasize the contingent nature of civil society's development. Its evolution cannot be understood in a vacuum or unidimensionally along a spectrum from dependence to autonomy. We must also pay attention to changes in political institutions, legal rules, and infrastructure, as well as to economic indicators such as urbanization, patterns of inequality, and unemployment. The development of civil society in China is tightly constrained by the institutions and structures outlined in this chapter. Yet by far the most constraining element is the ideology of the CCP, which continues to assert that it can encompass all legitimate interests and groups. Given the growing complexity of Chinese society, such encompassing power is surely in doubt. Thus it is likely that the realm of unofficial civil society will continue to grow. The CCP, consumed with the risk of legitimating "unruly" groups such as migrants, continues to ponder the risk of incorporation and acceptance. One hopes that China's leaders are also pondering the risks of inaction and excessive reliance on repression.

Notes

1. These are the so-called GONGOs—government-organized NGOs.

2. The civil society framework began to be applied to modern China in the late 1980s and early 1990s as a comparative framework between China and postsocialist countries in eastern Europe and as a way to understand the development and limitations of the prodemocracy movement of 1989. Timothy Cheek (1998: 219–52) summarizes the overall progress of the civil society framework. For a review of the civil society literature, see Gu Xin 1993–94. For key articles in this debate, see, e.g., Wakeman 1993; Strand 1990; Rowe 1990.

3. Those using state corporatist frameworks include Shue 1994; Pearson 1994; Chan 1993; White 1995; and esp. Unger and Chan 1995. See also Yijiang Ding 2001 for an explicit comparison of the corporatist and civil society aspects of Chinese associational life.

4. These debates are summarized and elaborated in Huang 1993.

5. This conclusion is overdrawn in that it simplifies European civil society. See Bermeo and Nord 2000.

6. The *xitong* is a vertical bureaucratic system; the *danwei* is the work-unit structure within which nearly all Chinese urban residents lived and worked; the *jiti* is the rural collective that structured rural work and life.

7. These were a comprehensive version of the provisional regulations issued in late 1989 in the aftermath of the student uprising. An English version of the regulations is included in Young 2001. For an analysis of the regulations, see Ge 2001.

8. This article of organization and several of the others cited can be found in "The Network of Foundations and Nonprofit Organizations" at http://chinanpo.org (accessed 3/7/2004), an informative, up-to-date website (in Chinese).

9. The funding of the All-China Federation of Trade Unions (one of the mass organizations under socialism), explained in the following case study, is somewhat different. Trade union branches are generally beholden financially to the enterprises in which they are based.

10. Double-posting occurs within the trade union branches at the firm as well, but it is slightly different, as explained in the following case study.

11. From the websites of these organizations. Nevitt's examination of private business associations in Tianjin also found the leadership positions filled with United Front Department cadres—paid by the CCP and appointed by party leaders to head these business associations (Nevitt 1996: 33).

12. Social organizations are dependent on the state and party because they copy their organizational structure from state bodies—leading to a highly bureaucratic structure that lends itself well to penetration by similar state and party institutions (Yuan and Sun 2001).

13. On the Three Represents, see Kynge 2002 and Saiget 2001.

14. In a survey of state-owned enterprise workers in 1993, some 46.5 percent believed that "the union doesn't play a large role." Other statements in the report on workers' attitudes reveal a cynical view of their position in the factory: "Now in reality it is the boss who has the final say." And on the union: "The union is part of the administration, we have no confidence in the union" ("Guanyu quanguo gongren jieji duiwu zhuangkuang de diaocha baogao" 1993).

15. For the effects this marginalization has had on political change in China, see Gallagher 2002.

16. Much of this analysis of the development of the Chinese trade unions under reform is drawn from my fieldwork in 1996–97, 1999, and 2001 (Gallagher 2001).

17. Attempts by workers and activists to establish independent unions and to mobilize workers have been dealt with very harshly, ending in long prison sentences for most labor leaders. Han Dongfang, a mainland labor activist in exile in Hong Kong, runs China Labour Bulletin. This organization follows attempts by mainland activists to mobilize workers as well as government policies and labor conditions. Radio Free Asia broadcasts a program with Han on Chinese labor issues into the mainland.

18. Interview, legal aid volunteer, Shanghai, China, October 26, 2003.

19. Extensive research has been done on Chinese urban entrepreneurs and Chinese business associations. There seems to be a general consensus in the literature that while Chinese business associations are developing quickly, the civil society framework is poorly designed

to capture the "mutually penetrated" nature of business associations and local state institutions. See, e.g., Solinger 1993a; Pearson 1997; Goodman 1999; Parris 1999; Wank 1995.

20. Dickson's study of private entrepreneurs and their relationship to the Chinese party-state is further elaborated in his book *Red Capitalists—The Party, Private Entrepreneurs, and Prospects for Political Change* (2003).

21. This point is expanded in Wank 2002 and linked explicitly to recent corruption scandals.

22. These points are elaborated in Foster 2001.

23. Many other types of organizations that deal with sensitive issues such as AIDS and religion are also severely restricted and monitored.

24. Rosenthal 2002. Wan Yanhai is China's foremost activist. His website, aizhi.org (accessed 3/7/2004 [in Chinese]), supplies information and support to those with AIDS. His detention in 2002 is representative of the harassment that some social activists experience in China.

25. By "inarticulate" I mean to capture the spontaneous and fleeting (but reiterated) resistance that occurs between Chinese social actors and the state. In some ways, this resistance is similar to James Scott's "weapons of the weak" and his focus on small acts of resistance by unorganized individuals rather than the organized and articulate expression of associations.

26. Ibid. For more information on this group, see also Solinger 1999: 270–72.

27. For a comprehensive examination of religion in China, see *China Quarterly*, special issue (2003).

28. As Richard Madsen and others have pointed out, Falungong was not unorganized. It was in fact a highly effective, albeit decentralized, organization. Its ability to organize and plan the spring 1999 demonstration was one reason for the state's ban and repression of the organization that began in July 1999.

29. For an optimistic view of civil society's future, see Johnson 2003.

30. Tsai 2002 finds also that temple associations and lineage groups increasingly play important roles in the provision of public services in many villages. She notes, however, that reliance on these traditional social organizations often has deleterious effects on state building and governance in the countryside.

31. It is not surprising that membership in Falungong, for example, attracted the losers in economic reform, including laid-off workers, the unemployed, and the sick and elderly. See Madsen 2000.

32. U.S. Department of State, Bureau of Democracy, Human Rights, and Labor, *International Religious Freedom Report 2002, China*.

33. See ibid., which notes that Falungong, otherwise known as Falun Dafa or the Wheel of Law, "blends aspects of Taoism, Buddhism, and the meditation techniques and physical exercises of qigong (a traditional Chinese exercise discipline) with the teachings of Falun Gong leader Li Hongzhi (a native of the country who lives abroad). Despite the spiritual content of some of Li's teachings, Falun Gong does not consider itself a religion and has no clergy or places of worship."

34. Naughton 2002.

35. These intellectual debates are well analyzed by Fewsmith 2001. There are also many articles and books on the resurgence of Chinese nationalism. Zhao 1997.

36. For an overview of the ebb and flow of the intellectual-state relationship, see Goldman 1996.

37. For an overview of attempts to form an opposition party, see Wright 2002.

38. There is now also much academic research on China's weak groups, see, e.g., Zhang Minjie 2003.

39. I believe that many groups have a fair degree of operational autonomy even given the government restrictions discussed above. Once a group engages in behavior that is deemed politically problematic, however, these restrictions become much more meaningful and can determine the group's future survival.

40. For other essays about the role of social groups in 1989, see Wasserstrom and Perry 1994.

Works Cited

Berman, Sheri. 1997. "Civil Society and the Collapse of the Weimar Republic." *World Politics* 49: 401–29.

Bermeo, Nancy, and Philip Nord, eds. 2000. *Civil Society before Democracy: Lessons from Nineteenth-Century Europe*. New York: Rowman & Littlefield.

Brook, Timothy, and B. Michael Frolic, eds. 1997. *Civil Society in China*. New York: M. E. Sharpe.

Chambers, Simone, and Jeffrey Kopstein. 2001. "Bad Civil Society." *Political Theory* 29(6) (Dec.): 837–65.

Chan, Anita. 1993. "Revolution or Corporatism? Workers and Trade Unions in Post-Mao China." *Australian Journal of Chinese Affairs* 29 (Jan.): 31–61.

———. 2000. "Globalization, China's 'Free' (Read Bonded) Labour Market and the Chinese Trade Unions." *Asia Pacific Business Review*.

———. 2001. *Chinese Workers Under Assault: The Exploitation of Labor in a Globalizing Economy*. Armonk, N.Y.: M. E. Sharpe.

Cheek, Timothy. 1998. "From Market to Democracy in China: Gaps in the Civil Society Model." In Juan Lindau and Timothy Cheek, eds., *Market Economies and Political Change: Comparing China and Mexico*. New York: Rowman & Littlefield.

Chen, Nancy. 2002. "Healing Sects and Anti-Cult Campaigns." *China Quarterly* 174 (June): 505–20.

Davis, Deborah, ed. 2000. *The Consumer Revolution in Urban China*. Berkeley: University of California Press.

Davis, Deborah, Richard Kraus, Barry Naughton, and Elizabeth Perry, eds. 1995. *Urban Spaces in Contemporary China: The Potential for Autonomy and Community in Post-Mao China*. New York: Cambridge University Press.

Dean, Kenneth. 2000. "Ritual and Space: Civil Society or Popular Religion?" In Timothy Brook and B. Michael Frolic, eds., *Civil Society in China*. Armonk, N.Y.: M. E. Sharpe.

Deyo, Frederic, ed. 1987. *The Political Economy of the New Asian Industrialism*. Ithaca, N.Y.: Cornell University Press.

———. 1989. *Beneath the Miracle: Labor Subordination in the New Asian Industrialism*. Berkeley: University of California Press.

Dickson, Bruce. 2002. "Do Good Businessmen Make Good Citizens? An Emerging Collective Identity Among China's Private Entrepreneurs." In Merle Goldman and Elizabeth J. Perry, eds., *Changing Meanings of Citizenship in Modern China*. Cambridge, Mass.: Harvard University Press.

———. 2003. *Red Capitalists: The Party, Private Entrepreneurs, and Prospects for Political Change*. Cambridge: Cambridge University Press.

Ding, X. L. 1994. "Institutional Amphibiousness and the Transition from Communism: The Case of China." *British Journal of Political Science* 24(3) (July): 293–318.

Ding, Yijiang. 2001. *Chinese Democracy after Tiananmen*. Vancouver: University of British Columbia Press.

Economy, Elizabeth C. 2004. *The River Runs Black: Environmental Challenges to China's Future*. Ithaca, N.Y.: Cornell University Press.

Feng, Tongqing. 1993. "Internal Relations and Structure of Chinese Workers Under Market Reform" (Zouxiang shichangjingjide zhongguo qiye zhigong neibu guanxi he jiegou). *Chinese Social Sciences* 3 (May).

Feng, Tongqing, and Zhao Minghua. 1996. "Workers and Trade Unions." *Chinese Sociology and Anthropology* 28 (Spring): entire volume.

Fewsmith, Joseph. 2001. *China After Tiananmen: The Politics of Transition*. New York: Cambridge University Press.

———. 2001. *China since Tiananmen*. Cambridge: Cambridge University Press.

Foster, Kenneth W. 2001. "Associations in the Embrace of an Authoritarian State: State Domination of Society." *Studies in Comparative International Development* 35(4) (Winter): 84–109.

———. 2002a. "The Organizational Evolution of Business Associations: Processes of Change in the Transformation of China." Paper presented at the annual meeting of the American Political Science Association, Boston.

———. 2002b. "Embedded Within State Agencies: Business Associations in Yantai." *China Journal* 47 (Jan.): 41–65.

Gallagher, Mary E. 2001. "Contagious Capitalism: Globalization and the Politics of Labor in China." Ph.D. diss., Princeton University.

———. 2002. "Why China's Economic Reforms Have Delayed Democracy." *World Politics* 54(3) (Apr.): 338–72.

———. Forthcoming. *Contagious Capitalism: Globalization and the Politics of Labor in China*. Princeton: Princeton University Press.

Gallagher, Mary E., and Junlu Jiang. 2002. "China's Labor Legislation: Introduction and Analysis." *Chinese Law and Government* (Nov.–Dec.): entire volume.

Garon, Sheldon. 2002. *The Evolution of Civil Society: From Meiji to Heisei*. Civil Society in the Asia-Pacific Monograph Series. Cambridge, Mass.: Program on U.S.-Japan Relations, Harvard University.

Ge, Yunsong. 2001. "Shehui tuanti de chengli" (On the establishment of social organizations). www.chinanpo.org/subpages/yanjiu.asp (accessed 11/1/2003).

Goldman, Merle. 1996. "Politically-Engaged Intellectuals in the Deng-Jiang Era: A Changing Relationship with the Party-State." *China Quarterly* 145 (Mar.): 35–52.

Goldman, Merle, and Roderick MacFarquhar, eds. 1999. *The Paradox of China's Post-Mao Reforms*. Cambridge, Mass.: Harvard University Press.

Goodman, David. 1999. "The New Middle Class." In Merle Goldman and Roderick MacFarquhar, eds., *The Paradox of China's Post-Mao Reforms*. Cambridge, Mass.: Harvard University Press.

Goodman, David, and Beverly Hooper, eds. 1995. *China's Quiet Revolution: New Interactions Between State and Society*. New York: St. Martin's Press.

"Guanyu quanguo gongren jieji duiwu zhuangkuang de diaocha baogao" (Report on the status of the national working class). 1993. In *Gonghui gongzuo tongxun* (internal trade union work report).

Gu, Xin. 1993–94. "A Civil Society and Public Sphere in Post-Mao China? An Overview of Western Publications." *China Information* 8(3) (Winter): 1–14.

Guo, Chengdu. 1995. "Fujian Province FIEs' Labor Disputes: Special Characteristics and Countermeasures"(Fujiansheng sanziqiye laozijiufen de tedian ji duice). *Research and Suggestions.*

Guthrie, Douglas. 1998a. *Dragon in a Three-Piece Suit: The Emergence of Capitalism in China.* Princeton: Princeton University Press.

———. 1998b. "The Declining Significance of *Guanxi* in China's Economic Transformation." *China Quarterly* (June): 254–82.

Haggard, Stephan. 1990. *Pathways from the Periphery: The Politics of Growth in the Newly Industrializing Countries.* Ithaca, N.Y.: Cornell University Press.

He, Baogang. 1997. *The Democratic Implications of Civil Society in China.* New York: St. Martin's Press.

Howell, Jude. 1990. "The Impact of China's Open Policy on Labour." *Labour, Capital, and Society* (Nov.): 288–322.

Huang, Philip. 1993. "Public Sphere / Civil Society in China: Paradigmatic Issues in Chinese Studies, III." *Modern China* 19(2) (Apr.): 216.

International Confederation of Free Trade Unions (ICFTU). 1995. Annual Survey of Violations of Trade Union Rights, 1995.

International Religious Freedom Report 2002: China. Released by the Bureau of Democracy, Human Rights, and Labor, U.S. Department of State.

Johnson, Chalmers. 1982. *MITI and the Japanese Miracle: The Growth of Industrial Policy, 1925–1975.* Stanford: Stanford University Press.

Johnson, Ian. 2003. "The Death and Life of China's Civil Society." *Perspectives* 1(3) (Sept.): 551–54.

Kang, Xiaoguang. 2001. "China's Social Organizations in Transition." In Chinese. www.chinanpo.org/subpages/yanjiu.asp (accessed 11/1/2003).

Kynge, James. 2002. "China's Capitalists Get a Party Invitation." *Financial Times,* Aug. 16, 17.

Lee, Ching Kwan. 1999. "From Organized Dependence to Disorganized Despotism: Changing Labour Regimes in Chinese Factories." *China Quarterly* (157): 44–72.

Li, Ling. 2001. "Towards a More Civil Society: Mingong and Expanding Social Space in Reform-Era China." *Columbia Human Rights Law Review* 33(149) (Fall): 149–88.

Li, Ning. 2001. "Guanyu woguo jijinhui touziwentide tantao" (Inquiry into the investment problems of China's foundations). www.chinanpo.org/subpages/yanjiu.asp (accessed 11/1/2003).

Li, Ping Sun, Jin Jun, and Jiangsui He. 2001. "Socially Reorganizing Social Resource: Study on the Process of Project Hope's Resource Mobilization." In Chinese. www.chinanpo.org/subpages/yanjiu.asp (accessed 11/1/2003).

Lindau, Juan, and Timothy Cheek. 1998. *Market Economics and Political Change: Comparing China and Mexico.* New York: Rowman & Littlefield.

Madsen, Richard. 1993. "The Public Sphere, Civil Society, and Moral Community." *Modern China* 19 (Apr.): 183.

———. 1998. *China's Catholics: Tragedy and Hope in an Emerging Civil Society.* Berkeley: University of California Press.

———. 2000. "Understanding Falun Gong." *Current History* (Sept.): 243–48.

Migdal, Joel, Atul Kohli, and Vivienne Shue, eds. 1994. *State Power and Social Forces: Domination and Transformation in the Third World.* Cambridge: Cambridge University Press.

Naughton, Barry. 2002. "China's Economic Think Tanks: Their Changing Role in the 1990s." *China Quarterly* 171 (Sept.): 625–35. This issue of *China Quarterly* includes several essays on the changing nature of research institutes in China.

Nevitt, Christopher Earle. 1996. "Private Business Associations in China: Evidence of Civil Society or Local State Power." *China Journal* 36 (July): 25–43.

O'Brien, Kevin. 1996. "Rightful Resistance." *World Politics* 49(1): 31–55.

Oi, Jean. 1999. *Rural China Takes Off: Institutional Foundations of Economic Reform*. Berkeley: University of California Press.

O'Leary, Greg, ed. 1997. *Adjusting to Capitalism: Chinese Workers and the State*. Armonk, N.Y.: M. E. Sharpe.

Overmyer, Daniel L. 2003. "Religion in China Today: Introduction," *China Quarterly* 174 (June): 307–16.

Parris, Kristen. 1999. "The Rise of Private Business Interests." In Merle Goldman and Roderick MacFarquhar, eds., *The Paradox of China's Post-Mao Reforms*. Cambridge, Mass.: Harvard University Press.

Pearson, Margaret. 1994. "The Janus Face of Business Associations in China: Socialist Corporatism in Foreign Enterprises." *Australian Journal of Chinese Affairs* 31 (Jan.): 25–53.

———. 1997. *China's New Business Elite: The Political Consequences of Economic Reform*. Berkeley: University of California Press.

People's Republic of China. Research Group of the Ministry of Labor. 1994. "Guanyu woguo xianjieduan laodongguanxi tiaozheng gongzuode baogao" (China's current work on the adjustment of labor relations). *Zhongguo laodong kexue* (China labor science), Mar. 20–23, 15.

Perry, Elizabeth, and Mark Selden, eds. 2000. *Chinese Society: Change, Conflict, and Resistance*. London: Routledge.

Read, Benjamin. 2001. "Democratizing the Neighborhood? New Private Housing and Homeowner Self Organization in Urban China." Paper presented at the annual meeting of the American Political Science Association, San Francisco.

"The Role of Protecting Rights by Union Representatives: Problems and Countermeasures." 1996. *Handling and Research of Labor Disputes* (Nov.): 15–16.

"The Role of the Union Representative in Protecting Rights During Collective Bargaining: Problems and Countermeasures." 1996. *Handling and Research of Labor Disputes* (Nov.).

Rosenbaum, Arthur Lewis. 1992. *State and Society in China: The Consequences of Reform*. Boulder: Westview Press.

Rosenthal, Elizabeth. 2001. "China Eases Rules Binding People to Birth Regions." *New York Times*, Oct. 23, A8.

———. 2002. "China's Top AIDS Activist Missing; Arrest is Suspected." *New York Times*, Aug. 29, A3.

Rowe, William. 1990. "The Public Sphere in Modern China." *Modern China* 16(3) (July): 309–29.

———. 1993. "The Problem of Civil Society in Late Imperial China." *Modern China* 19(2) (Apr.): 139.

Saich, Tony. 2000. "Negotiating the State." *China Quarterly* 161 (Mar.): 124–41.

Saiget, Robert J. 2001. "Chinese Leader under Fire over Capitalists in Communist Party." *Agence France Presse*, Aug. 14.

Schmitter, Philippe. 1974. "Still the Century of Corporatism." In Frederick Pike and Thomas Strich, eds., *The New Corporatism: Social-Political Structures in the Iberian World*. Notre Dame: University of Notre Dame Press.

Schmitter, Philippe, and Gerhard Lehmbruch, eds. 1979. *Trends Toward Corporatist Intermediation.* Beverly Hills, Calif.: Sage.

Shenyang City Union Investigative Office. 1995. "Shenyang Shi xiandaihua qiyezhidu shidianzhong gonghui cunzai de wenti ji duice" (The experimental modern enterprise system in Shenyang: Union problems and countermeasures). *Gonghui lilun yu shi jian* (Union theory and practice), Aug. 1.

Shue, Vivienne. 1994. "State Power and Social Organization in China." In Joel Migdal, Atul Kohli, and Vivienne Shue, eds., *State Power and Social Forces: Domination and Transformation in the Third World.* Cambridge: Cambridge University Press.

———. 2001. "State Legitimation in China: The Challenges of Popular Religion." Paper presented at the annual meeting of the American Political Science Association, San Francisco.

Solinger, Dorothy. 1993a. "Urban Entrepreneurs and the State: The Merger of State and Society." In id., *China's Transition from Socialism, 1980–1990: Statist Legacies and Market Reform.* Armonk, N.Y.: M. E. Sharpe.

———. 1993b. *China's Transition from Socialism, 1980–1990: Statist Legacies and Market Reform.* Armonk, N.Y.: M. E. Sharpe.

———. 1999. *Contesting Citizenship in China: Peasant Migrants, the State, and the Logic of the Market.* Berkeley: University of California Press.

Strand, David. 1990. "Protest in Beijing: Civil Society and Public Sphere in China." *Problems of Communism* (May–June): 1–19.

Thornton, Patricia. 2002. "Framing Dissent in Contemporary China: Irony, Ambiguity and Metonymy." *China Quarterly* 171 (Sept.): 661–81.

To, Lee Lai. 1986. *Trade Unions in China: 1949 to the Present.* Singapore: National University of Singapore Press.

Tong, James. 2002. "An Organizational Analysis of the *Falun Gong*: Structure, Communications, Financing." *China Quarterly.*

Tsai, Lily Lee. 2002. "Cadres, Temple and Lineage Institutions, and Governance in Rural China." *China Journal* 48 (July).

Unger, Jonathan, and Anita Chan. 1995. "China, Corporatism, and the East Asian Model." *Australian Journal of Chinese Affairs* 32 (Jan.): 29–53.

———. 1996. "Corporatism in China." In Barrett L. McCormick and Jonathan Unger, eds., *China after Socialism: In the Footsteps of Eastern Europe or East Asia.* Armonk, N.Y.: M. E. Sharpe.

Wade, Robert. 1990. *Governing the Market: Economic Theory and the Role of Government in East Asian Industrialization.* Princeton: Princeton University Press.

Wakeman, Frederic. 1993. "The Civil Society and Public Sphere Debate: Western Reflections on Chinese Political Culture." *Modern China* 19(2) (Apr.): 108–38.

Walder, Andrew. 1986. *Communist Neo-Traditionalism.* Berkeley: University of California Press.

———. 1991. "Workers, Managers, and the State: The Reform Era and the Political Crisis of 1989." *China Quarterly* (Sept.): 467–92.

———, ed. 1995. *The Waning of the Communist State: Economic Origins of Political Change in China and Hungary.* Berkeley: University of California Press.

Wang, Xu. 1997. "Mutual Empowerment of State and Peasantry: Grassroots Development in Rural China." *World Development* (25): 1431–42.

Wank, David. 1995. "Bureaucratic Patronage and Private Business: Changing Networks of

Power in Urban China." In Andrew Walder, ed., *The Waning of the Communist State: Economic Origins of Political Change in China and Hungary*. Berkeley: University of California Press.

———. 1999. *Commodifying Communism: Business, Trust, and Politics in a Chinese City*. New York: Cambridge University Press.

———. 2002. "Evolving Business-State Clientelism in China: The Institutional Organization of a Smuggling Operation." Paper presented at the annual meeting of the American Political Science Association, Boston.

Wasserstrom, Jeffrey N., and Elizabeth J. Perry. 1994. *Popular Protest and Political Culture in Modern China*. 2d ed. Boulder: Westview Press.

Weller, Robert P. 1999. *Alternate Civilities: Democracy and Culture in China and Taiwan*. Boulder: Westview Press.

———. 2001. "Civil Associations and Autonomy Under Three Regimes: The Boundaries of State and Society in Hong Kong, Taiwan, and China." MS.

———. 2002. "Worship, Teachings, and State Power in China and Taiwan." MS.

White, Gordon. 1988. "State and Market in China's Labour Reforms." *Journal of Development Studies* 24 (July): 180–202.

———. 1995. "Prospects for Civil Society: A Case Study of Xiaoshan City." In David Goodman and Beverly Hooper, eds., *China's Quiet Revolution: New Interactions Between State and Society*. New York: St. Martin's Press.

———. 1996. "Chinese Trade Unions in the Transition from Socialism: Towards Corporatism or Civil Society?" *British Journal of Industrial Relations* 34(3) (Sept.): 433–57.

White, Gordon, Jude Howell, and Xiaoyuan Shang. 1996. *In Search of Civil Society: Market Reform and Social Change in Contemporary China*. New York: Oxford University Press.

Wilson, Jeanne. 1990. "Labour Policy in China: Reform and Retrogression." *Problems of Communism* 39 (Sept.–Oct.): 44–65.

Womack, Brantly. 1991. "Transfigured Community: Neo-Traditionalism and Work-Unit Socialism in China." *China Quarterly* (July): 324–32.

Woo-Cumings, Meredith, ed. 1999. *The Developmental State*. Ithaca, N.Y.: Cornell University Press.

Wright, Teresa. 2002. "The China Democracy Party and the Politics of Protest in the 1980s–1990s." *China Quarterly* 172 (Dec.): 906–26.

Xinhua News Report 2003. "Beijing Eases Urban Residency Restrictions for Rural Workers." Feb. 26. FBIS-CHI-2003-0226, wnc.fedworld.gov (accessed Apr. 30, 2003).

Yang, Tuan. 2001. "Chinese NPOs Viewed from the Study of the Experience of the Hetong Home for the Elderly." www.chinanpo.org/news/findnews/shownews.asp?newsid=3175 (accessed 11/1/2003).

Yasumuro, Kenichi, ed. 1999. *Chugoku no roshikankei to genchi keiei* (China's labor-capital relations and on the ground management). Tokyo: Hakutoshobo.

Yi, Jianguang, and Yu Yong. 2001. "Zhongguo shehui zhuanxing shiqi de zhiyuanfuwu: Shenzhenshi zhiyuanzhe ji qifuwu de yanjiubaogao" (Volunteer service during China's transition: A research report on the volunteers of Shenzhen City and their service). www.chinanpo.org/ (accessed 11/1/2003).

Young, Nick, ed. 2001. *250 Chinese NGOs: Civil Society in the Making*. Special Report from China Development Brief. August.

Yuan, Shen, and Wusan Sun. 2001. "'Institutional Isomorphism' and the Transformation of Chinese Associations: Case Analysis of Chinese Youth Development Foundation and Its Overseas Contact." www.chinanpo.org/subpages/yanjiu.asp (accessed 11/1/2003).

Zhang, Li. 2001. *Strangers in the City: Reconfigurations of Space, Power, and Social Networks Within China's Floating Population*. Stanford: Stanford University Press.
Zhang Minjie. 2003. *Zhongguo ruoshi qunti yanjiu* (China's vulnerable groups studies). Changchun: Changchun Publishing House.
Zhao, Minghua, and Theo Nichols. 1996. "Management Control of Labour in State-Owned Enterprises: Cases from the Textile Industry." *China Journal* 36 (July): 1–21.
Zhao, Suisheng. 1997. "China's Intellectuals' Quest for National Greatness and Nationalistic Writings in the 1990s." *China Quarterly* 152 (Dec.): 725–45.
"Zhongguo siyingqiye guyongjilaodongguanxi baogao" (Report on Chinese private enterprise employment and labor relations). 1995. In *Zhongguo xinshiqi jiejijieceng baogao* (Social class and social stratum in China's new era). Liaoning: Liaoning People's Publishing House.
Zhou, Xueguang. 1993. "Unorganized Interests and Collective Action in Communist China." *American Sociological Review* 58 (Feb.): 54–73.

PART V

Conclusion

CHAPTER FOURTEEN

The Nonstate Public Sphere in Asia

Dynamic Growth, Institutionalization Lag

MUTHIAH ALAGAPPA

From the discussions in the preceding chapters, it is evident, not only that civil society organizations exist in Asia, but that, with their numbers growing exponentially in many countries, they have become a substantial and important force in politics. The nature and strength of these organizations, and their relationship to the state and political society, vary widely across countries and over time. Their roles in political change are also complex and changing, defying neat characterizations. The growing recognition in Asia of civil society as a distinct realm for organization and discourse does not, however, constitute acceptance in all quarters. Segments of the elite in certain countries remain suspicious of organizations and governance that are independent of the state. Through legal, financial, institutional, and coercive measures, these elites seek to curtail the space for the nonstate organizations and repress or co-opt those that exist. The rise of civil society (in conjunction with other factors) has trimmed the overbearing state in several countries, contributing to a restructuring of the relations among state, political society, and civil society. However, this has not significantly diminished the importance of the state in Asia. Assertions to the effect that civil society is replacing the "domineering" state as the center ground of contemporary political thought and practice certainly do not apply to Asia. For a number of reasons, the state still dominates the political thinking of Asian elites, including those in civil society. The paramount concern of civil society leaders has been to bring about change in the state and its policies; lesser attention has been devoted to the institutionalization of civil society or the development of governance that is independent of the state. From an analytical perspective, the civil society lens does yield certain key insights into the politics and political processes of Asian countries. But to use it as the only lens, or even the primary lens, can be misleading. A proper perspective on the political significance of the realm of civil society and the organizations that populate it requires that they be viewed in the context of specific circumstances and issues, as well as of their relations with other realms and actors, both domestic and international.

Drawing on the studies in this volume and other published works, the two concluding chapters address the questions posed in the Introduction with particular focus on the following two sets of questions.

First, what is the nature of civil society in Asia? Is it a realm of nonstate organization, a site of discourse and struggle, a realm of governance independent of the state, or a means to bring about change in the state, its agencies, and policies? What are the nature, composition, and dynamics of the organizations that populate the civil society space? How have these altered over time? What factors account for the development or nondevelopment of civil society? What are challenges confronting the institutionalization of civil societies in Asian countries?

Second, what is the connection between civil society and democracy? What is the contribution of civil society organizations to the development of the nonstate public sphere, and in promoting regime, government, and policy change in the direction of open, participatory, and accountable politics? What is the implication of the rise of civil society groups for the state and for state–civil society relations? What is the relationship of civil society to political society and how has the development of the former affected the development of the latter?

This chapter explores the first set of questions; the second set is explored in the final chapter. On the nature and development of Asian civil societies, the study advances six propositions. First, contrary to the claim in the abstract debates cited in the Introduction that the idea of civil society is alien to Asian cultures, civil society organizations not only exist in Asia but have experienced dramatic growth since the mid-1980s; in some cases, civil societies have relatively long histories. Second, the development of civil society is social-reality-specific; multiple factors have fueled the development of civil societies in Asia. Civil society in many Asian countries has its roots in opposition to colonial and repressive authoritarian rule and, as well, in social reform. Capitalist development, democratic transitions, international support—these too have stimulated the development of civil society. Contrary to the popular view in the democratization literature, civil society organizations have not become weaker or receded in importance in the wake of democratic transitions. In fact, they have become more numerous and even stronger. Third, civil societies in Asian countries are highly diverse in composition, resource endowment, and goals; they are arenas of power, struggle, and cooperation. With competing visions of politics and society, some civil society organizations have contributed to polarization in society; others have facilitated the development of crosscutting linkages and more pluralistic societies. Fourth, the composition and dynamics of civil societies have altered dramatically over time in several countries, and more change is in prospect.

Fifth, contemporary Asian civil societies display features of both the neo-Tocquevillean and neo-Gramscian frames. Which frame dominates and how different features combine are largely a function of the legitimacy of the state and its policies. As the state and its political institutions become more legitimate, the neo-Tocquevillean frame tends to dominate. Thus, as argued in Chapter 1, the framing of civil society is contingent on the social reality and must be inclusive to capture the dynamics and orientations of formal and informal groups operating not only in the legal space but also underground and in foreign countries. Finally, the dramatic growth in the number of civil society organizations has not, however, been accompanied by a comparable institutionalization of the nonstate public sphere. Individual and group rights necessary to construct and protect an autonomous realm are still not in place in several countries, including democratic ones. And even when these are enshrined in formal documents such as a constitution and basic laws, for example, the rules and institutions to enforce them (including an independent and effective legal system) are lacking or frequently violated with impunity. These six propositions are elaborated in the following sections.

Proposition 1: Burgeoning Civil Societies

Contrary to sweeping assertions that the idea of civil society is alien and inapplicable to Asian situations because of political, cultural, and other differences, the studies in this volume attest to the presence and growth of nonstate, nonprofit organizations in nearly every country, although their breadth, depth, and density have varied over time and across countries. Although accurate and comparable data are not always available, the mapping sections in the country chapters highlight the dramatic increase in the number of civil society organizations, especially since the mid-1980s. Japan in the mid-1990s had approximately 400,000 legally sanctioned civil society organizations and another 1.2 million groups without legal status. In India, it is estimated that the number of nonstate, nonprofit organizations exceeds one million. The number of civil society organizations in South Korea increased from about 9,500 in the year 2000 to more than 35,000 in 2003. Taiwan had 18,465 registered civil society organizations in 2001; in 1980, it had only 3,960. The number of registered organizations in the Philippines increased from about 27,000 in 1986 to between 60,000 and 95,000 in 2000. By 1998, a total of 29,754 organizations had registered in Malaysia under the Societies Act. In Sri Lanka, the Presidential Commission of Inquiry on NGOs reported 3,000 organizations in 1990. Pakistan had about 45,000 active, private, nonprofit, self-governing organizations in 2002. In China, there were over 180,000 officially registered social organizations in 1998, of which some 2,000 were national-level associations. It should be noted here that because of the many constraints still confronting them, a substantial number of nonstate organizations, especially in authoritarian and communist states, do not register or are not recognized by governments; others sometimes seek to circumvent regulations by registering as businesses or companies. Except for Japan, moreover, no reliable data are available on the number of civil society organizations without legal status—especially at the provincial and local levels. In all likelihood, the number of organizations is substantially more than that revealed by official statistics. The dramatic growth in the number of civil society groups in Asia has been observed in other studies as well (Salamon and Anheier 1996; Yamamoto 1995; Tsujinaka 2002, 2004).

This increase in the number of organizations has been accompanied by strategic and tactical alliances among civil society groups and with other domestic and international actors. To augment their expertise, resources, power, and influence, civil society organizations increasingly cooperate with other bodies and coordinate their activities as part of national and transnational umbrella organizations. In South Korea, for example, aspiring to lead a new wave of citizen involvement in politics and policy, thirty-nine citizens' groups formed the Korea Council of Citizens' Movements in 1994. This alliance included religious groups, environmental movements, women's groups, the consumer movement, the reunification movement, the movement for education reform, and organizations for the handicapped. Broad-based coalitions comprising political parties and civil society organizations from both the Left and Right were formed in the Philippines to oust authoritarian and corrupt rulers like Ferdinand Marcos and Joseph Estrada and to prevent changes to the constitution such as the elimination of term limits for the office of president. Several issue-specific umbrella organizations, such as the Congress for a People's Agrarian Reform (CPAR) and the National Coordination of Autonomous Local Rural People's Organization (UNORKA) focused on land reform have also been formed in that country. In Thailand, the Confederation for Democracy, comprising a broad range of groups, was formed to protest the military's attempt to regain control of political power in 1992. Environmental NGOs, academics, civic groups, and others joined by villagers affected by government infrastructure projects formed the Assembly of the Poor to stage major protests and rallies with a view to seeking change in policy and compensation for the affected. The primary purpose of most of these umbrella organizations appears to have been to increase their leverage over the state in demanding policy change.

Equally important is the expanding scope of civil society organizations and their active role in demanding, supporting, or preventing political change, in developing agendas for social reform and empowerment, in assisting the state in service delivery, and in formulating and implementing programs of their own. Civil society groups in Asia now function in a broad range of areas, including culture, religion, community development, social welfare, sports and recreation, language and education, medicine and public health, the physically challenged, labor, business, consumer protection, agriculture, the environment, economic development, social reform, minority and human rights, the media, economic justice, politics, foreign affairs, and security matters. As we shall see in Chapter 15, civil society organizations have been in the forefront in pushing for political liberalization, transitions to democracy, and measures to deepen and consolidate open political systems. Social movements have become more active in Asia on many fronts: demanding rights for minorities, women, lower castes, and migrant workers; promoting human rights, including the modification or abolition of repressive security laws; protecting the environment; advocating economic justice; and demanding greater transparency and accountability in government, political parties, and the bureaucracy. But certain civil society organizations have also constricted democratic space, undermined democratic institutions, and supported reversions to authoritarian rule.

Although there are substantial cross-country and temporal variations, it would be fair to say that civil society organizations have become more numerous and vigorous in Asia. Certainly, they have become an important force in the political and policy processes in many Asian countries. Their prominence is reflected in the acknowledgment of Asian political leaders and in their inclusion in calculations of legitimacy, distribution of political power, and formulation of public policy, including development policy, as well as in service delivery. Depending on their orientation and calculations, political leaders have sought to support and mobilize certain civil society organizations while coercing, suppressing, or co-opting others.

Proposition 2: Multiple Forces of Growth

Several factors explain the growth of civil societies in Asian countries: anticolonial mobilization, weakness of states, resistance to repressive rule, government sponsorship of organizations, increase in democratic space, economic growth and development, the information and communication revolutions, change in the international normative structure, and growing international support. The salience of these elements varies by country and over time—emphasizing the point that the development of civil society depends on the social reality.

Although there has been a surge in the number of civil society organizations since the mid-1980s, in many countries, their roots can be traced to the colonial period; in some cases, they predate colonial rule. Political life in the colonies was dominated by the metropolitan authority, but social, cultural, and certain avenues of economic life remained largely outside state control. In these relatively free areas, indigenous groups organized to regulate affairs, provide welfare, educational, religious, cultural, and economic services, and, when possible, make representations on behalf of their groups to the colonial authority. The number of groups increased sharply and their orientations altered substantially as mobilization against colonial rule gained ground and independence became a real option. India, for example, has a rich history of voluntarism. Until the colonial period, education, health, culture, and relief efforts remained largely the domain of the nonstate institutions affiliated with family, caste, trade guilds, and religion. Except in certain select areas—and even then only at certain levels—nonstate organizations continued in the colonial era to perform services and regulate public affairs in the social and cultural arenas. On matters subject to the British colonial rule, members of certain adversely affected sectors like agriculture organized to make representations to the colonial authority. Peasants, for example, "established a number of resistance groups, collected funds for litigation, and sent petitions to the British government of India" (Pandey 1988: 124). As the social reform and independence movements gained momentum, the number of organizations multiplied—many of them taking on a political hue as well.

Mobilization of the population in the struggle against Spanish and American rule in the Philippines, against Dutch colonial rule in Indonesia, and, to a lesser degree, against British rule in Malaysia spawned numerous and diverse organizations at the national, provincial, and local levels. In South Korea, Japanese colonial rule stimulated the development of a fractious and oppositional civil society. The nonstate public space during the struggle for independence was inhabited by both political and civil society groups; the distinction between them was not always clear. In the postindependence period, the development of civil society was connected to the legitimacy and strength (or weakness) of the state. The initial focus on the organization of the new state and political society—plus the high degree of legitimacy enjoyed by nearly all the postindependence governments combined with the expectation that government will provide all ideational, material, and status goods—contributed to a decline in the number and salience of politically oriented civil society groups. They did not disappear, however. Civil society organizations, especially those advocating social reform, survived. In countries like Indonesia and the Philippines, where the central governments were weak and had limited reach, civil society organizations actually flourished. In these countries these organizations not only grew in number but began to take on basic functions that would normally be the responsibility of the government.

Disaffection with government was a key factor in the growth of nonstate organizations in the postindependence period. In India, for example, institutional decay, the government's inability to deliver basic goods and services, and the accompanying crisis of governance contributed to a reinvigoration of civil society in the 1960s and 1970s. In Sri Lanka, civil society organizations based on language, ethnicity, and religion became stronger as they mobilized to influence the structure and politics of the state in a particular direction. Disenchantment with and the vulnerability of the incumbent UMNO-led Barisan Nasional government in the 1990s was a key consideration in the invigoration of oppositional civil society in Malaysia under the banner of Reformasi. Declining confidence in the scandal-ridden world of politics, especially in the much acclaimed bureaucracy, combined with prolonged economic stagnation and the state's unresponsiveness to the needs of the public (dramatically highlighted by the slow government response to the Great Hanshin earthquake) underlie the growing prominence of the nonprofit sector in Japan (Schwartz 2003: 14–15).

Repressive governments have both curtailed and stimulated the development of civil society. Leninist and totalitarian governments as well as absolutist ones allow virtually no legal space for organizations that are not in some way controlled by the party, dictator, or authoritarian ruler. While successful in denying legal space, such governments have also stimulated the development of informal and underground organizations within the country and formal organizations in the diaspora communities in foreign lands. This is most evident in Burma (see Chapter 12). Because certain legally sanctioned organizations were appropriated by the students in the prelude to the 1988 protests, the military junta that controls Burma allows virtually no legal space for independent organizations that it suspects may challenge its authority. This policy has severely limited the number of formally registered organizations and their functions. But it has also stimulated the rise of numerous informal organizations within Burma and the development of vocal Burmese groups in neighboring Thailand and in the United States, Canada, and the European Union countries. Control and repression in the contemporary PRC have resulted in a large number of unofficial organizations. Repression by successive authoritarian governments in South Korea stimulated the development of an oppositional civil society. In India, oppressive government during the 1975–77 emergency period stimulated the development of rights-oriented civil society organizations.

The development of Asian civil societies has also been encouraged by government sponsorship of certain groups with a view to countering independent organizations and assisting the state in governance (especially in local development, service delivery, and relief work). Such organizations have been pejoratively labeled GONGOs (government-organized NGOs). Many analysts would not regard GONGOs as "genuine" civil society organizations, because of their ties to government, but they do occupy nonstate public space and influence policy. In China, for example, most officially registered organizations are connected to government through legal and administrative guidelines, restricted financial autonomy, and the practice of "double-posting" (see Chapter 13). In addition to influencing policy and assisting in service delivery, in time these GONGOs can become more autonomous organizations taking on new issues and even contributing to political change. In 1989, some state-sponsored organizations were "captured" by students protesting in Tiananmen Square; such captures contributed to the spread of protests to other cities. In Burma, government-sanctioned organizations operating in legal space (bar associations, monasteries, community and alumni associations, medical associations) were appropriated by politically conscious activists in the prelude to the 1988 mass protest and its aftermath (see Chapter 12). In Taiwan, local groups established under the community renaissance program initiated by the Ministry of Culture under the direction of President Lee Teng-Hui gained social momentum of their own and began to take on new issues, such as the environment, with the purpose of shaping government policy (see Chapter 5). Members of such groups also became involved in local politics.

Civil societies in Asia experienced dramatic growth with the onset of political liberalization and democratic opening and, more generally, with the expansion of democratic space. Contrary to assertions in the democratization literature, civil societies in Asia have flourished in the wake of democratic transitions, although their salience and orientation sometimes changed substantially. As observed earlier, the number and scope of civil society organizations increased dramatically in the wake of democratic transitions in the Philippines, South Korea, Taiwan, and Thailand. With political opening, groups that had once operated informally and underground surfaced and organized themselves in a formal manner. Concurrently, new groups seeking to correct past abuses, broaden and deepen democratic opening, or advocate new policy agendas proliferated. Groups also began to function in hitherto forbidden areas: security, civil-military relations, corruption, and the judicial system. With decentralization of government, political opening led to the formation of provincial and local-level civil society groups as well. Political opening also facilitated the development of large umbrella organizations at the national level and the forging of ties with international bodies.

Economic growth and its socioeconomic and political consequences have been a major stimulant for the development of new civil society organizations. Sustained economic growth in South Korea, Taiwan, Thailand, and Indonesia, based on the export-led model, made for more complex and diversified economies that were heavily dependent on foreign investment and markets. This created more complex societies—empowering certain segments of the population and disempowering others. In time it also brought a host of new issues and concerns to the fore (the environment, labor rights, political participation, and more). Seeking to consolidate their power and influence, newly empowered groups (businesspeople, professionals, students, industrial workers) organized themselves politically and in the sphere of civil society. Deeply dissatisfied groups that bore the brunt of the cost of rapid growth (small farmers, peasants, blue-collar workers) also organized themselves (sometimes informally), often under the leadership of urban-based personalities and groups. New social movements emerged to protect the environment, promote economic justice, review government-business relations, and reform corporate governance, especially in the conglomerates. These movements proliferated and became more consequential when the opportunity structure opened up because of legitimacy concerns of the ruling elite, competition among ruling factions, resistance from below, or international pressure. In a few countries like

Singapore and Malaysia, sustained economic growth has not had these effects. But even in tightly controlled Singapore, legitimacy and innovation concerns led the government of Goh Chok Tong to encourage the development of "civic society." In Malaysia, economic slowdown in the wake of the 1997 financial crisis made the government vulnerable and empowered oppositional political and civil society groups.

From the late 1980s on, changing international conditions spurred the development of civil societies in Asia. The highly visible role of civil society organizations in the rapid collapse of the Soviet-dominated communist states in central and eastern Europe had a significant demonstration effect in Asia—as, for example, in China in 1989. Even more significant was the demonstration effect of the Philippines' People Power revolution in 1986 on civil society organizations in South Korea and Taiwan. Later the imputed role of civil society groups in the collapse of the Suharto regime in Indonesia had a contagious impact on the Reformasi movement in Malaysia. At the global structural level, with the termination of the Cold War and the emergence of the United States as the only global power, the promotion of free-market systems, democracy, and human rights worldwide became key goals of the Bush Sr. and Clinton administrations. The remaining communist and authoritarian governments in Asia—the PRC after the Tiananmen tragedy, Burma after 1988, Pakistan during 1999–2001, and Vietnam—confronted sanctions and pressure from the Western countries. A key element in the West's democracy enlargement and human rights strategies was the promotion of civil society. Concurrently—and in several ways connected to this changing international context—the world saw the proliferation of transnational social movements in the areas of the environment, human rights, humanitarian concerns, economic justice, violence against women, and peace and justice.

Changing international conditions combined with the global information and communications revolutions (discussed next) not only provided Asian civil society organizations with moral support but helped increase their expertise and resource base. The net effect was to empower civil society and put nondemocratic states on the defensive. International support was not always forthcoming, however. Burmese civil society groups, for example, felt badly let down by the West in their struggle against the military junta. Although the Western countries imposed economic sanctions, they had little leverage over Burma. Nor were they willing to invest a huge amount of political capital or take military action. Burma was not a vital interest. Sometimes international support has been a mixed blessing. Often it prevents the development of an indigenous support base and raises credibility problems, subjecting civil society groups to criticism by nationalist forces and other indigenous organizations. Furthermore, strategic and economic considerations still influence the foreign policies of Western states, especially in relation to major countries like China. Such considerations have become more pronounced under the

Bush Jr. administration, which accords the highest priority to the "global" war against international terrorism. For now, democracy, human rights, and the rest appear to have taken a back seat.

The development of civil society, especially in countries under authoritarian rule and with closed political systems, has been facilitated by the information and communications revolutions. The opportunity to organize in cyberspace and communicate through the Internet has helped dissident civil society organizations to circumvent government control and regulations. Despite their best efforts, governments are finding it difficult to regulate activities in cyberspace. The imperative to participate in the global economy and to benefit from the "positive" aspects of the globalization process makes this task even harder. In Singapore, for example, citizens are increasingly turning to the Internet for alternative sources of news and information. Criticism of government policy and making fun of the Singapore political system on the Internet have also become frequent (see Chapter 10). As illustrated by the examples of Think Center and SINTERCOM, there is an ongoing struggle in that country between the efforts of certain civil society groups to broaden political discussion through cyberspace and the desire of the government to control such groups and restrict political space. Dissident Burmese groups in exile such as the Free Burma Coalition (FBC) have effectively used the Internet to organize an alliance of student organizations in North America and to network with human rights and student organizations in twenty-eight Asian and European countries with very limited resources (see Chapter 12). Through these networks, the FBC has been successful in exerting pressure on multinational corporations from doing business with the military government. From the above discussion, it is evident, not only that multiple forces have influenced the development of civil societies in Asian countries, but that the weight of specific factors has been greater in certain countries and in specific times. Furthermore, the space for civil society is not confined to the formal arenas controlled by the state. Extralegal, transnational, international, and cyberspace have all been used to organize civil society organizations and their activities. These findings support the assertions in Chapter 1 that the framing of civil society is contingent and should be social-reality-specific, and that its conceptualization must transcend official national space.

Proposition 3: An Arena of Power, Struggle, and Cooperation

Civil societies in Asia are highly diverse in composition, resource endowment, and goals. In the colonial and immediate postindependence periods, civil societies were confined largely to the social, cultural, and, at times, economic (commerce, trade, agriculture) spheres. In time, however, several developments—the growing salience of manufacturing, finance, and knowledge-based industries in Asian economies; dramatic expansion in tertiary education; increasing political awareness and public participation in politics, combined with political liberalization and democratic transitions; the emergence or reemergence of religion and ethnicity as political forces; new social concerns; and dramatic increases in regional and international engagements—broadened the range of actors, contributing to highly diverse civil societies. Today, civil society organizations exist in almost every facet of life, employment, and government, and their political orientations span a broad spectrum. There are wide variations, too, in their size and capacity. Some like the Nahdlatul Ulama and Muhammadiyah in Indonesia claim memberships in the millions; others have very small or no real constituencies. Their financial resources, organizational capacity, expertise, autonomy, and functions vary widely as well.

The inequality arising from these wide disparities, combined with the totalizing goals of some organizations, make struggle a central feature of Asian civil societies. Certain organizations view civil society as a terrain for waging their battles against other segments of society and against the state. This was especially the case in the early postindependence period, when lack of agreement over national identity and the sociopolitical order was widespread. Civil society organizations often had communal, religious, or ideological foundations—and the goals of certain key organizations were highly incompatible, with no room for compromise. The intense zero-sum struggle among them deeply polarized civil societies. Indonesian civil society in the 1950s and early 1960s, for example, was fused with political society and dominated by four *aliran*s, or streams: two Islamic *aliran*s (Nahdlatul Ulama and Masjumi) that sought to establish a theocratic Islamic state or at least make sharia'ah law binding on all Muslims; the other two *aliran*s (nationalist and communist), drawing their allegiance from nominal Muslims, lower classes, and religious minorities, opposed this goal, with the communist *aliran* seeking eventually to create a communist state. Creating intense zero-sum struggles among the *aliran*s, the totalizing goals deeply polarized Indonesian civil society (see Chapter 2).

A similar zero-sum struggle continues to characterize the Sri Lankan civil society (see Chapter 9). The majority Buddhist Sinhala community associations and the two major Sinhala political parties advocate a unitary Buddhist state, with Sinhala as the only official language. Little or no protection is afforded to the minority Tamil community. In fact, it has been discriminated against and persecuted. In the 1980s, the Tamil community was subject to pogroms with the connivance of the state. The totalizing goal of the majority community and the like response of the minority community have produced an intense political and subsequently military struggle that has made for deep cleavages. The struggles in Indonesia of the 1950s and 1960s and Sri Lanka (still ongoing at the time of writing) were largely the consequence of a lack of agreement over the fundamental features of the state: the configuration and identity of the new nation-state and the nature of the sociopolitical order. Thus they transcended civil society to affect political society and the state. In Sri Lanka, the state has become an instrument of the majority community in the oppression of the minority community.

South Korean and Philippine civil societies suffered deep divisions as well. These divisions, however, were based not on ethnic or religious differences but on different ideological leanings—the radical, reform-oriented Left and the conservative Right, which supported the status quo. Left-leaning organizations formed the dominant civil society stream in South Korea at the time of its liberation from Japanese imperial rule (see Chapter 4). Peasants and workers who had successfully organized at the national level waged a class struggle for their rights and were also in the forefront in the nationalist independence movement against Japanese colonialism. Seeking to capitalize on these organizations, the Korean Communist Party helped establish several national federations and councils. In response, rightist elements in society organized their own groups, aided by the U.S. military government, which encouraged rightist and pro-Japanese segments to form social organizations, while banning "communist" organizations, parties, and newspapers. Rightist groups quickly rallied around the American anticommunism stance. At the inauguration of the Republic of South Korea in 1948, the tension and conflict between Left and Right translated into a confrontation between civil society (dominated largely by the Left) and the state (constituted largely by right-wing leaders who had served the imperial Japanese government in Korea and now were backed by the Americans). Adopting a confrontational attitude toward the state, the highly organized, militant civil society organizations emerged as the main bastion in the protracted struggle for democracy in that country.

In the Philippines too, civil society was divided, but along class lines. The elite-dominated Right has all along supported the status quo, which favors the landed, business, and professional strata of society. The Left for its part seeks to empower the poor and marginalized segments of society (see Chapter 3). The struggle between these two classes can be traced to the nationalist struggle against Spanish colonial rule. The Philippine elite have commanded the state and political society for much of the past fifty years. They also organized to dominate civil society. The Left continues to be grounded largely in civil society, with certain segments going underground to support violent struggles against the state—the Huk rebellion from 1946 to 1954 and the armed struggle waged by the New People's Army (the armed wing of the Communist Party of the Philippines) since 1969. Although civil society organizations from both classes cooperated to overthrow the authoritarian rule of Marcos, their collaboration was temporary and marked by deep distrust. The attempt to bring the Left into the Corazon Aquino administration failed. Philippine civil society continues to be divided along class lines, with each class articulating a different vision for the Philippine state and society. This situation was reflected most recently in their divergent responses to the administration of Estrada and his ouster. The class divide is likely to be an important factor in the 2004 presidential election.

Splits and struggles of varying intensities characterized civil societies in several other countries too, including Japan in the early postwar period, Thailand during the 1973–76 period, Pakistan beginning with the seizure of power by General Zia-ul-Haq in 1977, Taiwan under KMT party rule, Singapore before the PAP monopolized the political scene, Malaysia in the prelude to the 1969 racial riots and their aftermath, and, more recently, in India with the rise of Hindu nationalist forces. Splits and struggles have also been a feature of civil societies operating underground or in exile, like the Burmese ones. In countries like Japan, India, Malaysia, and Singapore, where avenues for political participation have been available, these struggles have not become violent. In Taiwan, Thailand, and the Philippines too, as they democratized, the struggles in civil society found expression in the political process. The key point is this: contentions over national belonging, identity, the sociopolitical order, and protection and expansion of rights and interests have made struggle a central feature of many Asian civil societies. As the state and the sociopolitical order become more acceptable, the dynamics of civil society are altered. Zero-sum struggles give way to competition, cooperation, and compromise. This has not been a one-way street, however. Reversals have occurred as well. In light of the broad and diverse nature of organizations and their competing and at times highly incompatible goals, Asian civil societies continue to be an arena of power, struggle, and cooperation. It makes little sense to treat civil societies in Asian countries as a single coherent entity. Civil societies are neither homogeneous nor static.

Proposition 4: Dynamic Civil Societies

The composition, dynamics, and orientation of civil societies have altered over the years, most dramatically in South Korea, Taiwan, and Indonesia. Although the divisions in civil society have not disappeared, they now find expression as competing visions of democracy in a political process that has become more legitimate. While segments of civil society still adopt a confrontational orientation toward the state, this confrontation is now centered on reform and rights (political reform, economic restructuring, media reform, labor rights) and is not intended to challenge the legitimacy of the state or the political order. Transition to democracy has altered the power and salience of groups—empowering issue-based groups that seek to improve socioeconomic equity and strengthen democracy by increasing transparency and accountability.

Losing ground, the traditional militant organizations in South Korea, for example, have begun to alter their goals and methods. Concurrently, Korean civil society is being infused with new dynamics arising from the generational divide, tension between nationalism and globalization, and concerns with new social issues. A similar transformation—from an oppositional civil society seeking system change to one that is less partisan and self-limiting with attention now focused on empowering citizens, demanding accountability in political society and the state, and advocating policy alternatives—has also occurred in Taiwan. Indonesian civil society has undergone dramatic change as well. The realm of civil society is no longer a terrain for bitter struggle among sociopolitical *alirans* with totalizing goals. Self-limiting organizations that now accept the state and sociopolitical order dominate civil society. In the Suharto era, the state became the primary focus of civil society organizations in their effort to change policy and redress grievances. Indonesia has witnessed numerous ethnic and religious conflicts in the wake of Suharto's ouster. These are largely local conflicts, however. Except in Aceh and Papua, they do not challenge the legitimacy of the state. The evolution of Indonesia's civil society can be traced to the policies of the Suharto government, including its ban on *aliran* politics, destruction of the Communist Party, and changes in the economic structure—all of which shifted the focal point of conflict away from local class clashes to contests between local groups and the faraway state—and the changing international context. These changes altered the dynamics and discourses in Indonesian civil society. There appears to have been no decisive break in civil society dynamics in Sri Lanka, the Philippines, and Burma. Communally polarized organizations continue to engage in a deep struggle over state identity and the sociopolitical order in Sri Lanka; class divisions and different visions of the state and the democratic order continue to inform the organization and struggles in the civil society realm in the Philippines; and circumventing the state and struggling against it characterize the state-civil society interaction in Burma. Features of the neo-Gramscian frame of civil society continue to be pronounced in these countries.

Proposition 5: Features of neo-Tocquevillean and neo-Gramscian Frames

Civil societies in the countries investigated in this study display features of both the neo-Gramscian and neo-Tocquevillean frames outlined in Chapter 1. Which frame dominates and how the different features combine appear to depend on the legitimacy of the state and the sociopolitical order. If the state and the accompanying sociopolitical order have a high degree of legitimacy and the state has a high capacity for governance, then the neo-Tocquevillean frame is dominant. If there is widespread lack of agreement or certain minority groups vehemently oppose the configuration and identity of the state and its political system, then civil society organizations (along with those in political society) are deeply divided, espousing totalizing goals that make for bitter contests. In these situations, civil society becomes the terrain for struggle and dominance. The neo-Gramscian frame dominates in these countries. The features and strengths of civil society hinge on the progress made in construction of legitimate national states, political institutions, and processes. As these are long-drawn-out processes and the countries in Asia are relatively new as modern nations and states, the composition, dominant features, and dynamics of civil societies are likely to continue to change. Civil society organizations are not, however, passive; they are active players in the state- and nation-building (or destruction) processes and in the construction of the system of governance.

The neo-Gramscian frame was dominant in South Korea, Taiwan, and Indonesia in the predemocratic era, especially in the lead-up to their democratic transitions. Features of this frame continue to dominate civil societies in Sri Lanka, the Philippines, and Burma. Opposing (or seeking to entrench) the domination of the state and political society by the upper classes, a certain ethnic community, or the military, some segments in these countries view the realm of civil society as the crucial battleground for waging their counterhegemonic struggles against other segments of society or the state. Civil society is the only available space in which oppressed segments can organize (formally, informally, or in the underground), inculcate values, construct counternarratives, and develop assets to recover their dignity and ensure their cultural, political, and economic survival. For those seeking to entrench their domination, civil society is the last remaining space to be won. Without a willingness to accommodate conflicting goals and forge a unifying worldview, the struggles intensify—leading frequently to the use of violence both to oppress and to resist. In these totalizing situations, struggles become bitter, and civil and political societies tend to fuse.

In many other countries—Japan, India, South Korea, Taiwan, Thailand, Indonesia, and, to a much lesser degree, Malaysia and Singapore—contemporary civil societies display features of the neo-Tocquevillean frame, although certain features of the neo-Gramscian frame are evident as well. In these countries, there is general but not complete agreement on national identity and the system of political order. Hindu nationalist groups in India, for example, challenge the secular identity of that country. The Acehnese, Papuans, and certain small Islamic groups challenge the configuration and identity of the Indonesian state. Some of these groups resort to violence to achieve their political ends. Such violence, however, is sporadic except in the case of minority groups that seek secession. By and large, civil society organizations do not fundamentally challenge the state or the political order. They are self-limiting and channel their demands through the political process. Their attention is focused on the state and political society—making demands for concessions, benefits, and policy change to advance their group's interests, broaden democratic space, and increase the accountability of government and political parties. Intermediation between society and state is a key if not primary function. Nonstate organizations in several countries—among them, India,

Thailand, the Philippines, and Malaysia—are also engaged in cultivating counternarratives, values, and assets in civil society, however, in order to deepen and broaden democracy and advocate alternative visions of social justice and development.

Proposition 6: Lag in Institutionalization

Although civil society organizations have become more numerous and consequential in politics, and the long-term trend is toward the development of the features of the neo-Tocquevillean frame, the institutionalization of the realm of civil society as a legally protected space for autonomous organization and site for critical reflection, discourse, and governance that is independent of the state has made comparatively less headway in Asian countries.[1] As observed in Chapter 1, institutionalization of civil society involves a guarantee of fundamental rights, which in turn calls for a constitution, separation of powers, and an independent judiciary; an independent and accessible media; devolution of power and resources to local levels and nonstate institutions; acceptance of nonstate institutions as legitimate; and financially secure organizations. When these conditions obtain, civil society becomes a legally protected sphere distinct from the state and political society.

Institutionalization of civil society as a legally protected realm has made significant progress in a number of Asian countries, but it confronts several challenges as well. The legal framework is broadly supportive of civil society in India and the Philippines, but the inability of the state to guarantee the rights to all citizens and the struggles in society limit institutionalization in these two countries. The legal framework is still constrained by the remnants of certain authoritarian-era laws in Taiwan, South Korea, Thailand, and Indonesia. Relatively effective states and enabling socioeconomic circumstances have contributed to a higher degree of guarantee of basic constitutional-legal rights to most citizens and civil society groups in Taiwan and South Korea, facilitating greater institutionalization of civil society in these two countries than, for example, in Indonesia.

The respective constitutions and basic laws of India and the Philippines clearly specify a broad and permissive space for legally sanctioned civil societies in a democratic setting. Articles 13 to 32 of the Indian constitution provide the framework for civil society as an integral part of democracy in that country. The rights to freedom of speech, expression, movement, residence, peaceful assembly, and to form associations or unions are enshrined in Article 19. Although violated, especially during the period of national emergency, many of the fundamental rights are now universally accepted and form the legal backbone for civil society organizations in that country. The press is free, and NGOs are recognized as legitimate actors. Despite the permissive constitutional and legal framework, and enabling conditions such as a free press and devolution of power to local government, institutionalization of the civil society sphere in India faces a number of challenges. Proliferating security laws have infringed significantly in some cases on individual rights and civil liberties. Even more significant, the rights provided in the constitution have not been available to a majority of Indian citizens; a cumbersome state with limited resources and a hugely backlogged and inaccessible legal system have not been able to guarantee the rights and rules to develop and safeguard an autonomous nonstate public sphere, especially at the regional and local levels. Even more fundamental are the political challenges to the development and institutionalization of civil society as a distinct and autonomous sphere. The rise of caste and religious politics and the intimate connection between civil society, political society, and the state blurs the distinction among them, fusing the three realms. The growth of organizations with totalizing goals and the ensuing intense struggles in civil society are also eroding the neo-Tocquevillean features of India's civil society.

A similar situation prevails in the Philippines. The civil society legal framework is rooted in the 1987 constitution. Formulated in the wake of the massive public–civil society uprising and a military mutiny that resulted in the ouster of Ferdinand Marcos, that constitution seeks to prevent future authoritarian rule, emphasize social issues and human rights concerns, and facilitate the development of autonomous civil society. The Declaration of Principles and State Policies (Article II), the Bill of Rights (Article III), Role and Organization of Local Government (Article X), and Social Justice and Human Rights (Article XIII) are among the important provisions in the constitution affecting the legal framework for civil society. As in India, the constitutional provisions are broad and supportive. However due to political and socioeconomic reasons and the limited reach of the central government and its institutional deficiencies, these rights have not been available to the vast majority of Filipinos. As observed by Jennifer Franco in Chapter 3, there are still a large number of subnational spaces where less than democratic conditions severely limit the legal framework for civil society. The constitutionally defined rights have also been frequently compromised to suit the political needs of particular governments. And certain legislations, like the Public Assembly Act, the Labor Code, and the Cooperative Code of the Philippines, contain provisions pertaining to civil society that can be abused. Nevertheless, the legal frameworks in the Philippines and in India are generally supportive of civil society; civil society organizations can and do rely on the framework to organize and pursue their rights and goals. They suffer many fewer legal inhibitions than do the civil societies in South Korea, Taiwan, Indonesia, Malaysia, Sri Lanka, Singapore, Pakistan, Burma, and China. Their primary challenges arise from the weaknesses of the state in enforcing fundamental rights and the many struggles in society.

Regime change in South Korea and the demands of civil society organization in that country have resulted in the enactment of rights, rules, and procedures that facilitate the development of a distinct and autonomous civil society sphere.

Among other things, civil liberties have significantly expanded, including the right of free expression and assembly, and restrictions on the political activities of civil society organizations have eased. The 1987 revision of the constitution eliminated the power of the president to declare an emergency and dissolve the National Assembly, which was frequently resorted to in the authoritarian period. The Basic Press Law enacted after the 1980 coup to censor the media has been abandoned, and laws that severely restricted labor rights have been overhauled. In 1999, the government recognized the previously suppressed Korean Confederation of Trade Unions. In 2000, the Non-Profit Civil Society Organizations Act was enacted to guarantee voluntary activities and to facilitate the development of civil society. Nonstate organizations are now accepted as legitimate actors. Concurrently, political prisoners and prisoners of conscience were freed, civilian control over the military increased, and domestic surveillance by intelligence agencies of dissident political and civil societies has terminated. These constitutional, legal, institutional, and political measures, and the effectiveness of the state in enforcing them, have significantly expanded the space, autonomy, and protection for nonstate organizations.

Such measures still have a tentative character, however; vigilance on the part of robust civil society organizations in South Korea continues to be essential to safeguard and further expand the protected legal framework. Several legal constraints remain in place. Although revision of the Law on Assembly and Demonstration, which was extensively used by authoritarian rulers to suppress antigovernment protests, has increased the space for political assembly and demonstration, there is an effort to strengthen the law to curb civil society protests against government policy failures. Similarly, although Election Law Number 87, which prohibits political participation by civil society organizations, was revised in April 1998, it still forbids them to engage in an array of political activities, including participation in election campaigns. Civil society organizations have been vigorously campaigning for the elimination of this legal restriction. More significantly, the National Security Law passed in the 1950s remains in place and contains a broad and vague definition of sedition that can still be deployed by power holders to suppress virtually any kind of political opposition (see Chapter 4).

In Taiwan too, significant steps have been taken to make civil society more autonomous, but the legal framework has not kept pace with the evolution of civil society in that country and remains constraining. In many instances, practice is several steps ahead of the legal framework. Under martial law, KMT decrees effectively curbed the right of assembly and association provision in the ROC constitution. Articles 11, 13, and 15 of the 1942 National Emergency Law on Civic Organizations granted the government the right to reject applications to form associations and gave it the power to dissolve organizations. Since the lifting of martial law in 1987, the law on civic organizations has been revised several times. In the post-1987 period, restrictions on the right to free speech, assembly, and political demonstration have been eased. In 1998, the Council of Grand Justice ruled that provisions of the Demonstration and Assembly Law that prohibited demonstrations promoting communism and Taiwan's separation from the mainland were unconstitutional. And in 1999, previous restrictions on the registration of groups that included "Taiwan" in their names were removed. In all these cases, legal amendments followed practice. The revised 1989 law that regulates civil society organizations, for example, still sets unduly high standards for membership and a rigorous application procedure that hampers registration of independent associations. Several government organizations and civil society groups are now working on a draft "Non-Profit Organization Law" to provide a new legal framework to facilitate an autonomous and accountable civil society in Taiwan.

Limited but significant steps have been taken in Indonesia to provide a more secure legal framework for civil society. Constitutional amendments have strengthened the right to associate, assemble, and express political opinion. Rules pertaining to certain sectors have been liberalized. It is much easier, for example, to establish labor unions, leading to the proliferation of hundreds of such organizations. The press is one of the freest in Asia; legislation has been passed to devolve power and resources to the district level; and NGOs are acknowledged as legitimate actors in most sectors. There has been a general attempt to strengthen the rule of law (including judiciary reform and the establishment of a constitutional court), which is crucial for the institutionalization of civil society. The major challenge in Indonesia (even more than in the Philippines) is to realize and be able to practice the rights and protection afforded in the constitution and laws. Political expediency and corruption, an inadequate and corrupt legal system, a corrupt police force, the use of extralegal militias and criminal gangs to break up unions and peasant organizations and intimidate journalists and publishers who expose corruption, and a resurgent military, among other things, imply that a secure legal framework is far from being a reality. NGOs, including human rights organizations that are active in areas affected by separatism and communal violence, are still subject to arbitrary and repressive state action. The commitment of the Indonesian government to a secure legal framework for civil society falls far short of the commitment of the governments of Taiwan and South Korea. The Indonesian state's ability to guarantee rights is limited even when it is positively disposed—and it is sometimes actually negative.

In the semi-democratic, military-authoritarian, and communist regimes investigated in this study, constitutional provisions and certain basic laws severely limit individual and group rights, as well as the nature and activities of organizations that populate civil society. In Singapore, the constitution guarantees basic freedoms: Article 14 guarantees freedom of speech, assembly, and association; and Article 15 guarantees freedom of religion, subject to regulations governing public order, public health, and morality. However, Article 9 states that such freedoms may be limited by law in the interest of security, friendly relations with other countries, public order, and so forth. Legislation thus can and has abridged civil rights. An array of laws, including the Societies Act, the Internal Security Act, the Newspaper and Printing Presses Act, and the penal code, limit the space for civil society. Furthermore, regulating agencies such as the Singapore Broadcasting Authority and the Public Entertainment and Licensing Units, and government links to key organizations, such as the National Trade Union Congress and CASE, permit close monitoring and oversight of legally sanctioned organizations. The Societies Act, first promulgated in 1889 to control or suppress the activities of secret societies, and subsequently revised in 1966, gives the Registrar of Societies high discretionary powers. Most recently, a new law to protect cyberspace from exploitation by "terrorist cells" has raised concerns in civil society groups. The press in Singapore is controlled, and power is vested in the executive and the bureaucracy. Nonstate actors are permitted in nonsensitive areas, but they are dealt with harshly if they engage in political activities or challenge core government policies. Except on the margins, it is difficult to speak of a legally protected autonomous civil society sphere in Singapore (see Chapter 10). There is relatively greater legal room for civil society in Malaysia, but even there, there are constitutional limits on basic rights such as free speech, the right to political assembly, and the right to form associations. As in Singapore, there is an array of legislation that can be selectively enforced when the government sees fit. In 1987, over a hundred activists and political leaders were charged with inciting racial animosity or showing Marxist tendencies; more recently the Internal Security Act has been used against suspected militant Islamists, many with connections to "opposition" NGOs (see Chapter 8). The major presses and broadcasting stations are all under some form of government or government-related control; and the independence of the judiciary has been severely compromised. In Malaysia and to a greater degree in Singapore, civil society organizations function at the pleasure of the government; the legal protection afforded to them is limited.

The legal framework for civil society is even more constrained in Pakistan. Six different laws, many dating back to the colonial period, govern the registration of societies: the Societies Registration Act (1860), the Trusts Act (1882), the Charitable Endowments Act (1890), the Cooperative Act (1925), the Voluntary Social Welfare Agencies Ordinance (1961), and Companies Act (1984). As Aqil Shah observes in Chapter 11, rather than facilitate the development of civil society, these laws make for an ambiguous framework that is made worse by the high discretion accorded government officials and their arbitrary application of laws. Recent attempts to streamline the legislative environment through a military-sponsored draft bill—the Non Profit Public Benefit Organization (Governance and Support) Act 2002—would extend government control over the finance and internal governance of nonstate organizations. The Non-Profit Organizations Commission that would be set up under the act would be empowered to initiate audits and liquidate noncomplying organizations. Obsolete and intrusive laws also inhibit trade union organization and activities. The print media have been a target of successive military governments; the judiciary has been emasculated and subordinated; and military governments have undertaken a systematic attempt to coerce and co-opt all possible arenas of contestation to military rule. Independent civil society in Pakistan has been allowed very limited legal space (in development, service delivery) and has little or no legal protection.

For all intents and purposes, a legally protected autonomous civil society realm does not exist in Burma and the People's Republic of China (PRC). Since assuming control in 1962, the Burmese military has sought to eliminate political organizations and politically inclined associations, and it closely monitors and harasses the few organizations that are sanctioned. The 1964 National Solidarity Act forbade the formation of political associations without government permission. Only the Burma Socialist Program Party and its affiliates were permitted under this law. And the government created several organizations to capture and control key sectors, including workers, peasants, youth, veterans, literary workers, and those engaged in the performing arts. Similarly, after the 1988 uprising, the government arrested hundreds of NGO members; enacted the 1990 Sangha Organization Act to outlaw politically oriented Sangha organizations; and created several new organizations and penetrated existing ones to mobilize support for itself and to monitor the activities of dissidents. In essence, there is no formal nonstate public sphere in Burma.

In the PRC, a realm exists between state and society; and with the withdrawal of the state from certain sectors, that realm is growing. However, the organizations occupying it are not autonomous. They are bound to the state by four mechanisms: legal and administrative regulations that issue the crucial legal standing for organizations, delineate their scope, and determine their proper relationship to the state and to the party; restriction of financial autonomy through government subsidy and limiting nonstate sources of revenue; the practice of "double-posting" government or party cadres to leadership positions in social organizations; and the required commitment to party ideology that subordinates the role of social organizations and their ability to speak on behalf of members (see Chapter 13). Constitutional and legal constraints, monopolization of power by the CCP, government control of the media, and a weak legal system: all these prevent the development of a legally protected autonomous civil society in China.

From the above discussion, it is evident that only democratic states acknowledge the ideal of an autonomous, legally protected civil society sphere. The legal framework is virtually nonexistent in communist and military authoritarian states and purposely limited in illiberal, semidemocratic ones. The type of regime and state capacity to guarantee fundamental rights are the crucial variables in explaining the delayed institutionalization of civil society in Asia. Although democratic Asian states recognize the legitimacy of an independent civil society sphere, even in these countries there are several constraints on its institutionalization. For example, in Japan, the leading industrialized democracy in Asia, administrative, legal, and financial provisions, and the practice of *amakudari,* constrain the development of an autonomous civil society. In democratizing countries such as South Korea, Taiwan, and Indonesia, several authoritarian era laws and practices are still in place or have not been fully overhauled. In yet others, such as India and the Philippines, where the legal framework is conducive, the inability of the state to guarantee the rights and rules of the legal framework inhibits the institutionalization of civil society. Several other factors, including political and socioeconomic ones discussed in the chapter, also inhibit and explain the lag in the institutionalization of civil society in Asia.

Challenges and Future Development

To conclude, civil society organizations have become more numerous and consequential in Asia. The nature and dynamics of civil society and the factors that fuel growth are multiple and country-specific; however, it is difficult to deny the growing universality of the idea among Asian elites and increasingly among the lay people as well. Civil society organizations are acknowledged as legitimate by democratic and pseudodemocratic governments and their public. Even certain military and communist governments see some value in a controlled civil society. The upward trend in the number of civil society organizations and the widening range of issues in which they are involved is connected to the spread of open political systems, market economies, and globalization. This trend cannot be easily reversed. Asian civil societies display features of the neo-Gramscian and neo-Tocquevillean frames. As states become more legitimate and consolidated, features of the neo-Tocquevillean frame become dominant.

Associational life in Asia, however, still confronts major constraints and challenges. The guarantee of individual and group rights necessary for the construction of a legally protected sphere still does not obtain in many countries. Even a relatively long-standing democracy such as Japan still has legislation in place that controls and inhibits the institutionalization of civil society. Two key variables in the growth and institutionalization of civil society are regime type and effective government. As regimes become more open and democratic, the space for civil society increases; and effective government helps guarantee the fundamental rights in practice. This does not imply that civil society is passive and dependent. As we shall see in the next chapter, civil society organizations can and do play important roles in political change.

Although not discussed in this chapter, it is important to observe that civil society associations in Asia suffer legitimacy, revenue, expertise, and accountability problems of their own. Legitimacy problems arise from connections to foreign governments, transnational civil society organizations and their agendas, close connection to their own government, or a lack of a local constituency. Many associations cannot survive without government subsidy or foreign support. Such dependence, especially on foreign support, makes them a legitimate target for nationalists and antigovernment forces. Along with other considerations, revenue shortfall limits the expertise of associations and their capacity. Leadership struggles, transparency, and accountability problems dog many civil society organizations as well.

Even so, highlighting constraints and challenges does not weaken the argument that civil society organizations have become an important feature in the political landscape and policy processes of most Asian countries. Their salience and role are explored in the next chapter.

Note

1. I would like to thank Sunhyuk Kim, Amitabh Behar, Jennifer Franco, Meredith Weiss, Neil DeVotta, Edward Aspinall, Suzaina Kadir, Yun Fan, and Mary Gallagher for their input in writing this section.

Works Cited

Pandey, Gyanendra. 1988. "Congress and the Nation, 1917–1947." In Richard Sisson and Stanley Wolpert, eds., *Congress and Indian Nationalism: The Preindependence Phase*. Berkeley: University of California Press.

Salamon, Lester M., and Helmut K. Anheier. 1996. *The Emerging Nonprofit Sector: An Overview*. New York: Manchester University Press.

Schwartz, Frank J. 2003. "Introduction: Recognizing Civil Society in Japan." In Frank J. Schwartz and Susan J. Pharr, eds., *The State of Civil Society in Japan*. Cambridge: Cambridge University Press.

Tsujinaka, Yutaka. 2002. *Gendai Nippon no Sibiru Sosaeti/riekidanntan* (Civil society and interest groups in contemporary Japan). Tokyo: Bokutaku-sha.

———. 2004. *Gendai Kankoku no Sibiru Sosaeti/riekidanntan* (Civil society and interest groups in contemporary Korea). Tokyo: Bokutaku-sha.

Yamamoto, Tadashi. 1995. "Integrative Report." In Tadashi Yamamoto, ed., *Emerging Civil Society in the Asia Pacific Community*. Tokyo: JCIE and Singapore: ISEAS.

CHAPTER FIFTEEN

Civil Society and Democratic Change

Indeterminate Connection, Transforming Relations

MUTHIAH ALAGAPPA

This final chapter explores the connection between civil society and democracy, the role of civil society organizations in promoting open politics, and the implications of the rise of civil society for the state and political society, and for interaction among actors and agencies in these three realms. In Chapter 1 it was noted that both neo-Tocquevilleans and the New Left associate civil society with democracy—one stream positing a connection among a dense civil society, a high stock of social capital, and robust democracy. Civil society has also been deployed as a key variable in explaining political liberalization and democratic transition, and its development has been advanced as a precondition for the consolidation of democracy. The studies in this volume present a much more complicated picture of the connection between civil society, democracy, and the role of civil society organizations in advancing change in the direction of open politics. Similarly, the growing political significance of civil society has had substantial impact on the structure, power, and reach of the state, but the development of civil society has been deeply influenced by the state as well. And civil society's interaction with the state in Asia is not necessarily confrontational; it spans a wide spectrum and is often multidimensional, incorporating elements of struggle, confrontation, coercion, co-optation, and interaction on the basis of mutual recognition and shared principles and norms. Moreover, the character of such interaction has altered over time in several countries. Likewise, the rise of civil society has not been negative for political society; there is much synergy between actors in the two realms. The democratic effects of civil society are enhanced when prodemocratic forces in the two realms act in concert.

The chapter advances ten propositions: four on the connection between civil society and democracy; four on the implications of the rise of civil society for the state and its relations with society; and two on the relations between civil and political societies. First, there is no necessary connection between the rise of civil society and democratic change. Civil society organizations have both expanded and contracted democratic space. Second, civil society supports democracy when its dominant discourse is rooted in democratic ideals and when it is not dominated by organizations with totalizing goals. Third, the specific democratic role of civil society is contingent upon a number of factors: the political opportunity and constraints, specific stage of political development, and the strength, orientation, and role of the state and political society in a country. Fourth, civil society is a necessary but not sufficient condition for democratic development. On its own, civil society has a limited effect; in fact it faces an uphill battle in promoting and consolidating democratic change. Deepening democracy requires a strong and responsive state, strong issue-based political parties and an independent and effective judiciary as well. Fifth, the rise of civil society has limited the power and reach of the state although the latter continues to be the most powerful institution in Asia. Sixth, the state has had a strong impact on the nature and development of civil society. Seventh, state-civil society interaction in Asia is not necessarily confrontational. The relationship varies widely across countries and has undergone transformation in several of them. Eighth, present civil society-state relations in Asia span a broad spectrum. Ninth, there is much overlap between civil and political societies; the boundary separating them is porous. Finally, the development of civil society is not necessarily detrimental to the development of political society; in fact there is much synergy between them. The rest of the chapter elaborates these propositions.

Civil Society and Democratic Change

Proposition 1: The Contingent Connection Between Civil Society and Democracy

Civil society organizations have been in the forefront in several countries (South Korea, Taiwan, the Philippines, Thailand, and Indonesia) in preparing the ground for or in fact taking the lead in advocating political liberalization, political reform, and democratic transition; and they continue to play important roles in deepening and broadening democracy in these and other countries. In Indonesia, resistance by civil society and the articulation of a democratic counternarrative undermined the ideological foundations of the state and undermined the legitimacy of the Suharto regime, laying the ground for the dramatic change in 1998 (see Chapter 2). Civil society organizations from the Left and Right in the Philippines have been in the forefront not only in preparing the ground for political change, but also in mobilizing the public, jointly leading democratic change, and resisting abuse of power (see Chapter 3). In South Korea, civil society organizations have made critical contributions to democratic transition (resisting authoritarian rule, recruiting and training future political leaders, and advocating political and economic reform); they continue to play a key role in deepening and broadening democracy in that country, focusing on political and economic reform agendas, greater transparency in government, preventing abuse of power, and so forth (see Chapter 4). Social movements in Taiwan led the resistance to authoritarian rule, initiated and nurtured the opposition political party, produced a counternarrative that emphasized Taiwanization, democracy, and the construction of the nonstate public sphere, and mobilized international support for democratic change. Civil society organizations in that country continue to play important roles in educating and empowering citizens to strengthen the nonstate public sphere, reform state agencies, increase government accountability, seek equal status for women, and eliminate local factions and patronage networks through community development (see Chapter 5).

Despite the key role of civil society organizations in these and other countries in democratic change, there is, however, no necessary connection between civil society and democratic change or between the density of civil society and the vigor of democracy. Not all civil society organizations are supportive of democratic development. Depending on their collective interests, adherence to totalizing missions, and, in some cases, resort to violence to achieve political ends, civil society organizations have also supported authoritarian governments or contributed to the closing of democratic space. Asia has a history of unbridled competition in civil societies contributing to democratic breakdowns and succession by authoritarian rule.

The social and political turmoil arising from the intense struggle between Left and Right in South Korean civil society contributed to the seizure of power by Syngman Rhee. Although civil society organizations from the Left and Right played a prominent role subsequently in ousting the Rhee government, their continuing struggle undermined the ensuing democratic government of Chang Myon. Similarly, the unrest arising from the bitter class struggle in the Philippines led to the imposition of martial law by Ferdinand Marcos, a clampdown that was welcomed by the elite and middle-class segments of civil society on the grounds of security, stability, and economic development. The continuing class struggle in that country, and the competing visions of state and society, impede the deepening and broadening of democracy, contributing to the development of what Jennifer Franco has called "authoritarian enclaves" at the local level (see Chapter 3). In Indonesia, the struggle among the four *aliran*s contributed to the breakdown of democracy, paving the way for Guided Democracy and eventually military-autocratic rule under Suharto. Certain segments of Indonesian civil society, especially Islamic and minority organizations, supported military rule well into the late 1980s. In Thailand, conservative rightist groups mobilized against the prodemocracy left-wing groups in the 1973–76 period, supporting the return to military rule in 1976 and subsequently the decade long semiauthoritarian rule under the leadership of

General Prem Tinsulanon. In 1991, middle-class organizations in Bangkok welcomed the military ouster of the democratically elected but massively corrupt Kriangsak government.

Even in the long-standing democracies of India and Japan, the democratic effects of civil society are not uncontroversial or unidirectional. Civil society organizations in India are simultaneously expanding and contracting democratic space (see Chapter 6). Sections of civil society, especially at the state and local levels, seek to broaden democracy by empowering the poor, ordinary, and marginalized citizens and to deepen it by limiting the Indian state and increasing its transparency and accountability. To make the society more just and equitable, some organizations articulate alternative visions as well as a model of development that is people-oriented and sustainable. The democratic effects of these organizations are countered by the substantial and growing religious segments of civil society that seek to make India a Hindu state. The totalizing goals of these organizations communalize state institutions—threatening the secular character of the country and universal criteria of citizenship and curtailing the rights of minorities. The tensions among religious and communal groups, which often erupt in violence, undermine trust in society and weaken the democratic foundations of the state. Such concurrent expansion and contraction of democratic space is also occurring in varying degrees in the Philippines, Indonesia, and Thailand.

In Japan, a huge number of small, face-to-face neighborhood associations have enhanced the government's performance at the local level, but with virtually no impact on the structure of the state, in limiting the influence of bureaucrats (who despite their poor performance record and scandalous conduct continue to wield enormous influence) or in demanding greater transparency and accountability from state and party officials (see Chapter 7). Contrary to the claims of theorists like Robert Putnam, the social capital produced by the small neighborhood associations has not strengthened democracy in Japan. Neither has the growing disaffection with the state and democracy as practiced in that country resulted in a more vocal civil society demanding political and economic reform at the national level.

In Sri Lanka, as observed earlier in Chapters 9 and 14, civil society organizations have played a key role in the rise of ethnic chauvinism and political violence—both of which have torn the social and political fabric of that country, resulting in the rise of illiberal democracy. The interethnic struggle has promoted sectarianism, communalism, insecurity, and institutional decay. Individual and group rights, transparency and accountability of government, all have been undermined; corruption and abuse of power are rampant; and the military and paramilitary forces of the government and the Liberation Tigers of Tamil Eelam dominate large swaths of territory and people. Although national elections have been held regularly, the liberal features of democracy have been jettisoned. Totalizing goals and the war have promoted the ethnic-bonding type of social capital to the detriment of interethnic bridging. Sinhala-only organizations have opposed concessions to the minority community and obstructed the peace process. Although multiethnic Malaysia has avoided a debilitating conflict like that in Sri Lanka, influential civil society groups in that country have basically supported the Malay-dominant political status quo and seek policy changes within the present framework (see Chapter 8). Even when certain organizations joined opposition political parties in the late 1990s to oust the incumbent Barisan Nasional government, the majority Malay-community organizations were more inclined to support the creation of an Islamic society and state; support for political liberalization and democracy was limited.

Moreover there is no uniform democratic impulse in the reaction to authoritarian rule. In Burma, civil society organizations inside and outside the country seek to isolate and sanction the military junta in the international arena in the hope of eventually bringing about democratic change. In Pakistan, by contrast, the religious right, developmental advocates, and liberal segments of civil society welcomed the 1999 military coup and support the Musharraf government (see Chapter 11). The rightist religious groups share the military's hostility to India and aversion to democratic politics. Influential developmental NGOs, sections of the print media, and the liberal intelligentsia welcomed the Musharraf military coup because of the rampant corruption, abuse of power, and the dismal performance of governments in the preceding eleven years of democracy. Many of these civil society organizations derive considerable power and benefit from the military-led state; some see it as necessary for modernization and as a bulwark against fundamentalist forces. Co-opted by the state, key organizations function as partners of the military government. In the post-Tiananmen PRC, official civil society groups, with much to gain from links to the state, appear to accept a communist regime that is committed to liberalizing the economy and increasing personal freedom (see Chapter 13). Although it is difficult to gauge the strength of unofficial groups in civil society, democratic forces inside and outside that country appear to have been marginalized. The complex picture presented here refutes the notion of undifferentiated connections between civil society and democracy.

Proposition 2: Propitious Conditions

As observed earlier, however, it is clear that certain civil society organizations at selected points in time have played key roles in the transition to democracy and its subsequent development. Investigating these propitious conditions will give us a useful insight into the contingent connection between civil society and democracy. Drawing on the studies in this volume, I argue here that civil society can be deemed to be supportive of democracy when the following two conditions obtain: first, civil society is not dominated by organizations with totalizing goals; second, the dominant discourse in civil society is rooted in democratic ideals or at least democratically oriented organizations have critical mass. The first condition does not imply that there is no conflict in civil society. Indeed, a central thesis of this study is to highlight the inequality, conflicting goals, and struggles in Asian civil societies and caution against treating civil society as a single harmonious entity. But competing goals and contention in civil society are not incompatible with democracy; in fact, democracy is enhanced by such competition so long as it is conducted within accepted rules. Struggle issuing from conflicting totalizing goals, however, is detrimental to democracy; often violent, it promotes antidemocratic forces and practices. As one can see from the Indonesian and Sri Lankan cases, totalizing goals make for bitter zero-sum struggles for survival, in which one party seeks the subjugation of the other, including through violent means. Intense struggle has also characterized civil societies in South Korea, the Philippines, and Thailand. Different segments of civil society in these countries have espoused competing visions of the state and society, but with few exceptions, they have not sought the elimination or total subservience of contending segments. A degree of compromise and cooperation was possible—especially in relation to their common purpose of ousting authoritarian and corrupt rulers. To support democracy, organizations with limited goals that rely on civil means must dominate civil society.

The second condition is important because narratives seek to define how the society thinks and acts, and discourses in civil society are not necessarily democratic. Alternatives emerge in civil and political societies when the state narrative is discredited. The content of such alternative narratives, however, hinges on several factors, including the content and resonance of the state narrative in the society at large, beliefs of civil society leaders, the available alternatives, and the reigning international narratives. In the early postindependence and Cold War periods, alternative narratives included socialism, communism, democracy, and nativism. With the collapse of the Soviet-led communist world—and the weaknesses or failure of alternative political and economic models—democracy and the free-market economy have become the central international narratives. This does not guarantee that democracy is always the alternative narrative, however. In Malaysia, for example, the dominant alternative to the state narrative of stability and development is not that of citizens' rights and democracy but of an Islamic society and state. Narratives based on Islamic society and state have appeal in Indonesia too, although they are not politically dominant. In democratic India, a Hindu nationalist narrative was on the rise. Confucian narratives had appeal in the 1990s, when East Asian countries were experiencing "miraculous" growth rates and were deemed to be on the rise.

The beliefs of civil and political society leaders, combined with the nature, performance, and legitimacy of the incumbent government, determine whether alternative narratives will emerge. In South Korea, Taiwan, the Philippines, Thailand, and Indonesia, the incumbent authoritarian governments and their legitimizing narratives were widely discredited. Despite differences in their visions of state and society, dissident political and civil society leaders in these countries articulated their group interests and couched their counternarratives largely in terms of democratic ideals. In Taiwan, for example, democratically inclined civil society movements and organizations constructed a subaltern or counter public sphere to escape the domination of public space by the KMT and articulated a counternarrative that had democracy as its central element. As it gained force, the narrative helped expose the shortcomings of the KMT narrative and delegitimate the authoritarian mainlander regime and its policies (see Chapter 5). Even segments of civil society that benefited from the status quo became disenchanted with the incumbent government and began leaning toward democratic narratives. The commitment of civil society leaders to democratic ideas and norms, however, varied widely in Asian countries. In some cases, the commitment was instrumental; others were underpinned by strong democratic beliefs. Such variations—combined with attachment to different features and configurations of democracy—have affected the subsequent unity, orientation, and role of civil society organizations.

Proposition 3: Democratic Roles of Civil Society

The role of civil society organizations in promoting political change in the direction of open politics depends not only on the attributes of civil society but also on the legitimacy and strength of the state and the specific stage of political development. In situations of legitimate authoritarian rule, they have been limited to seeking political liberalization and policy change within the prevailing framework; in a widely discredited regime, they have advocated and led system change; in transitional democracies, they have bolstered democratic forces to prevent reversals as well as to broaden and deepen the scope of democracy; and in long-standing democracies, they have sought to remedy procedural shortcomings, make democracy more substantive, and foster norms and habits that would make democracy the only game in town. Although we focus here on the democratic roles of civil society organizations, one should not lose sight of the fact that other forces in civil society with competing agendas simultaneously inhibit and in some cases block democratic development. Even democratic forces can undermine democracy because of the heavy burden they place on nascent democratic arrangements and fragile state institutions that are unable to cope with their many demands.

Political Change Within the Authoritarian Status Quo. The political arrangements in Singapore and Malaysia combine features of pluralism and authoritarianism—leading observers to label them as semi-, quasi-, or pseudodemocratic, or authoritarian-pluralist regimes. Despite shortcomings and grievances, these arrangements enjoy fairly widespread acceptance by their respective populations (Case 1995; Khong 1995). Allowing them limited legal space (more in Malaysia than in Singapore), these governments keep civil society organizations on a short leash.

Transgressing leaders and groups are punished severely. In a context of legitimacy combined with good performance and repression, civil society organizations have had limited room for maneuver. By and large they are confined to advocating policy changes in a limited range of nonsensitive areas and pushing for political change on the margins or change from within the system.

In Singapore, civil society organizations have been permitted space to operate in such areas as women's issues (domestic violence, equality in the workplace), the environment, and community development so long as they do not challenge the political status quo (see Chapter 9). The Association of Women for Action and Research and the Nature Society of Singapore, for example, have had some limited success in the Goh Chong Tong era in proposing new legislation, providing input into government policy, and modifying certain policies and projects. But organizations like the Association of Malay Muslim Professionals—which departed from the government-approved focus on education and welfare and challenged the government's policy on leadership selection for the Malay-Muslim community—are deemed to be venturing into the prohibited political arena. As a result of this transgression, government funding for this organization became more conditional. When civil society agendas and actions are considered unacceptable, the government does not hesitate to react quickly and strongly. The net effect has been to limit the civil society sector to organizations that are basically supportive of the status quo.

Opportunities for citizen participation in government are limited in Malaysia as well, although there is greater room for autonomous civil society there than in Singapore. And Malaysian civil society organizations have had much greater impact on the politics of the country, although not necessarily in a democratic direction (see Chapter 8). Civil society groups have brought about political change in Malaysia in several ways. First is the government's adoption of popular civil society agendas (like the popular Islamic revival movement in the 1970s) and co-optation of popular leaders like Anwar Ibrahim into the ruling party. In responding to Malay-Muslim criticism that the government is un-Islamic or not sufficiently Islamic, the ruling UMNO-led Barisan Nasional government introduced the policy of absorbing Islamic values in 1982. But the government also cracked down on Islamic groups that were deemed to be engaged in propagating deviant teachings and endangering national security and stability. Second, civil society groups have been active in advocating policy or lobbying for the adoption, abrogation, or modification of government policy on a variety of issues including education, women's rights, human rights, and environmental concerns. Ever mindful of the possibility of repression, such advocacy is often couched in the government's legitimating narrative, including its claim to democratic credentials and multiethnic accommodation. Only rarely do organizations enter sensitive areas or challenge the status quo. A third way in which civil society groups have attempted to bring about political change with some success is in the matter of developing counternarratives. Islamic organizations, some in cooperation with the opposition Islamic party, have been developing a counternarrative since the early 1970s. This narrative emphasizes Islamic law, society, economy, and state in contrast to the government narrative emphasizing Malay dominance, economic development, and stability in a multiracial and multireligious society. Yet another counternarrative articulated by certain segments of civil society in the 1990s under the banner of Reformasi emphasized citizenship, human rights, democracy, and multiethnic politics. It had limited appeal in comparison to the Islamic narrative. Today the Islamic-secular dimension has become the primary axis for political competition. The role of civil society groups in altering the terrain of political competition in Malaysia indicates their potential even in tightly controlled states. The change has not, however, been in a democratic direction.

There is even less autonomy for the official civil society organizations in the PRC (see Chapter 13). Nearly all of them are connected to, and benefit from, the party-state. Although the ideological basis of the party-state has severely eroded, the CCP's rule in the PRC, severely challenged in 1989, is not without legitimacy. Public acceptance of CCP rule rests on good economic performance, increasing personal freedom, nationalism, lack of alternatives, fear of the unknown, and fear of repression. In this situation, official civil society has not articulated a political or economic counternarrative. Its role in political change is limited and indirect. Official organizations have been allowed a policy role in such areas as the environment, scarce natural resources, and wildlife because they bring much-needed resources and expertise, and also because Beijing's tolerance of them mutes international criticism and raises its international standing (Elizabeth Economy, cited in Chapter 13). A more important avenue of change has been the transformation of politics from within the system—arising from the transition to a free-market economy, the rise of the private sector, and the accompanying interpenetration of wealthy leaders of business organizations and the party-state. The CCP's vanguard role has been redefined under Jiang Zemin's "Three Represents Theory" to comprise the productive forces of Chinese society, including business corporations. Party membership is now open to wealthy entrepreneurs. That this change in a key feature of the system came from within suggests a possible direction of system change in years to come. A third avenue of change would be a repeat of the 1989 prodemocracy movement when certain state-sponsored organizations and the public sympathized with or even joined student activists in demanding a more open political system. Such protest leading to change appears unlikely now, but it cannot be ruled out.

System Change: Democratic Transition. Civil society organizations have performed multiple functions, but here we discuss three key roles in the transitions to democracy in Asia: delegitimating authoritarian rule, constructing democratic counternarratives, and bolstering democratic forces. In a context of growing political consciousness and transformation of subjects and clients to citizens, civil society holds the key to the legitimacy of political arrangements and incumbent governments (Bratton 1994; Alagappa 1995). Even the most authoritarian governments claim that they rule on behalf of their nations and peoples—evident from their formal statements, their eagerness to attach the democracy label to their system of government (*barangay* democracy in the Philippines under Marcos, Pancasila democracy in Suharto's Indonesia, the Burmese Way to Socialism under New Win, and Thai-Style democracy under Sarit, Thanom-Praphat, and Prem), and their attempt to clothe themselves in popular legitimacy through elections that are often stacked and rigged to ensure their victory. Despite the obvious drawbacks, authoritarian rulers seek domestic and international validation through such elections, and not without success. Park Chung-hee and subsequently Chun Doo Hwan in South Korea, Ferdinand Marcos in the Philippines, Suharto in Indonesia, Prem Tinsulanon in Thailand, and the KMT governments in Taiwan all organized periodic elections to convince other strategic groups in society (and themselves) that they have the support of the people and rule on their behalf.

Civil society is the key site for the production of legitimacy that is essential for hegemony in the Gramscian sense. Both governments and opposition groups therefore struggle to dominate civil society in their efforts to entrench or resist hegemony. The need for rulers to clothe themselves in legitimacy provides civil society with a key weapon to resist the incumbent government and deny it legitimacy. Repeated social protests and massive mobilizations—like the 1986 People Power uprising in the Philippines, the massive rally in 1987 in South Korea, the 1973 student rallies and 1992 mass demonstration by the Confederation for Democracy in Thailand, and the mass demonstrations in 1998 in Indonesia—expose the moral bankruptcy of the incumbent rulers and often (although not in Burma and the PRC) lead to their ouster (as in the Philippines, Indonesia, and Thailand) or force them to accede to demands of civil society (as in South Korea and Taiwan).

Closely linked to delegitimation is the counternarrative role. It serves two functions: first, it exposes the deficiencies of the social and political structure, the hollowness of the claims of the incumbent rulers, and their abuse of state power; second, it offers an alternative framework for governance and the moral basis for organizing resistance. The content of the counternarratives is rooted in social reality and often includes many elements; democracy, however, is a central theme. The counternarrative in Taiwan, for example, included ethnic differentiation, self-determination, democracy, and social justice. Democracy was the predominant theme, however, both as an organizing ideology and because it was viewed as the vehicle to achieve ethnic differentiation and self-determination. The counternarrative—which also included socially progressive ideals like human rights, environmentalism, labor and consumer rights, and gender equality—exposed the shortcomings, abuses, and unsuitability of the KMT regime's mainland-oriented narrative and structure for

Taiwan. Faced with brutal repression and control of the print and broadcast media by the state, civil society groups used underground newspapers and magazines and relied on social protests in constructing and propagating the counternarrative. Similarly, the counternarratives constructed by civil society organizations in the Philippines, Thailand, South Korea, and Indonesia comprised features that were peculiar to each country, but democracy was a key theme in all of them.

Civil society organizations in these countries also bolstered democratic forces by creating alliances and umbrella groups in civil and political societies and by mobilizing domestic society and international opinion in favor of their democracy movements and alternative political leadership. Students played a key role in mobilizing the democratic forces in Thailand, South Korea, and Burma. In the Philippines, organizations in civil and political societies rallied around Corazon Aquino, the widow of Benigno Aquino who was assassinated by the Marcos government. In 1980s Taiwan, social movements joined force with the oppositional political elite to protect the infant Democratic Progressive Party. Subsequently, they acted in concert with democratic forces in political society to bolster the democratic movement. Students and immigrant communities in foreign lands (Taiwanese students and communities in Japan and the United States; Burmese students and communities in the United States and the European Union countries), assisted by transnational civil society organizations and the international media, mobilized international support for the democracy movements in their respective countries. All three roles of civil society in democratic transition—delegitimating authoritarian rule, developing a counternarrative, and especially augmenting the power of democratic forces—continue to be relevant in subsequent stages of democratic development.

Deepening and Broadening Democracy. Civil society organizations have played leading roles in broadening and deepening democracy in both transitional and relatively long-standing democracies like India and Japan. These roles have been diverse: giving voice to previously marginalized communities, furthering democracy education and socialization, widening the range of issues subject to democratic governance, intermediating, contributing to policymaking, participating in governance at the national and local levels, restructuring and monitoring state institutions, demanding greater transparency and accountability from government and political leaders, demanding and promoting transitional justice, monitoring elections, fostering the development of new political leaders, and bolstering democratic forces to prevent reversals. These roles are discussed in several chapters in this volume, especially those covering India, South Korea, Taiwan, Thailand, the Philippines, and Indonesia. Here we focus on a few selected cases.

Although the Indian constitution and laws have a well-developed notion of citizenship, in practice the rights of citizenship have been realized only by the educated and privileged. They have not been available to a majority of the population (see Chapter 6). Nevertheless, the constitution has become a reference point for a wide range of Indian organizations that seek to open democratic space for the poor and marginalized sections by securing for them the basic rights and entitlements guaranteed to all citizens in the constitution. In addition to making their collective voice heard through the political process and targeting state agencies in the formulation and implementation of policies, civil society groups have undertaken projects to elevate the socioeconomic well-being of the poor and marginalized sections of the population and to protect their cultural, land, and other rights. In the Philippines too, the rights of ordinary Filipinos, especially the rural poor, have been denied or compromised by the politically powerful landed elites who continue to dominate politics in that country. Segments of civil society have engaged in a deep struggle with the state and the landed elite on behalf of the traditionally excluded to obtain for them the "right to have rights" (Neil Harvey 1998, cited in Chapter 3). This struggle is most evident in the continuing push for land redistribution and agrarian reform. In a country where poverty is widespread and persistent and land continues to be a key source of political power, the fight for land reform waged by civil society organizations on behalf of the poor and landless has been an uphill battle, with only modest success. In Thailand too, civil society groups—specifically new social movements—are engaged in struggles with the state and conservative forces to realize participatory democracy by empowering local communities, the rural poor, women, and other disadvantaged sections of the population in their demands for social justice, human rights, improved environmental conditions, and a generally better life and the power to exercise their rights as citizens.

Civil society organizations in Thailand have also spearheaded political reform (Bungbongkarn 2001). Faced with growing political corruption, the increasing role of money in politics, and inaction on the part of the state, the national assembly, and political parties, prodemocracy civil society groups led the post-1992 political reform effort. A key feature of the reform agenda was drafting and guaranteeing the integrity of a new constitution. Civil society organizations were involved in every stage: making the case for an autonomous drafting body that included representatives from all provinces and strata of society and the necessary professional experts; influencing the orientation and substance of the constitution, including provisions for checks and balances; promoting society's involvement in public hearings; taking part in the intensive campaign to compel the national assembly to endorse the new constitution; and setting up agencies like the autonomous constitutional court and countercorruption committee. Civil society organizations in the Philippines played similar roles in drafting the post-1986 constitution. Groups such as Poll Watch in Thailand, National Citizens Movement for Free Elections (NAMFREL) in the Philippines, and the Citizen's Council for Fair Elections in South Korea have all been active in monitoring elections to ensure they are conducted in accordance with laws and in a relatively free and fair manner.

Increasing the transparency and accountability of the state and political parties has been another key focus of Asian civil society organizations. In South Korea, for example, the Citizens' Solidarity for Monitoring the National Assembly Inspection of Government Offices, comprising forty civil society organizations, monitored the national assembly on two issues: first, recording the attendance of lawmakers in various committees and evaluating their performance and, second, monitoring the assembly's consideration of 166 crucial reform tasks, such as ending corrupt practices in private schools and dealing with the problems arising from the implementation of the national pension system (see Chapter 4). Frustrated with the lack of cooperation from legislators and political parties and with only modest success in their legislative oversight role, civil society groups decided to focus on the candidates standing for election in 2000. The Citizens' Solidarity for General Elections (CSGE) produced a list of unfit candidates who should not be nominated because they had violated laws, had engaged in bribery, or had not discharged their legislative function effectively. Although the two opposition parties were not supportive and the ruling party was lukewarm, the majority of the general public was supportive, and several faith-based organizations endorsed the CSGE effort. In the April 2000 election, fifty-nine of the eighty-six candidates on the CSGE list were not elected. In the process of the campaign, the CSGE and its 975 affiliated organizations and more than 1,000 activists contributed greatly to increasing the political consciousness of the voters, promoting the emergence of a new generation of political leaders, and forcing a partial revision of the election laws. In India, the Majdoor Kisan Shakti Sangathan (MKSS), engaged in a struggle with the state of Rajasthan to empower rural workers and peasants, concluded that advancing its cause required exposing corruption in the state government; this in turn required access to information (see Chapter 6). Through a series of measures including networking, agitation, and exposés, the MKSS forced the state government to issue an order in 1995 declaring that citizens have the right to obtain copies of government documents pertaining to development projects in their areas. This measure was followed by a comprehensive bill passed by the state legislature giving citizens the right to information from all government departments. With ramifications for other states and at the national level, the effort of the MKSS represents a milestone in increasing transparency and accountability in the Indian system of governance.

Transitional justice has been a key concern of civil society organizations in South Korea, the Philippines, and Indonesia. In South Korea, civil society groups were in the forefront in demanding the trial of political and military leaders involved in the 1980 violent suppression of the democratic movement in Kwangju and the subsequent series of coercive "cleansing" campaigns. More than twenty generals were discharged or transferred, among them four who were tried for mutiny (defined to include couplike actions). Former presidents Chun and Roh were tried, convicted, and imprisoned for treason and corruption. The personnel and promotion systems were revamped to rid the South Korean military of factions. Civil society groups in the Philippines and Indonesia too were active in seeking trial of senior government and military leaders and officials and their families for past abuses, including massive corruption, human rights violations, and participation in coups d'état against legitimately elected governments. With a few exceptions, these attempts have been stalled for a number of reasons. Conservative forces—nationalists and the military, for example—have regrouped to fend off efforts to correct past abuses. In the process, conservative forces have also become stronger, making democratization more difficult in certain areas, such as civilian control of the military and security policymaking. Furthermore, although efforts to obtain transitional justice are essential, they have made political reconciliation much harder to achieve and intensified political struggles. In sum, it is important to observe here that although strong civil society organizations have contributed much to broaden and deepen democracy, their numerous and competing demands, their inability to prioritize, and their preference for quick remedial action have also hindered democratic development.

Undermining Democracy. Impatience on the part of democratically inclined civil society organizations (and in certain cases vested interests) has obstructed democratic practices and retarded development of the rule of law. The endorsement by urban groups of the 1991 military coup in Thailand to remove the corrupt but democratically elected Kriangsak government, for example, brought the military back into politics. When the military attempted to perpetuate its role, civil society groups had to resist through mass mobilization. The ensuing conflict resulted in bloodshed and intervention by the king to resolve the crisis. Although they may provide quick relief, mass protests to remove ineffective and corrupt governments—like the forced resignation of the Chavalit government in 1997 and the ouster of democratically elected Estrada in 2001—subvert the democratic process and rule of law. Political protest is a legitimate activity. But frequent resort to mass protest, especially to massive demonstrations, legitimizes street politics and encourages politics by protest and referendum. Such actions circumvent parliamentary politics and do unintended harm. The ouster of Estrada, for example, raised serious questions about democratic civilian control of the military in the Philippines and also the constitutionality of the presidency of Gloria Macapagal-Arroyo. Democratic development has also been hindered by the non-self-limiting nature of the goals and means of certain civil society organizations, by the inability of new and weak states to meet the many demands of nonstate groups, and by the lack of democratic practices and accountability on the part of the civil society organizations themselves.

Proposition 4: Civil Society's Influence

Clearly, civil society organizations in Asia have played an important role in democratic transitions, and subsequently in broadening and deepening democracy. But how significant were they compared to other domestic and international actors and developments? Not all the chapters in the volume investigate this question, but it is evident that even in cases where civil society organizations did play a crucial role, on their own, they could not have realized the democratic breakthroughs or been effective in advancing democratic development. The orientation and capacity of the state, cooperation with political society, the strength of political society, the international context, and support of international actors were essential as well. The relative weight of these factors and how they combine have varied by country, circumstance, and issue.

In Thailand, for example, mass mobilization and protest by civil society groups was crucial in exposing the moral bankruptcy of the military government in 1973 and 1992 and engendering crisis situations that commanded domestic and international attention. Resolutions of these crises and subsequent transitions to democracy, however, were a function of the split in the military in 1973 and intervention by the revered monarch in both cases. In the Philippines, the decision of segments of the military to defect from Marcos and throw their weight behind the People Power movement, combined with the withdrawal of American support, were key factors in Marcos's decision to go into exile. In Indonesia, civil society organizations lacking a mass base were too weak and ill suited to play the antiregime mobilization role. The democratic transition was driven by students and the urban poor, acting in ad hoc fashion in the context of the declining legitimacy of the corrupt Suharto regime, which was further eroded by an economic crisis with domestic and international roots. Withdrawal of military support was a key factor in Suharto's decision to hand over power to his vice president. The democratic transition in Taiwan was driven as much from below as from above by Chiang Chingkuo's decision to liberalize politics in order to secure the KMT's hold on Taiwan in the context of political and economic changes on the mainland and the international ascendance of democratic norms. It is pertinent to note here that a mass protest led by students resulted in the resignation of New Win and the organization of multiparty elections in Burma. The military junta, however, refused to transfer power to the National League for Democracy, which won an overwhelming victory in the 1991 election. Instead, it imprisoned popular political leaders and violently suppressed nonstate organizations. Similarly, the 1989 democracy movement in Beijing was suppressed by the CCP with the support of the military. The point here is not to downplay the significance of civil society organizations but to put them in proper perspective and highlight the need to understand their specific functions, possibilities, and limits in democratic transition.

Likewise, civil society is a crucial but not the sole or even the primary force in the democratization and consolidation processes. A responsive civil democratic state with the capacity to address the demands of society, a strong political society capable of aggregating and representing interests, a functioning legislature, an independent judiciary, and an effective bureaucracy and police force, combined with a commitment on the part of the political elite and state officials to democratic ideals and practices—these are key prerequisites for democratic development. If these institutions and commitments are weak or absent, civil society groups face an uphill battle in their democratization role. Their effectiveness will be limited and their results short-lived. This has been the case in the Philippines, in Thailand, and, to an even greater degree, in contemporary Indonesia. As noted earlier, civil society organizations in these countries have been active in widening political participation by empowering marginalized citizens and groups, narrowing the range of issues excluded from democratic governance, drafting constitutions, and restructuring and monitoring of the state and legislature. Despite the vibrancy of civil societies, democratic development in these countries has a checkered history of periodic setbacks. Political parties are weak, especially in the Philippines; legal systems are woefully inadequate; the judiciary is corrupt; and political power is still concentrated in the state and the highest political office.

Democratic development has made greater headway in South Korea and Taiwan, where there is greater agreement on the sociopolitical order, state institutions are stronger, and the democratic commitment is deeper and more widespread. From these cases it is evident that a vigorous civil society is a necessary but not sufficient condition for democratic development. The democracy-producing effects of civil society organizations are much greater and longer-lasting when these groups act in concert with others in political society and the state. There is a paradox here: civil society can play an important role in creating democratic institutions and processes; yet its effectiveness in promoting democracy hinges on the presence and functioning of such institutions and processes. But this paradox simply highlights the complex and interdependent relationship among them, especially between the state and civil society.

The Rise of Civil Society: Transforming the State and State-Society Relations

The growing political significance of civil society has had a substantial impact on the structure, power, and reach of the state but, as observed in Chapter 14, the development of civil society has been deeply influenced by the state and its policies as well. This section explores the propositions on the mutual influence of the state and civil society and examines how the relationship between them has been altered by the increasing power of civil society. Proposition 5 asserts that the proliferation of civil society groups and their activism in a wide range of areas have in several cases limited the state's power and reach and pressured governments to restructure and reform certain agencies. Combined with the widespread embrace of the free-market economic system and globalization, the rise of civil society has contributed to diffusion and decentralization of power, authority, and resources. This does not, however, imply a reduction in the salience of the state, which continues to be the most powerful institution. Nevertheless, traditionally strong states, especially in East Asia, are being compelled to adjust to changing circumstances as civil society becomes a key part of the political equation. Proposition 6 argues that the state is a major force in the development of civil society. The composition, dynamics, orientation, and functions of civil society have been shaped to a considerable extent by the type of state, its legitimacy, policies, and effectiveness. The next proposition posits that state–civil society relations have undergone dramatic change in many countries—and that further change is in prospect. The final proposition, on state–civil society interaction, asserts that the present relationship of civil society to the state in Asia spans a wide spectrum, ranging from confrontation through constructive engagement to partnership and co-optation. Furthermore, because civil society and in several cases the state itself are not cohesive entities and feature multiple actors and shifting dynamics, the relationship between nonstate groups and government agencies varies widely, even within the same country, by level, issue, and organization.

Proposition 5: Limiting the State's Power and Reach

The proliferation of civil society organizations and their increasing influence have had several powerful effects: they have limited the all-pervasive state and its extensive reach into society, compelled a restructuring of state agencies especially in the internal security arena, opened up the policy process to public input and scrutiny, and generally altered the calculations of the political elite. The limitation of state power and its reach in society is most evident in Taiwan and South Korea. In Taiwan, the KMT party-state penetrated and dominated every level and segment of society, and nearly every aspect of political and social life, leaving little space for organization and governance that are independent of the state. With the proliferation of civil society organizations, along with such developments as the rise of competitive political parties, the growth of the market economy, Taiwan's integration into the global capitalist economy, and the growing international embrace of the norm of limited government, the state-dominated space and influence in that country have shrunk. Checks and balances on the government have increased, with civil society organizations constituting an important check. Policy formulation and implementation are no longer the exclusive preserve of the state; public input and monitoring have become key features of the political process. A strong prodemocratic civil society has been instrumental in society's internalization of the norm of democratic civilian control of the military, contributing significantly to the creation of an environment conducive to restructuring civil-military relations (Lo 2001). Civil society bolstered the power of the civilian political leaders in their effort to restructure the command and control of the military, make it more professional, and make changes in defense department policies, including procurement. In South Korea, the state continues to be powerful but can no longer ride roughshod over public opposition without suffering political consequences. Pressure from civil society groups is increasing the transparency and accountability of the legislature and government agencies. They have also helped open up the policy process to public input and scrutiny in numerous areas—including hitherto forbidden matters like civil-military relations, security policy, government-business relations, and corporate governance in the conglomerates. As in Taiwan, the firm opposition of South Korean civil society groups to military-authoritarian rule was and continues to be significant in advancing civilian control and altering the calculus of the military itself (Jun 2001).

Demands of civil society organizations have contributed to the restructuring of state security agencies and their roles in several other countries as well, including Thailand, the Philippines, and Indonesia. Excluding the military from politics (or limiting its political role), reducing the military's role in internal security, creating a separate police force under the control of a different ministry, increasing the role of democratically elected leaders in security policymaking, increasing civilian oversight of the military—these are among the areas in which civil society organizations have had an impact (Alagappa 2001). This is not to say that the state has become less relevant or is on the decline—only that civil society groups have become an important component of the political equation (more salient in some and less so in others), with the power to affect the structure and process of government. Although political leaders and state officials in the traditionally strong states like South Korea, Taiwan, and Japan may not be positively disposed, they are being compelled to adjust to the growing significance of civil society organizations. Adjustment is facilitated in some cases by recognition of the legitimating potential of these organizations, the expertise and resources they can bring to the table, and the functions they can undertake in social service, relief work, and local development to relieve the burden on the state. Civil society leaders in several countries, including South Korea, the Philippines, Thailand, Malaysia, and Indonesia hold positions in government, have joined statutory boards, or act in an advisory capacity. The influence, however, has not been unidirectional.

Proposition 6: The Central Role of the State

Several chapters in this volume highlight the central role of the state—type, policies, and effectiveness—in the development of civil society. Democratic states in general have tended to provide legal space for autonomous organizations and to stimulate the development of self-limiting organizations that emphasize the intermediation function. Communal states have stimulated and reinforced communally based civil society groups. Authoritarian states have distorted and retarded the development of civil society, but they have also stimulated the development of democratic oppositional civil societies.

Although democratic states are in the main positively disposed, the development of autonomous civil societies has hinged both on the capacity of the state to guarantee the rights necessary to institutionalize the nonstate public realm and on the governance philosophy of the rulers. As observed in the previous chapter, effective states in Taiwan and South Korea have facilitated the development of institutionalized civil society, while relatively weak states in India, the Philippines, Thailand, and Indonesia have been less conducive to the development of a strong institutionalized nonstate sector. As illustrated by the case of Japan, however, a strong democratic state does not necessarily facilitate the development of strong nonstate organizations that emphasize interest aggregation, intermediation, and advocacy functions. The extensive role of the Japanese state in social and economic life, combined with legal regulations (power to permit, monitor, investigate, and punish) and bureaucratic practices has made it difficult for independent groups to grow large in Japan, and for the few large groups that do exist to remain independent (see Chapter 7). The state has effectively constrained the development of civil society organizations devoted to advocating policy. A more limited democratic state (as opposed to a weak state) like that in posttransition Taiwan has been more conducive to the development of such organizations and institutionalization of the sphere of civil society.

Communal politics and the communalization of the state in Sri Lanka and Malaysia—and the ongoing attempt in this direction by the BJP in India—stimulate and reinforce communal organizations in civil society. The domination of the Sri Lankan state by the majority Sinhala community, facilitated by the electoral system, as well as the ensuing ethnic conflict in that country, have polarized civil society along communal lines. In the process, the power of ethnically based organizations, especially those with grassroots support, was augmented, while that of organizations seeking to bridge the interethnic divide and promote human rights and liberal democracy was undermined (see Chapter 9). Ethnic bidding and state policies that favor the majority community have privileged ethnic bonding at the expense of interethnic bridging. Similarly, the Malaysian state (based on Malay political dominance and communal politics) and its Malay preference policies make it imperative for civil society groups to organize and articulate their demands along ethnic or religious lines. Attempts to form multiethnic parties and organizations in Malaysia have not been successful. In the majority community, the strong appeal of the entrenchment of Malay political dominance in the state structure explains, in part, the feebleness of the democratic and human rights discourses (which would advocate greater equality among citizens of different ethnic groups) and the greater attraction of the Islamic state and society discourse (which would continue to privilege the Malay community) in Malaysian civil society.

Authoritarian states and their repressive policies affect the development and dynamics of civil societies in several ways. First, they distort and retard the development of autonomous civil society through limitation of legal space, coercion, fragmentation, and co-optation. The classic example here is Pakistan under military rule (see Chapter 11). Under Generals Ayub, Zia, and now Musharraf, military governments severely curbed political and civil rights and liberties, suppressed political dissent, and coerced the press, intelligentsia, and autonomous organizations. At the same time, the generals, especially Zia, made overtures to Islamic and sectarian forces. To shore up their international legitimacy and ease their burden in local governance, the generals have been favorably disposed toward developmental NGOs. Through these and other manipulative measures, the military governments in Pakistan have fragmented civil society and made several segments heavily reliant on the state. The net result is a coerced and co-opted civil society in the service of an authoritarian state.

Second, severe limitation of legal space and constant government harassment and repression have driven civil societies underground and abroad. Today, the classic illustration of this effect is Burma. In responding to suppression by the military junta, some organizations altered their formal roles; some operated informally or went underground; some relocated to border areas where the government's reach was limited or contested; some moved to neighboring Thailand or formed associations in the United States and the European Union countries that have resident diaspora communities and a supportive environment. This was also the case in Thailand during 1976–77 and in Taiwan when it was under KMT domination. In addition to changes in their formal role and physical location, civil society organizations in these countries and in others, such as Singapore and Malaysia, have resorted to the use of cyberspace to circumvent government control. Despite their best efforts, governments have found it difficult to regulate the use of cyberspace—especially when they have to balance such controls with the benefits of opening and integrating their national economies into the global capitalist economy and more generally joining the globalizing world.

Third, authoritarian rulers and their legitimating narratives frequently stimulate the development of oppositional civil societies and democratic counternarratives.

In the Philippines, South Korea, Taiwan, and Indonesia, authoritarian rule spurred the development of oppositional civil society organizations that advocated democracy and had no stake in the status quo. Opposition to the authoritarian state was an important factor in mitigating conflict among rival groups and unifying them, at least temporarily, against a common adversary. And fourth, the tendency of authoritarian governments to support conservative groups and suppress left-leaning organizations as subversive threats to national security reinforced tensions in civil society. Competing visions of state and society contributed to the debilitating struggles between leftist and rightist organizations. In the Philippines, South Korea, Taiwan, and Thailand, such struggles also translated into confrontation between the state and certain segments of civil society—leading eventually to political change and transformation of state–civil society relations.

Proposition 7: The Transformation of State–Civil Society Relations

The relationship of civil society to the state in Asia has not been static. Although the more dramatic changes have followed the ouster of authoritarian governments, substantive changes have occurred in long-standing democracies and in semiauthoritarian and communist states as well. Following the 1987 democratic transition in South Korea, the legacy of oppositional civil society in constant confrontation with the state has gradually given way to a self-limiting civil society focused on engaging the elected government to broaden and deepen democratic governance. Tensions within civil society have not disappeared; certain segments still confront the state; but these are not the only or even dominating features in the current context. A similar transformation has occurred in Taiwan, where civil society groups are now focused on promoting public participation in the democratic process through education, developing political skills, and empowerment of the ordinary people, and in advocating policy change and demanding democratic accountability of the state and political parties. In the Philippines and Thailand too, state–civil society interaction has been transformed in the postdemocratic transition era. But the posttransition relationship in these countries, more so than in South Korea and Taiwan, combines features of confrontation and engagement. Confrontation becomes the predominant mode when key actors in civil society think the government has deviated seriously from accepted norms; in areas where there is broad agreement, engagement and even collaboration have become the central mode. In Indonesia, the state–civil society relationship has undergone two transformations: from a civil society engaged in bitter struggles among the different *alirans* in the context of a weak state to a civil society focused on a predatory state in the New Order era to the present relationship combining features of confrontation and engagement.

Substantive changes have featured in state–civil society relations in India and

Japan, Asia's two long-standing democracies, too. The end of the stranglehold on politics and society by the Indian National Congress—combined with the political rise of lower castes, regional forces, and Hindu nationalism, liberalization of the economy commencing in 1991, the gradual shift of power from the center to the states, and coalitional politics at the center—has unleashed new sociopolitical and economic forces that, among other things, are altering the dynamics and reconfiguring the relationship between the state and civil society. In the political arena, the rise of Hindu nationalism, for example, has created a seamless web among relevant segments in civil society (VHP, RSS, Shiv Sena), political society (the BJP), and the BJP-led coalition government in New Delhi. The VHP and the RSS appear able to exert considerable influence on government policy on core issues pertaining to national identity. For the Muslim and Christian communities, the BJP-led state is not an impartial guarantor of the rights of all citizens but an instrument of groups with totalizing goals bent on altering the identity of the state and relegating them to a subordinate status. In the economic arena, a shrinking state confronts competing pressures from civil society. Economic liberalization has unleashed private-sector groups pushing for even faster liberalization. Groups representing nationalist forces and those adversely affected by economic reform denounce liberalization for subjecting India to a new form of foreign invasion and domination and widening the socioeconomic inequity gap. Demanding social justice, they advocate policies that would slow or reverse liberalization, continue subsidies, cancel some major development projects, or provide compensation for those negatively affected. In a large, complex, diverse, and changing country like India, the relationship between civil society and the state is multidimensional and varies widely across groups, levels, and issues. In several ways, this diversity also characterizes state–civil society relations in Indonesia and the Philippines.

Japan, traditionally a strong state bent on dominating the small nonstate sector, has now been compelled to come to terms with its own weaknesses and accept the growing prominence of civil society organizations, especially with respect to social welfare and relief work. In the process the patron-client nature of the relationship is being redefined, though gradually. Some change in state–civil society relations is visible, as well, in semidemocratic Malaysia and communist China. Although it has not resulted in system change, civil society activism in Malaysia has affected the identity of the state (it has become more Islamic) and exposed the vulnerability of the UMNO-led Barisan Nasional government, making it more permeable to influences and input from civil society. Although elections continue to be the key source, government legitimacy increasingly turns on proper use of state power as well. Civil society's role in this process is becoming more significant. In China, the relationship is changing from one of domination of all "nonstate" organizations by the CCP (to mobilize the public behind the party to propagate its ideology and entrench its dominance) to a situation where the party-state still retains control but sees value in legally sanctioned quasi-independent social organizations in certain areas of governance. This is most visible not only in the economic-commercial arena but increasingly in the environmental arena as well. Such changes are gradually altering the relationship between state and civil society. In sum, then, state–civil society relations in many Asian countries have undergone substantive changes and more are coming. The nature of the state and civil society in many Asian countries, especially the authoritarian and communist regimes, is not a settled issue. As they alter, so too will the relations between agencies and actors in the two domains.

Proposition 8: A Broad Spectrum of Interaction

It is evident, then, that state–civil society relations in Asia span a wide spectrum, ranging from Burma and China at one end to South Korea and Taiwan at the other. Although nearly all Asian governments exercise a substantial degree of control over their official civil societies through legal, financial, organizational, and coercive measures, there is considerable variation across states in terms of state control, size of the legally protected space, and mode of interaction. State–civil society relations in the countries investigated in this study may be divided into three broad groups.

China, Burma, and Pakistan comprise one group. A high degree of state control over the legally sanctioned social organizations is the norm in China. Except on the margins, the interaction mode of such social organizations with the state is not confrontational, but one of interpenetration, mutual benefit, and cordiality. This, however, is not the case with unofficial civil society. Here the relationship is much more hostile and confrontational, with the state seeking to harass and eliminate such organizations. Burma allows almost no legal space for even quasi-autonomous civil society organizations. Confrontation is the only mode of interaction between unofficial civil society and the state. In Pakistan, the small liberal segment of civil society has been coerced and co-opted by the government, while the developmental and religious right organizations find it in their interest to cooperate with the military-led state, which has severely limited the space for civil and political society.

Singapore, Sri Lanka, and Malaysia comprise the second group. Although a few autonomous organizations are present in Singapore, most of its civil society groups, as in the PRC, are under the control of some government agency or government-linked body. Organizations that challenge the political status quo or government policies in sensitive areas are dealt with harshly. For the most part, civil society organizations are subservient to the state. The corporate model is an apt description of the current status of state–civil society relations in Singapore and the PRC. In Sri Lanka and Malaysia, although both states exercise a high degree of control over their civil societies, the predominance of the ethno-religious dimension has sometimes limited and sometimes increased state tolerance of civil society organizations and alternative discourses—making for multiple modes of interaction between the state and civil society. Considerations of race and religion have been deployed by incumbent governments to limit the space for civil society groups on grounds of security, stability, and development. But ethnic and religious bidding in the competition for political power among groups in the majority community has compelled states to tolerate certain opposition groups and alternative discourses. In the process, governments in these two countries have embraced certain organizations and agendas while repressing others.

Indonesia, the Philippines, Thailand, South Korea, Taiwan, and India comprise the third group. State–civil society interactions in these countries approximate that of the neo-Tocquevillean frame, although certain Gramscian features are present as well. Despite misgivings, lapses, and periodic setbacks, states and civil society groups acknowledge one another's legitimacy, interact on the basis of accepted norms and rules, and minimize resorting to violence. As observed earlier, varying degrees of progress have been made in guaranteeing legal space for civil society; organizations populating that realm in these countries by and large emphasize self-limiting goals and the intermediation function. Great diversity—coercion, resistance, confrontation, co-optation, and interaction on the basis of a mutually acknowledged framework—across and within countries characterize civil society interaction with the state in these countries.

Japan does not readily fit any of the three groups. It is an advanced industrialized democratic nation, but the Japanese state, despite the passage of the 1998 NPO law and the granting of tax privileges under the 2001 fiscal reform, continues to maintain a high degree of control over organizations in the nonprofit sector. Furthermore, Japan's civil society at the national level is small—almost minuscule compared to other developed countries and even some newly industrializing and developing countries in Asia. State domination and state-centered collaboration are still the predominant mode of state–civil society interaction in Japan. Although the preceding discussion highlights the wide differences between countries, it is crucial to note that variations in state–civil society relations occur *within* countries as well, depending on the issue and group.

Civil Society and Political Society

The democratization literature, as observed in Chapter 1, posits a dichotomy between civil society and political society—depicting the former as having a limited role in democratization and hindering the development of political society. Based on this premise, then, in the posttransition era, civil society should recede in importance as political society takes the lead in the ensuing democratization process. The studies in this volume do not, however, support such a sharp dichotomy between civil and political society; they suggest a mixed picture. The boundary between the two realms is porous, and the interaction of political and civil society organizations is characterized both by cooperation and by competition. There is a great deal of synergy between political and civil society organizations; often their roles and effectiveness are enhanced when they act in concert. When political parties are underdeveloped, weak, and insufficiently reform-oriented, civil society groups take the lead in initiating democratic reform. In the end, however, such efforts do not have long-lasting consequences if political society remains weak.

Proposition 9: Porous Boundary and Overlap

Political society and civil society are conceptually distinct. In practice, however, there is considerable overlap—especially in nondemocratic settings, when the two realms are undifferentiated and there is much fusion in the composition, leadership, and roles of organizations. This was the case through much of Asia during the colonial period and in South Korea, Taiwan, the Philippines, Thailand, and Indonesia in the era of authoritarian rule. As independence became a viable option, political society began to differentiate itself. In India, for example, the Indian National Congress debated its relationship with caste- and guild-based organizations and decided to exclude them from the party. But this was not always the case. Political and civil society groups did not differentiate themselves through much of the anticolonial struggle in the Philippines, South Korea, and Indonesia. At independence many political parties in these and other countries, such as Malaysia and Burma, in fact emerged from civil society organizations.

This was the case in the authoritarian era as well, when many political leaders and organizations found refuge in official and unofficial civil society. In their effort to depoliticize politics and emasculate the political realm, most authoritarian governments (and some semidemocratic and democratic ones too) enacted legislation and issued decrees to confine civil societies to the nonpolitical domain. Except in a few cases, such as Singapore and Burma, in the long run such efforts have not had the desired effect. In the prelude to democratic transitions, and in their wake, several social movements that stood apart from the state have evolved into political parties. The Democratic Progressive Party in Taiwan was created by leaders of social movements. Two major political parties in Indonesia—Partai Kebangkitan Bangsa and Partai Amanat Nasional—have their roots in the Nahdlatul Ulama and Muhammadiyah. The Barisan Alternatif and especially the Keadilan (Justice) party in Malaysia drew substantially on civil society organizations. Other organizations that cannot make the cut or, for whatever reason, cannot be registered as political parties, continue to function in the realm of civil society. Because of such origins, the distinction between political parties and civil society groups has been less marked in the posttransition era.

Even in a long-standing democracy like India and consolidating democracies like Taiwan and South Korea, the distinction between political society and civil society is not always clear. Many civil society organizations are ideologically linked to political parties or seek to affiliate with them on instrumental grounds. Ethnic and religion-based civil society groups in India are allied with the BJP, Congress, and other political parties. This is the case in Malaysia and Sri Lanka as well. In Taiwan, many civil society groups are politically driven. But civil society organizations in that country and in South Korea are becoming more issue-oriented and interest-based. As noted earlier, they seek to be less partisan and more intent on advancing democratic reform (both procedural and substantive) and new social agendas.

Proposition 10: Synergy and Mutual Reinforcement

Civil society organizations have been an important source of leaders, agendas, and support for political parties. The democratic roles of civil society discussed earlier–delegitimating authoritarian rule, constructing democratic counternarratives, and mobilizing democratic forces—have augmented the strength of political parties. The effectiveness of civil society roles has in turn required the support and cooperation of oppositional political society. When they combined forces and acted in concert, oppositional forces in the Philippines, South Korea, Taiwan, and Thailand were successful in commanding the moral high ground, ousting authoritarian rulers, and preventing rollback.

Synergy and mutual reinforcement, although reduced in the posttransition era, continue to be significant on several issues. The legitimation and balance-of-power roles of civil society have shored up prodemocratic political parties in their interaction with conservative forces. Acting in concert, prodemocratic forces from the two realms prevented a rollback of democracy in Thailand in 1992 and in the Philippines during the Aquino administration. Again acting in concert, they prevented change to the 1986 Philippine constitution. In South Korea, Taiwan, and Thailand, segments of political and civil society cooperated in advancing democratic reform and new social agendas. Although civil society organizations have taken the lead on several reform issues, their success (or failure) has hinged on cooperation with political parties and leaders in the legislature and the executive branch of government. Interaction of civil and political society organizations has also been characterized by tension—especially in the Philippines, South Korea, and Thailand, where conservative political parties and progressive civil society groups have clashed on issues of political and socioeconomic reform and economic development strategies. Rather than view such interactions negatively, it is possible to see them as part of the normal push and pull of democratic politics in which tension, conflict, intermediation, and compromise are normal occurrences. Perceived in this light, such interactions, within limits, reinforce rather than weaken the democratic roles of both civil and political societies.

The rise of civil society has been perceived in some quarters as having a negative effect on the development of political society. The weakness of political societies in the Philippines, Thailand, South Korea, and Indonesia, for example, is often attributed to the strength of civil societies. This proposition rests on the faulty premise that the relationship between the two realms is zero-sum. If one is vigorous, it is deemed that the other must be anemic. However, there are cases in Asia itself where both civil and political societies are vigorous, as in India and Taiwan, and cases where both are weak, as in Japan and Pakistan. A dynamic civil society may attract talent and resources. But there is no guarantee that in its absence, the talent and resources will flow to political parties. The weakness of political parties in the Philippines and South Korea, for example, is due to many reasons that go well beyond civil society. It is possible that the high profile of civil society actors in certain countries stems from the weaknesses and conservative orientations of political parties. When political parties are unable to lead, the initiative passes to civil society. But this is not a zero-sum game. There is ample space for organizations from both realms in a democratic system.

Future Prospects and Challenges

To conclude, civil societies exist in all the countries investigated in the study, and they have become an important feature of the political landscape. The legitimacy of civil society organizations is acknowledged in democratic states, and such organizations are not absent in other political systems. They exist and function as well in societies whose cultures—whether Confucian or Islamic—have been depicted as inhospitable. The legal framework for civil society, the number of organizations, their scope, the issues on which they focus, and their political roles, however, vary widely across countries and over time. The general trend in Asia is toward more complex and dynamic civil societies. The multiple factors that fueled the dramatic growth in the number of nonstate organizations—including the expansion of free-market economies, limitation in the economic and welfare functions of the state, the inability of the state to manage complex societies, increasing democratic space, individual freedom, and political awareness and participation by citizens, the growing force of the rule of law, increasing globalization, and the persistence of an international normative structure that favors democracy, human rights, and market economies—are still relevant. There can be setbacks in individual countries, but a major reversal of the trend toward open politics appears unlikely. Civil society is a cause and beneficiary of this trend.

Institutionalization of civil society, as observed in Chapter 14, has made less headway and is a major challenge for Asian countries. Effective institutionalization requires a more supportive and secure legal framework. In several democratizing countries, the laws in place are dated, lag behind practice, and constrain civil society activities. They have to be overhauled or new legislation enacted (see, e.g., the ongoing effort in Taiwan to enact a new NPO law) to create a more conducive legal framework for civil society. An equally important, and in many ways more difficult, task is for governments to develop the capacity and will to guarantee the rights and rules of the legal framework, namely, to make the framework a reality for most citizens and organizations. In semidemocratic, authoritarian, and communist states, the task is harder because of the type of political system and the negative inclinations of governments. Here civil society organizations may have to join forces with dissidents in political society to enlarge their operational space or engage in a struggle to bring about change in the political system, as was the case in the authoritarian Philippines, Taiwan, South Korea, Thailand, Bangladesh, and Indonesia.

A related challenge is to rethink civil society in Asia. Much of the effort of civil society organizations in Asian countries has been focused on the state: bringing about change in the type of state, restructuring state agencies, and demanding policy change. The agency dimension of civil society has tended to dominate. Although this study does not directly address the governance dimension, it is possible to infer from the country studies that relatively less effort has been made to develop civil society, an arena of democratic governance that is independent of the state. Such development in social, cultural, economic, educational, and other areas will devolve more power and resources to society, reduce the centrality of the state, and make civil society more rounded and robust. In other words, development of civil society must occur in all four dimensions of our definition—space for organization, site for critical discourse, site of self-governance, and the collective actions agency role dimension. Finally, the development of civil society must also effectively address the legitimacy, expertise, and financial problems of nonstate organizations, which have been highlighted in several chapters. Some of these can be dealt with through legal and administrative measures; but others will require effort on the part of civil society organizations to make themselves more credible and accountable to society.

Works Cited

Alagappa, Muthiah. 2001. "Asian Civil-Military Relations: Key Developments, Explanations, and Trajectories." In Muthiah Alagappa, ed., *Coercion and Governance: The Declining Political Role of the Military in Asia*. Stanford: Stanford University Press.

———. 1995. "Introduction" and "The Anatomy of Legitimacy." In Muthiah Alagappa, ed., *Political Legitimacy in Southeast Asia: The Quest for Moral Authority*. Stanford: Stanford University Press.

Bratton, Michael. 1994. "Civil Society and Political Transition in Africa." In John W. Harbeson, Donald Rothchild, and Naomi Chazan, eds., *Civil Society and the State in Africa*. Boulder: Lynne Rienner.

Bunbongkarn, Suchit. 2001. "Thailand." In Tadashi Yamamoto and Kim Gould Ashizawa, eds., *Governance and Civil Society in a Global Age*. Tokyo: Japan Center for International Exchange.

Case, William. 1995. "Malaysia: Aspects and Audiences of Legitimacy." In Muthiah Alagappa, ed., *Political Legitimacy in Southeast Asia: The Quest for Moral Authority*. Stanford: Stanford University Press.

Jun, Jinsok. 2001. "South Korea: Consolidating Democratic Civilian Control." In Muthiah Alagappa, ed., *Coercion and Governance: The Declining Political Role of the Military in Asia*. Stanford: Stanford University Press.

Khong, Cho-Oon. 1995. "Singapore: Political Legitimacy Through Managing Conformity." In Muthiah Alagappa, ed., *Political Legitimacy in Southeast Asia: The Quest for Moral Authority*. Stanford: Stanford University Press.

Lo, Chih-Cheng. 2001. "Taiwan: The Remaining Challenges." In Muthiah Alagappa, ed., *Coercion and Governance: The Declining Political Role of the Military in Asia*. Stanford: Stanford University Press.

Index

Index

In this index an "f" after a number indicates a separate reference on the next page, and an "ff" indicates separate references on the next two pages. A continuous discussion over two or more pages is indicated by a span of page numbers, e.g., "57–59." *Passim* is used for a cluster of references in close but not consecutive sequence.

The authorized representative in the EU for product safety and compliance is:
Mare Nostrum Group
B.V Doelen 72
4831 GR Breda
The Netherlands

www.ingramcontent.com/pod-product-compliance
Lightning Source LLC
Chambersburg PA
CBHW030632270326
41929CB00007B/48

* 9 7 8 0 8 0 4 7 5 0 9 7 4 *